Special Edition **Using**

MICROSOFT®
TCP/IP®

John Ray

201 West 103rd Street, Indianapolis, Indiana 46290

Special Edition Using TCP/IP

International Standard Book Number: 0-7897-1897-9

Library of Congress Catalog Card Number: 98-87538

Printed in the United States of America

First Printing: January, 1999

01 00 99
4   3   2   1

Trademarks

Warning and Disclaimer

EXECUTIVE EDITOR
Grace Buechlein

ACQUISITIONS EDITOR
Gregory Harris

MANAGING EDITOR
Brice Gosnell

PROJECT EDITOR
Kevin Laseau

COPY EDITOR
Anne Owen
June Waldman

PROOFREADER
Andrew Beaster

TECHNICAL EDITOR
Fred Soward

SOFTWARE DEVELOPMENT SPECIALIST
Jack Belbot

INTERIOR DESIGN
Dan Armstrong

COVER DESIGN
Ruth Lewis

LAYOUT TECHNICIANS
Brandon Allen
Tim Osborn
Staci Somers

Contents at a Glance

I ┃ TCP/IP and Networking

    1   Understanding Network Layers   7

    2   Integrating TCP/IP and OSI Network Layers   17

    3   Exploring IP Addresses   51

    4   Controlling Network Traffic   73

    5   Configuring Client Workstations   87

II ┃ TCP/IP Protocols

    6   Understanding TCP/IP Protocols   103

    7   Using Mail Protocols   109

    8   Using Document Delivery Protocols   129

    9   Investigating Other Useful Protocols   145

III ┃ TCP/IP Services

    10   Creating a TCP/IP Intranet   167

    11   Exploring Client OS File Server Capabilities   185

    12   Adding Email and Web Server Capabilities to Your OS   223

    13   Establishing Dedicated Servers   271

IV ┃ Connecting to the Internet

    14   Connecting Your Network to the Network   289

    15   Using Proxy Servers   297

    16   Using Proxy NAT Servers   337

V ┃ Managing Your Network

    17   Implementing Hardware Solutions   351

    18   Using Security Techniques to Protect Your Network and Data   361

    19   Managing TCP/IP Network Resources   379

    20   Configuring Networks with DHCP   393

    21   Using SNMP and Other Diagnostic Tools to Monitor Your Network   411

    22   Recognizing and Diagnosing Network Problems   437

VI | TCP/IP: Present and Future

23 Using and Administering Your Network Ethically   457

24 The Future of TCP/IP: IPng   467

A The TCP/IP Protocol Suite   477

B Using TCP/IP Remotely   707

Glossary   757

Index   765

Table of Contents

Introduction 1

Where We Were 1

How Far We've Come 2

Problems We Face 2

The Purpose of This Book 3

I TCP/IP and Networking

1 Understanding Network Layers 7

OSI by the ISO 8

OSI Network Model Overview 9

Inside the OSI Layers 9
 The Hardware/Physical Layer 9
 The Data Link Layer 10
 The Network Layer 11
 The Transport Layer 13
 The Session Layer 14
 The Presentation Layer 14
 The Application Layer 15

Where Do We Go from Here? 15

2 Integrating TCP/IP and OSI Network Layers 17

The Physical Layer 18
 Thinnet Cabling 18
 The Alternate Wiring Solution 20
 What Else Do They Call That? 21
 What's the Best I Can Buy? 22
 What Do I Plug This Stuff Into? 22
 What Will All of This Cost Me? 23
 Summary 23

The Data Link Layer 24
 Detecting Errors in Data 24
 Getting Data to Its Destination 25
 When Collisions Occur 27
 Other Methods of Connecting 28
 Summary 29

The Network Layer 29
 IP Addressing 30
 Fragmentation 31
 What Does an IP Packet Look Like? 31
 Communication Problems 32
 Summary 35

TCP/UDP and the Transport Layer 35
 Using Netstat to See Connections 38
 Summary 40

TCP/The Session Layer 41

Speaking in the Presentation Layer 42
 Summary 43

The Application Layer 43
 ICQ 43
 Hotline 44
 The Palace 45
 The CDDB 45
 PointCast 47
 VNC 47
 Java 48
 Quake 49
 Moving Forward 49

Other Information 49

3 Exploring IP Addresses 51

Why IP Addresses? 52

How the Hardware Address and IP Address Work Together 54

DHCP 56
 How Does DHCP Do Its Job? 57

Dial-In Connections 58

How Can I Tell What Method of Assignment I'm Using? 58

Subnets and the IP Address 60
 The Subnet Mask 61
 Smaller Subnets as a Solution to Routing Problems 62
 Private Subnets 63

Hostnames and DNS   64
Whatis Whois?   70

Other Information Sources   72

4 Controlling Network Traffic   73

Repeaters   74

Bridges   74

Routers/Gateways   74
Getting Information to Its Destination   75

Moving Packets Between Networks   77
Transparent Bridging   77
Routers/Gateways   78
Switches   82
Smart or Manageable Hubs   82

Monitoring Your Connections with SNMP   83

Broadcasting and Multicasting   83
MBONE   85
Broadcasting and Routing   85

Will I Need to Buy This Stuff?   85

Other Information Sources   86

5 Configuring Client Workstations   87

Configuring a Mac OS 8.x Computer to Use a TCP/IP Network   88
Open Transport Versus MacTCP   88
Configuring Open Transport   89

Configuring Windows 95/98   90
Installing TCP/IP   91
Configuring Windows TCP/IP   92

Configuring Red Hat Linux 5.x.   95

Other TCP/IP Configurations   98

Other Information Sources   99

II TCP/IP Protocols

6 Understanding TCP/IP Protocols   103

Telnet   104

Protocols and Protocol Development   105

Uniform Resource Locators   106

The Future of the File System   108

Let's Get Started   108

7 Using Mail Protocols   109

POP3   110
POP3 Authentication   111
Controlling Your POP3 Session   112
Optional Commands   114
Doing It by Hand   115

SMTP   115
Connecting to the SMTP Server   115
Sending Mail   116
Optional Commands   118
Doing It by Hand   119

IMAP   119
IMAP Authentication   120
Controlling the IMAP Session   121
Configuring IMAP Mailboxes   126
Doing It by Hand   127

Client Software and Other Information Sources   127

8 Using Document Delivery Protocols   129

Gopher   130
Connecting to a Gopher Server   130
Controlling the Gopher   131
Out with the Old   133

HTTP   133
Connecting to the Web Server   133
Using GET to Retrieve a Resource from the Server   133
Other HTTP Commands   139
Secure Web Connections   143

Client Software   144

Other Information Sources   144

9 Investigating Other Useful Protocols   145

Network News Transfer Protocol (NNTP)   146
Connecting to the NNTP Server   147
Client Software   150
Other Information Sources   150

Chatting on the Internet   151
IRC   151
Client Software   160
Other Information Sources   160

Less Friendly but Useful Protocols   160
FTP   160
NTP   163

III TCP/IP Services

10 Creating a TCP/IP Intranet   167

Setting Up and Understanding Your Hub   168
Using a "Crossover" Cable to Connect Two Hubs or Two Computers   169

Planning Your Wiring   169

Making the Connection   170

Using Ping to Check the Connection   170
Network Unreachable   171
Network Timeout   172

Exploring Your Basic TCP/IP Services   173

Basic Client Services   173
Mac OS Default Services   173
Windows 95/98 Basic Services   176
Basic Linux Services   182
Do I Need More?   183

11 Exploring Client OS File Server Capabilities   185

Sharing Files via TCP/IP   186

Using Mac OS to Share Files over a TCP/IP Network   187
Using Mac OS and AppleShare over a TCP/IP Network   191
Using Mac OS as a Peer on a TCP/IP Windows Network   193
Using Mac OS to Share to a Windows Network   196

Using Windows 95 or 98 to Share Files over a TCP/IP Network   198
Using Windows as a Peer on a Mac OS AppleShare IP Network   207

Using Linux to Share Files over a TCP/IP Network   209
Using Linux as a Peer on a Windows TCP/IP Network   215

12 Adding Email and Web Server Capabilities to Your OS   223

Providing Messaging Services Under Mac OS   225

Providing Messaging Services Under Windows 95 and 98 and Linux   235

Web Services   256
Delivering the World Wide Web Using Mac OS   257
Delivering the World Wide Web Using Windows   262
Delivering the World Wide Web Using Linux   265

13 Establishing Dedicated Servers   271

AppleShare IP   272

Windows NT   276

Linux (and Other UNIX OSes)   280

Now I'm Confused; What's the Best
Solution?   283
   Ease of Use   283
   Stability   284
   Services Provided   284
   Cost   284
   Scalability   284
   Security   285

IV Connecting to the Internet

14 Connecting Your Network to the Internet   289

Phone-Line Connections   290

ISDN   290

ADSL   291

Cable Modems   291

T1 Lines   291

What Should I Choose?   292
   Proxy Servers   292
   The NAT/IP Masquerading
   Solution   293

Other Information Sources   296

15 Using Proxy Servers   297

Controlling/Censoring Internet
Content   298

Proxy Servers   300
   Configuring Your Browser to Use a
   Proxy Server   300

Configuring Mac OS Browsers   301

Configuring Windows for Proxy Servers   303

Configuring Linux for Proxy Servers   306

Using Mac OS for Proxy Serving   308

Using Windows for Proxy Serving   321

Using Linux for Proxy Serving   329

16 Using Proxy NAT Servers   337

Using the Mac OS as a NAT Server   338

Using Windows as a NAT server   341

Using Linux as a NAT Server   345

Wrapping It Up   346

You're Connected!   347

V Managing Your Network

17 Implementing Hardware Solutions   351

What is a Secure Network?   352

Security in Stability   354

Ways of Securing Your Network   357
   Firewalls   357
   Packet Filtering Firewall   358
   Data encryption   358

Security and Your Network   359

Other Information Sources   360

18 Using Security Techniques to Protect Your Network and Data   361
   Using a Mac OS Computer As a
   Firewall   362
   Using Windows As a Firewall   364
   Using Linux As a Packet-Filtering
   Firewall   365
   Other Firewalls   365

Data Encryption As a Security Mea-
sure   366
   What Is RSA?   368
   Using PGPFreeware on Mac OS and
   Windows   369
   Using the UNIX-Based PGP on
   Linux   376

Security: The Final Word   378

Other Information Sources   378

19 Managing TCP/IP Network Resources   379

Where Things Go Wrong   380

Hardware   380
  Thinnet   380
  Twisted Pair   382

Software   384
  TCP/IP Settings   384
  Application Settings   388

Users   390

Somewhere in the Middle   392

20 Configuring Networks with DHCP   393

Configuring Your Client for DHCP   394
  Mac OS and DHCP   394
  Windows 95/98 and DHCP   396
  Linux and DHCP   397

Serving DHCP Using Mac OS   398

Serving DHCP Using Windows   402

Serving DHCP Using Linux   408

21 Using SNMP and Other Diagnostic Tools to Monitor Your Network   411

Monitoring Your Network Using Mac OS   412

Monitoring Your Network Using Windows   422

Monitoring Your Network Using Linux   428

Supplement, Don't Replace   435

22 Recognizing and Diagnosing Network Problems   437

Diagnosing User Errors   439
  Did Someone Mistype a Hostname (Fully Qualified Domain Name)?   440
  Is the Case Correct?   440

Is There a Space in the Name?   440

Diagnosing Configuration Errors   441
  Duplicate IP Addresses   441
  Nameserver Configuration Errors   442

Router Configuration Errors   446

Subnet Mask Configuration Errors   446

Diagnosing Software Errors   447

Diagnosing Cabling Problems   448

Netstat   449
  Spray   450

Diagnosing Network Hardware (Other Than Cabling) Problems   452

The Right Way To Do Things   453

VI TCP/IP: Present and Future

23 Using and Administering Your Network Ethically   457

Bandwidth   458

Information Sharing   461

Information Privacy   465

Don't Worry, We All Make Mistakes   466

24 The Future of TCP/IP: IPng   467

Enter IPv6   469

Addressing   469

Simplified Headers   470

Extensibility   472

Security   473

Quality of Service   473

Transitioning to IPv6   474

Other Resources   475

Wrapping It Up   475

A The TCP/IP Protocal Suite 477

B Using TCP/IP Remotely 707

Glossary 757

Index 765

About the Author

John Ray is an award-winning Web application developer and systems administrator for The Ohio State University. He holds a computer engineering degree from OSU and oversees network options for one of its colleges. There, he wrote a campus-wide database for maintaining TCP/IP information for a variety of machines. He has also created a beginning-level programming language known as Weaver, which is used in OSU's Extension News database, as well as in several other high-end applications. In his spare time, John provides customized TCP/IP programming solutions to businesses nationwide. You can reach him at jray@poisontooth.com.

Acknowledgments

Creating *Special Edition Using TCP/IP* has been quite an experience, and I have many people to thank for making the experience enjoyable. Gregory Harris, my acquisitions editor, and Fred Soward, the technical editor, were a pleasure to work with and were responsible for making this book straightforward to read and technically accurate. There's a good chance that I may now be able to write a sentence in the active, rather than passive, voice!

My work on *Special Edition Using TCP/IP* came at a rather tumultuous point in my life, and there is an entire cast of family and friends that I'd like to thank for getting me through everything:

My parents, of course, who aren't really sure what this book is about, but were supportive all the same

My brother, for reading and rereading each chapter and for his contributions to Chapter 22

Troy Burkholder and Russ Schelby, for forcing me to stop looking at the computer long enough to eat

Anne Groves, for constantly reminding me that there was something I was supposed to be doing and providing an endless supply of really bad candy

Kama Dobbs, for telling me to shut up every time I complained

Jack Derifaj, for his endless ramblings about life, the universe, and so forth

Kim Steinmetz, for being a constant source of entertainment and confusion for as long as I can remember

Thanks to all of you and to everyone else who helped make this book actually happen!

—John Ray

Tell Us What You Think!

As the reader of this book, *you* are our most important critic and commentator. We value your opinion and want to know what we're doing right, what we could do better, what areas you'd like to see us publish in, and any other words of wisdom you're willing to pass our way.

As an Executive Editor for the Operating Systems team at Macmillan Computer Publishing, I welcome your comments. You can fax, email, or write me directly to let me know what you did or didn't like about this book—as well as what we can do to make our books stronger.

Please note that I cannot help you with technical problems related to the topic of this book, and that due to the high volume of mail I receive, I might not be able to reply to every message.

When you write, please be sure to include this book's title and author as well as your name and phone or fax number. I will carefully review your comments and share them with the author and editors who worked on the book.

Fax: 317.581.4663

E-mail: opsys@mcp.com

Mail: Executive Editor
         Operating Systems
         Macmillan Computer Publishing
         201 West 103rd Street
         Indianapolis, IN 46290 USA

Introduction

TCP/IP Networking is a topic that has received more and more attention over the past few years. As the Internet has grown, people have taken notice of TCP/IP, perhaps without even being aware of it. Web browsers, email, and chat rooms are used by millions of people each day. TCP/IP silently keeps them all running.

Where We Were

Less than 10 years ago, computers were a novelty item to most people. They provided the service of a typewriter, calculator, and an entertainment center all-in-one. The concept of a computer network was entirely foreign to the average user. The floppy disk was the primary way of transferring information between machines. Computer bulletin board systems were the popular meeting grounds for owners of different systems. Word processors fit and ran off of a single floppy disk, many times without any hard drive, and a megabyte of memory was an extravagance. At that point in time, computers were not a necessity for everyday life. The ability to exchange data between your home PC and your computer at work was very rarely present and, in most cases, unneeded. Computers existed in their isolated little worlds, and humans were the carriers of information.

How Far We've Come

Today, computer networks fill classrooms, from kindergartens to college campuses. Email allows us to communicate across the planet instantly. Machine requirements are greater, but the cost of the technology has fallen dramatically. Computer technology is everywhere, and it cannot be ignored. Openness and information sharing now drive computing. Computer networks are the logical evolution of the information age. No longer do we need to manually move data from place to place. We can leave our computers at work turned on, and with a modem and phone-line connect to them, allowing us full access to the information they contain. Central repositories of shared data can be created and accessed by hundreds of people simultaneously. By giving machines a communications medium of their own, we allow information to freely flow and be shared across great distances; the computer network is born.

Problems We Face

In the early '90s, Tim Berners-Lee built the first Web browser on a NeXT Computer workstation. This was one of the first steps in solving what has been a long-standing dilemma with computer networks: how to share and represent data across different platforms. How do we present documents to the Macintosh user and make them appear identical to the PC User and the UNIX guru? If we allow proprietary standards to exist and perpetuate between platforms, we essentially build the modern equivalent of the tower of Babel: millions of different computers "speaking" in languages that millions of other machines don't understand. As far as cross-platform documents are concerned, that problem has been mostly solved by the constantly evolving HTML standard and cross-platform browsers such as Netscape and Internet Explorer. However, if you stop to think about it, for our Web browsers to work, we must already be sharing data between different types of computers. The cross-platform communication is already happening transparently on many of our computers, so how is this possible? The answer is TCP/IP.

TCP/IP was developed by the Department of Defense to link together individual networks forming what was called the ARPANET. These networks were built on a lowest-bidder contract basis and, as such, didn't necessarily have any way of speaking to anything outside of the LAN, or local area network. To overcome this, TCP/IP was designed to accommodate different hardware, software, and network configurations. The specification for TCP/IP is also an open specification, which means that anyone can write software that uses TCP/IP, as long as they follow the guidelines for the protocol. The robust and open quality of TCP/IP led to significant network software development using it as the primary communications protocol. ARPANET expanded its reaches to universities and beyond, and has now evolved into what we know as the Internet.

Why Is Cross-Platform Computing Networking Important to Me?

The concept of cross-platform network computing is extremely important in any environment where multiple types of machines, or even similar machines with different versions of the operating system, exist. Choices are made as to what sort of computing platform is employed to accomplish what job. Sometimes this is a personal choice; other times it is based on criteria necessary to accomplish a certain task. Religious computer wars are waged daily as people extol the virtues of the machines they have chosen to work with. There are diehard Apple Macintosh users who love the Mac's interface and ease of use. Windows 95/98 users have access to incredible amounts of commercial software. Windows NT/UNIX operators enjoy rock-solid stability. Choosing what system best suits your needs is a topic we'll discuss in a later chapter. There are many different computers with many different operating systems, and if we are to enjoy the freedom of choice that we currently have, these systems must be able to communicate. I am using an Apple Macintosh PowerBook to write this book. I'll be submitting the manuscript to an editor running a Windows operating system. Without cross-platform networking capabilities, submitting my work would be a bit of a problem. As it exists now, I simply attach the Word document to an email message and send it. TCP/IP and the email software take care of ensuring that it is received correctly on the other end. Another, more complex real-world example might be as follows:

> A publishing company may have a variety of computing solutions it uses in day-to-day operations. There may be graphic artists using Macintosh systems for design work. These machine may then, in turn, store all of their image files on a Windows NT server. This same server may also be used to store stories and text as they're entered on Windows clients throughout the company. The company may also have a Web presence that is served up through a UNIX-based computer that uses information generated by Windows clients, as well as the graphics images generated on the Macintosh machines.

There are thousands of possible arrangements like this, and each day, similar things are happening in businesses throughout the country. You may not know it, but your Windows network drive may be being served to you by a UNIX machine, or your Macintosh may be talking to an NT box. Until a computing platform exists that is everything to everyone, cross-platform computing will continue to be important. Taking it one step further, as more and more information is transferred to electronic media, and our "paperless society" continues to grow, so will the need for cross-platform networking. Within the span of our lifetimes, we've moved from using the command line to graphical-based systems. The rate of change of computer technology is probably the best argument for cross-platform communications. The operating systems and computers we have now will undoubtedly be replaced by new technologies in the future. TCP/IP provides our bridge between whatever machine we choose to use now, in the future, and everything else.

The Purpose of This Book

I'm writing this book with the hope of helping you accomplish the following goals:

- Gain a clear understanding of the underlying concepts of TCP/IP networking
- Learn the basics needed to configure a TCP/IP connection
- Understand how services you may take for granted, such as email, the Web, and so on, actually work

- Show you new and different TCP/IP services you may not be familiar with
- Help you pick, configure, and operate the services you want to provide
- Bring the Internet to a local TCP/IP intranet, and your intranet to the Internet
- Determine your security needs and evaluate different security options for your network
- Diagnose network problems that may occur
- Find out where the future of TCP/IP networking lies

You'll first learn the concepts behind TCP/IP, and then put them into practice. If you already have a reasonable background with computer networks, you may want to jump ahead to Chapter 3, where we'll look at TCP/IP specifics. If you come across information you don't understand, don't worry. There are hundreds of technical pages describing the TCP/IP protocol, and it's impossible to cover everything in the space of this book. You need only understand the concepts and reasoning behind the design of TCP/IP to put it into efficient use in your own network.

To successfully use the book, you should understand how to successfully install a network card in your computer. We'll look at configuring a working card with sample TCP/IP network configurations, but covering IRQs, I/O addresses, PCI versus ISA, and so on is a topic that would require its own book to completely address. You should have a good understanding of how to navigate through the different operating systems if you want to work with them. This means having the ability to find and open applications and control panels. If you're interested in the Linux configurations, you must have administrative root access to the system and a basic understanding of how to get to a "shell" and successfully run a text editor. It is also necessary for you to have Internet access, as many of the examples will demonstrate TCP/IP services over the Internet.

My focus will be on how a TCP/IP network works, what the configuration means, and how it relates to several different operating systems, not on configuring specific hardware systems or providing a reference for the day-to-day use of different operating systems. There are other books that address these topics in depth, and covering them here would simply reduce the amount of TCP/IP-related material we can talk about.

Throughout this book, I'll be stressing the cross-platform nature of TCP/IP and will provide examples and solutions for Macintosh, Windows, and Linux (Red Hat 5.x) computing platforms. Unfortunately, I cannot provide detailed information on the configuration of every TCP/IP service you may want to run (I would if I could, but there are hundreds of services that you could choose to operate if you wanted). Instead, I'll give an overview of the configuration and capabilities of the basic servers available on each platform. It's my hope that this book will provide information that will help you make timely and cost-effective decisions when setting up your own TCP/IP network, and allow you to join the growing group of people successfully running TCP/IP-based networks.

TCP/IP and Networking

Before you can understand TCP/IP, you must have an understanding of what a network truly is. Part 1 explores the definition of a network and builds a network model from the ground up. You will learn about the OSI network model, and how it relates to TCP/IP. From there, you will be introduced to the hardware that TCP/IP uses, and the common configuration information you'll need to get up and running.

1   Understanding Network Layers 7

2   Integrating TCP/IP and OSI Network Layers 17

3   Exploring IP Addresses 51

4   Controlling Network Traffic 73

5   Configuring Client Workstations 87

Understanding Network Layers

by John Ray

In this chapter

OSI by the ISO **8**

OSI Network Model Overview **9**

Inside the OSI Layers **9**

Where Do We Go from Here? **15**

Before discussing the specifics of building and using a TCP/IP network, it's important to learn a bit of the background on what a network really is and how it works. Fortunately, a number of real-world analogies can help us gain that understanding. We know, for example, that a car moves us from place to place. A network, similarly, moves data from place to place. A car also consists of several components, which, depending on our automotive background, can be abstracted in different ways. There's an engine, which provides power for the transportation, a passenger compartment that provides the storage for moving people and their belongings around, a transmission to control the speed, and braking system to prevent errors from occurring. A network behaves in much the same fashion and can be described much like our abstraction of a car. The trick is to come up with a network model that can be applied to any situation, whether you're building a TCP/IP network or a network using protocols that haven't even been created yet. There have been several attempts at providing such a model, but most have failed to cover all the aspects of defining all the components that can be considered part of a network. Luckily for us, there is one model that has been widely accepted internationally and can be used to describe both present and future network models in an abstract manner.

OSI by the ISO

What is the ISO?
The ISO, or International Standards Organization, is a group comprised of members from over 75 countries who work together to compile and maintain engineering standards from around the world. Interestingly enough, ISO is not an acronym; the ISO was named for the Greek word iso, which means "equal," so like chemical elements, the name ISO is consistent in all languages. The ISO created the network model we'll use for examining TCP/IP.

The International Standards Organization (ISO) recognized the need for a model that could be used when designing networking protocols. The Open Systems Interconnect (OSI, not to be confused with ISO) network model provides us with an abstract view of how a network functions, from the wiring that connects the computers to the programs we use to communicate. Layers are the key component to the OSI model. A layer in the network model is simply a functional piece of the whole network, like the braking system or engine is in our car model. Breaking the network down into layers provides us with a starting point for our definition of a network, and allows us to build up the components we need to create a network that does what we want. From a development standpoint, defining networking based on a layered model allows for the development of new technologies that take advantage of existing hardware and software by using underlying layers that are already in place. As you read about the OSI model, try to picture the relationship between each of the layers. I think you'll find that each layer has a distinct and necessary purpose. Together, the whole is truly greater than the sum of its parts.

OSI Network Model Overview

A total of seven layers are used in the OSI model to describe a network from the ground up. These layers, in order, are the Physical, Data Link, Network, Transport, Session, Presentation, and Application layers. Each layer builds on the next and would be completely useless by itself, or if one of the preceding layers was missing. It follows that each layer cannot exist in a vacuum; it must possess some knowledge of the layers that surround it and have a method of communicating to those layers. In its specification of the OSI model, the ISO does not bind any particular network standard, such as TCP/IP, to the model. By basing the layers on their function, rather than specific existing network standards, the ISO has provided a model that is robust, open, and can be used to explore existing network specifications and design the standards of the future (see Figure 1.1).

FIGURE 1.1
Each layer builds on the
layers under it.

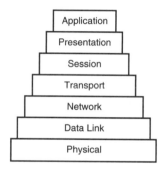

Inside the OSI Layers

As we look at a general overview of each layer, we'll compare it to a real world model when appropriate. You'll see how easily the OSI model lets us view the complex creature known as a network.

The Hardware/Physical Layer

This first layer provides the foundation that the following layers will build on. Hardware refers to the computer, network cable, satellite dishes, or any other physical devices you choose to use when linking two or more computers. This concept includes the actual physical wiring and the electrical signals that travel through them. For satellite hardware, the term would include the radio waves that pass to and from the satellites. The hardware must also have the capability of determining when a signaling problem has occurred and notifying upper levels of the trouble.

These tasks may sound a bit daunting, but they happen at a level that most of us don't need to worry about. The signaling properties are handled by the hardware we choose to link the computers; we don't need to design our signaling methods each time we set up a network. In a car, this action is equivalent to the engine's ability to translate fossil fuels into kinetic energy, which turns the tires. We don't necessarily need to know all the specifics of combustion to understand how it works; we just need to know that without an engine, there will be no motion. Furthermore, we don't need to be civil engineers to understand that without the road, our car isn't going to be traveling very far. Likewise, it's quite safe to say that if there isn't a Physical Layer, you're going to be having some serious problems getting a network up and running.

The Data Link Layer

Once we've made a physical connection at the Physical Layer, we need to be able to move data over the connection. The Data Link Layer accomplishes this purpose. Imagine a unit of data, called a frame or packet, is to be transmitted over our Physical Layer. The Data Link Layer must be capable of creating the packet holding our information, identifying the destination of the remote machine, or node, that will receive the data, and providing low level error checking to identify any problems that may have occurred and acting on those problems. The Data Link Layer is also responsible for regulating the transmission of data from the Physical Layer. Depending on the type of network you're setting up, there are certain conditions during which the machine must either wait its turn to transmit data, or wait for a certain length of time to pass before it can transmit again. An example of this behavior would be if two nodes on an Ethernet network attempted to send data at the same time. The result is a collision in which the information from the two nodes overlaps and is unintelligible. In the left side of Figure 1.2, two packets pass through the network juncture in sequence, with no collision. On the right side, however, the packets arrive at the juncture simultaneously, and a collision occurs.

FIGURE 1.2
Two packets that overlap are considered a collision.

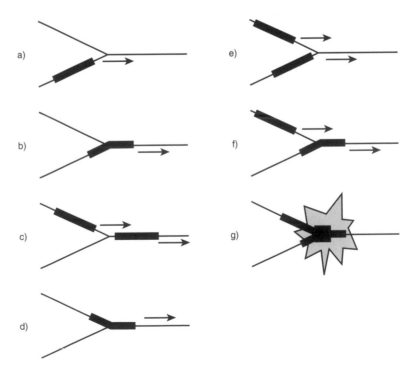

When a collision occurs, the Data Link Layer must make a decision on how to handle the problem. Should it retransmit the data immediately? If it did, and the Data Link Layer on the other node made the same decision, the result would be another collision… and another… and another, and so on. Later, in Chapter 2, we look at the Data Link Layer in relation to TCP/IP. You'll learn how this event has been well thought out, and precisely how the situation is handled. For now, just be aware that such problems can and do occur, and the Data Link Layer is responsible for keeping them to a minimum. The Data Link Layer provides the bridge between hardware and software. It must communicate directly with the Physical Layer, prepare data to be sent, and receive incoming data. Then, after verifying the correctness of the data, it must make it available to the next layer. In our car/road model, this component is analogous to a vehicle's tires. The tires provide an interface between the motion created by the engine and the road upon which the motion will take place. Remove the tires from the car, and it goes nowhere. Take the Data Link Layer out of the network, and data will cease to flow.

On your computer system, the Data Link Layer is typically represented by the Network Adapter driver and is supplied on a floppy disk when you buy your network card. In many cases, Windows and Macintosh systems arrive with network cards and drivers installed, so the Data Link Layer is often already present, will not be something you need to worry about, and will require minimal configuration if you need to set it up yourself.

The Network Layer

With the Data Link Layer in place, we have the necessary logic to transmit information to different nodes on our network. Networks are, however, not isolated entities. A network can consist of many different nodes, using many different hardware layers and Data Link Layers.

What is a Node?

A node is any device that is connected to a network. For our purposes, it usually refers to a computer.

Because network components can vary widely, how can one network communicate with another? At the Data Link Layer, a low-level addressing scheme identifies individual nodes and is specific to the hardware underneath it. For heterogeneous networks to exist, there must be a common way of identifying nodes at a higher level. The Network Layer provides this addressing scheme. Once a common addressing method is available, we need to worry about the most efficient way to communicate between our different networks. Once again, this is the responsibility of the Network Layer. For simple networks, this is not a problem. For an arrangement such as this, there are three distinct networks, or subnets, each with a single connection to each other. The data obviously must pass through subnet B to get to subnet C, or vice versa (see Figure 1.3).

FIGURE 1.3

In a simple network with single connections, traffic must pass through subnet B on its way from subnet A to subnet C.

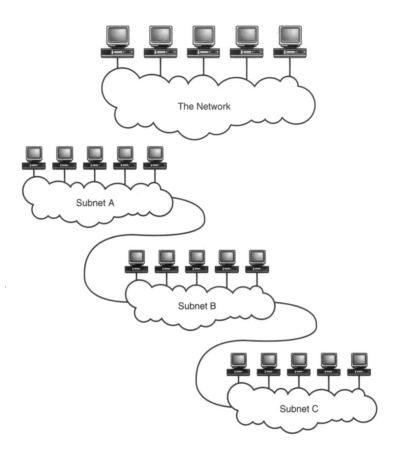

Now imagine four subnets, labeled A, B, C, and D, that are connected as shown in Figure 1.4, via Ethernet, phone dialup, and even satellite connections.

If a node on subnet B wants to send data to a node on C, it has two choices: send the data through subnet A or through subnet D. Obviously, if there is a fast connection all the way between B and D, and D and C, it makes sense to send the data by way of network D. Suppose that subnet D fails after a horrible lightning strike. In that case, the node in subnet B must also know that, if necessary, it can send information through the connection to A and still have it arrive by way of the slow phone connection at subnet C. Imagine this on a scale of magnitudes larger, with hundreds of individual subnets, and you have a typical business or university setting. Expand this to the Internet, and now there are literally millions of subnets to take into account. Moving data efficiently and reliably between them is a monumental task and is referred to as routing. Similar to looking at a map to find the best route to take in your car, and taking the appropriate detours when necessary, the Network Layer provides the same services in the network model.

FIGURE 1.4
Four subnet networks
with different speed
links.

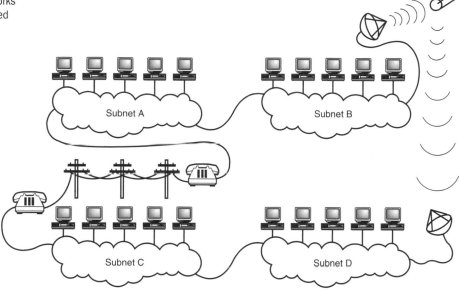

Subnet A is connected to B via a fast Ethernet link.
Subnet C is connected to D via a fast Ethernet link also.
Subnet A is connected to Subnet C by a dialup phone connection.
Subnet B is connected to Subnet D by a fast satellite connection.

The Transport Layer

Our model is now to the point where we can send information, and it will be able to find its way
from one node to another node sharing the same network layer; things become significantly
easier at this level and throughout the remaining layers. The primary concern of the Transport
Layer is that the data we receive is actually what we're supposed to be receiving. The amount
of data that can be transmitted on a network at a time is finite. The Transport Layer takes the
information to be sent and breaks it into individual Datagrams that are sent and reassembled
into a complete message by the Transport Layer at the receiving node. The Transport Layer
may also provide a signaling service for the remote node so that the sending node is notified
when its data is received successfully by the receiving node.

Unfortunately, networks are dynamic, and things do go wrong on a regular basis. Packets are
lost on bad wiring, connections are broken when people (very bad people) decide to rewire the
network in their office, and messages are scrambled as they are routed through different
subnets. Because of these sorts of problems, Datagrams are not guaranteed to arrive in a specific order. If an error does occur during transmission, it's up to the Transport Layer to reliably
correct the error. Depending on the network protocol in use, this correction does not necessarily mean that the data is exactly the same as it was when it was sent. This does mean that there
is no ambiguity in what happens to the data. A set of rules is followed that detail the handling of
the error and how to correct it. This correction may mean resending just the damaged data or

restarting from the beginning; but even if this involves discarding the erroneous data and continuing, it's still considered error correction. However, if an email is sent from your supervisor over a TCP/IP network with the message "You will never be fired" and arrives as "You will be fired," you can be assured that the Transport Layer is not doing its job. We'll drop our real-world analogy for this layer, as it is assumed that no one ever gets lost while driving his or her car.

The Session Layer

Most data transmitted over a network is not in the form of a single packet. Typically two or more nodes open connections between themselves and exchange multiple packets. As packets travel back and forth, they carry both the data that the end user wanted to send and extra information that is used by the protocol to help guarantee that the packets are delivered successfully. When the nodes are finished communicating, the connections are closed. It's also possible for multiple connections to be made to a single machine (think of how long you'd have to wait to download your favorite Web pages if the computer serving them to you could serve only one page to one person at a time). The Session Layer manages the opening and closing of connections, and assures the layers above it that each connection has its chance to send and receive data. If you ever open multiple connections to multiple Web sites, you're putting the Session Layer to use. Most of today's computers are capable of multitasking and providing many sorts of services over the Internet. They must call upon the session layer of the network in order to serve their data to other machines in an efficient manner. You can think of the Session Layer as the dividing lines on the highway: They define starting and ending points, and allow multiple lanes of traffic to flow along concurrently.

The Presentation Layer

With so many layers already in place, it may seem difficult to imagine that we still need two more before our model is complete. The Presentation Layer provides a simple service to the network model. It prepares data for its trip across the network and readies the data for use in an end user application when the journey is complete. Syntax for communicating with a remote machine may also be defined in the Presentation Layer. The Presentation Layer serves as a translator for the data that the Application Layer wants to send. Typing a URL into an application means nothing to the network. It's up to the Presentation Layer to translate that URL into an appropriately worded request that another machine will be able to recognize. The Presentation Layer makes data presentable to the applications that use the network and presentable to the network itself. A car has a steering wheel, brake pedal, and gas pedal. These can be connected to the components that perform the appropriate actions in a variety of different ways; however, they present themselves in a way that is recognizable no matter what kind of car you're driving.

A growing use for the Presentation Layer is to provide secure communications over a network. Data can be encrypted in the Presentation Layer before it's passed down to the lower layers for transmission. Similarly, data can also be compressed in this layer. Compressing the data before sending it can result in significant speed increases in transmitting and receiving. Why isn't all data encrypted and compressed before it's sent? Keep in mind that compressing and encrypting data is a time-consuming task, and a balance must be maintained between network speed and the rate at which the local and remote nodes can process the incoming data within the Presentation Layer.

The Application Layer

At last we arrive at the last part of the OSI model: the Application Layer. This layer provides the final interface to the network that we, the end users, use to access network services. You've interacted with the Application Layer of the TCP/IP protocol if you've used a Web browser, a mail reader, or anything else over the Internet. Netscape, Internet Explorer, Eudora, Outlook, and so on are all examples of the Application Layer. This layer is the final product that we've been building up to—the resulting application that hides all the inner workings of the network. Returning one last time to the car analogy, we're now in the driver's seat of our 1998 Volkswagen Beetle, and the open highway is in front of us.

Where Do We Go from Here?

At this point, you should have a good understanding of each level in the OSI network model. In the following sections, we'll show how TCP/IP fits within this model, and then move on to configuring each layer to suit your network needs.

Intergrating TCP/IP and OSI Network Layers

by John Ray

In this chapter

The Physical Layer **18**

The Data Link Layer **24**

The Network Layer **29**

TCP/UDP and the Transport Layer **35**

TCP/The Session Layer **41**

Speaking in the Presentation Layer **42**

The Application Layer **43**

Other Information **49**

Now that we know what the OSI network layers do from a general functionality standpoint, let's integrate our knowledge of the network model with TCP/IP. First, let's flesh out our existing layered network diagram and include specific TCP/IP information, as shown in Figure 2.1.

FIGURE 2.1

The layered network model now includes components of the TCP/IP suite.

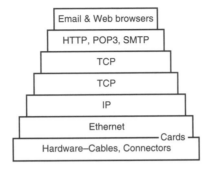

Why is TCP/IP Called a Suite?

TCP/IP is often referred to as suite. This is because it can be broken down into individual sub-protocols, with these lower level protocols making up a suite of protocols. Syntactically, you may refer to TCP/IP as a protocol suite, or as a singular protocol.

The Physical Layer

The Physical Layer, as we learned earlier, makes up the basic underlying connection of the network. In most TCP/IP networks, this layer will be a form of wiring. It's also possible to build a TCP/IP network with components such as microwave and radio transmitters, but these items are generally used in highly specialized situations where networks must be linked over long distances.

Thinnet Cabling

A common Ethernet wiring scheme—in fact, once the standard practice—is coaxial cable, called *coax* or *thinnet*. This cable is usually found in buildings that were wired 10 to 15 years ago. It's very similar to the wiring that your cable TV box uses. Although this form of wiring is the most common, it's also the most problematic. Coax cable is laid out in a string, and network devices are connected to it in series. The loose ends at either end of the string are *terminated* by placing a 50ohm resistor on either end. This terminator assures that there won't be signal reflection on the line, which would make data transmission unstable, or more likely, impossible. To visualize what signal reflection does, imagine a friend and a piece of rope. You ask your friend to hold the end of the rope tightly, and then take the other end of the rope and give it a shake. You'll see a wave travel down the length of rope, and, upon reaching your friend, bounce back along the length of the rope. On a computer network, this reflection happens at the speed of light, or 186,000 miles per second. Packets that your own computer creates are themselves reflected, and that reflection creates a collision with the original packet. This situation can bring an entire network, consisting of hundreds of computers, to its knees in seconds.

The 50ohm terminators absorb the signal at the end of the wire and prevent the reflection problem from occurring. This type of network is called a *bus* topology.

A typical thinnet network appears in Figure 2.2.

FIGURE 2.2

A bus network with several stations connected to the network with T connectors and terminators at the ends.

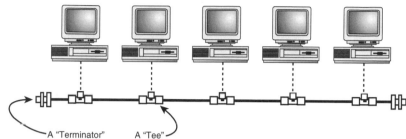

A "Terminator"   A "Tee"

A single strand of thinnet cable can be up to 185 meters (approximately 630 feet) long before signal degradation occurs, and computers can be connected along this length as close as six feet to each other. At each device along this network strand is a "T" connector. These are sometimes referred to as BNC (British Naval Connector) connectors (see Figure 2.3).

FIGURE 2.3

There are three failure points for each thinnet connection.

The *T* splits the wire and provides a connection point for the device to plug into the network. Unfortunately, because of the splitting of the wire at each connection point, this leads to three potential points of failure for each network connection: each side of the network wire and the connection of the T into the network device. If any portion of a T connection fails completely, the network cable can be considered to be split, and the network ceases to be correctly terminated. What follows is generally a complete failure of the entire length of wire. It's the same effect as pulling a light out of an old string of Christmas tree bulbs. If one light goes out, they all do. Imagine the problems of diagnosing a failure in this type of network. Potentially hundreds of points of failure, and until the failure is solved, hundreds of angry users spouting hundreds of potentially non-pleasant words.

I would not recommend thinnet for networks with more than a handful of devices connected. Coax cable is cheap and extremely simple to set up, but costly and time-consuming to diagnose and repair. I personally have to deal with a building of approximately 400 to 500 people, all network connected, and all using thinnet. A company that no longer exists strung the wiring throughout the five floors of the building. There are no maps of how the wire was strung; in some places it loops back on itself, jumps across halls and between floors. It's entirely common for someone to upgrade their computer in the building and unplug their existing computer from the network, remove the T connector and leave the wire dangling unconnected by their desk. Then, as if to seal the fate of the network, they'll leave on vacation and lock their office.

Another seemingly bizarre problem is that of the disappearing terminator. Terminators, as I just mentioned, are 50ohm resistors at the ends of the thinnet cable. They're a rather nice weight and are either polished steel or a bright green color. One or more of these attributes seems to attract the common "terminator snatcher" who, as near as I can tell, is building a nest out of these things somewhere. Terminators disappear off of network lines on a daily basis, never to be seen again.

Sometimes it takes days for me to completely locate and solve network problems when they occur. As you might infer, I am not a fan of thinnet for networking on a large scale. I use it myself in my apartment, but only to connect two computers and a printer. If I accidentally disconnect one of the wires, there are very few places I need to check for failure; furthermore *my* terminators seem to stay where I leave them.

The Alternate Wiring Solution

The increasingly common, and thankfully so, standard in wiring is *twisted pair*. Twisted pair resembles a very wide phone line and doesn't suffer from the problems of thinnet. In a twisted pair network, each device has its own strand of wire that runs from the machine to a central point called a *hub*. The hub has several ports, and each port can feed a network device, or perhaps even another hub. The network layout for twisted pair networks is called a *star topology* because the physical layout of the wiring looks somewhat like a star, as shown in Figure 2.4.

FIGURE 2.4

A standard hub configuration using 10BASE-T; if the machines were spaced around the hub, the star configuration would be more obvious.

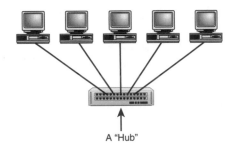

A "Hub"

There's no need for terminators on a twisted pair network, as signal termination is handled internally by the hub and the computer's network card. In addition, most hubs have the capability to detect excessive unusual activity on a port and isolate it from the rest of the network. This isolation can keep a single computer from bringing down the rest of the network. Each section of twisted pair wire, from hub to computer, can be up to 100 meters long, so the potential distance between the furthest connections on the network is about 680 feet—100 meters each way. While this distance is nearly the same as thinnet, the star topology allows machines to be placed anywhere within 100 meters of the hub. This allows a single hub 10BASE-T network far greater reach then a single strand thinnet network.

Okay, I See Some Really Expensive Twisted Pair Wiring, and Some That's a lot Cheaper; Which Should I Buy?

Twisted pair wiring comes in a variety of configurations. In addition to the normal "Cat-5" (Category 5) UTP (unshielded twisted pair) cabling that is used in most normal installations, there are specialty types of wiring that are necessary, for example, if your network will be exposed to high levels of electrical noise. You may also find Cat-3 cabling—usually at a significantly lower cost than Cat-5 cabling. Cat-3 cabling is only capable of handling 10Mbit/sec traffic. It generally is a bad idea to build a network with Cat-3 cabling as it would be necessary to remove and replace all Cat-3 cabling with Cat-5 cabling if you decide to install 100Mbit/sec network hardware in the future. For most normal installations, Cat-5 UTP cabling should serve well.

Despite the obvious benefits of twisted pair, things can still go wrong. Remember the building with 400 to 500 people and thinnet strung throughout? There are a few offices in the building that have been rewired with twisted pair. Unfortunately, the people who handled the rewiring chose to connect the hubs to the same thinnet line that everyone else is connected to. Once again, if the thinnet goes offline, the twisted pair hub goes with it. Thinnet will usually prove to be the weak link in a network that contains several wiring schemes.

What Could Go Wrong?

A very big problem with 10BASE-T networks is the similarity of the wiring to a standard office phone line. In fact, the plugs are so similar that they are interchangeable. I often have users walk into my office and complain that their computer has no network access. One of my first questions is, "Have you rearranged your office or moved your phone?" If they have indeed moved their phone, my next question is, "Is your phone working?" The usual response, after a few moments of silence, is "no." Undoubtedly, they have switched their phone wire with the network line. A slightly different but related problem is that users will attempt to extend their network cables. They notice the similarity of 10BASE-T to their phone line and replace the network cable with more easily available phone cable. In some cases, this substitution does work, but it will be extremely slow and may cause corrupt information to be sent to the network. Most network problems are simple to solve and generally involve human error rather than software or hardware failure.

What Else Do They Call That?

Thinnet is also called 10BASE-2. The "10" refers to the transmission speed that the wire can handle. In this case, it is 10 megabits (10^3) per second. This equates to 1.2 megabytes per second. In real life, transmission speeds don't actually reach this speed, but it's the theoretical maximum. The "2" is the maximum length of the wire in hundreds of meters. Thinnet can be nearly 200 meters in length. Twisted pair is also known by the similar name *10BASE-T*. The only difference in the naming is the "T"; this letter designates "twisted pair" as the style of wiring. Depending on whom you're talking to, they may use the wiring names interchangeably. Lastly, twisted pair is also sometimes referred to by its acronym, *UTP*, or *unshielded twisted pair*. If you're going to set up your own network, feel free to use whatever names you feel comfortable with. If you choose to use thinnet, you'll probably come up with some very creative names on your own.

What's the Best I Can Buy?

The emerging standard in networking is *100BASE-TX*. 100BASE-TX, as the name implies, is a 100 megabit connection, which makes it 10 times faster than standard wiring. If you're building a high traffic network from scratch, you'll want this option. You'll need to buy higher rated wiring and slightly special network hardware, but, in five years, you'll be patting yourself on the back as everyone rushes to move over to 100BASE-TX.

What Do I Plug This Stuff Into?

In most cases, you'll need to purchase an *Ethernet card* to connect to the wiring of the network. Ethernet cards come in a variety of models. There are combo cards that contain ports for thinnet wiring and 10BASE-T. Some may include an *AUI port*, which can handle an extremely old wiring standard called Thicknet, or, with an adapter that plugs into the AUI port, 10BASE-T. Your best bet is to buy a combo card. They're priced similarly to the cards that have a single port and can handle either of the common wiring standards. Remember to also look for 100Mbit Ethernet cards if you like the idea of building a really fast network. 100Mbit cards look like normal 10BASE-T cards but generally have a port that automatically detects the speed of the line that is plugged in. If you order your computers pre-built, the manufacturer should be able to supply you with several different network card configurations. If you happen to be purchasing a Macintosh, chances are it already has an Ethernet card built in.

If you're building a network based on twisted pair, you'll need to buy a hub. Hubs come in a variety of configurations, from 4 ports to 32 or more. You can buy hubs that also have a thinnet BNC port in case you want to integrate a 10BASE-T network with thinnet. Fast Ethernet (100BASE-T) hubs are significantly more difficult to integrate with slow Ethernet networks (either 10BASE-T or thinnet) because of the speed difference between the lines. The hub must provide a *step down* service for outgoing data if it is to be able to communicate with the slower devices.

Newer model Macintoshes, laptops, and other preconfigured computers may have only a 10BASE-T port. If that's the case, is it possible to connect to a thinnet network without installing another Ethernet card? The answer is yes, but at a cost. The solution is to buy a 10BASE-T hub that includes a BNC port. The 10BASE-T from the computer plugs into a 10BASE-T port on the hub, and then the BNC connection on the hub is used to connect to the rest of the network, as shown in Figure 2.5.

Unfortunately, this solution is the only available option. It costs a bit more but doesn't require another Ethernet card to be installed, which may not even be possible with some notebook computers.

FIGURE 2.5
Using a 10BASE-T hub to connect to a thinnet network.

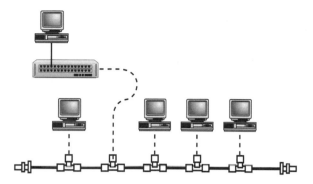

What Will All of This Cost Me?

The price of network devices has fallen significantly in recent years. This table should give you an idea of the price ranges you'll be looking at when purchasing your network equipment.

Hardware	Price
BNC/UTP cable	$.50/foot
Pre-built cables (BNC/UTP)	$1.00/foot
Ethernet cards (10MB)	$40–75
Ethernet cards (100MB)	$85–100
4–5 port UTP hubs	$50
8 port UTP hubs	$80
8–12 port UTP/BNC hubs	$100–150
8 port (100mb) UTP hubs	$250

As you can see, building a 100Mbit fast Ethernet network will require almost double the money investment of a 10Mbit network, but remember, for only twice the cost, you're getting 10 times the performance.

Summary

This review completes the implementation of the Physical Layer. You may have noticed that there isn't anything at all in this layer that is specific to the TCP/IP protocol. The reason for this generality is that at this level, you're simply forming a physical connection. This information given for the first layer is valid for almost any network configuration: AppleTalk, NetWare, TCP/IP, NetBEUI, and so on. It isn't until you reach the third layer that you'll begin to learn how TCP/IP plugs into the big picture.

The Data Link Layer

In most cases, you'll be connecting your network with Ethernet cards. *Ethernet* is a standard in and of itself. It provides the basic communication that most of the world's TCP/IP local area networks are built on. Because of this prevalence, we'll focus on Ethernet as the primary connection type for the Data Link Layer.

Data is transmitted across an Ethernet network in the form of discrete pieces of information. These pieces are known as *packets* or *frames*. A frame has a structure that identifies where the information is going, where it is headed, the type of information contained in the frame, the data to be transmitted, and a *Cyclic Redundancy Check (CRC)* that helps detect errors that occur in transmission. A graphical representation of a frame is shown in Figure 2.6.

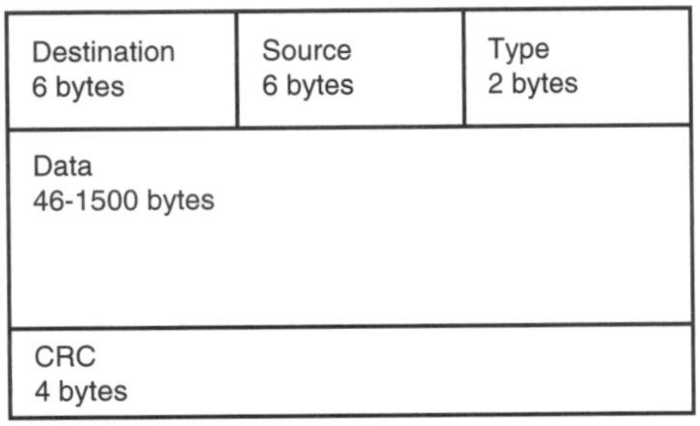

FIGURE 2.6

Here's a graphical representation of an Ethernet frame.

Destination 6 bytes	Source 6 bytes	Type 2 bytes
Data 46-1500 bytes		
CRC 4 bytes		

As you can see, the amount of data transmitted in each frame is extremely small. To transmit a file of 100K, it would take more than 68 packets of the maximum size of 1500 bytes. As you move up through the network layers, there will be more and more information that each layer must add to each frame that's sent. You'll find that there is quite a bit of overhead created by the other layers, and that it will actually take quite a few more than 68 packets to send our 100K file.

Detecting Errors in Data

With such a large number of packets being sent back and forth, it's extremely likely that data will, at some point, be corrupted. This likelihood is where the CRC comes into play. A Cyclic Redundancy Check is often used to determine if data has arrived at its destination unharmed. A CRC is a unique number that's generated from the data stored in the frame. Upon receiving the data, the receiving computer calculates a CRC based on the data in the frame and compares it to the CRC information that's sent with the frame. If the numbers match, the data is assumed to be correct. If not, there has been an error in transmission, and the data will need to be retransmitted. There is always a small chance that the CRC itself would be corrupted in the process of being sent, or that the data in the frame is corrupted in such a way that it generates the same CRC as the correct data. The chance of this duplication actually happening in practice is vanishingly small. Furthermore, as we move up the network layers, you'll see that almost all the layers have their own error checking procedures, so if something is corrupt in the frame, the error will be found.

Getting Data to Its Destination

As you may have noticed, there is a source and destination address in the frame. Every Ethernet device on a network has a unique identifying address called a *hardware address*, or *MAC address*. This address is 48 bits long and is assigned by the manufacturer of the network device. It is *the* defining address for the basis of Ethernet network communications. You can usually find the address for your network hardware silk-screened onto the network card or labeled on the outside of the device. The address is most likely displayed as a six-part hex number, sometimes separated by colons. For example, the address of the PowerBook I'm using to type this is

Part
I

Ch
2

    00 00 94 7b 75 7f

There doesn't exist, anywhere, an Ethernet device with the same address. This address is mine and mine alone. The first three segments of the address identify the manufacturer. Some common manufacturers and their corresponding identifiers are

    00608C 3Com
    080007 Apple
    00805F Compaq
    08005A IBM
    00AA00 Intel
    00004C NEC
    00000F NeXT
    080079 Silicon Graphics
    0080F3 Sun

When data is transmitted over the Ethernet, it travels along the line, and the individual network devices examine each frame as it passes. If a device's hardware address matches the destination address on the frame, the network device reads the rest of the information from the frame and passes the information up through the network layers so that it can be processed by whatever software is appropriate. If you have an Ethernet card in your computer, you should easily be able to determine your hardware address.

Windows 95/98 users, choose Run from your Start menu, and then type **\winipcfg.exe**. (If nothing happens, you can add the path C:\WINDOWS\winipcfg.exe.) You'll see a screen similar to the one shown in Figure 2.7 that shows you various information about your network configuration, including the hardware address.Macintosh owners can get similar information by going to their TCP/IP Control Panel and choosing Get Info from the File menu. You'll see a dialog box similar to the one shown in Figure 2.8.

FIGURE 2.7

The winipcfg program displays information about your computer's network settings, including the all-important hardware address.

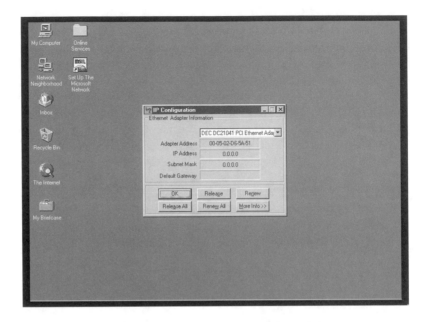

FIGURE 2.8

Macintosh users can obtain their computer's IP address by opening the TCP/IP Control Panel.

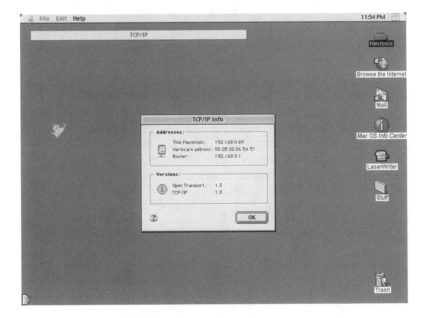

Lastly, Linux users can view their hardware address in the dmesg file that contains information about the system configuration as determined at boot-time. You'll see information that looks like this:

```
> grep "eth0" /var/log/dmesg
eth0: Intel EtherExpress Pro 10/100 at 0xe000, 00:A0:C9:1F:09:16, IRQ 9.
```

When Collisions Occur

As I mentioned earlier, there are special circumstances that can and do occur that the Data Link Layer must deal with cleanly. Collisions happen when frames of data are transmitted simultaneously on the network. Transmitting machines monitor the Ethernet line and send their frames only when they see that the line is inactive. Unfortunately, if more than one station sees the network as being inactive and both need to send data, it's likely they'll both send the data at the same time and cause a collision. Collisions are part of the design of Ethernet; they aren't indicative of an error in the network. They are a common occurrence on an Ethernet network and must be handled in a manner that reduces the likelihood that they'll reoccur.

Ethernet uses what is called a *backoff* algorithm to determine what to do when a collision takes place. The name backoff is descriptive of action that's taken to eliminate the problem. The devices that were involved in creating the collision back off from sending data and wait a random number of microseconds, and then attempt to retransmit their data.

Here's an example of a collision and the backoff algorithm in action:

Computer A transmits at the same time as Computer B, and a collision occurs. This process is shown in Figure 2.9. Both machines then back off from sending data for a random number of microseconds, in this case 10[mu] for A and 5us for B.

FIGURE 2.9

When computers send information packets simultaneously, a collision occurs. Then a backoff algorithm forces each to resend the packets after a random interval.

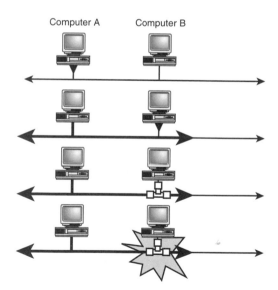

Computer A   Computer B

When Computer B's timeout backoff period expires, it retransmits its information. Computer A is still in a wait state. Finally, Computer A finishes waiting and sends its data, as seen in Figure 2.10.

FIGURE 2.10

After waiting a random number of microseconds, the computers resend their packets, which this time do not pose the risk of collision.

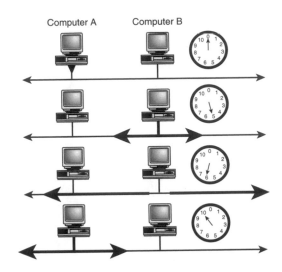

If consecutive collisions take place, the amount of time each device waits before retransmitting increases. If the failures continue, the frames may eventually be discarded, and it's left to the software at upper layers to deal with the error that has taken place.

Other Methods of Connecting

While Ethernet is the logical and most prevalent choice for wiring a local network, there are other types of connections you're probably already familiar with that are equally valid ways of connecting to a TCP/IP network. The two other Data Link methods we'll look at briefly are SLIP and PPP; both are commonly used to dial into a network from a remote station.

SLIP   *SLIP*, or *Serial Line Internet Protocol*, was designed specifically for transmitting TCP/IP data over serial lines. It's a simple protocol that defines a way of transmitting individual frames over a serial line. It does nothing more than define a start and stop sequence for each frame that's to be sent over the line. SLIP is not a very well-defined protocol and can be implemented in ways that are incompatible with other variations. The largest packet size is 1006 bytes, which is significantly smaller than the largest Ethernet packet. Because of its inability to adapt to other network protocols, SLIP has fallen out of favor in lieu of the more versatile PPP protocol.

PPP   *PPP*, *Point to Point Protocol*, provides services that reach far beyond SLIP. PPP is capable of providing a transport for essentially any network protocol, including our favorite: TCP/IP. These protocols can run simultaneously over the same link without interfering with each other. It's not uncommon for PPP servers to simultaneously transmit TCP/IP and protocols such as IPX and AppleTalk over a single connection. Because there's no set specification that a PPP server must carry certain protocols, it's likely that a server will support certain protocols that a client won't, and vice versa. All popular PPP clients, however, seem to support TCP/IP, which is, after all, the one we're interested in.

Besides being extremely flexible, PPP was also designed to make configuration as easy as possible. Configuration information can be stored on the PPP server and transmitted to the client at connection time. Depending on the implementation of the server and client, there may be nothing to configure on the client but a name, number, and password. PPP also contains provisions for *PAP*, or *Password Authentication Protocol*. This protocol enables user authentication to take place without the use of scripts that SLIP connections usually require.

Summary

There are other ways of connecting TCP/IP networks besides Ethernet and SLIP/PPP, but these two methods are the most common for end users. MacOS 8.x, Windows 95/98/NT, and Linux 5.x support PPP and Ethernet in their default shipping state.

We'll discuss a few of the alternate connection methods—Cable Modems, ADSL, and ISDN later—but for now Ethernet will suffice for illustration purposes.

Now that you understand the basis for communications on our network, it's time to begin implementing TCP/IP in the model.

The Network Layer

The Network Layer implements the "IP" in TCP/IP. The Internet Protocol allows packets to be routed across different types of hardware and Data Link Layers. It allows SLIP connections to talk to PPP connections and PPP connections to talk to Ethernet devices. The protocol does not take into account data reliability, ordering of data, or other necessities of networking. It provides an addressing scheme and a mechanism to fragment packets for transmission across networks that allow very limited frame sizes.

Each frame of information that's processed by this layer of the network is considered a separate and unique item. There is no concept of a continuous connection. The IP module takes data from the TCP module, applies the appropriate addressing information to the data, and delivers it to the Data Link Layer. The concept of a connection will be introduced later in the chapter in the Transport and Session Layers.

As data moves along a TCP/IP network that's comprised of several smaller networks, decisions must be made about the path that the data takes along its trip. The data will travel through devices called *Routers* or *Gateways* which provide the necessary links to the other networks. It's the responsibility of these devices to find the next logical step that the data takes on its journey (see Figure 2.11).

The IP protocol includes information in each packet that these gateways can use to select the route the data will take. Other useful information may be included with the data as well, such as timestamps and security information.

FIGURE 2.11

Three subnets are connected by a gateway.

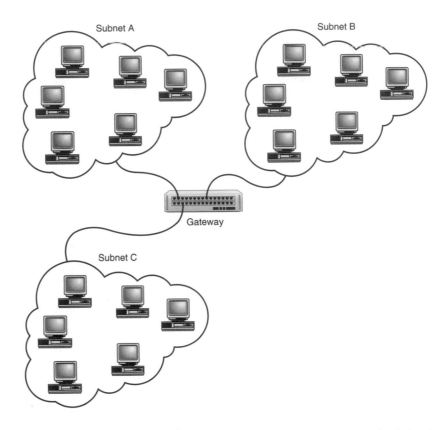

Included in the IP data is a parameter called the *Time To Live* or *TTL*. This is a time limit that is set for the data to reach its destination. As the data passes through each gateway, the Time To Live is reduced. When the time reaches zero, the data is discarded. Because an electrical signal cannot be destroyed, it's simply no longer transmitted to other networks, and its journey stops when the signals reach the network's termination. If the TTL did not exist, it would be possible for a packet to live forever, traveling in loops around a network.

Lastly, the IP module provides its own error checking with a *checksum* of the data it sends with each packet. A checksum is simply a numeric sum of the data that needs to be verified. If a receiving device, such as a remote computer or a gateway, notices that the checksum it calculates differs from the one that's contained in the frame, it will discard the frame.

IP Addressing

Addresses, which we'll discuss further in the next chapter, are currently 32 bits long and are commonly refereed to as *IP Addresses*. They are most commonly represented as four eight-bit numbers separated by periods. An example of such an address (courtesy, once again, of my PowerBook) is

140.254.85.2

It's possible for a single host to have multiple IP addresses for a single network connection. This capability is commonly called *virtual hosting* because the machine is acting as several virtual devices, although it is only one physical device. Similarly, it's also possible for a single host machine to have multiple real connections to a network, such as multiple Ethernet cards, each with a different IP address, or multiple IP addresses assigned to a single card. This practice is called *multihoming*. Usually, however, your machine will have one IP address. If it's connected to the Internet, it will have one IP address that's its very own IP address, and no other machine connected to the Internet anywhere in the world will have the same IP address. If your machine is not connected to the Internet, your IP address must still be unique among all the machines connected to your LAN (local area network).

Fragmentation

The IP module handles *fragmentation* of packets as it sees necessary. Although causing fragmentation seems like something that should be avoided, it's a common occurrence and is needed for TCP/IP to be effectively implemented across a variety of networks.

Fragmentation must take place as packets move from a network that allows large packet sizes to one that has a lower limit on the size of the data. Packets are split into a number of pieces that are flagged as being fragmented. When the fragmentation takes place, information about the source and destination addresses is copied to each of the newly created packets. Information is also stored with each packet that allows the receiving device to reassemble the fragmented packets into their original sequence. It's possible for data to be sent with a "Don't Fragment" flag set. In these cases, the data will be discarded before it's forced to be fragmented.

What Does an IP Packet Look Like?

Now that you have an idea of the basic services that the IP layer provides, let's take a look at how it stores this information. Each packet contains an *IP header* that stores the pieces of information we've just discussed. While there is no need to delve too deeply into this topic unless you're writing low-level TCP/IP services, it's useful to have an idea of just what information is being sent back and forth as computers communicate on the network.

The IP header contains the following fields, which we'll define below: Version, IHL, Type of Service, Total Length, Identification, Flags, Fragment Offset, Time To Live, Protocol, Header Checksum, Source Address, Destination Address, Options, and Padding (see Figure 2.12).

FIGURE 2.12

A graphical representation of an IP packet, as specified in RFC 0791.

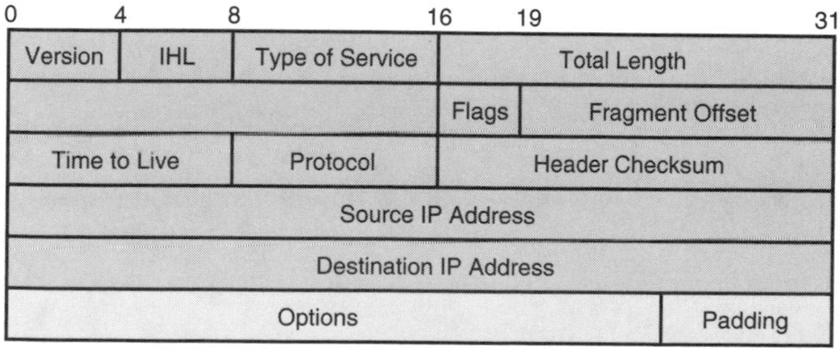

- Version—This field provides information about the version of IP that's being used to build the packet. The current standard is IP version 4. Later in the book, I'll discuss the upcoming IP v.6 and the benefits it offers over the current standard.
- IHL—This number is the total length of the header in 4 byte units. The minimum length of an IP header is 5, or a total of 20 bytes.
- Type of Service—This field provides a request for a certain quality of transmission. Depending on the type of network that the data is traveling through, this field may be used or ignored. For example, with the appropriate settings in this field, requests for qualities such as High Throughput or High Reliability can be made.
- Total Length—The length of the entire packet being transmitted.
- Identification—Used in reassembly of fragmented packets.
- Flags—These flags are used to set if a packet is part of a fragment or if it can be fragmented at all.
- Time to Live—As I mentioned earlier, this byte is our "timeout" value for a packet. It's a single byte that stores a number in seconds. As each device, such as a gateway, passes the packet, it must decrease this value by at least one.
- Protocol—The field specifies what protocol was used in the data portions of the packet. We'll look at TCP and UDP, although there are others.
- Header Checksum—Once again, this number provides a check to make sure that the information contained in the header is still intact.
- Source/Destination Address—These digits are our 32-bit IP addresses to identify our machines across different network segments.
- Options—Options can carry a variety of data, including routing information. It's possible to record the route a packet takes as it travels across networks by setting an option in this field.
- Padding—The IP header must be evenly divisible by 4 bytes (32 bits). Zeros are "padded" onto the end of the header to ensure that the header meets this condition.

Communication Problems

The IP layer provides a basic mechanism for allowing information about errors and routing to be communicated between devices. This capability is called *ICMP*, or the *Internet Control Message Protocol*.

If a gateway can't forward a packet to its destination network, or for some reason a packet can't reach its destination, an ICMP message may be sent. The device making this determination discards the packet and returns an ICMP message to the source. Usually, the machine making this decision is a router or gateway. Gateways may also send ICMP messages to hosts to inform them of a shorter route they can use to send data to their destination. In the event of an error, a typical ICMP message that might be sent is "Destination Unreachable"—or, if the Time To Live for a packet expires, a "Time Exceeded" message may be sent. This capability does not, however, ensure reliable communications. There is no guarantee that every error that occurs will be reported with a corresponding ICMP message.. It's left to the next layer to provide a method for ensuring that data reaches its destination in its original form.

From a structure standpoint, ICMP consists of an IP header, like any other IP packet. The data portion of the packet consists of several ICMP fields that are used to specify a message type, details about the message, and a checksum for the ICMP data itself.

There are a total of eight different messages that can be sent, each giving different information related to the network "condition":

- Destination Unreachable—This message may be sent if a gateway cannot determine the route data needs to take to reach its destination. A remote host may also invoke it if it can't accept incoming data.

- Time Exceeded—If the Time To Live field has been reduced to zero, a gateway sends this message to the host that originated the packet. The message may also be sent by a receiving device if portions of a fragmented packet have not arrived within the Time To Live of the packet.v

- Parameter Problem—If there is a problem with the IP header in a packet, this message may be sent along with information that identifies where in the header the error occurred.

- Source Quench—This message is sent from a gateway or host to a machine that's sending packets faster than they can be processed. It asks the source machine to slow down its transmission to prevent packets from being discarded.

- Redirect—The redirect message is sent to a host by a gateway if it detects that there's a shorter path to the destination network other than by way of itself.

- Echo—A useful message that, much later, we'll use to help diagnose network problems, the echo message is sent to a specified address, which then replies with an "Echo Reply" ICMP message. The reply can be used to determine information about the state of the network.

- TimeStamp—Similar to the Echo, the sender sends a timestamped message to a destination. The destination adds a "received" timestamp to the message and sends it back. As it travels back, gateways change a "Transmit" timestamp to indicate the length of time it spent returning.

- Information Request—Used by a source machine to request information about network of the packet.

Using Ping to Send an ICMP Request   To see a quick demo of ICMP in action, we can use the *ping* program to send an echo request to a remote computer. Assuming you have an active connection (a dial-in Internet connection is fine), you can use ping to bounce a signal off a remote computer much like the sonar signal for which the program gets its name.

Bring up a command window on your Windows 95/98/NT machine, or a shell window on a UNIX-based system. Macintosh owners, unfortunately, don't have access to a built-in ping program with the supplied system software.

How Do You Use Ping from A Macintosh?

If you're using a Macintosh and want to use ping, take a look at IPNetMonitor from Sustainable
Softworks:

`http://www.sustworks.com/`

IPNetMonitor will provide several of the network services available natively on other platforms we'll be
looking at later in the book. The software provides a very nice interface to traditionally command-line
applications.

Once you've opened a command/shell window, type the following:

`>ping 140.254.85.75`

This command will result in ICMP echo request packets being sent to the address
140.254.85.75. We can expect, barring failure of the network, to see a response from the remote
machine:

```
PING 140.254.85.75 (140.254.85.75): 56 data bytes
64 bytes from 140.254.85.75: icmp_seq=0 ttl=255 time=0.8 ms
64 bytes from 140.254.85.75: icmp_seq=1 ttl=255 time=0.8 ms
64 bytes from 140.254.85.75: icmp_seq=2 ttl=255 time=0.6 ms
64 bytes from 140.254.85.75: icmp_seq=3 ttl=255 time=0.7 ms
64 bytes from 140.254.85.75: icmp_seq=4 ttl=255 time=0.7 ms
— 140.254.85.75 ping statistics —
5 packets transmitted, 5 packets received, 0% packet loss
round-trip min/avg/max = 0.6/0.7/0.8 ms
```

Here you can see some of the information we've been discussing displayed in a readable format. Your screen may look slightly different, depending on the version of ping, and whether
you're using Windows or Linux. The information will be similar, however. In this example, our
computer has sent five echo request ICMP messages to the machine 140.254.85.75 and has
received a reply from each message that was sent. The packet sequence numbers are listed in
the `icmp_seq=` portion of the display. As you can see, all of our packets were received, and
received in the appropriate order. Also displayed is the Time To Live of each packet (TTL). The
Time to Live of all the replies we received is 255; this is the maximum possible TTL that can
exist. This number is high because the machine I'm pinging is located on the same network as
my client computer, so no gateways have been passed through, and the value has not been
decremented at all. You can also see that response time is a fraction of a millisecond, another
indication that I'm about 15 feet from the machine I am pinging. When you perform this test
from your machine, you'll see very different values, which will indicate your relative distance,
network-wise, from the destination machine. If I ping a different machine, this time located on
the other side of the city from my local client, you can see the difference.

```
PING 204.210.240.191 (204.210.240.191): 56 data bytes
64 bytes from 204.210.240.191: icmp_seq=0 ttl=59 time=160.3 ms
64 bytes from 204.210.240.191: icmp_seq=1 ttl=59 time=10.0 ms
64 bytes from 204.210.240.191: icmp_seq=2 ttl=59 time=11.4 ms
64 bytes from 204.210.240.191: icmp_seq=3 ttl=59 time=12.2 ms
64 bytes from 204.210.240.191: icmp_seq=4 ttl=59 time=12.2 ms
— 204.210.240.191 ping statistics —
5 packets transmitted, 5 packets received, 0% packet loss
round-trip min/avg/max = 10.0/41.2/160.3 ms
```

Now, the Time To Live has obviously been reduced, and the response time is greatly increased. The network connection still appears to be good, as the icmp_seq value is in order, and there is 0 percent packet loss on the network. Later in the book, we'll revisit ping and use it to help diagnose problems that may exist on TCP/IP networks.

Summary

With the Internet Protocol providing a method of addressing and transmitting information across networks, and the ICMP portion of the layer providing status information about the network, you should understand the basic addressing and messaging of the TCP/IP network. Now we add the TCP to our picture with the Transport Layer.

Part

I

Ch

2

TCP/UDP and the Transport Layer

Although we're discussing TCP/IP networks, let's first take a look at the transport protocol known as *UDP*, or *User Datagram Protocol*. UDP is important because it's used extensively on TCP/IP networks and is generally considered part of the TCP/IP protocol. The primary difference between UDP and TCP is that UDP does not necessarily provide reliable data transmission. In fact, there's no guarantee by the protocol that data will even arrive at its destination. Although this may seem like a strange "requirement" for a protocol, it's actually quite useful. When the goal of a program is to transmit as much information as quickly as possible, where any given piece of the data is relatively unimportant, UDP is used. Applications that transmit video, for example, are interested in getting the video stream to its destination as quickly as it can. It doesn't matter if a pixel or two are scrambled, just that the video is as smooth and fluid as possible. This sort of communication is also used in many Internet games. When playing a multiplayer game over the Internet, it's unlikely that every single piece of position information is necessary for the game to function properly; therefore, data is sent out as quickly as possible, and what doesn't arrive in its original form is discarded. Many programs will use a separate TCP connection as well as a UDP connection. Important status information is sent along the reliable TCP connection, while the main data stream is sent via UDP (see Figure 2.13).

The purpose of TCP is to provide data transmission that can be considered reliable and to maintain a virtual connection between devices or services that are "speaking" to each other. TCP is responsible for data recovery in the event that packets are received out of sequence, lost, or otherwise corrupted during delivery. It accomplishes this recovery by providing a sequence number with each packet that it sends. Remember that the lower Network Layer treats every packet like a separate unit; therefore, it's possible for packets to be sent along completely different routes, even though they're all part of the same message. This routing is very similar to how the Network Layer handles fragmenting and reassembling packets, only at one level higher. To ensure that data has been received correctly, TCP requires that an acknowledgement, called an ACK, be received from the destination machine upon successfully receiving the data. If the appropriate ACK is not received within a certain time limit, the packet is retransmitted. If the network is congested, this retransmission leads to duplicate packets being sent. The receiving machine, however, uses the sequence number of the packet to determine if it is a duplicate and discards it if necessary.

FIGURE 2.13

UDP versus TCP: packets sent singly and reliably (left) or fast with data loss (right).

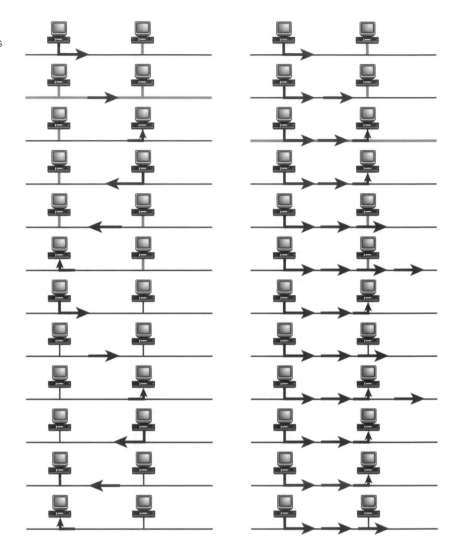

TCP also allows the receiver to specify the amount of data it wants sent to it. By specifying acceptable sequence numbers after the last received sequence, the sender can be informed that the receiver is only capable of receiving a very specific set of data, and will not blindly send data and then wait for acknowledgement.

TCP and UDP introduce the concept of *ports*. A port is a virtual outlet that can be opened on a network device. Ports are generally predetermined and are related to a particular service that's running on a machine. Some common ports, and the services that run on them, are listed here:

FTP	21 and 20
telnet	23
SMTP	25

| http | 80 |
| POP3 | 110 |

By specifying ports and including port numbers with TCP/UDP data, the process of *multiplexing* is achieved. Multiplexing allows multiple network connections to take place simultaneously (see Figure 2.14).

FIGURE 2.14

Multiplexing is a single computer connecting to multiple sources.

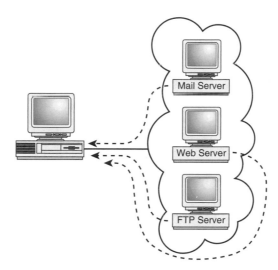

The port numbers, along with the source and destination addresses for the data, determine a *socket*. Each machine that communicates using TCP will open a socket to the receiving machine. Once the sockets are connected, the machines may speak across the connection reliably. A single machine may open multiple sockets and handle many incoming or outgoing connections at once.

During the lifetime of a connection, there are several states that the communicating devices can be in. TCP controls these states and makes the information available to the upper network layer in case it wants to act based on the status of the connection.

The states that can exist, as defined in the TCP RFC 793, are as follows:

LISTEN—A device is "listening" for a connection request from a remote device.

SYN-SENT—A connection request has been sent, and the device is waiting for a corresponding acknowledgement.

SYN-RECEIVED—The corresponding request has been returned, and the device is now waiting for a final confirmation of the connection.

ESTABLISHED—A connection exists, and the data can be transmitted and received reliably.

FIN-WAIT-1—The device is waiting for a request that the connection be terminated or acknowledgement that its request for termination has been received.

FIN-WAIT-2—The device is waiting for connection termination request from the remote device.

CLOSE-WAIT—The device is waiting for a connection termination request from the upper network layer.

CLOSING—The device is waiting for connection termination acknowledgement from the remote user.

LAST-ACK—The device is waiting for the final acknowledgement of connection termination from the remote machine.

TIME-WAIT—The device is waiting for a timeout period to be sure that the remote device has received its acknowledgement of connection termination.

CLOSED—There is no connection.

As you can see, the majority of the states are related to the closing of a connection. While this preponderance may seem a little strange, it's particularly important that machines know when a connection is closed so they can free the resources (memory, server processes) that a particular connection may have been using. There's a common type of hacking attack on TCP/IP-based servers called "Denial of Service" attacks. These attacks exploit the failure of some TCP/IP implementations to correctly detect when a connection is finished. The attacker will open many simultaneous connections to a given machine, and then close them without going through the appropriate messaging procedure. While there is generally some global timeout period where a machine will determine that a port is no longer connected, it's possible to open so many ports and leave them sitting in a FIN-WAIT state that the server slows to a standstill. All connections come at a price of CPU time and memory; with enough connections open at a time, these resources can be depleted, and the attackers can shut down a server remotely. It should thus be obvious that it's extremely undesirable for well-intentioned programs to inadvertently cause similar attacks—thus, the extremely detailed procedures of closing connections.

Using Netstat to See Connections

On Windows and Linux clients, you can use the program *netstat* to get a snapshot of the current state of connections on the machine. This state includes outgoing as well as incoming connections—any TCP/IP traffic that's currently being processed by the computer. Netstat will become useful later on to help determine network problems, but for now, it should let you see how the machine monitors the state of each connection. Macintosh users will need to refer to IPNetMonitor's Monitor function in order to see similar data. In a command or shell window, type the following:

```
>netstat
```

(Windows users must type **C:\WINDOWS\netstat.exe** in place of netstat.)

For example, I'm running netstat on the main campus Web server. Hopefully, we'll see some traffic as Web browsers access the pages.

```
Active Internet connections
Proto Recv-Q Send-Q  Local Address           Foreign Address          (state)
tcp        0      0  leviathan.80            207.224.67.124.1070      SYN_RCVD
tcp        0      0  leviathan.80            intrance.ag.ohio.2302    ESTABLISHED
tcp        0      0  leviathan.80            intrance.ag.ohio.2301    ESTABLISHED
tcp        0      0  leviathan.80            intrance.ag.ohio.2297    FIN_WAIT_2
tcp        0      0  leviathan.80            usr4-09.mor.nj.w.1438    ESTABLISHED
tcp        0      0  leviathan.80            usr4-09.mor.nj.w.1437    ESTABLISHED
tcp        0      0  leviathan.80            usr4-09.mor.nj.w.1436    ESTABLISHED
tcp        0      0  leviathan.80            usr4-09.mor.nj.w.1435    ESTABLISHED
tcp        0      0  leviathan.80            usr4-09.mor.nj.w.1434    TIME_WAIT
tcp        0   1532  leviathan.80            208.11.185.5.1213        ESTABLISHED
tcp        0   4096  leviathan.80            208.11.185.5.1212        ESTABLISHED
tcp        0    158  leviathan.23            dub240191.columb.61180   ESTABLISHED
tcp        0      0  leviathan.80            208.11.185.5.1211        TIME_WAIT
tcp        0      0  leviathan.80            ppp-207-214-180-.1082    FIN_WAIT_2
tcp        0      0  leviathan.80            ppp-207-214-180-.1081    FIN_WAIT_2
tcp        0      0  leviathan.80            ppp-207-214-180-.1080    FIN_WAIT_2
tcp        0      0  leviathan.80            ppp-207-214-180-.1079    FIN_WAIT_1
```

Yep, there's a bit of traffic on the system. (This listing represents about a tenth of the total number of connections that were online.) In the column labeled "Local Address," you can see the name of the receiving machine (leviathan) followed by the port number that the remote (Foreign Address) computer is speaking to. In all cases but one (a telnet connection), they're connected to port 80, which is the http Web server port. In the column labeled state, we can see the different connection states of the machines, precisely as they were defined above. Because Web connections are rapidly changing, if we were to rerun netstat, we would get an entirely different display.

Before moving on, let's take a look at the TCP header format as we did with the IP layer. By seeing the amount of data that's transmitted for each layer of the network model, you should begin to gain an appreciation for the amount of information that each layer must process and decode. It's also interesting to see how much "extraneous" data is sent with every packet that travels over the network.

A TCP packet consists of the following information: Source Port, Destination Port, Sequence Number, Acknowledgement Number, Data Offset, Reserved, URG/ACK/PSH/RST/SYN/FIN, Window, Checksum, Urgent Pointer, Options, and Padding, as shown in Figure 2.15.

- ■ Source Port—A 16-bit number that specifies the port that the data is coming from. When the receiving machine replies, it will use this as the destination port for the reply.
- ■ Destination Port—The port number on the receiving device that the data is intended for.
- ■ Sequence Number—Specifies in what order a particular packet belongs. Used for arranging out of sequence packets and removing duplicates.
- ■ Acknowledgement Number—Identifies the sequence number expected next.
- ■ Data Offset—Specifies where the data begins and the header ends.

Part
I

Ch
2

■ Reserved—No current use.

■ URG/ACK/PSH/RST/SYN/FIN—Single bit flags set to indicate certain conditions that are present in the connection:

- URG: Data contained in the urgent field is significant and shouldn't be ignored.
- ACK: Data contained in the Acknowledgement field is significant and shouldn't be ignored.
- PSH: Push.
- RST: Resets the connection.
- SYN: Synchronize sequence numbers.
- FIN: No more data from sender.

■ Window—Defines the amount of data that the sender will receive.

■ Checksum—Yet another check for correctness in the data. Notice that at each level, a separate error check exists.

■ Urgent pointer—Identifies data that should be considered urgent.

■ Options—The options can be used to specify extra information about the TCP connection.

■ Padding—Functions the same as in the IP header. It's used to fill out the TCP header so that it's is an even multiple of 4 bytes (32 bits).

FIGURE 2.15

This graphical representation shows a TCP/IP packet as specified in RFC 793.

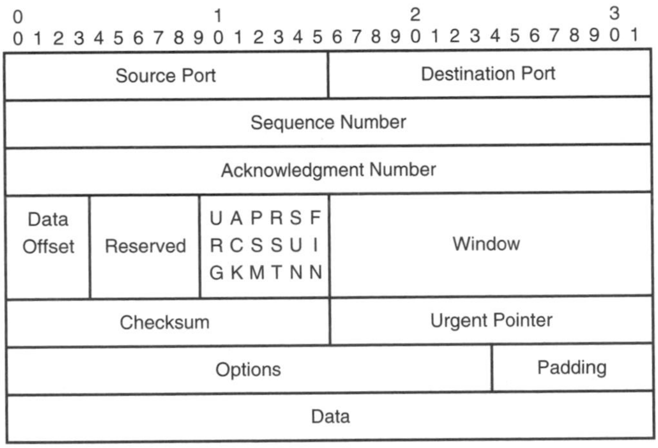

The TCP header format as shown in RFC0793

Summary

Before we continue with the next layer, I'd like to clarify a point that might seem a bit confusing. Each layer builds on the layers prior to it, and as it operates, it passes its own data down through the different layers. In the Data Link Layer, we defined a frame or packet and the data that it contained. Then we defined a packet of IP data and finally a packet of TCP data. These are *not* to be thought of as separate units. Each is processed by the underlying layer to fit into that layer's master plan. Think of it as being similar to the little dolls that fit inside one another, as shown in Figure 2.16.

FIGURE 2.16
Each protocol fits into the data structure of the layer beneath it.

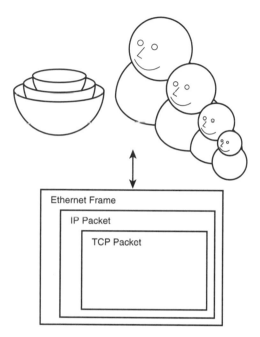

Ethernet Frame
IP Packet
TCP Packet

The TCP packet information is placed inside the IP packet, which, in turn, fits inside the Ethernet frame. The final piece of TCP/IP information that's transmitted (over an Ethernet network) is an Ethernet frame from the Data Link Layer. Everything else is squeezed into this frame (or, more likely, into multiple frames). I hope this analogy helps clarify the relationship of the layers to each other and shows how they independently carry out their own function without needing to know too much about the layers that are underneath them.

TCP/The Session Layer

As we defined earlier, the Session Layer is responsible for maintaining point-to-point communications within the network model. TCP provides this connection functionality in the form of sockets, as we've seen from the last layer. Two sockets connect to provide our virtual circuit between two devices, and thus a session. This structure is an example of how it is sometimes difficult to fully expand a network standard to the OSI Network Model. In the case of TCP/IP, TCP extends across both the Transport Layer and the Session Layer, providing a full range of services. We've already covered TCP and its capabilities, so we've inadvertently covered the Session Layer without even knowing it. That was rather quick and painless, wasn't it?

Now we're ready to move on to the layer that's very close to the top of the network model. We're no longer worried about packets, headers, and data reliability. Instead, our concern is deciding what sort of language we'll be using to communicate over our reliable TCP/IP connections.

Speaking in the Presentation Layer

The Presentation Layer is simple to understand but provides so many services that it may be a bit surprising how much variation exists in this layer. Continuing our automobile analogy from Chapter 1, when you take your car to a mechanic, you need to be able to effectively communicate with the mechanic about what's wrong with your vehicle. Similarly, if you're talking about computers with your co-workers, you employ a different set of rules to successfully communicate with them. You use the right language and vocabulary for the right job. The Presentation Layer does exactly the same thing. It defines the languages that computer programs will use to communicate when they're speaking across a network.

If you have email, you may have seen acronyms such as POP or SMTP server in your configuration files. These are essentially languages, or TCP/IP protocols, that your computer can speak to send and receive electronic mail information to and from other machines. Each of these languages usually operates on a uniquely defined port number, a few of which we saw defined in the transport layer. We'll have an in-depth look at the actual communications process that exists for these applications to talk to one another later in Chapter 6. Understanding the vocabulary of these "languages" can help us diagnose problems in client software and provide insight to some of the error messages you may see pop up from time to time. For now, here are some of the common presentation layer protocols, the ports they run on, and a general description of what they do:

FTP	20/21	File Transfer Protocol, used to exchange files with remote machines.
Telnet	23	Provides a terminal connection to a remote system.
SMTP	25	Handles sending and storing email.
Gopher	70	The menu-driven precursor to the WWW.
HTTP	80	The World Wide Web.
POP3	110	Remote access to email.
IMAP	143	Another remote email access method.

Each of these Presentation Layer protocols speaks a different language, and there are hundreds of others. If you begin TCP/IP programming, you can develop your own services and run them off of your own port numbers. You need to make sure that you aren't using a preassigned port and that your "language" is defined well enough that client software can be written to take advantage of the services it provides.

Summary

When working with protocols running under the Presentation Layer, we can breathe a sigh of relief because we have underlying reliable TCP/IP connection running underneath, and there is no need to worry about data sequencing, duplicate packets, or any of the other problems we've discussed. They're all handled transparently by the underlying layers. I find it fascinating that you can talk to email servers and Web servers with the knowledge of just a few simple commands. When you see what actually goes on behind the scenes of a Web browser, you'll be surprised to see just how simple the networking portion of the World Wide Web really is.

The Application Layer

Finally, we reach the top of the network model with TCP/IP fully implemented underneath. The Application Layer provides the friendly face we're used to seeing when we use our computers. Programs running in the Application Layer will usually extend into the Presentation Layer as well. They implement both the user interface and the language that the interface must translate its data into in order to speak on the network. On some operating systems, the OS may provide key features, such as the ability to speak to email servers, and so on. In cases such as this, all the Application Layer is used for is creating "added value" and a useable interface that can talk to the OS-supplied services.

You're undoubtedly familiar with TCP/IP applications such as Netscape, Eudora, Outlook Express, and others. These applications are rather well known and are not very exciting to discuss in terms of how they handle TCP/IP. Instead of using this space to discuss Web browsers or the like, I'd rather use this space to introduce some applications you may not have heard of, which I find to be both fun and useful. All of these applications use TCP/IP to accomplish their network communications and provide a good demonstration that there's a great deal more to a TCP/IP network than the World Wide Web. With the hype surrounding the Web, it's easy to overlook many of the other services that TCP/IP applications have to offer. All of these applications are available to download for free but may require you to pay under the shareware concept if you find them useful. They're applications I've found to be useful and have survived more than a few days without being erased from my hard drive. This is a good time to take a break, download a few of these programs, and enjoy yourself.

ICQ

The first program, which is a definite must-have for anyone who uses the Internet for communications, is called ICQ (I Seek You) by Mirabilis Communications. The ICQ software is currently free and is available for Windows, Macintosh, and UNIX machines. There's also a Java client that will run anywhere Java runs. Upon installing the software, you'll be given a unique ICQ number that identifies you on the Internet. This number is equivalent to your email address in that it can be used by anyone, anywhere, to communicate with you over the network. ICQ allows you to build a list of friends who also are registered with the ICQ service and chat with them online. It's unique in that you can see, in real-time, when people on your list log into the network, as their names change from red to green (see Figure 2.17).

FIGURE 2.17

ICQ in action; the system will let me know when Crew Man logs on and other users can see I'm available.

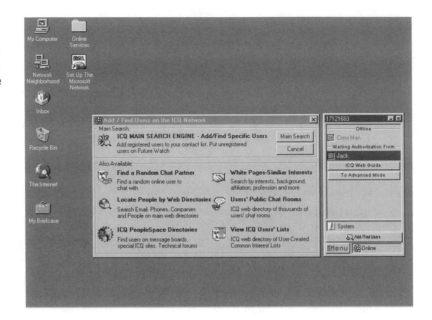

Once connected, you can chat directly with fellow users and exchange files with them. You can even leave messages for friends who are offline that will be displayed when they next log in. Even better, you can install ICQ on multiple machines and activate your account from whatever machine you're on. This allows your friends to reach you from your single ICQ number, no matter where you're logged onto the Internet. You have complete control over whether a person can see you're online, or even if a person can add your address to their list of friends. For private online chatting and messaging, ICQ is well worth a download.

You can check out ICQ at:

http://www.mirabilis.com/

Hotline

Another fun social Internet application is Hotline. Hotline is the '90s Internet equivalent of the '80s bulletin board. The software provides an instant connection to hundreds of Hotline servers throughout the Internet. Everything is simply a matter of point and click. Available servers, with a display of the information they contain, are listed automatically by clicking on a tracker button. Hotline bulletin boards have online news, which you can post and read, online chatting, and file transfers (see Figure 2.18).

All actions are fully multithreaded, fast, and performed without ever touching a single key. Hotline was designed and programmed for the Macintosh computer systems; however, it also exists in a Windows version and an unsupported UNIX client. Because it has Macintosh origins, Hotline sites are still mainly oriented towards Mac users, but a growing number of servers dedicated to other operating systems exist.

FIGURE 2.18
The Hotline client software, MacOS version.

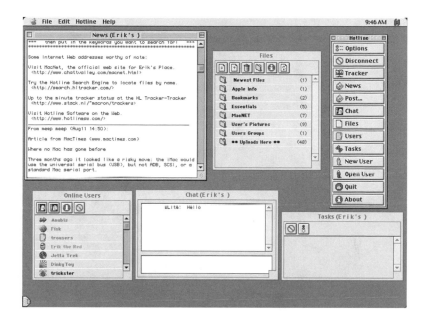

Hotline is available from:

`http://www.hotlinesw.com/`

If you want to run a Hotline server, you can also download the server software from the same location. Although we won't be covering Hotline servers in the scope of this book, you'll find that you can be serving your own Hotline bulletin board within minutes of downloading the software.

The Palace

Continuing our theme of TCP/IP software for group collaboration, the Palace is a completely fun piece of groupware. You enter a virtual Palace in which you can move from room to room and chat with other occupants of the Palace. The users appear as cartoon-like avatars, and it's just plain fun to play around with the software (see Figure 2.19).

The Palace is available for Windows, Macintosh, and Java based clients at this address:

`http://www.thepalace.com/`

The CDDB

The CD database (CDDB) is yet another interesting application of shared cross-platform data. It's a collection of CD information, such as CD Titles, song titles, and artists. The fun starts when you download a CDDB-compliant CD player for your computer system. If you use a CDDB client to play a CD in your computer, it will identify the CD and show you all the pertinent information about the CD (see Figure 2.20).

FIGURE 2.19

The Palace provides Internet chat in a virtual reality setting.

FIGURE 2.20

TitleTrack 1.5, by Riversong InterActive, is an example of a Mac OS CD player that accesses the CDDB.

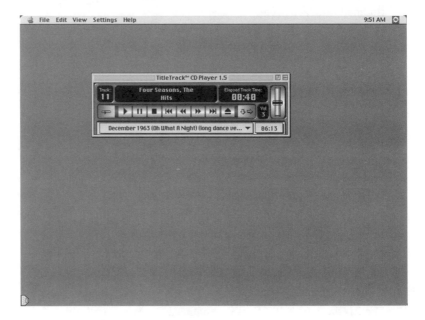

The software is free or shareware, and is available for Macintosh, UNIX, and Windows clients. Try it out on your system, and forget about the days of having to remember what track your favorite song is on.

http://www.cddb.com/

Next, let's move on to some "serious" fun...

PointCast

With the recent Browser Wars over push technologies, it's hard to believe that a company other than Microsoft and Netscape could possibly have the upper hand in the battle to send information directly to user's desktops. If you're unfamiliar with push technology, the idea is that the user doesn't need to interact with the program to have new and useful data downloaded to their computer. PointCast downloads up-to-date weather maps, stock quotes, headline news, and so on to your desktop without disrupting your work or requiring you to start up a Web browser. The software will also act as a screen saver and flash news headlines on your screen when it's asleep (see Figure 2.21). It's nice to see that despite the wars being waged by the big boys of the browser world, a small company can still make a product that actually delivers on push technology.

Part
I

Ch
2

FIGURE 2.21
PointCast displays weather information for cities around the world.

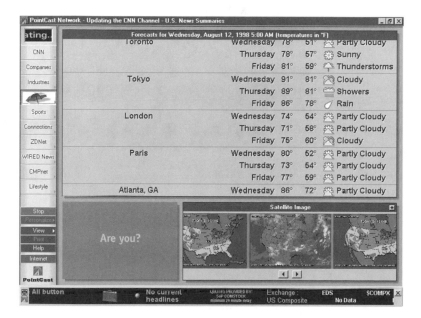

PointCast is free, exists in Macintosh and Windows versions, and is available from:

`http://www.pointcast.com/`

VNC

Have you ever wished you could control your work computer from home? There are a number of commercial packages that accomplish this, but the licensing fees for installing them on more than a few computers could be expensive. There's an entirely free alternative called VNC, or Virtual Network Computing, from Olivetti Research Laboratory. The VNC is a cross-platform solution that allows you to control remote stations from within a window on your local computer. It lets you control your Linux or NT server from your 95/98 machine or Macintosh. You can collaborate with remote sites by allowing multiple people to share a screen at once (see

Figure 2.22). This package is especially useful for UNIX machines in that it allows multiple desktops to exist and be shared from a single machine. If you're using a software package on UNIX, this can provide a true thin-client environment that is significantly faster than using X Window.

FIGURE 2.22

VNC is being used under Windows 95 to control a remote Linux computer.

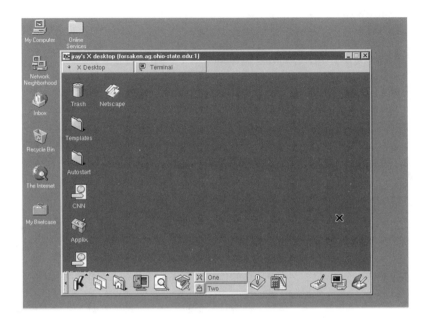

UNIX, Macintosh (client only), Windows, Java (client only), and source code for the software is available from

`http://www.orl.co.uk/vnc/index.html`

If you have multiple computers you need to control, or a single monitor you must share between multiple computers, this will make your life much easier.

Java

While Java is not exactly a program or protocol, it provides a wealth of networking capabilities to the programmer that enables him or her to quickly create unique TCP/IP applications. These applications can then be easily made available over the Web. If you're interested in writing network software, Java is an excellent place to start.

Developed by Sun Microsystems, Java has been ported to every platform imaginable. If you have a recent Web browser, you are already capable of running Java applications. Point your browser to this location and take a look at vast amount of network-enabled Java software:

`http://www.gamelan.com/`

Quake

I can't possibly close the discussion of the Application Layer without mentioning Quake. Quake, and its sequel, Quake 2, are multiplayer network games in which players either hunt each other down in a dungeon-like setting or cooperate to escape from a variety of monsters. There is no real redeeming value of Quake, except that it's extremely fun to fight your co-workers in a virtual battle to a virtual death. You can play quake with friends on your local network or over a TCP/IP network with an opponent located on the other side of the planet.

Quake is a commercial package but is available in a level-limited version for Windows, Macintosh, and UNIX computers at

`http://www.idsoftware.com/`

Part

I

Ch

2

Moving Forward

While you're trying out these software packages, be aware that they're using TCP/IP to accomplish all of their networking. Be sure to take time to appreciate all of the different network layers as they work together to build up to this end user experience. After all, you're here to learn, be sure not to enjoy yourself too much!

The preceding discussion completes the OSI network model in relation to TCP/IP. You should now understand the components that make up TCP/IP, the services they provide, and how they accomplish their tasks. The next few chapters will expand on the ideas of addressing and routing, and put the concepts we've discussed so far into practice.

Other Information

Much of the information contained in this chapter is available in a series of highly technical papers called *RFC* (*Request For Comments*) documents. These are the actual, official specifications for the various protocols we've discussed and are not light reading. However, if you're interested in learning more about the topics we've discussed so far, check out the RFCs available at the following addresses. There are several mirrors of the RFCs online; these URLs happen to point to a mirror that is extremely close to me. If you have trouble connecting to these sources, perform a search for the RFC number. You'll have no problem locating hundreds of copies of this information.

Where Do RFCs Come from?

As the name Request For Comments might imply, these documents are the result of a public collaboration to define an Internet standard. RFCs are constantly changing and evolving as new features become necessary and are discussed and agreed upon. Adhering to these standards when implementing software that uses them is extremely important. RFCs allow protocols to expand to include functionality that end users need, not what companies think they need.

The Internet Protocol	RFC 0791 `http://www.cis.ohio-state.edu/htbin/rdc/rfc0791.html`
Internet Control Message Protocol	RFC 0792 `http://www.cis.ohio-state.edu/htbin/rfc/rdc792.html`
User Datagram Protocol	RFC 0768 `http://www.cis.ohio-state.edu/htbin/rfc/rfc0768.html`
Transmission Control Protocol	RFC 0793 `http://www.cis.ohio-state.edu/htbin/rfc/rfc0793.html`
SLIP	RFC 1055 `http://www.cis.ohio-state.edu/htbin/rfc/rfc1055.html`
PPP	RFC 1661 `http://www.cis.ohio-state.edu/htbin/rfc/rfc1661.html`
Host Requirements	RFC 1122 `http://www.cis.ohio-state.edu/htbin/rfc/rfc1122.html`
Host Requirements, Applications	RFC 1123 `http://www.cis.ohio-state.edu/htbin/rfc/rfc1123.html`

I will continue to provide "Other Information" links to RFCs and other useful information at the end of each chapter.

## CHAPTER 3

Exploring IP Addresses

by John Ray

In this chapter

Why IP Addresses? **52**

How the Hardware Address and IP Address Work Together **54**

DHCP **56**

Dial-In Connections **58**

How Can I Tell What Method of Assignment I'm Using? **58**

Subnets and the IP Address **60**

Hostnames and DNS **64**

Other Information Sources **72**

In Chapter 1, we discussed how the IP Layer uses your IP address to uniquely identify your computer across interconnected TCP/IP networks. This address is the most critical component of the software portion of a TCP/IP configuration. Without it, your machine cannot speak to other network devices, even if they're directly connected to the same wire your computer is on.

You may remember that at the Data Link Layer, there's also a hardware address that's assigned to your network device and also a unique number that's used to help data reach your computer. The relationship between the hardware address and the IP address is simple: The IP address is for locating your computer across any number of individual networks, across the Internet, from anywhere in the world. Gateways pass packets toward their destination based on the IP address. Not until the data arrives on the local network does the hardware address become important.

Why IP Addresses?

You may be wondering why you can't just use one address and make life easier. Let's give it a shot, using the hardware address as our "definitive" network address, and see what happens.

First of all, a sending machine does not have any knowledge of the hardware address of the remote machine; neither do the gateways that information must pass through to reach the destination. For the hardware address to be used as a definitive address, gateways would need to know where, geographically, different addresses existed. Because the hardware address is assigned by the manufacturer, and the manufacturer has no way to tell where a product will be sold or deployed, it's quite impossible to predict the physical location of a particular network device (see Figure 3.1).

Without that information, it's impossible to pass packets in the correct direction from the source. Communications would be impossible.

Now, how about using the IP address as our single address? This scheme, at first glance, might seem to work. The gateways know how to pass IP packets toward their destination based on the IP address. However, once the packet reaches its local network, there's a bit of a problem. Each machine would need to have IP addresses implemented at the data link layer for them to recognize packets that are intended for them. Great, you say, so the people who designed TCP/IP messed this all up. They should have talked to me first. You have a point, but there's still a drawback to this scheme. Think of what would happen under this system if two different machines had the same IP address on the network. Both machines would receive and process information as it came in (see Figure 3.2).

FIGURE 3.1

A gateway is trying to decide where to send data to machine 13 based on a hardware address.

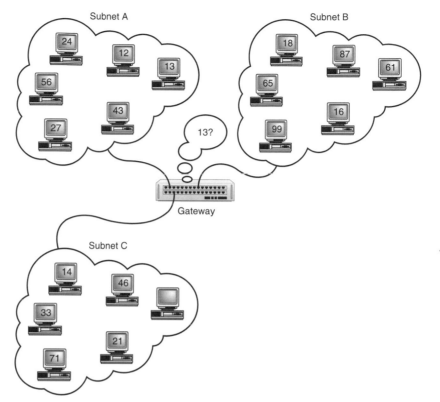

The result would be network traffic that's a big jumbled mess, with essentially no way of identifying the problem. That's because the only unique thing about the machines would be the IP address, and, in this case, even that wouldn't be unique. This would give a malicious network user (yes, they're out there, believe it or not) the ability to assign his or her IP address to be the same as your companies main server's address and bring the network to its knees. Although this might result in a few days of freedom from work, it would probably not be looked upon by many as a good thing. It's already possible for someone to assign a duplicate IP address on a network; however, it's also possible to identify the hardware address that the duplicate packets are coming from, identify the manufacturer of the device, and track down the culprit. It would be a guessing game if the hardware address weren't present.

Part

I

Ch

3

FIGURE 3.2
The gateway is still trying to decide where to send data based solely on an IP address.

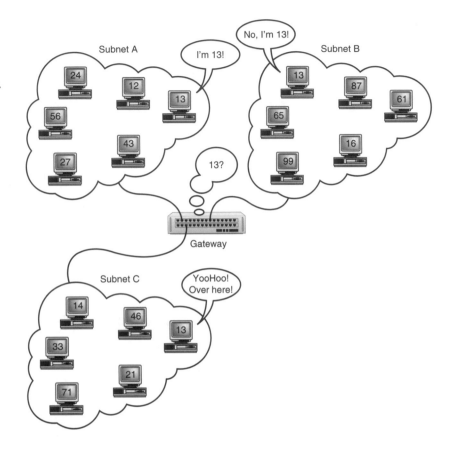

How the Hardware Address and IP Address Work Together

We'll get into further detail on how this works in Chapter 4, but for now, just the basic details of the relationship between the hardware and IP address will serve our purpose. The biggest question you should have right now is how does the hardware address come into play on the network?

As packets come into the network from the outside, they pass through a gateway for your local network. The gateway provides a translation service between the IP addresses and hardware addresses. It can do this by maintaining a list of all the hardware addresses on the network and their corresponding IP addresses, or by a more dynamic lookup process that will be discussed later. Individual machines on the network also maintain a similar list of information about machines that have recently talked to them, or that they have talked to. When an IP packet arrives and the hardware address of the destination is unknown, it's looked up from the table and added to the packet's header (see Figure 3.3).

FIGURE 3.3

A gateway fills in the hardware address to a packet as it goes by.

With the added hardware address information, the local network device with the corresponding hardware address can then receive the packet.

Where does my IP address come from?

If you have any sort of intranet or Internet access, while you're connected to the network, you have an IP address. If you have a Macintosh or Windows computer, you can display your IP address using the same techniques used to find your hardware address, as discussed in Chapter 2. Linux users can find out their address by reading their network interface configuration file, usually /etc/sysconfig/network-scripts/ifcfg-eth0.

Your IP address is assigned on a network-basis, meaning that other computers that are physically located on the same network with your machine probably have numbers that are similar to yours. The portions of your IP address that you share with your fellow network users determine your local network. This portion is your subnet, which we'll discuss very shortly. If you poke around enough, you can probably find a gateway device, which all the computers must eventually talk to in order to reach the outside world. If you investigate even further, you'll find that the numbers on the other side of the gateway are not as similar to yours. They're being used to define a network that's considered remote to your own.

Traditionally, IP addresses have been assigned to individual workstations by a network administrator. The administrator is responsible for being sure that unique addresses are assigned and tracked for each computer that he or she oversees. This, if done correctly, is a perfectly legitimate way of managing a network, but, as you'll soon see, is sometimes a bit more responsibility than a single person might want.

For the past three years, I've maintained a database of over 1,500 IP addresses spanning eight different buildings. When I took over the task, the database was located on a single computer, accessible by only one person: myself. Each building has its own network administrator, but they had to contact me to have an IP address assigned. As a result, some people got lazy and decided to maintain their own IP address database and assign numbers themselves. I gladly handed the responsibility over to them. Within six months, they came back, begging me to take over the database again. During that time period, they had assigned duplicate addresses and caused enough network conflicts to drive their users crazy. To keep track of the addresses they had assigned, they chose the revolutionary "back of an old envelope" database method to write changes and additions to the network. It then, once again, became my responsibility to reorganize the database and reintegrate their database with my own. I spent countless hours surveying their buildings, going from machine to machine to find out what IP addresses really existed in the buildings. Since that time, I've written an online IP database that allows the building administrators to connect and instantly request an unused IP address for a computer. This has eased my headaches considerably. If you'd like to take a look at this database, feel free. You won't be able to assign any addresses, but you can see the sheer volume of information that administrators have to manage.

`http://www.ag.ohio-state.edu/~jray/cgi-bin/ip.cgi`

As computers move between different users, and users move between different rooms, it becomes a real challenge to keep track of who and what is where. The usual result from this sort of confusion is that IP addresses are copied from machines and reused by people who have drastically different job titles than network administrator. As we discussed previously, it's possible to use hardware addresses to locate machines with duplicate addresses, but even with that information, it isn't something that could easily be considered fun or productive. Trust me.

DHCP

Recently, people have begun to use a different technique to assign IP addresses to client machines. This technique is called *dynamic assignment* and is handled by a machine running what is called a *DHCP (Dynamic Host Configuration Protocol)* server. DHCP Servers can be configured to automatically set up a user's TCP/IP configuration when they power up their computer. It also gives the administrator the power to remotely adjust the configuration of client machines. In a later chapter, we'll look at setting up a DHCP server. While this solution may seem ideal for a problem such as the one I described, there are also drawbacks, which, in my mind, make it an almost even toss-up between the two different assignment techniques.

The advantages of DHCP are obvious: No end-user configuration is required and no maintaining a huge unwieldy database of IP numbers. DHCP frees the network administrator from a time-consuming and rather non-productive task. However, it can also limit his or her ability to troubleshoot problems for individual users. Addresses are refreshed on the basis of a length of time called the DHCP *lease* time. Machines are leasing addresses from the server. Once the lease expires, the number can be reassigned to the same machine or can be assigned to a different computer. It's up to the client to attempt to renew its lease on the assigned IP address when half of the lease time has expired. Usually, the address can be leased indefinitely. If a lease expires and isn't renewed. it's possible for a DHCP server to serve different IP configurations to the same machine. This action creates a network where a network administrator doesn't have any convenient way of telling who has what address at a given point in time, other than a list of IP addresses and the hardware addresses they're assigned to.

While lease lengths and other options are controllable from the server, the more effort you put into controlling it, the closer you come to maintaining a database of static addresses. On a Windows network, a Windows NT server running DHCP can determine the individual machine's Name and store it with the leases, so you can look up who has leased what. However, this scheme is specific to the Windows platform, and it isn't the case for a generic DHCP server.

In an ideal world, it wouldn't matter what address a user had, as long as they could successfully access the network. This convenience, however, is not reality, as it becomes the network administrator's responsibility to be able to identify users who may be performing malicious actions on the network. A few years ago, a user on our network emailed the White House and threatened the life of one of the Presidential Pets. Secret Service members arrived at our network operations center and demanded that email be traced back to the person who sent it. Despite the absurdity of the situation, these things happen, and it's much more comfortable to have the information needed to trace down problems than to reply with an "I don't know."

How Does DHCP Do Its Job?

Because the machine that's being configured does not yet have an IP address, the DHCP server must communicate with it using the hardware address, as shown in Figure 3.4. The first step (a) is for the client to send a DHCP request to the network. This packet is broadcast to the network (b), and is recognized by the DHCP Server as a DHCP Discover packet. Upon receiving a request, the DHCP server will offer an address (d) to the client computer. The server sends a packet back to the hardware address contained in the original request. The Offer packet from the DHCP server contains an available IP address that the computer can use. The client now must respond (e) to the DHCP server and request to use the offered address. First, it assigns the offered address to its network device to make life a bit easier (see Figure 3.4).

The DHCP server then has the option of acknowledging the request or denying it. If the request is denied, the client must start the process over again. This process is instantaneous from the point of view of the user.

There are other methods of assigning an IP address that you may run across, such as BOOTP (Boot Protocol), but the modern standard is DHCP. DHCP is very similar to BOOTP and, in fact, is an extension of the original BOOTP protocol. The advantage of DHCP is that it can be run from one server across several different subnets. BOOTP must have a separate server for each network that needs to be configured.

FIGURE 3.4
A client and DHCP server negotiate an IP address

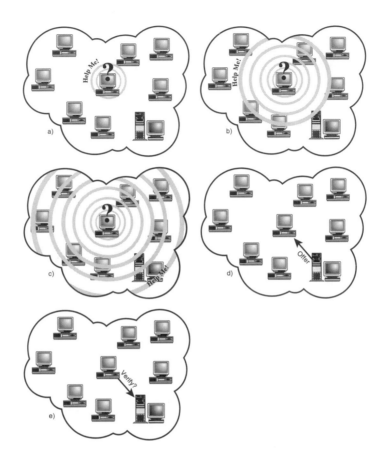

Dial-In Connections

If you're dialing into a network, you're probably being dynamically assigned a number by the machine that you're connecting to. This dynamic assignment is probably not a function of DHCP, rather the PPP server itself. Generally, the server will have a statically assigned IP address for each port or dial-in connection it supports. Upon connecting to a given port, you're assigned that port's address and automatically configured to use the network by way of your PPP client software.

How Can I Tell What Method of Assignment I'm Using?

When setting up the networking on your computer, it must be prepared to handle DHCP TCP/IP configuration or a statically assigned address. If you have a local network connection, you can find out how your IP address is configured by looking at the TCP/IP setup screens. If you're running Windows 95/98, open your Network control panel, and then double click the

TCP/IP protocol. If the Obtain an IP address automatically button is highlighted in the resulting window, you're using DHCP. Otherwise, you have a statically assigned address. In Figure 3.5, you can see that this Windows machine is configured to use DHCP.

FIGURE 3.5
You can tell if you're using DHCP in the Windows TCP/IP Properties Screen.

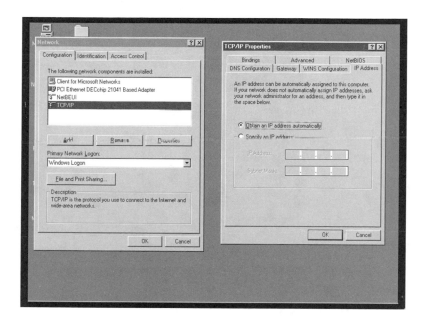

Part

I

Ch

3

Macintosh users can open their TCP/IP control panel, which is functionally identical to the Windows counterpart. If your screen reads Configure: Using DHCP, you're using a DHCP server. If, instead it says Configure: Manually, you have a statically assigned IP address. Figure 3.6 shows a Macintosh with a static address assignment.

Linux users can determine how their address is assigned by looking at the contents of their Ethernet card's configuration file, usually /etc/sysconfig/network-scripts/ifcfg-eth0.

```
>grep "BOOTPROTO" /etc/sysconfig/network-scripts/ifcfg-eth0
```

The result may read: BOOTPROTO=dhcp.

This notation indicates that this particular system is using DHCP to configure its network interface upon booting. If the command doesn't return anything, you're running with a statically assigned address.

Now you should have a pretty good idea of how you came about having an IP address and what it's good for, but we still haven't looked at the address itself or what it's numbers mean. We'll do that now.

FIGURE 3.6
The Macintosh TCP/IP Configuration screen also reveals your DHCP status.

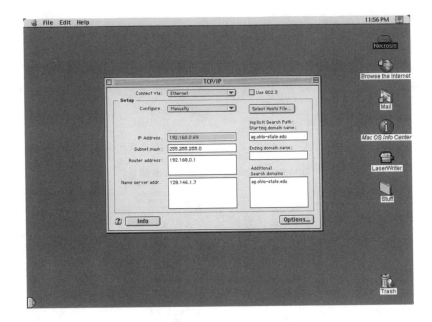

Subnets and the IP Address

As we've learned, an IP address is a 32-bit number that's usually represented as four separate 8-bit numbers separated by periods. These periods break the IP address into components that help make sense of what the address as a whole means. You can think of the numbers as representing the network you're a part of and your individual computer, or node on the network. The first one, two, or three segments of the IP address generally will be your network identifier. The remaining digits identify your individual machine on the network.

For a real-world example, let's look at the IP address my PowerBook uses when I'm at work. My address is broken down as follows:

```
140     .   254    .   85          .   2
---------------------           ------
The network I am part of,       My computer's
Specifically, Vivian Hall at      unique identifier
The Ohio State University.       Within Vivian Hall
```

Earlier, we touched on the concept of a "subnet" as being a portion of a larger network. 140.254.85.xxx is a subnet of The Ohio State University's entire network. A machine must know what subnet it's on so that it knows if another machine it's communicating with is on the local network. If the two machines are not on the same subnet, the packets must be routed through a gateway to reach the remote device.

In classical TCP/IP networking, there are three primary classes of networks: Classes A, B, and C.

Class A addresses were designed for large networks. A class A address uses the first 8 bits of the IP address to determine the network. If we define this number as a class A address, the breakdown looks like this:

```
126.            0.  0.  1
----            ------------
Our network     My node on the network
```

Class B addresses split the 32-bit IP address in half and use 16 bits for the network and 16 bits for the host.

```
128.128          0.  1
------           ------------
Another network    The node
```

Lastly, *Class C*, which is the most common addressing, uses the last 8 bits to determine the node and the first 24 bits to determine the subnet. This scheme is identical to the configuration of my personal computer, as shown here.

```
128.128.128.       1
------             ------------
```
Another network   The node

The Subnet Mask

While subnet classes form a definition of a network's relationship to the world, they're rarely used for configuration purposes anymore. These days, administrators complete the configuration of the network class by setting a *subnet mask* in the TCP/IP configuration. The subnet classes are rarely referred to anymore, as people decided they needed to divide the 32-bit addresses up with a bit more flexibility than what the three subnet classes allowed. The use of a subnet mask gives us the ability to determine precisely which bits of the IP address identify the subnet and which identify nodes on the subnet.

The subnet mask is another 32-bit number that looks very similar to an IP address. We can easily map the traditional subnet classes to nodes to subnet masks by looking at how subnet masks are formed. For a Class A address, the first 8 bits of the address determine the subnet. Correspondingly, the default subnet mask will mask the first 8 bits of the address to show that they determine the subnet. It creates this mask setting bits to 1 that are part of the subnet. For a Class A address, this numbering works out to

```
    Class A subnet:
11111111.00000000.00000000.00000000
      255    . 0    . 0      .0
```

So, for Class A addresses, the subnet mask is 255.0.0.0. Apply the same logic to Class B and C addresses:

```
    Class B subnet:
1111111.11111111.00000000.00000000
        255   .   255   .   0   .   0

        Class C subnet:
        1111111.11111111.11111111.00000000
        255     .   255   .   255   .   0
```

The subnet masks for Class B and C addresses are 255.255.0.0 and 255.255.255.0, respectively.

What does a misconfigured subnet do?

If you have a network problem where your computer can talk to a distant computer without any trouble but fails to communicate with machines on your local network, the prime suspect is the subnet mask. Your local machine uses the subnet mask to determine which devices are local and which must be communicated with via a gateway. Many default TCP/IP configurations will have an improperly set subnet mask. The result is often the ability to communicate with remote machines while local traffic is lost. We'll discuss configuring client's gateways in Chapter 5.

Smaller Subnets as a Solution to Routing Problems

One of the reasons that subnet masks were created was to solve a problem that was originally unforeseen with the class system of subnetting. There was no foresight during the early days of the Internet that it would ever grow beyond the capacity of the hardware that ran it. Recent years have shown, however, that the Internet is now growing at an almost exponential rate, with thousands of network devices being added daily. The problem that arises from this growth is that as new devices are added, new subnets must be formed. The most common form of subnet is the Class C subnet. If each subnet is considered a separate entity to the gateways that provide service of getting packets to their destination, then these devices have to maintain huge tables of information about the appropriate paths to send packets along. The amount of memory needed to store this information, as well as the processing time required to look up path information for each incoming packet, is extremely limited. If more routes exist than can be held, portions of the network become unreachable. If a router cannot keep up with the number of requests it receives, information is lost. To help alleviate this problem, subnets are grouped together into larger subnets. Routers can then keep track of the larger subnet, which in turn handles routing to the smaller subnets.

For example, consider five subnets: A, B, C, D, and E. If the outside world considers each of these subnets as a separate entity, they must maintain routing information about all five. This redundancy is a waste of valuable memory for the router, as shown in Figure 3.7.

FIGURE 3.7
A router routing
information to five
subnets.

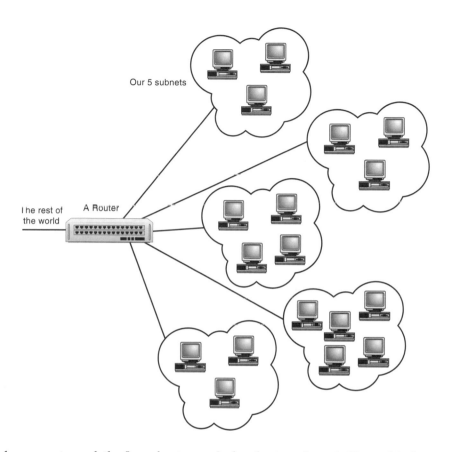

If instead, we were to mask the five subnets as a single subnet, as shown in Figure 3.8, the router can then maintain a single entry for all five, which, in turn can provide their own routing amongst themselves.

This is a far more efficient method of handling multiple subnets and has given us some breathing room in terms of allowing Internet technology to catch up with Internet growth.

Private Subnets

There are addresses reserved for subnets that will never be connected to larger networks. These subnets are safe to use for your own networks. If you later expand your network to have access to outside networks, you don't risk the chance of having chosen a subnet that is in use in the real world. When I set up my first local TCP/IP network in my apartment, I made up a subnet and IP addresses because I never expected to have the network connected to the outside world. Later, when I decided that I really needed to connect to my computer at work, I opened a connection to the outside world. After trying hopelessly to connect to a Web site, I finally realized that the subnet I had randomly chosen overlapped with the real-world addresses. The result was that when I tried to reach the remote network, my network thought that I was trying to reach a local machine and couldn't find the server I was attempting to contact. With three machines, it isn't hard to reconfigure settings to fix a problem like this. But with 30 devices, you'll wish you had planned ahead. The following subnets are designated for use in private networks:

```
10.0.0.0   (Class A)
172.16.0.0 (Class B)
192.168.0.0 (Class B)
```

FIGURE 3.8
Router routing to a single subnet that has five internal subnets.

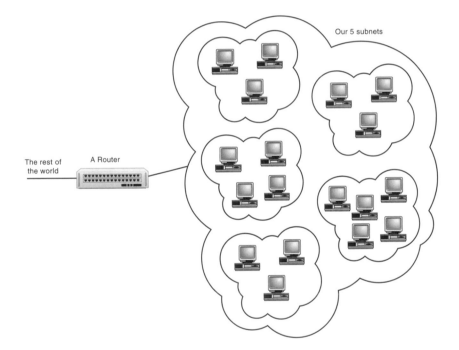

Our 5 subnets

The rest of the world

A Router

Hostnames and DNS

You may have noticed that you rarely use numbers when contacting remote machines. Your email address, for example, must specify a unique computer that will receive mail that's sent to you, but it doesn't have an IP address in it, does it? What it has instead is a *hostname*.

Hostnames, like IP addresses, have different parts, separated by periods, referred to as the *host* and the *domain* name. The host is the first portion of the hostname, and the parts that follow determine the domain name. In my machine name, `pointy.poisontooth.com`, the host is `pointy`, and the domain name is `poisontooth.com`. You can interpret some information about the particular host from the ending of the domain name; this "ending" is called the *top level domain* or *TLD*.

The common TLDs are

.com—Commercial domain

.edu—Educational institution

.org—Non-profit organization

.gov—U.S. government

.mil—US military

.net—A second commercial domain (often an ISP)

Recently, a controversial plan to add several more TLDs was approved. This plan essentially completes the commercialization of the Internet by adding new "public" domains to the existing domains and removing government control over domain names. Many people have been against this move, because it's viewed as the final nail in the coffin for the Internet as an information tool, rather than a giant online catalog. Take a look at the new domains and decide for yourself:

.firm—Firms and businesses

.shop—Firms and businesses that are selling goods online

.web—Groups related to the Web

.arts—Sites offering cultural and entertainment information

.rec—Organizations offering recreation and entertainment activities.

.info—Informational services

.nom—Anyone wanting a personalized Web presence

There are also specific domains to identify hosts in countries outside the United States. Examples include

.ky—Cayman Islands

.cl—Chile

.fr—France

.de—Germany

.jp—Japan

.nl—Netherlands

.uk—United Kingdom

.zm—Zimbabwe

Being able to refer to a machine by its hostname gives us a few very significant benefits. First, people who must access a remote server are much more likely to remember that they're connecting to the server `poisontooth.com` (my personal Linux machine), rather than `204.210.240.191`. It's easier to attach recognizable words to various IP addresses than to assign IP addresses within a subnet that have some meaning. Secondly, if a server is referred to by a hostname, it can be reconfigured to a different IP address, even an entirely different network, without causing users to lose access. Lastly, in terms of logging, it's convenient to assign hostnames to individual users that help identify that user. That way, when `evil-bob-smith.poisontooth.com` attempts to access and erase your hard drive remotely, you can easily identify the remote computer and user.

The server that allows you to look up hostnames is called a *DNS server*, or *Domain Name Service* server. There should be both a primary and secondary (backup) DNS for your network. The DNS server can handle several types of different requests that return portions of its hostname database. All of this request handling occurs transparently to the user, as all well-behaved TCP/IP programs will look up the IP addresses for a given hostname automatically.

Domain Name Servers do not each individually contain information about all the computers available on the Internet. Instead, they have authority over certain subnets and contain hostname information only for these subnets. They also have the capability to look up information from other DNS servers so they can provide answers to requests for machines over which they do not have authority. To minimize network traffic, most DNS servers will cache information from other servers and respond to requests directly, as if they are authoritative over the remote subnets; however, it must identify its response as being *non-authoritative*. To keep information held in the DNS cache "up to date," each entry in the DNS database has a specific time to live (TTL) value. Once the TTL has expired, the entry is deleted from the cache. The TTL is usually set to several hours, because hostnames tend to be relatively stationary.

Name resolution can be a costly process in terms of processing time. Although most names are resolved in a fraction of a second or two, the actual processing time is entirely dependent on how quickly a domain's primary DNS servers can respond to a request. My department's Wb server is accessed by about 100,000 different IP addresses weekly. Each Sunday evening, an automated routine generates statistics for the server, during which the server looks up each IP address that accessed it and stores the corresponding hostname. If the stats start at 10 a.m. Sunday morning, it usually takes until 2 p.m. or 3 p.m. Monday afternoon for all of the names to be resolved. To cut back on the name server load, a caching-only server can be set up on a network to help take the load off of the primary servers.

Although most hostname resolutions will be handled transparently, sometimes it's useful to be able to perform direct lookups on a name server. If you happen upon an IP address in a log file, it's nice to be able to look up the machine name or information about the subnet the machine is on. Some common requests you can make of the server are for

Address records (A):	The most common type of lookup, the address record is the IP address of a given hostname.
Canonical Name (CNAME):	The CNAME provides an alias for the machine's hostname. For example, I might want to provide FTP service from a machine named `www.poisontooth.com`. I can set a CNAME of `ftp.poisontooth.com` to my `www` hostname and both with resolve to the same address.

Mail Exchanger (MX): | Mail exchanger records are used by mail servers to allow messages sent to a certain hostname to be di rected to a different name. For example, if I want mail sent to `poisontooth.com` to actually go to mail.`poisontooth.com`, I can set an MX record for poisontooth.com that points to `mail.poisontooth.com`.

Why Do I Need MX Records?

If you have a mailserver, it's a good idea to have MX records set to point to the server for all the computers on your network. This would allow mail to be sent to any computer in your organization, and it would still go to the main mailserver, regardless of how it was addressed.

Name Server (NS): | Given a domain name, an NS lookup will return the name servers that are registered for that domain.

Start of Authority (SOA): | The SOA record returned for a hostname gives infor mation on which nameserver is the authoritative nameserver with control over this name and all ma chines in the same subdomain as this name. It also gives e-mail contact information for the subdomain and various information regarding data refresh time peri ods and how recently this data has been updated.

There are other types of name server records, such as the Host Information (HINFO) record, that are rarely used. The Host Information record can be used to store information about a particular computer's hardware and operating system configuration. This storage presents a security risk because the name server could be queried to determine vulnerable operating systems and the information used to target machines for attack.

```
To perform name lookups on your client computer, you'll need resolver software
that can speak to a name server. For Mac users, the IPNetMonitor that you,
hopefully, downloaded after its reference in Chapter 1 will work nicely. Linux
users and users of Windows 95, 98, and NT can run the command line utility
NSLOOKUP to determine their machine name.
```

Let's go ahead and send some queries using nslookup under Linux. Macintosh and Windows users can follow along with their graphical counterparts.

Part

I

Ch

3

Start nslookup from within your Linux shell by typing

```
>nslookup

Default Server:  ns1.net.ohio-state.edu
Address:  128.146.1.7
>
```

nslookup is running and waiting for your first command. Let's send an address request query. Doing so is as simple as typing the hostname you'd like an address for.

```
>www.poisontooth.com

Non-authoritative answer:
Name:    www.poisontooth.com
Address:  204.210.240.191
```

The address for `www.poisontooth.com` (204.210.240.191) returns within a few seconds. Similarly, we can look up a CNAME record by typing in the IP address as our request:

```
>204.210.240.191

Non-authoritative answer:
Name:    www.poisontooth.com
```

Notice that the response is labeled as non-authoritative. This label appears because the nameserver I'm using is not the server that contains the official records for my `poisontooth.com` domain. Thus, it's considered non-authoritative for the query we've sent. To find out what the authoritative nameserver is, we can send a request for the NS records for `www.poisontooth.com`:

```
> set querytype=NS
> poisontooth.com

Non-authoritative answer:
poisontooth.com nameserver = CMHC.CMHCSYS.COM
Authoritative answers can be found from:
CMHC.CMHCSYS.COM        Internet address = 207.87.223.37
```

This query shows that my authoritative nameserver is `CMHC.CMHCSYS.COM` (207.87.223.37).

Lastly, let's check for a mail exchange record for a machine that doesn't exist on OSU's campus. I'm intentionally using this example because it shows how a name that doesn't resolve to an IP address can have an MX record that will allow email to be sent to it.

```
> set querytype=MX
> ag.ohio-state.edu

ag.ohio-state.edu       preference = 10, mail exchanger = leviathan.ag.ohio-
state.edu
leviathan.ag.ohio-state.edu     Internet address = 140.254.85.75
```

The mail exchanger for `ag.ohio-state.edu` is returned as `leviathan.ag.ohio-state.edu`. Thus, email sent to `jray@ag.ohio-state.edu` will automatically be routed to `jray@leviathan.ag.ohio-state.edu`.

If you're running a private network, you can run your own DNS server and create your own domain names as you see fit. If you're using an Internet-connected network, a domain name must be requested from an organization called the *InterNIC*, which keeps a database of domain names, including contact information and the DNS servers for each domain. It's easiest to work with your Internet Service Provider (ISP) to arrange for new names to be assigned. Your ISP will probably be able to provide you with DNS services as well. You can make requests directly from the InterNIC, but the process is slightly more complicated. There's a cost associated with registering a Domain Name with the InterNIC (this cost applies whether you deal directly with InterNIC or with your ISP). I recently registered my domain name `poisontooth.com` for the cost of $70 for 24 months.

Beware the Domain Name Scam!

Beware of Internet sites offering domain names at bargain prices. The InterNIC is currently the only source for these names. Other companies must buy names from the InterNIC, the same as you. They may sell you a domain name but share it amongst multiple people. It's best to go directly to the InterNIC for your names, or work directly with your ISP. If an offer appears too good to be true, it probably is—even (or perhaps especially) on the Internet. Because of the fluid nature of the Internet, the InterNIC may not be the only source for names in the near future. Domain names have been a topic of great discussion and debate, and determining who runs what is still up in the air.

Where Do IP Addresses Come From?

IP subnets are usually allocated from the company that's providing your TCP/IP connectivity. Once a subnet is allocated to an individual or organization, they may assign the IP addresses on that subnet as they see fit. On a larger scale, IP addresses for individual service providers are allocated from Arin http://www.arin.net.

If you're interested in registering a machine name without having a fun domain, take a look at the free DNS registration service offered by Monolith services. Monolith maintains a huge database of DNS entries in the domains `dyn.ml.org` and `ml.org`. For absolutely no cost, you can apply for a user account and a machine name that will appear in either of these domains. Via a Web interface, you then configure your hostname entry and IP address. I have registered `poisontooth.dyn.ml.org` for my personal use. The `dyn.ml.org` domain is mainly for the use of people who have IP addresses changing on a constant basis. The TTL value for cached entries in the `dyn` domain is only 10 minutes. This duration means you can have your IP address change, update Monolith to point to the new IP address, and all cached entries will be correct within 10 minutes of the change. This service is really nice if your only source of a network connection is a dial-in line, and you want to provide some sort of connection service for friends, and so on. The Monolith service can be reached, applied for, and configured at:

```
http://www.ml.org/
```

Whatis Whois?

One last resource related to DNS is the *whois* service. A whois request queries the databases that contain domain registration information. Utilities exist for all platforms to perform a whois request on a domain, but it's only natively available under Linux. Luckily, there are several Web interfaces to the whois service that allow anyone to easily perform a lookup by way of a Web browser. The results from a whois query contain information you can use to contact the owner of a domain. This information is extremely useful if you notice irregular network activity and want to find out who is responsible for the machines causing you trouble. Let's take a look:

```
http://www.internic.net/
```

This address is for InterNIC, which has a whois query engine directly on the homepage. To perform a lookup, fill in a domain name into the Search field on the page, and then click Search, as shown in Figure 3.9.

FIGURE 3.9

The InterNIC Web page allows you to perform a "whois" query on a domain.

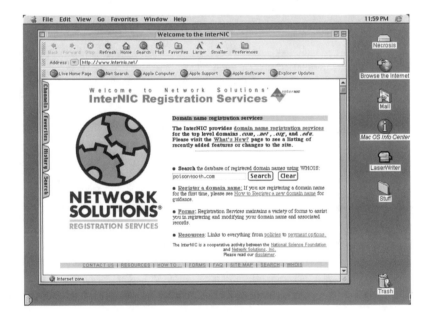

I'm going to perform the search on my own domain poisontooth.com:

```
The result is below:
Registrant:
      John Ray (POISONTOOTH-DOM)
          7879 Rhapsody Drive
          Dublin, OH 43016
          US

      Domain Name: POISONTOOTH.COM
      Administrative Contact:
        Ray, John  (JR10134)   jray@DIFFERENT.AG.OHIO-STATE.EDU
        614-555-9597
```

```
Technical Contact, Zone Contact:
    Grimble, John  (JG2463)  mrjohn@CMHC.COM
    614-555-0143 (FAX) 614-555-0362
Billing Contact:
    Ray, John  (JR10134)  jray@DIFFERENT.AG.OHIO-STATE.EDU
    614-555-9597

Record last updated on 16-Jun-98.
Record created on 16-Jun-98.
Database last updated on 6-Aug-98 04:06:34 EDT.

Domain servers in listed order:
CMHCSYS.CMHCSYS.COM          207.87.223.39
CMHC.CMHCSYS.COM            207.87.223.37
```

Part

I

Ch

3

The results of a whois lookup will appear identical whether you choose to use a client for your OS or use the Web interface. As you can see, the whois request generated a wealth of data that identifies…well, a startling amount of information about myself. Most of the information is self explanatory: my address, the administrator of the domain (me), the domain's technical contact (the person who is contacted regarding technical questions about the domain's name servers, and so on), a billing contact (you can guess what that means), and lastly, the two name servers that will resolve queries for the poisontooth.com domain. I've chosen not to run my own name servers and am currently having DNS service provided by a friend, thus the technical contact is not myself, and the name servers are running from cmhcsys.com. You may find it interesting to try running your own whois queries. It gives a human face to the thousands of anonymous domain names out there.

If you don't want to officially register a domain name but would still like to refer to your computers by a name, you do have an option. An alternative to using a DNS server is to use a hosts file that's located locally on each client computer. The hosts file provides an immediate lookup point for the computer. It lists hostnames and corresponding IP addresses in a table. When the machine wants to find out a hostname, it looks in the file and sees if it can find a matching entry. If the searching computer finds the hostname it's looking for, it uses the name. If not, it then goes on to consult the DNS server if one is available and the client is configured to use it.

On a network of 10 computers, it would be very effective to use a hosts file to entirely replace the functionality of a name server. This substitution equates to 100 entries spread across 10 different files on 10 different computers. Not too bad. On a network of 100 machines, we're looking at 10,000 entries spread across 100 different files and computers. Because each of these files must be updated manually, it becomes a high-maintenance task to keep all the hostnames and IP numbers correct on a network that's at all dynamic. In all cases, however, it's actually useful to have a hosts file on each client that contains the names of the local servers, along with the name of the client machine itself. This allows the network to continue to function even if DNS services fail. It also allows an individual machine to quickly identify all possible aliases to itself without having to perform a lookup, and on UNIX often provides for a single configuration point for a machine's IP address information as well. In Chapter 5, we'll look at how to configure the hosts file on our three sample platforms as we configure each machine's TCP/IP network interface.

You've just finished a relatively complete overview of IP addresses, subnet masks, and DNS servers. They make up most of the information you'll need to communicate on a TCP/IP network; in fact, it's all the information you'll need to communicate over a local network. The missing piece of information is the gateway your computer will use to speak to remote networks. Once that information is in hand, I'll take a few moments to show how to configure our various client machines with the complete set of TCP/IP parameters. The following chapter will contain information on gateways, routers, switches, and all the devices used to connect different subnets together. It will be the last chapter of mainly theory before we switch into a full hands-on mode. Keeping that it mind, you might want to curl up somewhere comfortable for the next several pages, because after you're finished with them, there's going to be a bit of typing to do.

Other Information Sources

The Internet Protocol   RFC 0791 `http://www.cis.ohio-state.edu/htbin/rfc/rfc0791.html`

Domain Name System   RFC 1034 `http://www.cis.ohio-state.edu/htbin/rfc/rfc1034.html`

The InterNIC Domain registrations `http://www.internic.net/`

Arin IP address allocation `http://www.arin.net/`

Controlling Network Traffic

by John Ray

In this chapter

Repeaters **74**

Bridges **74**

Routers/Gateways **74**

Moving Packets Between Networks **77**

Monitoring Your Connections with SNMP **83**

Broadcasting and Multicasting **83**

Will I Need to Buy This Stuff? **85**

Other Information Sources **86**

By this point, you probably have a good idea of what a router/gateway is and does. We've discussed the idea of subnets and how they can be combined into a larger TCP/IP network. The devices that accomplish combining these networks into one larger network are known by a variety of names, such as routers, bridges, or gateways. Generally, if you hear someone refer to a device as a gateway, and another person refers to it as a bridge, they're both probably right. The distinctions between these different pieces of hardware have blurred in the past few years, and it isn't at all easy to come up with a good explanation as to how to really tell them apart. We are concerned with devices, no matter what the name, that interconnect different subnets. Let's take a look at the traditional definitions of these devices.

Repeaters

First, the simplest network linking device is a *repeater*. Repeaters work entirely at the physical level and provide a simple service to the networks they connect. As the name implies, a repeater "repeats" packets across two or more networks, effectively linking them. It has no capability to process the information that it moves; it simply copies a signal from wire to wire. This duplication allows networks to be extended beyond the distance limitations of the wiring.

Repeaters and hubs are essentially the same device. A repeater will take an incoming line and repeat the signal across one or more outgoing lines, the same as a hub. The naming convention that seems to be used the most is that hubs seem to be associated with twisted pair/10BASE-T wiring, while repeaters are used with thinnet. In both cases, the end result is the same.

Bridges

Second, we will look at *bridges*. Bridges operate at the Data Link Layer of the network. This means that they do not have any information on the upper-level protocols that are running across them. A bridge links two or more networks at the lowest possible level. If a bridge is connecting two Ethernet networks, it is concerned solely with transmitting Ethernet frames between the two networks. Bridges make all their routing decisions based on the information contained in the Ethernet frame header, which in turn is based on hardware addresses, not on the IP address or any other protocol-based data.

Bridges also provide the ability to filter packets based on source information and other parameters in each frame. They can be used to reduce traffic from broadcast packets (packets sent out to the entire network) and multicasting, which we will discuss shortly. Because of this, bridges are commonly used to isolate high-traffic networks from one another.

Routers/Gateways

Finally, *routers* and *gateways* are also (almost—see sidebar) the same device and may be used interchangeably, as undoubtedly you've seen me do in what you've read so far. The router is a much more sophisticated device than either the repeater or the bridge, yet it can also perform the same services that either of the lower-level tools provide. Routers operate on the upper layers of the network, providing services that are specific to TCP/IP networks. Because routers understand the upper-level protocols, they can be used to combine subnets with different physical layers into a common TCP/IP network. Bridges and repeaters are generally used to move data between subnets that are based on a similar hardware layer. Routers, on the other hand, are concerned with the information contained in each packet and have the capability to examine it to make decisions. This capability allows routers to use TCP/IP addresses to move the packet toward its destination. It also allows very specific traffic to be screened out, or routed, in an extremely configurable manner. IP addresses, ports, and so on can all be looked at by the router and used to filter data.

Wait a minute—I hear some people say routers are gateways, and some people say they aren't. Who's right?

In common usage today, you'll see router and gateway used interchangeably. Configuration screens variably ask for Default Router or Default Gateway. In both cases, they mean the same thing. If you're interested in the technical details, properly, a gateway is a device that provides connection and translation services between differing protocols or physical layers. In certain circumstances, a gateway can even be used to translate between two different protocols being used on a single network. Routers, on the other hand, are properly devices that provide interconnection of different networks.

Getting Information to Its Destination

As data moves from network to network, it is said to make a *hop*. Hops can occur at the hardware level for devices being linked by bridges, or at a higher level with a gateway/router. If we look at the number of hops being made across a TCP/IP network, be aware that there may be several smaller hops across bridges that take place in order for data to reach each router. Before getting into the technical background of how routers/bridges accomplish their tasks, let's take a look at how many hops it takes to move a piece of information across a TCP/IP network. The program we will use to do this is called traceroute (/usr/sbin/traceroute) on Linux machines, or TRACERT.EXE under Windows. The Macintosh will need to rely on IPNetMonitor's interface to trace the packet's route in order to perform these tests. I'm going to take a look at the number of hops a piece of data must make to go between my computer here at work (primal.ag.ohio-state.edu) and at home (www.poisontooth.com). We should be able to see several hops in action as the packet travels from OSU to my home.

Start up a shell or MS-DOS prompt window, and then type the following (Windows users, remember to substitute "TRACERT.EXE" for "/usr/sbin/traceroute"):

```
>/usr/sbin/traceroute    www.poisontooth.com
```

The traceroute program will take a few moments to run and will give us a listing of the gateways/routers the packets traveled through. You will undoubtedly see a different display, but you should notice at least one similar gateway at the end of your display. This common gateway is the final one that the packet must pass to reach my machine. Each hop brings the packet closer, at least in terms of the network's point of view, to its final destination.

```
traceroute to poisontooth.com (204.210.240.191), 30 hops max, 40 byte packets
 1  kh1-eth1-5.net.ohio-state.edu (128.146.143.1)  1.736 ms  1.688 ms  1.611 ms
 2  kc2-atm0-0s10.net.ohio-state.edu (164.107.1.222)  1.684 ms  1.681 ms  1.793
ms
 3  mciws-fddi6-0.ohio-dmz.net (192.148.245.41)  1.679 ms  1.599 ms  1.762 ms
 4  204.210.252.70 (204.210.252.70)  3.347 ms  2.787 ms  3.588 ms
 5  dub240191.columbus.rr.com (204.210.240.191)  325.665 ms  10.988 ms  7.881 ms
 6  * * *
```

As you can see, our packet was routed five times before it reached its destination. While this may seem excessive, it is actually a very short route. The route that a packet takes does not, in any way, need to be the shortest physical path to a computer. For example, I also use an ISP that is located here in Columbus. Let's do a traceroute to their web server, www.netset.com.

```
>/usr/sbin/traceroute www.netset.com
```

```
traceroute to dilbert.netset.com (206.183.227.13), 30 hops max, 40 byte packets
 1  kh1-eth1-5.net.ohio-state.edu (128.146.143.1)  1.739 ms  1.621 ms  1.624 ms
 2  kc2-atm0-0s10.net.ohio-state.edu (164.107.1.222)  6.130 ms  1.938 ms  1.634
ms
 3  krc2-atm0-0-0s1.ohio-dmz.net (192.88.192.6)  1.335 ms  1.316 ms  1.350 ms
 4  sot3-atm4-0.columbus.oar.net (199.18.202.23)  1.878 ms  1.917 ms  1.931 ms
 5  bordercore2-hssi0-1-0.Atlanta.mci.net (166.48.49.253)  23.442 ms  23.390 ms
27.668 ms
 6  core3.WillowSprings.mci.net (204.70.4.25)  121.718 ms  450.003 ms  69.181 ms
 7  ameritech-nap.WillowSprings.mci.net (204.70.1.198)  719.905 ms  149.178 ms
698.667 ms
 8  aads.fnsi.net (198.32.130.64)  62.901 ms  69.000 ms  69.827 ms
 9  core1-hssi88.Columbus.fnsi.net (206.183.239.25)  99.642 ms  95.698 ms  108.0
35 ms
10  NETSET.Columbus.fnsi.net (206.183.239.74)  126.288 ms *  93.904 ms
11  dilbert.netset.com (206.183.227.13)  75.014 ms  73.993 ms *
```

Wow! A big difference, huh? And all three of these computers are located in the same city! In fact, poisontooth.com, my home machine, is located about 10 miles away, while the second is only about 5 miles away. Take a close look at traceroute's response. Remember, I am transferring data from one machine in Columbus, Ohio, to another machine in Columbus, Ohio—not a huge leap, you'd imagine. Look at hop #5 in the results. Do you see anything strange? The domain name for the gateway that my data passed through is Atlanta.mci.net. A packet from my computer, located five miles away, travels from Ohio, down through Georgia, and then back to Ohio again before arriving at its destination. You might imagine that this meandering route slows things down significantly, but not necessarily. Routing decisions are made based on a number of conditions, including current network speeds, network outages, and so on. The routers work to provide what they consider to be the fastest and most reliable path to the destination. When we are dealing with the speed of light, a quick trip to Georgia won't be noticed and may actually provide a more reliable connection than taking a shorter and less stable routing configuration. Your network may have one or more gateways or routers, depending on its configuration.

Now that we've seen some TCP/IP routing in action, let's look at how decisions are made as to where data will go. We'll start with bridges and then look at gateways/routers. Repeaters are omitted because they do not apply logic when making their decisions. They are purely hardware devices, while bridges and routers utilize some programming to control how they process packets.

Moving Packets Between Networks

To begin to get an understanding of how packets reach their destination, let's look at how a bridge does the job of locating its destination. Remember that a bridge does not have knowledge of the TCP/IP protocol, so we will be working strictly at the Data Link level with Ethernet. The type of bridging that is used in an Ethernet network is called *Transparent Bridging*.

Transparent Bridging

Transparent Bridging uses an idea called a *spanning tree*. You may picture this concept quite literally as a branching tree, with bridges located at the joints of branches, and individual networks located in between. The base of the network spanning tree is referred to as the *root*. The root is either determined automatically based on the hardware address or is chosen by the person designing the network layout. Because we need to know definite paths between any two points, if there are bridges that form circular routes in the network, these are detected and deactivated. The need to remove routes will lead to conditions where it is possible to remove more than one route to solve the problem. In these cases, the route that is the greatest number of hops away from the root is deactivated (see Figure 4.1).

Once the spanning tree is constructed and loops are removed, the network begins operating by broadcasting packets it receives to all the bridges connected to it. As hosts receive and send data, the bridges build a table of the hardware addresses that are communicating with each of its interfaces. In essence, it learns about its surroundings. The bridge uses this table to determine where it will send data. The larger the table gets, the more specific a route the bridge can choose for each frame. After enough time passes, the bridge will contain information that allows it to successfully route any frames it receives to the appropriate destination without broadcasting extraneous information anywhere.

A drawback to this approach is that the bridged network, once it builds its tables, cannot be reconfigured without the same process happening again. If a subnet is attached to the network, the spanning tree is changed, and the broadcasting of all data on the network must reoccur. This is potentially a concern for a dynamic network environment, as changes in topology might happen on a very regular basis. The good news is that transparent bridging is precisely what its name implies: transparent. As a network administrator, you must simply deal with configuring your subnets and attaching the bridge hardware between them. The bridge itself takes care of determining the correct routes to take and reconfigures itself to fit the network. All bridge operations are transparent to the administrator and user.

FIGURE 4.1

This diagram illustrates a network spanning tree.

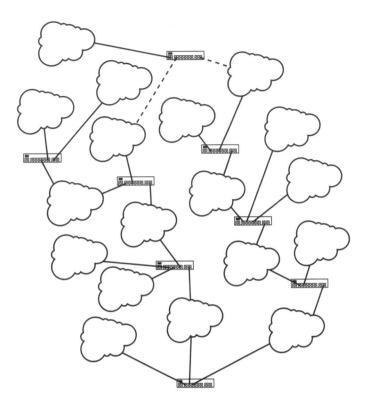

Routers/Gateways

Routers and gateways, which "know" about particular protocols, are used to link different subnets (which, as you now know, are internally linked by bridges) to form large TCP/IP networks. Routers must be able to determine the physical address of devices on the local network to which they are attached, as well as have knowledge of the outside network to move outgoing data to the correct destination. Computers that are sending data also need to be able to determine the hardware addresses of the devices to which they are sending data for inclusion in the generated frames. However, if a computer on a local network wants to send data to a remote IP address, it does not need to determine the remote machine's hardware address. Instead, it uses the address of the network's router in the frame that it sends. Upon receiving this data, the router will follow the exact same process of the computer originating the transmission. It will determine the appropriate next hop for the data, replace its hardware address in the frame with the address of the next appropriate router (we'll soon see how it determines what the appropriate router is), and then transmit the frame.

You may be wondering how computers can locate the hardware addresses of devices on its local network. The answer is called an *ARP* request.

ARP Requests *ARP*, or *Address Resolution Protocol*, is used by devices to ask for another device's hardware address. Each network device maintains an ARP cache. This cache contains a list of devices it is communicating with or has communicated with recently. It eliminates the need to send an ARP request every time a frame is sent. We can display the contents of a computer's ARP cache by using the `/sbin/arp -a` command under UNIX and `arp.exe` under Windows. Unfortunately, I have not been able to locate software to display the ARP cache maintained on Macintosh computers. To display the ARP cache currently held on your machine, use the following command in a shell or command window:

```
>/sbin/arp -a
```

This is a listing of what that command returned from our primary mail server. As you can see, it isn't really talking too much right now, and its ARP cache is rather empty.

```
Address                   HWtype  HWaddress           Flags Mask        Iface
kh1-eth1-5.net.ohio-sta   ether   00:00:0C:04:9D:83   C                 eth0
meine.ag.ohio-state.edu   ether   08:00:2B:E5:34:67   C                 eth0
```

The two entries in the file are the gateway device for our network, which is to be expected, and one of our departmental web servers, which shares data with the mail server. Just for fun, we can force an entry to be included in the ARP cache just by talking to another machine. To do this, I will ping a host on our local network. Let's try one of our NT servers: `oasis.ag.ohio-state.edu`.

```
>ping oasis.ag.ohio-state.edu
```

The results of the ping operation are unimportant; what is important is what happens when we run the `arp` command again.

```
>/sbin/arp -u
```

```
Address                   HWtype  HWaddress           Flags Mask        Iface
kh1-eth1-5.net.ohio-sta   ether   00:00:0C:04:9D:83   C                 eth0
meine.ag.ohio-state.edu   ether   08:00:2B:E5:34:67   C                 eth0
oasis.ag.ohio-state.edu   ether   00:A0:C9:26:EB:D3   C                 eth0
```

The entry for oasis is indeed now in the ARP cache! I used a similar technique to quickly create a database of the hardware addresses of local networks that is stored as part of the online IP database. ARP cache entries eventually time out and are removed from the cache after a short period of time. If you are using `arp` from a machine that has dialed into a network and has no local Ethernet connection, your ARP cache will be empty. This is because the dial-in network interface does not use Ethernet hardware addresses for its communications. It is up to the device handling the dial-in to provide the Ethernet connectivity and maintain ARP information.

Choosing a Route Now we will take a look at how the routers actually decide what the most appropriate path for a packet to take actually is. Each router and each computer maintains a table that identifies the IP address of a destination, the address of a gateway, (or in the case of data being sent to the same network, the same address as the destination), and information about whether the route is up or not. When a packet comes into the router, the router consults this table, chooses the appropriate destination router, and forwards the packet. The size of this routing table can be many megabytes in size; keeping track of where information needs to travel is not a trivial task.

Part

I

Ch

4

For routers to keep their tables current, they can communicate with other routers and exchange routing information. By doing this on a frequent basis, routing information is propagated, and new routes are added on a continuing basis. One of the most common protocols for communicating this information is the *RIP*, or *Router Information Protocol*. RIP information is broadcast between routers every 30 seconds, A broadcast can contain information on if a route is currently up and the number of hops needed to reach a destination. There can be many redundant routes that a packet can take, so this information is used by the router to figure out what the best possible route is at that given point in time. When a router updates its tables based on a RIP broadcast, it will then broadcast the changes down the network. The changes propagate throughout the entire network.

Another protocol used by routers is the *Open Link State Protocol*. The *OSLP* is a transaction-based communication protocol for routers, as opposed to RIP, which is a simple broadcast of information. OSLP connections allow routers to exchange configuration information and even build routing tables from scratch by downloading an entire database about an existing router's database.

Tunneling with Routers Another function a router can perform is *tunneling*. Tunneling is the process of encapsulating data within the packets of one network protocol, transmitting them by using that protocol, and then unencapsulating them on reaching their destination. For example, AppleTalk originally was not a TCP/IP-based protocol, which means that AppleTalk services stop wherever the local subnet stops. AppleTalk offers extremely easy-to-use file and printer sharing and browsing, and it's nice to be able to use these features from a remote site. To do this, we must tunnel AppleTalk through a protocol that can be transmitted between each site. The obvious tunneling choice is TCP/IP. By placing a router on a local AppleTalk network, and a similarly configured router on a remote network, they can communicate with each other and pass AppleTalk packets between the networks using TCP/IP as the carrier of the information. When the router on the local network sees an AppleTalk packet, it creates a TCP/IP packet that contains the AppleTalk data. This packet is then transmitted to the remote router. The remote machine decodes the AppleTalk data from the TCP/IP data and rebroadcasts the AppleTalk packet. To local and remote networks, this is transparent. It simply appears that it is one big AppleTalk network. Using the same tunneling process, we can transmit any protocol we want over the network, even if it was only designed to operate on a local network (see Figure 4.2).

A benefit of doing this sort of tunneling is that the router can modify packets before they are sent to the remote destination. The most common use for this is encryption of packets to form a secure network. If there is sensitive data, which must be transmitted between local and remote destinations, it is entirely possible for that information to be sniffed or read from the network as it is being passed along. If we are dealing with data being sent over a TCP/IP connection, we can create a tunnel using TCP/IP that *carries* TCP/IP. While this may sound a bit strange, it isn't. We are simply extending our TCP/IP subnet to a remote destination and securing the communications in the process.

FIGURE 4.2
Tunneling between two networks works like this.

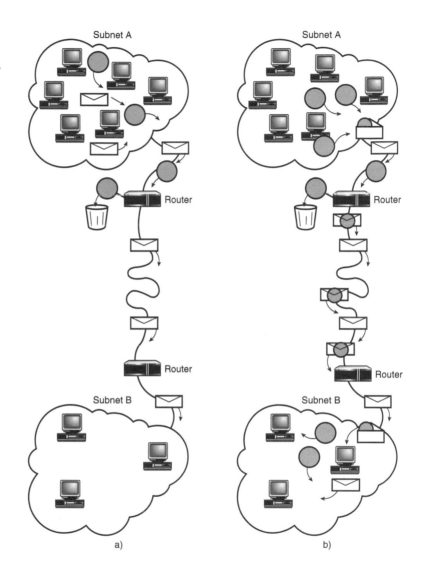

a)

b)

High Functionality, High Price Routers, obviously, are rather intelligent devices that must process huge amounts of data on a continual basis. They must operate 24 hours a day, handle thousands of packets a second, and make decisions for each individual packet they process, based on consulting a database containing thousands of entries. If a router is also performing encryption and tunneling, its processing time is much higher. It's a bit hard to imagine the magnitude of the job these devices are entrusted with. Because of the extreme requirements, routers are expensive devices and should be purchased based on quality, not price.

Part

I

Ch

4

Switches

Switches are a type of connecting device that can be deployed to help reduce traffic on an Ethernet. This is called switched Ethernet. Switches work by segmenting local networks. The main network feeds the switch, and then several subnets plug into it. As a packet arrives at the switch, the switch looks up the destination device from an internal ARP cache and switches the packet to the appropriate subnet. This device is similar to a bridge and also operates on the Data Link Layer, making it useful for segmenting LANs running any protocol. Switching is generally used on a smaller workgroup level to divide individual networks within a building or department.

Switches usually use two different technologies to provide their services. The first is called *cut-through*. Cut-through switching analyzes incoming frames for the hardware address and then immediately sends the frame to the appropriate destination. This is essentially offering the functionality of a slightly more advanced repeater. *Store-and-forward* is the other type of switching technology, which stores the entire incoming frame before resending it. This allows the switch the chance to look for errors or other problems with the packet and discard it if it finds a problem.

In cases where there are thousands of interconnected network devices, it is likely that from time to time a device will fail and send up a broadcast storm. A year ago, a network printer here at Ohio State took down computers in several buildings when it decided to send out garbage packets as quickly as it could. In some cases, computers had to be physically removed from the network cable before they became usable again. The campus network had originally been designed to act as one gigantic subnet, so all packets were broadcast everywhere. With appropriately configured bridges or "store-and-forward" switches, this problem wouldn't have affected anything but the local network of the printer. Instead, it brought several hundred machines to a screeching halt.

Smart or Manageable Hubs

We've already discussed the purpose of hubs and dismissed repeaters as being similar to hubs, but there are also *smart hubs*, which are a bit more interesting than the components we have seen so far. A smart hub performs all the services you would expect, but it also provides informational services to the operator. Smart hubs can report things such as network traffic and collision information to its administrator. The administrator, in turn, has control over the hub's ports and can deactivate individual stations remotely if he or she notices unusual network activity or an unusually high number of collisions. Ports may also be configured to pass only certain kinds of traffic. These devices are useful for a network environment that requires precise control and monitoring of individual stations. It is far simpler to remotely determine and disable which workstation that is causing 50 percent of your network traffic than it is to monitor the entire network, determine the hardware address of the renegade machine, match that to a port on a hub, and physically unplug that port.

Monitoring Your Connections with SNMP

All the devices we've mentioned so far, with the exception of repeaters/hubs, usually offer remote configuration and monitoring. Because hundreds of these devices can exist on a single network, it would become very tiring to try to physically monitor each device. It would also be a bit disturbing if each device offered its own software package for managing its functions. Several hundred devices combined with several hundred programs would not be a good thing. Luckily, there is a standard management protocol that most network devices follow, called *SNMP*, or *Simple Network Management Protocol*. In Chapter 21, "Using SNMP and Other Diagnostic Tools to Monitor Your Network," we look at using SNMP to manage different devices; for now, let's take a look at how SNMP works.

SNMP was designed to provide a temporary solution to the problem of communicating with different network devices. However, it has persisted and become the network configuration standard. The SNMP consists of a set of protocol specifications that cover all the bases of network administration and is not taxing on the network system itself. SNMP works by exchanging messages with devices; these messages contain variables, their names, data types, if they can be changed, and their current values. SNMP messages can be sent to read data from a device, to set data on a device, and to monitor network SNMP broadcasts that devices send as they change their network state, such as coming online or shutting down. These messages are referred to as gets, sets, and traps, respectively.

The simplicity of the protocol has made it very popular among hardware manufacturers. It is simple to create devices that follow these specifications, and it is equally easy to write software that can manage them. SNMP can also be expanded easily as different needs become known.

Running SNMP consists of running a *manager* and an *agent*. Each SNMP-compatible node on the network runs the agent. The job of the agent is to collect information for its device and make it available to be read or modified. The manager polls the agents for various information and can set variables on the agents if the appropriate permission is given. SNMP management/ monitoring software often provides a full graphical interface to the network and allows point-and-click monitoring and configuration of network devices. UNIX machines generally come with SNMP agent software, as do Windows computers. The Macintosh system had SNMP agent capabilities under MacTCP, but these were removed with the introduction of Open Transport, which we will discuss in the next chapter. By the time this book is published, Mac OS 8.5 will be available, and SNMP agent capabilities will return to the operating system.

The largest problem with the original SNMP specification is that there is a lack of security provisions. Although there is a basic password control scheme in SNMP, it is possible for a malicious user to gain access to SNMP devices. A recent revision to SNMP, SNMPv2, provides a comprehensive authentication security, but SNMPv2 has yet to actually be deployed.

Part
I

Ch
4

Broadcasting and Multicasting

Up to this point, we've talked about TCP/IP traffic as a point-to-point method of communicating. Two computers open a connection between each other and send data back and forth. In most applications, this two-way traffic is all that is needed. However, there are some instances where this is a highly inefficient way to send information.

Consider the transfer of video over the Internet. If live video of an event is being sent from a single source to thousands of clients, imagine the implications: The server must open and maintain a connection with each client computer. As a new frame of video is made available on the server, it must, in sequence, send that frame to each of the machines, essentially duplicating the same action thousands of times. You can imagine the load this would put on the server. As each new client connected, the performance of the server would degrade because of the added CPU and memory requirements needed to maintain the connection. At the same time, the network capacity itself would be taxed because of the thousands of times the same piece of data was being transmitted. Obviously, this is not an optimal solution for this sort of situation.

A more vconvenient scheme might be to create a system similar to the one that delivers your TV signal now. A single signal travels out from the source, and our television sets receive and display the results. Luckily, a similar technique exists for the computer network called, appropriately, *broadcasting*. When a computer broadcasts to a network, it sends out a packet that isn't addressed to any computer in particular. The address that the packet contains is called the *broadcast address*; it is usually calculated automatically by your operating system. We'll see exactly how it is calculated when we configure Linux (which doesn't automatically perform the calculation) in the next chapter. A packet addressed to the broadcast address is looked at by all the computers on the network that happen to be paying attention. If a client computer wants to receive the packet, it does so, like any other packet; if not, it ignores the packet. By using this technique, a server can send the same information to an entire subnet just by sending a single packet.

Unfortunately, this technique applies only to a single subnet, or multiple local subnets if the bridges are configured correctly. You can imagine what would happen if all routers and bridges passed broadcast packets between themselves. A single packet sent out on the Internet would propagate through all the network devices in the world. This situation would be very bad, to say the least! A single computer could flood the Internet and disrupt global communications. No, not good at all. Because of this, routers and bridges do not pass broadcasts unless they are specifically configured to do so.

A broadcast packet contains a port number, so it is possible for some types of broadcasts to be allowed, while others are filtered out. A common reason for a bridge to be enabled to pass broadcasts is to allow platform-specific file sharing protocols like Windows NetBEUI and MacOS's AppleTalk to take place between different buildings, and so on. Both of these protocols rely on broadcasts to alert other computers of the presence of a new network device. Unfortunately, this also means that a problem on one Macintosh Network will also exist on the other network, and one misbehaving computer could potentially take down all subnets that it can broadcast to. When a computer generates broadcasts at a tremendous rate, this is called a *broadcast storm*. For these very reasons, broadcasting can be a rather dangerous activity.

We now understand how broadcasting can help us to communicate large amounts of information to a group of clients on a single network, but what about over a large TCP/IP network? Is it possible to broadcast from a remote site over the Internet? The answer is yes, and the solution is TCP/IP *multicasting*—broadcasting to multiple different subnets. This is accomplished, at a high level, by allowing clients to join a broadcast group that is then simultaneously sent a packet from the server. You might think that this still requires the server machine to maintain a list of all the IP address and to communicate with each of them individually, but a clever protocol has been designed to make life much easier for the server.

MBONE

MBONE, Multicast BackBone, is the most prominent technology for performing broadcasts over TCP/IP. MBONE works by creating a tunnel between different MBONE servers located on different networks. This tunnel works along the same principal as the tunnels we discussed earlier. However, in the case of MBONE, the goal is to create an entire virtual network linked by these tunneling servers. The tunnels will be used to carry the broadcasts to the clients.

When a client wants to receive a broadcast over MBONE, he or she joins the server closest to his or her location. As the server generates broadcasts, they are sent out over the MBONE network through each of the tunnels to the receiving MBONE server nodes. The receiving MBONE servers then rebroadcast the signal to the clients that have joined the broadcast. There is still slowdown as each of the endpoints in the MBONE network can be required to serve multiple clients, but the primary load of the server is far less than if it had to directly broadcast to each individual client.

Broadcasting and Routing

I've chosen to discuss multicasting in the routing section because of the role that routers play in broadcasting packets. Depending on the needs of you network, you must take into consideration the amount of broadcasting you'll be doing and control your traffic accordingly. Be aware of the problems associated with routing broadcasts, and avoid unnecessary protocols, which can result in broadcast storms.

Will I Need to Buy This Stuff?

Unless you're designing a network for a large company or would like to join networks between different buildings, chances are you will not need to worry about buying routers and bridges yourself. The purpose of this chapter is to give you an idea of the hardware that's available and what you might need if you want to accomplish a specific networking task. If you're setting up a network for a small office group (20 to 50 clients), you may want to purchase a switch to help segment high-load workgroups within your office. The devices we've looked at here are considered serious networking devices and are priced in the hundreds to thousands of dollars. For most small networks using 100BASE-TX, this will be sufficient for anything you'd like to do. My office is running non-switched Ethernet, cabled with 10BASE-T. We have an Internet connection and support around a million accesses to our servers each month without any problem.

Part
I

Ch
4

Other Information Sources

Routing on the Internet `http://www.scit.wlv.ac.uk/jphb/comms/iproute.html`

Internet Standard Subnetting Procedure RFC 950 `http://freesoft.org/CIE/RFC/950/index.htm`

Address Allocation for Private Internets RFC 1918 `http://freesoft.org/CIE/RFC/Orig/rfc1918.txt`

Simple Network Management Protocol RFC 1157 `http://freesoft.org/CIE/RFC/1157/index.htm`

LAN Switches

`http://www.cnetusa.com/wplanswitch.html`

Tunneling

`http://www.byte.com/art/9707/sec6/art3.htm`

The MBONE Information Center

`http://www.mbone.com/`

Configuring Client Workstations

by John Ray

In this chapter

Configuring a Mac OS 8.x Computer to Use a TCP/IP Network **88**

Configuring Windows 95/98 **90**

Configuring Red Hat Linux 5.x. **95**

Other TCP/IP Configurations **98**

Other Information Sources **99**

So far, this book has covered the different devices that make up a TCP/IP network and the corresponding pieces of information used to configure TCP/IP on a network device. Now, you will put this knowledge to use by following the configuration process for a Windows 95 or 98 computer, Mac OS, and a Red Hat Linux client. Once again, no matter what platform you choose to use, you should realize that TCP/IP networks connect many different types of machines. If you are working with a TCP/IP network, it is extremely likely that you will spend time on more than one platform. We will work through our client configuration in order of difficulty, from easiest to most difficult: Mac OS, Windows, and Linux. For each configuration, we will set up a standard configuration with these parameters:

Data Link Layer	Ethernet	
IP Address	192.168.0.2	
Gateway	192.168.0.1	
Primary DNS	192.168.0.250	
Secondary DNS	192.168.0.251	
Subnet Mask	255.255.0.0	
Domain	poisontooth.com	
Hostname	mymachine	
Hosts	Server1	192.168.0.10
	Server2	192.168.0.11

These settings are just an example. You should use these IP addresses only if you are practicing setting up machines for a private network; they will not work for a real-world configuration. As you may have noticed, I'm using the 192.168.xxx.xxx subnet, which is one of the subnets reserved for private networks.

Configuring a Mac OS 8.x Computer to Use a TCP/IP Network

We start with the supposition that your Macintosh already has an Ethernet card installed. For almost all Macintoshes shipped within the past five years, this is usually the case. If you do not have an Ethernet card, you might want to check out Asanté at

http://www.asante.com/

Asanté has an extensive inventory of Macintosh (and PC) networking products that should cover every network-capable Macintosh. Installing a network card is a simple matter of plugging it in, running a driver installer program that is included with the card, and rebooting your computer.

Open Transport Versus MacTCP

In the past three years, Apple has drastically changed their network software architecture. With the introduction of Mac System 7.5.3, networking moved from a TCP/IP driver called

MacTCP to an entirely different package called Open Transport. Open Transport provides an open network architecture on which different protocols can be implemented, such as TCP/IP. We will look exclusively at Open Transport, which is installed by default in System 7.6, and Mac OS 8.x. You can tell if you're running Open Transport by looking for the presence of a control panel called "AppleTalk." If it exists, you are indeed using Open Transport.

Configuring Open Transport

Setting up Open Transport's TCP/IP configuration is simple. By default, the necessary files for TCP/IP access are installed when you install your system software. There is no need to worry about extra drivers; everything you need is already on the system. All configuration takes place from one control panel, called TCP/IP. Open the control panel now. If your display looks different from what you see in Figure 5.1, choose the User Mode... selection from the Edit menu, and be sure that you're set to the Advanced or Administrative user mode. The different modes allow you to specify some extra configuration data, as well as lock the settings so they can't inadvertently be tampered with.

FIGURE 5.1

The Mac OS TCP/IP Configuration screen lets you enter information about your machine, including its IP address.

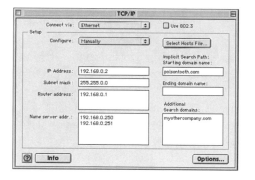

Part

I

Ch

5

You should recognize most of the fields you see. Starting from the top, let's configure the client using our hypothetical network information.

- Connect via—Select the Data Link Layer you will be using from this drop-down menu. Our connection method is Ethernet, so this should be your choice. PPP is usually also listed as a selection; choose it if you're configuring a dial-in connection.

- Use 802.3—There is a slightly different specification for the Ethernet frame used on some networks. If your network uses this type of frame, you need to click this box. It is highly unlikely, however, that you will be using this option.

- Configure—This selection allows you to specify you want the client computer to be assigned an IP address. We're assigning a static address, so we want to choose Manually from the menu. You can see that several other methods of assigning an address, including DHCP, are selectable from this screen.

- IP Address—The statically assigned IP address for the computer. Simply type **192.168.0.2** in this field to configure the client's IP number.

- Subnet Mask—Our subnet mask for the client is 255.255.0.0, so type that here.
- Router Address—Here we specify the gateway for our network, 192.168.0.1.
- Name Server Address—The addresses of our name servers should be typed here, separated by returns. Our servers are 192.168.0.250 and 192.168.0.251.
- Starting domain name—When you type the name of a machine you want to connect to, usually you type the hostname to identify it uniquely on the network. This field allows you to specify what will happen if you type only the name itself of a computer. Specifying search domains will attempt to contact a host by that name in each domain you list. For example, if I specify a starting domain of poisontooth.com, and then attempt to connect to a remote machine by just using the name server, the TCP/IP software will automatically append poisontooth.com to the name I've used. Hopefully, it would then successfully locate a machine called server.poisontooth.com. In our example, it would be nice to be on a first-name basis with other machines in our domain, so type **poisontooth.com** into the starting domain.
- Ending domain name—This allows you to specify the domain name for a larger domain that includes your domain. If a computer cannot be located using the starting domain you specified earlier, the value in this field will be tried as well. For our setup, however, we'll just leave this blank.
- Additional search domains—Any other domain names you want to use to search for a machine. These can be anything, not necessarily related to your domain. We'll be leaving this blank, but you can feel free to fill in whatever domains you like.
- Select Hosts File…—This allows us to select a file containing our hostname/IP address mappings. You can create this file in a text editor (simply include a line with an IP address, followed by a space, and then the hostname, for each of our servers). Remember to include the IP address and hostname for this machine as well.

Entering this information should complete your configuration of the Mac OS's version of TCP/IP.

Upon closing the TCP/IP control panel window, the Macintosh will scan the information you entered for correctness. If an error is found, you will be asked to fix it before saving. Once you've saved, the network configuration is immediately available for use. This is another nice feature of Open Transport: no rebooting required!

Configuring Windows 95/98

Setting up TCP/IP in Windows 95/98 is similar to the Mac setup, but the information is not all contained on a single screen. Furthermore, TCP/IP is not installed by default when there is a network adapter in your system. There is a good chance you'll need to add TCP/IP to your available protocols before you can configure it.

Installing TCP/IP

To start, open the Network control panel. You can access the Network control panel by clicking the Start button, selecting Settings, and then clicking Control Panels. An alternate method is to double-click My Computer, and then open the Control Panels folder. Once the Control Panels folder is open, double-click the Network icon. The resulting Network dialog box will display a list of all of your installed network devices, and the protocols that they are configured to use, as shown in Figure 5.2. Assuming you have an Ethernet card installed, you should see it listed, followed by its protocols.

FIGURE 5.2

You configure Windows 95 and 98 TCP/IP settings through the Network control panel.

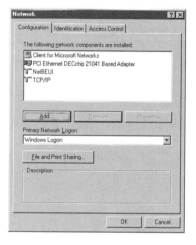

In this example, you can see that I have a DEC Ethernet card installed and have TCP/IP listed as one of the protocols. By default, Windows installs NetBEUI and IPX protocols to perform local networking. We are not interested in these non-TCP/IP protocols, so you can select them and click the Remove button. If TCP/IP is not listed, you will need to add it. Click the Add button to invoke a dialog box, shown in Figure 5.3, that will allow you to pick components you want to add to the system. If TCP/IP is already installed, skip ahead to the section "Configuring Windows TCP/IP."

Part

I

Ch

5

FIGURE 5.3

You can add new protocols in the Select Network Component Type dialog box.

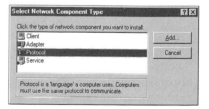

Choose the Protocol icon and click Add…. You will then be prompted to choose a protocol manufacturer (this is simply the company that wrote the driver, not the organization responsible for designing the protocol). Choose Microsoft as the Manufacturer, and TCP/IP as the protocol you want to install, as shown in Figure 5.4.

FIGURE 5.4

Use the Select Network Protocol dialog box to choose the appropriate protocol.

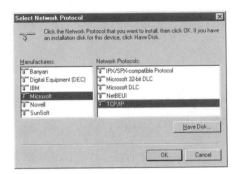

You will need to have your Windows installation CD at hand, because the system will need to install additional software before the system can use TCP/IP.

After you click OK, you should be back to the list in Figure 5.2. From here, you can configure your TCP/IP settings. Read on to see how to do so.

Configuring Windows TCP/IP

From the dialog box listing the adapters and protocols, highlight the TCP/IP selection and click Properties. If you are using a machine that has multiple Ethernet cards, or a dial-up adapter (for remotely connecting to a network), you will probably see multiple listings for the TCP/IP protocol, each followed by the name of the device that will use them. Be sure to choose the TCP/IP protocol that is followed by the type of Ethernet card you have installed; otherwise, you may inadvertently configure your dial-in connection to have a static IP address, in which case it would fail. Once you have opened the TCP/IP configuration dialog box, ensure the IP Address tab is selected, and you should see a familiar set of options, as shown in Figure 5.5.

By default, the IP Address tab should be selected. If not, select it now. Here there are three items that will require your attention.

- Specify an IP address—Be sure that this button is selected; otherwise, the computer will attempt to contact a DHCP server in order to set up its TCP/IP configuration.
- IP Address—These fields should be filled in to form the IP address 192.168.0.2. Take note that while each segment of the IP address is stored in a separate segment of the field, you can simply type the "." (period) in the appropriate place to move between the fields. This is something you will learn to appreciate as you fill in similar fields on a repeated basis.
- Subnet Mask—Here you enter the subnet mask for your network; that is, 255.255.0.0.

FIGURE 5.5

In the TCP/IP Configuration dialog box, use the IP Address tab to enter the settings for your machine.

You've now completed the basic identification of the computer's IP address and subnet. However, you must still configure the DNS server information and gateway before our setup becomes entirely useful. To set up the DNS, click the DNS Configuration tab located at the top of the window to access the dialog box shown in Figure 5.6.

FIGURE 5.6

Now select the TCP/IP Configuration dialog box's DNS Configuration tab.

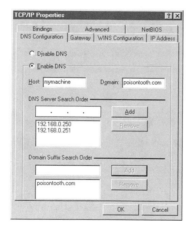

In the DNS Configuration tab, you'll want to check the following settings:

■ Enable DNS—You will want to enable DNS service on the computer. Be sure that this button is selected.

■ Host—This is the host portion of the machine's hostname. In our sample network, we will use mymachine. Entering the host here does not mean that it will automatically be recognized by other machines across a TCP/IP network. The hostname must still be officially registered with a DNS before it is useable. This field tells the Windows machine what its hostname is, so that a DNS lookup can be avoided if the information is needed by a piece of software.

Windows and DNS/WINS

Windows offers a few services that are a bit different from most TCP/IP implementations. First, in a Windows-only network, the hostname will be resolved if it is located on the same subnet. Windows also offers WINS, The Windows Internet Name Service, which resolves machine names to IP addresses. WINS servers are similar to DNS servers but do not contain the depth of information located on DNS servers. It can be used to offer network browsing services across different subnets. Both Windows NT and Red Hat 5.x offer WINS serving features out of the box. WINS, however, does not integrate well into cross-platform networks.

- Domain—The domain name for the network the computer is located on, poisontooth.com.

- DNS Server Search Order—Fill in this field with the primary DNS server, and then click the Add button. You will see it appear in the list of DNS servers directly below the entry field. Do the same thing with the secondary name server. Make sure that when you fill out information in this field and fields that are similar (a main entry line, followed by a list of entered values), you always press the Add button once you are done entering data. If you type in an address without using Add, it will be discarded once you close the configuration window.

- Domain Suffix Search Order—Like on the Macintosh, adding domain names to this list will allow you to connect to machines in these domains by simply specifying the base name for the host. Enter **poisontooth.com** and click the Add button.

Now that you've configured your computer's DNS information, it's time to move on to the second-to-last configuration option of our Windows TCP/IP setup, the gateway. Click the Gateway tab to go to this final settings screen, shown in Figure 5.7.

FIGURE 5.7

You'll finalize your TCP/IP Configuration settings in the Gateway tab.

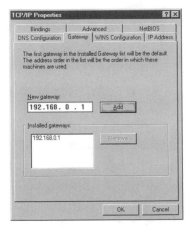

Once you've selected the Gateway tab, enter the appropriate information into the following text boxes:

■ New gateway—Type the gateway for this computer into this field, and then click Add. You will see it appear in the list of installed gateways.

Lastly, let's configure our hosts file for the Windows client. Use edit or WordPad to edit the text file called HOSTS that is located in your WINDOWS directory (usually C:\WINDOWS). The format of the file should be identical between platforms and consist of an IP address followed by a hostname. Include both the servers and our machine's hostname when you create the file.

You are now finished with the Windows TCP/IP networking setup. This configuration will allow you to communicate with similarly configured machines on a TCP/IP network. Click the OK button to save your changes, and activate your settings. You will probably need your Windows 95 CD at this point, and you will be prompted to reboot your computer.

Is the HOSTS File Necessary?

If you've configured TCP/IP before, you probably haven't edited the HOSTS file. In fact, these examples are more of an exercise than a necessity. Defining your HOSTS file eliminates DNS lookups for the computers you define. If you have a working DNS, you don't need the file, but it can speed things up. If you're working only on a single subnet, chances are you don't need a HOSTS file at all.

My display doesn't quite look like yours; is something wrong?

No, you're probably running the first version of Windows. The primary tabs that you need to be concerned with are the IP Address, DNS Configuration, and Gateway tabs. The other tabs are used to configure Windows-specific TCP/IP properties.

Part

I

Ch

5

Configuring Red Hat Linux 5.x.

Linux is the most difficult of the three clients to configure for TCP/IP. If you're running the Red Hat distribution of Linux, you have several useful tools that allow you to easily change configuration information, just like a Macintosh or Windows computer. Unfortunately, these tools, although nice, are distributed only with Red Hat Linux, and there are several different distributions of Red Hat available. Although I'm using Red Hat 5.x as my reference platform, I am also attempting to keep my examples as generic as possible so they can be applied to other Linux distributions and other UNIX variations when possible. For that reason, I'm going to be showing you the nitty gritty information behind a Linux TCP/IP configuration and how to change it by hand. Don't worry, it isn't too bad—just a little bit more convoluted than our other examples.

Linux stores its TCP/IP configuration information in text files that, unfortunately, are scattered around the system. The good news is that they're easy to configure, once you know where they are. The bad news is that there are several you'll need to edit to accomplish the same thing that one configuration dialog box did in our previous two examples.

Let's start by setting up one of the best-hidden parts of the TCP/IP configuration, the DNS server. Many unices will allow you to set up IP, gateway, and subnet information in a single location, and will then leave you entirely in the dark as to where you set the DNS server. Typically, you accomplish this task in a file in /etc called resolv.conf (yes, the "e" is supposed to be missing). This file specifies the domain name of the host as well as a list of name servers it uses. It isn't uncommon for this file to be missing entirely on UNIX systems, which will nonetheless function perfectly but require an IP address, or a name and IP definition in another file, /etc/hosts, to reach any other TCP/IP device. To edit the DNS configuration and set our domain, simply open /etc/resolv.conf in a text editor such as emacs, and add the following lines:

```
Domain          poisontooth.com
Nameserver      192.168.0.250
Nameserver      192.168.0.251
```

Naturally, you'll substitute the appropriate information for your own machine. Don't worry about the spacing when editing the file; just make sure you have at least one space between the different words (Domain and poisontooth.com, and so on). Linux will figure out what you mean. Finally, save the file, making sure you're saving it in the /etc directory (otherwise, the machine will not notice its existence). That wasn't too bad, was it?

The next step will be setting the hostname so the machine will know what to call itself. The first place you will do so is in the hosts file (once again, in the /etc directory). Open the /etc/hosts file and configure it to look like this:

```
127.0.0.1           localhost localhost.localdomain
192.168.0.2           mymachine.poisontooth.com
192.168.0.10        server1.poisontooth.com
192.168.0.11        server2.poisontooth.com
```

The first line specifies what is called a loopback interface; this line will already exist in the file. It allows the machine to talk to itself using TCP/IP, even if it isn't on a network. The second line contains our IP address, followed by the host name of our computer and the domain name concatenated together into a fully qualified domain name (FQDN). You may add additional lines to this file with other IP addresses and hostnames. We'll add the addresses of our two servers to the bottom of the file, and then save the results.

Now, you get to some of the more critical files. When editing these files, make sure you type carefully. The computer uses them when initializing the TCP/IP configuration, and a typo may cause your computer to behave strangely. The previous two files can contain errors without causing too much harm. Start with the file network which is located a bit deeper in the Linux directory structure: /etc/sysconfig/network. Here you will configure the machine's hostname (again), domain name, and gateway. Open the file in your text editor now and enter the following information:

```
NETWORKING=yes
FORWARD_IPV4=false
HOSTNAME=mymachine.poisontooth.com
DOMAINNAME=poisontooth.com
GATEWAY=192.168.0.1
GATEWAYDEV=eth0
```

What happens if my hostname here doesn't match the one I put in /etc/ hosts?

If you accidentally put different hostnames in your /etc/hosts and your /etc/sysconfig/network files (for example, if you change hostnames and forget to change one), your machine may behave very strangely. It's likely to respond to one hostname at its console, and to another from the network. All in all, a situation guaranteed to cause both you and your network administrator unwanted stress.

There's also a way to get your machine to believe it has one IP address at the console but to respond to another on the network interface; discovering this is left as an exercise for the terminally curious.

Each line defines a separately configurable field for the network configuration. Here's a brief summary of the various settings:

- NETWORKING=yes—This tells Linux to initialize its networking at startup. If NETWORKING were set to "no," any network devices in the machine would be disabled.

- FORWARD_IPV4=false—For now, we'll leave this set to false. Later, when we discuss various ways of providing server services to your network, we'll discuss IP Forwarding.

- HOSTNAME—Simple enough, this is the entire hostname (machine name + domain name) of our machine. To fit our sample configuration, it should read `mymachine.poisontooth.com`.

- DOMAINNAME—The name of the domain the machine is located in: `poisontooth.com`.

- GATEWAY—Make sure this is set to the gateway for the computer. Ours is 192.168.0.1.

- GATEWAYDEV=eth0—If you were to have multiple Ethernet cards in your machine, you would need to tell it which card talks to the gateway. For a simple one-card machine, the name of the primary Ethernet card for all network activity is eth0.

Lastly, you'll want to look at the configuration file that specifies the final pieces of information needed for our network interface. This file is called ifcfg-eth0 (interface configuration file for the default Ethernet controller) and is located in /etc/sysconfig/network-scripts/. Go ahead and open the interface configuration file now and make the following changes:

```
DEVICE=eth0
IPADDR=192.168.0.2
NETMASK=255.255.0.0
NETWORK=192.168.0.0
BROADCAST=192.168.255.255
ONBOOT=yes
```

Again, each line can be considered a field value that controls a specific setting for a specific network device. Here's an explanation of the settings:

- DEVICE—The device we're configuring. Once again, eth0 is the default Ethernet card for a Linux system. If there are multiple Ethernet cards, you may also have eth1, eth2, and so on. These configurations would be contained in the files ifcfg-eth1 and ifcfg-eth2, respectively.

- IPADDR—The IP address to be assigned to this network device. The IP address for our sample configuration is 192.168.0.2. Be sure that if you change your IP address in this field, you also change it in the /etc/hosts file.

■ NETMASK—The Network mask: 255.255.0.0.

■ NETWORK—Specifies the subnet directly. You may think of this as the IP address, with "0" filling the bit positions that would be occupied by nodes on the network. Our network is 192.168.0.0.

■ BROADCAST—Packets sent to this address can be read by any machine on the network. This is used to send out requests for information when the exact address of a server isn't known. It's the same as the network address, except the bit positions that define network nodes are filled with 1s rather than 0s. For the network 192.168.0.0, the broadcast address is 192.168.255.255.

Why don't I configure a broadcast/network address under Windows or Mac OS?

Under the previous two operating systems, the broadcast and network addresses are computed automatically for you. Linux, on the other hand, requires a separate configuration.

■ ONBOOT=yes—Controls whether this network interface will be initialized on boot. If you were to set this to "no," the computer would not read this configuration file when it's started. You can, however, manually start a network interface once the machine is running. The most common reason that this value would be set to "no" is if the network connection is a dial-in network device. You, most likely, would not want your computer dialing into a remote network every time you turned it on.

That's the worst it gets, so if you made it this far, you'll have no trouble with anything else on the Linux side of things.

Other TCP/IP Configurations

You now have the knowledge to successfully configure three different types of TCP/IP clients for your network. Although each of these setups was purely an exercise to help you become comfortable with where information is located within different operating systems, you will apply this information later in the book to set up a small network.

You've seen a few possible TCP/IP setups, but there are hundreds of other possible configurations. You may have assumed, until now, that a network device is a computer, but this isn't always the case. There are TCP/IP printers, dedicated web servers, cameras that serve their images directly over the network without requiring a connection to a computer, and the list goes on. The number of network-ready devices has increased quickly since the explosion of the Internet. You should see similarities between the different configurations you just set up. Keep in mind that there are four key pieces of information needed to successfully set up a TCP/IP network:

■ An IP address

■ A subnet mask

■ A DNS server

■ A gateway

Before long, you'll be able to set up any TCP/IP device you stumble across, whether you are familiar with it or not.

Other Information Sources

Apple's Open Transport Information `http://developer.apple.com/dev/opentransport/`

Linux Configuration and Troubleshooting `http://www.redhat.com/support/`

Windows Networking `http://support.microsoft.com/support/windows/howto/98/networking.asp`

Part

I

Ch

5

II

Part 2: TCP/IP Protocols

TCP/IP is a protocol in and of itself, but there are also numerous protocols built on top of the TCP/IP presentation layer. Everytime you check your email, or send a message to someone else, you're probably using a TCP/IP protocol. In part 2, you'll look at several of the common TCP/IP protocols and how they work. Web pages aren't the "magic" they sometimes appear to be. Take a look at the HTTP protocol and find out how they really work. Once you've finished part 2, you'll understand what goes on behind the scenes.

6   Understanding TCP/IP Protocols 103

7   Using Mail Protocols 109

8   Using Document Delivery Protocols 129

9   Investigating Other Useful Protocols 145

## CHAPTER 6

Understanding TCP/IP Protocols

by John Ray

In this chapter

Telnet **104**

Protocols and Protocol Development **105**

Uniform Resource Locators **107**

The Future of the File System **108**

Let's Get Started **108**

In this and the following several chapters, we'll look at a couple of ways of using TCP/IP at the protocol level. You'll learn the underlying messages that pass between your computer and the various servers you may communicate with, such as email and Web servers. This knowledge, in turn, will give you a better understanding of error messages you may encounter when providing your own TCP/IP services. If you come from a programming background, you may even want to take a stab at writing your own client software for some of these protocols. The world can always use another Web browser!

To follow these examples, we'll be connecting to a number of different services and manually carrying on dialogs that would usually be handled automatically. Some of this might not make much sense at the outset, but if you work through the instructions as given and think about what we're doing in each, you'll come away with a much better understanding of how these programs work their magic. Most of the examples will require a telnet client on your computer. Such a client is available as a DOS command under 95/98/NT and can be accessed by bringing up an MS-DOS Prompt window and then simply typing **telnet**. The standard Windows telnet is shown in Figure 6.1. Under Linux (UNIX), you must open a shell and again type **telnet**.

FIGURE 6.1

Telnet is commonly used to connect to mainframes or run remote text-based programs.

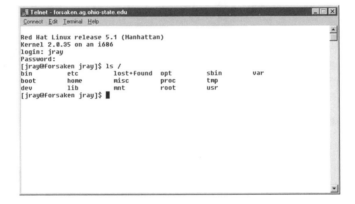

Macintosh computers do not come with a telnet client, but client software is readily available online. The most feature-filled Macintosh telnet client is "BetterTelnet" and is available from:

`http://www.cstone.net/rbraun/mac/telnet/`

Once you have a telnet client installed on your Macintosh, you may follow the examples by selecting "Open" from the client's file menu and entering into the connection dialog box any information following the word *telnet* in the examples I'll provide shortly.

Telnet

Because we're going to be using Telnet extensively, it might be helpful to have a bit of background on the telnet protocol and why we'll be using it so extensively in this section. Telnet was designed to provide the service of a terminal that could be used over a network. It can connect to a remote TCP/IP host and provide a two-way communications stream between the local and remote hosts. Port 23 is the port that has been predefined for telnet connections.

Telnet clients usually connect to telnet servers, which run by default on UNIX machines and are available for Windows and Macintosh machines as well. The server allows a telnet client to remotely operate a shell on the host machine.

A variety of low-level information is passed back and forth between a telnet server and telnet client when they first connect. These communications are part of the presentation layer and are referred to as DOs, DON'Ts, WILLs and WON'Ts. They allow the two machines to communicate information about themselves, such as the rate at which information is transferred, character sets used, and so on.

When a telnet client wants to offer a particular feature, it will send out a WILL XXX command to indicate its willingness to use that feature. The second machine may respond with DO or DON'T, depending on whether it wants to activate the function. Similarly, one of the machines can request that a feature on the other machine be turned on by sending a DO request. The other may respond with a positive WILL or negative WON'T.

Although these negotiations take place by sending a few unrecognizable (to human eyes) bytes back and forth, it's still easy to understand the simplicity of the protocol. We'll discuss a few other protocols that use an unreadable language in their presentation layer at the end of this chapter. We'll start with some of the most frequently used protocols, which actually are very easy to understand. Telnet will be used to connect to the ports that these protocols run on; it doesn't need to talk to a telnet server to be useful. Telnet can open a connection to any TCP service on any port and allow you to communicate directly with the remote server.

Protocols and Protocol Development

As you might have guessed, we cannot even begin to scratch the surface of the number of available TCP/IP protocols we can use on our networks, but we'll be looking at some of the most common. These protocols, in turn, can be advanced with other protocols, and so on. For example, we can expand our email protocols with TCP/IP-based secure authentication. An extension to a Web server protocol can allow client browsers to upload entire files to a server. There is a protocol in use daily called *RPC* (*Remote Procedure Calls*) that allows programmers to execute portions of their programs on different machines, enabling a network to work together to process information more quickly.

Streaming video and sound is one of the hot topics on the Internet today. Unfortunately, there are many different multimedia protocols competing for user acceptance. Each has its advantages and disadvantages, and there is no clear winner. Because a standard has yet to be determined, we're forced to download client software (usually plugins for our browsers) to support each of the different protocols we want to use. Undoubtedly, you've used Netshow, RealVideo, or even Quicktime to view video over the Internet. These are just a few of the many competing streaming standards. This fragmentation of the user base is the primary disadvantage to proprietary protocols.

Protocols discussed in RFCs are owned by the network population as a whole. We can make comments and critique protocols as they're being developed. We actually have a chance to interact with the people developing the standards, rather than being shielded from them. If you come up with a modification to a standard, you can submit your thoughts and suggestions in an RFC of your own, and, if there is enough support for the changes you suggest, it might very well become a standard.

Unfortunately, even with the RFCs, there are problems. People can and do make changes to the accepted standards when they're implementing their own client software. This can be just as bad as creating a proprietary protocol. Obvious examples of this are the browser-specific HTML tags that are not recognized by different Web browsers. Although HTML is a rigidly defined standard, browser authors decided that the language didn't quite live up to their expectations. Rather than submit their requests to the public for open discussion, they chose to implement their own tags that enabled the functionality they desired—often without apparent forethought regarding the consequences of these additions. The end result of this is that when we visit Web sites, we see banners such as "Best Viewed With So-n-So's Browser." The purpose of HTML is not to force a particular visual representation on data display, but to make certain that all data is completely and "properly" (based on the user's preferences) displayed. If HTML is truly to be a standard, Web pages must present the same information on any browser we use to view them. As we all know, this just isn't the case.

As you work more with TCP/IP, you'll come to appreciate how robust and extensive the services it can offer really are. Keep in mind, however, that it's the open specification that made TCP/IP what it is today, and it will be open specifications that allow it to grow into the future.

Uniform Resource Locators

Before we begin our discussion of protocols, let's take a few moments to review the commonly misunderstood *URL*. While not a protocol itself, a URL is a way of referring to protocols and the information that can be retrieved over them. URLs, as I'm sure you know, are the little addresses that you use to specify a Web site. They are commonly thought to be directly related to the World Wide Web, but, in fact, they are destined to serve a far more significant role with TCP/IP. *URL* stands for *Universal Resource Locator*, and its purpose is to do precisely that: universally locate and identify resources to be accessed.

Today we commonly use a variety of different directory structures on different platforms to access data. For example, let's take a look at the location of the HOSTS file we edited on each platform during the TCP/IP configuration process in Chapter 5, "Configuring Client Workstations."

On the Macintosh, the file path is specified as:

`MacintoshHD:SystemFolder:hosts`

Under Windows 95/98, we must look at:

`C:\WINDOWS\HOSTS`

On the Linux machine, we edited the file:

`/etc/hosts`

How can the Macintosh have a file path?

Macintosh users are probably scratching their heads after seeing the file path specified for MacOS. After all, the Macintosh has no command line, so it's impossible to specify a file path. That's true. However, when programming the Mac, file paths must be used, and they are denoted by the path taken to reach the file through the folder hierarchy, with the names of the individual folders separated by ":" (colons).

The goal of URLs is to provide a common method of specifying any file on any operating system. Imagine what a Web address would look like if it had to contain the path to each of its files as denoted by the operating system of the server. It would be next to impossible to remember addresses, because you'd also have to memorize whether you were using colons, forward slashes, back slashes, or, heaven forbid, the entirely evil directory structure of the OS known as VMS. Let's take another look at our HOSTS files, this time as they would be referenced using a file URL.

Macintosh:

`file:///MacintoshHD/SystemFolder/hosts`

Windows:

`file:///C/WINDOWS/HOSTS`

Linux:

`file:///etc/hosts`

This system is obviously a bit more consistent and easier to understand than using the native file reference techniques. But wait a second, what's with the `file://`? Shouldn't that be `http://`? Nope. This is the beauty of the URL. It was made to be able to specify any source of resource, no matter where it is stored, or what protocol must be used to access it. The most common place we see URLs is in reference to Web sites, but that is just the tip of the iceberg. A URL consists of two things: an access method and a resource path. The access method is specified by the pattern `qqqqq://` (where `qqqqq` is a mnemonic for an access method), and the resource path is the remainder of the string. Let's take a look at the common access methods that can be specified in a URL:

- `file://`—This denotes a file that exists on the file system of the local machine. Any file on your local hard drive can be specified using this syntax. In our example, you may have noticed that there are three forward slashes following the `file://` access method. This is because the path to the file starts at the top of your directory structure, which is always `/`, and works down.

- `http://`—A resource that is accessible using the HTTP (Hypertext Transfer Protocol) transfer protocol commonly used with the World Wide Web. This is the most common URL we see and is often mistakenly assumed to be the only valid type of URL.

- `nntp://`—A resource located on an NNTP (Network News Transfer Protocol) server newsgroup.

- `ftp://`—A resource accessible through FTP (File Transfer Protocol).
- `gopher://`—Ever used a gopher server? You will soon. It's a bit old, but even it has its own URL access method.

There are also methods of specifying URLs for files that exist on Macintosh and Windows networks using the AppleTalk and SMB protocols. These URLs are proprietary, so they aren't of great interest to us here.

The Future of the File System

As with many recent technologies, despite encompassing more than just the Web, URLs have had to rely on the popularity of Web browsers to gain importance. The future could be very exciting if URLs are allowed to live up to their full potential: the abstraction of the methods for accessing data. Imagine the convenience if we could open a file on a remote machine just by typing the URL into our word processor, or edit an online image by supplying its URL to a paint program. This sort of functionality is beginning to appear in the three major office suites (Corel WordPerfect, Lotus SmartSuite, and Microsoft Office), and a few other products. Linux users will want to check out the KDE desktop system for UNIX systems at:

`http://www.kde.org/`

KDE is a free desktop and application environment with precisely this sort of information location abstraction. It is very nice to be able to edit and save files directly on an FTP server. KDE can do this today. Hopefully, within the next few years it will be a common capability of all operating systems.

Let's Get Started

My hope is that the upcoming three chapters will give you a greater appreciation for the ways in which high-level TCP/IP communications take place. You should also be able to interact with a number of TCP/IP services without the use of client software, which will allow you to diagnose problems as they occur between clients and servers. If you're interested in learning about other protocols that exist, I highly recommend that you take a look at the index of available RFCs and spend some time clicking through them. They are an excellent source for technical information as well as a wonderful way to become more acquainted with what TCP/IP protocols exist, why they were created, and where users think they should evolve:

`http://freesoft.org/CIE/RFC/rfc-ind.htm`

My first experience with TCP/IP was being asked to take over administration of a DOS and UNIX network. I had no background in TCP/IP, UNIX, or even networking. It was not a pleasant introduction to the topic. I don't want your first look at TCP/IP to leave you feeling the way I did. If you are at all uncomfortable with the concepts of IP addresses and TCP/IP configuration, please take this time to look back over Chapters 3 and 5 before continuing into the protocol descriptions. The rest of the book will be concerned with the setup and configuration of actual services on your own TCP/IP network. Get ready, the fun stuff is about to begin.

Using Mail Protocols

by John Ray

In this chapter

POP3 **110**

SMTP **115**

IMAP **119**

Client Software and Other Information Sources **127**

In the previous chapter, we prepared to study TCP/IP protocols by firing up our Telnet program and discussing Uniform Resource Locators and the development of open protocol standards. Now we will begin our exploration of the common TCP/IP protocols by looking at some of the most popular protocols. In particular, I'm talking about the protocols used in transferring electronic mail. For each protocol, we'll discuss an authentication procedure that is used in the initial connection, and then the commands that we can issue after we have authenticated. I'll also provide examples of the use of the commands to make their use clear.

POP3

To begin our look at the session layer mail protocols, we'll look at the POP3, or Post Office Protocol. You're probably already very familiar with using POP3 if you regularly use an email client such as Eudora or Microsoft Outlook to read your mail.

The purpose of the POP3 server is to provide a pickup point for your email. Your computer connects to the POP3 server through a TCP/IP connection on port 110. It then issues a series of commands that identify who you are, collects information about the messages you have, and then retrieves the messages to your local computer. POP3based email was developed to help ease the load of multiple sustained connections on a mail server. Previously, clients had to log directly into a mail server and use software, generally command-line driven, on the server to read email. For a corporation or university of any reasonable size, this scheme would place quite a load on the server (and still does, in some cases). Furthermore, once you had read your mail, it was not automatically removed from the server. You could leave it on the server for as long as you saw fit. POP3 eliminates these problems by making short, fast connections to the server, during which the email is moved from the server onto the local client machine. Server resource requirements are significantly reduced when using the POP mail system.

If I Use POP3 for Reading My Email, Do I HAVE to Remove the Mail from the Server?

No, not really. The intent of POP3 was to reduce the load—both on computational resources and on storage—for the server. It's a rather controversial protocol in that many feel it was designed to serve the needs of administrators, and that the needs of the users were barely considered all. While most POP clients are set to remove mail from the server automatically by default, and most server administrators would prefer that you did, you'll find an option in most clients to allow you to leave your email on the server.

When learning to communicate with this and other protocols, we'll enter commands to the server and react to the server's responses. One thing you'll notice with POP3 and many of the other TCP/IP protocols is that they use very understandable and English-like syntax in the commands. This is not always the case, but, in a surprising number of instances, you can almost guess the commands you'll need to use.

POP3 Authentication

For the example of the POP3 protocol, I'll connect to my personal email account. You'll need to use your own POP3 server to follow the example fully. In general, your POP3 server is the machine name that follows the @ symbol in your email address. For me (jray@poisontooth.com), the POP3 server is poisontooth.com. Depending on the email server you choose to use, the responses will probably be slightly different from what you see here, but will still contain the same information. Figure 7.1 shows a sample Telnet-based POP session.

FIGURE 7.1

A POP3 session is controlled here via Telnet.

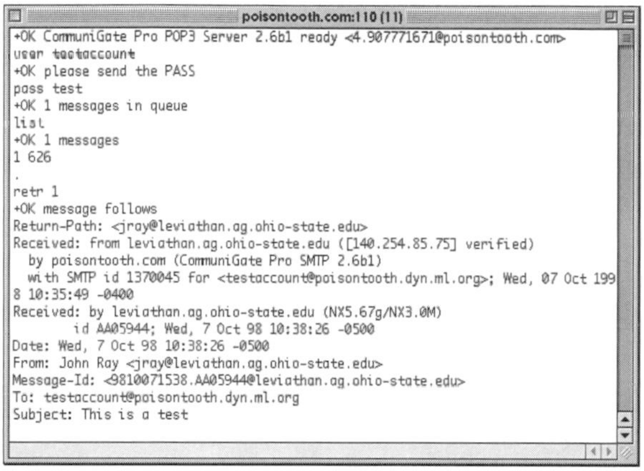

```
+OK CommuniGate Pro POP3 Server 2.6b1 ready <4.907771671@poisontooth.com>
user testaccount
+OK please send the PASS
pass test
+OK 1 messages in queue
list
+OK 1 messages
1 626
.
retr 1
+OK message follows
Return-Path: <jray@leviathan.ag.ohio-state.edu>
Received: from leviathan.ag.ohio-state.edu ([140.254.85.75] verified)
   by poisontooth.com (CommuniGate Pro SMTP 2.6b1)
   with SMTP id 1370045 for <testaccount@poisontooth.dyn.ml.org>; Wed, 07 Oct 199
8 10:35:49 -0400
Received: by leviathan.ag.ohio-state.edu (NX5.67g/NX3.0M)
         id AA05944; Wed, 7 Oct 98 10:38:26 -0500
Date: Wed, 7 Oct 98 10:38:26 -0500
From: John Ray <jray@leviathan.ag.ohio-state.edu>
Message-Id: <9810071538.AA05944@leviathan.ag.ohio-state.edu>
To: testaccount@poisontooth.dyn.ml.org
Subject: This is a test
```

With your information in hand, the next step depends on your operating system. Linux users access a command shell. Windows users should launch an MS-DOS Prompt window, while Macintosh owners select Open from inside your Telnet client. At the command prompt, type the following, substituting your POP3 server name for poisontooth.com:

```
>telnet poisontooth.com 110
```

This command will connect you to port 110 on the machine with the name you specified; port 110 connects you to the POP3 server. You should see a message indicating that the POP3 server is ready to accept commands:

```
+OK POP3 dub240191.columbus.rr.com v4.47 server ready
```

There are two commands we'll now issue to the POP server: USER and PASS. The USER command will identify a username on the server that points to a particular mailbox. As you might guess, PASS will allow us to specify the password for the mailbox.

USER My user account is jray (from jray@poisontooth.com), so I will send a command that looks like this:

```
USER jray
```

The POP3 server can now respond with either an +OK message that indicates that the username has been accepted, or +ERR that will be shown if there is an error.

```
+OK User name accepted, password please
```

Part
II

Ch
7

PASS My user name was accepted successfully, so I can now finish logging in. To do this, I'll use the PASS password command followed by my email password. The password will be displayed as clear text (I'm substituting asterisks to keep my password secret, so make sure no one is watching when you type yours:

```
PASS ********
```

At this point, the POP3 server will indicate a successful login, once again using this +OK convention, or, if the password is incorrect, +ERR.

```
+OK Mailbox open, 4 messages
```

I am now successfully connected to my mailbox, and I can proceed to issue other POP3 commands.

Controlling Your POP3 Session

Once logged into the POP server, there are several basic commands you can use to manipulate messages in your mailbox. These commands may be used in any sequence, so feel free to mix and match as you see fit.

STAT The STAT command is used to determine information about the mailbox we're connected to; specifically, the number of messages available and the number of bytes of storage space they use. The response will be in the form of +OK x y, where x is the number of messages, and y is size of the messages. It's possible that the server will return other information in response to the STAT command, but it's unlikely.

Example:

```
STAT
+OK 4 4522
```

This shows that we have four messages in our mailbox, occupying a total of 4522 bytes.

LIST Message-Number The LIST command can be used by itself or followed by a message number. Before anything, it will return a +OK response, followed by the number of messages in the mailbox. If used by itself, LIST will display a listing of all the active messages in your mailbox. The format of the list is a message number followed by the size of the message in bytes. If the LIST command is used in conjunction with a message number, it lists only information about that message. In the case that a message number that doesn't exist is specified, LIST will return -ERR no such message.

Example:

```
LIST

+OK 4 messages
1 2895
2 2275
3 15295
4 3269
```

RETR Message-Number This will retrieve the message number specified, including the message's header information. If a message number that doesn't exist is used, it will display `-ERR no such message`.

Example:

```
RETR 1

Received: from different.ag.ohio-state.edu (different.ag.ohio-state.edu
[140.254.85.74])
Date:    Tue, 21 Jul 1998 12:41:17 -0400
To:      jray@poisontooth.com
From:    Jack Derifaj <jackd@xxxxx.net>
Subject:    Address For SDK
Mime-Version: 1.0
Content-Type: text/plain; charset="us-ascii"
Status: RO

        Now how far did you get in that book?
        Jack
```

DELE message-number Marks the message number specified in the command as being deleted. Any other attempts to retrieve of obtain information about this number will generate an error message. Success is indicated by +OK message deleted.

Example:

```
DELE 1
+OK Message deleted
```

NOOP Performs "no operation." This does absolutely nothing on the POP server except generate an +OK response. A client might use this command to make sure that the POP server is still responding to requests.

Example:

```
NOOP
+OK cool
```

RSET Resets any message marked as deleted to their original state. The only response is +OK.

Example:

```
RSET
+OK markers cleared
```

QUIT The QUIT command ends the clients connection to the server, and removes any messages that have been marked for deletion.

Example:

```
QUIT
+OK CommuniGate Pro POP3 Server connection closed
```

Part
II

Ch
7

Optional Commands

You have now seen the basic POP3 commands that can be issued to any POP3 server. There are additional commands that, depending on your server implementation, may be useful. These are not required by the POP3 specification, and may not work for you.

TOP *Message-Number Number-of-Lines* The TOP command can be very useful for finding out information about messages without reading them. TOP will return the header information for the message number specified. The second parameter indicates the number of lines of the message body itself that TOP will display. This must be a non-negative number and must be specified, even if it is zero. The server will respond with an +OK message and the desired header, or an error -ERR no such message.

Example:

```
TOP 1 0

+OK Top of message follows

Received: from different.ag.ohio-state.edu (different.ag.ohio-state.edu
[140.254.85.74])
Date:    Tue, 21 Jul 1998 12:41:17 -0400
To:      jray@poisontooth.com
From:    Jack Derifaj <jackd@xxxxx.net>
Subject:   Address For SDK
Mime-Version: 1.0
Content-Type: text/plain; charset="us-ascii"
Status: RO
```

UIDL message-number The "Unique ID Listing" may seem a bit strange at first, but it has a very practical purpose. It will generate a list of the message numbers in your mailbox, followed by a unique identifier. This unique identifier is a sequence of letters and numbers computed by the server and guaranteed to be unique. In your email program, you may have seen the option to leave mail on server; UIDL is used in this case. For the email client to know if it has downloaded a message already, it stores the unique IDs, as generated by the server. If it sees a matching unique ID on the server, it will skip the message during downloading, thus saving you from having extra copies of the message in your email client. The server will respond to this command with a +OK message followed by a listing of messages with their IDs. If a specific message number is given, the result will be OK+ followed by information about that message, or an error -ERR no such message.

Example:

```
UIDL

+OK Unique-ID listing follows
1 35b2d5960000008a
2 35b2d5960000008b
3 35b2d5960000008f
4 35b2d59600000091
```

Doing It by Hand

So how does this information help us? Can't we just continue using Eudora and never see these commands? Although email clients are used most of the time, there are several instances where connecting directly to the POP server is helpful.

It's not uncommon for an email client to have problems retrieving a message if the message is malformed or corrupted. In these cases, the client generally "hangs" once it reaches the offending message. Using what you now know, you can connect to the server, erase the message and the problem with it.

Now, suppose you are connected to the network with a 28.8 or, perish the thought, slower modem. You start downloading your email only to discover that someone has sent you a 10-megabyte attachment that will take several hours to download. Most email clients allow you to skip large messages, but how do you remove it permanently from the server? It's entirely possible that there might be a quota on your email account, and the evil attachment could be causing important incoming messages to be rejected. Using the LIST and DELE commands, you can determine a message's size and delete it from your mailbox.

Knowing the POP3 commands allows you to access your email from anywhere via a basic TCP/IP connection. You don't need access to anything more than a Telnet client, which, as we mentioned in Chapter 6, "Understanding TCP/IP Protocols," comes with Windows 95, 98, and NT as well as UNIX, and is freely available for the Macintosh.

SMTP

We've covered reading our email via a direct connection to a POP3 server, but how about sending email? Some POP3 servers and clients can actually send email from within a POP3 connection, but this operation is not to be considered the norm. Most clients connect to a separate TCP/IP service called SMTP to send messages.

SMTP, or Simple Mail Transfer Protocol, is the backbone for all email. It accepts incoming mail on port 25 and stores it in individual mailboxes, or transports the mail to another machine for delivery.

Connecting to the SMTP Server

To demonstrate SMTP at work, we compose and send a message by talking directly to an SMTP server. You can generally identify your SMTP server from the SMTP Host line in your email client. In many cases, it will be the same machine as your POP3 server. Once again, in our examples, I will use poisontooth.com as my SMTP server. You should substitute your SMTP host for poisontooth.com.

```
>telnet poisontooth.com 25
```

Once connected, you should see a welcome message from the SMTP server:

```
220 poisontooth.com ESMTP Sendmail 8.8.7/8.8.7; Mon, 3 Aug 1998 23:50:25-0400
```

***Saying* "HELO"** The HELO command identifies your domain name to the SMTP server. This should be what comes to the right of the @ symbol in your email address. I will be using poisontooth.com.

```
HELO poisontooth.com
250 poisontooth.com Hello [192.168.0.2], pleased to meet you
```

Strangely friendly, isn't it? You may now send the commands that will identify the message's sender (you) and the recipient, as well as the body of the email.

Sending Mail

Once connected to the SMTP server, you can issue commands much like you did with the POP3 server. In this case, however, the command structure is slightly more rigid, and we must send the commands in the correct order; otherwise, the server will respond with error messages.

MAIL FROM: sender-email-address First, we need to specify the sender (you) of the message using the MAIL FROM command. I'm using my address (jray@poisontooth.com). You should use your own address in place of mine; otherwise, you'll be inadvertently forging a message from my email account. The server will respond with a 250 Ok message if the sender address is accepted as valid.

Example:

```
MAIL FROM: jray@poisontooth.com
250 jray@poisontooth.com... Sender ok
```

Can Email Messages Truly Be Forged?

I just advised you not to use my email address when logging into the SMTP server to avoid seeming to forge an email message from me. But if you had nefarious intentions, is it possible to forge an email from someone? Not without considerable effort. Looking at the SMTP protocol, you're probably thinking that you can specify any sender that you'd like, and your identity will be hidden. This, however, is not the case. Headers that are stored with each email message will trace the message back to the machine that originated the connection to the SMTP server. While a message may appear to be from a person other than the actual sender, there are mechanisms in place to keep track of the path an email takes to reach its destination.

RCPT TO: receiver-email-address Now we use the RCPT TO command to specify a recipient for the message we're going to send. I'm using the address of a friend; you can use any address you'd like, although it's a bit easier to confirm that everything worked okay if you use your own address. If the server accepts the given recipient, it will reply with a 250 OK message. If not, it will return a 550 Failure. You may specify multiple recipients with this command by simply using it multiple times. In this example, I'll name three recipients, two of which are valid, and a third that isn't.

Example:

```
RCPT TO: jackd@qqqqqq.net
250 jackd@qqqqqq.net... Recipient ok
```

```
RCPT TO: mrsandman
550 mrsandman... User unknown
RCPT TO: jray@bigmac.ag.ohio-state.edu
250 jray@bigmac.ag.ohio-state.edu... Recipient ok
```

There are some cases where the recipient of the email will be considered a special case on the server. Besides the positive 250 message and the negative 550, there are two other messages the server might want to send at this point:

- 251 Non-local user, will forward—The server knows that the user is not located on this machine but will attempt to forward the email message to the appropriate destination. No user interaction is required.

- 551 Non-local user, please try recipient-email-address—Once again, the server recognizes that the user does not have a local mailbox. In this case, however, it refuses to forward the message and provides the appropriate address to the client to use to reach the recipient.

DATA Now's the time to enter in the data (that is, the message body) for the email we want to send. I'm going to send a short message to a friend of mine; you can send anything (within reason!) that you'd like. The message must be entered one line at a time and is considered complete when you type a "." (period) on a line by itself. The server will return a 250 OK message upon successfully processing the message.

If you want to specify header information such as the Date or Subject, you must add these lines to the body of your message. They're not part of the standard SMTP generated headers and will not be present in the final message unless entered manually.

Example:

```
DATA

354 Enter mail, end with "." on a line by itself
Hi Jack,
    How is it going?
John
.
250 WAA04771 Message accepted for delivery
```

The SMTP server will now look at the recipient's address and determine if it is a local address. If it is, the server will store the message in the user's mailbox. If it isn't, it will look at the hostname specified in the recipient's email address. It uses this hostname to look up the MX (Mail Exchanger) record for the hostname, which, if it can't find, will assume is the same as the hostname itself. This is the SMTP server for the remote mailbox. Our SMTP server will then contact the remote SMTP server using the same communications procedure we just used and will deliver the message to the remote server.

Within a few minutes, your message, assuming it was correctly addressed, will be delivered to its destination. You can use your knowledge of the POP3 protocol to connect to your POP3 server to verify that the message was delivered successfully.

QUIT The QUIT command closes the connection to the SMTP server. A successful exit is indicated by a 221 message.

Example:

```
QUIT
221 poisontooth.com  closing connection
```

Optional Commands

There are additional commands that provide added functionality to the SMTP command set, much like the added commands of POP3. Let's look at a few of these commands now.

RSET This command resets the information that has been entered into the SMTP server. It will clear out the sender, recipients, and any data that has been entered. The server will respond with a 250 OK message.

Example:

```
RSET
250 Reset state
```

HELP *Command-Name* If used without an option, HELP displays a list of the available commands. If used with a command, it will give information about the syntax and use of the command.

Example:

```
HELP

214-This is Sendmail version 8.8.7
214-Topics:
214-    HELO    EHLO    MAIL    RCPT    DATA
214-    RSET    NOOP    QUIT    HELP    VRFY
214-    EXPN    VERB    ETRN    DSN
214-For more info use "HELP <topic>".
214-To report bugs in the implementation send email to
214-    sendmail-bugs@sendmail.org.
214-For local information send email to Postmaster at your site.
214 End of HELP info
```

VRFY `recipient-email-address` VRFY verifies an email address as being acceptable by the system. This command can be used before the RCPT TO: command to confirm the validity of email addresses. It will either issue a 250 OK message or any of the other error messages that can be generated by the RCPT TO: function.

Example(s):

```
VRFY jray
250 John Ray <jray@poisontooth.com>
VRFY mrsandman
550 mrsandman... User unknown
```

Don't be surprised if your SMTP server does not support the VRFY command. The first step that hackers take when attacking a network computer is to try to determine valid usernames on the system. Once a name is found, they can progress to trying to hack the user's password.

The VRFY command is a quick method of determining if a username exists on a system and is often disabled by security-conscious system administrators.

I've Heard of Sendmail Security Issues; Is There Anything Else I Should Know?

And how! Sendmail, the program that most commonly implements the SMTP protocol, is an amazingly complex and convoluted piece of software. System administrators can commonly be heard muttering about the "Sendmail bug of the week," and not without some cause. By virtue of the tasks that Sendmail must perform, it is provided unparalleled access to the filesystem, and over the years has provided what is almost without a doubt the greatest number of security holes in the UNIX environment. Properly configuring Sendmail and maintaining it in a functional and reasonably secure condition requires a significant and ongoing commitment and is well beyond the scope of this book. For further information, point-and-click your way to http://www.sendmail.org/, where you should find up-to-the-minute information on configuring your server for the best performance and security.

EXPN alias-name This command expands an alias and returns a list of the recipients that the alias will send mail to. Depending on the configuration of the mailing list, and the mail server, this command might not provide the results one would expect.

Example:

```
EXPN    webmaster

250-<hlaufman@xxxxxx.ag.ohio-state.edu>
250 <jray@poisontooth.com>
```

Here we see that email, which is sent to webmaster, is expanded by this SMTP server to go to both hlaufman and myself. (We both maintain the campus Web server) Once again, if the EXPN command is disabled on your server, don't be surprised. The EXPN command is potentially more dangerous than VRFY, because it allows an entire list of usernames to be discovered.

Doing It by Hand

Once again, knowledge of the SMTP command set is useful when diagnosing problems sending messages. You may have noticed that sometimes you can check mail without any trouble, but sending mail fails—or vice versa. This is because, as you now know, the service that sends mail is entirely separate and isolated from the one that delivers mail. Connecting directly to an SMTP server and manually attempting to send a piece of mail that is causing a problem for your email client is likely to return an error message that is far more useful than what the client itself can tell you.

IMAP

The IMAP, or Internet Message Access Protocol, is a recent addition to the TCP/IP mail protocols, and one of the most useful. It allows clients to connect to an IMAP server and remotely manipulate mailboxes as if they were located locally on each client. IMAP is designed to eliminate the frustration many people have with POP mail: too many copies of messages in too many places. POP-based email is effective when dealing with a single client computer. However, if you have a computer at home and one in the office, and share an email account between them, you're bound to run into some problems. I frequently receive help requests while I'm at home reading my mail. When I was still using a POP3 server, I would go to work and completely forget (until the phone rang) that I had gotten the email. IMAP eliminates this by keeping all your email on a server and allowing you to access it the same way, wherever you are. When I start Outlook Express at home, my mailboxes look exactly the same, message for message, as they do at work, and vice versa. Some IMAP servers will even allow you to configure rules to process your incoming IMAP messages into different mailboxes automatically.

Because of its rather large functionality, IMAP has a more extensive command set than the other protocols we've seen so far. Once again, we will start with the basic connection to the server, and work our way through each of the main functions. IMAP works much like the other protocols we've seen, with a small exception. When we send commands to the IMAP server, we must prefix the command with a unique tag. For our examples, we'll simply use a count and increase it as we go along (1,2,3, and so on). The use of this tag is necessary because IMAP servers can process more than one command at a time. When the server returns its results, it adds the tag that was used when the corresponding command was sent; this allows the client to determine which command (if multiple commands have been sent) is being replied to. Figure 7.2 shows a sample IMAP session that is being controlled through Telnet.

FIGURE 7.2

IMAP, like POP, can also be accessed and explored from within Telnet.

IMAP Authentication

IMAP servers run off of port 143. Let's go ahead and use our Telnet client to connect to an IMAP server now. Your mailserver may not be running IMAP, which you will quickly see if you can't connect to port 143. If this is the case, I strongly suggest you request that your ISP or network administrator install IMAP. It has proven to be a lifesaver on many occasions, and I couldn't even imagine going back to using a POP3 server.

This example will assume you're using simple login names and passwords to authenticate. IMAPv4 supports multiple authentication methods, including Kerberos—the holy grail of network security.

Kerberos? What's Kerberos?

Kerberos is a user authentication scheme that uses public-key encryption. Kerberos is generally thought of as less-than-friendly to install (and deriving its name from the three-headed canine guardian of the gates of Hades, one might actually expect this), but provides the best value in user authentication and security currently available. To learn more about Kerberos, point-and-click your way to the MIT Kerberos homepage at: http://web.mit.edu/kerberos/www/. To learn more about public-key encryption, see Chapter 18, "Using Security Techniques to Protect Your Network and Data."

```
>telnet poisontooth.com 25
* OK poisontooth.com IMAP4rev1 v10.223 server ready
```

CAPABILITY CAPABILITY displays special capabilities of the IMAP server, as well as the authentication method it supports. You don't need to send this command, but I'll do so to verify that my server is using the standard LOGIN authentication method, rather than a Kerberos database. Remember that we must prefix this and every command to the server with a tag.

```
1 CAPABILITY

* CAPABILITY IMAP4 IMAP4REV1 NAMESPACE SCAN SORT AUTH=LOGIN THREAD=ORDEREDSUBJECT
1 OK CAPABILITY completed
```

LOGIN The LOGIN command will allow me to send my username and password to the server. If a successful login occurs, the server will return the tag number I sent, along with an OK message.

```
2 LOGIN jray *****
2 OK LOGIN completed
```

We are now authenticated with the IMAP server and can proceed to send it commands to manipulate our mailboxes.

Controlling the IMAP Session

The IMAP server uses commands similar to the POP3 server to retrieve mail and information about messages. Because it also offers the ability to keep multiple mail folders per account, it must also provide commands to work on different folders and the messages they contain.

SELECT/EXAMINE mailbox-name This command will select a mailbox to be used on the server. You can work with only one mailbox at a time, so before you can read any messages, you must tell the server which mailbox the messages will be coming from. The default incoming mailbox on an IMAP server is called INBOX. You should use that for this example. If you choose to use the EXAMINE command instead of SELECT, you will open the mailbox in a read-only mode. Otherwise, SELECT and EXAMINE are identical.

Example:

```
3 SELECT INBOX

* 226 EXISTS
* OK [UIDVALIDITY 900912534] UID validity status
* OK [UIDNEXT 919] Predicted next UID
```

Part

II

Ch

7

```
* FLAGS (\Answered \Flagged \Deleted \Draft \Seen)
* OK [PERMANENTFLAGS (\* \Answered \Flagged \Deleted \Draft \Seen)] Permanent
flags
* OK [UNSEEN 50] 50 is first unseen message in /home/jray/mbox
* 1 RECENT
3 OK [READ-WRITE] SELECT completed
```

From the 226 EXISTS line, you can infer that there are a total of 226 messages in your mailbox. There is a single RECENT message that has not been viewed. That message is number 50, which is determined from the UNSEEN 50 indicator. The UIDNEXT 919 shows that a unique identification of 919 will be used for the next arriving piece of mail (remember how the POP3 server used this?). Also shown are the flags that supported in the mailbox, as well as the permanent flags that the user can set. Quite a bit of information from just selecting a mailbox, huh?

Notice that in the last line of the server, the mailbox is shown to be READ-WRITE, indicating that you have the ability to create and read messages in the mailbox. You may ask yourself, why would there be a mailbox that I can't write to? With IMAP's multiple mailboxes come some exciting new ways to look at email. It's possible under IMAP to have a shared mailbox that exists under many accounts. A group mailbox could contain company announcements and other information, and, to keep the information valid, it might be set to READ-ONLY for everyone except the person maintaining the information. That way no one would inadvertently delete or modify a message intended for everyone.

STATUS mailbox-name (option1 option2…) STATUS returns basic statistics on the given mailbox. You can view this status before selecting a mailbox to determine if there are new messages waiting. The options specify what data you're interested in returning.

The valid options are:

- MESSAGES—The total number of messages in the mailbox
- RECENT—The number of unread messages
- UIDNEXT—The next unique identifier that will be assigned to an incoming message
- UIDVALIDITY—A unique identifier for this mailbox
- UNSEEN—The total number of unread messages

Example:

```
4 STATUS INBOX (MESSAGES RECENT)

* STATUS INBOX (MESSAGES 229 RECENT 2)
4 OK STATUS completed
```

FETCH message-set (data-item-names) The FETCH command provides the meat of the message retrieval capabilities of IMAP. It can return all or portions of a message or range of messages from an IMAP server. The message set can be a message number, or a range of messages in the format of x:y, which would select all the message numbers between x and y. You must have issued the SELECT command for a mailbox before the FETCH command will work. There are a huge number of parameters that can be used with the FETCH command, so I'll provide two useful examples. You may want to read the RFC to construct your own FETCH commands that return the information you feel is important.

The first example will display a list of messages between 1 and 4, showing the `date`, `from`, and `subject` fields in the header.

Example:

```
5 FETCH 1:4 (FLAGS BODY[HEADER.FIELDS (DATE FROM SUBJECT)])

* 1 FETCH (FLAGS (\Seen) BODY[HEADER.FIELDS ("DATE" "FROM" "SUBJECT")] {109}
Date: Tue, 21 Jul 1998 13:58:10 -0400 (EDT)
From: devseed@apple.com
Subject: Apple FTP Site Access Code
)
* 2 FETCH (FLAGS (\Seen) BODY[HEADER.FIELDS ("DATE" "FROM" "SUBJECT")] {113}
From: Jack Derifaj <jackd@xxxxxx.net>
Date: Tue, 21 Jul 1998 13:09:58 -0700
Subject: I need to buy a Mac
)
* 3 FETCH (FLAGS (\Seen) BODY[HEADER.FIELDS ("DATE" "FROM" "SUBJECT")] {117}
Date: Tue, 21 Jul 1998 15:19:16 -0400
From: Will Ray <ray@anime.com>
Subject: Happy Day
)
* 4 FETCH (FLAGS (\Seen) BODY[HEADER.FIELDS ("DATE" "FROM" "SUBJECT")] {129}
Date: Tue, 21 Jul 1998 15:30:35 -0400
From: Abull Industries <abull@bigmac.ag.ohio-state.edu>
Subject: Large Salad
)
```

The result is self-explanatory. Message information is returned, as we requested, with the header fields we wanted. The flags set for each of these messages are also shown—in this case, all of these messages have the (`\Seen`) flag set, which indicates that they have all been read.

Now, let's use the FETCH command in another example to return the entire body of message number 2 from the list:

```
6 FETCH 2 BODY[]

* 2 FETCH (BODY[] {1959}

Received: from xxxxx.net by xxxxx.net
        via smtpd (for [193.70.128.146]) with SMTP; 21 Jul 1998 18:09:04 UT
Received: from ccMail by XXXX.NET
  (IMA Internet Exchange 3.0 Enterprise) id 001F6F04; Tue, 26 May 98 13:11:
MIME-Version: 1.0
Date: Tue, 21 Jul 1998 13:09:58 -0700
Message-Id: <001F6F04.eval@xxxxx.net>
Subject: I need to buy a Mac
To: John Ray <jray@different.ag.ohio-state.edu>
Content-Type: text/plain; charset=US-ASCII

    Hey John,

    I need to go ahead with the purchase of that iMac.  My other computer just
died again.
I need to get started with the programming again, and figure I'll try something
different this time.
```

```
Jack
)
6 OK FETCH completed
```

STORE message-set item-name-to-set (value-to-set) STORE allows us to update the flags stored in each message. The message-set is defined as in the FETCH command: a message number or a range of numbers separated by a ":" (colon). The item-name-to-set consists of either FLAGS or FLAGS.SILENT. The SILENT option will not return an updated status message from the server; otherwise, it's identical to the FLAG item. Both of these options must be preceded by a "+" or "-" to indicate whether you will be setting or unsetting a flag. The value-to-set is a list of flags that you want to set or unset. The flags you have to choose from were listed in the response message when we SELECTED the mailbox. Most often, you would be using this command to set the deleted flag (/Delete), so that is what you will do in the example. You will set the deleted flag for message number 2.

Example:

```
7 STORE 2 +FLAGS (/Deleted)

* 2 FETCH (FLAGS (\Seen \Deleted))
7 OK STORE completed
```

The results confirm that message number 2 is now flagged as Seen and Deleted.

EXPUNGE Appropriately named, the EXPUNGE command will remove all messages in the current mailbox that are flagged as Deleted.

Example:

```
8 EXPUNGE

* 2 EXPUNGE
* 230 EXISTS
* 1 RECENT
8 OK Expunged 1 messages
```

Message number 2, which we flagged as Deleted, is now permanently removed from the server.

SEARCH searching-criteria The SEARCH command is an extremely nice function of the IMAP server. It allows you to search for messages matching certain criteria, and it will return a list of those that do. This functionality would normally be implemented in the email client software; however, because IMAP email is kept on the server, the client would have to download all of the email before it could be searched. If we perform the search on the server itself, the client doesn't have to do anything. Once again, the number of options that can be sent to the SEARCH command is huge, so we'll look at only a few here.

First, let's start with a search that displays unanswered messages that have been received since August 1st, 1998.

Example:

```
9 SEARCH UNANSWERED SINCE 8-Aug-1998

* SEARCH 206 207 208 209 210 211 212 213 214 215 216 217 218 219 220 221 222 223
9 OK SEARCH completed
```

The numbers that are returned are message numbers that match our search. The parameter UNANSWERED is a tag that indicates one of the flagged states of the messages. Here are some of the options that can be used with the search:

- UNANSWERED—Messages that have not been replied to
- ANSWERED—Messages that have been replied to
- DELETED—Messages that are marked as deleted
- UNSEEN—Messages that have not been read
- SEEN—Messages that have been read
- NEW—Messages that have just arrived

We can also directly search the body text of messages for a particular word or phrase by using the TEXT parameter, followed by the string we want to search for. If you'd like to confine the text search to just the subject of the message, just replace TEXT with SUBJECT.

Example:

```
10 SEARCH TEXT "TCP/IP"

* SEARCH 28 33 87 129 130 132 138 152 198 208
10 OK SEARCH completed
```

This extremely powerful tool can quickly identify messages meeting a wide variety of parameters. The search capabilities that can be performed directly on the server are probably more extensive than what can be done with the help of an IMAP client.

CLOSE CLOSE will close the current mailbox and automatically EXPUNGE all messages that are tagged as Deleted. To perform further actions on the server, we'll need to use SELECT again to open a mailbox. The connection to the server is maintained.

Example:

```
11 CLOSE
11 OK CLOSE completed
```

LOGOUT Logout completes the IMAP session with the server returning a BYE response.

Example:

```
12 LOGOUT

* BYE poisontooth.com IMAP4rev1 server terminating connection
2 OK LOGOUT completed
```

Configuring IMAP Mailboxes

Rounding out our overview of the IMAP command set, we'll look at the commands that modify mailboxes on the server. We can create new mailboxes, move mail between them, and delete them.

CREATE mailbox-name CREATE will create a new mailbox with the name `mailbox-name`. If the mailbox already exists, an error message will be returned, and the existing mailbox will be untouched. Let's try creating a mailbox called `NewStuff`.

```
12 CREATE NewStuff
12 OK CREATE completed
```

To verify that the mailbox has been created, SELECT it.

```
13 SELECT NewStuff

* 0 EXISTS
* OK [UIDVALIDITY 902630810] UID validity status
* OK [UIDNEXT 1] Predicted next UID
* FLAGS (\Answered \Flagged \Deleted \Draft \Seen)
* OK [PERMANENTFLAGS (\* \Answered \Flagged \Deleted \Draft \Seen)] Permanent
flags
* 0 RECENT
13 OK [READ-WRITE] SELECT completed
```

The server indicates that the mailbox does indeed exist, with 0 messages inside. The next message ID to be stored in NewStuff will be number 1, showing that no other messages have been stored here.

COPY message-set mailbox-name With multiple mailboxes, it only makes sense that we should be able to store information in them. The COPY command allows us to save a message, or range of messages, to a particular mailbox. We must first SELECT the mailbox containing the messages that are being copied. In our example, we'll select the standard INBOX and COPY messages 1–4 to the new NewStuff mailbox. Finally, we will re-SELECT NewStuff, which should then have a message count of 4.

Example:

```
14 SELECT INBOX

* 229 EXISTS
....
14 OK [READ-WRITE] SELECT completed

15 COPY 1:4 NewStuff
15 OK COPY completed
16 SELECT NewStuff
* 4 EXISTS
....
16 OK [READ-WRITE] SELECT completed
```

It looks like it all worked! Four messages are now stored in NewStuff. Presumably, they're the same messages we copied from INBOX.

RENAME old-mailbox-name new-mailbox-name RENAMEs an existing mailbox to a new name. Renaming INBOX is possible but behaves differently from what one might expect. If the INBOX is renamed, a new INBOX will be created in its place and continue to receive incoming mail. New mail will not go to the renamed mailbox. We cannot rename a mailbox we're currently using. Because I'm currently using the NewStuff mailbox, I'm going to close it before I attempt to rename it. An error may be returned if the mailbox being renamed doesn't exist, or if the new mailbox name is already in use.

Example:

```
17 RENAME NewStuff OldStuff
17 OK RENAME completed
```

DELETE mailbox-name A mailbox and all of its associated messages can be deleted with the DELETE command. There is no confirmation given when using this function, so be careful. You can't be using the mailbox being deleted when issuing the command. Errors will be returned if the mailbox-name doesn't exist or if it's in use.

Example:

```
18 DELETE OldStuff
18 OK DELETE completed
```

Doing It by Hand

As with POP3 and SMTP, it's extremely useful to have a background of the IMAP commands. I've been using IMAP for a few months and have found it useful to log into the server to manually delete mailboxes when my client has failed. With any Application Layer client, there are always conditions that can exist where the client and the server don't communicate properly, and manual intervention is the quickest solution to the problem. The search capabilities of IMAP make it extremely easy to log in to the server, search for messages containing attachments, and delete them, without ever having to display them in your email client.

Client Software and Other Information Sources

For each TCP/IP protocol discussed, I'll also provide a few clients that use the protocol. You're learning how the protocols work by hand, but once you've set up your own network, your clients will probably want to use something slightly more user-friendly. This list is not meant to be all-inclusive, or indicative of an endorsement of the software.

Netscape Communicator (Windows, MacOS, Linux) POP3, IMAP, SMTP:
http://www.netscape.com/

Microsoft Outlook/Outlook-Express (Windows, MacOS) POP3, IMAP, SMTP:
http://www.microsoft.com/ie/

Eudora Mail Clients (Windows, MacOS) POP3, IMAP (Windows client only), SMTP:
http://www.eudora.com/

The Post Office Protocol v3 (POP3) RFC 1939:
`http://freesoft.org/CIE/RFC/Orig/rfc1939.txt`

Simple Mail Transfer Protocol (SMTP) RFC 821:
`http://freesoft.org/CIE/RFC/821/index.htm`

Internet Message Access Protocol v4 (IMAP) RFC 2060:
`http://freesoft.org/CIE/RFC/Orig/rfc2060.txt`

—

## CHAPTER 8

Using Document Delivery Protocols

by John Ray

In this chapter

Gopher **130**

HTTP **133**

Client Software **144**

Other Information Sources **144**

While every protocol exchanges information, there are a few that have been used to allow people to easily access information in a "point and click" manner. Before the advent of the World Wide Web, there was a protocol known as Gopher. Here we'll look briefly at the Gopher protocol for historical reasons, and then at the HTTP protocol. The command sets for these protocols are smaller than those of POP3, SMTP, and IMAP, which we covered in the preceding chapters, so the next few pages will be somewhat easy, but hopefully informative, reading. Unlike the mailserver samples, you may follow these examples exactly as they appear, and your results should be close to identical.

Gopher

The Gopher protocol was designed to allow computers to navigate stored information in a user-friendly and platform independent manner. Data is arranged in a hierarchical format with different directory levels that the user can move into and out of. On a typical client, these levels are represented as menus. Selecting a menu option can do one of three things: redirect you to a different Gopher server, take you to a submenu of the menu you are on, or display or download a document. Because of its capability to redirect a client to a different server, the Gopher system behaves much like a simple World Wide Web browser. The difference between a Web browser and Gopher, however, is the structured and directed interface. The World Wide Web browser is usually an abstract and highly graphical tool, while Gopher systems provide information in a straightforward and text-based fashion. Web servers, however, can structure their data in the same hierarchical standard as the Gopher server, and Web browsers can act as Gopher browsers. Because of these reasons, Gopher servers are becoming increasingly rare.

Connecting to a Gopher Server

Gopher is run off of port 70 on servers that are still providing the service. My department maintains a Gopher server, as it has proven extremely fast and useful for providing text-based service bulletins to the world. Let's take a look at the OSU Extension Gopher server now.

```
> telnet gopher.ag.ohio-state.edu 70
```

How Do I Make This Work Again?

Remember, if you're using Windows, you need to be in a DOS Prompt window to issue this command.
If you're on Linux in a shell window, Mac users need to select Open Connection in their Telnet client.

Upon connecting, the server will not display a status message. This behavior is normal. Gopher was designed to be a quick-and-dirty, very low resource server and protocol. One way to reduce server resource requirements is to offload smarts from the server to the client, and to make the protocol stateless and connectionless. That is, the server doesn't keep any information regarding the state of the client—where the client is, what it has retrieved, or where it has been. Nor does the server maintain a connection with the client; clients connect, grab a piece of information, and are immediately disconnected. In this model, which is, incidentally, also the model on which HTTP is based, all of the apparent interconnectedness and continuity of the data or site as you experience it is a result of a very smart browser. The browser makes every-thing look interconnected by making repeated connections to a very trivial server that doesn't remember from one second to the next that your client even exists. Because you're here to learn about how these things work, you don't get to use one of these super-smart browsers right now; but once you're done with these chapters, you should have a new appreciation of the sophistication that can be achieved with a very simple set of instructions.

So let's get connected; issue your Telnet command, and if a connection is successfully made, you can begin issuing commands to the server.

Controlling the Gopher

Gopher commands are quite straightforward. The Gopher command set was created to be as fast and efficient as possible, and the responses as short and to the point as they can be. Go-pher connections are limited to one command per session. This means that for each example, you'll need to reconnect (reissue the Telnet command) to the server to issue your command. I will not be repeating the Telnet command, so be sure that you remember this!

Getting a Listing of Available Resources

Once connected, let's get a list of the available resources on the server. Because we are at the root or start level of the Gopher server, we do this by simply pressing the Return (or Enter) key.

Example:

```
<return>

1About this Information Server  1/about leviathan.ag.ohio-state.edu     70
1Calendar of Events     1/calendar      leviathan.ag.ohio-state.edu     70
1Information  1/connections   leviathan.ag.ohio-state.edu    70
1Organizational Resrcs       1/orgres        leviathan.ag.ohio-state.edu     70
1Administrative 1/admin leviathan.ag.ohio-state.edu     70
1People 1/peoples      leviathan.ag.ohio-state.edu     70
```

This is a list of the resources that are available on the Gopher server. The list contains informa-tion that identifies the type of information, its name, and where it is located. The first character "1" of the line identifies each of these resources as being another directory, similar to this directory. A "0" indicates the selection is a document, while a "7" is the Gopher search service that will search the text in a directory for matching documents. The second portion of the listing identifies the directory on the server that each resource is located in, while the third and fourth pieces indicate the server and port number the data is on. For the first directory item, About this Information Server, we can see that it points to the 1/about directory on leviathan.ag.ohio-state.edu, port 70. (Incidentally, leviathan.ag.ohio-state.edu is the same machine as gopher.ag.ohio-state.edu, just under a different name.)

Viewing Other Directories
Now let's send a command to view the contents of the About this Information Server directory. You do this by sending the name of the directory you want to see, followed by a forward slash (/) and a return. Remember, if you followed the example above, you'll need to reconnect to the server to issue a new command.

Example:

```
1/about/
```

```
1/about/
0Welcome to the Ag. Gopher!      0/about/welcome.txt      leviathan.ag.ohio-
state.edu    70
1Documentation for the GN server          1s/about/docs    leviathan.ag.ohio-
state.edu    70
0Gopher Usage Report (Updated Hourly)   0/about/greport.txt
leviathan.ag.ohio-state.edu      70
```

As you can see, we now have reached a directory that contains information files, indicated by the "0" in front of Welcome to the Ag. Gopher! and Gopher Usage Report. These two titles point to the files 0/about/welcome.txt and 0/about/greport.txt, respectively.

View a File

Since you've come this far, go ahead and view one of the files on the server. I'm interested in seeing the Gopher statistics report, because I'm quite positive I shut the statistics down over a year ago. To retrieve this file, I'll use the same syntax as viewing a directory, except I will not add a "/" to the end of the resource name.

Example:

```
0/about/greport.txt
```

```
12500 records processed.
OSUE Gopher Log Analysis                          Page: 1
Client Domains by Frequency of Use

Host Domain or IP Address                  Calls    %     Cum
-------------------------------------------------  -------  ----  ----
ag.ohio-state.edu                           6612   52.7   52.7
128.146.140.                                 975    7.8   60.4
ix.netcom.com                                175    1.4   61.8
ipt.aol.com                                  166    1.3   63.2

...

            Starting date: Thu Dec 14 10:34:01 1995
            Ending date: Thu Feb 22 11:01:13 1996
```

Yep, that looks like it's a few years old. Obviously, even my die-hard Gopher server no longer gets the respect and attention it deserves.

Hey, I Didn't See That In My Telnet Client; Is Something Wrong?

Probably not; if all you see is a few lines, you just need to check your scroll-back buffer (see "saved lines" or a similar field in your preferences if you don't have a scroll-back buffer) to see the rest of the data. If you see something completely different, either our server is broken, or perhaps you've mistyped the command. Give it another try, and if it still doesn't work, go play a game of Quake or something similarly relaxing. It's more fun than looking at outdated Gopher statistics anyway. If you're still curious when you get back, you can take a look at the same thing by asking your Web browser to talk to our Gopher server; you should be able to see the statistics page by entering

```
Gopher://gopher.ag.ohio-state.edu/about/greport.txt
```

on the URL line; but of course, you won't get the enjoyment of knowing that you got to it by hand, the hard way.

Out with the Old

Gopher servers, for their time, offered an extremely useful cross-platform method for sharing information files. They were high on content and low on "fluff." Times have changed, for better or for worse, and the World Wide Web has unseated the Gopher server from its once proud perch. Let's look at how the Web differs from Gopher in the way it handles information.

HTTP

The Web is often looked upon as an amazing creation, but just how amazing is the networking that makes it happen? The answer will probably surprise you. The HTTP protocol specification is extremely large and encompasses a huge number of conditions that can exist between the server and client; however, it also is conceptually easy to follow and demonstrate.

Connecting to the Web Server

At its most basic level, the HTTP protocol consists of a connection and single command delivered to a Web server. Web servers, by default, listen for connections on port 80. Let's start by connecting to my poisontooth.com Web page.

```
>telnet www.poisontooth.com 80
```

Usually, the server will simply open a connection and give no other indication that it's ready to receive your commands. In some cases, it may identify the server software it's running. Once connected, there are a few relatively simple commands we can use to request data from the server.

Using GET to Retrieve a Resource from the Server

Start by giving it a command to display the main Web page. To retrieve a resource over the HTTP protocol, you use the GET command, followed by the resource you want to have sent to you from the server. Lastly, you must specify the protocol version number you want to have the information sent with. To get the root-level home page, you'll want to ask for the / resource. You can figure out what to specify for this parameter by looking at the corresponding URL and removing the http://hostname.whatever.com portion.

For example:

```
http://www.poisontooth.com/
```

This URL will obviously return the poisontooth.com home page. To find out the resource name you want to request from the server, remove the `http://www.poisontooth.com` portion of the address. You're left with simply `/`.

If you wanted to manually retrieve a document at this location called

```
http://www.poisontooth.com/test.html
```

you would use `/test.html` as the resource to request from the server.

In our examples, we'll be using an older version of HTTP, 1.0, to get the page. If the server responds and indicates that it supports the 1.1 protocol, we'll use it in further examples. Knowing this, we can now type the appropriate command and see the results. Note that you must follow the command by two carriage returns before the server will carry out the action.

```
GET / HTTP/1.0
```

The Web server should return the top-level Web page along with a header containing status information for the server software.

```
HTTP/1.1 200 OK
Date:Wed, 05 Aug 1998 03:18:08 GMT
    Server: Apache/1.2.5
    Last-Modified: Wed, 05 Aug 1998 03:17:52 GMT
    ETag: "688d0-b3-35c7cee0"
    Content-Length: 179
    Accept-Ranges: bytes
    Connection: close
    Content-Type: text/html

<BODY BGCOLOR="#FFFFFF">
<CENTER>
<IMG SRC="Poisontooth.gif">
<BR>
<FONT FACE="Arial" SIZE=2>
</FONT>
</CENTER>
</BODY>
```

Figures 8.1 and 8.2 demonstrate the differences between viewing a Web page as through a standard Web browser and through a Telnet session. Granted, the Web browser display looks a bit better, but we can see what's really going on in the Telnet window.

From this returned information, you can gather that the server is running Apache, version 1.2.5, and supports HTTP version 1.1. Because of the great number of type of documents that an HTTP server can serve, the header is very important. The information contained in the header allows the client computer to correctly render the page or perform another action on the data that is returned.

FIGURE 8.1
A standard Web browser displays a Web page like this.

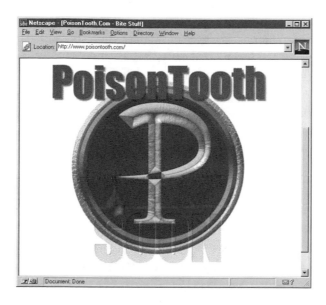

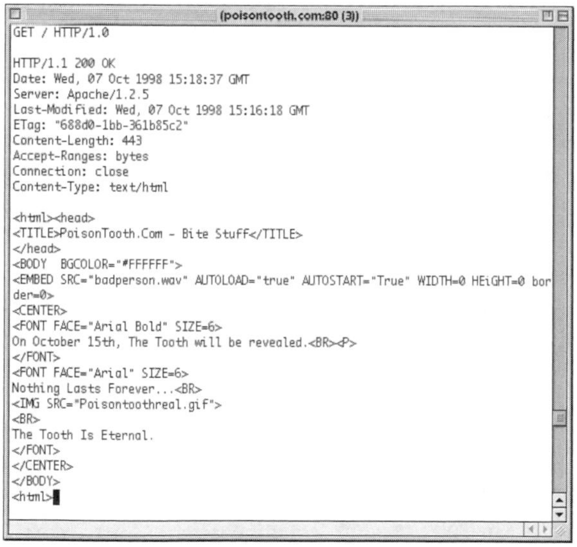

FIGURE 8.2
The same Web page in Figure 8.1 is seen here through a Telnet client.

What Is Apache?

Apache is a free Web server that's widely used on UNIX servers and is also available for Windows 95 and NT. A commercial form is available for the Macintosh. According to an independent and ongoing survey by Netcraft, Apache is the most popular and fastest growing Web server on the planet. You can check out the Netcraft survey for yourself at http://www.netcraft.com/Survey/.

Interpreting the Header   Let's take a look at some of the information that was returned, what it means, and why it's important. First and foremost is the server's identification that it can use HTTP 1.1 as its primary communications protocol. Because you can use version 1.1 of the HTTP protocol, let's take a look at what that ability provides.

HTTP 1.1 (HTTP/1.1)   For several years, HTTP 1.0 has persisted as the primary protocol used between Web servers and their clients. The HTTP/1.0 protocol suffers from several problems, though, which make it significantly more wasteful than version 1.1. The HTTP protocol has progressed through three different versions since 1990. Version 0.9 simply served to transport data based on simple requests. Version 1.0 expanded 0.9 to allow data to be sent in a format that identified its contents and also specified methods to send data back to the server. Version 1.0 is still widely used today in older (Netscape 2.0, Internet Explorer 2.0, and so on) clients, which may be installed by default with early distributions of Windows, and so on. Server software has actually lagged behind the clients, although most popular packages now speak the 1.1 protocol as well.

One of the largest differences between version HTTP/1.0 and 1.1 is the use of persistent connections. In version 1.0, a client could send one request per connection. You saw this sort of behavior when you used the Gopher protocol. Each request you made required you to Telnet back into the server. In the Gopher system, this made sense; one request returned one entire piece of data. In the Web model, it's an entirely different story.

In the request you sent to www.poisontooth.com, you requested the root level Web page, and the HTML that makes up that Web page was indeed returned. However, there really isn't anything on the page except an image, and that image certainly wasn't returned in the response you received. So how do you get the image? Under HTTP v1.0, you must reconnect to the server and request the image in a separate connection. Each connection requires resources on the client and server to set up and connect. This redundancy can lead to many connections for a single Web page to be downloaded. A quick look at CNN's Web page (http://www.cnn.com) reveals at least 30 different images on the page. Each of these images would require a separate connection to be made to the server. Take into account the ability for pages to now have embedded sounds, movies, fonts, Java applications, and so on, and it becomes quite clear that a single-connection based transaction system might not be the ideal form of communications for the Web. You may have heard individuals quote claims of how many "hits" their Web page or Web site has received. In general, they are referring to the number of individual connections that their server has returned, not the number of actual pages, in their entirety, that have been served. That little trip to CNN's page a few minutes ago may very well have resulted in over 30 hits to their Web server, depending on the version of HTTP they're running. The next time someone brags to you about the number of hits they've received, ask them how many of the hits came from unique hosts (unique IP addresses). Chances are they will change the conversation topic rather quickly.

We obviously need a way to talk to a Web server without having to connect to it 50 different times per page. The HTTP 1.1 protocol saves the day by allowing the client to specify multiple requests within a single connection. This capability saves CPU time for the server and client and network bandwidth. It's also useful for further expansion of the HTTP protocol, because it could allow negotiations between the client and server in order to identify the feature sets that each supported. Persistent connections are the default type of connection under 1.1. The server will assume that it should keep the connection open unless otherwise indicated by the client (usually by not sending an HTTP 1.1 request, like you did earlier.)

Another new feature in HTTP 1.1 is the capability to provide virtual hosting without using extra IP addresses. Virtual hosting is generally used to give a person or organization Web space that appears to come from an individual server but is actually a shared resource. For example, our campus Web server currently holds over 350 different Web sites. Many of the owners of these sites want a cute name to go along with the site. Rather than setting up a separate server for each of these requests, we can simply set up a virtual host. For example, these two addresses, although they have different hostnames, actually both point to the same IP address:

http://jray.ag.ohio-state.edu/ (My OSU Web page)

http://ohioline.ag.ohio-state.edu/ (Ohioline News)

Being able to assign a virtual host allows the client's Web site to appear as an individual entity, not as part of a conglomeration of Web sites. It also leads to URLs that are easier to remember and fit nicely onto the space of a business card.

Virtual hosting has been present before HTTP 1.1 but has had some special requirements. For virtual hosting to work under HTTP 1.0, a separate IP address had to be assigned to the server, and the appropriate virtual host's hostname assigned to that IP address. Because the server can look at a packet and identify the destination IP address of the packet, it was extremely simple to select and serve specific Web pages based on the IP address that the machine was being called by. Remember how I mentioned that our Web server has more than 350 accounts on it? This machine is located on a class C subnet that can hold 254 different IP addresses. For us to provide virtual hosting to all of our clients under HTTP 1.0, we would need to expand to a new subnet or redefine our existing subnet to have a larger address range. All of that, just so a few Web sites can have their own customized URLs. If we had gone that route, it would have been an extremely poor use of IP resources (which you will later learn are becoming an increasingly valuable commodity), and a big pain to keep track of.

Once again, HTTP 1.1 solves the problem in an elegant manner. When an HTTP 1.1 client machine connects to a Web site and requests a resource, it now specifies the hostname that it wants the resource delivered from. This eliminates the problem of hostnames that are all pointing to a single address cannot be told apart. The client itself makes this distinction for the server. The end result is that with HTTP 1.1, we can now specify a single IP address for a server and assign as many names as we want to that address. HTTP 1.1 server software can then be configured to map these hostnames to the individual sites, thus eliminating the need for multiple IP addresses, and huge subnets.

N O T E Although you might expect a class C subnet to have 256 IP addresses for hosts, it can use only 254. One number (x.y.z.0) is reserved for the subnet itself and one (x.y.z.255) for the subnet broadcast address.

Web Server Status (200 OK) Because of the large number of documents that can be served by HTTP, and the robust nature of the interconnections it offers with other servers, it's logical that the server would have an extremely large amount of status information it can use to communicate information to the client. You undoubtedly have seen some of these status messages in your travels and have perhaps even cursed aloud when the dreaded 404, File Not Found error has appeared. Let's take a look at some of those messages now. You'll see that at times your Web browser might be doing more behind the scenes than you had previously thought, such as automatically fixing a broken link.

- 101 Switching Protocols—A client can request that the server use a newer version of HTTP to communicate. If the server can comply, it responds with this message.

- 200 OK—Indicates that the client's command was understood and processed successfully. When you requested the www.poisontooth.com Web page, you received a 200 OK response, indicating that everything was A-Okay.

- 301 Moved Permanently—The resource that the client is attempting to access has been moved to a new permanent location, which is also returned along with the message. Most Web browsers will automatically point to the new location without any user interaction. Links that are coded to this location should be manually updated to point to the new location.

- 400 Bad Request—Simply indicates that the command sent to the server was not understood and not processed.

- 401 Unauthorized—The client is attempting to access a protected resource that requires authentication. The authentication mechanism used by the server software is usually configurable to be as simple as a plain text password file to a Kerberos authentication database.

- 403 Forbidden—The page being accessed cannot be served to the client. This could occur if the client has been blocked from accessing a particular resource of if the Web server's file permissions are set incorrectly.

- 404 File Not Found—The file resource requested is not on the server. No redirection information is available.

- 408 Request Timeout—Common in the persistent connections of HTTP 1.1, Request Timeouts occur when the server decides it has waited long enough without the client sending any requests.

- 500 Internal Server Error—An error has occurred when processing the client's request. This often happens when running programs on the server that are misconfigured and do not return the appropriate results to the server software.

- 503 Service Unavailable—Might be indicative of a large load on the server, causing it to deny requests for resources, or any other condition that results in requests being denied.

- 505 http Version Not Supported—The version of the HTTP protocol that the client is using is not supported by the server software.

Last-Modified Date   Also returned in the header is the last-modified date for the Web page. This information is extremely useful because it can be requested from the server without downloading the entire Web page. Most Web clients keep track of the last-modified date for Web pages, and, if on returning to a Web page the modification date has not changed, the browser can use a cached copy of the information, rather than downloading it from the network again.

Content-Length   Because it's now possible for multiple requests to take place on a single connection, it's important that we know the length of the data we'll be receiving. The content-length portion of the header specifies the length of the resource we've requested, in bytes.

Content-Type   The content-type portion of the header is perhaps the most important piece of information the Web server can return. It specifies what is called a "MIME-Type" for the data, which the client can then display or process accordingly. MIME, or Multipurpose Internet Mail Extensions, are a way of specifying the content of a document. They are typically used in email programs to allow attachments to be identified and processed with standard email. The HTTP protocol uses "mime-like" content-types, which are not considered to entirely follow the MIME standard but are generally very close. Some common types returned by Web servers are

> text/html—An HTML document
>
> text/plain—A plain text file
>
> image/jpeg—jpeg graphic file
>
> image/GIF—gif graphic file
>
> image/TIFF—A TIFF format graphic file
>
> application/rtf—Rich text format document
>
> application/zip—A PKZIP or WinZIP compressed file
>
> video/mpeg—An mpeg video clip
>
> video/quicktime—QuickTime video file

Hundreds of types have been defined for use over the Internet, from Microsoft Word and WordPerfect document types to Macintosh Pict image files. With such a huge number of different types of files, it may seem hard to believe that any browser could handle processing all of them. They don't. You're probably familiar with "helper" applications in your browser and various browser plug-ins that are available. To process types of files it doesn't understand, a Web browser will download the file to disk, and then trigger a helper application that understands the file type to open the document. If a plug-in is available that understands a certain file type, it might be used instead.

Other HTTP Commands

Now that we've learned a bit about the HTTP protocol and the information returned by the server, let's try to send a few more commands to it.

GET, Revisited   Because you first sent the GET command as an HTTP 1.0 protocol command, now try sending it using version 1.1. Because you're using the 1.1 protocol, you must also specify the hostname of the virtual host you're asking to return the data (remember, it's just one server pretending to be many different servers; now you've got to tell it which server it needs to pretend to be for your request). Look closely at the two following examples. I'm using the same GET command but requesting the root level Web page from two different hostnames (both of them point to www.poisontooth.com). Remember to follow each request by two carriage returns. I'll leave off most of the returned information for brevity's sake.

Example 1:

```
GET / http/1.1
Host: www.poisontooth.com

HTTP/1.1 200 OK
<TITLE>PoisonTooth.Com - Bite me</TITLE>
<BODY BGCOLOR="#FFFFFF">
...
</BODY>
```

Example 2:

```
GET / http/1.1
Host: michaelk.poisontooth.com

HTTP/1.1 200 OK
<TITLE>Mike's Page</TITLE>
<BODY>
...
<H3>Thanx John</H3>
</center>
</body>
```

The result is precisely what you would expect; although the GET commands were identical, you've returned two different root Web pages from the same machine, just because you specified the hostname according to the HTTP 1.1 protocol.

Using the HEAD Command to Retrieve a Page's Status   If we're interested only in information about a page or resource, not in retrieving the entire resource itself, we can use the HEAD command. HEAD is used in precisely the same way as GET, but it does not return the body of the Web page. This command can be used (and is used in some browsers) to notify you when a Web page has been updated. It could also allow a browser to make a decision about whether to download a page based on its size. Unfortunately, I'm not aware of any currently available browsers that have such flexibility.

Because you now know what HTTP 1.1 is, I'll continue to use 1.1 syntax for the remaining example. Let's also take this opportunity to verify that you can indeed send multiple consecutive commands to the Web server. Here I'll retrieve HEAD information for the Web page at michaelk.poisontooth.com and the main www.poisontooth.com page, all from within a single connection. Again, I'll leave out most of the header information to save space.

Example:

```
HEAD / HTTP/1.1
Host: michaelk.poisontooth.com

HTTP/1.1 200 OK
Date: Sun, 09 Aug 1998 21:23:12 GMT
...
Content-Length: 656
Content-Type: text/html

HEAD / HTTP/1.1
Host: www.poisontooth.com

HTTP/1.1 200 OK
Date: Sun, 09 Aug 1998 21:23:34 GMT
...
Content-Length: 393
Content-Type: text/html
```

Sending Data to the Server   Besides transferring data from a server to a client, HTTP also has the capability to send data from the client to the server. There are two common methods that transfer information to the server: POST and GET.

Wait a second—doesn't the GET request data *from* the server, not send information to it? While it may seem slightly confusing that GET can be used to send data to the server, the manner in which it does so is extremely simple. You may have seen URLs that look like this

```
http://www.poisontooth.com/proc.cgi?name=jray
```

in your Web browser before, perhaps after you've completed a form or search request on a Web site and submitted it.

This URL will send data to a program called proc.cgi that is located on my Web server. Returned to proc.cgi is also the information name=jray, which is a piece of data that a Web page wants to send to the server. The variable name is set to the value jray. Multiple pieces of data can be sent by separating them with the "&" character, like this:

```
http://www.poisontooth.com/proc.cgi?name=jray&age=12
```

This would pass the value jray in the variable name and 12 in the variable age (no, that isn't really my age) back to the server. Kinda sneaky isn't it?

One of the problems with using GET as a method to transfer information to the server is that information is passed in plain sight on the URL/Location line of your browser once you submit a form. It's also highly likely to be stored in a viewable history file for your particular browser. If you're submitting sensitive information, you might not want this information to be so easily accessible. Another problem with GET is that the resulting URL, after having submitted a form, is often extremely huge. If you fill out some basic information about yourself on an online form (using GET) in order to join a Web site, then submit it to enter the site, the resulting URL is likely to be a bit unwieldy. You also might not want to give out the URL to anyone else, because it contains personal information about yourself on it. Even if you did, they might not want to spend the time typing in a 200-character URL just to see the latest presidential scandal or other hot Web topic.

These problems are overcome by using the POST command to send data, instead of GET. POST is a command sent to the server outside of a GET command. It is simply a list of variables and their values that the server will then pass to whatever program needs them. This command is a much cleaner and friendlier way of submitting information to a server. The client is not made aware of the mechanism of the data transfer as they are when using GET, and are probably better off for it. It would be difficult to demonstrate a POST command here, so, in the future, watch what happens when you submit data over the Web. If you see URLs filled with "?"s and "&"s, you're dealing with a Web page that is using GET. If you submit a form and see a nice, clean URL, you've just used a POST command.

The Evil Covert Cookie Method of Sending Data to a Server

If you've used the Internet, you've heard someone complain about "cookies" and how they are stealing information from their computer. There seems to be a general misconception in the public as to what a cookie is, what it does, and the information it can transfer. Let's take a look at cookies and how they are set.

A cookie is nothing more than a small piece of information that a Web server has politely asked your Web browser to store for it. It's not intended to, and should not be capable of, storing binary data, so you can forget about it carrying viruses and horrible Trojan horses to your computer.

Are Cookies Safe?

In general, cookies should not cause you any alarm. They were invented and are generally used to enhance your Web-browsing pleasure. It is, however, up to the individual browser software to implement cookies in a safe fashion, and up to Web site administrators to make reasonable and responsible use of them. If your browser writes the cookie data to a file, then, for fun, decides to try running the file, it is not a safe implementation. Likewise, if an online shopping-mall decides to store your credit card number in a cookie, and then allows that cookie to be retrieved in a non-secure fashion, your MasterCharge number could quickly be public knowledge. If you frequent online shopping sites, you may want to have your browser warn you before a cookie is set, or even set it to refuse all cookies. (Look in your Web-browser's security preferences for cookie acceptance options; if you set it to "refuse all," don't be too upset when a lot of sites that remember who you are between visits or that use online shopping-carts stop working for you.)

Servers generally store things such as your name, or other identifying information, so that they can pull up a profile on you when you return to their site. The public perception seems to be that cookies contain your credit card information. I have done a fairly large about of Web browsing and have never had credit card information stored in my cookie file. Of course, it is indeed possible for a Web site to store that information, but it has not been my experience that anyone is doing so on a regular basis. If you're worried about what is being stored, you can turn on options in your browser to ask you before writing a cookie, or keep cookies from being written at all. An extremely nice feature of Internet Explorer is that it allows you to browse all of the cookies that are on your computer, the Web sites that set them, and what they contain. If you don't like something you see, you can instantly remove it.

Cookies themselves consist of a variable name, the value of the variable, the machine that set the cookie, and a date after which the cookie will expire and be discarded. When a client browser returns to a site where a cookie has been set, it passes the cookie information back to the server, which then makes it available to whatever software might want it. So how does a cookie get set? The Web server software sends a `Set-Cookie` command to the client as part of the header message.

Example:

```
Set-Cookie: name=jray; expires=Fri 12-Nov-99 3:59:59 GMT
```

This would set a cookie on the remote browser called `name` with the value `jray`. The cookie would be set to expire on Friday, November 12, 1999 at 3:59 GMT. If a server decides that it wants to get rid of the information stored in a cookie, it can reset the cookie information with another `Cookie-Set` command, or it can cause a cookie to expire by setting the expiration to a date that has already passed.

Example:

```
Set-Cookie: name=jray; expires=Fri 1-Jul-98 3:59:59 GMT
```

Setting this cookie will actually result in the "unsetting" of the original cookie, because the expiration date has already passed. Keep in mind that cookies are read, set, and reset by specific URLs. Not every URL can read every cookie.

I use cookies occasionally on my server to try to make life a little easier for some users, and most other Web sites use them for the same reason. A message board system that I wrote, for example, uses cookies to remember what user account a user belongs to. That way, they can go straight to the board and begin posting, and all of their information is immediately available. There is no login process necessary. This is what cookies were intended for and what, for the most part, they are used for. I find them to be a huge time-saver when they're put to good use.

Secure Web Connections

Commercial Web sites often have the need to keep data secure while it is being transferred from a client's browser to the server. Credit cards, Social Security numbers, and other sensitive information can easily be stolen over insecure connections.

There are currently two different methods that a server and client can use to communicate securely. The first is *SSL*, or *Secure Sockets Layer*. The SSL was developed by Netscape to provide secure communications for its servers and browsers. It has since been adopted by other companies and is available in several free implementations. SSL provides a secure connection between the client socket and the server socket. All data that is transmitted between them is encrypted. This data can include pictures and any other information coming for the server.

One drawback to this approach is speed. While using a secure server, you may notice a slight delay when receiving data. This delay occurs because of the encryption and decryption process that takes place.

The second secure method is known as S-http and was developed by Enterprise Integration Technologies, which was later bought by Verifone, Inc. S-http is an extension to the HTTP protocol that allows individual messages to be sent securely. Using this method, only critical data needs to be encrypted, while unimportant information is sent using the standard HTTP protocol. The obvious advantage is speed.

SSL is in place in all major browsers and is supported by Web servers from Netscape, Microsoft, and Apache. It is the leading technology used to secure Web communications.

How Secure Is Secure?

While both SSL and S-http do their jobs admirably, it's still within the processing power of desktop computers to crack and decode the encrypted information. What might be most surprising is that your primary security concern when sending data over the network should not be the protocol that is being used to send it to the remote site, but what is done with the data once it is received. You're far more likely to have credit card information stolen from a receipt in your trash or from someone looking over your shoulder in a checkout line than you are having them intercept it over the Internet—even without a secure connection. However, once the data reaches its destination, it's probably stored in a database of some sort. The security of that database is extremely important. A hacker is much more likely to go for a whole pot of gold (cracking a database of thousands of credit card numbers) than a single coin.

Client Software

Netscape Navigator/Communicator (Windows, MacOS, Linux) Gopher, HTTP: `http://www.netscape.com/`

Microsoft Internet Explorer (Windows, MacOS, HP-UX) Gopher, HTTP: `http://www.microsoft.com/ie/`

Opera (Windows, MacOS (soon)) Gopher, HTTP: `http://opera.nta.no/`

Other Information Sources

The Gopher Protocol RFC 1436 `http://freesoft.org/CIE/RFC/Orig/rfc1436.txt`

HyperText Transfer Protocol v1.1 RFC 2068 `http://freesoft.org/CIE/RFC/2068/index.htm`

Secure Sockets Layer FAQ `http://www.consensus.com/security/ssl-talk-faq.html`

Cookie Central – Information on Web Cookies `http://www.cookiecentral.com/`

Chocolate Chip Cookies (yes, real cookies!) `http://www.diamondwalnut.com/dess01.htm`

## CHAPTER 9

Investigating Other Useful Protocols

by John Ray

In this chapter

Network News Transfer Protocol (NNTP) **146**

Chatting on the Internet **151**

Less Friendly but Useful Protocols **160**

The protocols we've already seen—such as POP3, SMTP, IMAP, Gopher, and HTTP—account for most of the traffic on the Internet. However, there are many other protocols that are equally important and notable, only a little more obscure. This chapter is dedicated to them. Because we'll move back and forth between things that have very different functions, I've included an "Other Information' section directly following each protocol, so you should easily be able to find client software and references for what you find interesting. We'll begin this final protocol chapter with a look at NNTP.

Network News Transfer Protocol (NNTP)

Falling somewhere in between email and the World Wide Web is *NNTP*, the *network news transfer protocol*. NNTP is a very large information repository consisting of discussion groups that are contributed to by millions of people around the world daily. NNTP delivers messages in an email-like format but allows you to browse through relevant information and download the articles you find useful. Like IMAP, all the information is maintained on a separate server, and messages are returned only when you specifically request them. One of the interesting things about NNTP is its distributed nature. There are thousands of NNTP servers throughout the world comprising a public news network known as USENET News. Messages that are posted to a single server propagate to other NNTP servers and are available within minutes globally. Each server maintains its own local storage for the messages so they can be quickly retrieved by clients that access that server. Messages are categorized into newsgroups; servers can decide if they want to carry newsgroups on an individual basis. If you run a news server, you might want to carry a news feed with just technical newsgroups on it. Most ISPs will provide as extensive a news feed as they can to their customers and use it as a selling point. If you haven't used newsgroups before, I'd advise you to take a look. Like Web pages, you'll need to do some searching to find newsgroups that interest you, but you will undoubtedly find several that match your interests or needs. Figure 9.1 shows Microsoft's Outlook Express for Mac OS accessing a news server. We're going to be looking at the underlying protocol, but it's nice to know you can use a nifty client program to access news via point and click if you need to!

Where Did the USENET Come From?

USENET, or User Network, was originally conceived by two college students in late 1979 on the UNIX platform. The protocol was further refined by other students in 1981. It continues to be advanced by the input of the public today. It is truly the network by and for the user. If you'd like to learn more about the history of USENET, check out http://www.amdahl.com/internet/events/usenet-history.txt for a complete look at its history.

FIGURE 9.1.
Outlook Express is one of many graphical USENET readers.

Part II
Ch 9

Connecting to the NNTP Server

As with the other protocols we've discussed, NNTP is controllable from a Telnet session. Port 119 hosts the NNTP service. Your ISP should have provided you with an NNTP or news server address to use to retrieve news. I will be connecting to OSU's news server for the examples, which is available only to my local subnet. Most news servers will not require authentication to connect unless you're trying to access them from a network they don't recognize. You'll need to use your own news server if you'd like to follow along. The service I'm connecting to is limited to OSU addresses only.

```
>telnet nntp.service.ohio-state.edu 119

200 magnus.acs.ohio-state.edu InterNetNews NNRP server INN 1.7.2 08-Dec-1997
ready (posting ok).
```

The server responds with a welcome message once a connection is made. Because we don't need to log in, we can start sending commands immediately.

Sending Commands to the NNTP Server   You send commands to the server on a line by line basis, as you did with the other protocols. The server will respond with one of five types of messages for each command that it attempts to execute:

100—A message to the user; no action needs to be taken.

200—The command is okay.

300—The command has been processed successfully; the client may complete the operation.

400—An error occurred while attempting to complete the command.

500—The operation is not valid on this server.

There are variations of these messages, but they will all fall within these five main categories. We'll start our look at the NNTP vocabulary with the LIST command.

LIST It makes sense that after connecting to a news server we would want to see a list of the newsgroups it has. If you're connected to the Internet using a modem, *do not* run this example. The OSU news server has several thousand newsgroups, and even that great number is only a small subset of the total number of groups your server might offer. My local service provider offers over 15,000 different groups. Waiting for 15,000 different groups to list won't be much fun on a slow connection, so you may want to skip this step. I'll show a tiny portion of the total amount of information returned. If I were to show you the entire results, the book would end with this command.

Example:

```
LIST

215 Newsgroups in form "group high low flags".
alt.2600 0000467188 0000442572 y
alt.2600.codez 0000066884 0000062034 y
alt.2600.crackz 0000259071 0000256648 y
alt.2600.hope.announce 0000012407 0000012358 y
…
comp.games.development.audio 0000000120 0000000060 y
uts.disted 0000000002 0000000001 y
de.comm.software.mailreader.misc 0000000000 0000000001 y
```

As the first line of the response indicates, the listing is in columns with the group name, the highest message number, the lowest number, and a flag that indicates if you're allowed to post to that group. The 215 does not indicate that there are 215 newsgroups; it's one of the 200-series of messages, which indicate that the command completed successfully.

NEWGROUPS date time The list of available newsgroups is growing on a continuing basis. New topics are added daily. Rather that relisting the entire selection of newsgroups that are available, and then figuring out what's new, we can use the NEWGROUPS command. NEWGROUPS takes a date, in the format YYMMDD, and a time, in the HHMMSS format. The command returns a list of newsgroups that have been created since that time. Let's see how many have been created since the first of July 1998. (In the date formatting we'll use, 980701 is July 1st, 1998; 000000 is midnight.)

Example:

```
NEWGROUPS 980801 000000

231 New newsgroups follow.
uts.disted 2 1 y
de.comm.software.mailreader.misc 0 1 y
```

GROUP newsgroup Now that we can locate newsgroups we might be interested in, either from the LIST command or by browsing new groups with the NEWGROUPS function, it's time to start interacting with the groups. The first command we'll look at is GROUP. GROUP selects a newsgroup and returns the first and last message numbers in a group, as well as an estimate of the number of messages that are available. Shouldn't that just be the first message number subtracted from the last message? NNTP allows messages to be deleted by authors and administrators, so there may be messages missing between the first and last message numbers.

Rather than keep track of how many messages are available at any given point in time, the server can choose to just give an estimate.

Example:

```
GROUP comp.games.development.art

211 57 45 103 comp.games.development.art
```

Again, the 200-series response indicates that the command completed successfully. The second number, 57, is our estimate of the number of messages posted to the newsgroup, while the third and fourth numbers are the first and last message identifiers, respectively. Now that we have selected the `comp.games.development.art` newsgroup, we can read messages from it.

ARTICLE/HEAD/BODY message-number   The article command will return a message from the selected newsgroup. If the message number does not exist on the server or is not retrievable for any reason, a 400-series error message will be generated. Because the GROUP command revealed the first message in our sample newsgroup is 45, let's go ahead and try reading it.

Example:

```
ARTICLE 45

220 45 <6q37oq$kkv$1@xxxxx.net> article
Path: magnus.acs.ohio-state.edu!news.cis.ohiostate.edu!nntp.sci.cmu.edu!
bb3.andrew.cmu.edu!pitt.edu!portc02.blue.aol.com!howland.erols.net!news2.ais.net!
jamiais.net!ameritech.net!uunet!in1.uu.net!xxxxxxx.net!not-for-mail
From: "Mr. Jack E. Derifaj" <jackd@xxxxx.net>
Newsgroups: comp.games.development.art,comp.games.development.design
Subject: Re: A game of Abstract Expressionism?
Date: Sun, 2 Aug 1998 19:39:52 -0700
Lines: 20

Hi Guys,
Just finished up the latest version of the figures.  Hope you like them!
--Jack
```

Not a very exciting message, but it worked nonetheless. You might want to take a look at the header line `Path:`. It shows the news servers that the message passed through to reach the server I'm using. Because each server has its own copy of messages, the path will look different depending on the server you're reading it from. We can also tell from the `Newsgroups` line that the message was cross-posted to `comp.games.development.art` and to `comp.games.development.design`. Cross-posting means that the message, although only stored once on the server, is listed under both of these newsgroups.

If we had wanted to retrieve only the header or the body of the message, we could simply replace the ARTICLE command with BODY or HEAD.

Example:

```
HEAD 45

221 45 <6q37oq$kkv$1@guysmiley.blarg.net> head
Path: magnus.acs.ohio-state.edu!news.cis.ohio-state.edu!nntp.sei.cmu.edu!
bb3.andrew.cmu.edu!pitt.edu!portc02.blue.aol.com!howland.erols.net!news2.ais.net!jamiais.net!
ameritech.net!uunet!in1.uu.net!xxxxxxx.net!not-for-mail
From: "Mr. Jack E. Derifaj" <jackd@xxxxx.net>
```

```
Newsgroups: comp.games.development.art,comp.games.development.design
Subject: Re: A game of Abstract Expressionism?
Date: Sun, 2 Aug 1998 19:39:52 -0700
Lines: 20
```

NEXT/LAST The NEXT and LAST command make browsing messages on a news server extremely simple. Once we retrieve a message, a pointer to that message number is set on the server. If we want to get the message immediately following the message we've retrieved, we use the NEXT command. If, instead, we want the message preceding the current message, the LAST command will do the trick. These commands are used without any parameters. If NEXT or LAST attempts to access a posting that doesn't exist, the server will return a 400-series message indicating an error with the command.

Example:

NEXT

223 63 <6q8ej5$60e$1@guysmiley.blarg.net> Article retrieved; request text separately.

The server responds that the next article has successfully been selected. You can now use the ARTICLE, BODY, or HEAD commands *without* specifying a message number. The selected message (or portion of the message) will be displayed.

QUIT QUIT closes the connection to the NNTP server. A 200-series completion message is returned.

Example:

QUIT

205 .

Client Software

Netscape Navigator and Communicator (Windows, Mac OS, Linux): http://www.netscape.com/

Microsoft Outlook and Outlook Express (Windows, Mac OS): http://www.microsoft.com/ie/

Multi-Threaded NewsWatcher (Mac OS): http://www.best.com/~smfr/mtnw/

NN-TK (Linux, X Window): http://www.general.uwa.edu.au/u/toivo/nn-tk/

Other Information Sources

Network News Transfer Protocol RFC 977: http://freesoft.org/CIE/RFC/977/index.htm

Chatting on the Internet

If you're like me and you mainly use the Internet for email and Web access, you may scratch your head when you hear someone talk about participating in Internet Chat Rooms. What they're probably referring to is yet another protocol called IRC, Internet Relay Chat. The first Internet chatting protocol was called"talk" and allowed two people to talk to each other in real-time across a TCP/IP connection. IRC is far more capable than that.

IRC

Internet Relay Chat, or IRC, was developed to be the ultimate Internet chat protocol, and it has proven to be precisely that. IRC is the MBONE of Internet chatting. The IRC is a group of interconnected servers that allow thousands of clients to connect simultaneously and converse with one another. Much like MBONE, the multimedia backbone of the Internet, IRC interconnects servers around the world. As messages are sent to one server, they're rebroadcast throughout the IRC network.

Using an IRC server might be a bit confusing at first, but this is because there has yet to be client software written that completely hides the IRC protocol. Most clients require you to actually understand most of the IRC command set in order to use it efficiently. IRC servers define channels and operators. Channels are the notorious chat rooms that we have all heard so much about. Anyone can create a channel once logged into an IRC server. If you create a channel, you'll probably want to become the operator for that channel. Being an operator of a channel gives you the ability to control users who try to join your channel. You can ban them, kick them out of the group, and a variety of other things. You can even exchange files with other users, directly through the IRC interface. A word of warning, however: The IRC is huge and has a number of hidden features and loopholes. Experienced IRC users can wreak havoc on your channel if provoked; they can even deploy bots that will cause trouble without them being present. The IRC is an excellent place to meet for group collaboration but is also the primary meeting ground for many hackers.

If you would like to provide chat services for your organization and like what you see in the IRC protocol, you don't have to join the existing network of IRC machines. Each IRC server can provide standalone chat services as well as link into the global IRC network. The simplest (and often most useful) IRC server configuration is to operate in this standalone mode.

What Is a Bot?

Because of the open standard of IRC, programmers have been able to exploit its capabilities in ways that were never intended. One of these exploits is the creation of bots. A bot is a piece of software that connects to an IRC server like any user but is entirely automated. A bot could watch for new channels to be created, and then grab operator permissions from the real owners before they have a chance to set themselves as the operator. This sort of activity is all too common on IRC. The code of conduct on the IRC is to mind your own business. If you don't misbehave in someone else's channel, you should be fine.

We'll take a close look at the IRC protocol and its many features. Connecting to IRC servers directly, as we'll be doing now, is actually the preferred method of some IRC users. Really!

Connecting to an IRC Server As with the other protocols we've looked at, we'll be connecting directly to the IRC server port, usually 6667. There are actually several different IRC networks you can connect to—often divided geographically. A partial list of the available networks and servers on those networks is available from

```
http://www.irc.net/servers/index.html
```

For our examples, I'm going to be using a server that is located somewhere at MIT. You can use this one or any other server you'd like, and the results should be similar.

Let's go ahead and connect to the IRC server now. Issue the command

```
>telnet irc-2.mit.edu 6667
```

No response will be given upon a successful connection, but we can start talking to the remote IRC server. If we do not issue commands relatively quickly, the server will time out and kick us off.

Registering a Connection on the IRC Server The first thing we'll need to do once connected to the IRC server is register ourselves as a user on the IRC network. This process consists of specifying a password for the connection, a nickname that you'll be using during chatting, and information to identify your real identity.

PASS connection-password First, let's set a password for the session with the PASS command. Most servers will not require any password. It's possible, however, for some authentication to take place based on this value. For our purposes, just use anything you'd like, and you should be fine.

```
PASS    TheLargeAntelope
```

The server will not return any status messages, and you might think you've done something wrong. Don't worry; this lack of response is entirely normal. The IRC protocol only sends status messages when it needs to—usually to inform the user of an error or that a change has taken place.

NICK nickname The IRC uses nicknames to identify users during conversations. This can be anything you'd like. I generally use"Doorknob" as my nickname (it's a long story). The next step in registering with the server is to supply this nickname using the NICK function.

```
NICK Doorknob
```

Once again, the server will not return any information. If we want to verify that we have indeed set a nickname, let's go ahead and change the nickname to something else. This will force the server to tell us that the old nickname has been updated.

```
NICK John
```
```
:Doorknob NICK :John
```

Sure enough, the server indicates that the user Doorknob has changed his nickname to John. We weren't just talking to ourselves after all! (By the way, for future examples, I'll change my nickname back to Doorknob.)

USER username hostname servername :realname Because we've now identified ourselves to the server under a nickname, it would probably be polite to identify ourselves as a real person. Supplying this information to the server will allow it to announce our presence throughout the IRC network.

The username and hostname portions of the USER command should be set to your email username and email hostname. Other IRC servers use the servername to indicate which server we're connected to. Lastly, the realname parameter is your real name, prefixed with a colon (:).

```
USER jray poisontooth.com irc-2.mit.edu :John Ray
```

This process will complete our registration with the IRC network and will, finally, result in an actual message being sent to us from the server. This message, called the "MOTD" or Message Of The Day, is a welcome message that identifies the server, its operators, and any rules that it might have. Here is a portion of what the server returned after I completed my registration:

```
:irc-2.mit.edu 001 Doorknob :Welcome to the Internet Relay Network Doorknob
:irc-2.mit.edu 002 Doorknob :Your host is irc-2.mit.edu[rastro], running version
2.8.21+CSr29
:irc-2.mit.edu 003 Doorknob :This server was created Mon May 26 1997 at 12:19:34
EDT
:irc-2.mit.edu 004 Doorknob irc-2.mit.edu 2.8.21+CSr29 oiwsfcukbdl biklmnopstv
:irc-2.mit.edu 251 Doorknob :There are 29 users and 22 invisible on 1 servers
:irc-2.mit.edu 252 Doorknob 1 :operator(s) online
:irc-2.mit.edu 254 Doorknob 41 :channels formed
:irc-2.mit.edu 255 Doorknob :I have 51 clients and 0 servers
:irc-2.mit.edu 250 Doorknob :Highest connection count: 96 (95 clients)
:irc-2.mit.edu 375 Doorknob :- irc-2.mit.edu Message of the Day -
:irc-2.mit.edu 372 Doorknob :- 20/5/1998 1:48
:irc-2.mit.edu 372 Doorknob :- Welcome to irc-2.mit.edu (dedicated to dog3)
:irc-2.mit.edu 372 Doorknob :- Comments, questions, problems to <irc-admin@MIT.E
DU>.
```

We gather from this message that there are 41 channels on the server, 51 clients connected to the server, and no (0) other IRC servers networked with this server.

Controlling a Basic IRC Server Chat Session   Once registered with the server, we can begin using commands to create and join discussion groups, and interact with other users. You can issue the following commands in any order you'd like, so feel free to play around. Let's start by taking a look at joining and participating in a chat session.

LIST channel-name   Before we can carry on a discussion, we need to have an idea of what the different channels are that we can join. The LIST command will return a listing of all the current channels, along with an optional description. If we give the LIST command an existing channel's name as an argument, it will display information on that channel alone.

Example:

```
LIST

:irc-2.mit.edu 321 Doorknob Channel :Users  Name
:irc-2.mit.edu 322 Doorknob #danubius 1 :
:irc-2.mit.edu 322 Doorknob #nofx 1 :
:irc-2.mit.edu 322 Doorknob #Anthill_99 1 :
:irc-2.mit.edu 322 Doorknob #hamlet 1 :
:irc-2.mit.edu 322 Doorknob #Tomjencorp 1 :
:irc-2.mit.edu 322 Doorknob #sci_fi 1 :
:irc-2.mit.edu 322 Doorknob #ragtime 1 :
:irc-2.mit.edu 322 Doorknob #gemini 1 :
:irc-2.mit.edu 322 Doorknob #TwilightZONE 1 :
:irc-2.mit.edu 322 Doorknob #irchelp 1 :
:irc-2.mit.edu 322 Doorknob #france 1 :
:irc-2.mit.edu 322 Doorknob #macintosh 2 : Macintosh discussion group
…
```

Channels are usually prefixed with the pound sign (#). We can see that there really isn't much going on in the groups from the low user count on each channel. All of the channels appear to have only one user in them, except for the #macintosh channel. The #macintosh channel also has a description that indicates that it's a Macintosh discussion group. (What a surprise!) Let's go ahead and join #macintosh.

JOIN channel-name(s) channel-password(s)   Use JOIN to connect to a channel, or multiple channels, by specifying the channel name or names in a comma separated list. If a channel has a password (most don't), you can specify a matching list of passwords immediately following the channels. On most client software, joining multiple channels will open a different window for each channel. Because we're communicating with the server through one window, it would be confusing to try to carry on multiple conversations on different channels at the same time. We'll connect to a single channel in our examples.

Example:

```
JOIN #macintosh

:Doorknob!~jray@leviathan.ag.ohio-state.edu JOIN :#macintosh
:irc-2.mit.edu 353 Doorknob = #macintosh :Doorknob HWD DannyMac @Frankie
:irc-2.mit.edu 366 Doorknob #macintosh :End of /NAMES list.
```

The server responds by automatically issuing the NAMES command, which displays all the users on the channel. There are now four users in this channel: myself (Doorknob), HWD, DannyMac, and @Frankie. If we sit back and wait, we should see the conversation unfold:

```
:DannyMac!dannymac@somewhere.net PRIVMSG #Macintosh :k i'm here
:HWD!~hermann@somewhereelse.net PRIVMSG #macintosh :do you know some URLs about
learning to use irc better than i do now
:DannyMac!dannymac@somewhere.net PRIVMSG #Macintosh :i dunno what you're saying?
:HWD!~hermann@somewhereelse.net PRIVMSG #macintosh :sorry - do you know some web
sites explaining irc?
```

Not the most exciting group of people, but it demonstrates that we can indeed join a group and listen to the conversation. But how do we send a message to the discussion ourselves? Read on to find out.

PRIVMSG receiver(s) :message   One way we can communicate with other users on an IRC server is by using the Private Message function. PRIVMSG allows us to specify a comma separated list of receivers, which can be either channel names or users' nicknames, and a message to be sent, prefixed with a colon (:). If a channel is given as one of the receivers, the message will be displayed to all the members on the channel. In our previous example, we can see that each user is using PRIVMSG (probably without even knowing it) to send a message to the receiver #macintosh. Let's go ahead and try the same thing for ourselves and see what happens. If you chose to use a user's name instead of a channel, PRIVMSG will send a message to that user alone.

```
PRIVMSG #macintosh :Hello all.
```

At first, we won't get any response from the server, because it doesn't have anything new to tell us. If we're lucky, one of the other channel users will decide to talk to us.

```
:DannyMac!dannymac@somewhere.net PRIVMSG #Macintosh : Hi Doorknob, you in ohio?
:DannyMac!dannymac@somewhere.net PRIVMSG #Macintosh :i'm from kentucky!
```

The Internet certainly brings us closer together, doesn't it?

PART channel-name   We've probably caused enough paranoia on the #macintosh channel by now, so it's time to leave. Joining a channel and not contributing to the conversation is called *lurking* and is looked upon as an invasion of privacy by many channel operators. I've been connected to #macintosh for almost an hour now and have only said "Hello." Chances are that the other channel members are a little curious about what I'm doing, so we'll use PART to leave the channel.

Example:

```
PART #macintosh

:Doorknob!~jray@leviathan.ag.ohio-state.edu PART #macintosh
```

QUIT   If you're done using the IRC server, you can use QUIT to disconnect from the network. The server will return an error message, which indicates that the connection has been closed. Because this is precisely what you want, it isn't exactly an error.

Example:

```
QUIT

ERROR :Closing Link: Doorknob[~jray@leviathan.ag.ohio-state.edu] (Doorknob)
```

Creating and Controlling Your Own Channels   Now that we've seen how to carry on a basic conversation using the IRC protocol, let's use it to do something useful. Let's create our own discussion group and learn the basic administration commands to control it. There are far more IRC commands than are needed to grasp the concepts of the protocol, so we'll not discuss all of them here. If you're looking for a specific function that would be useful for your needs, don't assume that IRC does not already have the capability. Consult the RFC mentioned at the end of this section for a complete list of commands that IRC servers can support.

Revisiting JOIN channel-name As you now know, the JOIN command is used to join a channel or channels, and prepare to converse over that channel. What do you think happens, however, if you specify the name of a channel that doesn't exist? Let's go ahead and try that right now. I'm going to choose #TheLargeTableofToothpicks as the name of the channel I attempt to join. I'm guessing that it is a relatively safe bet that this channel isn't already in use on the server.

Example:

```
JOIN #TheLargeTableofToothpicks

:Doorknob!~jray@leviathan.ag.ohio-state.edu JOIN :#TheLargeTableofToothpicks
:irc-2.mit.edu 353 Doorknob = #TheLargeTableofToothpicks :@Doorknob
:irc-2.mit.edu 366 Doorknob #TheLargeTableofToothpicks :End of /NAMES list.
```

Interesting, no error message! In fact, the command we just sent was entirely valid. We have now created our own channel (with a rather strange name) that users will see if they use the LIST command. As the result from the server shows, there is only one user currently connected:ñ Doorknob (me).

TOPIC channel-name :topic Because no one is going to understand exactly what a channel called #TheLargeTableofToothpicks is really about, we'd better set a description, or topic, for it. The TOPIC command allows us, assuming we have the appropriate permission, to set the description for a channel that we have joined. Let's go ahead and set a topic for our new channel. Be sure to prefix the topic text with a colon (:).

Example:

```
TOPIC #TheLargeTableofToothpicks :A Dentistry Discussion

:Doorknob!~jray@leviathan.ag.ohio-state.edu TOPIC #TheLargeTableofToothpicks :A
Dentistry Discussion
```

We can verify that the topic has been set by using LIST to display information about our channel.

```
LIST #TheLargeTableofToothpicks

:irc-2.mit.edu 321 Doorknob Channel :Users   Name
:irc-2.mit.edu 322 Doorknob #TheLargeTableofToothpicks 1 :A Dentistry Discussion
:irc-2.mit.edu 323 Doorknob :End of /LIST
```

Sure enough, there it is. We can now sit back and wait for the thousands of people interested in discussing dentistry to join and chat with us.

MODE channel-name mode-options <limit> <user> Because we're now facing a certain flood of curious dentists (and dentist groupies) to our channel, it's time that we seize control of the channel and set up some ground rules. The MODE command allows us to customize certain parameters of a channel to make it suit our needs. There is an extensive list of the different mode options that can be set or unset for a channel by placing a + or - in front of the corresponding option. Here are a few of the options that are available:

o—Assign operator privileges to a user. If a user is assigned as an operator, he or she has access to this same set of commands and can effectively take over a channel.

i—Set the channel to be an invite-only group. This will keep random people from joining. For an IRC user to become part of the discussion, they must be invited with the INVITE command.

t—Specifies if only the operator can set the channel's topic. Generally, you'll want to set this option for your channel. Failure to do so could result in a playful user turning our"Dentistry Discussion" into something less exciting.

l—Allows you to set a limit to the number of users on the channel. Although we've seen only a group with four members in it so far, it's entirely possible for hundreds of people to join. Do we really need to be lectured on the importance of flossing by a hundred dentists?

b—Bans a user, or group of users, from the channel. If someone in the discussion is misbehaving, or is simply unwelcome, that person can be banned from the group.

k—Sets a key or password for the channel. Only users who know the password can join the discussion by sending the JOIN channel-name password command.

s—Turns the group into a secret channel. Secret channels are not listed by the LIST command, so an IRC user must know the name of the channel in order to connect.

n—Disables users who haven't joined a channel from sending messages to the channel. Normally the PRVMSG command can send a message to a channel whether or not a user has actually joined it.

There's quite a bit that you can do with your channel, isn't there? Let's go ahead and apply some of these modes in examples. You need only make use of the modes that suit your needs. If you want to have a free-for-all, anything-goes channel, there is nothing else you need to set. If not, read on.

The first thing you'll want to do after creating your channel is to set yourself as the operator. This might seem slightly obvious, but it's usually overlooked because it would make sense that the server automatically set a channel's creator to be the operator, which is not the case. Use the MODE +o command to make yourself the operator for our channel. There will be no server response generated from this request.

Example:

```
MODE #TheLargeTableofToothpicks +o Doorknob
```

Next, because we don't want anyone to mess with the channel topic we've set, let's go ahead and use MODE +t to disable other people from changing it.

Example:

```
MODE #TheLargeTableofToothpicks +t

:Doorknob!~jray@leviathan.ag.ohio-state.edu MODE #TheLargeTableofToothpicks +t
```

Finally, because we don't want to be overloaded by thousands of chatting dentists, let's set a limit on the number of connections our channel supports.

Example:

```
MODE #TheLargeTableofToothpicks +l 10

:Doorknob!~jray@leviathan.ag.ohio-state.edu MODE #TheLargeTableofToothpicks +l 10
```

We have now successfully created an IRC channel with a limit of 10 users, in which we are the operator. The topic cannot be modified except by us or others we configure as having operator privileges.

WHOIS nickname   Once we're successfully running our channel, we may want to manage users who join it. One of the first commands you'll need is the WHOIS command. WHOIS identifies the remote user, the client machine they're using to connect to the IRC server, and the length of time they've been connected. The server software itself determines this information, so the client's hostname cannot easily be hidden. Let's see what the WHOIS command returns about my nickname.

Example:

```
WHOIS Doorknob

:irc-2.mit.edu 311 Doorknob Doorknob ~jray leviathan.ag.ohio-state.edu * :John
Ray
:irc-2.mit.edu 312 Doorknob Doorknob irc-2.mit.edu :Massachusetts Institute of
Technology
:irc-2.mit.edu 317 Doorknob Doorknob 7 902863163 :seconds idle, signon time
:irc-2.mit.edu 318 Doorknob Doorknob :End of /WHOIS list.
```

The server correctly returns the information I entered when registering with the IRC network. It also shows that I am using `leviathan.ag.ohio-state.edu` to access the server, despite the fact that I never specifically told it that `leviathan` was my hostname.

KICK channel-name nickname   If you've decided that a user on your channel is no longer welcome, you can forcibly remove the malcontent from the channel with the KICK command.

Example:

```
KICK #TheLargeTableofToothpicks Doorknob

:Doorknob!~jray@leviathan.ag.ohio-state.edu KICK #TheLargeTableofToothpicks
Doorknob :Doorknob
```

Upon completion of the KICK command, the user is ejected from the channel, but they can immediately rejoin. If you want to keep a user out of a channel, you must follow the KICK command with a MODE ban command. (To ban myself, I'd use MODE #TheLargeTableofToothpicks +b jray@leviathan.ag.ohio-state.edu.)

USERHOST nickname(s)   Like the WHOIS command, the USERHOST command returns information about a nickname or a list of up to five nicknames (separated by spaces). Because you can look up multiple nicknames at once, this might be a more convenient way to gather information about people using your channel.

Example:

```
USERHOST Doorknob DeepBlue

:irc-2.mit.edu 302 Doorknob :Doorknob=+~jray@leviathan.ag.ohio-state.edu DeepBlu
e=+Renrorer@1Cust119.tnt2.mail.net
```

The IRC server returns all the information for the two nicknames (Doorknob and DeepBlue) on a single line. Though the information might appear to provide email addresses for the users, this is not necessarily the case. The server is simply concatenating the username with the hostname that the user is currently on. In most cases, it's unlikely that this is the same hostname the user's email is stored on.

ISON nickname(s)   The ISON command is the last IRC command we'll look at in the protocol. Despite our delay in getting to it, ISON is actually one of the more useful commands. The IRC is often used as a meeting place for groups working together from remote locations. It's also a social gathering place for friends. Whatever your use for it, you will soon find yourself gathering a list of nicknames of people you talk to on a regular basis. The ISON command lets you check a list of nicknames against all the users on the IRC network, and will let you know who in the list is currently logged into the server.

Example:

```
ISON Doorknob MrPuddles DeepBlue

:irc-2.mit.edu 303 Doorknob :Doorknob DeepBlue
```

The server responds to show us that two out of the three users are indeed online (Doorknob and DeepBlue).

HELP   Before we leave the topic of IRC completely, let's take a look at one other command: HELP. HELP displays a list of the available commands on the server. Because we can't discuss every command, using HELP can at least give you an idea of just how huge the IRC protocol really is. Of the protocols we've discussed, IRC has, by far, the largest vocabulary of the TCP/IP protocols I describe in this book.

Example:

```
HELP

:irc-2.mit.edu NOTICE Doorknob :PRIVMSG
:irc-2.mit.edu NOTICE Doorknob :NICK
:irc-2.mit.edu NOTICE Doorknob :NOTICE
...
:irc-2.mit.edu NOTICE Doorknob :DNS
:irc-2.mit.edu NOTICE Doorknob :REHASH
:irc-2.mit.edu NOTICE Doorknob :RESTART
```

Although they are not all displayed here, the MIT server returned over 50 different commands that can be sent to the server. That should keep you busy for quite awhile! If all of this information is a bit overwhelming, you might want to take a look at ICQ, which I mentioned in Chapter 2. ICQ is a very quick and easy-to-use chat system (http://www.mirabilis.com/).

Part

II

Ch

9

Client Software

Of the three operating systems we've been looking at, Linux is the only one that comes with its own built-in IRC client, IRCII. IRCII is a full-screen, text-based client, which, despite not running in a graphical environment, is considered by many to be the premier IRC client. In fact, IRCII has even been ported to Windows. Linux users can access the IRC instantly by typing `irc` at a shell prompt. If you don't happen to be running Linux, don't fret; there are more than enough clients to go around. Here are a few of them and the Web addresses where you can download them or get more information.

Ircle (Mac OS): `http://www.xs4all.nl/~ircle/`

MacIRC (Mac OS): `http://www.macirc.com/`

CIRCus (Linux): `http://www.nijenrode.nl/~ivo/circus/`

PIRCH (Windows): `http://www.bcpl.lib.md.us/~frappa/pirch.html`

mIRC (Windows): `http://www.mirc.org/`

Other Information Sources

Internet Relay Chat RFC 1459: `http://freesoft.org/CIE/RFC/Orig/rfc1459.txt`

Less Friendly but Useful Protocols

You've now seen a wide variety of protocols and the vocabularies they use to communicate. There are other useful protocols that are important, but they use commands that are not readily readable. Because these protocols cannot be demonstrated directly with examples, this section will be typing free. Enjoy this time while you can; once we complete this chapter, we're going to start looking at setting up our own TCP/IP network and services, and things will start moving very quickly.

FTP

FTP is a network workhorse used to transfer files over TCP/IP connections. Servers and clients have been written for every imaginable platform, and, despite the popularity of using HTTP to transfer files, FTP has remained the king of direct cross-platform file transfers.

If you've never used FTP, one of the first things you'll notice is that it's very fast. The protocol was designed to be extremely simple and to transfer data as quickly as possible. Try copying a file to a remote computer by using FTP, and then by using a protocol specific to your computer's operating system. Chances are, you'll be quite surprised at the difference in speed.

FTP employs a different method of communication from the protocols we've looked at up to this point. We *can* communicate with an FTP server through a Telnet connection, but not completely. The reason for this is that a single FTP session maintains a connection on two separate ports. Port 20 is called the "data connection," and port 21 is the "command connection." As you might expect, commands are sent to port 21. Data being delivered to the client from the server is sent by way of port 20. If we were to attempt to connect to the server and issue commands to control it, the server would eventually return an error:

```
425 Can't build data connection: Connection refused.
```

(Feel free to try this later as an exercise.) The reason for the error is because the second connection on port 20 doesn't exist, so the server can't send the data the client needs.

A benefit of the unique dual-port structure of FTP is that the data connection doesn't necessarily have to be to the same machine as the control connection. A client computer, for instance, can open command connections to two different remote systems, and then open a data connection between the remote machines. It can use the command connections to cause the remote computers to exchange data between themselves. This eliminates the need to transfer the data from the remote host to the client, and then from the client to the second remote machine.

The FTP Command Set   Although we cannot successfully use all of the FTP command set, I'll present just a small subset of the commands here. Most FTP programs allow you to view a plain-text log of the commands as they are sent back and forth to client. In some cases, they'll allow you to use the commands directly. You'll see, once again, that the vocabulary is remarkably friendly.

USER username   The USER command puts the FTP server into authentication mode and specifies the username for the connection. You can use this command multiple times during a single command connection in order to log into multiple accounts on a system. It's usually followed immediately by the PASS command, which I'll describe now.

PASS password   PASS allows the user to specify his or her password for the connection. Doing so will complete the authentication process and allow the client to begin transferring files and directory information.

CWD directory-name   CWD, Change Working Directory, is the command sent to the server to switch to a new directory. Rather than using the commands that are native to the operating system that the server is running on (such as CD in DOS), FTP uses its own command set, thus enabling it to be successfully used across platforms.

I've Used Command-line FTP before, But I Remember Using Different Commands. What's Going On?

What you're using is simply a text-based client that accepts commands and translates them into what the FTP protocol accepts. For example, you don't often use CWD to change directories from a command line FTP session; you probably issue the CD command. Even so, the CWD command is being executed behind the scenes. The same goes for LIST, which you often call by typing DIR or ls inside the command-line client.

LIST directory-name   LIST displays a directory listing for the specified directory or the current directory if a directory name is not given. This information is passed on the data-connection.

Part
II

Ch
9

PASV PASV places the server in passive mode. This allows the server to listen on a different data port other than port 20. Normally, the server will attempt to contact and open a port for data transfer on the client. In passive mode, the server will wait for the client to contact it. This is useful for instances when your computer is on a secured network. Some security systems will not allow incoming connections to machines on the network. This, in turn, will cause FTP to fail. Using passive mode FTP allows the client to create the connection and carry on the conversation with the server—something that is generally allowed on secured networks.

TYPE type-code TYPE identifies the type of the file that's going to be transferred. The two most common options are "I" and "A," for Image and ASCII. Setting the server to Image will allow binary file transfers (programs, images, and other data) to be transferred. ASCII transfers will allow only basic text files to be transferred. A nice feature of using the "A" type is that transferring text files between different platforms results in an appropriately converted file. One of the most common errors made when using FTP is transferring binary data using an ASCII transfer. The result is a file that is unusable.

What Is an EOL?

Different operating systems use different characters to mark the end of a line (EOL) of text. Our three sample operating systems—Mac OS, Windows, Linux—all have different EOLs. Opening a file created on a Linux machine under Windows or Mac OS will look slightly strange, and vice versa. Transferring the files using FTP's ASCII transfer mode rewrites the EOL character to be appropriate for the client's computer system.

STOR filename The server begins storing data that arrives on the data connection to the given filename. The client sends this command when it wants to transfer a file to the server. The file type specified with the TYPE command is used for the upload.

RETR filename This command retrieves the given filename from the server using the data connection.

QUIT This command terminates the connection to the FTP server, closing both the data and command connection.

Client Software Both Windows and Linux come with command line FTP programs built in (type `ftp` at a command/shell prompt). They're not graphical clients, but they allow you to interact directly with the server and can be quite educational. Web browsers function well as FTP clients but are rather bare-bones as far as graphical FTP interfaces go. Finally, you can download and run a number of FTP clients for various platforms. Here are some examples:

Netscape Navigator/Communicator (Windows, Mac OS, Linux): `http://www.netscape.com/`

Microsoft Internet Explorer (Windows, Mac OS): `http://www.microsoft.com/ie/`

Fetch (Mac OS): `http://www.dartmouth.edu/pages/softdev/fetch.html`

Anarchie (Mac OS): `ftp://ftp.share.com/pub/peterlewis/anarchie-pro-30.sit.bin`

WS-FTP (Windows): `http://www.ipswitch.com/products/ws_ftp/index.html`

Other Information Sources   File Transfer Protocol RFC 959: `http://freesoft.org/CIE/RFC/959/index.htm`

NTP

FTP introduced the first protocol we've looked at in this chapter that doesn't exist in an entirely human-readable format. However, FTP is still a very high-level TCP/IP protocol. We can still see the commands that are being sent back and forth to accomplish tasks on the network. Our examples have shown that many protocols work based on a model of client request and server response. It is important to realize that not all protocols follow this model. You may not have realized it, but we actually looked at two such protocols earlier: SNMP and DHCP. Let's take a look at one final protocol that's fun, useful, and not based on a human-readable protocol format: NTP, the Network Time Protocol.

I have two computers that, together, perform a relatively important function on my network. For the software I've written to work correctly, it must be started at a regular interval on each machine. If the programs start as much as 30 seconds out of sync, they cannot do their job, and the program will abort. The problem with this situation is that computer clocks are only as accurate as any other digital clock. In some cases, they can be terrible, losing several seconds a week, especially as their rechargeable batteries get old. What can I do to keep the computers successfully talking to each other as their clocks drift apart? The answer is supplied by NTP.

NTP provides a mechanism by which a network device's internal clock can be synchronized with the clock of an NTP server. The NTP server's clock is considered to be an authoritative source for the time, even though it's not necessarily accurate itself. (In other words, you're synchronizing the clocks, but not necessarily to the correct time.) To avoid this pitfall, many NTP servers synchronize themselves by connecting to other NTP servers that are directly linked to atomic clocks; you can't get much more accurate than that. By having both of my computers connect to the NTP server periodically, I can assume that their clocks will remain in sync, and my software will continue to run as it should.

Even in a standard workgroup situation, NTP is useful. If users collaborate and share files, it might be confusing if a file's modification time appears to be a few minutes in the future for one user, and several minutes in the past for another. Each computer on the network could talk to an NTP server and synchronize their clocks to within a tiny fraction of a second.

To work its magic, an NTP server must be able to reply to a client request with a packet (sent using UDP) that contains the server's local time at the time the packet will reach the machine. The server must, therefore, be capable of determining the amount of time it takes for a packet to reach the NTP client before it can reply. It also includes an estimate of the amount of error that may be included in the calculations.

The client, upon receiving the NTP packet, will adjust its clock accordingly and send another request to the NTP server containing its new local time. The process will continue until the difference between the clock on the client and the clock of the server is zero. NTP is capable of synchronizing clocks within a millisecond of each other.

It should be obvious that this sort of precision requires messages to be sent as quickly as possible. Therefore, the protocol consists of sending small packets containing only the necessary time information to update the clock. Rather than implementing an entire vocabulary to control the process, the client and server recognize one form of packet and can generate one response based on its contents.

Client Software   Although software does exist to synchronize the Mac OS clock to an NTP server (one of which is listed below), you may want to invest in Mac OS 8.5.x instead. Mac OS 8.5 has the capability to synchronize with an NTP server automatically from its Dates and Times control panel.

Vremya Clock Synchronization (Mac OS): `http://www.lava.net/~kirill/software/vremya.html`

NTP32 (Windows): `http://desktop.ucdavis.edu/software/freeware/ntp/ntp32.exe`

Other Information Sources   Network Time Protocol RFC 1305: `http://freesoft.org/CIE/RFC/Orig/rfc1305.txt`

TCP/IP Services

By now you know how TCP/IP works, and how to configure your client computers to use TCP/IP, but what services can you provide over your network? Part 3 investigates the TCP/IP capabilities built into the client operating systems, as well as how to extend them. By the end of Part 3, you will have learned how to set up Web servers, mail servers, and file servers that can be used across a variety of different platforms. Can Windows and Mac OS truly get along? Sure they can, just read Part 3!

10 Creating a TCP/IP Intranet 167

11 Exploring Client OS File Server Capabilities 185

12 Adding Email and Web Server Capabilities to Your OS 223

13 Establishing Dedicated Servers 271

## CHAPTER 10

Creating a TCP/IP Intranet

by John Ray

In this chapter

Setting Up and Understanding Your Hub **168**

Planning Your Wiring **169**

Making the Connection **170**

Using Ping to Check the Connection **170**

Exploring Your Basic TCP/IP Services **173**

Basic Client Services **173**

By this point, you've seen what goes into setting up a TCP/IP client, and some of the protocols that run on TCP/IP. Now you'll begin putting it all together to set up your own TCP/IP network. In Chapter 5, you configured three different clients for the operating system: Windows 95 or 98, Linux, and Mac OS. Using this knowledge, it's time to look at connecting these machines to form your own TCP/IP intranet. Later (in Chapter 14), you'll connect this intranet to the Internet.

I'll assume that the first network you would want to build is a 10BASE-T or 100BASE-TX network. These are both the cheapest and most useful network setups you would want to consider. You might be able to save a few dollars by going with a thinnet network, but, in the long run, life will be much easier for you with a twisted pair configuration.

Go ahead and get started with configuring your intranet. The first thing you'll need to do is pick a range of IP addresses that you'll use for your network. For the sample configuration, I chose 192.168.0.xx as my private subnet, so let's continue to use it. This time, however, let's start assigning IP addresses at a higher range than 192.168.0.1. Depending on the size of your network and your plans for dedicated services that you might want to offer, you might want to skip the first 10 to 15 addresses on your subnet and reserve these for your servers, routers, and so on. Be sure to keep a list of the IP addresses you use on your network and what machines they belong to. Later, you'll be setting up a software-based gateway or router that will connect your little network to the Internet, but, for the time being, you will not set a gateway device. Besides not setting a gateway, you will also hold off on setting a name server address. Even without this information, you'll still be able to communicate between your computers. You won't, however, be able to communicate with the outside world. You can create hosts files for the machines if you'd like, but it's unnecessary for your particular configuration, unless you would like to run a TCP/IP based email service immediately. If you're simply adding computers to an existing TCP/IP network, then be sure to get the appropriate addresses and gateway information from the network administrator. Never choose IP addresses just because you know they'll work (unless you're the administrator, of course).

Setting Up and Understanding Your Hub

After configuring the client computers, you will plug them into a hub. Your local computer store should have several makes and models of hubs to choose from. For a basic small network, there is little reason not to go with the cheapest you can find. Larger, more expensive hubs offer a variety of features that might be useful for a big network, but most five- to eight-port hubs offer the same basic features. You should be looking at paying $50 to $75 for a good five- to eight-port hub. You should notice several LEDs on your hub. Most hubs will have a green light for each port, which will be lit if a network client is attached correctly. You might also notice a red or orange collision light. This light will flash as collisions are detected on your wire. Don't be alarmed if you see this flash on a frequent basis. These LEDs are provided to give you an indication of excessive collisions, in which case the LED will be lit almost constantly. Seeing the light flash once or twice a second is quite normal. More expensive hubs will also include a light for each port that indicates traffic on that port. As a device attached to the port sends packets, you'll see the light flash correspondingly. This is a useful feature if there's a misconfiguration on your network and a device is broadcasting packets faster than it should be. A quick glance at your hub, and you can quickly determine the culprit. Most hubs contain a feature that detects irregular activity on a port that might affect other ports and will disable the port if such a condition exists. The process of disabling a port is often referred to as *partitioning*. If a port is partitioned, it will be completely unusable, even if the condition that caused the partitioning is resolved. In this case, the hub will either have a reset button that will remove any partitions that it has set, or you will need to power down the hub.

Using a "Crossover" Cable to Connect Two Hubs or Two Computers

You may notice a different port on your hub called a *crossover* port. The crossover port is used to connect two hubs, allowing you to extend your network. You cannot use this port to connect to a computer, because the wiring is slightly different from a normal 10BASE-T wire. In some cases, your hub will not have a crossover port, and you'll need to make a crossover cable to connect to another hub. You can also use a crossover cable to connect two computers together without a hub. If you'd like to create a two-computer network without buying a hub, this is how you do it. A crossover cable is wired as shown in Figure 10.1.

FIGURE 10.1
Crossover cables are wired like this.

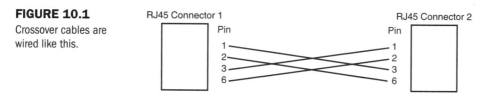

If you're not experienced with making cables, I recommend that you buy a crossover cable. Using an improperly wired cable can introduce errors into your network.

Planning Your Wiring

When laying out your network, if it's going to be spanning multiple rooms, it's best if you first create a scale overhead view of the area that will be on your network and position the hub where wires will adequately cover the range you need. Remember, 10BASE-T wiring can be a length of around 100 meters. Although keeping wiring out of sight is a common goal for network planning, it's even more important to keep the wiring away from other electric wires, including light fixtures. Laying your network cable in the same path as standard electrical wiring could result in an induced current being created in the wiring. This might cause network instability, as well as potentially causing currents in the wiring that could damage your hubs and Ethernet cards. You also want to avoid making kinks in the cabling as you lay it. This may damage the wire, and partial reflections could be created.

Making the Connection

Once you've laid your wiring and positioned your hub, you can connect your computers or other network devices to the hubs. Simply plug them in and turn then on. You should notice a light become active on your hub for each of the machines you've plugged in and turned on. The light does not indicate that a proper TCP/IP configuration has been set up; it simply means that the hardware layer is successfully connected and working. Be sure that you connect your 10BASE-T cables to your computers before booting up the computers. If you're using "combo' Ethernet cards, the card may be designed to detect the port that the wiring is connected to when the machine first powers up. If the twisted pair wiring is not connected, the card may default to using a different port and will not work correctly once it is connected. Rebooting your computer will cause the card to be reinitialized, and it will redetect the wire it's connected to.

Using Ping to Check the Connection

Assuming you've connected your computers to the hub, configured them according to our IP numbering scheme, and turned everything on, you're ready to see if your network is actually working. To do that, you'll use ping again. You should be able to ping each of your nodes from each of the other nodes. You only need to test this from one computer, however, because the ping command sends an ICMP echo request to the receiving computer. If the receiving computer is correctly configured, it will send a return echo packet back to the sending machine. If it incorrectly configured, your ping request will time out, and there will be no response.

Go ahead and try this now. If you recall, you can run ping from within a command prompt in Windows, or within a shell window in Linux. You will need to use the IP addresses you have specified in the individual configurations, because you haven't set up a DNS. If you've created a hosts file on each machine, you can use the hostnames specified in the files. Windows users should be able to ping any local host by hostname regardless. If you're using Linux to ping the remote station, it will run ping continuously until you press Control-C. You will probably want to run at least five pings, just to be sure everything is working.

Isn't Pinging Bad? I've Heard of the "Ping of Death."

Pinging is not bad at all. There are a few cases where an abnormal ping can cause problems, however. The most famous of these situations is "The Ping of Death," which sends abnormally large packets to a remote host and can cause it to crash. Most operating systems (all three we're reviewing) have been updated to withstand Ping of Death attacks. Another potential problem caused by ping is a flood ping. A flood ping can fill the network with a large amount of traffic, overloading the destination machine. Both of these attacks are inappropriate uses of ping and can't be triggered by the type of pinging we're doing here.

```
>ping 192.168.0.21
PING 192.168.0.21 (192.168.0.21): 56 data bytes
```

```
64 bytes from 192.168.0.21: icmp_seq=0 ttl=64 time=0.5 ms
64 bytes from 192.168.0.21: icmp_seq=1 ttl=64 time=0.4 ms
64 bytes from 192.168.0.21: icmp_seq=2 ttl=64 time=0.4 ms
64 bytes from 192.168.0.21: icmp_seq=3 ttl=64 time=0.4 ms
64 bytes from 192.168.0.21: icmp_seq=4 ttl=64 time=0.4 ms

-- 192.168.0.21 ping statistics --
5 packets transmitted, 5 packets received, 0% packet loss
round-trip min/avg/max = 0.4/0.4/0.5 ms
```

You can see that there is an extremely low response time, of around 0.4ms, for each ping you sent. You should expect response times of 1ms or lower for a local network that's running from a single hub. As you add other hubs, the ping time may increase slightly. On a regular day, I can ping a machine in a building that is approximately a quarter of a mile from my office and is separated by two bridges from my office machine, and still have a response time of 1ms. If you notice consistent jumps in the response time or if there are any dropped packets (the sequence number does not increase by one for each packet), then there is most likely an error in your hardware layer. Make sure your cabling is securely plugged in and is not kinked or damaged in any way. Also, be aware that activity on the remote machine can affect the ping time. Software running on the destination computer is what is generating the ping response. If there is something else running that's using a large amount of your CPU time, you'll see response times jump around drastically. It's best to test your network and confirm the connections before the clients are put into active use.

Why Does the First ping Response Always Take Longer than the Rest?

Because the implementation of the ICMP echo response is in software, the machine receiving the ping doesn't necessarily have to have that portion of the software in memory all the time. Usually the first ping packet wakes up the remote computer, which determines how it needs to respond, and then responds. Sending subsequent ping requests is faster because the remote computer is now prepared to respond.

Usually excessive ping times and dropped packets are indicative of a cabling or hardware problem, not a software configuration issue. There are two other situations where ping may return messages that point to a misconfiguration of the TCP/IP settings on the clients.

Network Unreachable

If you see an error message saying `Network unreachable` or `Destination host unreachable`, this means that your computer is probably misconfigured, or you mistyped the IP address of the device you were trying to test. The Unreachable message means that your computer believes that the other computer is on a different subnet, and it would need to speak to a gateway in order to talk to it. To correct this, verify that you entered your IP address and subnet mask correctly. A simple typo is usually the culprit. Figure 10.2 shows an example of a misconfigured gateway.

Part
III

Ch
10

FIGURE 10.2

The Destination host unreachable message is indicative of a gateway misconfiguration.

In extreme cases, an Ethernet card that is incorrectly configured may generate similar errors. This, however, is a more serious problem, which must be diagnosed for each individual PC.

Network Timeout

A Timeout error is precisely what it sounds like. Your computer has sent a ping request, and it has given up, or timed out, while waiting for a response. If this happens, it may mean that your computer's IP address is incorrectly configured. Figure 10.3 illustrates a timeout during a test ping.

FIGURE 10.3

If your ping request times out, make sure your IP address configuration is correct.

It's also possible, although less likely, that you typed the destination address incorrectly. Typing a destination on the local subnet that does not exist will give you the same error message. Double-check the configuration of the computer sending the ping requests, and then move on to check the configuration of the remote machine. Once you have successfully pinged a computer on your network, this is positive proof that your network configuration is working and is stable. You can then use one of the successfully configured computers to ping the rest of your network. If an error message is returned, you can be sure that the problem is with the remote computer's configuration.

Be sure to use ping to check each connection as you install it; never assume that the network is completely functional until you have. Often the task of setting up machine after machine with the same information can lead to silly mistakes being made, no matter what your experience level.

Upon verifying all of your connections, you can give yourself a quick pat on the back; you have now successfully set up your TCP/IP network!

Exploring Your Basic TCP/IP Services

Without installing any special software on your computer system, you can immediately begin providing some basic TCP/IP services to your network. We'll look at configuring several TCP/IP servers later in Chapters 11 and 12, but for now, let's see what you can do without installing anything additional. We'll take a quick look at the basic services for each OS and provide information on how to use them. My hope is that by providing this approach, you can easily determine what you need for your network. There are three possibilities for providing TCP/IP services that I'll cover, in this order:

Part
III

Ch
10

> Client OSes and the TCP/IP services they provide by default
>
> Extensions that can be made to the Client OS to provide additional services
>
> Dedicated server solutions

It's entirely possible that for your needs, you'll require only what is supplied with, or easily added to, your client operating systems.

Basic Client Services

Because both the Mac OS and Windows 95/98 are both considered "client" OSes, they provide a limited number of TCP/IP services by default. While there are programs that can serve information from both Mac OS and Windows, they're usually limited in speed and in the number of clients that they can handle. Linux, on the other hand, is often used as both a client and a server operating system. It provides a large number of services out of the box, and therefore I'll discuss it when we look at our heavy-duty servers and as we examine the clients.

Mac OS Default Services

Mac OS, by default, includes only a single TCP/IP client: a Web browser. However, it does have the capability to provide the functionality of a basic Web server and file server. Included in Mac OS 8.x is a control panel called *Web File Sharing*. If you do not have this control panel, rerun the Mac OS Installer from your system CD; you will be able to activate Web File sharing by performing a custom installation from the CD.

Using Mac OS Web Sharing   *Web File Sharing*, as you might have guessed, is a method of sharing files from your Macintosh out to the world over a TCP/IP connection using the HTTP protocol. There are two modes of operation for Web File Sharing: Web server mode and the Web "Finder" mode. In the Web server mode, the Web File Sharing acts like a normal Web server. You can select an HTML page on your computer, and it will be served when people connect to your computer. A very nice feature of the Web server mode is that it can instantly translate SimpleText files into Web pages.

What Is SimpleText?

Macintosh owners are usually extremely familiar with SimpleText. It's a small styled-text editor that is installed on every Macintosh system. It's also included with many software packages. The rationale behind this is that most Mac users don't need SimpleText and throw it away, so the people producing the software product want to be sure that it's installed so that any README files can be read. The reality of the situation is that most Macintoshes have several dozen copies of SimpleText installed.

This feature allows users who have no knowledge of HTML to quickly create Web pages using software that is already on their machines. Simply use SimpleText to visually create your Web pages, save them, select them in the Web Sharing control panel (shown in Figure 10.4), and they're online.

FIGURE 10.4

You can give other users on the network access to Web pages on your machine.

The second Web-sharing mode is called the Web file server mode. This mode allows you to share out files over the Internet and download them from other machines. To activate this mode of operation, you simply select a directory to share instead of a file. A user connecting to your machine will then see a listing of the directories within the directory you specified, as shown in Figure 10.5.

Clicking on a file will download the file from the remote computer. You may notice that some files do not show up as being clickable. This is because the control panel server does not recognize the appropriate MIME type for the document on your computer. If you want to allow that document to be recognized, you can add to the MIME types that the machine recognizes by editing the Web Sharing MIME Types file, located in the System Folder. (You might use SimpleText to edit the file—another use for that program!) If you want to be able to download files that aren't clickable, you'll need to make additions to this file, as shown in Figure 10.6.

FIGURE 10.5

Web file sharing mode lets users access the contents of a folder on your machine.

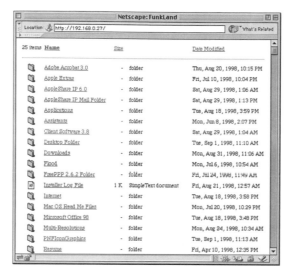

FIGURE 10.6

You can edit the Web Sharing MIME Types file in the System folder to add to the number of recognized files.

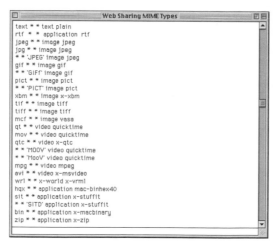

Now, with your new ability to share files from your computer, you have new problems that must be addressed. With respects to Web file sharing, you have opened up your computer to your entire network, and that might not be something that you truly want. You need some way to protect the information that is being sent out from your machine. On a three-node network like the one you're building, this really isn't necessary. But even on a network of 10–20 people, it's unusual that all the people will need access to all the data. To protect your Web file sharing, you can use the control panel to turn on protection for your pages. Web file sharing uses the same access-control system that standard Mac OS file sharing uses: the Users and Groups control panel, shown in Figure 10.7.

You can use the Users and Groups control panel to create a Web Users group that has access to all your Web resources. To do this, first open the Web Users control panel. Create a new user by clicking on the New button and filling in a username and password for the individual. Continue doing this until you have created all the users who will need to access your Web page. Now, you'll want to create a new group to contain all your users. Do so by clicking on the New Group button. Name your group something descriptive for the purpose it will be serving, such as Web Users. To add users to your group, simply drag the user names onto the group icon. You can view the users in your group at any time by double-clicking the group's name in the Users and Groups control panel. At any point in time, you can see the changes you've made to your settings by launching one of the included browsers on your system. Mac OS installs Internet Explorer by default and, at the time of this writing, also includes Netscape. To connect to your local machine, you can simply use localhost as the URL you want view.

FIGURE 10.7

The Users and Groups control panel lets you restrict file access on your shared computer.

What Is the Localhost?

The localhost entry is the hostname for the loopback address, which you learned will connect to your local computer whether or not your network adapter is set up properly. You can use localhost to refer to your computer as if it were an assigned hostname.

The Mac OS, by default, does not include any other TCP/IP server capabilities with the default-installed system. It does have built-in file sharing and networking called AppleTalk (or EtherTalk), which can be used over your Ethernet network, but is not based on TCP/IP. I'll introduce AppleShare IP later, which allows AppleTalk to be used over TCP/IP. This is a separate server product and is not part of the standard Mac OS operating system. We'll look at software that can supplement each operating system after we cover the default capabilities that each can provide out of the box. For now, let's take a look at the default Windows 9X capabilities.

Windows 95/98 Basic Services

Windows is on the opposite end of the spectrum from Mac OS: It includes several TCP/IP clients but no default cross-platform serving capability. Depending on the version of the OS you have installed, you may have a Web serving function that is similar to the one in Mac OS. The default installation of Windows 95 does not include this feature, however. When the TCP/IP protocol is installed, Windows also installs several useful TCP/IP applications. Telnet, ping, netstat, traceroute, Internet Explorer, and ARP are all installed as part of the default Windows TCP/IP networking suite. From the client standpoint, this is an excellent collection of utilities that can be used to diagnose connection problems on the network. Because Windows 95 and 98 are designed to be clients, this situation is perfectly acceptable.

Windows does provide one TCP/IP service by default, but it is of limited value to us on a cross-platform network: Windows SMB file sharing. *SMB* is a file serving system that is proprietary to the Windows platform. But with the help of the transport protocol *NetBIOS*, it can run over TCP/IP. There are Mac OS and Linux clients, but they require extra software to work. If you're running a Windows-only network, this is fine, as is a Windows-Linux network. Unfortunately, the Mac clients are not free and will cost you for each workstation you want to connect to the network. We'll look at connecting a Macintosh to a Windows network after we finish discussing the basic features that are included in each OS.

Using Windows TCP/IP Filesharing   Let's take a look now at setting up a shared TCP/IP volume in Windows. Before you actually set up your computer to share resources, you must make sure that NetBIOS is enabled for use over TCP/IP. To do this, open the Network control panel and double-click the TCP/IP protocol in the listing. Click the NetBIOS tab, and verify that the "I want to enable NetBIOS over TCP/IP" check box is selected. If it isn't, select it now. You can now proceed with configuring the computer to share local resources across the network.

The first thing you need to do is assign a common workgroup to all your Windows clients. A workgroup is simply an organizational unit that contains computers that are all in the same office, or working on similar projects. You can arbitrarily create workgroups for each machine, but it makes most sense to group computers together by function when assigning the workgroups. To set your workgroup in Windows, go to the Network control panel and click the Identification tab. You'll see a dialog box similar to the one in Figure 10.8.

Part
III

Ch
10

FIGURE 10.8

Configure workgroups in the Network control panel.

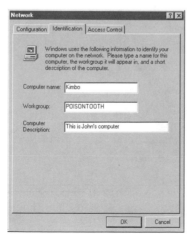

Here you can identify your computer with a name that will be displayed to other Windows' clients on your TCP/IP network. The name I have chosen is "Kimbo." You can also set a description for your computer, as well as the workgroup that we've just been discussing. I've chosen "POISONTOOTH" for my workgroup, but you can choose anything. These values do not have any relation to the hostname or domain name that your computer may have assigned; they're used only for the Windows networking protocols.

Once a workgroup is set, you can start configuring the file sharing services. Click the Configuration tab in the Network control panel, and then click the File and Print Sharing button. The File and Print Sharing dialog box will appear, allowing you to select the resources you want to share from your computer. I've chosen to share both printers and files from my computer. You may choose to do the same or only provide one or the other. Remember, however, that although you're providing this service on a very small scale at this point, if you were to plug your little intranet into the Internet, you could potentially be giving everyone on the Internet access to your files or printers!

The last step in setting up our file sharing is to choose the way you protect your files from people you don't want connecting to your system. Click the Access Control tab. You can now choose between a share-level access control and user-level access control, as shown in Figure 10.9. Share-level control lets you specify a password for the individual folders you'll be sharing out over the network. User-level control allows you to specify a list of users who have access to your resources. Most people use the share-level control, because it's easier to set up and configure. If you need further control over access to your files, you'll need to look at a full dedicated-server solution, such as Windows NT. For the purpose of a small TCP/IP network, share-level control should be sufficient.

FIGURE 10.9

Choose between share-level and user-level access control to your computer's resources.

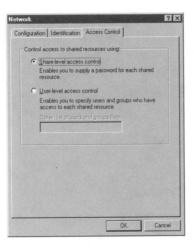

These steps should complete the basic configuration needed to start sharing files over TCP/IP. Click the Configuration tab in your Network control panel dialog box. The display should now look similar to Figure 10.10.

If there are extra protocols listed, such as NetBEUI or IPX, you may remove them. Once you're finished with the configuration, click the OK button, and Windows will finish setting up your computer for file sharing. This process will usually require you to have your Windows 95 or 98 CD handy, and will ask you to reboot your computer to finish the installation. Go ahead and do so now.

FIGURE 10.10
After configuring access control, you should see a new element in the network component list.

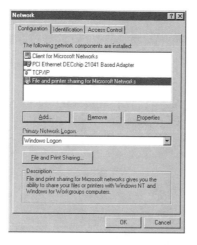

You can now select a folder that you want to share and set it up for access over your intranet. The easiest way to do this is to right-click on the folder and chose Sharing from the resulting pop-up menu. You can then configure the access privileges that will be used to determine who can and can't connect to your resource, as shown in Figure 10.11.

FIGURE 10.11
Use the Sharing tab to grant rights to your computeris folders.

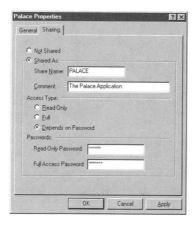

In Figure 10.11, I have chosen to share the Palace folder that is located on my C:\ drive. I can share it out under any name I wish; however, the default PALACE name is fine with me. I have also set the shared folder to have read-only access if one password is entered, or read-write access if another password is used. You can set up your share similarly, or set it to be read-only or full access, depending on the state of the buttons you chose. Once you've set your options, click OK. The icon for your shared folder should now be updated to reflect that it's being served over the network (it'll display a little hand holding the folder), as shown in Figure 10.12.

FIGURE 10.12

The hand under the Palace folder indicates itís shared.

Your files are now available over your network!

There are two different ways that other users can connect to your shared resource. The quickest way to do this is to right-click on the Network Neighborhood desktop icon and select Map Network Drive from the pop-up menu. A small dialog box, shown in Figure 10.13, will appear. This dialog box should allow a user to connect directly to the resources that you've shared.

FIGURE 10.13

You can choose to map a shared folder as a network drive.

You must type the information to access your share in a special Windows "share path" format, specifically:

```
\\COMPUTERNAME\RESOURCENAME
```

> **CAUTION**
>
> Be very car-eful of the direction of the backslash (\)characters in the share path. They do not slant in the same d-irection as the slash (/) characters you use to type a URL. Furthermore, the backslash character is located in- different places on different keyboards.

Because I've shared out Palace from my Kimbo machine, I've typed `\\Kimbo\Palace`. I've also told the computer to connect this remote resource as Drive D. If I select the Reconnect at logon option, I'll be automatically reconnected to this resource (if it's available) the next time I restart Windows. If you're connecting to a resource that you'll use on a regular basis, it will save time to select this option. Connecting to the drive each time you boot will not cause an extra load on the network. Once I've typed in my share path, I click OK, and I should be able to see the shared resource connected to my machine as Drive D.

Another way to connect to the network drive is by using the Network Neighborhood icon directly. Double-clicking the icon will show a list of all of the available resources in the same workgroup as the computer you're using. If you want to see resources in other workgroups, you'll need to double-click the Entire Network icon. You can navigate through the listed servers in the same way that you navigate through your computer's file system. An icon of a computer represents individual computers on the network. Double-clicking that icon will reveal a list of the shared resources available on that computer. If you want to connect to one of the resources, simply right-click on the resource name and choose Map Network Drive or go to the File menu and choose the menu selection with the same name.

Using the LMHOSTS File to Share Across Subnets   A question you may be asking yourself at this point is, "How far can I browse?" If you're connected to the Internet, can you browse to every single other computer that's connected to the network? It seems unlikely, and for good reason. The Windows browsing mechanism relies on a computer called a *Browse Master*, which exists for every Windows network. The Browse Master contains a list of all the available servers on the Windows network. When a computer connects and wants to get a list of what is available, it broadcasts a packet to the network, and the browse master responds with a list of servers. The client then contacts the desired server for its list of resources. This can only take place across a local TCP/IP subnet. There are methods to link subnets together, but they're often more trouble than they're worth. One possible solution is to create a WINS server that runs on an NT server. *WINS*, or *Windows Internet Naming Service*, is a Windows-only service that's very similar to DNS.

An acceptable solution for small networks that need to connect to a few remote resources is to create an LMHOSTS file in the Windows directory. An LMHOSTS file is similar to the HOSTS file that you already know about, except that it provides a mapping between a Windows computer name and an IP address. If you want to connect to a computer called WORKSTATION (and more specifically, its shared folder called DOCUMENTS) that's located in another state, or even another country, it's impossible for Windows to determine where \\WORKSTATION\DOCUMENTS is actually located. For our local network, this isn't an issue. Once you're connected to the world, it becomes a very real problem. To quickly give yourself the capability of mapping this share path, you must first determine the IP address of the computer you want to connect to. This information should be available from the administrator of the remote network.

If the IP address of the remote station is 140.254.85.77, create an LMHOSTS file (no extension) in your Windows directory (usually C:\Windows) that contains the following entry:

```
140.254.85.77    WORKSTATION
```

That's it! Your computer will now know where to go when you attempt to map a share path of \\WORKSTATION\DOCUMENTS. This has proven to be one of the most useful pieces of knowledge that you can have when doing basic file sharing over a Windows TCP/IP network. You can quickly configure your computer to access a remote station without requiring your NT administrator to add an entry to his or her WINS database.

Part
III

Ch
10

What Is lmhosts.sam File?

You may see a file called lmhosts.sam in your Windows directory. This is a sample LMHOSTS file that you can edit for your specific needs. It might be easiest to copy this file to LMHOSTS (by selecting the Start menu, clicking Run, and typing **COPY LMHOSTS.SAM LMHOSTS**) to give yourself a starting point for building your own file.

You may wonder why you can't simply type the IP address in the share path, like this:

```
\\140.254.85.77\DOCUMENTS
```

Surprisingly enough, you *can* do this under Windows NT 4.0 Server and Workstation, but the capability has been left out of Windows 95. It seems only logical that you should be able to use an IP address to connect to a remote TCP/IP computer over a TCP/IP network. However, for some reason, the designers of Windows 95 omitted this feature.

Although there are no built-in cross platform TCP/IP sharing capabilities in Windows, it's still extremely valuable to have file sharing that can work over TCP/IP. If you're only worried about interacting with other Windows computers, SMB over TCP/IP is an ideal method of sharing resources.

Basic Linux Services

Linux is difficult to classify as either a server or a client operating system. There is a growing number of applications and extremely easy-to-use desktop environments that run under Linux. Linux machines are also often used for their X Window capabilities to run remote applications from other UNIX systems. At the same time, Linux-based computers are used in a large number of ISPs, can provide stable, fast, and cost effective Web and file serving, and costs next to nothing. Red Hat Linux comes with FTP, Web, DNS, Mail, Samba (SMB), and other services that, whether you know it or not, are probably already up and running. Try testing some of these out.

From another computer on your network, or from your Linux machine, try connectingI~services (client);Linux;Apache Web server> to the Apache Web server that comes with Linux. The URL `http://localhost/` will connect to the server from your Linux machine, but you'll need to supply the IP address of your Linux computer if you're connecting from a different node.

You can also trying FTPing to your Linux machine, as FTP is another default service that should be running.I~services (client);Linux;FTP>

The Linux services that are installed can also be considered server quality services, because the Linux OS is designed with all the qualities of other dedicated servers—namely extremely high throughput and the capability to handle a load of many simultaneously connected clients. Configuring Linux's services is not to be considered easy; I'll cover this topic throughout the remaining chapters. I'll also address the integration of Linux with other operating systems as we begin adding new TCP/IP features to Mac OS and Windows.

Linux is an operating system that is finally coming of age and becoming increasingly popular. It has a potential of offering excellent client services, as well as offering full serving capabilities. The biggest challenge facing Linux is that it is a publicly developed operating system that no one person or agency is truly responsible for. There is, however, a growing number of companies offering support services for Linux, and the support available over the Internet is unparalleled. You will begin seeing Linux computers showing up on more desktops in the future as more and more people recognize the benefits that this free operating system offers. For more information on Linux (and to see where to download a free copy of the operating system), visit `www.linux.org`.

Do I Need More?

You should now have a complete picture of what each of our client systems offers in the default installation. Mac OS and Windows can probably provide the services you need if you're going to communicate with a handful of computers running the same operating system. Chances are, however, that you need more.

Software can be added to Windows, Mac OS, and even Linux to make them into systems that can provide a variety of other services for local networks. You can add the ability to run email servers, Web servers, and cross-platform file sharing to each of our client OSes. In some cases, this software takes over the system and provides the capabilities of a dedicated server. More often, it works in the background to provide simple capabilities that are not available with the basic operating system. Don't assume that adding these extensions to your operating system will turn your computer into a machine that can handle all of your company of 10,000's email traffic. Installing software does not change the basic structure of the underlying client operating system and was not designed to provide heavy-duty serving capabilities.

When making the decision of whether you want a dedicated serving solution or want to use your basic OS with some extensions, there are several factors you need to take into account.

First and foremost, consider how many users you're expecting to connect to support. Depending on the service you would like to offer, your operating system can support either a handful or potentially several hundred users. File sharing, including FTP, can cause a serious load on your system, especially if you're running applications from a shared drive. Do not expect to support more than 10 simultaneous connections on your computer without serious slowdown. Web serving is an entirely different matter. If you would like to run a Web site on your network and expect only a handful of connections, a non-dedicated Web server should be sufficient. Remember that a Web connection usually lasts only a few seconds. You can potentially serve thousands of hits an hour without ever having more than a single connection at a time. POP mail serving is also an extremely low-cost service that can easily be provided. POP connections are also limited to only a few seconds and occur on a relatively infrequent basis. I have served over a hundred POP accounts on a non-dedicated Mac OS server without any problem.

Be sure to consider the stability of the services that you need to provide. If you're serving your company's email from a server that's also used for word processing and as a general-purpose workstation, you're probably taking a risk. Applications crash, and client OSes are not guaranteed to provide 24-hour, 7-day-a-week serving capabilities. The crash of a word processor can take out your company's email capabilities. This would probably not be looked upon as a good thing! Even worse, if your officemates rely on your computer to share an application that everyone uses and your computer crashes, you'll be the object of much derision. Dedicated servers provide a level of stability that is unobtainable in non-dedicated servers. A simple Web server that's used for serving a few homepages isn't likely to require its own server and is a different matter entirely.

An extremely important aspect you should give a great deal of thought to is the growth you expect your network to experience. A simple client-based server solution might be everything you need for this stage in the development of your TCP/IP network. However, what about a year from now, or two years from now? You should identify the primary services your network will provide to your organization and, if you're planning on any sort of expansion, use a dedicated server OS to provide those solutions. Migrating services from one serving solution is not necessarily a trivial matter. As this book is being written, my department is in the process of migrating 1,500 email accounts located on a VAX system to a new dual Pentium Pro Linux server. The VAX has simply not kept up with the growth of our network and is being retired. The problem is, there is no simple way to pull the email accounts from the VAX and move them to the Linux computer. I've written a piece of software to help the migration along, but already the amount of work hours that have been exhausted moving accounts is phenomenal. If we had paid closer attention to the network growth and its effect on the VAX, we could have begun migrating when there were only 500 active accounts on the machine. These are the sorts of decisions you need to make early on in the design of your network. If you're bound by cost, you need to prioritize the services you intend to offer. Determine what is mission critical and run those services from a dedicated server or servers. Use your client OS-based computers to provide the additional services your network needs.

Lastly, ease of use should be a consideration. Will the services you're providing be maintained on a regular basis by a network administrator, or will the upkeep be the responsibility of several people? There are many classes that are taught regarding Linux/UNIX and Windows NT. These operating systems can be a bit daunting to someone who wants to provide casual TCP/IP services without having any background on server operation. Mac OS-based servers, such as AppleShare IP (which you'll look at later), offer stable, easy-to-use services that can fill most needs but falls a bit short on scalability. You must consider what is important for your operations. The cost of employing a network administrator full-time for NT and UNIX work can cost as much as $60,000 to $80,000. You may wish to start with a lower-priced server system, such as AppleShare IP, and re-evaluate your needs as the demands of your network increase. Budgeting a large amount of money for the maintenance of a full-blown server OS is often a poor investment for smaller companies and, in the long run, might have been better spent on a few non-dedicated server products.

## CHAPTER 11

Exploring Client OS File Server Capabilities

by John Ray

In this chapter

Sharing Files via TCP/IP   **186**

Using Mac OS to Share Files over a TCP/IP Network   **187**

Using Windows 95 or 98 to Share Files over a TCP/IP Network   **198**

Using Linux to Share Files over a TCP/IP Network   **209**

In the previous chapter, you created an intranet using the built-in TCP/IP capabilities of three popular operating systems. You also saw how to configure folders on individual computers to share files and documents with other computers on the network. In this chapter, you begin to extend your operating systems to take full advantage of the inherent cross-platform capabilities of TCP/IP. Mac OS comes with a basic Web server that can be used to share files in a rather simplistic manner across a network. Windows allows you to share files with other Windows machines anywhere on a connected TCP/IP network. Linux…well, Linux does everything, so it requires the least attention on extending. The important point with Linux is getting it to play nicely with other operating systems on our network. This chapter examines the capabilities that you can offer over TCP/IP and considers how you can apply them to each platform so that your network computers and devices can interact with each other.

Sharing Files via TCP/IP

The first, and most obvious, place to start is with file sharing. Sharing information between computers is the goal of any network, and so far, you've only seen how to do it by using Windows networking. You've looked briefly at the FTP protocol, which is fully cross-platform and can also be used for sharing files, but is not included as a default server except under Linux.

What types of file-sharing capabilities are right for your network? Should you provide FTP services, or should you use SMB, or how about AppleShare IP? The answer to the question is based on your individual needs. Let's look at FTP first. FTP is a fast and effective method of allowing other people to access your files and transfer files of their own to your computer or FTP server. However, FTP is exactly what the name implies: a File *Transfer* Protocol. Files are transferred from one place to another; they are not shared from a single location. A potential problem with this arrangement is that multiple copies of the same file might end up on different machines. In some cases, this method of operation might be better than having everyone make changes to a single file. In other cases, it might lead to some serious confusion. A definite disadvantage to FTP is that you cannot run software from an FTP server. You could potentially transfer a program from the server to your own hard drive, but you can't execute it remotely. Again, you must choose your route according to your individual needs.

I use FTP frequently to provide a location where people outside my department can place files for other employees. Internally, the files can be accessed by connecting to a shared folder or directory on one of the department's servers. Providing a public share that anyone in the world can connect to is dangerous and potentially a break-in point for hackers. FTP provides a rather more secure drop-off area for files and lives peacefully side by side with other file-sharing services. AppleShare IP and SMB both constitute full file-sharing systems that enable users to run applications from a centralized location. Although I haven't fully discussed AppleShare IP yet, you can probably guess that it offers the capability to use Apple's file-sharing capabilities over TCP/IP.

Using Mac OS to Share Files over a TCP/IP Network

This discussion of the extension of file sharing in the client operating systems begins with a look at Mac OS. The goal here is to show you how to set up an FTP server that you can access from your other client computers. An extremely popular FTP server for the Macintosh is the shareware program NetPresenz. In addition to offering FTP services, NetPresenz includes a Web server and a Gopher server. This fully integrated package is well worth its small price tag. To begin, go ahead and download NetPresenz from the author's Web site:

```
http://www.stairways.com/
```

Install NetPresenz by dropping the resulting archive onto the Stuff-It Expander icon, which should be located in your Internet folder under System 8.x. NetPresenz runs as a background "faceless" application on the Macintosh. You use the NetPresenz Setup program to configure it. Go ahead and start NetPresenz Setup now. The initial NetPresenz control panel is shown in Figure 11.1.

FIGURE 11.1

You configure NetPresenz in its control panel.

As you might have deduced, the place to start for setting up FTP services is the FTP Setup button located on the left side of the setup bar. Click the button now to bring up the FTP Setup dialog box shown in Figure 11.2.

FIGURE 11.2

The FTP Setup dialog box lets you configure FTP host settings for your Macintosh.

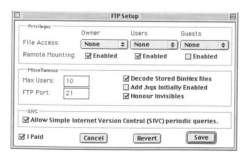

The first settings to look at are the File Access privileges. These privileges pertain to the owner of the machine, as listed in the File Sharing control panel; the users, as defined in the Users & Groups control panel; and a guest, or anonymous, user. These settings represent the highest access level that each individual could possibly have. For example, you can define a folder that a guest has no permission to read from or write to; however, the setting in this dialog box might still allow a guest to upload to the server. In other words, you are allowed to define a folder that a guest can upload to. Similarly, you could define a folder that has guest privileges, but set your guest account to None in this configuration screen. In that case, the guest would not be able to log in to the server. Allowing guest access to your server is sometimes asking for trouble, so be sure that *anyone* really needs to connect to the server before you decide to give any privileges to the guest account. You can also set Remote Mounting privileges for each type of user. If you click the Enabled button under any of the user types, that user can send a command to the server that mounts your network drive and enables FTP access to it. This process is sometimes extremely slow, resulting in a performance drop on your machine, and usually should be disabled.

Next, you need to configure a few other options, including the number of users who can connect to the server. The default setting for the Max Users field is 999. Chances are, though, you want it to be something significantly smaller. If 999 users were to connect simultaneously to NetPresenz, your machine would slow to a crawl and your connected users would have nearly zero throughput. You might have attempted to connect to an FTP server, only to be notified that the number of allowable users would be exceeded. The Max Users field determines this setting for your Mac. You probably do not need to change the FTP Port setting for your FTP server. In fact, many clients do not allow the user to specify which FTP port to connect to. If you change this setting, such clients would be unable to use your server. One potential reason for running on a port other than 21 is "security through obscurity." If you'd like to provide private FTP service, but don't want anyone poking around and accidentally finding your service, you can run it from a different port. This method doesn't guarantee a secure FTP server by any means; it is just a bit more difficult for intruders to locate by guesswork. The Decode Stored BinHex Files option allows the server to store files from other Macintoshes in a more efficient format. There's no reason why this should not be activated. Add .hqx Initially Enabled is another useful option if you are running a Mac-only FTP server but will confuse matters if other computers are connecting. Do *not* activate this option. The Honour Invisibles option should remain checked. Doing so keeps invisible files that your computer has stored from showing up in the file listing. Click Save to apply your changes.

Now you want to configure some actions that happen when particular users log in to the machine. To do so, click the FTP Users button in the main NetPresenz Setup dialog box. The user configuration screen, shown in Figure 11.3, appears.

FIGURE 11.3

Use this dialog box to configure actions your server takes when users log in to the FTP server.

Every user or category of users should be listed in the User drop-down menu. You can provide different settings for each default login folder and specify which commands are processed upon login. The first three listed users in the menu are Owner, Users (meaning any users defined on the system), and Guests (anyone who logs in anonymously). For example, rather than set a login directory for each user, you can set a directory to Users in general, which then applies to everyone who has a user account. A typical setting might be for Guests to be automatically logged in to a directory called /Incoming in which they can place files. You can specify the pathname of the Login Directory manually, or you can click Choose to use the Macintosh file system interface to graphically select the directory. In the Login Commands field, you can type any commands that you want the server to execute when a user connects. The most useful command to place here is the File Listing command, which displays a list of available files to the user who has successfully logged in to the server. However, in a world that increasingly uses graphical clients to connect to FTP servers and the like, the value of this feature is questionable, so feel free to leave this field blank. Click the Save button to save any changes you made and to return to the NetPresenz Setup screen.

The last thing you need to do before deciding which folders to share over FTP is to set some basic security options for the site. Click the NetPresenz Setup dialog box's Security button now.

In the General Security portion of the Security dialog box, shown in Figure 11.4, you can configure the server to Log Actions to File. This setting is extremely important for any FTP server on any system. Activating it creates a log of all the users accessing your system and the IP addresses from which they are connecting. You can also select the Hide Log in Background option, which keeps the log view hidden while you use the computer for other tasks. The third General Security option, which can be quite dangerous, is Allow Clear Text Passwords. This setting applies to the FTP server's capability to mount remote AppleShare volumes using a "clear text," or nonencrypted, password. Potentially, a rather devious hacker could use this permissiveness as a method of collecting passwords to Apple file servers by observing passwords as users enter them.

Part

III

Ch

11

FIGURE 11.4

This vital dialog box lets you establish security options for your FTP server.

Look now at the User Restriction settings. These relatively self-explanatory settings govern which commands you want users to be able to execute on your server. Note, again, that if a user has Allow Delete activated, it does not necessarily mean he or she can delete any files. Users can only delete files to which they have write access. If users do not have Allow Delete selected, they cannot delete files from any location, including directories to which they can write or files that they have uploaded to the system. You can change these settings as you like. I generally leave them all on.

The final two options control Owner Restrictions. If multiple users share the computer's owner account, you might want to turn off these options because they allow users logged in with the owner password to control server operations.

You might also want to set the Connection Sounds option to one of its two active settings if you plan to use the computer while the server is running. Depending on the style of connection sounds you set, your computer either speaks to you as connections are made or makes a sound to indicate an access to the NetPresenz FTP server.

Click Save, and if you'd like, select the File menu and choose Quit to exit the Setup application. NetPresenz is now ready to begin serving files, using FTP. However, you still need to do a few things with the operating system itself before your computer is entirely prepared. If you are using AppleShare file sharing, you can immediately start using NetPresenz by double-clicking the NetPresenz icon. NetPresenz uses the standard AppleShare file-sharing permissions to determine which folders are available over FTP and which users can access them. If you have not configured any sort of file sharing previously, you need to do so now. First, open the File Sharing control panel and click the command to start file sharing. This procedure generally takes a few minutes. You then need to set up the folders that you want to share. Doing so is simply a matter of highlighting a folder you want to share and then selecting Sharing from the File menu. You can also Control-click (*not* command-click) on the icon to bring up a contextual menu containing a Sharing option.

As you can see in the dialog box in Figure 11.5, you can pick the permissions you want to set for the folder. You can choose which user owns the folder and which changes the owner can make to the contents. You can also assign permissions for another user or group of users. Last, you can set guest privileges. If you want to set up a place for anonymous users to upload, you need to make the folder writeable by Everyone. You can learn more about the Apple file-sharing setup process in your System 8.x owners manual. In the previous chapter, I briefly talked about creating users and groups for the Web file sharing, which uses the same user database.

FIGURE 11.5

Use this dialog box to assign file-sharing privileges to a folder.

One last change is to decide whether you want guest users to connect. Mac OS has a special user called Guest in its Users & Groups control panel. If you want to allow anonymous guest access, you need to open the Users & Groups control panel, edit this account, and then click the Allow Guests to Connect to This Computer button, as shown in Figure 11.6.

FIGURE 11.6

If you want to allow anonymous FTP access, edit the Guest account in the Users & Groups control panel.

Remember, because this change affects file sharing as well, other Macs on your local network can browse through the folders where you have set some sort of access for Everyone.

You can now start the NetPresenz program, and other users should be able to FTP successfully into your Macintosh. That's all there is to it. You can move files back and forth between your Mac OS-based computer and the other network boxes (Windows, Linux, and so on).

Using Mac OS and AppleShare over a TCP/IP Network

Sometimes it is far more convenient to have direct access to the files on your network rather than to transfer them with FTP. It is very nice to be able to edit and collaborate on files that are in a centralized location. In the case of a Web server, being able to edit the files and see the changes online in real time is a wonderful time saver. You can already enjoy this level of convenience with Mac OS on a local network with other Macintosh computers, but how about over different subnets? And how about with other Macs over the Internet? To communicate across subnets, you're going to need to use AppleShare IP rather than the default version of AppleTalk that is included with the operating system. But, you might ask, how do I share files with people using Windows? Don't worry, you'll get there! First, though, let's take a look at sharing with your fellow Macintosh users.

One way to use AppleShare over TCP/IP is to buy the AppleShare IP file server, which is covered in the dedicated server section later in this chapter. This rather costly piece of software might not be necessary for simple file sharing. An alternative solution is a small program called ShareWay by Open Door Networks. ShareWay runs in the background on a Mac and provides the translations necessary to enable the AppleTalk protocol to be used over TCP/IP. This software does not replace AppleShare IP, but it can be used in cases where a high-powered server isn't entirely necessary. Three versions of the ShareWay IP software are available:

- A personal edition that allows a single Mac OS computer to run the software and share its files over a TCP/IP network
- The standard edition that allows a single Mac OS computer to provide the appropriate translation for *any* Mac OS AppleShare computer on your network
- A professional version that allows a single Mac OS machine to provide TCP/IP translation for any number of AppleShare servers

Part
III

Ch
11

Interestingly, this software works with *any* AppleShare server. Because Windows NT 4.0 provides basic AppleShare services, the standard or Pro version of ShareWay IP Gateway can turn an NT AppleShare volume into something that is AppleShare IP accessible. This section covers the standard version of the software, but the other versions configure very similarly. The pricing for the software ranges from around $80 to several hundred dollars, depending on the version you select. Substantial educational discounts are available.

You can download a 10-day demo version of any of the ShareWay products from http://www2.opendoor.com/gateway/.

The package consists of one program and some documentation files. To follow the example, download the trial version and then jump right in by double-clicking the ShareWay IP icon.

The configuration of ShareWay IP is quite simple. Before starting the server, you must pick the AppleShare server that the ShareWay IP Gateway will provide translation services for. If you want to provide the service for the Macintosh that this software is running on, simply select the Server on This Macintosh setting. If you want to make another AppleShare server accessible over TCP/IP, then select the Server on AppleTalk volume. You can then click the Choose button and pick the server you want to use. In the selection screen shown in Figure 11.7, I've chosen John's Kicker to share out with ShareWay IP.

FIGURE 11.7

You select the server you want to provide translation services for in this dialog box.

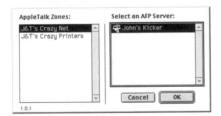

You're now ready to start sharing! Click the Start button, and you're in business. When you're up and running, your display should resemble the display in Figure 11.8. The IP Address that remote computers need to connect to is shown in the ShareWay IP Gateway Status dialog box. The IP address is the address of the computer that ShareWay IP Gateway is running on, even if the AppleShare server is a remote server.

FIGURE 11.8

When your IP gateway is active, you'll see a dialog box resembling this one.

The reason for the use of this particular IP address is that the software itself is acting as the front end for the server. The software communicates with the server, provides the appropriate translation, and then essentially "reshares" the volume over TCP/IP. You can now open the Chooser from the Apple menu of any Macintosh on your network and connect to the server.

Connecting to any AppleShare IP server is as simple as selecting the AppleShare icon in the Chooser and then clicking the Server IP Address button. In Figure 11.9, I'm about to connect to one of my machines at work by providing its IP address.

FIGURE 11.9
Type the IP address of the computer you want to connect to.

Type the IP address or hostname of the server into the dialog box and click Connect. You will quickly be connected to the remote server, as if you had connected to it over a local network. This connection process is usable over any TCP/IP connection and from anywhere, as long as TCP/IP connectivity is available. To avoid having to reenter the IP address each time you want to connect to the server, you can make an alias to the server volume. Then you can double-click the alias to reconnect to the server at any time.

How do I make an alias?

To create an alias of a drive, or any other file, simply select the icon and choose Make Alias from the File menu. Alternatively, select the icon you want to alias and then drag it while holding the command and option keys. When you release the mouse button at the end of your drag, an alias will be created.

Using Mac OS as a Peer on a TCP/IP Windows Network

As you can see, extending Mac OS file sharing so that it works across a TCP/IP network is a fairly simple process. However, it still remains proprietary to the Macintosh platform. The choices are to provide AppleShare IP services under Windows or to provide Windows SMB sharing under Mac OS. Because this discussion covers extending the Mac OS, I'm sure you can guess which one we're going to look at now. Later we examine a Windows AppleShare IP client. Your decision on which to purchase should probably be based on whether you have more Windows machines, or more Macs.

Thursby Software Systems produces a Macintosh-based Windows-compatibility program for the Macintosh; the program, called DAVE, is priced at around $150. DAVE provides full integration of your Macintosh into a Windows network, including the capability to connect to Windows 95 or NT shares and Windows PostScript printers and to share local Mac volumes and Mac printers to a Windows network.

DAVE is an extremely configurable program, enabling you to configure the NetBIOS protocol at a level that even most Windows users aren't accustomed to. You can download a fully functional 10-day evaluation version of DAVE from `http://www.thursby.com/`.

Here's a quick look at DAVE. After downloading DAVE, you should notice several additions to your system, including three extra control panels: NetBIOS, DAVE Print Client, and DAVE Sharing. You also have a DAVE Access under your Apple menu and a DAVE Client in the Chooser. Before doing anything with your newfound cross-platform compatibility, you need to configure your NetBIOS settings. Start by opening the NetBIOS control panel, which is shown in Figure 11.10.

FIGURE 11.10

After installing DAVE, you have a new NetBIOS control panel.

Remember how you configured file sharing under Windows in the previous chapter? Does anything look familiar? It should. Here you can provide a name for your computer (I've chosen metz), a workgroup (POISONTOOTH), and a description of the computer. Although it looks like a configurable option, the Transport Protocol section can only be set to TCP/IP, so there's no need to adjust that setting. You can also set up WINS servers for your computer. WINS is similar to DNS in that both allow a computer name to be resolved to an IP address. If you have a WINS server running, make sure the WINS check box is selected and type the server's IP address or hostname into the Primary field. If you are running a secondary server, you can include it in the Secondary field. If no WINS services are running on your network, don't worry; you probably won't need them. The DHCP check box allows a DHCP server to automatically configure your NetBIOS settings if your network is running a DHCP server and the DHCP server supports this sort of configuration. Chances are, you won't need this setting checked either. The Info button allows you to look at some network information and to perform lookups from a WINS server. The Admin button allows low-level changes to be made to the NetBIOS protocol's timing. You should not need to modify this portion of the control panel for normal operation. Consult the DAVE owners manual if you wish to experiment with any of these settings. That's it! You're now a node on the Windows network.

Now, go ahead and see how you can connect to a Windows share. If you are trying to connect to a share that is using a User Level access control, then be sure to set your username in the File Sharing control panel. Windows users would use the same username to log in to their Windows 95 or 98 computer. To become a client to a Windows network, select the Chooser from the Apple menu and click the DAVE Client icon to bring up the connection controls, as shown in Figure 11.11.

FIGURE 11.11

Choose DAVE Client in the Chooser to invoke this connection control dialog box.

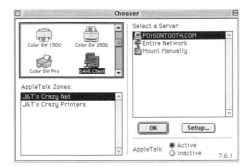

A delay occurs when opening the client while DAVE searches your network for a "master browser" to supply your Mac with a list of the available Windows (or now Mac!) resources on the network. If your computer cannot find the master browser, don't worry; you won't need one if you know the IP address of the computer you want to connect to. If you have computers with SMB shares already on your local subnet, they appear in the listing on the right side of the Chooser. You will be able to see the machines in the same workgroup as your computer by default. If you want to browse other computers, you can double-click the Entire Network item in the Select a Server list. This procedure is precisely the same as under Windows. If you see a server that you want to connect to, select it from the list and click OK. I've just completed a connection to a Windows resource in Figure 11.12.

FIGURE 11.12

A successful connection to a Windows server looks like this.

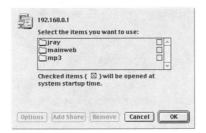

You are now presented with a list of the shared resources on the server you have connected to. You may select resources, and if you want to have the resource mounted at start, click the check box to the right of the resource name. If you've used Mac OS file sharing before, you should feel very comfortable using DAVE; the operation is very similar. With the volumes you want to mount selected, you may click the OK button; the shared volumes then appear as local disks on your desktop.

If the resource you want to connect to is not located on the local network, then you can connect to it manually. Double-click the Mount Manually selection in the Chooser. Figure 11.13 illustrates the results of this action.

FIGURE 11.13

Double-click Mount Manually to mount a network resource not available in the local network.

Here you can enter in a server name—either computer name, which can then potentially be resolved by a WINS server, or the hostname/IP address of the server you want to connect to. You must also enter the name of a share you want to use. If you have chosen to enter a hostname or IP address for the server, you need to select the DNS or IP radio button. Otherwise, be sure that NetBIOS is selected. Clicking OK connects you to the share you selected.

A particularly nice feature enables you to add commonly used servers to your server list automatically. Simply click the Setup button from within the Chooser, as I've done in Figure 11.14.

FIGURE 11.14

DAVE lets you automatically add commonly used servers.

Click the Add button to type in a server name or IP address. The servers you add automatically show up in the main DAVE client listing.

Obviously, the client has other features that you haven't touched here. This brief coverage should, however, give you a good idea of what you need to do to access a shared volume. Now, how about actually sharing a Macintosh volume with Windows users? It's just as simple. DAVE provides full NetBIOS client and SMB server TCP/IP capabilities. In fact, you can even use DAVE to share files between other Macintoshes. It makes sense to adopt a common protocol for your network, because doing so makes it easier to diagnose network problems as they occur. DAVE certainly gives you that capability.

Using Mac OS to Share to a Windows Network

To share files, you use the DAVE Sharing control panel, shown in Figure 11.15. Go ahead and open the control panel now.

FIGURE 11.15
The DAVE Sharing control panel lets you establish a common file-sharing protocol for your network.

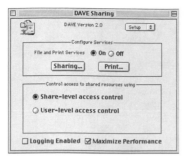

The first obvious step is to toggle File and Print Services to On. You can also select the Share-Level Access Control option, which allows you to specify a password to access a shared folder or the User-Level Access Control option. For the latter, you must also specify a domain to provide your authentication. For simple file sharing between machines, you should use share-level control. If you were using an NT server, you could use its ability to be a domain controller to authenticate. With the basic options set, you can click the Sharing button to pick a resource you want to share. First, a list of the shared resources is displayed, as illustrated in Figure 11.16.

FIGURE 11.16
DAVE displays a list of shared resources.

Click the Add button to bring up the standard Macintosh file selection dialog box. You can now navigate to the folder you want to share, highlight it, and click the Select button.

As Figure 11.17 shows, DAVE prompts you for the name you want to share the resource as. This step is useful because the Mac OS often uses special characters in its folder names that do not necessarily translate well to a Windows computer. You must also select the passwords that users use to connect to the shared folders. Use the pop-up menu to select whether you want to provide Read Only, Read/Write, or Both passwords and then type the desired passwords into the corresponding fields. You do not need to specify any passwords at all, but an omission allows anyone to connect to your computer. Click OK to accept your settings. You may now add or remove your shared resources, or click OK to begin sharing.

Part
III

Ch
11

FIGURE 11.17

Assign passwords to control user access.

At this point, you should be able to connect your Mac OS computer to a Windows TCP/IP network and use it as a client or a server. It's just as easy to provide printer-sharing services to your Windows network by using the DAVE Sharing control panel and selecting the Print option or to use a shared Windows computer by accessing the DAVE Print Client control panel. DAVE is a very flexible program that offers excellent performance and complete integration of Mac OS and Windows networking. To investigate more of DAVE's many features and options before you buy, the entire DAVE manual is available for download from the Thursby Web site.

Using Windows 95 or 98 to Share Files over a TCP/IP Network

You've seen how the Mac OS can be adapted to provide TCP/IP solutions across a network. Now it's time to take a look at the Windows side of things. Windows 95 and 98 can already share over TCP/IP with other Windows machines or with Macintosh computers running DAVE. However, being able to run an FTP server is still useful when you need to connect quickly to a machine and transfer files. One of my main reasons for using FTP is to transfer installation files to client computers. Given the size and complexity of the network that I work with, I rarely know what sort of computer I'm being called in to look at. Keeping an FTP server running with copies of all of the drivers and patches I might need has been a godsend. FTP is the lowest common denominator in terms of file sharing, but that does not, in any way, make it a less significant tool.

One of the most popular free FTP servers for Windows 95, 98, and NT is called the War FTP Daemon, or War FTPd. You can download the latest version from http://www.jgaa.com/.

The War FTPd comes in a self-extracting and self-installing archive. After FTPd extracts itself, it guides you through the setup procedure in a straightforward manner by using the wizard shown in Figure 11.18. Begin the setup by clicking INSTALL. Several steps during the installation configure the server to match your system, which means that you can be up and running in a matter of minutes. These steps are critical to the operation of your server; I'm covering them in detail here to avoid digging around War FTPd's huge configuration system later.

FIGURE 11.18
WarFTPd provides an
easy-to-follow
installation wizard.

What is a daemon?

As you learn more about servers and begin installing your own servers on your network, you will notice that many of them are referred to by the protocol that they use, followed by a d. The d stands for "daemon" and is usually pronounced as "demon." It can sometimes be a bit confusing to hear a conversation where individuals are referring to an http demon. You might think that they are discussing a very enthusiastic Web surfer, but in fact, they are discussing a Web server. The term daemon refers to a background server process and is mainly used when discussing UNIX-based servers. Windows typically refers to its server processes as services. Even so, you will often see software, like War FTPd, that uses daemon or at least the d in daemon as part of its name. Don't be afraid—a "daemon" is an entirely good demon.

The first step is to tell War FTPd whether you are upgrading a previous version of the program or are performing a new installation. Unless you are already using War FTPd, click New Installation and Next to access the configuration screen shown in Figure 11.19.

FIGURE 11.19
Specify the server
name in this dialog
box.

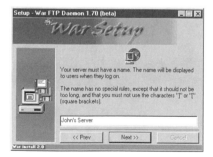

Now you need to specify the name of the server, which can be anything you like. When you connect to an FTP server, the server usually identifies itself by name. I'm going to name my server John's Server and break the "poisontooth" mold for the moment. Click the Next button when you're ready to access the screen shown in Figure 11.20.

FIGURE 11.20

The next step is to choose whether to run automatically as a system service.

You can now choose whether WAR FTPd should run automatically when the serving computer is booted. By default, this option is selected, but be sure that this mode of operation is actually what you want. If you only run FTP to transfer files to a few people on a rather infrequent basis, constant operation can pose a security risk to your system. It is best to provide services only when they are needed. On the other hand, if you plan to run a full-time FTP server, go ahead and make sure Run as a System Service is selected. Then click Next to access the dialog box shown in Figure 11.21.

FIGURE 11.21

Now you can provide a tag for WarFTPd to identify itself to Windows.

WAR FTPd uses a special tag to identify itself to the Windows system. You can either specify a tag here or use the default. There is no reason to change this setting. Click Next to go on to the dialog box shown in Figure 11.22.

FIGURE 11.22

Choose a root directory for your FTP file system.

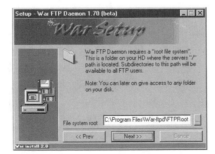

Now you must decide from where you will be sharing files. If you already have a directory prepared, select it now. Otherwise, a directory will be created. This directory is considered the "root" directory of the FTP server. All other directories that you want to make available to your FTP clients branch from the root. This entry does not affect any directories that you may have shared; only the directories that the FTP server allows access to are shared from this root. After you decide which directory to use as the root, click Next to go on to the dialog box shown in Figure 11.23.

FIGURE 11.23

You have several options about what kind of file access to allow.

If you need to have anonymous users connect to your system, click the Allow Anonymous Access check box on this Basic Security setup screen. This setting allows someone without an FTP account to connect to your computer. Again, think carefully about this decision before allowing anonymous access. Although it is indeed useful to allow guests into your server, you must also be careful not to allow them to access anything that they shouldn't. You can also choose the permissions that are set for a public upload directory on your system. By default, both of the available options are set to No. This setting means that a person can upload, or send, a file to a public upload directory on your system, but other users will not be able to download or view the files. Leaving these default settings alone is a powerful security tool. FTP servers that are left open and allow public uploads and downloads often end up being used by pirate and hacking groups to store and trade files. If miscreants can't download or see files after they have been uploaded, their activity becomes pointless. You, as the administrator, have full control over when the files become visible to the public. Click Next when you are ready to continue to the step in Figure 11.24.

FIGURE 11.24

Create a password for yourself as an administrator.

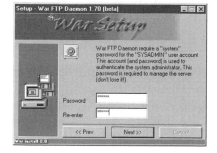

Part
III

Ch
11

To administrate War FTPd, you need to set a password for the system. This password should be something that only you know and *must* be kept private. A user that discovers this password could potentially cause a great deal of harm to your system. Click Next to go on to the step shown in Figure 11.25.

FIGURE 11.25
You can provide your
email address so users
can reach you if
necessary.

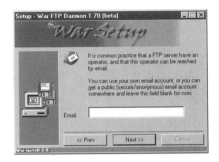

You're almost done, but you still need to provide a few more settings. In this dialog box, you can specify an email address that is displayed to users logging in to the server. This feature is not necessary, and if you expect to provide a large volume of publicly accessible resources, it can be more trouble than it's worth. I recommend leaving this field blank and clicking Next to access the step shown in Figure 11.26.

FIGURE 11.26
Specify your FTP port
here.

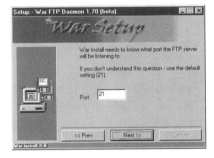

Last but not least, you can change the default port that FTP operates from (usually 21). As I mentioned when setting up the Macintosh FTP server earlier in the chapter, changing the port can provide some "security through obscurity," but there are very few other reasons for changing it. Click Next, and you're done. WAR FTPd is now ready to configure and install itself based on the settings that you have given. Click the Next button again to begin the install. You need to click through a few more screens to finish the installation, but no other settings need to be made now.

Now you are ready to customize the setup to suit whatever application you intend to use the server for. Upon completing the installation, War FTPd immediately starts its administrative tool, War Daemon Manager. This tool is also available under the program group Jgaa's freeware in the Programs section of the Start menu. The War FTPd manager is unique in that it allows you to control a War FTP server over the network, rather than just on the local machine.

To begin administrating, you must set the connection properties. When you start War Daemon Manager, it should display a screen very much like Figure 11.27.

FIGURE 11.27

Opening dialog box for War Daemon Manager.

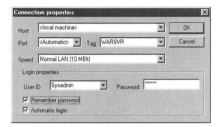

Here you can either select a host machine that you want to administrate or, if you are controlling a server on the same machine as the manager software, use the default <local machine> setting. If you have changed the FTP port, you should specify the port that the server is running on. You must also enter the tag that you chose when the server was installed. If you didn't change the default tag, you won't need to configure anything. The Speed selection should be set to accurately reflect the type of connection between the manager computer and the server computer; if it is the same machine, choose Local Machine.

Now, complete the remaining connection configuration by typing the password you used to secure the server during installation. If you did not write down the password or have forgotten it, you unfortunately need to reinstall the WAR FTPd package. Checking Remember Password automatically enters the SysAdmin password when you run the manager software again. Activating the Automatic Login setting goes one step further and connects you to your server when you start the management software. Click OK when you're satisfied with your settings.

The War FTPd software is an incredible package, as you will soon see, and offers a wide range of options that are unavailable on most FTP server implementations. The range of options exceeds even Microsoft's NT FTPd implementation, and thus NT administrators often use War FTPd. The number of features and the complexity of the configurations that can be generated are indeed overwhelming. Take a look at the important features you need to have a properly functioning FTP server. Feel free to explore the additional features after you are comfortable with the basic setup.

The initial display after you have connected to your server should look similar to Figure 11.28. A graph of server activity is located on the right, showing both the number of users that are connected and the number of characters per second that are being sent. Both of these values are displayed in comparison to unit time. On the left side of the screen, you can see a display of tabs labeled Sessions, Servers, Users, Hosts, Select, Files, and Log. You need to use a few of these tabs to administrate the server effectively, so let's check out how they work.

Click the Sessions tab to see a list of users that the server is currently hosting, as shown in Figure 11.29. You can click on a session to learn more about an individual user. For example, you can find

- The IP address a user is connecting from
- The date and time a user logged in

- The amount of idle time since the user's last command
- The user's CWD (which stands for current working directory)
- The last command the user sent to the server

FIGURE 11.28
The initial server-connection display.

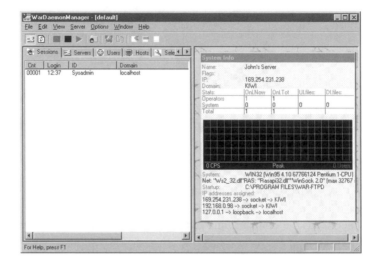

FIGURE 11.29
You can use the Sessions tab to keep tabs on individual users.

This information can be used to monitor problem users and potentially remove them from the system if you notice any suspicious activity. To disconnect a user at any time, simple select the session you want to remove and click the boot icon on the toolbar. You have several options as to what you want to do to the user. With War FTPd, you can disable a user account or even ban a user from connecting from the machine he or she is on.

Another useful view is the Log view, located on the far right of the tab bar. In Figure 11.30, you can see the War FTPd manager with the log view fully expanded.

The log allows you to quickly see what actions are taking place on the server and to identify any problems that the server might have recorded. Pay close attention to your log files and *never* disable logging on a server that has public access. Over the past few years, I have had the pleasure of tracking down several groups of people who stumbled on our servers and used them to store pirated software. Keeping extensive logs of any publicly accessible resource protects both you and your users and may very well be presented as evidence in your defense if a crime is committed on your network.

FIGURE 11.30
The Log view summarizes system activity.

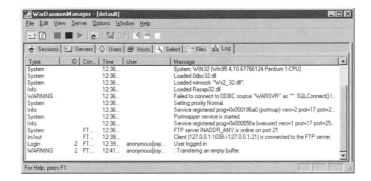

Before you can truly do anything useful with the server, you need to turn on a few more features. Right now, you potentially have anonymous access enabled and a Sysadmin account. You will almost certainly want to add your own users to the server. To do so, click the small User Manager icon (a folder with a person's head in front of it) at the center of the toolbar. The User manager actually manages far more than just basic user settings, but right now you need to concentrate on getting your server up and running in a usable configuration.

The User manager is based on a hierarchical system, much like Windows Explorer. When you open the manager, you will see System listed on the right, with a plus mark beside it. Click the plus mark to display the different types of users that can be added to the system. Your display should now resemble Figure 11.31. Most likely, you will want to add users to the system. You can do so by right-clicking on the User folder and selecting Add User. You are asked for a username and then a password. After you enter this information, the new name appears under the expanded User folder. Select the name and double-click the FTP Access line so that the Allow setting changes from No to Yes. The user can now log in to your system. You can continue to add as many users as you want, including users with Administrative privileges and other "guest" user accounts.

FIGURE 11.31
The User manager view lets you create users and groups.

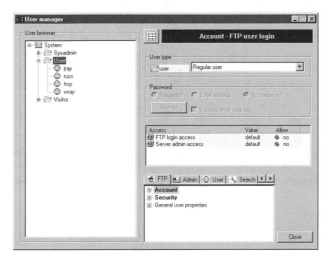

Part
III

Ch
11

One step remains before your FTP server can serve your basic needs: You still need to set up the capabilities for each user. For each user, or user class (represented by the folders that contain the user accounts), you can set basic server properties. Go ahead and highlight a user or class now. After you have selected a user, click on the User tab in the lower left of the display. You will see a list of hierarchical settings that control the capabilities of the user. For example, if you choose the Security setting, your screen should look a lot like the one in Figure 11.32.

FIGURE 11.32

You can assign security settings to a user or class of users.

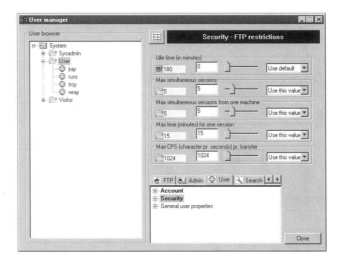

Here you can set the length of time a user can remain idle while still staying connected to the server and the number of simultaneous times a user can be logged in. Users who want to download more than one file at a time often log in several times. This situation is a drain on resources, and you should probably limit the simultaneous connections to a single session. You'll notice that you can change the simultaneous sessions in two places, once for *any* simultaneous sessions and again for sessions from a single machine. If you have distributed a group username and password that multiple people will be using, you will want to allow them to log in simultaneously, so you will need to set the first setting to a number higher than one. The setting for simultaneous sessions from a single machine does a sufficient job of cutting off most people who are making multiple connections to your machine, as they are probably doing it from a single source. Other settings include the number of minutes that a user can be logged in and the number of characters per second that the user can transfer. The latter setting is extremely useful for keeping your network traffic to a minimum. If you are planning to serve files to a large number of people via FTP, your network could come under extreme load if they all connect and data is sent as quickly as possible. A low number here limits the bandwidth that each connection uses and keeps your network from being easily overloaded.

You should now have enough background to set up your own Windows FTP server and administrate it for several users. War FTPd lies in a gray area between a dedicated server and an add-on to the Windows OS. It can exist peacefully on a computer that is used for everyday work or can be set up as a full-blown server. The software is extremely capable and is of higher quality than most commercial products.

Using Windows as a Peer on a Mac OS AppleShare IP Network

You saw that the Mac OS can easily integrate into a PC network with the help of DAVE software. This setup is fine for a network consisting mostly of PCs and a few Macs, but what about the opposite configuration? If you have a largely Mac network with only a handful of PCs, it isn't economical to reconfigure all your Macs to talk using Windows protocols. The answer is a very simple and easy-to-use piece of software called COPSTalk. COPSTalk is an implementation of the AppleShare (including AppleShare IP) protocol for the Windows platform. You can download a demo version of COPSTalk from (appropriately enough) http://www.copstalk.com/.

If your organization has purchased AppleShare 5.x, you may already own licenses to COPSTalk. You can contact COPS customer support if you are unsure. COPSTalk arrives in a self-installing package, which installs the appropriate AppleTalk protocols onto your client machine, but does not add the protocols to your network setup. To add the protocols to your network setup, open the Network control panel on the client machine (the COPSTalk installer does this step for you when you first run it). Then click the Add button, select Client from the list of components that can be installed, and click Add again.

Now you can select COPS, Inc. from the list of manufacturers and the Client for AppleTalk Networks (COPSTalk) client; then click OK. Your screen should look exactly like the screen in Figure 11.33. Be certain that your AppleTalk protocol is bound to the correct network adapter (it may be bound to your Dial-Up adapter). When you are done, your Windows computer reboots; when it starts again, it is a member of the local AppleTalk network. You are now prompted for a login to the AppleTalk network, as well as for your standard Windows network login (if you had a Windows login before). Do not be overly concerned with what you provide for your login name and password; these are simply the defaults that are filled in when you attempt to connect to an AppleShare server. You can change the values when you connect; there is no need to log in to Windows with a different username and password to connect to different shares.

Part

III

Ch

11

FIGURE 11.33

Install the COPSTalk client to a Windows machine on a largely Macintosh network.

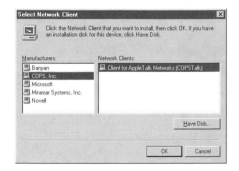

COPSTalk fully integrates the AppleShare file-sharing system with standard Windows 95 or 98 networking. You use the Network Neighborhood display to mount AppleShare volumes exactly as you would for native Windows shares. If you are connected to a network with active Apple file sharing, go ahead and open the Network Neighborhood window now. To access Macintosh shares, double-click the Entire Network portion of the Network Neighborhood. The Macintosh zone now shows up as its Windows equivalent, the workgroup. You can navigate through the zones and computers precisely as you would on a Windows-only network. To your computer, it is exactly the same as working in a Macintosh zone. You will notice a zone that doesn't actually exist on your network, called AppleShare IP Hosts. These computers are running AppleShare IP and have been configured to appear from within COPSTalk.

To add an AppleShare IP share, you must know the IP address or hostname of the server. COPSTalk installs a utility called AppleShare IP Host Editor inside of its program group. The Host Editor allows you to enter an IP address and a resource name, which then appears in the AppleShare IP Hosts zone, as shown in Figure 11.34.

FIGURE 11.34

After you enter an IP address in the AppleShare IP Host Editor, your Macintosh zone appears in the Network Neighborhood window.

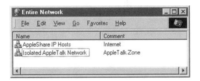

This feature is not available in the demo; however, the demo does come with a few sample public AppleShare IP servers installed. You should be able to connect to them from your computer. You can also use COPSTalk to connect to an AppleTalk printer, the same way that you would connect to a Windows network printer. Although COPSTalk is not TCP/IP based, the software provides a full range of cross-platform capabilities for your local subnet as well as the larger TCP/IP network.

COPSTalk is an excellent and easy-to-use product that requires very little setup time and very little configuration. Its sole drawback is that it is not capable of sharing files from Windows computers; it acts only as a client to an AppleShare network. If you need to share files from a PC to a Macintosh using AppleShare or AppleShare IP, you should look at the product PC MACLAN by Miramar Systems. Miramar also offers several version of PC MACLAN for Windows 95, 98, and NT. You can download a demo from http://www.pcmaclan.com/.

Unfortunately, PC MACLAN does not enable you to share files over TCP/IP. If a Macintosh is located on the same network as a PC running PC MACLAN, you can always use the ShareWay IP Gateway software to provide AppleShare IP services from your PC.

Using Linux to Share Files over a TCP/IP Network

As you know, Red Hat Linux comes, by default, with an FTP server up and running. It also arrives with anonymous FTP access turned on, which is not necessarily a good thing. In this section, you learn how to customize the FTP server for your needs.

The Linux FTP process (wu-ftpd) runs as the user FTP and stores its files in the FTP user's home directory. The FTP account is not an actual user of your system, but simply the owner of the FTP process. Other client operating systems don't really have a sense of ownership for files or processes. Linux is a full-featured, multiuser, UNIX-like system, which requires the concept of ownership. The administrator of a UNIX computer is usually called the root user. It is generally a dangerous practice to allow root to be the owner of any server processes. If you ran FTP with root permissions, a flaw in the FTP server could result in an outside user being able to grab access to your entire system as the root operator. Because FTP runs under its own user account, it has the permissions of that account only and cannot do any more damage than a standard user.

By default, anonymous login is allowed under Linux and is easily configurable, as you will see shortly. However, because of the complexities of a multiuser system, anonymous login requires very special permissions to be set in the ftp directories. If you log in as a standard user to the system, FTP can use your account permissions to run UNIX utilities to show you file listings and so on. However, if you are an anonymous user, FTP must provide a special configuration that allows the same programs to be run for the guest user. To view the home directory for anonymous logins, type the following:

```
>ls -al ~ftp

total 6
drwxr-xr-x   6 root      root        1024 Jun 11 18:39 .
drwxr-xr-x   8 root      root        1024 Jun 23 00:49 ..
d--x--x--x   2 root      root        1024 Jun 11 18:39 bin
d--x--x--x   2 root      root        1024 Jun 11 18:39 etc
drwxr-xr-x   2 root      root        1024 Jun 11 18:39 lib
dr-xr-sr-x   2 root      ftp         1024 Nov  6  1997 pub
```

As you can see, even though you are looking in the FTP directory, the root user owns all the files. Only the pub directory is accessible by members of the FTP group (which would be the FTP process). These directories are critical for a working anonymous login setup. Even if you do not want to allow anonymous login at this time, *do not* delete the directories. If you change your mind, you'll end up digging through the FTPd documentation to figure out precisely how the directory structure and the files that it contains are set up. If you want to make files available to the public through anonymous FTP, place them inside the pub directory. Everything you add to the server should happen from within the pub directory. Although it is possible to create new directories at the same level as the pub directory, doing so is not common practice and should be avoided. The pub directory has the so-called sticky bit set for the group, which means that any directories you create inside the pub directory are automatically set to the appropriate FTP group to allow anonymous access.

Part

III

Ch

11

What Are File Permissions?

File permissions usually exist only in multiuser operating systems such as Linux and Windows NT and allow files to be owned by users, groups, or both. If a file or directory is to be shared by several people, they can all be assigned to be members of a group that owns the file. The permissions that a file can have are divided into three categories: the owner, the group, and everyone else. Each of these categories can then have read, write, or execute permissions for the file. UNIX also has special permissions that can be set; they are called sticky bits. The commands that set file permissions are chown, which changes the file's owner; chgrp, which changes a file's group; and chmod, which changes the permissions given to the file's owner, group, and everyone else. As with any UNIX function, you can learn more about these commands by looking at their man pages. Simply type man chmod at a command line to get complete instructions on the command's use.

To create a directory where users can upload, you simply create a new directory that has write permissions for the group FTP inside the pub directory. If you are logged in as root, you can simply type:

```
>mkdir ~ftp/pub/incoming
>chmod g+w ~ftp/pub/incoming
```

This command creates a new directory on the server; the directory, called incoming, can be written to by the FTP group. Red Hat Linux ships with the capability to overwrite files turned off for anonymous users, so those two simple commands should be all you need to provide a drop-off point for anonymous users. If you want to provide service for taking files from the server, you can do something similar:

```
>mkdir ~ftp/pub/outgoing
>chmod g-w ~ftp/pub/outgoing
```

The permissions are very close to what you had set previously except that this time you want to be sure that the directory does not have write permissions, so you remove them. You can now store files in the outgoing directory, and they will be available to the anonymous users. Be sure that the files you are serving have the appropriate group set so that FTP users can access them. For example:

```
>chgrp ftp ~ftp/pub/outgoing/myfile.txt
>chmod g+r ~ftp/pub/outgoing/myfile.txt
```

These lines change the group of myfile.txt to FTP; now, because the FTP user is a member of the FTP group, he or she will have access to the file. The example also changes the file permissions on myfile.txt so that the file's group (FTP) has read permissions.

Now that you've looked at setting up directories for anonymous access, what can you do to allow individual users to access the server? The easiest way to allow individuals to access the server is to create user accounts on the system, using the /usr/sbin/adduser command. Each user, by default, can use FTP to log in to the system. Rather than being transferred to the anonymous login directory, a user logs in to his or her account's root directory. From there, the user can navigate through the entire file system—or as much as he or she has permission to view. For anonymous users, the FTP user's directory is the entire world. They cannot move out of the anonymous directory and explore the system. So it is simple enough to provide basic sharing services under Linux, but you need a bit more control.

Like War FTPd, wu-ftpd has many features that can be controlled. Lets take a look at a few basic settings that you might want for your server.

One thing that you might notice immediately when trying to FTP to your Linux computer is that it is impossible to FTP into the machine as root. This security feature protects your administrator password from hacking attacks. You should never leave open any method of quickly hacking on the administrator's password. For the same reason, you cannot telnet to a Linux machine as root either. However, I've run into some special situations in which I need to activate the root account so that I can use it with FTP. Doing so is simple enough; it just requires editing the /etc/ftpusers file, which contains a list of all of the accounts that are not allowed to log in to the system. Here's a list of FTP user restrictions:

```
>cat /etc/ftpusers

root
bin
daemon
adm
lp
sync
shutdown
halt
mail
news
uucp
operator
games
nobody
```

An interesting list, to say the least. Each of these names exists as a user account on the system, probably with its login disabled as well. As you saw with the FTP user, these users were also created to be the owners of special processes and files on the system. Because they are not actual people (except root), they do not need the ability to connect to the system. Thus they are listed in the /etc/ftpusers file. If you want to allow root to log in to your system through FTP, simply remove the root name from the list. Similarly, if you have set up other users who have no need to connect to the system, you can place their account names in this file to keep them from logging in to wu-ftpd.

Now, how about providing some security and control over the people who you are allowing to connect? Simple enough: The main configuration file for wu-ftpd is located in /etc/ftpconf. Here is a sample configuration file for my poisontooth.com Linux machine:

```
>cat /etc/ftpaccess

class   badnet anonymous 140.254.85.*
class   local  real *
class   remote anonymous *
```

```
limit badnet 0 Any
limit remote 2 Any
limit local 10 Any

deny !nameserved

e-mail root@poisontooth.com

loginfails 3

message /welcome.msg          login
message .message              cwd=*

chmod           no            anonymous
delete          no            anonymous
overwrite       no            anonymous
rename          no            anonymous

log transfers anonymous,real inbound,outbound

passwd-check rfc822 warn
```

Don't for a second think that the settings we are discussing are a complete representation of what you can do with wu-ftpd. Like War FTPd, wu-ftpd offers so many configurations that it would take many chapters to describe all its features. You might never need more than the settings described here, but don't hesitate to explore further commands by typing the command **man ftpaccess** on your Linux computer to access its documentation.

First, wu-ftpd uses the idea of classes of users. A class, based on a set of rules that classify the type of connection that the user has made, is assigned to a user when he or she first logs in to the FTP server. In my example configuration, I have defined three classes with the class command. The first class, the badnet class, checks to see whether a user is logging in anonymously, and from an IP address in the 140.254.85.* subnet. If a connection matches those criteria, it falls into the badnet class. The second class, local, checks for real users (users who have real system accounts) who are logging in from any IP address and classifies those connections as being local. The third class is the remote class, which is assigned to anyone connecting anonymously from any IP address. You may define as many classes as you want, and the list of IP addresses or subnets is not limited to a single address. You may want to create a class for users from one particular subnet, or a class that contains users from several subnets.

After a class is defined, you can place limits on the connections that members of that class can make. Because classes are determined for users before they have completely logged in, you can make decisions on how to handle their connection (or if you want to accept the connection) before they are allowed access. I've defined three limits for my three classes. The first limit limits the number of incoming connections for the class badnet to zero (none) at any time of the day. In terms of the class definition, this restriction means that no anonymous logins are allowed from the 140.254.85.0 subnet. If you have logged suspicious activity from a particular IP address or subnet, you may wish to make your own badnet class to lock out of your system users from the suspect site. The second limit defined in the example is a limit on the remote class. This limit allows only two anonymous connections at a time. If you plan to allow anonymous access to your machine, you should put a reasonable limit on the number of people who can connect, especially if you are providing the ability to write to your drive anonymously. The goal of every software pirate is to find an open FTP site that allows unlimited anonymous connections and to set up shop using your resources. If you limit the number of simultaneous anonymous logins, your server becomes far less attractive to those pirates. The last limit, as you have probably already determined, limits to 10 the number of users with accounts on the machine who can connect at once. To view the status of the logins on your ftp server at any time, you can use the `ftpwho` command. Here's a sample of the command with a couple of active connections to my machine:

```
>ftpwho

Service class badnet:
    -    0 users (  0 maximum)

Service class local:
  4237  ?  S     0:00 ftpd: barney.biosci.ohio-state.edu: jray: IDLE
    -    1 users ( 10 maximum)

Service class remote:
  4267  ?  S     0:00 ftpd: soyokaze.biosci.ohio-state.edu: anonymous/jray@: IDLE
    -    1 users (  2 maximum)
```

If you see any connections that you want to disconnect, the number in front of each connection is the wu-ftpd process ID. You can simply issue a `kill` command to shut down that process and end the connection.

The next setting, the deny !nameserved option, is useful for maintaining tight site security. This setting prevents users from connecting if they do not have a valid hostname for their computer. Most well-managed networks and ISPs provide hostnames for each node or dial-in line on the network. If a name hasn't been assigned, it is potentially an address that someone has chosen to use for hacking purposes. A nonregistered name is much harder to track, because you do not have a domain name to go by. Many hostnames also identify the owner of the machine or provide some sort of information that helps to identify the owner. For example, the hostnames on the OSU network are assigned on a building-room basis. So a hostname of kh-100.ag.ohio-state.edu tells me that the host is in room 100 of Kottman Hall. By disallowing connections from unnamed hosts, you provide a basic level of security in that you can potentially track down the machine that a connection came from.

On the next two lines, the message options define messages that are displayed to the user at login and when they switch to other directories. Although this information is lost in some graphical clients, it is still useful for people connecting through a command-line FTP or from a Web browser, most of which display any welcome messages directly above the file listing. The file paths listed from these messages are relative to the root of the anonymous FTP directory—that is, the FTP user's home directory, /home/ftp.

The commands `chmod`, `delete`, `overwrite`, and `rename` are all relatively self-explanatory. You do not want to allow anonymous users to change file permissions or modify existing files in any way.

Part
III

Ch
11

Next, logging is activated for the system. I cannot stress enough the need to maintain good log files for all the services you run. You will quickly learn that you are held responsible for all of the activities that take place on your servers. If something happens that is illegal or at all harmful, you must be able to track down the people who committed the act and you need a record of precisely what they did and the steps you took to counter their actions. I have set my FTP server to log two types of information. First, it is set to log all incoming and outgoing transfers for both real users and anonymous users. At the very least, you should always log transfers. I have also enabled the logging of commands for all the anonymous users. This information allows me to keep a close watch on how they are using the server and if they are sending any commands to try to hack it. Watch closely for anonymous users trying to create directories or change file permissions. If you see any, quickly add their subnet to the badnet class.

The final option I have specified is the Password Check setting. Anonymous logins usually require the anonymous user to enter his or her email address as the password. This information is simply for logging purposes. However, there is no way of knowing whether the information is correct, so the most that can be done is to print a warning or deny access to the user if his or her email address does not meet the specifications for an email address as defined in RFC 822. Even if your setting denies access to an improperly formed email address, you cannot force the user to enter in a valid address. FTP has no way of enforcing such an action. The user could enter `bogus@hacker.com`, and FTP would accept the address as valid.

The final option that you might want to set for the Linux FTPd is the timeout period that must pass before a user is disconnected. By default, wu-ftpd has a 15-minute timeout period, which the client can reset to be as long as 2 hours. Depending on your traffic, it is a waste of system resources to allow users to connect and then stay connected for hours. I usually set a relatively short timeout period on my servers. This approach provides another point of discouragement to would-be pirates because they must maintain some level of activity on your server to avoid being cut off. (In contrast, their ideal situation is a long-term timeout during which they occasionally check for new files that are being sent.) To configure the timeout for wu-ftpd, you need to provide a new command-line option to the server when it is started.

The Linux FTPd starts a bit differently than other daemons on the Linux machine. It is activated on a connection basis—meaning that it does not run in the background constantly waiting for connections. Instead, Linux waits for an attempt to connect on the FTP port and then launches a copy of wu-ftpd for each connection attempt. The file that controls this activity is `/etc/inetd.conf`. Open this file in a text editor and look for a line that starts the ftp server. It should look like this:

```
ftp     stream tcp     nowait root     /usr/sbin/tcpd  in.ftpd -l -a
```

Change that line to include a -T timeout option (specified in seconds; the T must be uppercase). My timeout is set for 5 minutes:

```
ftp     stream tcp     nowait root     /usr/sbin/tcpd  in.ftpd -l -a -T300
```

You need to reboot your computer, or restart the inetd process, for your changes to take effect.

Although the Linux FTP service is a bit more complicated to configure than other FTP servers, it is very powerful and has many more configuration options. Also remember that because you are running Linux FTP under an operating system that can be justifiably considered a server OS, this service can handle a far greater load than can either NetPresenz running under Mac OS or War FTPd running under Windows 95 or 98.

Using Linux as a Peer on a Windows TCP/IP Network

Okay, so Linux is obviously well equipped to provide FTP services to a network, but how easily can it join in directly shared files from Windows or Mac OS systems? Once again, Linux comes through. Connectivity is a built-in feature in every Red Hat 5.x system. In fact, you actually have two ways to connect to Windows shares. The first program you can use to connect is smbclient. It is part of the UNIX Windows connectivity package known as Samba. Samba is a free implementation of the SMB file-sharing system and the NetBIOS transport. It comes preinstalled in Linux. To learn more about Samba and pick up the latest version, visit the Samba Web site at http://samba.anu.edu.au/samba/.

The smbclient software is similar to an FTP program, except that the former connects to an SMB share and allows you transfer files to and from the share. To use smbclient, all you need to do is specify a share name exactly as you would in Windows. Because of the way that UNIX shells escape characters with the backslash (\) (allowing you to specify unprintable characters), you probably need to give the share name an extra "\" and put it in quotes. For example, a share name that I have is \\pointy\jray, but I'm going to connect to it with this command:

```
>smbclient "\\\pointy\jray"

Added interface ip=204.210.240.90 bcast=204.210.240.255 nmask=255.255.255.0
Server time is Sun Aug 23 20:10:16 1998
Timezone is UTC-4.0
Password:
Domain=[JOHNLAND] OS=[Unix] Server=[Samba 1.9.17p4]
connected as guest security=share
smb: \>
```

You are now connected to the file share and can begin sending commands to control the server. The first thing that you probably want to do is get a directory listing. Do so with the ls command, just like FTP:

```
Smb: \> ls
    What is a network            A    1039872  Sun Aug  9 10:46:36 1998
    usings~1.doc                 A     164352  Wed Jul 15 16:48:12 1998
    .ncftp                       DH         0  Wed Aug 19 11:03:01 1998
    Temporary Items              D          0  Sun Jul 26 21:15:45 1998
    festival                     D          0  Fri Aug 14 17:07:39 1998
    new                          D          0  Tue Aug 18 12:34:35 1998
    MacAmp 1.0b5 %C4             D          0  Fri Aug  7 01:35:49 1998
    imap-4.1.BETA-11.i386.rpm        787297  Mon May 11 16:25:00 1998
    .mailboxlist                 H        172  Wed Jul 22 00:32:20 1998
    .mlbxlsttmp                  H        138  Tue Jul 21 10:12:32 1998
    utils                        D          0  Sat Aug 22 10:28:37 1998

        58110 blocks of size 32768. 1859 blocks available
```

Part

III

Ch

11

Files are listed as you would expect, including the filename, type of file (A=Archive, D=Directory, H=Hidden), size of the file, and modification date. Now try switching to another directory, using the cd command (again, this command matches the FTP command set).

```
smb: \> cd utils

smb: \utils\>
```

Next, try transferring a file from the server, using the get command. You can also use the mget (multiple get) command and a list of files, or wildcards, to get multiple files at once. I'm going to transfer all the files that begin with john in the utils directory.

```
smb: \utils\> mget john*

smb: \utils\> mget john*
Get file johns_filters? y
getting file \utils\johns_filters of size 700 bytes as johns_filters (9.23774 kb
/s) (average 9.23775 kb/s)
Get file johns_filters.log? y
getting file \utils\johns_filters.log of size 396419 bytes as johns_filters.log
(595.581 kb/s) (average 535.651 kb/s)
Get file johns_filters~? y
getting file \utils\johns_filters~ of size 631 bytes as johns_filters~ (25.6754
kb/s) (average 519.288 kb/s)
```

Pretty simple, huh? If you'd like to avoid having to type Y for each file in a multiple file transfer, you can use the prompt command to toggle the prompting on and off. To return a file to the shared directory, use the put (or mput for multiple files) command. Here I send a file called mbox to the file server.

```
smb: \utils\> put mbox

putting file mbox of size 2543728 bytes as \utils\mbox (696.414 kb/s) (average
696.414 kb/s)
```

That should be sufficient for you to communicate with an arbitrary share on your network. If you need to talk to a server that isn't on your local network, you can use the hostname or IP address as the computer name when you are connecting. It will be resolved correctly by the smbclient software. When you're finished using the software, you can use the quit command to exit smbclient.

If you're wondering why you can't connect a share directly to your computer instead of transferring files back and forth using smbclient, the answer is that you can. The reason that a piece of software such as smbclient is necessary is because of the way the UNIX file system operates. UNIX has a single-tree file system. All drives that are mounted on the UNIX system are mounted as part of the larger file system. The result is that mounting any sort of resource into the UNIX file system requires root privileges. Being able to mount a resource without root permission could lead to a situation in which many users have unintentional access to files. If you have root permissions (which I've assumed you do up to this point), you can use the /usr/sbin/smbmount command to directly mount a shared resource on your computer. To use the command, you must specify both the server in the same manner that you did with the smbclient command and a mount point. The *mount point* is the directory to which you want the resource to attach. I'm going to mount my \\\poisontooth.com\jray resource on a directory called /home/jray/johnstuff. You probably also need to specify a client name; otherwise, smbmount attempts to use the hostname of your computer as the client name, which is often longer than valid Windows names. In this example, my client computer's name is forsaken.

```
/usr/sbin/smbmount "//POISONTOOTH.COM/JRAY" /home/jray/johnstuff -c forsaken
```

If all goes well, the smbmount command will exit without any messages. You will immediately be able to access all of the files as if they were part of your local file system, and, in fact, they now are. As I mentioned earlier, remember that your mounted directory is now part of the entire UNIX file system. If you have mounted the files on a part of the file system that is publicly accessible, you could inadvertently be giving access to the files to everyone with an account on your Linux machine.

The smbmount software is not part of the Samba server suite; rather, it is distributed with a package called smbfs. You might want to check the smbfs Web site (http://samba.SerNet.DE/linux-lan/) often to make sure that you are running the latest version with the latest security fixes.

Connecting to an SMB share from Linux is, as you've seen, surprisingly simple. The only other problem you need to solve is how to serve to the Windows network. At this point, the rest of the Samba package comes into play. The Samba server suite is very extensive. It is capable of providing file-sharing services on a large scale to many clients. This is, once again, one of the charms of Linux. It takes a bit more to configure than an NT or AppleShare IP server but is every bit as capable and, again, is provided at no cost with the Red Hat Linux distribution.

The Samba configuration options are stored in the file /etc/smb.conf. There are *lots* of options and many ways of serving your data. This section looks at only a small subset of the Samba configuration. The entire command set is viewable by entering the command **man smb.conf** at a command prompt. The online documentation itself is 71 pages long and is in a summary format. Luckily for us, the default configuration file that is provided with the Red Hat distribution is useable almost immediately without any changes.

Before you begin configuring the server, be sure that you really want to do so. It is very easy to set up multiple servers on your network, and as your network grows, it is very easy for all of the servers to become a convoluted mess. If you need a few files shared out to a handful of people and you have a Mac or Windows computer on the network, by all means use them to serve the files. Samba is likely to require a bit of tweaking before it works entirely the way you want, and unless you want to take the time to learn the Samba suite in depth, you may end up very frustrated. I do not mean to discourage the use of Samba, only to point out that, depending on how serious your server needs, you might want to use something else. If you plan on serving a large number of files to a large number of people and expect a large volume of server activity, Samba will work well for you.

Now that you are probably terrified, take a look at the configuration file. Most configuration options are either Share or Global. The Share options can be changed for each shared resource from the computer. These options involve items such as valid users for the resource and file permissions for files that are created on the share. Global options affect the operation of the

Part
III

Ch
11

entire server or set a default that you can then override if you need to. The server name and server description are examples of global options. Start by looking at a basic configuration of the server itself, without any resources shared. This example is actually a truncated version of the basic configuration. I've left the file's comments intact, as they should help explain the configuration as you read through it.

```
>cat /etc/smb.conf

[global]

; workgroup = NT-Domain-Name or Workgroup-Name, eg: REDHAT4
    workgroup = JohnLand

; comment is the equivalent of the NT Description field
    comment = John's Samba Server

; Uncomment this if you want a guest account
    guest account = nobody
    log file = /var/log/samba-log.%m
; Put a capping on the size of the log files (in Kb)
    max log size = 50

; Options for handling file name case sensitivity and / or preservation
; Case Sensitivity breaks many WfW and Win95 apps
      preserve case = yes

; Security modes: USER uses Unix username/passwd, SHARE uses WfW type passwords
;         SERVER uses a Windows NT Server to provide authentication services
    security = user
; Use password server option only with security = server
;     password server = <NT-Server-Name>

; Domain Control Options
; OS Level gives Samba the power to rule the roost. Windows NT = 32
;         Any value < 32 means NT wins as Master Browser, > 32 Samba gets it
    os level = 33
; specifies Samba to be the Domain Master Browser
    domain master = yes

; Windows Internet Name Serving Support Section
; WINS Support - Tells the NMBD component of Samba to enable it's WINS Server
;         the default is NO.
    wins support = yes
; WINS Server - Tells the NMBD components of Samba to be a WINS Client
;         Note: Samba can be either a WINS Server, or a WINS Client, but NOT both
;     wins server = w.x.y.z
```

If you've read along as you've set up Windows file sharing, some of this code should look familiar. Let's quickly run through the options that were used in this configuration. Everything you're looking at now is a global option. Here's a summary of the options:

■ Workgroup —The workgroup setting controls the Windows workgroup or domain that the server will appear in. My Linux computer is set to appear in JohnLand. (There's nothing wrong with a bit of vanity.)

- Comment—The comment is simply a description of the server. You do not need to specify a comment, or if you do, it can be anything you'd like.

- Guest account—If you plan on having guest users connect to your system, you must provide a username that the connection will use. This name should be a nonprivileged account on your UNIX machine—the nobody account is generally a safe choice.

- Log file—Again, it is important to keep a good log of the activity on your server. The log file setting should be the path to the file where you want to store your log. In this configuration, the log filename is followed by %m, which automatically adds the machine name that is connected to the server to the end of the log file name. The result is an individual log for each client accessing the server.

- Max log size—Log files can fill up very quickly, and, in extreme situations, may fill your hard drive and disrupt running services. Samba allows you to limit the amount of log information that is stored. When the limit is reached, older log data is removed.

- Preserve case—As files are stored on the server, the filename can be stored in a single case (lowercase). If the Preserve Case option is selected, files are stored in the same case as on the client computer. It is also possible to specify case sensitivity for filenames. In UNIX, files are case sensitive, so test and Test are two separate files. Windows 95 and 98 are not case sensitive and turning on sensitivity might confuse applications that expect to open files in a non—case-sensitive manner. You probably want to use settings similar to mine.

- Security—Samba has three security options. *Share* protects resources on a share-by-share basis. *User* protects shares by requiring a valid username and password (based on the UNIX logins). *Server* uses an NT server to provide authentication information. I've chosen the user level of control. If you do choose to use server security, you need to specify a password server using the Password Server option.

- OS level—Windows provides resource-browsing services through the use of a master browser machine that maintains a list of the available resources on the network and replies to broadcast browse requests. This machine is not a dedicated server, and the function is performed transparently to the users of the network. The master browser is determined by an election process on the network. Depending on the level of the operating system, an individual computer might have a greater chance to win the election than another. Windows NT, for example, has a higher OS level than Windows 95 or 98 and would win the election. Samba allows you to specify its advertised OS level. You can set Samba as high as 255, but anything greater than 32 guarantees victory over Windows NT machines.

- Domain master—Enabling the Domain Master option tells Samba to try to become the master browser. Whether or not to enable this option is entirely up to you. If you have other Windows machines on your network, having Samba as your master browser probably won't make a noticeable difference.

- WINS support—This option enables or disables Samba's abilities to act as a WINS server for your Windows network. If you do not want to use Samba as a WINS server, it can be a client to another WINS server, which is specified with the WINS Server setting.

Part

III

Ch

11

That run through should give you a basic, useable Samba server configuration. Now you can get down to the business of sharing out resources. One of the nicest features of Samba is its ability to configure itself to share out each user's home directory automatically. Rather than having to specify each directory you want to make available, you can simply use the Homes option, which applies to all home directories.

```
[homes]
    comment = Home Directories
    browseable = no
    read only = no
    preserve case = yes
    create mode = 0750
```

Adding these lines to the /etc/smb.conf is all you need to do to start the home directories. Normally, the name of the share that you are creating is placed within the square brackets. This, however, is a special case—you cannot connect to a share called homes on the server. The shares that this option does create are named after the user accounts. If I start the server with this configuration in place, I will be able to connect to \\pointy\jray and have access to my entire UNIX home directory. Here's a list of the new options that you've now introduced into the Samba setup:

- [Homes]—All shares begin with square brackets around a share name. In this case, homes is a special reference that shares all of the server user's home directories at once.

- Browseable—The browseable option toggles whether this share is viewable inside the Windows network browser. Because letting the user browse all the home directories is a security risk (you'd essentially be giving out a list of all the usernames on the system), you set browseable to no for the [homes] share.

- Read only—If you want users to be able to read files from the shares, but not be able to save to them, you would set this option to yes.

- Create mode—As files are created on the system, they need to be mapped to the UNIX permission scheme. Because Windows 95 and 98 do not understand the concept of owners and groups, this option helps create the UNIX files with permissions that make sense. In this example, the creation mode is 750, which is exactly the same as running chmod 750 to set the permissions on each file that is created. The meaning of 750 breaks down as full owner permissions, read-execute permissions for the files group, and no permissions for anyone else. Other modes you might want to use are 700 (full access for owner only) and 755 (full access for the owner and read-execute permission for everyone else).

That's all it takes to put all of the user accounts from your server online. Keep in mind that although you can establish a setting of read only = no to enable connections to write to the shares, the UNIX permissions still apply. If some files in a shared directory do not belong to the user that is connected, the user won't have any more access to the files than they would under UNIX.

The next example shows you how to create a public share that only a few users can access. I often create shares like this one so that team members can collaborate on projects, such as

Web sites.

```
[ranking]
   comment = Goth Stuff
   path = /home/movies
   valid users = agroves6 ganwar7
   public = no
   writable = yes
   create mask = 0755
```

You've introduced a few new commands now, so take a look at the new options:

- `valid users`—The Valid Users option enables you to create shares that are accessible by a select number of people. I've made the ranking share accessible to users agroves6 and ganwar7.

- `public`—By default, this option is set to `no`. I've used it here because I could easily turn the share into a public share by commenting on the valid user's line. The public option, when set to `yes`, allows guests to connect to the share.

- `writable`—`writable` is simply another form of the read-only option that you've already seen. Setting the Writcablc option to `yes` is identical to setting the Read-only option to `no`. Use whichever one makes you happy.

One final option that I'd like to share with you that I've found very useful is the `force user` command. For example, I can specify the command `force user=jray` for a share from my machine. This command forces all connections to a share to be made as the forced user. Moving back and forth between using files directly on the UNIX/Linux computer and having to deal with a handful of users who are connecting to a share and creating files that are set with their ownership can be inconvenient. Sometimes it's just simpler if all actions that take place on the server take place as a certain user. You can still control the valid users of the share, but you no longer have to worry about having access to the files that they create.

You can use this information to create as many shares from your Linux computer as you'd like. Take time to read over the man pages for smb.conf, as you will find a wealth of services that you can provide.

This information should give you the skills you need to connect a Windows network and Macintosh clients using DAVE to a Linux server. What about an AppleShare IP server for Linux? Such a creature does indeed exist; however, it is far more difficult to configure than Samba is and relies on your Ethernet card drivers to have certain broadcast capabilities, which it might not. Two free AppleTalk products for UNIX are currently available: netatalk and CAP. Both require extensive configuration and are not included by default with the Linux operating system. If you'd like try running them, you can find more information at `http://www.cs.mu.oz.au/appletalk/cap.html`

You should now see how various operating systems can communicate with one another. Even if you don't use the tools discussed here, it's nice to know that they are available. Networks are dynamic creatures—a Macintosh-only network can suddenly change as Windows PCs are introduced, or vice versa. Having the tools to deal with a new configuration is a comfort.

Adding Email and Web Server Capabilities to Your OS

by John Ray

In this chapter

Providing Messaging Services Under Mac OS **225**

OSProviding Messaging Services Under Windows 95 and 98 and Linux **235**

Web Services **256**

With the ability to share files across a TCP/IP network now within your grasp, it's time to move on to two other features that are useful in a TCP/IP network—namely, messaging (email) and Web serving. This chapter starts with the more complex of the two: messaging.

Messaging is an extremely important feature for a network of any reasonable size. We looked at the POP3 and IMAP protocols, and you probably use email on your computer right now. In an office of four or five people, setting up a mail server might not be necessary. Add 10 or 15 more employees, though, and it's a necessity. Email servers that run under your client operating systems can serve a relatively large number of people. Dedicated servers should be able to handle thousands of user accounts. Non-dedicated servers can usually handle several hundred accounts without any trouble.

With a mail server comes extra system requirements. In a small office situation, this extra load is not really a concern. If you have a few hundred accounts, or more, you must pay close attention to the amount of disk space that the server uses. Today's email is often "media rich" and can include video, sound, and usually two or three lines of text. If a company memo is sent to 100 people and it contains the famous Dancing Baby video (if you don't know what this is, consider yourself lucky), your mail server will suddenly lose 200MB of storage. Some slightly more intelligent mail servers would store only a single copy of the message, but never assume that the one you're communicating with works this way!

To service around 1,500 accounts, our VAX dedicates 8 gigabytes of storage space to mail. On more than one occasion, the system has been brought to a halt because of a few pieces of huge email that were sent to every account. You'll need to purchase the appropriate amount of disk space to serve your accounts. If you are also using the mail server as a workstation, remember that files you save on that machine affect the amount of available storage. Creating a condition in which all of your company's email is bouncing because you felt like drawing a few pictures in Photoshop is not likely to win you very many friends.

Aside from simply running mail functions, you might also want to provide mail-related services such as mailing lists. *Mailing lists* are a method of distributing a message to a large number of people. Rather than addressing a piece of email to hundreds of people, you send a single message to the list, and that message is distributed to the subscribers. Depending on the complexity of the software handling the mailing list, you may be able to greatly customize your list. At its basic level, a mailing list is nothing more than a method of automatically forwarding messages. Good mailing list software allows a list to have an owner who controls who can post to the list. The members of the list are subscribers who can remove themselves from the list by sending an unsubscribe command to the list server. Advanced software can create *digests* of mailing lists, which summarize the messages that have been posted during a time period and send the summary, rather than the messages themselves, to subscribers.

Mailing lists are a useful method of communicating with groups of people within an organization. If you have more than a handful of individuals on your network, you will soon find yourself building groups of users within your email client. These groups could easily be replaced with a mailing list, and, as a list, would be usable by another person who also needed to contact the same individuals. Even if you don't see a need for a mailing list in the near future, be aware that the software exists and of the features it can provide.

Following the pattern established for file sharing in Chapter 11, "Exploring Client OS File Server Capabilities," this chapter examines ways of extending our client's capabilities to be mail servers. For email to work, this discussion assumes that your network already has a name server running or that all your computers have an appropriate hosts file installed.

Providing Messaging Services Under Mac OS

Several free email servers for the Macintosh can handle a reasonable load without stressing your computer. The best product that I have found for Mac OS-based email service is called SIMS, or Stalker Internet Mail Server. Stalker produces a large number of server products for the Mac OS and provides SIMS as a free starter. Stalker's flagship Macintosh server product, called CommuniGate, is also available in a demo version and provides enhanced email services, including the IMAP protocol. You can download SIMS (or the CommuniGate demo version) from http://www.stalker.com/

SIMS unarchives into a few files. Before you can start using SIMS, you also need to download the CommuniGator application so that you can configure SIMS. CommuniGator works with many of the Stalker products to provide a consistent configuration front end. While SIMS and CommuniGator are downloading, you can set up the Postmaster account that will control your server. You must create a Postmaster user in the Users & Groups control panel. Be sure to set the password to something secure. This account allows a user have remote access to your email functions, so you want to keep it private. You need to give the Postmaster account the capability to link to programs on the computer. Select the Show pop-up menu while you are creating your Postmaster user and switch it to Sharing. Make sure the option under Program Linking is checked. As a final step in the preparation of SIMS, open the File Sharing control panel and turn on Program Linking, as shown in Figure 12.1. You do not need to have file sharing enabled to use SIMS.

Part

III

Ch

12

FIGURE 12.1
Turn on Program Linking in the File Sharing control panel.

After you download and de-archive CommuniGator, start the server by double-clicking the SIMS icon. Notice that SIMS starts with very little fanfare. In fact, if you select Monitor & Control from the File menu, a greeting message tells you to control the software with CommuniGator or your Web browser. After you configure SIMS with CommuniGator, you can use your Web browser for all further configurations. Now start the CommuniGator application.

The CommuniGator application allows you to configure Stalker products that are running anywhere on your AppleTalk network. Thus the first thing you need to do is find the product that you want to configure. Usually, the connection screen is displayed when you launch CommuniGator. If not, select Connect To from the File menu. You should see something similar to Figure 12.2. Navigate through the available AppleTalk zones (if you do not have any zones on your AppleTalk network, your display will be slightly different). The CommuniGator screen provides a Chooser-like view to your AppleTalk network. Simply navigate through the zones and available computers until you find the system that is running SIMS. Select SIMS and click OK to begin configuring it. You are prompted for a login name—use the Postmaster name—and the password you assigned it in the Users & Groups control panel.

FIGURE 12.2

CommuniGator's opening dialog box.

Because SIMS offers Web administration as one of its primary features, you can use a Web browser for most of the configuration. Whenever I reconfigure SIMS, I am rarely on a machine that has CommuniGator installed, but almost all networked computers do have a Web browser. Before you can use a browser, however, you need to set up the internal HTTP server that is included with SIMS. To do so, select HTTP from the Server menu. You are now be in HTTP configuration mode and a new HTTP menu appears. From this menu, choose Service Settings to open the dialog box shown in Figure 12.3.

FIGURE 12.3

You configure TCP/IP channels for HTTP clients in this dialog box.

Here you set up the defaults for your Web administration interface. You can choose the level of logging for all HTTP connections, as well as the number of TCP/IP clients that can be connected and the port to which they will connect in order to configure the server. There is no reason to set the TCP/IP setting higher than 5 or 10 unless you are planning on a large number of people accessing the Web interface simultaneously. The default setting is 0, which disables the Web interface entirely. I set the server in this example to 10. Next, you can set the port to anything that is easy to remember. If you are running another Web server on the same computer as the email server, be sure that the ports do not overlap. If they do, one or both of the servers will probably be inoperable. My port is set at 8010, the default. Click OK when you are satisfied with your settings. You can now quit from the CommuniGator application and begin to configure the server via the Web interface.

To use the Web interface, you obviously need a Web browser. You can start a browser on the same machine or use any computer on your network. My server is located on a machine called primal.ag.ohio-state.edu, and I have configured it to run its HTTP server from port 8010, so I will be using the URL `http://primal.ag.ohio-state.edu:8010/` as my method of connecting to the server. Go ahead and make the initial connection to the server now. Your browser should look a lot like mine, shown in Figure 12.4.

FIGURE 12.4
Your Web browser will look like this when you connect to the SIMS Web interface.

Assuming that you have correctly set up the Postmaster account and password, you can now click the Enter hypertext link to reach the main menu. You are prompted for your username and password (which is the Postmaster username and password) before the connection is made.

You are greeted with the General Settings configuration screen, shown in Figure 12.5. The buttons along the left side of the window take you to other setting screens and allow you to control the server operation. If, at any time, you want to return to the General Settings screen, simply click the General button.

Part
III

Ch
12

FIGURE 12.5

After you enter your username and password, you are greeted by the General Settings configuration options.

You can configure the following options from this screen:

- Log—Usually the Problem level that is selected by default provides enough logging information for your server. You can change the level of logging with the pop-up menu. Be careful, however; on a server with only five accounts and a moderate amount of activity, I log between 1MB and 2MB of data each day. Over time, this amount of data can take a significant amount of space.

- Main Domain Name—This option specifies the primary name for which the computer will accept mail. If your computer is registered under a variety of aliases, you might want to change the default domain name to something else. For example, if my computer is registered as www.poisontooth.com, and mail.poisontooth.com is an alias, I would probably want to put the mail alias in this field. Initially, mail to other domains will be rejected.

- Delete Failed Messages—If, for any reason, a message is not delivered, you can tell the server when to delete that message.

If you make any changes to the server settings, you must click the Update button to apply the changes. You don't need to stop or restart the service.

Now that the server is up and running, it would probably be useful to create some email accounts on it. You do so by clicking the Accounts button to access the screen shown in Figure 12.6.

From User Accounts screen, you can see the existing accounts, which, in the case of your initial server setup, is just the Postmaster account. The current size of the user's mailbox is also listed, as is the time the mailbox file was last changed by incoming mail or messages being delivered. If you have a large number of email accounts, you can use the Filter field to provide a string that identifies the accounts you want to view. Clicking the Display button applies the filter. If you click Display without any filter specified, the default display lists all the accounts.

FIGURE 12.6
You can add or edit accounts in this screen.

To create a basic account, fill in a username in the New Account field. This entry should be a valid email account name, which can't include spaces. Next, click the Create button. The screen refreshes, and your new account appears in the account listing. Before the account is usable, however, you're going to need to change some of its settings. Each username is a hyperlink to a configuration page for that user. I want to click the jray account that I just created and configure it for use. Figure 12.7 shows a portion of the user configuration screen (the important stuff!), but several options are out of view.

FIGURE 12.7
Editing an existing email account invokes this screen.

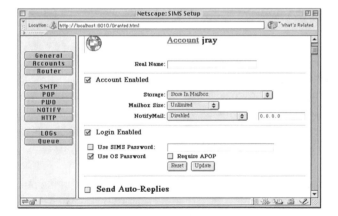

You can set a wealth of information for each user. The following options are useful for this network:

■ Real Name—The real name of the person who holds the account. Although this entry may seem obvious, it is quite easy to overlook setting this field. Your email system may grow from 10 or 20 users to several hundred. If you neglect to store the real name of the user along with each account, a time will come when you want to identify a user named superguy392 who has a 100MB mailbox file and you won't have any record of who it actually is.

■ Account Enabled—To quickly disable a user from receiving mail on the system, you can deselect this box. A large volume of mail arriving for the individual could be the result of that person being stuck in a mail loop. Disabling the account until the problem is resolved is a potential solution.

■ Storage—You can choose where you want messages for this account to go. They can be stored in a folder on your system, in a single mailbox file, or both. I've used Store in Mailbox for my configurations.

■ Mailbox Size—You can choose the amount of storage space that is dedicated to the user on your mail server. The default Unlimited is not a good idea. You will want to change this setting to a smaller amount. One technique for crashing a mail server is to fill up mailboxes with large amounts of junk mail. Setting a limit to the amount of mail that a mailbox can hold helps protect your system and your users.

■ NotifyMail—NotifyMail alerts your client computer every time new mail arrives on a mail server. This interesting product is available for Mac OS and Windows from `http://www.notifymail.com/`. This option enables the server to speak to the NotifyMail program. By default, it is disabled. If you choose to enable it, you can have it contact the notification program at the Last IP Address that was used to contact the server, a Fixed IP Address, or through an AppleTalk connection.

■ Login Enabled—Deselecting the Login Enabled setting makes the account inaccessible to the user. The account can still receive mail, but the user is unable to connect.

■ Use SIMS Password—If you select this option and enter a password in the field to the right, you can use that password to connect to the system. Selecting this option is one of the first things you do when you create an account because initially no password is set.

■ Use OS Password—If a user account exists on the system in the Users & Groups control panel that matches the username that you have created in SIMS, you can use the Users & Groups password to access the SIMS account. If the user is not defined in the control panel, this setting has no effect.

■ Require APOP—Setting this option requires the email clients to use special authentication when connecting to the server. The clients must be configured to use APOP if this option is selected.

■ Send Auto-Replies—Checking Send Auto-Replies and filling out the accompanying textbox tells the SIMS software to automatically reply to all incoming messages. Whatever is typed in the textbox is sent out immediately as an email message. For example, if you have a help email account that users can send inquiries to, you may want to send an immediate "Help request received" every time you receive a message.

■ Mirror to List—You can redirect any incoming messages to another address using the Mirror to List option. This option is useful for forwarding messages to other accounts.

That's quite a number of options that you can set for a single user, isn't it? When you have completed the setup for a user, click the Update button at the bottom of the form to send the changes to the server.

To help in the creation of future user accounts, you can use an account template to set some defaults to carry over to each account that is created. To do so, click the Template link from the user accounts screen to display a form that looks identical to the user configuration screen. You can use this template to set the initial values you want to use for future users. For example, if all users are created with a certain mailbox size or an initial default password, you can use the template to quickly and easily establish these settings as your default.

The next settings to look at are the router settings for the server. An email router allows you to redirect incoming mail to different domains or different accounts. In the case of a simple email server, the default settings are usually adequate. In fact, a misconfiguration in the router settings could cause mail to be bounced or delivered to the wrong address. To access the SIMS router, click on the Router button.

Again, you are greeted with an option to control the extent of the logging that the system should perform. There is also a nice big text box that you can use to set up your routing table. My biggest use for this option is to provide email aliases and to make sure that mail sent to other domain names is delivered correctly. For example, I have a mail server running at primal.ag.ohio-state.edu. That same server is also known as bigmac.ag.ohio-state.edu and abyss.ag.ohio-state.edu. In this case, I want mail that is addressed to any of those aliases to be delivered directly to a differently named server. The following rules implement this change:

```
bigmac.ag.ohio-state.edu=different.ag.ohio-state.edu
abyss.ag.ohio-state.edu=different.ag.ohio-state.edu
```

These settings tell SIMS that incoming mail for abyss and bigmac actually need to go to the primal.ag.ohio-state.edu domain. Figure 12.8 shows how I configured my primal machine. If your mail server has different aliases and you do not set up the appropriate routing table, mail will be bounced. If you suspect that your system is rejecting mail, you can check the log files (which are covered shortly) to make sure that the system is behaving correctly.

Part
III

Ch
12

FIGURE 12.8

I've created rules that automatically reroute messages sent to two email addresses to yet a third.

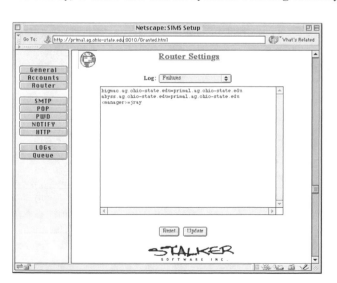

Another basic routing feature enables you to set up an email alias. You can use this feature to create vanity accounts for users, to set up multiple email addresses that are all stored in a single account, and to create a simple mail forwarding system. For example, if I want to create an alias that allows people to email me as `manager@primal.ag.ohio-state.edu` but have the actual email go to my `jray@primal` account, I can do so with a simple line:

```
<manager>=jray
```

Carrying that example one step further, I don't even need an account on the machine to have mail forwarded to me. If I want messages that are addressed to `manager@primal.ag.ohio-state.edu` to be delivered to `jray@poisontooth.com`, I can modify the routing table entry to look like this:

```
<manager>=jray@poisontooth.com
```

There are many other routing options you can explore and configure using the SIMS routing table. If you want to read the SIMS help, you can do so online by clicking the large heading hyperlinks at any time. Click Router Settings to go to the Stalker Web site, which gives you a complete background on the available router options. Be sure to click Update if you make any changes to the routing table.

That step completes the basic setup of the server. The remaining options configure the server's communication protocols. These five buttons—SMTP, POP, PWD, NOTIFY, and HTTP— allow you to set up basic networking properties for the protocols. This section describes these protocols and then examines the settings for the most complicated member of the group, SMTP.

- SMTP—If you read about the SMTP protocol in Chapter 6, "Understanding TCP/IP Protocols," you know that SMTP handles incoming messages and forwards them to the appropriate destination.
- POP—The POP3 protocol server. POP3 is used by Eudora, Outlook, and many other email clients to pick up messages from a remote server.
- PWD—PWD is not implemented by all email servers, but it provides a very nice service when it is. Through the use of PWD, a user can change his or her password by way of a graphic interface. Eudora and other email clients have a Change Password selection that talks to the PWD server.
- NOTIFY—NOTIFY refers to the NotifyMail program mentioned earlier, which allows the email server to directly notify clients as new email comes in.
- HTTP—If you're using a Web browser to configure SIMS, you know that the HTTP protocol provides the Web interface that you are using.

Three of these protocols (POP, PWP, and NOTIFY) have relatively similar configurations; SMTP and HTTP are the exceptions. Remember how we initially configured the HTTP module to allow 10 TCP/IP connections and to run from port 8010? That is precisely what you can do now by clicking on the HTTP button. The POP, PWD, NOTIFY, and SMTP protocols also allow you to specify the number of TCP/IP channels that can be opened at a single time. They also let you configure the number of AppleTalk connections that can use that service and the level of logging that the server will perform for each of the protocols. The default values for each protocol are probably sufficient for most applications, but the SMTP settings provide a bit of extra functionality that is extremely nice. Go ahead and bring up the SMTP settings now by clicking the SMTP button.

As you can see in Figure 12.9, you can set the number of TCP channels to be used for sending email (AppleTalk can't be used for sending via SMTP) and the number of TCP/AppleTalk channels for receiving email.

FIGURE 12.9
The SMTP Settings window lets you configure the mail transfer protocol.

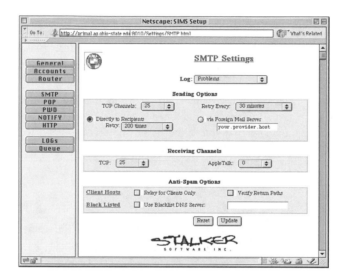

The Sending options control what happens when email leaves the server. For example, if email cannot immediately reach its destination, the server can be configured to retry a certain number of times, waiting for a length of time between attempts. The defaults are to retry sending messages 200 times and to resend every 30 minutes. If you want to take the outgoing email load off your server, you can set the Via Foreign Mail Server option to point to another SMTP server to deliver your email for you. The default settings should be sufficient for most cases.

Part
III

Ch
12

What Is Spam?

If you have an email account, you've been face to face with spam. As you travel the Internet, your email address becomes public. Some companies grab your email off Usenet postings you make, Web pages you create, anything. Companies even scan university computer systems to gather email addresses for everyone affiliated with the university and scan online services for member addresses. These lists are then sold to other companies or used to send large quantities of advertising email to the people on the list. This email is entirely unsolicited , and it often arrives in massive amounts. (In some cases, users log in to their mailbox for a brand-new account only to find spam waiting for them there.) To compound the affront, these messages usually are nothing but harebrained get-rich-quick schemes, bogus stock tips, phony diet cures, and advertisements for adult Web sites. This junk email is popularly—or unpopularly—known as *spam*. It will be your worst enemy as you run your mail server.

continues

continued

When you can, fight back. Spammers are using your resources for their financial gain. If you can trace spam, contact the ISP of the host from which the spam originated. We may have full legal recourse against spammers. For now, however, spamming remains a very gray area that is on the edge of legality, despite being ethically wrong.

By the way, if you're interested in an estimate of how much money spam costs Internet users, check out Bright Light Technologies' Spam Calculator at `http://www.brightlight.com/cgi-bin/spamulator2.cgi`.

You enter the monthly cost of your ISP and the number of seconds it takes you to delete each spam message, and the Web page calculates what spam costs you each year. Bright Light estimates that spammers send more than nine billion messages a year for an annual cost to users of $255 million!

One of the best features of SIMS, which isn't available in many other free servers, is the Anti-Spam Options for SMTP. If you have an email account, I'm sure you've seen the results of spam: worthless messages that you cannot—and should not—reply to and garbage advertisements that clutter up your mailboxes (see sidebar).

CAUTION

Sometimes spam message offer an email address that you can send a message to, requesting to be taken off the mailing list. For legitimate mail lists like the ones I described a little earlier, this technique works. Often with spam, however, you're merely sending the unintentional message that the user at that email address read the spam and responded to it, instead of deleting it right off the bat. Your email account will then be targeted for more spam, not less.

Email spammers often protect themselves by using other SMTP servers to send their mail, thus not needing to set up a server of their own. It also helps hide their identify, because the email ends up looking like it came from the SMTP server that merely relayed the email. SIMS offers some protection against this sort of nastiness, which you can configure in the Anti-Spam Options settings. You can configure the following options to protect your server:

- Relay for Clients Only—If you select this option, it will only allow clients that you list to send email. Click the Client Hosts link to bring up a screen in which you can enter a list of clients that can use the SMTP server. This is an excellent form of protection, but it requires you to know up front which clients will be using your SMTP services. If you have users that are dialing in through their own ISPs, but would like to use your server to send mail, their IP addresses would not be listed, and the mail would be rejected.

- Verify Return Paths—If email spammers have forged a fake return path to the sending computer, this option can be set to refuse messages for which the return path is not verifiable.

- Black Listed—Rather than create a list of clients that are allowed to use the server, it might be easier to put together a list of known spammers' domains and not allow connections from those domains. Lists that contain spammers' domains are published on a regular basis; simply feed in the list, and you're protected. Click this link to supply the Black Listed domains.

- Use Blacklist DNS—Checking this option and putting an IP address in the field to the right causes the server to use a "blacklist" DNS. This special DNS maintains a list of known spammers and resolves their domain names into an invalid IP address that identifies it as being black listed.

You've now successfully set up your first email server, and it should be fully usable. Try sending yourself some email; it should work. If it doesn't, you can always look at the LOG files. To do so, click the Logs button. You'll see the screen shown in Figure 12.10.

FIGURE 12.10

Logs can help you track down the source of any problems.

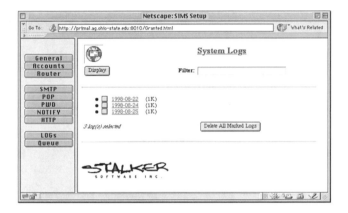

Logs are saved on a daily basis, and depending on the amount of logging that you select, they can be quite large. You can delete log files by selecting the check box in front of the log (or logs) you want to delete and clicking the Delete All Marked Logs option. To display a log, click on the date of the log file. If you choose the current day's log, SIMS does something very neat—it keeps the HTTP connection open and displays additions to the log as they are created. Any problems that you might have with the server should be detailed in the server logs.

The last option for monitoring the server is the Queue button. Select Queue to display all of the messages that are waiting to be sent. If something is going wrong and you find that your server is not delivering mail, the queue might be huge, indicating mail is simply backing up in the queue. This condition might be the result of an email spammer's use of your SMTP server. Clicking the hyperlink for each item in the queue tells you about the messages that are waiting to be sent, such as the send, subject, and return path. You can then click the check box in front the queued message to delete it from the server. That's all there is to it! You can now configure, control, and monitor your own Macintosh email server.

Providing Messaging Services Under Windows 95 and 98 and Linux

If you've read the Mac OS messaging section discussing SIMS, you're probably thinking, Wow, wish I could get that for Windows. Guess what—you can, only better and from the same company, no less! Stalker has recently released one of the best pieces of email serving software that I have ever seen. We're in the process of moving email from a dying VAX computer to a new UNIX-based system. Before the migration, I reviewed several email packages before I looked at the Stalker CommuniGate Pro suite. CommuniGate Pro works under Windows 95 and 98, as well as under NT and many versions of UNIX, including Linux. This email package is similar to War FTPd in that it will perform well under your client operating system and is robust enough to use as a dedicated server under NT of Linux. CommuniGate Pro is available from Stalker software, makers of the SIMS package at http://www.stalker.com/.

You can download the Win32 version, which has a standard Windows installer, or if you plan to use it under Linux, the gzipped tar file. This section covers the installation process under Linux first because it is more involved than the Windows installation. Even so, this process is remarkably simple. The first step is to disable Linux's built-in mail serving software.

Out-of-the-box (or CD-ROM, if you please) Linux has a POP, IMAP, and SMTP server. You may, in fact, be able to immediately send and receive messages from your Linux-based PC with no further configuration at all. The problems arise when any sort of variance from a normal configuration occurs or you need to configure the SMTP server to do any sort of protection. The piece of software handling SMTP connections is known as *sendmail*. If you were to ask anyone with experience in UNIX to configure your sendmail server for you, chances are that he or she would run away, very quickly, screaming. There are volumes of sendmail documentation, many books dedicated solely to the software, and probably a few sendmail-anonymous recovery groups. If you want to use sendmail for your system, feel free—it will be a valuable job skill if you're looking for a UNIX administration job. Sendmail is considered the pinnacle of email serving software. It is powerful, robust, scalable—and very, very complex. I've found that using a product such as CommuniGate Pro results in far less sleep lost due to configuration errors and disgruntled users.

Red Hat Linux 5.x ships with sendmail "dormant," but if it has been configured to run, it will conflict with CommuniGate Pro's own version of SMTP. To disable sendmail, you can use Red Hat's runlevel editor from within X Window. The runlevel editor allows you to disable certain services that are started when the system boots. I prefer to give Linux instructions at a command prompt level; this approach enables you, the administrator, to make changes from remote terminals or from a machine that isn't necessarily capable of running X Window. To quickly remove sendmail from the startup configuration, you need to delete it from your current runlevel. If your computer is booting directly into a graphical login screen, you're running at runlevel 5. To disable sendmail from runlevel 5, simply type:

```
>rm /etc/rc.d/rc5.d/S*sendmail
```

This statement does not delete anything important; it just removes a link from the sendmail startup script to the runlevel 3 directory. If you are not running X Window at boot, you're probably at runlevel 3, so you need to change the command just slightly to remove the sendmail link:

```
>rm /etc/rc.d/rc5.d/S*sendmail
```

Both of these commands are safe to run, even if sendmail is not running on your machine. They disable sendmail if it is there and do nothing if it isn't.

With sendmail safely disabled, you still need to remove two other Linux services: the IMAP and POP servers. These services are started by a connection to the port that each occupies (143 and 110, respectively). The file that controls this configuration is the /etc/inetd.conf file. Go ahead and open the inetd.conf file now. You should be able to find a set of lines similar to the following lines, but missing the pound sign (#) in front of the three protocol lines:

```
# Pop and imap mail services et al
#
#pop-2    stream  tcp     nowait  root     /usr/sbin/tcpd ipop2d
#pop-3    stream  tcp     nowait  root     /usr/sbin/tcpd ipop3d
#imap     stream  tcp     nowait  root     /usr/sbin/tcpd imapd
```

Notice that the POP-2 protocol is also disabled. POP2 has long since been replaced by POP3 and is not used by any clients. CommuniGate Pro does not provide a POP2 server, but you shouldn't need one. To apply the changes, you need to reboot, or restart the inetd process.

To install the CommuniGate Pro archive, you need to gunzip and tar to unarchive the files.

```
>gunzip CommuniGate Pro-Intel.tar.gz
>tar -xf CommuniGate Pro-Intel.tar
```

After unarchiving, a single installer script takes care of the entire installation process.

```
>./install.sh

Copying the CommuniGate Pro application folder
Application folder has been copied to  /usr/local/sbin

Installing the start-up launcher...
```

The entire installation takes only a few seconds and prepares CommuniGate Pro to be launched every time you boot your computer. If you want to start CommuniGate Pro, you can reboot your computer or, under Linux, run its initialization script (/etc/rc.d/init.d/CommuniGate). If you're installing under Windows 95 or 98, you don't need to worry about the process I just described—simply run the self-extracting installation program. CommuniGate Pro installs itself as a startup item in the system Registry under Windows 95 and 98 and registers itself as a service on an NT server.

As soon as CommuniGate Pro is running, you need to set your Postmaster password so that you can log in to the administrative interface. Under Linux, the default location for the Postmaster account is

```
/var/CommuniGate/Accounts/postmaster.macnt/account.settings
```

During the Windows installation, you are asked to select a base directory for CommuniGate. You need to edit the same settings file as Linux users do, but the installation location depends on what you have chosen. Go ahead and open the account.settings file now. You can change the generic password in the default file to anything you want. For example, my settings file now looks like this:

```
{ UseAppPassword = YES; Password = groves2;}
```

Part

III

Ch

12

Thus my password for this example is groves2. Set the password to whatever you want, but remember, it will be used to configure your entire email system, so it should be something relatively secure. Also, passwords are case sensitive, so groves2 is not the same as Groves2. When your users call and say they can't get the mail server to accept their password, the first words out of your mouth should be, "Is your CAPSLOCK on?" The response is usually, "Hey, yeah! Could that be the problem?"

That's it as far as low-level setup of the server goes. You're now to the point of being able to set up the server through a Web browser. This process is very similar to SIMS, and you'll probably notice a lot of visual, as well as functional, similarity. The administrative port is 8010, and if you have the server up and running now, you should be able to connect. My CommuniGate Pro server is running on poisontooth.com, so I'm going to connect to `http://poisontooth.com:8010/`, as shown in Figure 12.11.

FIGURE 12.11

You use a Web interface to configure CommuniGate Pro.

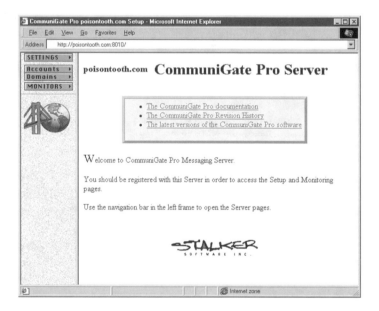

CommuniGate features a menu down the left side of the screen, just as SIMS does. This menu, however, is a hierarchical menu that can be expanded by clicking one of the four buttons: Settings, Accounts, Domains, or Monitors. Clicking on one of the lower-level buttons brings up a password dialog box. You can log in using the postmaster username and the password you set. The postmaster username is lowercase, so make sure you type it correctly. As you click around and explore the options, you are likely to be prompted more than once for your password and username. The reason is that you'll be able to create accounts with different security levels. To implement each security level, the software must authorize you for its different features. Internet Explorer offers the option to save the logins and passwords for Web pages, so this option might be useful if you'll be accessing the server's administrative features often.

CommuniGate Pro and War FTPd share a robust nature and the capability to run as a dedicated server. Similarly, they both have multiple configuration options, and, again, I do not cover everything that you can set up CommuniGate Pro to do. I do, however, cover the basic options you need to set up a successful server, and look at some of the features that you'll wonder how you lived without. Forgive me if you find a lot of this information redundant. CommuniGate Pro and the SIMS server have many similarities, so many of their elements overlap.

To start, click the General button, located under the Settings hierarchy. If you read through the SIMS section, the screen shown in Figure 12.12 should look familiar.

FIGURE 12.12
Begin by configuring CommuniGate Pro's general settings.

CAUTION
Whenever you change configuration settings in CommuniGate Pro's Web interface, be sure to click the Update button. Your settings won't be saved if you don't.

Here we can set the primary domain for the server, which should be the name that is used most commonly for the server (if your computer has multiple aliases) or just the name of the machine itself. You can also set the level of logging that the server uses when it saves information about itself. Each module of the server can have a different level of logging. You don't, for instance, have to turn the POP3 module logging up to the maximum level if you want to diagnose problems for users sending mail—you can just use the SMTP module's logging level.

Our next important setting is the router settings. If you read about the Mac OS SIMS server, you know that router settings allow you to redirect mail as it arrives at the server and to set up aliases for different user accounts. If you happen to have more than one name or alias assigned to your server and you wish to allow the server to receive email at any of its names, you need to set up some router settings. Click the Router button to configure your settings. The router settings consist of a single text box that you can use to enter a table of values, as shown in Figure 12.13.

Part
III

Ch
12

FIGURE 12.13

You can use the router settings to create account aliases.

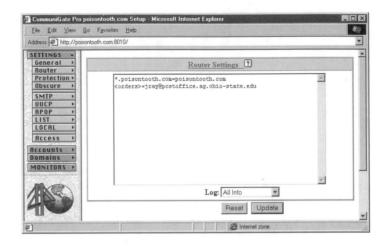

For my personal CommuniGate Pro server, which has the domain name poisontooth.com, I want to be able to receive mail at the hostname mail.poisontooth.com. For that particular case, I'm going to enter a line like this:

```
mail.poisontooth.com=poisontooth.com
```

If I want to receive email on poisontooth.com if it is sent to any of my machine's aliases, I can use a wildcard character to match any hostname:

```
*.poisontooth.com=poisontooth.com
```

This is just the beginning of what you can do with the router settings. You can also use them to redirect mail sent to a specific username to an account with a different name. I have an alias called orders, which people in my unit, including me, use when placing departmental orders. The mail that is sent to the alias account is rerouted to my account through one simple entry. There isn't even an "orders" account on my system.

```
<orders>=jray
```

The router can also redirect email to a completely different server. Just include the entire email address instead of a username.

```
<orders>=jray@postoffice.ag.ohio-state.edu
```

One last thing you might want to do is completely disable email from a domain. (This is a good anti-spam tactic.) If you are constantly getting email from a domain called meanbigfoot9.com (don't ask), you can use the router to completely remove email from this domain with this simple line:

```
meanbigfoot9.com=error
```

Always remember to click the Update button on each screen if you make any changes. Because the CommuniGate Pro interface is a Web interface, changing a field doesn't directly change anything on the server. You need to send the data to the server by submitting the form—that's what the Update button is for.

CAUTION

If your server is not behaving as you intended, check to make sure that your settings are configured correctly. It's extremely easy to fill in the fields on the Web interface and then forget to press the Update button.

You just saw one simple technique in the router section to disable email from a domain. As I mentioned, this procedure is a form of spam protection. CommuniGate Pro has other spam protection methods that are available by clicking the Protection button. You can see these options in Figure 12.14.

FIGURE 12.14
CommuniGate Pro offers additional spam protection.

The following anti-spam measures are available:

- Blacklisted IP Addresses—If you know an IP address or a range of addresses that spammers use, you can list the offending addresses here. They will not be able to use the SMTP functions of the server.

- Use Blacklisting DNS—A Blacklisting DNS server responds to a hostname lookup with either an appropriate response or an invalid IP address. In the case of the invalid IP address, the hostname that is being looked up has been "blacklisted" on the DNS server. This setting is a way of keeping a universal list of blacklisted hostnames that can be accessed by any program that can use this type of DNS. The only drawback to a blacklisting DNS is that it requires the server to make an extra hostname resolution. Depending on the number of connections being made to send email, this option might slow down mail delivery.

- Client Hosts IP Addresses—You can list your valid SMTP clients' IP addresses in this text box.

Part
III

Ch
12

When I was talking about SIMS earlier in this chapter, I mentioned that one of the problems with specifying all of your client's addresses is that if they are dialing in on a remote connection, they might have a changing IP address. CommuniGate Pro has a special way of letting you overcome this difficulty: the Authenticated Users Become Clients option. This option allows users who have connected successfully to the server using their username and password to then use the SMTP server to send email. You can choose the length of time during which they will be authenticated—from 10 seconds to an hour. This solution is a lot easier than listing all the possibilities for the IP addresses that your clients could connect to.

To look at the SMTP settings themselves, click the SMTP button in your Settings hierarchy. From this screen, shown in Figure 12.15, you can control the amount of email that CommuniGate Pro accepts from incoming connections and how it attempts to redirect the email.

FIGURE 12.15

Configure how CommuniGate Pro accepts incoming SMTP messages in this screen.

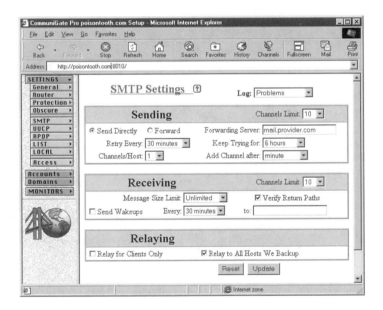

You've already seen how to protect the server by disallowing connections from parties that shouldn't have access, so you can assume that any connection accepted by the SMTP server is a valid user. The SMTP settings enable you to control how the server attempts to send and receive mail. As with every part of the CommuniGate Pro system, you can set the level of logging that you require for SMTP connections. In addition, you might want to adjust other settings for your system, depending on its speed and how you want to provide your email services. Here's a quick rundown of these settings:

■ Channel Limit—Each time you see the term *channel* in the CommuniGate Pro configuration, simply think of it as a TCP/IP connection. For each protocol, you can specify a limit to the number of simultaneous connections that the server can handle. The default for CommuniGate Pro's SMTP module is 10, which should be sufficient for medium-load networks.

- Send Directly or Forward—If you want the server to handle delivering messages to remote SMTP servers, then you need to choose the Send Directly option. If you have another SMTP server on your network, you can use that server to deliver mail and simply have CommuniGate Pro forward its SMTP queue to the other server. If you select this option, be sure to fill in the Forwarding Server field with a valid SMTP server; otherwise, mail may be lost.

- Retry Every or Keep Trying For—If the server fails to contact a remote SMTP server for delivery, by default the server does not immediately discard the messages. Email is usually a very reliable method of communications because the server is very persistent in trying to get a piece of mail to its destination. With the Retry setting, you can tell CommuniGate Pro to attempt to retransmit the message every few minutes, up until the time limit set by the Keep Trying For configuration.

- Channels/Host—If the server needs to deliver multiple messages to a particular server, it sends them one by one. This process can take quite a long time. To speed things up, the server can open multiple connections to the remote machine and send multiple messages simultaneously. The Channels/Host option puts an upper limit on the number of simultaneous connections that can exist between the server and the remote host.

- Add Channel After—Rather than immediately using all the possible connections to communicate with a host, CommuniGate Pro can ease into the load by adding a channel after a certain length of time. For example, if 10 messages are destined for the same remote server, it doesn't make sense to immediately dedicate all 10 SMTP channels to delivering those messages, because a single channel can probably deliver them in a few seconds. Instead, if they seem to be taking a long time to deliver, the server can add a channel every so often until the Channels/Host limit is reached.

- Message Size Limit—In the Receiving options, you can tell the server the upper limit that a message should be. For security reasons, it might be a good idea to set an upper limit of a few megabytes for this setting. Take into account the size of attachments that your users might get, because if you set the limit too low, messages with large attachments might be bounced. If you keep the default setting, Unlimited, you risk having your mailbox storage space filled by people who maliciously send 100MB attachments in an attempt to crash email servers.

- Verify Return Paths—Another anti-spam feature, this option allows CommuniGate Pro to discard incoming messages if the path of the message is invalid. All messages have a return path that identifies the computer from which the message originated and the servers that it passed through to reach its destination. If the return path is invalid, the message is almost certainly a forgery and is from a spammer.

Part
III

Ch
12

A few other settings in the SMTP configuration are probably not of immediate value to your system, as they are related to backup SMTP servers. If this is your first server, you probably don't have a backup server! A backup server receives messages for your primary server if it goes offline. In fact, your primary server could be connected with only a dial-in connection, and the backup server would collect messages until the primary server came online. CommuniGate Pro has a few options that allow you to send Wakeup messages to the secondary server that trigger it to transfer its email to your primary server immediately. Otherwise, depending on the backup server configuration, it could take several hours before the backup server attempts to contact the primary server. CommuniGate Pro supports the necessary *Remote Queue Starting Command* (RFC1985) to allow it to operate as a backup SMTP server.

The next CommuniGate Pro feature to consider is the RPOP, or Remote POP, module. This unique and highly useful feature is one of CommuniGate Pro's outstanding elements. RPOP allows users to access remote POP accounts through the CommuniGate Pro server. This feature can be used if the server does not have a continuous connection to the Internet and user's email is stored on a remote server that supports the POP protocol. If you have arranged with your ISP for a domainwide account, which is an account that holds all the email that is sent to it no matter what the To address is, then you can use this account to seed the entire CommuniGate Pro server. If not, then individual users can specify the POP accounts from which they want to retrieve mail, and the server automatically makes the necessary connections and retrieves the mail. Even if your server has a full-time connection, this functionality can be useful if users have several accounts but want to check their email from a centralized location. Allowing CommuniGate Pro to use RPOP to retrieve POP-based email enables the user to use all of CommuniGate Pro's features— such as the IMAP capabilities—to read all their mail. Click the RPOP button to configure the RPOP module via the screen shown in Figure 12.16.

FIGURE 12.16
CommuniGate Pro's RPOP module is one of the software's unique and outstanding features.

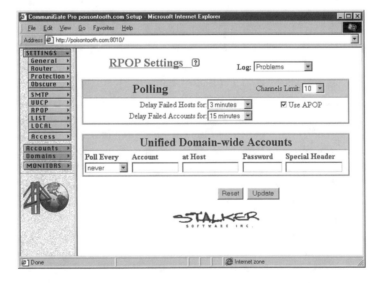

Let's take a look at some of the RPOP settings:

- Delay Failed Hosts For or Delay Failed Accounts For—If the server attempts to connect to a remote POP server and fails, or for some reason can connect to a server, but not to a specific account, you have set a delay before it makes another attempt to retrieve the messages.

- Use APOP—This option tells CommuniGate Pro to use the APOP authentication scheme for connecting to the POP servers. The standard POP authentication uses plain-text passwords, which can be easily cracked. This setting adds some extra security if the remote POP servers support APOP.

To set up a domainwide account to be polled, you must type the appropriate POP configuration information into the fields supplied in the Unified Domain-Wide Accounts section. Here you can choose a rate at which the POP accounts are polled, their hosts, passwords, and the header that contains the real username for the email.

For domainwide accounts to work, a special configuration needs to be in place at your ISP or on another server (CommuniGate Pro itself can be used to create domainwide accounts). This server rewrites the message header for any incoming mail for a particular domain and stores it under a single account. To find the original recipient and deliver the mail, a special header is added to each message. This header is usually X-Real-To but might change from system to system. Ask the account's administrator what the header is, and specify it for each domainwide RPOP account that you create. You must be in the User manager portion of CommuniGate Pro to configure individual RPOP accounts for users. We'll get there shortly.

Now you can click the Access button to view the access settings, shown in Figure 12.17. This screen simply lets you configure the number of channels that each module can use.

FIGURE 12.17
The access settings let you limit the number of channels you want clients to use.

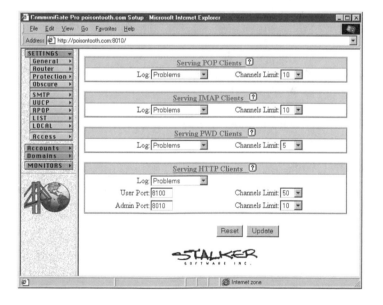

If you plan on having a high-volume server, you probably want to increase the number of simultaneous connections that can be made to the server. If not, the default settings should be fine. Increasing the number of connections can lead to a higher usage of system resources, so don't immediately put everything to its highest number setting—just in case. On a mail server of more than 1,000 accounts, you rarely have more than five or so simultaneous connections. Don't equate the number of connections to the number of users on your system. A connection usually lasts only a few seconds; you will probably never need to allow the maximum number of channels.

Much of the "meat" of the CommuniGate Pro server is accessed through the Accounts screen. Most of your configuration work takes place here. Click the Accounts button now, and you should see a list of all of the users on your system, as shown in Figure 12.18.

FIGURE 12.18
Use this screen to create and edit your user accounts.

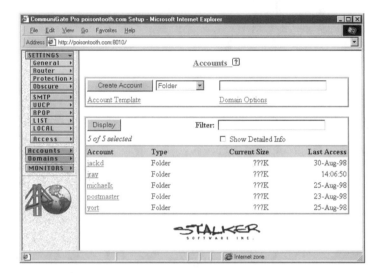

In the figure, I've already set up several email accounts on my system. To create an account, type the username for the new account in the first field, select whether you want to create a folder account or a text mailbox, and then click the Create Account button.

Why would I want a folder account?

The difference between folder accounts and text mailboxes is simple. Folders store your mail in a folder, whereas a text mailbox is a single text file on the system. The reason to choose a folder account is that it enables you to use features like the IMAP server to create subfolders and sort your mail. If you do not create a folder, then the server has no place to create other mail folders and won't be as useful. If you intend to access the user data files directly, create folder accounts. This approach leads to a much cleaner and more organized Accounts directory.

Accounts that have been created are listed immediately below the Account creation section. You can easily see the last time users logged in to the system and how much space they are using. If you have a large number of users, then you can use the Filter field and Display button to show only those users who match a certain substring. If you've just created an account, click the username to display the configuration options that are available for that user. I've clicked my username, jray, and have brought up my configuration screen, shown in Figure 12.19.

Be sure to immediately type in a real name for your user and then click the Update button to save the changes. About the time you have 50,000 accounts and are trying to figure out who the mrsmith account belongs to, you'll be glad you did. (Yes, I'm repeating what I said in the configuration of SIMS—I'm glad you're paying attention!)

FIGURE 12.19

Clicking on an individual user brings up that user's configuration information.

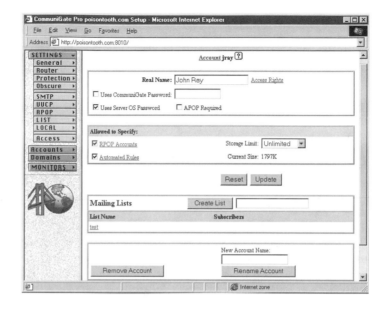

Now you get to the good stuff. From the user configuration screen, you can do four very important tasks:

- Set Access Rights—The Access Rights link lets you set how much of the server the user has the right to control. For large servers, it is very nice to be able to allow multiple administrators to control the system. We often hire interns to help us keep up with user account additions and changes, and we'd rather not let them use our personal administrative accounts. This feature allows you to give certain privileges to other people so that you don't have to set up everything yourself. By default, a user account has no special access rights, so if you desire to be all powerful, you don't need to change a thing.

- Configure RPOP Accounts—Remember how you set up domainwide accounts that fed email to the entire system? But you still haven't seen how an individual user can have remote POP accounts that are retrieved. This feature enables you to do so.

- Make Automated Rules—One of my favorite features of CommuniGate Pro is the automated rules feature. If you've ever set up your email client to filter messages to certain mailboxes, then you should have a basic understanding of what the rules do. They can automatically store mail in certain folders, delete garbage email, and even forward messages automatically to other accounts. When automated rules are used with the IMAP server, you get all the benefits of rules on your client, but they are available everywhere! I have a set of rules that moves mail from various lists to appropriate mailboxes. Because the rules exist on the server itself, I don't need to create any sort of custom configuration of my client software. Wherever I go, the mail is presorted and waiting for me. A pet peeve that I have with most email clients (well, all that I've used) is that they report incoming messages even if they have been filed. So, whenever my Web server sends me a status report (which is quite frequently), even though the message is immediately filed in a Reports mailbox, my client still tells me that I have new mail. I prefer to be able to have unimportant email delivered to mailboxes without being constantly notified that it is happening. The combination of CommuniGate Pro, automated rules, and IMAP make this system a reality.

■ Create List—This feature is the biggie. CommuniGate Pro has a full mailing list system that is both powerful and easy to use. Any UNIX user who is familiar with the intricacies of trying to configure majordomo or listserv will want to check this out. With as little as two or three clicks, you can create a mailing list and have it ready to use. Mailing lists, as I discussed earlier, are a way of distributing a discussion through email. Lists can have subscribers, owners, or moderators and can usually deliver their information in several formats. CommuniGate Pro provides all these features, plus an excellent interface for configuring them.

Wow, quite a bit can be done in the user configuration screen! Let's go ahead and take a more detailed look at each of these options, so you can see the feature set more clearly. Start by clicking the Access Rights link, which immediately follows the Real Name field. Access rights are easy to configure, as you can see in Figure 12.20.

FIGURE 12.20

You'll use this screen when you want to grant users access rights.

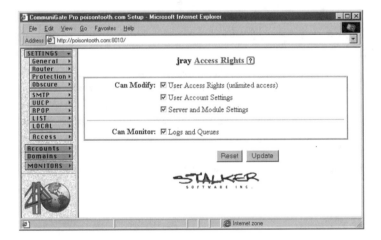

Three levels of access enable the user to modify settings on the server:

■ User Access Rights—Lets the user configure everything, including access levels for other users. If this option is checked, the account is a full, unlimited administrative account.

■ User Account Settings—Gives access to account creation and modification, but no other server settings. If other people are handling account creation for you, you probably want to give them this level of access.

■ Server and Module Settings—Everything we've looked at to this point (SMTP settings, RPOP configuration, and so on) falls under this category. Giving a user the ability to modify these settings enables him or her to modify the basic settings controlling the protocols that the server supports. Give this control only to co-administrators or other trusted users.

You also have the option of letting users have access to the Logs and Queues. If you select the Logs and Queue setting, the user will be able to monitor the server operation. The one tiny caveat here is the logs may very well contain plain-text versions of account passwords from POP3 connections. Don't assume that this setting is safe for anyone unless you've configured your logs to not store any sort of login information. When you are finished with your Access Rights settings, click the Update button to immediately apply the changes.

> **CAUTION**
>
> Remember, whenever you change configuration settings in CommuniGate Pro's Web interface, you must click the Update button. If you don't, your settings won't be saved.

Moving right along, suppose you want to specify a few remote POP accounts that your user will have retrieved. Click the RPOP Accounts hyperlink to bring up the configuration screen shown in Figure 12.21.

FIGURE 12.21

Configure remote POP accounts in this screen.

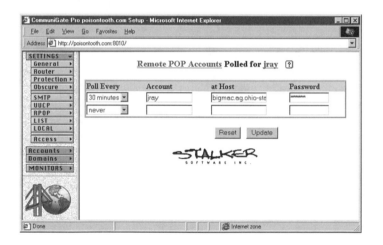

Nothing too complicated here—just some basic POP account settings. You can select the rate at which the POP account is polled, the account name (this entry is your username for your POP account), the POP3 server, and your password. Click Update to save your changes. You can use the same techniques to add more accounts.

When you're ready for something a bit more interesting, click back to the main user account configuration screen and follow the Automated Rules link. You will be taken to an interim screen that allows you to create a new rule and prioritize it. A higher priority means that the rule set is processed before rules with lower priorities. You can also delete and edit existing rules. I'm not providing a screenshot here because the interface should be self-explanatory, and the most important portion of the Automated Rules configuration is the definition of the rules themselves. Go ahead and create a rule set and then click the Edit link for that rule to bring up the rule programming screen. In Figure 12.22, I've set up a rule that discards messages from a certain address.

Part
III

Ch
12

FIGURE 12.22

Tired of spam? You can configure CommuniGate Pro to discard email from known spammers.

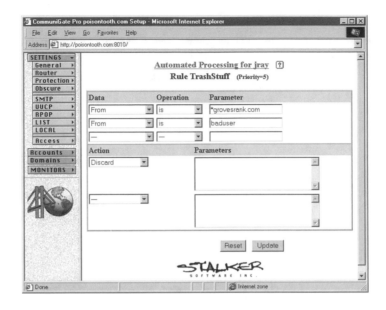

Creating new rules is very simple. You simply select a portion of the message to look at (From, Subject, and so on) from the drop-down menu under Data and then select a comparison operation from the Operation menu. Now you need to add something to the Parameter field. You can use wildcards if you don't want to specify an exact match. The final step is to select an Action to be performed on the piece of mail that is being processed. Actions include forwarding mail, deleting mail, storing it in a mailbox, and so on—everything you're used to seeing in standard email filter programs. In the Parameter field, you may need to enter data that will be used by the Action. For example, if you are forwarding or redirecting the message, you need to enter the destination addresses in the action Parameter field. If you need more rules to fully set up your action, you simply click the Update button and you will be given a new blank rule that you can fill in as well as another action that can be performed. If you aren't sure how you can use this feature, here's an example: You want to discard email from users named advertisement, but only if it comes from adomain.com. However, you want to accept other email from the adomain.com domainemail. In this case, you would set up the first rule to look for the name advertisement in the From field. The corresponding action for the first rule is to continue processing (because we haven't arrived at any conclusion about what to do with the message yet). You can then write a rule that matches the domain adomain.com, also in the From field. Finally, in this second rule, you would discard the message. You should be able to develop sets of rules that can handle just about any sort of filtering you need.

The final user account option is the configuration of mail lists. The mailing list manager has a very extensive configuration but creates a usable list by clicking a single button. Mailing lists are controlled by their owners; that's why you're configuring this option under a user account, rather than in another module. If you are an administrator, you can also access list configurations by clicking the Lists button under the Settings button hierarchy. This alternative brings you to the same configuration screen that you will be looking at shortly. To create a list, type a name for the list in the field to the right of the Create List button. Your new list shows up immediately under the Mailing Lists list. Click the list name to go to the list configuration screen. A subset of the configuration is shown in Figure 12.23.

FIGURE 12.23

CommuniGate Pro lets you configure mail lists.

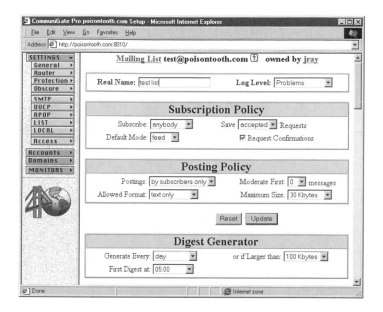

Because of the length of the configuration screen, the figure shows only a subset of the many settings. This section provides a brief overview of the various features; I'd almost need another book to describe them all.

- Subscription Policy—When a user subscribes to a list, the server does certain things when processing the subscription request. The Subscription Policy settings control these actions. You can limit a list with the Subscribe command so only people who have accounts on the CommuniGate Pro server are subscribed or so that anyone anywhere can send in a subscription request. You also have the ability to keep a log of all of the requests that are sent to the server and select the default mode that the server uses. CommuniGate Pro defines three different modes:

  - Feed mode—Messages sent to the list are immediately distributed to the list recipients.

  - Digest mode—Instead of being sent to the recipients directly, messages are held until certain conditions are met (we'll get to that shortly). At that time, a table of contents is generated, and the messages are concatenated to it. What is finally sent to the list subscribers is a large message containing all the messages that have been sent to the server since the last digest was mailed.

  - Index mode—Resembles digest mode except only a table of contents is sent to individual subscribers.

Choose whichever mode you want to set as the default for subscribers. They can later change their subscription mode if they want. One other nice feature that is offered by the subscription policy is the request confirmation. If you have selected this option, the server emails the address that is attempting to subscribe to the server and confirms that the subscription request is real. A common attack by mean, evil people is to write programs that automatically subscribe the victim to hundreds of lists. By requiring a confirmation before accepting a subscription request, CommuniGate Pro can keep your list server from being used in this sort of attack.

- Posting Policy—In addition to having a subscription policy, CommuniGate Pro also applies policies when a request to post to the list comes in. The Accept Postings configuration is the most important of the posting policies. You can tell the server to accept postings from anyone, from subscribers only, the owner only, or to run in a moderated fashion. A moderated list infers that all messages sent to the list must pass through the list owner before they are posted. The owner simply redirects the messages back to the list, and they are distributed. If you have a very sensitive mailing list, it might be wise to moderate it. A related setting is the Moderate First setting, which works only when Postings is set to From Subscribers. If you set the Moderate First selection, the server automatically moderates the first few messages that the user posts. After someone successfully posts (through the moderator) the number of messages you've chosen, that user is allowed to post freely to the list. Other policy options include limiting the size and type of messages that are distributed through the list.

- Digest Generator—Here you control how often your list generates digests. You can set the frequency of digest creation based on time or on accumulated size of messages submitted. You can also pick the time of day when the first digest is sent out.

- Bounce Processor—The bounce processor handles the way CommuniGate Pro deals with bounced messages. If a message is sent to a user on the list and bounces back to the server, the user's email server could be offline or the account may not even exist anymore. The bounce processor enables you to set a limit to the number of bounces that the server accepts from an account before suspending or removing the account from the list of subscribers. The server also maintains a count of the number of errors that have occurred for a given account. The server also sends email to accounts that have experienced an error at an interval that you specify. To clear out the error count, the user must respond to the message.

The other settings on the list configuration screen primarily customize response messages that the server uses when it sends a confirmation message to the user. The default messages should be fine for most purposes.

Now that your list is configured, how do you use it? Creating a list creates several new email addresses that you can use to communicate with the list. Here's a summary of these addresses and their functions (naturally, you substitute your actual list name and domain):

- `listname-on@yourdomain.com`—This address subscribes a new user to the list. Simply send email to the name of your list, followed by `-on`, and you'll be subscribed. Or if you're already subscribed, this address confirms your subscription mode.

- listname-subscribe@yourdomain.com—Does the same thing as the listname-on command, but the syntax is different.

- listname-feed@yourdomain.com—If you aren't subscribed to the list, this address subscribes you in the feed mode. If you are subscribed, this address switches you over to feed.

- listname-digest@yourdomain.com—Same as the preceding entry; subscribes or switches you to digest mode.

- listname-index@yourdomain.com —Subscribes or switches a subscription over to the index mode.

- listname-off@yourdomain.com—Removes you from the mailing list.

- listname-unsubscribe@yourdomain.com—Same as listname-off.

- listname-admin@yourdomain.com—You can use this address to contact the list administrator. Mail sent to this account goes to the administrator's personal account.

Given the complexity of most list servers, these commands are pretty darn simple! The CommuniGate Pro package is extremely nice because of its consistent interface and integrated features. You may think that you have now seen everything, but you still have not explored an important feature of the server: monitoring and logging.

First, take a look at the logging features (I think that the monitoring stuff is really neat, so I'm saving it for last!). Click the Monitors button in the left frame to expose the monitor and logging hierarchy. Next, click the Logs button. You should see a list of the logs on the server, similar to Figure 12.24.

FIGURE 12.24

CummuniGate Pro lets you access email logs on the server.

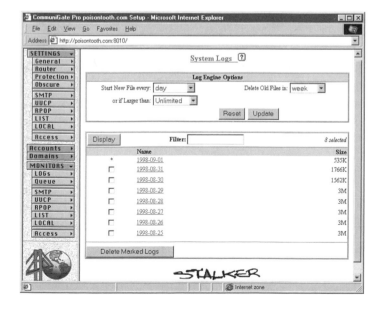

If you read the description of the SIMS server, you know that I warned you about letting your log files grow too quickly. Fortunately, CommuniGate Pro automatically handles the log file situation for you. You can tell CommuniGate Pro the maximum length of the log files to generate before it starts a new log, as well as specify how often (daily, weekly, and so on) to do so. The best option is for CommuniGate Pro to automatically delete log files after they have been on the server for a certain length of time. This approach keeps log files from eating up space on your server and growing out of control. If you're working with a limited amount of disk space, it's a pain to constantly have to log in to the server and delete log files. You can, by the way, delete files manually by selecting the check box in front of them and clicking the Delete Marked Log button. To view a log, click the name of the log file (which is set to the creation date). If the log is the current log, new additions to the log file are displayed immediately. Give it a try; it's pretty neat.

The rest of the options under the Monitors button enable you to monitor system functions. You can view SMTP activity in real time by clicking on the SMTP button, or you can track POP3, IMAP, and Web client access by clicking the Access button, as shown in Figure 12.25.

FIGURE 12.25

This screen tracks POP3, IMAP, and Web client access of an email server.

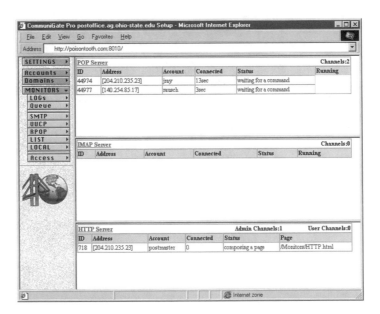

Although you view these statistics through a Web browser, it refreshes at a rate of about once every 2 or 3 seconds, fast enough to catch any connections to the server. I'm still quite impressed by this feature, because it provides better monitoring functions than some servers with dedicated configuration utilities.

Despite the promise of the IMAP protocol, I often want to access my email from a remote location. Usually I'm in front of a computer that isn't mine, and I would have no business reconfiguring the email client to point to my email account. I eventually wrote a Web-based

POP3 client called Majora that allows me to read my email through a Web interface. If you're interested in Majora, or would like a peek at the source code, it is available from `http://jray.ag.ohio-state.edu/`.

My implementation of POP3 has many limitations, and as a result, even Majora couldn't quite live up to what I needed. CommuniGate Pro filled in the gaps.

CommuniGate Pro supplies an incredible Web-based client to the email server, which is part of the entire integrated server suite. The Web server running the client is internal to CommuniGate Pro, so you don't need any extra server software for your system. The client itself is as fully featured as many desktop clients, such as Eudora or Outlook Express. It offers multiple mailboxes, the capability to move email around between mailboxes, attachment support (both receiving and sending), auto-reply vacation messages, and the list goes on. Figure 12.26 shows a sample session with the server, listing all the current email in my account.

FIGURE 12.26

You can use CommuniGate Pro as an email client, too!

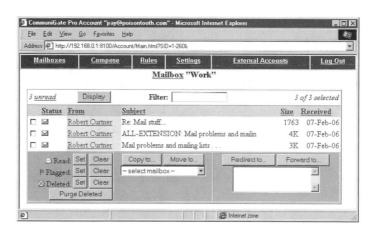

Carrying this concept one step further, CommuniGate Pro's remote POP account access allows the server to bring in all of your email to the server machine. Consequently, connecting via the Web interface enables you to access all your email, anywhere.

I've found that performing some operations under the Web interface are actually faster than trying to use a client on my own computer. For example, when I try to forward messages using Outlook Express, I select a group of messages, click Forward, and each message opens a new window so that I can specify the recipient addresses for each one. If I'm attempting to forward all the messages to another account, this process can be a bit time-consuming. Under CommuniGate Pro, I simply flag all the messages that I want to forward, supply a single forwarding address for all of them, and click the Forward To button. Because of nifty little features like this, at times I find myself using the Web interface even if I have a client ready to go on my computer.

To top all of this off, the CommuniGate Web interface is completely customizable if you know HTML. The HTML code and graphics are not internal to the server and can be changed as easily as editing any Web page.

In summary, CommuniGate Pro is an excellent server that you can use to expand a Windows 95 or 98 machine or run as a dedicated server under Linux or Windows NT. If you have a new model Macintosh, a version of CommuniGate Pro is available for the Mac OS X Server system software. SIMS, however, remains a free product, whereas you have to pay for CommuniGate Pro.

Web Services

You have now looked at file sharing and dabbled in email servers—so what's left? Web servers, of course! Even if you do not like the Web, it is far too important to ignore. Running a Web site is a very important means of promoting yourself or your business. Although the phrase "everyone has to have a Web page" has become a tired cliché, Web sites do reach thousands of people, and many people begin their searches for products or services on the Web. If you plan to run a high-volume Web site, you'd probably be best served with a dedicated solution running under UNIX or NT. If you want to run a server from your Macintosh, you can do it, but you need to dedicate a machine to the task.

An Internet discussion in which I recently took part claimed that the Mac OS is the most secure serving solution because of its single-user nature. There are no accounts to crack, for example. Several contests were run to test a particular server's security, and the Mac proved uncrackable at first; later, however, it *was* broken into, and its Web pages were modified. The server software itself was not insecure; rather, an extension to the server was configured incorrectly. Subsequently, the argument was raised that the single-user nature of the Mac OS explains why it is *not* a secure server solution— because Mac OS isn't a multiuser system, each program has full root access to the system and, if misconfigured, can erase anything on the drive. My disagreement with this statement is that the same thing applies to any Web server: If you configure the server incorrectly, you can lose data on any platform.

Setting up a common gateway interface (CGI), which is a program that processes data and dynamically generates results for a Web server, requires the CGI to run with permissions that will not enable it to access parts of the system that it shouldn't. If the system administrator mistakenly sets the program to run as the root or Administrator user, then any misbehavior by the software could result in anything at all—from creating files in directories they shouldn't be allowed in or erasing your entire file system. Security depends entirely on the software you are running and how it is configured. In fact, configuring server software to run under NT or UNIX is easier to louse up than configuring the software to run under the Mac OS. Developers creating software for multiuser systems rely on the administrator to correctly set the user who will run the software. Under Mac OS there is no question of which user will be running the software, so it is developed to be secure from the start, not to rely on the security (or lack thereof) of the underlying operating system.

Web servers are usually rather easy to set up because the Web serving protocol itself is so simple: A request is made for a resource, and if it's available, it is returned. The complexity of httpd servers appears when they are extended to offer additional features such as database access and online secure ordering. You can spend minutes setting up a Web server but hours learning to administrate all the features you'll eventually use. The next section considers how to get a Web server up and running on your client platforms.

Delivering the World Wide Web Using Mac OS

As you've seen, Mac OS already comes with a built-in Web server called Web Sharing. In System 8.0 and 8.1, this server was relatively simple. The newly released System 8.5 boasts several new features, including the capability to run plug-ins to add extra functionality to the server. However, Web Sharing remains a low-volume solution to Web serving and should not be used in a high-traffic Web site. You may have also noticed that the NetPresenz server that was provided with FTP service in Chapter 11, "Exploring Client OS File Server Capabilities," also has a built-in Web server. This is another low-volume serving solution, which can't reasonably handle more than a few simultaneous connections.

The big cheese of the Mac OS Web serving world is WebSTAR from StarNine, Inc. WebSTAR is a very-easy-to-administrate server that can handle medium- to high-load serving from a dedicated Mac OS computer. If you don't like the FTP solution provided with NetPresenz, WebSTAR even provides its own FTP plug-in service. You can download a demonstration version of WebSTAR from the StarNine Web site at `http://www.starnine.com/`.

WebSTAR is extremely simple to get up and running. After installing the software, you will have a new directory called WebSTAR (appropriately enough!) on your computer. Inside this directory are your two most important tools for running the server. First, you have the server itself, which starts with a simple double-click of the WebSTAR icon. At startup (and, if it is your first time running the product, typing in a serial number), you are greeted with the WebSTAR log screen, shown in Figure 12.27.

Part
III

Ch
12

FIGURE 12.27
When you run WebSTAR for the first time, it displays an activity log.

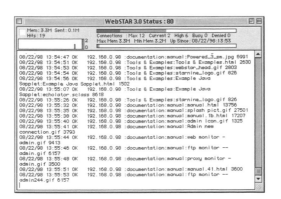

Here you can watch as thousands of eager Web browsers flow to your site. The screen shows a variety of status information about the server, including the amount of memory that is in use. As more people connect and more services are put into use, memory consumption increases. Being a Mac user, you should be familiar with increasing the amount of memory that the OS gives to a certain application. This display should help you determine whether you need to dedicate more memory to WebSTAR. You can also monitor connections as they occur and fine-tune the resources that the server uses. By default, the server starts by allowing 12 simultaneous connections. Our UNIX Web site serves more than a million hits a month but rarely has more than 2 or 3 simultaneous connections, so 12 should be more than enough. Although most capabilities are provided through the administrative interface, you can (and need to) perform some tasks from the server. As soon as you start the server, immediately set a password for the administrative interface by going to the Edit menu and selecting the Admin Password option. This password will be used for administrating the server with the separate WebSTAR Admin program. Under the Options menu, you can set a few simple options that might be handy:

- Verbose Messages—If you want more logging information than WebSTAR provides by default, you can pump it up a bit by turning on the Verbose Messages.

- Suspend Logging—Turns off the logging features of the Web server. If, for some reason you want to stop tracking server messages , select this option.

- Hide Window in Background—Keeps the WebSTAR monitor window hidden as you use other software on the computer. This option does not affect the operation of the server at all.

- Refuse New Web Connections—Disables Web service.

- Restrict CGIs to CGI-BIN—Rather than allowing CGIs to run from any place in the server directory structure, this option allows them to run only from the CGI-BIN directory. This restriction is a good idea on most multiuser systems for security reasons, though I question its necessity under Mac OS. Still, it's better to be organized than to have software running from all over.

- Flush Cache—WebSTAR keeps frequently retrieved documents in cache memory for speedy access. If you want to delete everything in the cache, choose the Flush Cache option.

That's about everything you can do from the server itself. If you haven't already, try connecting to your Web page. If your network is up and running, the WebSTAR Web page should pop up. This initial page is stored as Default.html within the server directory. You can edit that file to include your home page, add the rest of your linked HTML files, and bingo! Your Web site is online!

Now that you're online, you're still going to need a bit more control over what's going on with the server. Don't worry; there's a lot more that you can do, and it's just as simple as everything you have done so far. When you start the WebSTAR Admin program, it prompts you for the server you want to control and for the administrative password. You can run this program from any Mac on your network and have full remote administration and monitoring capability. When you connect to your server, monitors for all the server's services appear on your screen.

By default, WebSTAR runs a Proxy Server, an FTP Server, and the main Web Server. Because the focus here is on providing Web service, I have disabled the services I don't want to use. If you want to do this yourself, quit both the server and the administration utility and open the Plug-Ins folder that is inside your main WebSTAR folder. Drag the Proxy and FTP plug-ins out of the folder to disable them.

N O T E   The WebSTAR server architecture works on the idea of plug-ins. Rather than requiring a separate program to run for each new feature you want to add, you can add a plug-in, which extends the feature set of the server. This approach is far more efficient than the context switching that has to take place when running separate software.

After you remove these extra features, restart the server and reconnect to the Web server with the WebSTAR admin software. You'll now only see a Web server monitor. This monitor offers a subset of the features of monitor on the main server but still allows you to get a good idea of what is going on with your server. The menu choices under the Options menu mirror the choices in the server's Option menu, and their functions are identical.

Now that you're connected and talking, you can actually control some of the basic operations of the server. To do so, select Server Settings from the Edit menu. If you've removed the FTP and Proxy plug-ins as I have, your interface should be very much like Figure 12.28. If not, the Proxy and FTP services will be listed in the hierarchy.

FIGURE 12.28

If you disabled the FTP and Proxy plug-ins, your status screen should look like this.

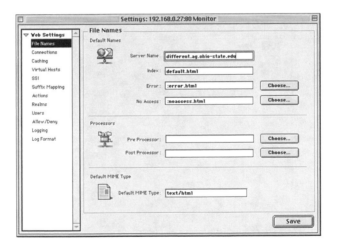

Part
III

Ch
12

There's a lot you can do with WebSTAR, so take a quick look at the important stuff. Here are some of the settings you might need to get the server working the way you'd like:

- File Names—This is the initial screen that is displayed when you are setting up the server; you should be seeing it now. One of the first settings you might need to change is the server name, which is the name that the server uses to identify itself to clients. For my server, which is named leviathan.ag.ohio-state.edu, I actually want it to identify it as www.ag.ohio-state.edu, which is an alias to leviathan. To do this, I would enter the full www alias name in the Server Name field. You can't just pick any value for the name, however; it *must* be registered with a name server. In this dialog box, you can also set the files that are displayed when clients connect to the machine. The Index file is the initial file shown when connecting to the base server URL, such as http://different.ag.ohio-state.edu. Error messages can be configured in the Error field, and when a user is locked out of the system, you can choose what message he or she sees in the No Access setting field. Each of these settings should point to an HTML file, so you'll need to be familiar with HTML or have a decent HTML editor on your machine to customize the settings. Other settings include a Pre and Post processor that can provide extra services to the client and server end of operations by running before and after a client Web connection. Last, the default MIME type is set to return an HTML document. Because you are presumably serving HTML from your server, there is no need for this setting to change.

■ Connections—The Connections settings, shown in Figure 12.29, allow you to configure the load that the server can handle. Remember that increasing the capability of a server to handle more connections means something has to change (otherwise, all servers would immediately be able to serve the maximum number of connections). This change usually results in a consumption of more memory and an increase in the number of processes that are listening and responding to connection requests.

FIGURE 12.29

Configure the number of active connections in this dialog box.

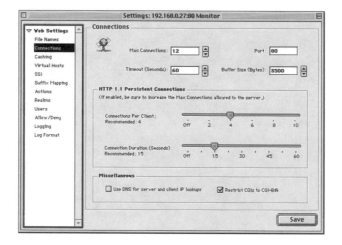

The Web server is, by default, configured to handle 12 simultaneous connections. From this dialog box, you can increase the Max Connections setting to as many as 500. Five hundred is an incredibly impractical number, but it *is* available if you really think you're going to get that many connections at a single time. You can also change the port that server operates on and the timeout before the server releases a connection. As I mentioned previously, a potential denial-of-service attack could be launched on the server if this number is set too high. If a hacker writes a program to open as many connections to the server as possible, that attack can use all of the server's available resources and service is denied. Keep the timeout set at 60 seconds, or even lower. Remember, HTTP 1.1 supports persistent connections, which enables a client Web browser to transfer several requests during a single connection. You can set a limit to the length of time of these persistent connections and the maximum number of simultaneous connections that are allowed per client. One last, very important setting is the Use DNS for Server and Client IP Lookups option. If you check this option, your server resolves all

IP addresses into hostnames for the log. Although this feature might sound good, it can cause serious slowdown. Each unique connection to the server causes WebSTAR to contact a remote DNS server to find the hostname. In this situation, you are entirely dependent on the speed of your network and name server to keep up with incoming Web requests.

- Virtual Hosting—Because WebSTAR is a full HTTP 1.1 server, it also has virtual hosting capabilities. You can easily set up virtual hosts by setting a hostname, IP address, and root folder for each of the hosts that you want to create. In the sample server shown in Figure 12.30, I've created a virtual host for bigmac.ag.ohio-state.edu and abyss.ag.ohio-state.edu.

FIGURE 12.30

You can create a virtual host for your Web server.

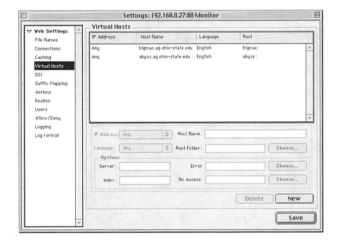

Each virtual host behaves like a separate server. You need to set the options for the virtual hosts so that they all have their own unique home pages and error files. If you've assigned multiple IP addresses to your computer, then the virtual hosting does not have to operate based on HTTP 1.1 and is compatible with older browsers. This is a waste of IP addresses, however, and should be avoided. Still, both IP addresses in the figure are configured identically, except for one setting. For IP-based virtual hosts, the IP Address selection is set to the IP address for the server. For HTTP 1.1–based virtual hosting, set it to Any.

Other features (and there are many) of WebSTAR include a full user management system to restrict access to portions of your server; an SSI, or Server Side Include, option that dynamically changes the contents of Web pages on-the-fly as they are being served; a plug-in for connectivity to Apple's dynamic WebObjects development environment; full support for CGIs written in any language, and on and on. The WebSTAR interface is one of the cleanest and most consistent interfaces I've seen. It enables you to get a Web server up and running quickly and expand its capabilities as you become more familiar with the software. WebSTAR even carries its easy-to-use administrative interface to the Web by allowing most of its features to be configured from within a Web browser. This full-featured server is ready for real-world serving solutions. Because WebSTAR is running on the Macintosh, it is an ideal choice for publishing and print houses that have Macintosh clients. Artists can connect to the server without any additional tools and quickly change the content while the server is running. However, like most Mac applications that must take on a heavy load, WebSTAR must be used on a machine that is dedicated to serving Web pages. However, if you are planning on serving a low-volume site, it will happily coexist in the background as you run other applications. The speediness of a Web site is one of the first things a person notices, your operation might look better if you give WebSTAR its own dedicated server machine.

Delivering the World Wide Web Using Windows

OmniHTTPd, the Windows Web server that we examine next, is from Omnicron Technologies and has won recognition for its ease of use and functionality. Two versions of the software are available: a free version and a professional version. Because the free version is actually very similar to the professional version, this section focuses on the free software. (After all, free is good!) The professional version offers a bit more in the way of features and comes at a low cost, so be sure to check it out if you need more than what OmniHTTPd offers for free. Either way, you get a high-performance Web server that runs under Windows 95 or 98 and as a service under NT. You can download OmniHTTPd from http://www.omnicron.ab.ca/.

OmniHTTPd arrives as a self-extracting archive, and the painless installation process does not require any configuration of the server until you get to the last step. And then all it does is ask whether you want to run the server at startup. If you do, click Yes and OmniHTTPd will start serving each time you start up your computer. To start OmniHTTPd, click the Start menu, choose Programs, and then select the OmniHTTPd group. There should be a single executable program controls the entire Web server. If the server is already running (check your taskbar's system tray for a small globe icon), you should click its icon in the tool tray to access the configuration screen. Running the executable again from the Start menu might result in multiple copies of the application running, which could mean that none of the copies will work.

If OmniHTTPd is running, you're serving! Open the administration interface to see how you can configure the server. The first thing to notice about the server is that very few settings can be changed from the menus. The Admin menu has a few features that are useful, however:

- Accept Connections—If you want to disable your server completely without shutting it down, deselect the Accept Connections menu option.
- Available—Without shutting down the server, you can warn people that it is unavailable. Deselect the Available menu option, and now Web browsers will see a Site Is Unavailable message when they connect to your server. You might use this feature if you're changing your Web pages and don't want anyone to access them until their ready.
- Shutdown Server—Does the obvious: shuts down the Web server.

The initial status screen shown when you start the server is minimal, as you can see in Figure 12.31.

You can monitor the amount of data sent to and from your server, as well as maintain a count of the total number of requests.

Now the good stuff. Select Properties from the Admin menu, and you are ready to configure the low-level server settings. Figure 12.32 shows the default Properties window with the Network tab selected. From here you can select the number of simultaneous connections accepted by the server, the port number of server, and various server timeouts.

FIGURE 12.31

When you run OmniHTTPd, the program window is minimal.

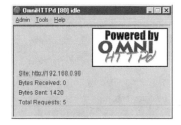

FIGURE 12.32

Choose Properties from the Admin menu and click the Network tab to access these settings.

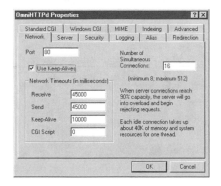

Note that the timeouts are specified in milliseconds, not seconds. The default times are 45,000 milliseconds, or 45 seconds, which is entirely reasonable. You also have the option of allowing Keep-Alives or persistent connections. The default settings should be fine, but you might want to enable keep-alive connections.

The Server tab provides a few more settings that you can use to personalize the server, as shown in Figure 12.33.

FIGURE 12.33

The Server tab lets you personalize your Web server.

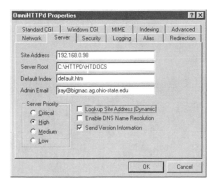

Part

III

Ch

12

As with the Mac server covered earlier, you need to set a name for the server if it is not the default name for the server's IP address. The server's root directory, or where the root-level HTML files are located, is also selectable. By default, this entry is set to HTDOCS within the directory where OmniHTTPd was installed. The Default Index file is the name of the file that is served when only a directory name is specified. Here's an example: If you have a directory called mypages and you want to serve it from a URL like http://www.yourdomain.com/ mypages, you need to tell the server what file to display by default for the mypages directory. Providing this information is precisely what this setting does. Under most UNIX servers, and in OmniHTTPd, this file is index.htm or index.html.

The other settings here adjust the amount of processing time OmniHTTPd is given (Server Priority). You can also ask OmniHTTPd to dynamically determine its own site address if you are on a connection where the address changes (such as a dial-in connection). Do *not* enable this option if you are on a connection with a static IP address. More important, and I stress this with each server I discuss, do *not* enable DNS Name resolution unless it is absolutely necessary. DNS resolutions can take a great deal of time and put an extra load on the network. Most people want to track hostnames for the purpose of logging, but most server statistics programs will also resolve hostnames for you, so your server does not have to do that job.

Another nice feature offered by OmniHTTPd is the aliasing capability. Click the Alias tab to view the aliases that are set on the server. By default, only the ICONS alias is entered, as shown in Figure 12.34.

FIGURE 12.34

You can use the alias feature to organize your Web site without creating a complex directory structure.

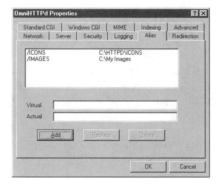

Aliasing allows administrators to organize their Web site's files without creating a nasty directory structure, which, in turn, would translate to a nasty URL for the end user. If you want to store all your images in a directory called My Images but then have them accessible to the Web server through a simple /IMAGES URL, you can set an alias to the directory that contains them. Simply put, this technique is a way to create the equivalent of a Windows shortcut, only have it apply to Web space rather than the Windows file system.

Feel free to explore the other options that OmniHTTPd has to offer. You don't need most of them to run your server successfully. OmniHTTPd is fast, easy to configure, and takes up very little in the way of system resources. If you want to run a Web server and don't want to take up tens of megabytes of space with something like Windows NT's Internet Information Server (IIS; of course, you'd also need to be running Windows NT for that), then take a serious look at

OmniHTTPd. A few things that are missing from the free OmniHTTPd version are included in the professional edition, for example, Virtual Hosting. If you're interested in Virtual Hosting, test the professional version. It is priced far below competing products and, like the base OmniHTTPd product, is a simple, elegant, Windows-based Web server.

What about IIS? I've Heard That It Is the Windows Web Server?

IIS, or Internet Information Server, is a free Web server that runs under Windows NT. It offers reliable, fast, and secure service. You'll learn a little more about IIS in Chapter 13, "Establishing Dedicated Servers." For many cases, however, IIS is overkill, and a simpler solution, like OmniHTTPd, may be more appropriate.

Delivering the World Wide Web Using Linux

So, you've installed Red Hat 5.x on you computer and you want to run a high-performance Web server and you want to do it now. Guess what—you're already doing it. If there haven't been any modifications to your system since Red Hat was installed, then you're already running Apache, which was named the most popular and fastest growing Web server on the planet in a recent survey.

Apache has gained its popularity because it is free and the source code is available, much like Linux itself. It is a grassroots effort that has gained much attention in the press and among IT professionals everywhere. Unfortunately, you are going to have to look at some configuration files again to do some tweaking, but you should actually already be up and serving. Try connecting to a Linux Red Hat machine through a Web browser; you should see the It Worked! page if Apache is installed correctly. The latest versions of Apache and extra add-on modules for it are available from `http://www.apache.org/`.

Within the past few months, Apache has been ported to work under the Win32 architecture, allowing it to run under Windows 95, 98, and NT. I chose not to discuss Apache for Windows, because my guess is that if you currently use a heavily graphical operating system, you probably would be most comfortable using applications that were also graphical. I encourage you to take a look at Apache because it is a very solid serving solution. Apache has even been ported to the Mac OS in a product called WebTop. The interface, however, still leaves much to be desired.

Here's what is running so far: By default, the Red Hat server directory is `/home/httpd/html`. Inside that directory, a file named `index.html` contains the default Web page for your server. This page is the root Web page that is returned when a client first visits your site. It should provide links to other files and so on. User accounts are also immediately accessible to the Web if they have a public_html directory created and it is world readable and executable. To create a directory for a user named username to serve his or her Web pages from, do this as the root user:

```
>cd ~username
>mkdir public_html
>chmod 755 public_html
>chown username public_html
```

This will change to the user's home directory, create the public_html directory, set it to the appropriate permission, and make sure that it is owned by the user, rather than by the root. Now, to serve from that directory, all the user needs to do is create an `index.html` file that holds his or her Web page inside of public_html. The page is then immediately accessible from the root server URL, followed by `/~username`. For example, my user account on www.ag.ohio-state.edu is jray, so my home page's URL is `http://www.ag.ohio-state.edu/~jray`.

Because you already have a fully functioning server, there's little else you need to do, but there's a great deal that you can do. The Red Hat Apache configuration is stored in the `/etc/httpd/conf` directory. Three files there roughly equate to these configurations:

- `httpd.conf`—Server configuration settings. Control the basic features of the server, number of connections, and so on.
- `access.conf`—Set privileges for the directories on the server. Define what can and can't happen within a particular directory structure, such as CGI execution.
- `srm.conf`—Define MIME types and the default document names that are served. For example, the index.html file is the default name for a file served when only a directory name is given.

Go ahead and take a look at some of the more important options that you can configure in the `httpd.conf` file. The file supplied with Red Hat is a bit lengthy, so I'm just showing a few excerpts from it. I've left in various comments from the original file because they do a good job of explaining the settings.

```
# ServerType is either inetd, or standalone.

ServerType standalone

# If you are running from inetd, go to ServerAdmin.

# Port: The port the standalone listens to. For ports < 1023, you will
# need httpd to be run as root initially.

Port 80

# HostnameLookups: Log the names of clients or just their IP numbers
#   e.g.   www.apache.org (on) or 204.62.129.132 (off)
# You should probably turn this off unless you are going to actually
# use the information in your logs, or with a CGI.  Leaving this on
# can slow down access to your site.
HostnameLookups off
```

The default setting for your server is standalone. If you are planning on serving a large number of requests, then this configuration is appropriate. If the Web server is secondary and you don't want it eating up your system resources, you might want to switch it to an inetd configuration. An inetd server starts only when requests come in on the Web server port (also shown here to be 80, as expected). This is extremely inefficient for a high-volume server because it has to start a copy of the software each time a connection occurs, which takes some time. You need to edit your /etc/inetd.conf file to include an entry for the HTTP service. You can also see that Hostname Lookups are off. As I mentioned with the other servers, this option can be very costly to enable. My very first experience with Apache was under a UNIX-like OS that didn't support multithreaded hostname lookups. Consequently, only a single name could be processed at a time, and if it took 2 minutes for the DNS server to respond with a "name not found" message, then the entire server was frozen for 2 minutes. Apache would accept connections and then just sit there while the OS waited for the name server. Obviously, this situation is a worst case scenario, but it should still demonstrate the risky nature of the setting.

Let's continue on a bit further in the http.conf file:

```
# ServerName allows you to set a host name which is sent back to clients for
# your server if it's different than the one the program would get (i.e. use
# www instead of the host's real name).

ServerName www.ag.ohio-state.edu
```

If you have multiple aliases for your server and the name you want your Web server to go by is one of them (as opposed to being the actual hostname), you should set the Servername option to the appropriate name of your Web server. If you don't, the server responds to clients under its true hostname.

```
# Timeout: The number of seconds before receives and sends time out

Timeout 300

# KeepAlive: Whether or not to allow persistent connections (more than
# one request per connection). Set to Off to deactivate.

KeepAlive On

# MaxKeepAliveRequests: The maximum number of requests to allow
# during a persistent connection. Set to 0 to allow an unlimited amount.
# We recommend you leave this number high, for maximum performance.

MaxKeepAliveRequests 100

# KeepAliveTimeout: Number of seconds to wait for the next request

KeepAliveTimeout 15
```

Apache, like the other servers discussed here, lets you specify timeout periods for the connections. If you have many Web connections that seem to stay connected forever (you can monitor this possibility by running netstat from the command line), you might want to lower the timeout period to 60 seconds or so. You can also shut off the persistent connections, which are part of the HTTP 1.1 spec. This may keep your server from being overwhelmed by connections that never end, but it also means a slower loading time for people accessing your Web pages. If you do leave KeepAlive on (which I'd recommend), you can set an upper limit on the number of requests that can be made during a connection, as well as a timeout period for between requests.

Now, take a look at some of the settings that determine how your server is going to perform under a load.

```
# Server-pool size regulation.  Rather than making you guess how many
# server processes you need, Apache dynamically adapts to the load it
# sees -- that is, it tries to maintain enough server processes to
# handle the current load, plus a few spare servers to handle transient
```

Part
III

Ch
12

```
# load spikes (e.g., multiple simultaneous requests from a single
# browser).

MinSpareServers 8
MaxSpareServers 20

# Number of servers to start -- should be a reasonable ballpark figure.

StartServers 10

# Limit on total number of servers running, i.e., limit on the number
# of clients who can simultaneously connect -- if this limit is ever
# reached, clients will be LOCKED OUT, so it should NOT BE SET TOO LOW.
# It is intended mainly as a brake to keep a runaway server from taking
# Unix with it as it spirals down...

MaxClients 150

# MaxRequestsPerChild: the number of requests each child process is
#   allowed to process before the child dies.

MaxRequestsPerChild 100
```

In this portion of the configuration, you can set up the number of servers that are started when Apache is initialized (StartServers), as well as a limit on the number of simultaneous server processes that can run (MaxClients). Apache is an intelligent server; if it needs 150 processes running to handle the load, it starts them. If the load decreases, Apache decreases the number of running processes accordingly. Apache also keeps a pool of Spare Servers to handle sudden spikes in the number of requests.

A particularly nice feature of Apache is the MaxRequestsPerChild setting. This entry limits the number of requests that a process can fill before it is killed. The main reason that computers crash is because of memory leaks in programs that are running, or because of a problem with the operating system itself. Over time, more and more memory is used up until the operating system no longer has memory for its own operations. Of course, all software developers try their best to make sure their software doesn't leak, but inevitably, there are always a few bugs. To get past this potential problem, Apache kills its server processes after they have filled a certain number of requests. This process clears out all of the memory that they were using, thus rendering most memory leaks harmless.

The last setting to look at is the creation of Virtual Hosts, using HTTP 1.1 under Apache. This process is really quite simple, and I use the feature constantly to create custom hostnames for users' Web sites. To create a virtual host, you use the Apache Virtual Host directive, like this:

```
<VirtualHost michaelk.poisontooth.com>
ServerAdmin michaelk@poisontooth.com
DocumentRoot /home/michaelk/public_html
ServerName michaelk.poisontooth.com
ErrorLog /home/michaelk/logs/error.log
TransferLog /home/michaelk/logs/transfer.log
</VirtualHost>
```

Here I've created a virtual host called michaelk.poisontooth.com with an administrator michaelk@poisontooth.com. The server's root directory is different from the main server's root directory, which I have chosen to set to the same directory as the michaelk user's Web page directory. Apache also creates separate Error and Transfer logs for the virtual host. The result is that the user michaelk on my www.poisontooth.com Web server can use two techniques to access his Web pages. He can go through the standard URL to his Web page, `http://www.poisontooth.com/~michaelk`. Alternatively, he can go through the new virtual host at `http://michaelk.poisontooth.com/`.

Which would you rather put on a business card or give out over the phone?

Apache has a far greater command set than you've seen here. The Apache Web pages detail all the available directives and also contain a wealth of modules that you can plug into Apache to give it new features. The Apache development team addresses bug and security fixes very quickly, and with its availability for Windows and just about every variation of UNIX, Apache rightfully deserves its top spot in the Web server market.

Regretfully, we've come to the end of our discussion on extending the client operating system. You've only seen a tiny fraction of the number of servers and extensions that are available. The servers that I have discussed are software packages that I use and find to be stable, friendly, and just downright good. You may well find other software that you like better, which is perfectly fine. This survey is not meant to provide a definitive list of what you *should* run, but is rather an introduction to what you *can* run. If you've read through the examples, you can see that the information is similar for the different servers, and although the configuration interfaces may vary, the result is the same. I truly wish that I could cover everything that could be of use to your TCP/IP network, but unfortunately the resulting book would be far too long, weigh too much, and I would be a very old man by the time it was done.

Part
III

Ch
12

## CHAPTER 13

Establishing Dedicated Servers

by John Ray

In this chapter

AppleShare IP **272**

Windows NT **276**

Linux (and Other UNIX OSes) **280**

Now I'm Confused; What's the Best Solution? **283**

In the previous several chapters, you've seen how our operating system clients can be expanded to provide a lot of TCP/IP services. I've discussed the many TCP/IP programs that come with Mac OS, Windows, and Linux. But even they might not be enough to fill your needs. It may be in your best interest to buy a dedicated server solution rather than piecing together everything you need from third-party utilities. Sometimes, however, the third-party programs can actually be better than the ones that come with the server. Don't think for a second that because a product comes with a big name behind it that it's the best solution for your particular application. This is a personal decision that you should make very carefully based on your needs. As has been said time and time again, don't believe the hype! Make your own decisions based on what makes you comfortable and does what you need. If you've just finished reading Chapter 12, "Adding Email and Web Server Capabilities to Your OS," don't stop until you finish this chapter. It's relatively short and should wrap up any loose ends.

AppleShare IP

The first piece of software we look at is Apple's AppleShare IP server. AppleShare IP is a software addition to the basic Mac OS 8.x operating system. Although we've discussed Mac OS as a client OS, AppleShare IP also makes changes to the basic operating system functions that allow it to perform as a very effective server. AppleShare IP will appeal to anyone who is accustomed to using the Mac interface. Users and Groups are handled in the same fashion as the basic Mac OS, as are file permissions. It also adds file owners and groups to the system, just like UNIX and Windows NT (which we'll be going over shortly). The latest versions of AppleShare IP even share natively to Windows computers and offer a Web interface for administration. After installing AppleShare IP, you'll notice that some of your computer's default services are no longer accessible. AppleShare IP takes over certain portions of your system and replaces them with enhanced functionality.

FIGURE 13.1

You control AppleShare IP Manager from this dialog box.

Let's take a look at some of the components that make up the AppleShare IP software suite. Then you can decide if they'll fill the functions you need. AppleShare IP can be thought of as consisting of a few integrated programs: an FTP and file server, an email server, and a Web server. All of the action is controlled through a single dialog box, as shown in Figure 13.1, from which we can choose what services we want to control.

The file sharing system integrates FTP and the new Users and Groups manager. The concept of Users and Groups builds on the basic Mac OS idea and operates in the same way. Because we're now providing Internet services through AppleShare IP, one of the additions to the user specification is the ability to give each user an "Internet Alias," as shown in Figure 13.2. This is a single-word username that will be used in email addresses. Users can use either their normal "full" name or the Internet alias to log into file sharing services.

FIGURE 13.2

You can assign an Internet alias to users.

Web serving, FTP, and file sharing are all handled by the main AppleShare IP module. All file permissions used by FTP and AppleShare file sharing are identical. If you configure your settings once, all you need to do is click a single button to immediately make your files available via FTP or native file sharing. A status display lets you see all the users who are currently connected to your computer and how much of the machine's resources are being used. You can adjust the processor time that is available to users by dragging a simple slider bar. Besides being able to share to a Macintosh network, AppleShare IP 6.x introduces a wonderful new feature to the AppleShare product line: Windows file sharing. Figure 13.3 shows the new Windows sharing setup.

FIGURE 13.3

AppleShare IP version 6 and later lets you add Windows file sharing.

Part

III

Ch

13

The latest versions of AppleShare IP support full sharing to Windows clients. There is no distinction made on the server as to whether clients are Mac OS or Windows based, so the same file permissions apply to both. Given the increasing number of Windows machines popping up in formerly Mac-only environments, this is an extremely nice feature. My department employs a number of graphic artists and page layout personnel. The vast majority of them use

Macintosh systems. From time to time, people involved in Web site development need access to the graphics files stored on our servers. Many of these people use Windows 95 and NT. Up until AppleShare IP 6.x, we were limited to exchanging disks or using DAVE or COPSTalk, which I discussed in Chapter 11. Now, I can create accounts for the Windows users on the same server that the Mac folks use, and everyone can connect and share files directly. AppleShare IP can also register itself with a WINS server, which helps it share files with Windows machines over a TCP/IP network.

Besides file sharing, AppleShare IP also includes a mail server, shown in Figure 13.4, that is easy to use and that shares both IMAP and POP3 capabilities. Once again, the AppleShare IP mail server employs the user accounts that have been created through the AppleShare IP management system. You have full control over the size of messages that can be received, hosts that can connect, how incoming messages are processed, and so on.

FIGURE 13.4

AppleShare IP's mail server contains both IMAP and POP3 capabilities.

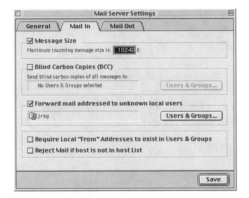

Like the SIMS server, AppleShare IP also supports the NotifyMail program to trigger your email client to check your account as soon as new messages arrive. Throughout the entire AppleShare IP system, consistency and ease of use are paramount. The email serving system provides excellent operator control and configuration, but does so in a way that allows you to be up and running with a default *useable* setup within a matter of minutes.

To fully provide TCP/IP services, and email services in particular, AppleShare IP comes with its own DNS server: MacDNS. MacDNS can provide name resolution services to your network with very little setup difficulty. Unfortunately, although MacDNS is not hard to use, it does not provide the full level of integration that the other AppleShare IP services offer. The version being supplied with AppleShare IP 6.0 has not been updated in more than two years. It does not share a common interface with the rest of the AppleShare IP package and appears to have been added as an afterthought. Quite frankly, it is not the best product to provide full DNS service from a Macintosh. An excellent DNS solution for Mac OS, which will run under AppleShare IP with no problem, is a commercial product called QuickDNS Pro from Men and Mice. The creation of domains is simplified through the use of assistants (the Mac OS version of Windows " wizards), and the interface is uncluttered and very user-friendly.

In my opinion, you probably won't want to provide DNS services using MacDNS. I've experienced unexplainable crashes while using MacDNS that have led me to believe that it is perhaps a bit too buggy to be used as a full-time solution. Your results, of course, may vary. If you'd like to check out QuickDNS Pro, you can visit the Men and Mice Web site at http://www.menandmice.com/.

So, what else can you do with AppleShare IP? There is still one service provided that's useful on some networks: a print server. Because most Macintosh printers are already network printers, it might seem a bit strange that we'd want to serve a printer out to the network twice. However, think about the last time you sent a large print job to a network printer from your Macintosh (if you have one!). The program probably spooled the file you were printing out to your hard drive and proceeded to print it from there. This, although allowing you to continue to do some work in the background, can be a bit annoying as your computer slowly crunches away at the file and sends it to the printer. Your machine will slow down; it's just a question of how unusable it will become. If you don't have Background Printing turned on in the Chooser, you won't be able to do anything while your job prints. By providing a print server, AppleShare IP eliminates this problem. Files to be printed are sent immediately to the print server and are spooled to the printer from there. You experience only a slight delay as the file is passed to the print server. A secondary benefit to using a print server is that it can identify individual jobs and print cover pages to separate them. In a lab of several hundred computers, trying to separate individual print jobs from a continuous stack of papers can be quite a challenge.

So you can see what AppleShare IP does do, but what *doesn't* it do? Probably the biggest problem with AppleShare IP is that it is still based entirely on the Macintosh operating system - it just "adjusts" it a bit to provide fast service. There are underlying problems with the Mac OS that limit its capability to be an effective server for large networks. The biggest problem you'll find with AppleShare IP is that although there are many services provided, if you expect a lot of traffic, you're probably going to end up having to use different servers for handling the different services. The Mac OS is not a *preemptive multitasking* environment; it is a cooperative environment where each program must voluntarily give up time to other programs for them to do their jobs. If your mail server is extremely busy, it might not be able to give enough time to your file sharing services, or vice versa. Rather than experiencing gradual slowdown of the system as more resources are used, you're likely to find some services running fine, while others are crawling. It will take quite a bit for your network to reach this state, but be aware that it can.

Another problem with the Mac OS is that it does not have *protected memory*. Protected memory enables each application that runs to have its own memory "space" that does not overlap with any other programs or any system resources. Without this protection, applications can corrupt one another's active memory and crash. The AppleShare IP software is tested extensively by Apple to make sure that all the components work together and do not have any sort of conflicts (except, apparently, the MacDNS software). Unfortunately, Apple cannot check the server software against every other program you might want to run on the server. I have an AppleShare server sitting behind me on a desk at work; from time to time, I need to quickly pull up a Web browser and check something out. If I do it on the file server and, for some reason, the browser crashes (I'm sure we've all been there), it can bring down the entire system. Your users will not be happy to find out that the files they've been working on have been destroyed because you decided to take a quick gander at the new South Park Web site that everyone has been talking about. If you plan on running an AppleShare IP server, plan on dedicating a machine to running the software and nothing else. This is usually good practice no matter what operating system you're using, but it's especially important in the case of AppleShare IP.

By the time you read this, Apple will have introduced a new operating system that was first known as Rhapsody and was recently renamed to Mac OS X Server. Mac OS X Server is the precursor to an entirely new Macintosh operating system that will just be called Mac OS X. These new systems support all the advanced features that Mac OS is currently lacking and will be robust enough to use as both a client and server. Hopefully in the near future, Apple will provide an implementation of AppleShare IP that runs under Mac OS X. Apple has a knack for providing reliable hardware and easy-to-use software; they just need to get the software to the point of being as reliable as the hardware itself.

Windows NT

If you haven't heard of Windows NT, I'm betting that you don't own a television, radio, computer, or any magazine subscriptions. (But thanks for buying this book!) Windows NT is the current "king" of operating system hype. Not to say that this hype is unfounded, but it is a bit exaggerated. Windows NT, like AppleShare IP, provides a wealth of different services—in fact, a great deal more than AppleShare IP. Windows NT is a multiuser system, which means that it uses the concepts of file permissions, owners, and groups. Because these concepts are an integral part of the operating system, an NT server system uses its database of users and groups throughout all the services it offers. From logging into the system to protecting Web page access, the server relies on its user database. Like the Mac OS and AppleShare IP, the addition and maintenance of user accounts is done through an entirely graphical interface, shown in Figure 13.5.

FIGURE 13.5

Windows NT lets you manage users and groups as part of its built-in capabilities and through a graphical interface.

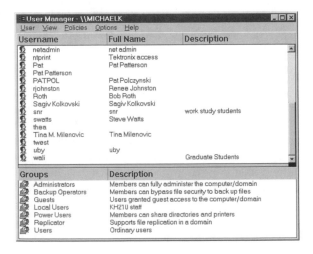

File-sharing services take place in a manner that's very similar to Windows but offer additional functionality. NT introduces the idea of domains to the Windows-sharing architecture. A domain is a collection of resources a user may be granted access to if the user is a member of that domain. As a user logs into the system, NT can execute login scripts that can mount volumes, and so on, on the remote user's computer. This gives NT great power to be a central network administration point. Like AppleShare IP 6.x, NT also offers services for "the other guy"—in this case, the Mac OS (see Figure 13.6).

FIGURE 13.6
Windows NT supports services for Macintosh computers.

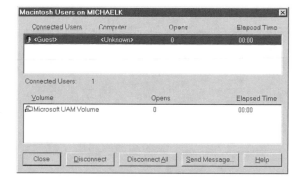

Unlike AppleShare IP, however, the Mac OS volumes are shared from a different administrative interface than everything else. The current release of NT does not support AppleShare over TCP/IP, but this limitation can be rectified with ShareWay IP, which we looked at earlier. Windows NT, surprisingly enough, offers better printer sharing to Macintosh clients than AppleShare IP offers. NT can "capture" a Windows printer and share it out to the AppleTalk network as a PostScript printer. Because any Macintosh can print to any PostScript printer, this special feature enables Mac users to take advantage of printers that weren't even designed for their system!

Robust file and print sharing is only the beginning of the features offered by NT server. NT server also comes with one of the fastest Web servers available: the Internet Information Server, or IIS (see Figure 13.7). IIS actually includes more than just a Web server; it also features SMTP, NNTP, and an FTP server.

FIGURE 13.7
Windows NT comes with its own Web server, the Microsoft Internet Information Server.

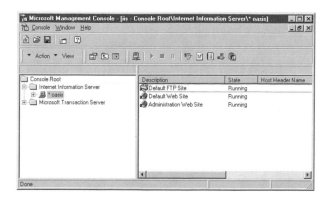

These applications all operate out of root directories the administrator can configure, unlike AppleShare IP, which uses the same structure as its file sharing. A few clicks, and you're running an FTP server. A few more, and your Web server is on the Net. A single administrative control lets you set permissions on individual directories and choose the authentication methods users will need to connect to your resources.

Two services that are implemented extremely nicely in the NT system are the DHCP service and DNS service. DHCP, if you recall, allows computers to be dynamically configured to the appropriate TCP/IP settings without any human interaction. The inclusion of this in the default NT server installation is a big plus for people working to manage a large TCP/IP network. The interface is, for the most part, easy to understand, and you have full graphical control over lease lengths and statically mapped leases.

The DNS server is similar. It doesn't offer the full wizard capabilities of QuickDNS Pro on the Mac, but then again, it's offered as part of the NT package; unlike the DNS server that come with AppleShare IP 6.0, I've had absolutely no problems with it. A few DNS entries are illustrated in Figure 13.8.

FIGURE 13.8

Windows NT also comes with a solid DNS Manager.

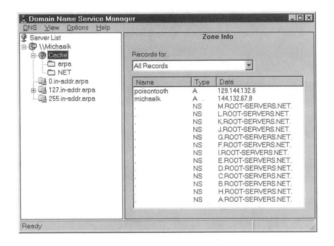

I could go on and on about NT's built-in serving capabilities. NT can function as a router. It provides PPP dial-in support for clients, remote administration from other Windows machines, PPTP encrypted tunneling to allow you to securely link two networks, and many other fine features. When it comes to system stability, NT is very good and even offers fail-safe features such as disk striping and software-based RAID (Redundant Array of Independent Disks) to secure your data.

One of the biggest reasons for Microsoft's success with NT has been the integration of all the Microsoft NT components. You can purchase the Microsoft SQL Server software to use with the Web server and quickly integrate databases with your Web site. Microsoft products tend to allow you to easily build solutions from templates or wizards without any programming knowledge. Microsoft's Active Server Pages and ActiveX give programmers the ability to build dynamic Web applications in record time. You can buy the Microsoft Exchange Server to provide email and collaboration services to your network. All these components integrate with the operating system to form what should be, and often is, a seamless administrative experience.

There are a few problems, however, with this seeming utopia of operating systems. The first is cost. Client licenses and other members of the Microsoft BackOffice suite (such as the SQL Server) can cost thousands of dollars. Hardware capable of running the Exchange Server or SQL Server at a reasonable speed is going to be expensive. We had originally tried to run an Exchange messaging server for its scheduling capabilities on a 233 MHz DEC Alpha with 64MB of RAM. The machine crawled. Because NT supports multiple processors (another plus!), it's possible to build or buy a system that can run most of the services you'll need, but plan on budgeting a reasonable sum of money to build your serving solutions.

The second problem with NT comes from one of its greatest strengths: It tries to do and be everything. In many instances, it succeeds; but in others, it fails. Being such a young operating system, NT is bound to have faults; the rate that people have been accepting it into mission-critical roles and the rate Microsoft has been adding new features have allowed some very serious bugs to creep into the system. Last year, hackers found a hole that allowed you to connect to a port on an NT server (or a Windows 95 machine) and send a single packet that would immediately lock the machine up if it were running TCP/IP services. Within hours of this being discovered, programs called *winnuke* and other fun names were distributed across the Internet, and hackers swept entire subnets with the winnuke programs, crashing everything they came across. What makes this scenario particularly scary is that even though Microsoft patched this hole very quickly, within a week a similar flaw was found, and it started all over again. The integration of the operating system with all the TCP/IP services, such as the Web server, has enabled a whole new generation of attacks that do everything from upload files that should be protected off of a server, to execute software on clients' computers without them even knowing it. NT is the new kid on the block, and it's currently getting picked on quite a bit. While this, in the long run, helps NT become a stronger system, you might not want your data to be part of the "learning process." On the positive side, however, NT does offer the preemptive multitasking and protected memory that Mac OS-based servers lack. You can safely run your browser and know that if it crashes, your users aren't going to be booted from the system.

Lastly (and this is no fault of NT, rather of the public perception), NT is not an entirely point-and-click environment. Things do go wrong: Patches need to be installed, hot fixes need to be run, and registry settings need to be tweaked. I've seen more than one person claim to be an NT administrator because they have successfully set up Windows NT. If you choose to run NT, *please* take the time to learn how to use it properly. When NT is running smoothly, everything works like a dream, but there are problems that can and do occur, and it's beyond even Microsoft to provide a wizard that can get you out of every little crisis you might encounter. Furthermore, because of the wealth of services you can run, it's possible for ignorance to create problems without even knowing it. An extremely common occurrence on the OSU network is for someone to set up an NT server and tell it that they want to provide services for Macintosh. We have a good mixture of Windows-, Mac-, and UNIX-based computers, so it makes sense that they'd want to do this. However, there is a single check box in the Macintosh service configuration called "Act as AppleTalk router." Clicking this box can completely dis-

Part

III

Ch

13

rupt an AppleTalk network. This is rather fresh in my mind, because I spent a good portion of my workday a few days ago walking through one of the OSU medical buildings trying to find an NT server with this exact setting. When I did find the culprit, the owner simply shrugged and said, "I didn't think it would hurt anything." This person should not have been running an NT server without appropriate training. If you're a Macintosh or Windows 95 user and you think you'll be able to immediately set up an NT server with no experience, you're probably right. However, when the time comes to make it do something different from its default configuration, or to diagnose a network problem, please be sure you have the appropriate skill set before you try.

Linux (and Other UNIX OSes)

I'm sure that there are some die-hard command line users out there who are screaming, "Who cares about those silly GUI systems; bring on the big boys!" There's no denying it; for sheer power out of the box, UNIX is tops. That doesn't mean that it has to rely on its command line interface to be configured. As we discussed the client OSes, I showed how Linux could be used to provide TCP/IP services along with the other clients. At the same time, however, I was showing you how to configure Linux as a server operating system. Linux blurs the line between client and server by offering the best of both worlds. A rapidly maturing operating system based on UNIX, Linux has several user interfaces that will seem friendly to anyone who has used the Mac OS or Windows. Being mostly a grassroots effort, much of the software available for Linux is entirely free. Unfortunately, the public perception has often been that "free" equates to "not worth anything." This is entirely untrue. I have a very soft place in my heart for Linux, because the people who write it and support it do so because they believe in it and love it, not because they think it will make millions of dollars for them.

Because we've already spent a great deal of time looking at configuring Linux at a basic level, let's take a quick look at how Linux can be brought to a level that makes it a little less intimidating to the average user. The best example of how this can be done is by installing a graphical interface called KDE, or the K Desktop Environment. KDE is, of course, entirely free and can be downloaded from `http://www.kde.org/`.

For administrating your Linux computer, KDE offers a full graphical user and group manager, as shown in Figure 13.9. This greatly decreases the amount of time you have to spend maintaining text files with the corresponding information. It's just as simple to use as the Mac OS or NT user manager, and is a free upgrade to an already free operating system.

For file sharing services, a Samba configuration tool is currently in development. Soon you'll be able to graphically create your shared directories that will be made available to your Windows computers (or DAVE-equipped Macs) without having to learn a single bit of the syntax of the smb.conf file. Pretty nifty, isn't it?

FIGURE 13.9

KDE provides a graphical user and group manager for Linux's built-in networking capabilities.

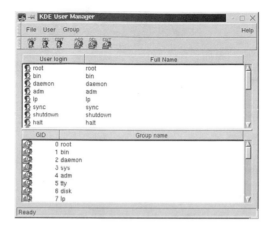

Shown in Figure 13.10, KDE includes a runlevel editor that is very much like the Windows service manager managing servers. From the runlevel manager, you can start, stop, and restart services running on your computer. Dragging and dropping the icons of the services allows you to change the order in which they start when your computer is booted. Drag an icon to the trash can, and it will no longer start automatically on your server. Doesn't seem too bad at all, does it?

With each passing day, the number of new utilities for Linux grows. Earlier this year, several large database companies, including Oracle, announced support for Linux in 1999. This will prove to be an important milestone for the operating system as it continues to work its way onto people's desktops and into their server closets. KDE provides an excellent environment with both client applications and server capabilities. It also provides a number of useful utilities for Linux itself, as shown in Figure 13.11.

FIGURE 13.10

KDE also includes a runlevel editor that lets you start and stop various services.

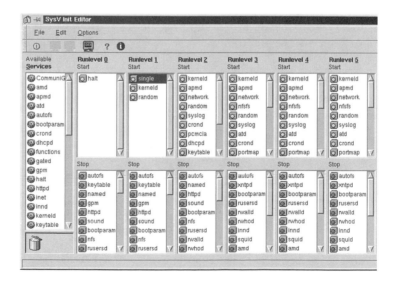

Part
III

Ch
13

FIGURE 13.11

Besides providing a graphical environment, KDE supplies many useful Linux utilities.

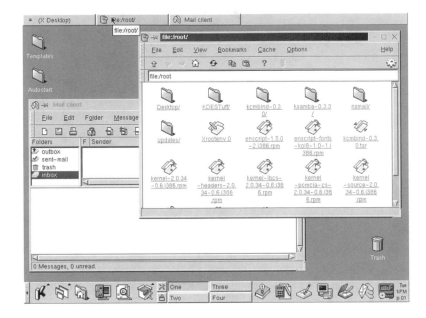

One of the biggest problems I've faced when recommending Linux solutions is the misconception that Linux doesn't "play well with others." This just isn't the case. I recently set up a Linux server running mySQL (a SQL Server) to serve a large database of personnel information. The data was linked directly as an ODBC datasource into a Windows Access database. A colleague built a front end to the data in this Access database, and we distributed it to the clients who needed it. The immediate assumption was that we were using a Microsoft SQL Server with NT to deliver the solution. In fact, we were using a very low-end Pentium and an entirely free piece of software (including the ODBC drivers for Windows) to deliver the same functionality that would have cost us several thousand dollars more. You can even use a Linux server as a back end to NT's Active Server Pages—any place an ODBC datasource is needed. That's the beauty of open protocols and TCP/IP!

What Is ODBC?

Open database connectivity (ODBC) is a standard designed by Microsoft to allow network databases to be shared among client computers. Designed as a cross-platform standard, ODBC requires that a driver for a particular data source be installed in your operating system. Once the driver is in place, you can use any ODBC-friendly program to access the remote data.

Now you're probably wondering how you could go wrong with an almost free (or entirely free if you download it) operating system and tools like KDE. The answer is that like Windows NT, you can point and click your way to some successes, but you're going to need to learn a lot more about the operating system to fully exploit its features and not cause problems. Linux will require knowledge of the command line and how to use it. You'll have to edit configuration files to fine-tune its operation. To use Linux as a router or as a tunnel, you'll need to recompile the kernel. In recompiling the kernel, what you're doing is actually rebuilding the very basic components of the operating system from its source code. If this sounds scary, it should. If something goes wrong during the installation of the new kernel, you may not be able to reboot your system. Linux gives you more than enough rope to hang yourself. You control every aspect of the system, and it does not make any attempt to protect you from yourself.

Compounding the you're-on-your-own problems of Linux is the fact that you have little recourse if problems do occur that are not your fault. Microsoft responds quickly to correct flaws in NT as they're discovered; this is because the users demand it. A single person, Linus Torvalds, originally designed Linux. You aren't going to get very far if you attempt to call Linus on the phone and complain that your Ethernet card isn't working or that a driver is crashing the kernel. Thankfully, there are some companies that will now enter into support contracts for Linux. I've not personally used any of these services, so I can't vouch for the quality or timeliness of their responses. It is, however, an indication that things are moving in the right direction for Linux to be a viable corporate tool. Even though Linux has very limited commercial technical support, you'll find that the online community provides a level of support that exceeds, in most cases, commercial offerings. It's very likely that if you're having problems with a particular driver, you'll be able to actually email the person who wrote the driver and correspond with that person to find a solution to the problem. This is the kind of openness that's the driving force behind Linux. Its the way things *should* be. Once again, however, even with the public support, Linux needs to have commercial support options available for it to become more widely accepted.

If you're interested in saving your company money, it makes good sense to investigate the features Linux has to offer. If you're unfamiliar with UNIX operating systems, take classes, or buy a *Using Linux* book. The costs of learning the operating system will generally be offset by the amount of money that will be saved running its services. It *is* harder to learn Linux than NT (and a lot harder to learn than AppleShare IP), but the experience is worthwhile, and you'll gain a far greater appreciation for the word *free*.

Now I'm Confused; What's the Best Solution?

I've probably now completely confused the situation by saying both good and bad things about each of the server solutions we've looked at. I'm not being wishy-washy; I'm trying to convey the reality that there is no perfect solution you can pick up in a box and throw online. Microsoft would like you to believe that Windows NT is the ultimate solution. It isn't. Apple wants the same for AppleShare IP, and Linux users worldwide will advocate their OS as the perfect server. They aren't. You've got to make some decisions based on what you need, based on your valuation of some simple criteria.

Ease of Use

How much time do you plan to spend maintaining your server? If you want a solution that will provide medium-load services to your network in a very easy-to-use fashion, look into AppleShare IP. If you're planning on serving a larger number of people and would still like to have a generally easy-to-use system, NT will fill your needs nicely. Lastly, if you need to serve a large number of people and you don't care if you have to get your hands a bit dirty, choose Linux.

Stability

Linux and UNIX systems in general still lead the pack in stability. Looking at one of our Linux mail servers, I see an uptime of over 200 days. Most UNIX machines only go offline when there is a power outage or a system upgrade. The operating system has been around for more than 20 years and has had an opportunity to be refined year after year.

Windows NT comes in second place with far greater stability than Window 95 or 98, but, as I mentioned earlier, a variety of security concerns have led to somewhat disastrous consequences due to the malicious actions of others. NT still has some memory leaks but is getting better. I have some personal concerns about the stability of the upcoming NT 5, given the large amount of new code that's going into the system, but I'll reserve final judgment for the shipping product.

Mac OS, in its current form, takes a distant third to Linux and NT. Although the AppleShare IP server suite is very stable and runs for months without any problems, it's extremely susceptible to problems caused by third-party utilities. You might think that the answer is to simply avoid running anything that isn't part of the AppleShare IP package, and that will usually work. It's unlikely that you'll be able to actually get away with this for long, however, because, at the very least, you should be using backup software on your computer to secure your users' data.

Services Provided

If you need basic out-of-the-box TCP/IP services, AppleShare IP has enough functionality to get Web, email, and FTP services online within minutes. Linux also includes these capabilities, but configuring the Linux email server (sendmail) can take far longer than one might like. On the other hand, NT also offers Web and FTP services, as well as DHCP, PPP, and others. Conspicuously lacking is a mail server system, because Microsoft also sells the Exchange mail server as an add-on to NT. This could make it slightly less desirable than Linux or AppleShare IP.

Cost

The clear winner is again Linux. With a cost of $0, or around $30 for one of Que's books that include the operating system on CD, you can't beat Linux's price. AppleShare IP is a somewhat costly piece of software but provides email services that NT is lacking and does not require per client licensing. Windows NT can provide a wealth of services for a low cost but can become quite expensive as you expand the capabilities. AppleShare IP and NT are tied in this category.

Scalability

Although NT supports multiple processors, it still doesn't scale as well as UNIX. NT does not perform as well as it should when running in multiprocessor setups. This is something that's being addressed, and Microsoft is promising far greater system scalability in the future. While Linux is a UNIX derivation, multiprocessor support is still considered to be in development, although I have few complaints with its performance. Linux and NT are currently on equal footing in this area; which one springs ahead is entirely up to the respective development teams. Mac OS, unfortunately, provides no support (except in very special applications) for multiple processors. This will almost certainly be changed in the upcoming Mac OS X operating system, but, for now, the only way to make a Mac faster is to buy a faster Mac.

Security

Windows NT is currently the most secure choice for serving among our choices. There are commercial UNIX solutions with security ratings higher than NT, but they are also priced to match. Linux is second and comes with some security features, but does not offer the data encryption services of NT. This doesn't mean that you can't upgrade the operating system to provide these features, just that it's not an integral part. Lastly, Mac OS is still a single-user operating system but has some additions to give it the capability to handle file owners and basic permissions. The fact that it remains a single user system at its core is significant. It means that there is no protection on the machine itself. A single user still technically controls all the files on the machine. Anyone sitting down in front of the server can trash all the files on the machine within seconds. In a closed office environment, this shouldn't be a problem. If the server is in a public area—look out!

Overall, each of the dedicated server solutions does a nice job in its own area. Only you can decide what will suit the needs of your network and what will make you feel comfortable using it. Mac OS users and Windows users have obvious choices, but they should not feel as though they can't look at the other options. Each of these server systems can coexist and complement each other. I run all three servers and am pleased with the capabilities that each offers me. There are days when I'm frustrated by each, and days when they all do exactly what they're supposed to.

Perhaps the perfect solution is to buy all three. I've mentioned several snags I've run into on my network that integrates machines of all three types, but I know I have the capability for almost anything somewhere on the network.

Connecting to the Internet

Once you've established a TCP/IP network of your own, the next logical step is to extend it to the Internet. This is actually much easier than it sounds. Part 4 looks at several different methods of providing Internet connectivity to your entire network in an economical fashion. If you happen to have an old computer gathering dust, you'll want to read this section to learn how that computer can provide connectivity to the Internet for your entire network.

14   Connecting Your Network to the Internet 289

15   Using Proxy Servers 297

16   Using Proxy NAT Servers 337

## CHAPTER 14

Connecting Your Network to the Internet

by John Ray

In this chapter

Phone-Line Connections **290**

ISDN **290**

ADSL **291**

Cable Modems **291**

T1 Lines **291**

What Should I Choose? **292**

Other Information Sources **296**

You can create a network, but how can you make it talk to the outside world? The Internet is nothing more than a huge TCP/IP network with thousands of subnets, gateways, routers and bridges. To connect to the Internet, you're going to need to provide some sort of gateway service to connect you to the world. Depending on the level of your needs, you're going to be looking at choosing one of several different types of connections. It's simply a matter of finding one that's available in your area and that meets your connection speed needs. Let's go ahead and look at the different ways people use to connect to the Internet, starting with the slowest and ending with something speedy. This won't be a complete list by any means, rather some of the most common.

Phone-Line Connections

Today, by far, the most used method of connecting to the Internet (for individuals) is using a modem to dial into a network server. Over the years, modem speeds have progressed from a little over 30 characters per second to the blazing fast 57Kbps modems of today. What took hours to transfer in the late '80s can be done in a matter of minutes. This is not, however, even remotely close to the speed of most direct Internet connections. Running at 10Mbps, an Ethernet LAN can transfer files over 200 times faster than the fastest modem. Because of the analog nature of telephone lines, modems cannot even connect at the highest speeds because of line noise. There is also a limit to the range of frequencies that can be carried on a phone line. This, in turn, limits the amount of data that can be carried and keeps modem technology from being able to match digital signaling. The average monthly cost of modem Internet service is $20, with a startup cost of around $100 for a decent modem.

ISDN

ISDN, or *Integrated Services Digital Network*, has been around for many years but has not been accepted by the public as rapidly as its supporters had hoped. Initial high equipment costs and restrictions on the distance a user can be from the telephone company have not helped it to gain widespread adoption. A common reading of the acronym ISDN is "It Still Does Nothing," which describes how many of the early supporters feel about it. Essentially, ISDN eliminates the analog problem of the telephone line and provides you with digital data channels you can use to connect to a network. The most common ISDN service provides two 64kbit channels the user can combine to get a 128kbit connection to a remote ISDN PPP server. This is more than twice the speed of the fastest analog modem. I've used ISDN service for the past two years, and rather than using both channels for data, I've chosen to use one channel for voice, and another for data—thus limiting me to a single 64kbit connection. I've since moved to something a bit faster. ISDN will cost you around $100 for installation, between $200 to $350 for a good ISDN "modem" (it isn't really a modem, but since it provides the interface to the digital line, it serves the same purpose as a modem on a phone line), and $25 to $35 a month of an ISDN PPP dial-in account. If you choose to use an ISDN channel for voice communications, you should check with your telephone company for extra charges. In some states, ISDN usage costs are far greater than a standard telephone line. Call your local phone company if you're interested in

ISDN service; the service isn't available in all areas and may cost extra depending on your location relative to your local phone company sub-station. Also, make sure that your local ISP provides ISDN dial-in accounts. There is no point in buying into ISDN if you can't use it.

ADSL

ADSL, or *Asymmetric Digital Subscriber Line*, is another somewhat older technology that is finally catching on, and may become a standard for future home connectivity. ADSL provides connection speeds in excess of a megabyte per second and uses the standard wiring already present for your telephone lines. ADSL maintains a constant connection to the Internet, so there is no need to dial into the network. This service is slowly being introduced into cities across the country and is currently only held back by availability. Costing only around $30 to $50 monthly, including the price of renting an ADSL network adapter, ADSL delivers extremely high-speed access at a very low cost. Once again, check with your telephone company and see if the service is available. If it is, buy it!

Cable Modems

Like ADSL, the *Cable Modem* provides a low cost, high-speed connection to the Internet. Cable Modems are currently non-standard, meaning there are several different variations in use. In some instances, a cable modem has a very fast download rate—around the same speed as ADSL, but uses a very slow connection to upload data to the network. This is fine for users who are only interested in downloading information off of the Internet to their PCs, but it does not meet the needs of those who want the ability to transmit data at high speeds. Luckily, cable modems are increasingly moving to high-speed transmission as the cable companies rewire their networks using fiber optics. I'm currently using a cable modem for my Internet service and couldn't be happier. For roughly $40 a month (on top of my already premium-station-laden cable television bill), I have download transmission speeds that are indistinguishable from the local Ethernet network at OSU, and upload speeds that are fast enough to serve reasonably high-volume Web pages. The machine you've been seeing referenced throughout this book, "poisontooth.com," is actually my cable modem connection. I run email and Web servers over this connection with no problem at all.

T1 Lines

A *Trunk Line Level One* is a high-speed connection that is capable of carrying data at a rate of 1.5Mbps. This line is a dedicated connection that is used to transmit voice and data. Each T1 line is divided (much like ISDN) into different channels. A single T1 line can carry 24 channels that are used for voice or data communications, each channel supporting data rates of 64kbits per second. Buying T1 access to the Internet will cost between $1,000 to $2,000 a month, or possibly even more, depending on your location. It's possible to buy the use of only a few channels for your data communications; the use of only a segment of a T1 line is called fractional T1 access. This plan will cost less money but will still far exceed the price of the other access

Part
IV

Ch
14

options discussed. If you're interested in buying T1 service, my advice is to shop around. There may be local ISPs in your area that can provide you with special rates on T1 service. Check your local ISPs and the local telephone companies. If you're lucky, you might be able to find T1 service offered at prices in the low-$1,000 range. Another potential solution, if you're in a shared office building, is to share the cost with another group. Several small companies should be able to share the bandwidth of a T1 line without any noticeable slowdown. There are still larger capacity lines called "T3" lines, which carry even more data channels. You can expect to pay between $5,000 to $10,000 a month for dedicated T3 access. I'll stick with my $40 cable modem until I win the lottery.

What Should I Choose?

The biggest problem you face in connecting to the Internet is price. The cost of buying a high-speed connection and an entire subnet of IP addresses will cost several thousand dollars a month. If you can afford it, great! But small business and offices that want to expand their network are likely to find that buying dedicated high-speed access lines is far too expensive. Luckily, two solutions will lower your cost to only the price of a single Internet connection.

Proxy Servers

The first solution is called *proxy* serving. A proxy stands-in for something—in this case, a server. Imagine a single computer on your network that alone has access to the Internet; this could be through a dial-in line, a dedicated connection, ISDN, or whatever you can afford to make the link. This is called the proxy server. It will run special software that allows a client computer on your network to make a request for something such as a Web page. The client computer, rather than trying to go directly through the Internet to the Web site it wants to retrieve, will instead pass the request to the proxy server. The proxy server, in turn, will download the Web page and pass it on to the client. This all happens in a manner that is entirely transparent to the user.

FIGURE 14.1
A proxy server works by accepting requests from a computer on the internal network, relaying them to outside hosts, and then relaying any response to the original machine.

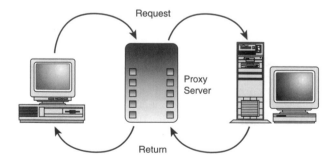

Proxy servers can be used to provide more than just Web service; they simply pass protocol information for a given protocol to the outside world, and then send the results back to the client. The problem with proxies is that they need to exist for every protocol you want to run over your network. This is a bit of a problem for protocols such as streaming video and audio.

You can only hope that a proxy server exists for the protocols you want to offer on your network. If a user downloads a TCP/IP program that is designed to work across the Internet, there's a good chance it isn't going to work through a proxy server. The software will even fail if it uses a protocol that is available through the proxy server, but it hasn't been programmed properly to take advantage of proxy servers. Other problems occur on pages that require some sort of interaction between the server and the user. Some proxy servers have a hard time passing data back and forth correctly to the client. Java applications are very likely to fail if they must communicate with a server while they are running.

Despite the limitations, there are some advantages to proxy serving. Most Web proxy servers are caching proxy servers. This means that they keep a copy of the information they're sent to fetch. If more than one user on your network requests the same Web page, it won't have to be fetched multiple times. It can also be delivered at the maximum speed of your local network from the cached file. So if there is a Web site that many people need to access daily, you could set up a simple caching proxy server that uses nothing more than a phone line to connect to the Internet. After the Web pages are loaded once over the slow connection, the rest of the network will be able to retrieve them very quickly from the cache. Some proxies will also allow you to use them to block access to certain sites that are objectionable for whatever reason. You simply give a list of site names or TCP/IP addresses to the program, and any attempt to reach them will be rejected.

Proxy servers are likely to be used as a means of connecting to the Internet from small, controlled organizations. They're useful in schools and in situations where the people running the network have complete control over the software that their users are running. They aren't only used in situations where they're the key to connecting to the Internet. Proxies can also be used by a company to provide services to their employees but limit the amount of access employees have to network services. Either way, proxy servers allow users to access Internet services by providing a middleman between the Internet and the internal network. Whether the limitation of only being able to run certain programs on the client is a benefit or a hindrance is entirely up to your perspective as a network administrator.

The NAT/IP Masquerading Solution

There are no small flying insects involved with using NAT. *NAT, or Network Address Translation* (sometimes called IP Masquerading), is a fast and extremely cost effective technique for connecting a local TCP/IP network to the Internet. The best part about using NAT is that it's entirely transparent to your internal network. Client computers can use whatever protocols they want to speak to the outside world, and, except in a few cases, they will succeed. There is no special configuration for the clients, no special software, nothing. To your internal network, the Internet will appear as if they were each directly connected. The limitation comes when looking at your network from the point of view of the Internet. The Internet will see your internal network as a single IP address when you're using NAT; all connections to outside machines will appear to come from one address, and all responses will be returned to that address. The beauty of it is that this is entirely transparent and actually secures your network from outside attack. The only drawback is that, without special configuration (which we'll discuss shortly), there is no way to provide services to the Internet from a computer on your internal network. All services must run on the computer that is running NAT.

FIGURE 14.2

NAT transparently routes packets between your internal network and the outside world. To the Internet, your entire network is represented as a single IP address.

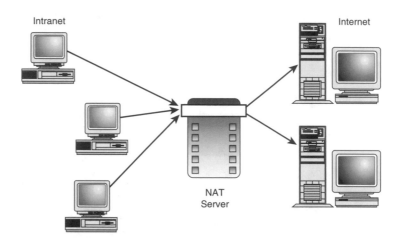

NAT works similarly to the way that hardware or MAC addresses are translated back and forth into IP addresses at routers and bridges. Client computers are configured to view the NAT server as a gateway (which indeed it is). When a packet is sent out from a client, it reaches the gateway, which places its own IP information in the packet, replacing the original IP address. Because this computer has some sort of connection to the Internet, this is a reachable address—unlike the private subnet addresses used on the internal network. When a response packet arrives, the gateway replaces the destination address with the address of the computer that sent the original packet. Besides just translating the address, NAT must translate header information as well as packet checksums.

A technique similar to NAT is called *IP masquerading*. IP masquerading is often used interchangeably with NAT. The primary difference between the two is the number of machines that can be served by the software. NAT allows an essentially limitless number of clients; IP masquerading does not. For most purposes, NAT and IP masquerading will be interchangeable solutions, and you can infer that comments about one will apply to the other. For the sake of clarity, I will refer to both Network Address Translation and IP masquerading as NAT. While not entirely technically correct, they both accomplish the same task and are configured identically to each other. We will look at a NAT solution under Windows and IP masquerading software for Mac OS and Linux in Chapter 16.

If you want to provide services to the Internet based on a computer on your local network, and you're using NAT as the method of connecting to the Internet, you'll need to make some special modifications. As we've seen, all TCP/IP communications take place on a certain port. If a computer on the Internet makes a request to retrieve a Web page from your network, it will request the document from your gateway NAT computer. If you want to run a Web server on the NAT machine, this is entirely fine and will work precisely as you expect; however, it's unlikely that everything you want to run can be served from a single computer. To solve the problem of allowing internal machines to respond to requests from the outside world, most NAT solutions will let you map a port number to an internal computer's IP address. For example, on my NAT machine, I map incoming connections on port 80 to an internal IP address of 192.168.0.50. Any and all incoming requests to port 80 on the NAT server are automatically, and transparently, forwarded to the machine running the Web server. This is the only fault of NAT. You connect to the network with a single IP address for your entire IP network. It hasn't proven to be a problem for several offices I've configured to use NAT servers, and, in fact, I've never had a single problem that a few moments of configuring NAT didn't solve.

Another big advantage to using NAT is that there are NAT servers that run with minimal hardware requirements. If you have an old 486 lying around, you can set up a DOS or Linux NAT machine using your old hardware. In fact, you can even run a server on a machine with as little as 640K of memory and a floppy drive. This is a big benefit of running a NAT server because it requires very little investment to start out. Proxy servers often have steeper requirements because they offer a specialized service for each protocol, not a low-level translation service like NAT.

Imagine this: providing close to T1 speeds to an entire network for around $40 a month. If you're purchasing a dedicated line, you're not going to find any sort of price that can compare. This is precisely the service that I am providing to my home network using a cable modem and a NAT server. I'm running a dedicated Web server, email server, and have several Windows shares that I mount on my computers at home and work. The speed is incredible, and I have to pay for only a single connection, yet I have service provided for several computers. If you don't want to buy dedicated Internet service for your network and you need more expandability, then NAT is a perfect solution.

One decision you'll need to make when creating a NAT solution is whether you'd like to use one or two Ethernet cards. If you choose to use two cards, you'll be employing a technique called *IP forwarding*. IP forwarding is the process of moving IP packets from one interface to another. One of your Ethernet cards will represent your internal network, while the other will be your connection to the rest of the world. Packets from one network will be forwarded from one interface to another. Your computer becomes, for all intents and purposes, a router. The reason you would want to choose two network cards is because otherwise your NAT packets will be sent across the network wire twice. For example, a packet is broadcast from your local network to NAT server. If the outside world is connected to the same card (such as a cable modem being plugged into a hub, and the hub being connected to the computer), then to reach the outside, the packet is modified and rebroadcast to the same card. The result is that you're essentially cutting your network bandwidth in half. A second problem with this approach is that your internal packets are potentially going to be seen by the rest of the world. This could be a security risk for your network. With a two-network card configuration, packets intended for your internal network are not forwarded to the outside network, which is connected to a separate Ethernet card. Local and remote communications are isolated and only connected when information needs to move between the two networks. I've run a handful of machines with a single card connection with no obvious problems, but I've since moved to a dual card configuration myself. If you don't want to fight with multiple cards and a slightly more complex situation, use a single card. If high-throughput is a must and you have a large internal network, choose two cards. If security is a significant issue for your network, you'll need to go with two cards, regardless of the size of your internal network. I'll try to include information in our setup examples that will show both types of configuration.

NAT Sounds Almost Illegal; Is It?

As I said, I'm paying for a single cable modem connection but am providing Internet service to several computers. The cable modem service provider also sells multiple IP addresses if I want to hook up multiple computers, but I choose to use NAT and pay for one. I'm paying for a single connection and am using the bandwidth that is reserved for that connection. If I were using multiple IP addresses without paying for them, then, yes, that would not be fair. It's important to note that in some cases, ISPs may not be happy to know that you're powering an entire network through a single low-cost connection—especially if you're using a huge amount of bandwidth and are constantly connected. If you're planning on using NAT on a large scale, check with your ISP first. Whatever the case, when you pay for bandwidth on a network, use it as efficiently as possible. NAT allows you to get your money's worth in a way that expands your capabilities far more than a standard connection. If you have more than one computer you need to serve, use NAT.

Upcoming chapters focus on proxy and NAT solutions we can use on our network. If you'd like to get Web browsing access to your network in a flash and that's your primary concern, then focus on the proxy serving information. If you'd like to connect your entire network to the Internet and allow a variety of services both in and out, then NAT is what you need. There are packages available for any operating system that make NAT and proxy serving extremely easy, so even if the concepts sound a bit confusing, you should find the implementation very straight-forward.

Other Information Sources

NAT, Network Address Translation, RFC 1631

http://www.cis.ohio-state.edu/htbin/rfc/rfc1631.html

Proxy Server Information

http://www.cedpa-k12.org/databus-issues/v36n1/proxy.html

ISDN and Data Networking (from 3COM)

http://www.3com.com/nsc/500606.html

ADSL Information and Resources

http://www-dos.uniinc.msk.ru/tech1/1997adsl/adslmain.htm

Cable Modem 101

http://www.catv.org/modem/cablemodem/

All You Wanted to Know About T1 But Were Afraid to Ask

http://www.dcbnet.com/notes/9611t1.html

## CHAPTER 15

Using Proxy Servers

by John Ray

In this chapter

Controlling/Censoring Internet Content **298**

Proxy Servers **300**

Configuring Mac OS Browsers **301**

Configuring Windows for Proxy Servers **303**

Configuring Linux for Proxy Servers **306**

Using Mac OS for Proxy Serving **308**

Using Windows for Proxy Serving **321**

Using Windows for Proxy Serving **329**

We've been building up to actually creating a connection to the Internet for some time now. You've learned how to share files over TCP/IP, set up Web servers, mail servers, and so on. But the real excitement begins when the services you've created become available to everyone in the world, and your users can access systems far beyond the reaches of your local network. In this chapter, you're going to learn how proxy servers can be used for Internet connectivity and how to configure your software to take advantage of proxy servers. In Chapter 16, "Using Proxy NAT Servers," you'll learn about NAT and its uses for connecting. With a connection to the Internet, however, comes added responsibility. Sometimes you'll need to protect your network from prying eyes. Other times, you'll want to limit what *your* users can see. Before we get down to business, I'd like to discuss one of the more controversial topics of the Internet: censorship. With your connection to the Internet comes the ability, and sometimes *responsibility*, to control the information people view on the network.

Controlling/Censoring Internet Content

Although censorship may seem like a rather strict term to apply to controlling what your users can and can't view on the Internet, recent laws have tried to push constitutional rights well beyond merely controlling what is appropriate to view. A recent attempt was made to pass a communications act that would have prohibited adult material to be shown on the Internet. This smut law was an attempt to help parents control what their children were viewing, and to clean up the Internet. Unfortunately, the wording of the act also made sites illegal that discussed important issues, such as breast cancer. The Internet is a dynamic global community and is not controllable by a single organization or government. Yet that is precisely what the U.S. government tried to do with the various incarnations of the Communications Decency Act. Undoubtedly, this will be an area that is explored repeatedly in the upcoming years. Take an interest in it, and don't assume that such laws will do nothing but wipe out pornography. They might just outlaw information that you have published online.

Still, there are reasons why content needs to be controlled. In some large businesses, it might be necessary to limit the amount of browsing employees can do on the job or limit the sites they can visit during high-traffic times of the day. For schools, the content that's made available could depend on the age group of the children, or the classroom. Personally, I find that the most effective strategy for the business world is to educate the employees rather than to try putting a wall between them and the data they want to access. If they understand how the extra traffic affects the network, or how their private browsing might affect co-workers, chances are they'll be happier, and you'll be happier in the long run.

It's really quite simple to get past most proxy server restrictions anyway. For example, although I didn't even intend it, one of the first cute Web-based programs I wrote, called LinkCheck, can be used to defeat proxy security. LinkCheck allows you to interactively browse and check hypertext links on Web pages to be sure that they're still working. You browse the Web as you would normally, except when using LinkCheck, you'll see status icons by each link, showing you whether the link is a good link, a bad link, or if the remote computer isn't even responding. If you're interested, feel free to give it a trial run by running it from my Web page at `http://jray.ag.ohio-state.edu`.

I haven't updated the code in over a year, so please ignore any glaring errors you might find, or drop me an email by clicking the link on my page.

One unintended side effect of my program is that it can be easily used to bypass a filtering proxy. (I discussed proxy servers in Chapter 14, "Connecting Your Network to the Internet.") LinkCheck works by dynamically grabbing the contents of the URL you want, on your local computer, and then rewriting it on-the-fly to include status icons. The resulting page has all the content of the original, but its source is local, not the original site. It is unlikely that an OSU Web server would be mapped out as a bad or forbidden server on a proxy. As long as someone can reach my Web page, they can then use it to browse the Web past their proxy server. Obviously, this is not why I wrote the program, but it does appear to be a common use for it. There are many other programs that work similarly to LinkCheck and can be used in the same manner. Some sites will translate pages into different languages and then spit them back out to the browser; others will reverse the images to make the mirror images of the original Web pages. These programs are all written for fun or utility purposes, but, at the same time, they allow people to bypass proxy security measures. It's just a matter of time before one person finds a way around the company proxy and tells a co-worker, and so on.

Classrooms, on the other hand, are far more controlled environments, and it is far less likely that a student will find a proxy bypass in a classroom. The main purpose of a proxy in a classroom is to restrict the ability of a student to follow links that might be inappropriate and that the teacher doesn't know about. In this sort of a controlled environment, a proxy server will work wonderfully and will let the instructors breathe a bit easier. On the other hand, left unattended, and with a goal in mind, don't discount the ability of students to find their ways into places that they shouldn't be. Effectively running a proxy server for filtering purposes will always require some sort of supervision.

NAT servers that allow content control suffer from the same problems. This isn't a failing of the software but rather an issue with the way the World Wide Web itself operates. The Web enables us to link resources from around the world into a single location. Trying to keep up with what information is located where is largely an impossible task. Content filtering can limit access to most inappropriate content, but will never be 100 percent accurate in determining bad sites, or in blocking access through *back door* services. In some cases, proxy filtering can be downright annoying. I recently received a call from a local school that was trying access one of our Web pages but couldn't connect. Upon examining the URL they were trying reach, I noticed it had xxx in it. (There were a series of directories on the Web site that were named using three of each letter of the alphabet: aaa, bbb, and so on). The content filtering software was convinced that this page, which was actually a gardening resource, was a source of inappropriate material due to the xxx.

With all the different products available for filtering, it quickly became apparent that a standard was necessary for specifying filtering content. There are several small software packages that will give a parent the ability to restrict the Web viewing their children do. Unfortunately, each package uses a different format for its filter files, so each manufacturer has to provide its own updates, and they are useable only with that specific product. In response to this situation, the PICS labeling format was introduced.

PICS, or *Platform for Internet Content Selection*, provides an interesting way of looking at labels. Strangely enough, PICS does not provide a rating system at all, nor does it attempt to classify data. Instead, it lets the site owner, or rating distributor, define the site's own rating system. This is an entirely arbitrary scale. Any system of classification can be used. Sites may then tag their pages according to a particular classification and, depending on the rating scale, will limit the user's level of access.

Separating the rating system from the software that controls access lets the developers concentrate on their strong points. Software developers develop interfaces and support for PICS into their software programs. Other people specializing in content can provide rating services that any PICS-compliant software can use. Unfortunately, PICS is just one standard in a sea of several ranking products. As I've mentioned, most use their own proprietary system, which is less than ideal. For an interactive tutorial on PICS, check out this Web site: http://w3c1.inria.fr/PICS/951030/AV/StartHere.html.

Proxy Servers

Let's go ahead and start with setting up a proxy server. Proxy servers can be as simple to run as starting a single program. Unlike the TCP/IP services we set up in the last few chapters, proxy and NAT servers are not as easily available on all the platforms. However, once obtained, proxies are usually easy to configure, thus their appeal. NAT, however, is the more complete solution, so, if you can't use proxy service because of platform reasons, a NAT solution will be available. Interestingly enough, there is a popular proxy server you might be using without even knowing it. Connectix produces a popular single client proxy server for MacOS- and Windows-based computers called SurfExpress. SurfExpress is a caching-Web proxy. To speed up your Web browsing, SurfExpress caches Web sites you visit and downloads new information to your cache. When your browser visits a Web site, it talks to the SurfExpress proxy engine, which delivers the data. It's an interesting use of a Web proxy server.

Even though NAT and proxy servers can be used to accomplish similar tasks, they can also be used together. You might still want to run a Web-caching proxy server (the most common form of proxy server) on a NAT-based network. This could speed up your Web browsing, as well as cut down on traffic that must travel between your intranet and the Internet.

If you implement a proxy server on your network, your users' Web browsers need to be configured to use it. Read on to see how to do it.

Configuring Your Browser to Use a Proxy Server

It's very simple to configure most browsers to use a proxy server, rather than trying to contact a remote computer directly. These days, the two standard browsers are Netscape and Internet Explorer, so let's see what it takes to get them set up correctly. The only information you'll need beforehand is the IP address or hostname of the proxy, as well as the port that the service is running on. The proxy servers we're looking at will be running on ports 8000 and 80, as seems to be common with most Web proxies. If you already have a proxy but don't know the port it's using, try the common ports. If that doesn't work, contact your network administrator, who should have a record of the correct ports to use.

Configuring Mac OS Browsers

The Mac OS browsers look a little different from the Windows versions, which look different from the Linux version, so I'll go through configuration of each of the operating system's browsers for clarity. To configure Netscape under the Mac OS, choose Preferences from the Edit menu. Scroll through the list of available preference settings on the left until you see the Advanced selection. If it's not expanded, click the arrow to display the hierarchy of advanced settings you can configure. You should see Proxies in the list. Click it now. If you've found the correct configuration area, it should look a lot like Figure 15.1.

FIGURE 15.1

To configure your proxy settings in Netscape for Macintosh, use this Preferences dialog box section.

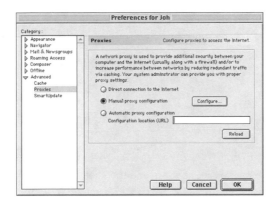

Select the Manual Proxy Configuration radio button, and then click the Configure button. Netscape lets you configure proxies for all the services it supports (Web, email, FTP, and so on). If you have other proxy servers running, be sure to fill them in appropriately. Otherwise, only fill in the HTTP proxy field and port, as shown in Figure 15.2.

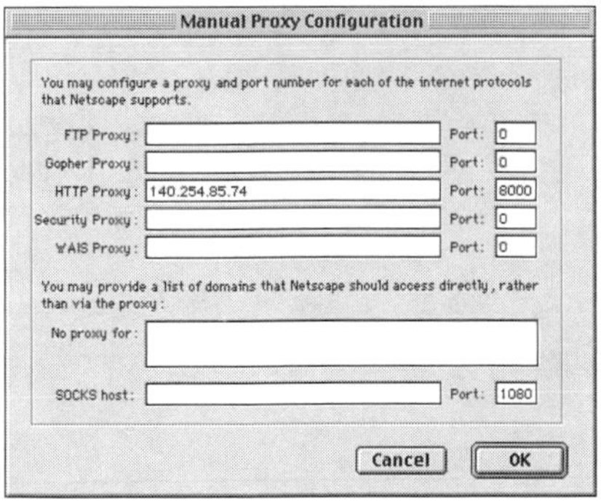

FIGURE 15.2

Enter the proper HTTP proxy address and port in their respective fields.

As you can see, my browser is set to 140.254.85.74 and port 8000. Don't try to use these values for yourself; they won't work. Click the OK button to save your changes, and then click OK again to exit the Netscape configuration screen.

If you're using Internet Explorer 4, which is now the default browser on the Mac operating system, you'll need to set it up a bit differently. Once again, go to the Edit menu and choose Preferences. The resulting configuration screen will look very similar to the Netscape preferences screen. Scroll to the Network options and expand them by clicking the triangle next to the word *Network*. Click the word Proxies to show the proxy setup screen seen in Figure 15.3.

FIGURE 15.3

You configure your Macintosh Internet Explorer proxy preferences in this dialog box.

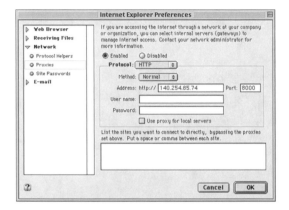

You'll want to click the Enabled radio button, and then set the protocol you're configuring a proxy server for. I'm setting up the same proxy server that I configured for Netscape (140.254.85.74, port 8000). Your configuration should look pretty close to mine, except for slightly different numbers, when you're done.

A feature of the new Mac OS 8.5x is that Internet preferences can all be configured in one dialog box. This might not work with all browsers, but, by the time you read this, most software should use this configuration. To use the system-level Internet controls, go to the Internet control panel (don't confuse this with the Microsoft Internet Configuration control panel, which is installed on some systems when setting up Internet Explorer and Outlook Express). The main screen will initially be missing the options we need to use, so you're going to have to change your user level to let you set up proxy servers. Go to the Edit menu and choose User Mode. You should switch your settings to Advanced by clicking the appropriate radio button, as shown in Figure 15.4

FIGURE 15.4

Before configuring your Internet settings, you need to select the Advanced user lever.

You can also choose the Administration mode if you want. The difference between the two is that the Administration mode lets you set a password and lock certain fields so that the machine's user can't change them. Most of the network settings on the Macintosh are changing to this format (different user levels). Once you've set the user mode for the Internet control panel, you should see an Advanced tab appear. Click the tab, and your display should be similar to the one shown in Figure 15.5.

I See Lots of Control Panels with Advanced Mode. What Do They Do?

Many of the Macintosh network control panels have an Advanced and an Administration mode. You'll find that you can set a wide variety of options that are otherwise hidden from view. In System 8.5, for example, the Internet control panel allows you to configure helper applications and other information in Advanced or Administration mode. Sometimes, however, you need to be careful what you configure. The AppleTalk control panel, once in Advanced mode, will allow you to set AppleTalk mode information for your computer. This could potentially disrupt your file sharing services. The best rule of thumb is, as always, if you don't know what it does, don't mess with it!

FIGURE 15.5
After choosing the Advanced user level, you'll have many more configuration options.

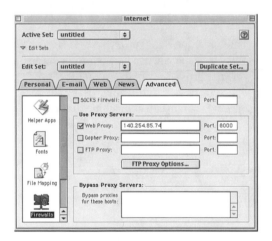

To set the system up to use a Web proxy server, simply check the Web Proxy button and type in the appropriate IP address and port. You can see how I've set mine up the same as I've done with the two browsers. Now hopefully any browser I use will automatically use the proxy I've set here. At the time of this writing, the Mac OS 8.5 Internet control panel successfully changes the settings for Internet Explorer; Netscape ignores it.

Configuring Windows for Proxy Servers

Once again, because you have two primary browsers in Windows, you have two different ways of configuring proxies. Let's start with Netscape again and follow up with Internet Explorer. Netscape should configure very similarly under Windows as under the Macintosh version. Start Netscape, and then choose Preferences from the Edit menu. Expand the Advanced settings by clicking the tiny plus box at the extreme left, and then select the Proxies subsection. Your screen should now look like Figure 15.6.

FIGURE 15.6

You configure a proxy server in Netscape 4.x for Windows in this dialog box.

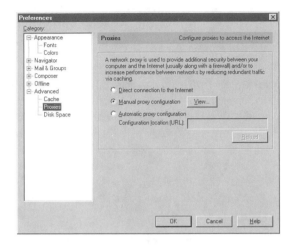

Click the View button to configure your HTTP proxy server. Here, as in the Mac version, you can configure the proxies that Netscape will use for the protocols it supports. Fill in the HTTP field to reflect the settings of your proxy server. I've set mine for the server 140.254.85.74, with the port 8000, as seen in Figure 15.7. As with the other examples, this server is not a functional proxy server that you can use. It is simply a test machine that I'm using during the writing of this book. You'll notice the entry 1080 in the Socks field. This is the standard port number for SOCKS service, which is a widely supported type of proxy.

FIGURE 15.7

Use the Manual Proxy Configuration dialog box to, well, configure your proxy manually.

Click OK to save your settings, and then click OK again to finish the configuration. Netscape should now be able to successfully contact your proxy server and return Web pages.

Configuring Internet Explorer 4 to use a proxy can be done in one of two ways. Internet Explorer 4.x will install an Internet applet in the Windows Control Panel that allows you to configure options in a manner identical to selecting Internet Options from the View menu within Internet Explorer itself. Selecting Internet options from within Internet Explorer itself is, of course, the other option. Whichever way you choose to access the configuration settings will be fine; you'll be seeing exactly the same settings. Once you open the control panel or Internet Options dialog box, click the Connection tab. You should now see a network configuration screen much like the one in Figure 15.8.

FIGURE 15.8

Internet Explorer offers you two ways to configure your Internet options.

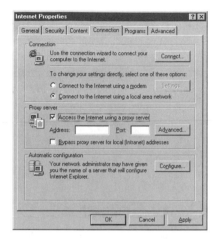

You'll want to check the Access the Internet using a proxy server check box, and then click on the Advanced button. You *could* specify a single proxy server in the space provided on this screen, but it's possible—in fact likely—that your network might end up having multiple proxy servers. Using the Advanced button, you can configure a different server for each of the different IE protocols, as shown in Figure 15.9.

FIGURE 15.9

You can configure multiple proxy servers for a variety of Internet Explorer protocols.

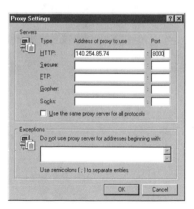

You should recognize my settings from the previous examples, and, as before, you shouldn't use them for your own computer. That should do it! Realize that changing the options in the Internet control panel will only update the settings within Internet Explorer. Even the Control Panel applet is not meant to configure programs other than the Microsoft Internet software.

What Are These Do Not Use Proxy Server for These Addresses Options?

You've probably already noticed two options that keep showing up when you configure your proxy servers. The first, Do not use Proxy Server for such-and-such Addresses, lets you set an address or range of addresses that the browser will bypass the proxy server to access. If your network is not configured to allow access to the outside world except through the proxy, then this option won't work. However, if you're just using the proxy to speed up access, you can set addresses. You might need to use this if you find a Web page that just isn't acting right through the proxy server. Some software has difficulty running through a proxy server, and your computer must talk to it directly. Another similar option you might encounter is Don't use Proxy for local hosts. Selecting this option will bypass your proxy server when you attempt to access any hosts on your local network. This setting should work regardless of your network connection and is probably reasonable to activate. Speeds will be faster accessing local servers directly, and you can most likely trust any servers that are running internal to your organization. This is especially useful on corporate intranets with links and permitted access to the outside.

Configuring Linux for Proxy Servers

Last but not least, let's take a look at Netscape under Linux. Netscape, once again, should be mostly consistent with the MacOS and Windows versions. To configure Netscape under the Linux, choose Preferences from the Edit menu. Scroll through the list of available preference settings on the left until you see the Advanced selection. If it is not expanded, click the triangle to display the hierarchy of advanced settings. You should see Proxies in the list. Click it now. If you've found the correct configuration area, it should look a lot like Figure 15.10.

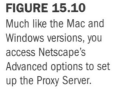

FIGURE 15.10

Much like the Mac and Windows versions, you access Netscape's Advanced options to set up the Proxy Server.

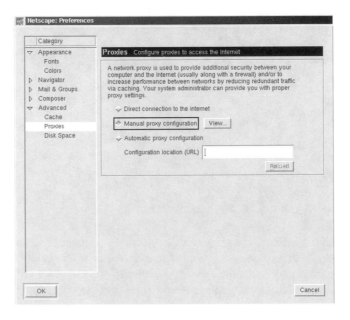

Click the Configure button to set up the proxy server for your network. Once you've set your proxy, click the OK button to save your changes, and then OK again to exit the configuration screen. Figure 15.11 shows the configuration for my proxy server at 140.254.84.74, port 8000.

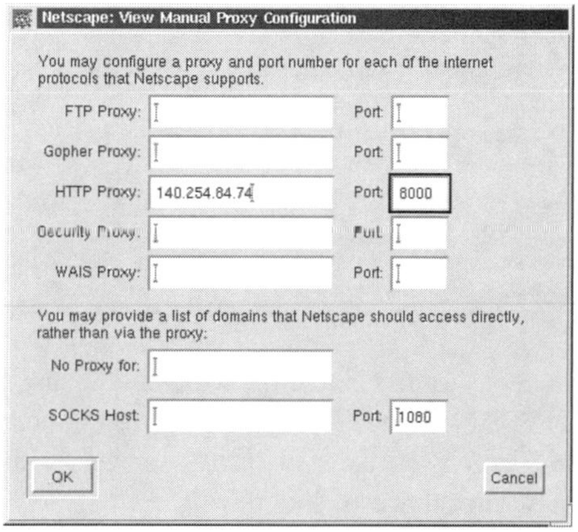

FIGURE 15.11

Netscape's proxy server setting is configured to 140.254.85.74, port 8000.

Because Internet Explorer is not available for Linux, we don't need to look at it. However, I'd be personally disappointed with myself if I didn't also include the information you'll need to config- ure the UNIX Lynx browser. Lynx is a text-only, command-line browser that is available for Linux and installed by default under Red Hat 5.x. I know what you're thinking: "Why in the world would anyone ever want to use a text-based browser?" Well, until you've used Lynx, you can't truly appreciate how fast a Web browser can be. Lynx supports forms, HTTP 1.1, and all the other features of modern browsers. If I have to download a file with the HTTP protocol and I'm on a slow connection, I can Telnet into a Linux machine on a fast connection and use Lynx to download the file, and then transfer it to my machine whenever I want. Another use I've found for Lynx is using it to retrieve Web pages without writing my own HTTP client. In Perl, I can call Lynx and have the output of a Web server returned to my program in one single state- ment. (Besides, we need to encourage Web authors to include text alternatives for their image files!) So, in short, don't discount a program simply because it doesn't have flashy graphics. Nevertheless, I digress; the real task here is configuring Lynx so it can be used with a proxy server. The Lynx configuration file is typically stored in /etc/lynx.cfg. If you edit the file, you should be able to find these options, currently disabled with the # character in front of them, which means it is a comment line rather than an action:

```
# Lynx version 2.2 and beyond supports the use of proxy servers that can
# act as firewall gateways and caching servers.  They are preferable to
# the older gateway servers.  Each protocol used by Lynx can be mapped
# separately using PROTOCOL_proxy environment variables (see INSTALLATION).
# If you have not set them externally, you can set them at run time via
# this configuration file.  They will not override external settings.
# The no_proxy variable can be a comma-separated list of hosts which should
# not be proxied, or an asterisk to override all proxy variables.
# Note that on VMS they are set as process logicals rather than symbols,
# to preserve lowercasing, and will outlive the Lynx image.
```

```
#
#http_proxy:http://some.server.dom:port/
#https_proxy:http://some.server.dom:port/
#ftp_proxy:http://some.server.dom:port/
#gopher_proxy:http://some.server.dom:port/
#news_proxy:http://some.server.dom:port/
#newspost_proxy:http://some.server.dom:port/
#newsreply_proxy:http://some.server.dom:port/
#snews_proxy:http://some.server.dom:port/
#snewspost_proxy:http://some.server.dom:port/
#snewsreply_proxy:http://some.server.dom:port/
#nntp_proxy:http://some.server.dom:port/
#wais_proxy:http://some.server.dom:port/
#finger_proxy:http://some.server.dom:port/
#cso_proxy:http://some.server.dom:port/
#no_proxy:host.domain.dom
```

For our configuration, we're just going to change the `http` and `https` proxy lines. Most HTTP proxy servers can handle HTTPS (secure HTTP) proxy requests, including my 140.254.85.74 test proxy. To set up Lynx to correctly speak to my proxy server, I'll simply uncomment the `http/https` lines or add in new lines that look like this:

```
http_proxy:http://140.254.85.74:8000/
https_proxy:http://140.254.85.74:8000/
```

As with the other graphical browsers, you can configure proxy servers for other protocols as well as use the `no_proxy` line to set sites that will not be accessed through the proxy server.

Using Mac OS for Proxy Serving

If you tried out the WebSTAR Web server on the Mac OS, you've probably noticed the WebSTAR proxy module. This is a full proxy server that comes with the WebSTAR package. The current crop of Mac OS-based proxy servers are only Web proxies, so, if you'd like to run services other than the HTTP protocol, you'll need to use a different operating system for the proxy service. As of version 8.1, the Mac OS does not support multiple active network interfaces. This means that you cannot use a proxy server connected to a modem to serve an internal network. The proxy server must exist on the same network as the computer itself. This is likely to change by the time you read this, as Open Transport will be going through some major revisions with the upcoming Mac OS 8.5 System software. I'm still going to talk about a Mac OS proxy server, because, for the most part, you'll probably want to use a proxy for reasons other than making a network connection (you can use NAT for that).

The proxy server I'm going to look at here is WebDoubler from Maxum software. It's fast, easy to configure (both locally and remotely), and can serve large workgroups. As with most Web proxy servers, it also caches the data to speed up transfers to your local area network. WebDoubler allows you to use PICS browsing restriction profiles that limit the Web sites that users are allowed to visit. Restrictions can be made on a client computer basis; this is an extremely useful feature for schools needing a proxy server. WebDoubler is available from `http://www.maxum.com/webdoubler`.

The software is very easy to get up and running. In fact, simply double-clicking the WebDoubler icon will start your proxy server. Most of WebDoubler is configurable from within the application itself; however, in its current form, a large portion of the configuration is available only through the administrative web interface. Because of this, I'm going to show most of the configuration as seen through a Web browser. I generally prefer this mode of administration anyway. Using the Web as an interface to real-world applications is one of best uses of the Web, in my opinion. Most people prefer to use their own system for its interface but don't really care if the software they're using is running on their machine or somewhere else. In the case of the Web-enabled application, the interface travels to wherever and whatever platform the user is using. Where the software itself is running is of no real importance. Anyway, the first thing you'll need to do with WebDoubler is to configure the administrative Web user interface. To do this, start the WebDoubler application. With the program running, access the initial configuration shown in Figure 15.12. Choose Configuration from the Server menu.

FIGURE 15.12

Configure WebDoubler from this screen.

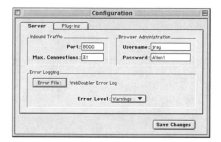

From here, you can change a few of the basic settings that the proxy server uses for its networking.

You may choose the port number that the proxy server uses and the maximum number of simultaneous connections it will allow. Many proxy servers operate off port 8080, so you might want to change the default to 8080, or even just 80. The maximum number of connections may need to be raised depending on the number of people you expect to be using the proxy server. The default setting (31) should be fine for most small workgroups. The settings we're most interested in here are the Browser Administration fields. Here you can change the username and password that will be used over the Web to control the proxy server. Change the default values to something you'll remember, and then click the Save Changes button. You're now ready to begin the web-based configuration process.

Start your Web browser, making sure it's configured to speak to your WebDoubler proxy server, and then connect to the following URL: http://your.domain.com/webdoubler.admin.

You'll need to supply the username and password you just set from within WebDoubler itself. Once connected, you'll be greeted by the main WebDoubler configuration screen, as shown in Figure 15.13.

FIGURE 15.13

You'll see this screen when you connect with WebDoubler.

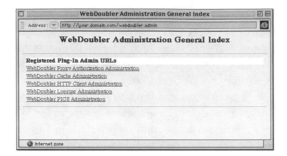

The current default installation of WebDoubler comes with five plug-ins you can configure. Here's a description of the plug-ins and their general functions:

- WebDoubler Proxy Authorization Administration—Lets you create and edit users and ranges of IP addresses that can use the proxy server.
- WebDoubler Cache Administration—Lets you create, manage, and delete proxy caches on the proxy server machine.
- WebDoubler HTTP Client Administration—Lets you control the amount of traffic and other network functions of the server.
- WebDoubler Logging Administration—Lets you set the level of logging on the proxy server.
- WebDoubler PICS Administration—Lets you create, edit, and manage PICS security profiles for the server. This is the most complex of the areas you'll be seeing. The PICS filtering provided by WebDoubler is powerful, but simple enough to set up in a few minutes.

Let's go ahead and start with the Proxy Authorization module. Click the link to the Proxy Authorization Administration module from the main WebDoubler administration screen. You should arrive at the authorization screen, which will look similar to the one in Figure 15.14.

From here, you can set up user accounts to access the server as well as ranges of IP addresses that will be able to use the proxy. The Access Control has two options: Allow any client to access WebDoubler, and Restrict WebDoubler access.

Obviously, the Allow any client to access WebDoubler option does precisely that: lets anyone use your WebDoubler proxy server for his or her proxy service. On a closed internal network, this setting would be fine, but leaving your server open to the public might result in a few problems. If the address of the proxy server leaks from your company, you might find that a larger number of people are benefiting from the speed increase of the proxy server than you thought.

FIGURE 15.14
You'll see this authorization screen when you click the Proxy Authorization Administration link.

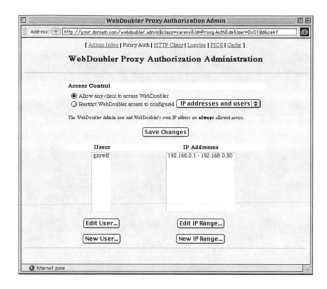

The Restrict WebDoubler access option lets you place limitations on the people who can access the server by specifying ranges of IP addresses, a list of users, or both. If you're using User authentication, each user will be asked to enter in a username and a password before they're allowed to connect to the server. The server will use the same authentication method it uses to determine if you're allowed to administrate the server. To add a user, click the New User... button, or if you already have users entered, you can select one and edit his or her settings with the Edit User... button. In Figure 15.15, I'm editing my growlf user.

FIGURE 15.15
You can edit access settings for an individual user.

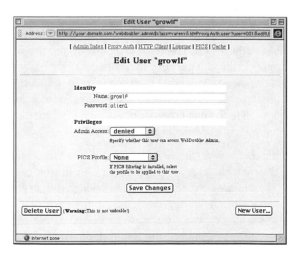

In the Identity portion of the configuration, you can set the username and the password that will be used to access the proxy server. In Privileges, you can use the Admin Access option to allow the user you've created to administrate the server. You can also select a PICS Profile for the user. This is a rather nice feature, because you can create a PICS profile for a particular user rather than having to apply a blanket policy to everyone who connects. There are usually a few special cases you'll need to work around for some users; the ability to provide a separate profile on a user-by-user basis is an excellent way to get around this problem. Because we haven't created any PICS profiles yet, there won't be anything we can set the profile to, but keep this screen in mind for future configuration. If you don't want to have to specify usernames for each of the people who should have access to the server, you can also use the IP address ranges to set up zones that can connect to your server. Click the New IP Range… button to set a new range of IP addresses that can access the server. In Figure 15.16, I'm adding a range of addresses for my local workgroup at work.

FIGURE 15.16

Rather than edit individual users, you can add a range of addresses.

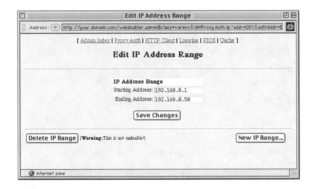

The drop-down menu in the Restrict WebDoubler access option lets you choose whether to use usernames and passwords for authentication, IP address ranges, or both. Be sure to select the radio button by the authentication method you want; otherwise, you might be a bit confused when your usernames/IP addresses are ignored by the program.

Now that you've configured the clients that can connect to the machine, let's continue and set up the caching options of the server. The *cache* stores data from the Web servers that the proxy connects to, thus eliminating the need to reconnect to these servers if other requests are made. You can reach the cache configuration screen (shown in Figure 15.17) by clicking the cache hyperlink at the top of any of the configuration pages, or by selecting the Admin Index link, which will return you to the main menu. I'm working through the options in the order of the main menu, just in case you're wondering.

From the cache configuration screen, you can set up the amount of disk space reserved for the caching and where the cache files are stored. You can even disable caching completely (which you should try only if there are very large problems loading Web pages). You can also set the logging of the cache module and the Aggressiveness of the caching. Caching is an intelligent process. Only pages matching certain criteria are cached, and each cached page has a certain lifetime, after which it will expire and be removed from the cache. The Aggressiveness levels control some of the brains behind the cache. The currently defined levels of aggression are

- Conservative—Follows the HTTP 1.1 standard as it currently exists. This is the first setting you should try for your caching and is the default setting.
- Ultra conservative—This is the same as conservative, but it doesn't cache things like searches, and so on.

- Aggressive—Netscape reloads will come from the cache, while shift-reloads (super reloads) bypass the cache. This is not the correct method of caching but might be useful.

- Very Aggressive—Caches longer than the other options and serves as much information from the cache as possible. If you access mainly static information, this might be useful for your network and should greatly cut down on the amount of network traffic to external Web sites.

FIGURE 15.17
Configure WebDoubler's cache settings in this dialog box.

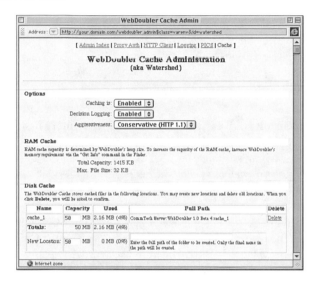

You'll also notice the RAM Cache setting, which you cannot change from within the Web interface. The WebDoubler proxy server can also use part of your Macintosh's memory to cache Web information. If you have a large amount of memory, you can greatly speed up the proxy server's performance by increasing the amount of RAM that the proxy uses in its cache. To do this, you'll need to quit WebDoubler and find the icon on your desktop. Select the icon without opening it and choose Get Info… from the File menu. You could also press Command-I to accomplish the same task. If you're using System 8.5 or later, you'll need to Select Memory from the pop-up Show menu in the resulting window. If you're using an earlier version of the OS, the memory information appears in the main Get Info window. Figure 15.18 shows the display as it appears under System 8.5.

You can leave the Minimum memory setting alone; it is mostly used in cases when an application's default memory setting does not provide enough memory. If you want to force a certain amount of memory to be reserved for WebDoubler, you can do it here. The setting that's best to change is the Preferred Size. This tells the machine how much memory you *want* to have reserved, but MacOS will not fail to launch the program if it can't allocate all the memory. Add as much memory as you can spare to the preferred setting, and then restart WebDoubler and reload the Cache Administration Web page. You should see that the capacity of your RAM Cache has increased by close to the amount of memory you reserved for the application. This memory-cache trick is a common thing to do for most Macintosh applications. In fact, if you're running other server software, you may want to check the documentation to see if increasing its memory allocation also increases internal caching performance.

FIGURE 15.18
WebDoubler displays
and lets you configure
its memory require-
ments.

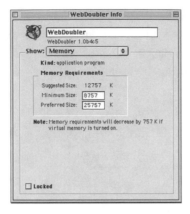

No matter how much memory you have, you certainly have more hard drive space you can use as a cache. You'll want to set up a disk-based cache for your proxy server. In the Disk Cache section of the cache administration page, you can do just that. You'll need to specify a size for each cache you create, as well as specify the entire path that leads to the cache folder you're creating. Be careful when you do so; the Macintosh is not the easiest machine to specify a path on, mainly due to the fact that special characters (trademark symbols, and so on) can be used (and often are) within a path. Click the Save Changes button when you've defined a new cache or changed any of the options and want to save them. Clicking the Delete link that's beside any of the cache locations will delete the cache from your hard drive.

The next area to take a quick look at is the HTTP client configuration. Click the HTTP Client link at the top of the screen, or return to the main menu and follow the link from there to reach the HTTP Client Administration screen, shown in Figure 15.19.

FIGURE 15.19
From this screen, you
configure your HTTP
proxy client.

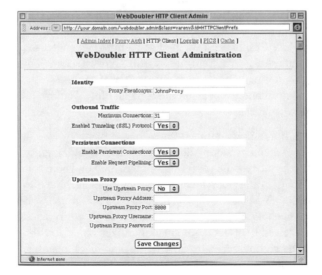

Most, if not all, of the options here can be left alone. The HTTP client module is used to retrieve Web pages that will be fed back to the client machine. It is the lowest level (network-
wise) of the different modules. Let's go through these settings now. The identity of the proxy
server is simply an identifying name for your WebDoubler machine. Set it to whatever you'd
like, or leave it in the default configuration. The Outbound Traffic section lets you choose the
number of connections that can be made to the server and enable SSL (Secure Socket Layer)
communications through the proxy. Under Persistent Connections, the server will let you shut
off the ability for a client to maintain a connection to the server. This will degrade performance
as multiple connections will need to be made to the server for each resource being retrieved.
Lastly, you can give the address and connection information for an Upstream Proxy. This is a
proxy for the proxy; unless you already have a proxy server set up on your network, you won't
need to use this option.

Before we get to the somewhat complicated PICS configuration, let's take a look at the second-
to-last configuration screen that's available to us: the Logging configuration. Once again, you
can reach this from the Logging link at the top of your screen, or from the Log Administration
item on the main menu. Shown in Figure 15.20, there isn't very much you can do on the Log
Administration page.

FIGURE 15.20

WebDoubler's Log
Administration screen
isn't very interactive.

You can see the number of hits that have been made on the server, the total amount of bytes
that have been transferred, and the average size of each proxy hit. You can also disable logging
if you'd like, or change the path to the log file that's being used. Once again, be careful when
setting the log path; Mac filenames often include characters that might be rather difficult to
specify through the Web interface. These settings should be pretty obvious, so let's take a
quick break, and then continue on to look at the last module, the PICS Administration module.
When you're ready, click the PICS link from the top of your screen or from the main configuration menu. The initial display should look like the screen shown in Figure 15.21.

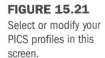

FIGURE 15.21

Select or modify your PICS profiles in this screen.

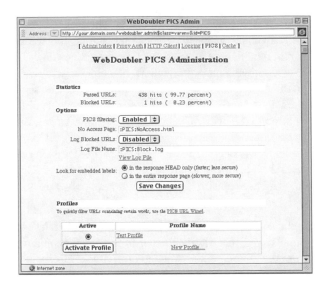

WebDoubler is configured with PICS profiles. Each profile can contain many individual filtering criteria. By default, there is no initial profile applied to the proxy server, and all data requested by the clients is retrieved. On this initial page, you can see some statistics on the number of URLs that have passed successfully through the proxy server and the number that have been blocked. You can also use the PICS filtering menu to disable PICS entirely and set the Web page that's displayed to users when they attempt to reach a page they do not have access to. If you choose to log the URLs that people are trying to access, you can enable that here as well. Because PICS uses labels that are embedded in Web pages themselves, you're given the option of determining *where* in the Web page WebDoubler looks for PICS rating labels. Ratings should be obtainable in the header of each HTTP response but are sometimes encoded throughout the HTML document. If you're willing to sacrifice some speed for more thorough checking of the Web pages, set the Look for embedded labels option to in the entire response page. Now, on to the profiles. Go ahead and click the New Profile... link so that we can define a new set of filtering criteria. Your screen should look very much like the one in Figure 15.22.

The first thing you're going to need to do when setting up a new profile is to identify the profile and its purpose. You do so in the Identity section of the profile creation screen. If you have many different PICS profiles created, it becomes very useful to know what the differences are between them. Because you can apply PICS profiles on a user-by-user basis, you potentially could have only slight variations from a main profile. In addition, you can move profiles around. If you create a profile and want to distribute it to other schools or other departments, the description will come in handy for the recipients.

Next, you're probably going to want to tell the PICS profile what rating system you're going to be using on your server. You might want to research PICS service providers other than the ones included by default with the WebDoubler package; there might be specialized ratings that would be of more use to you than the stock settings. To set up a new rating server, click the New Service link in the Services section. Figure 15.23 shows the resulting service selection screen.

FIGURE 15.22
Establish new filtering criteria in this dialog box.

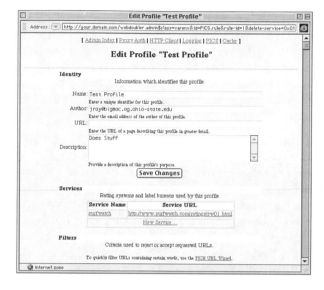

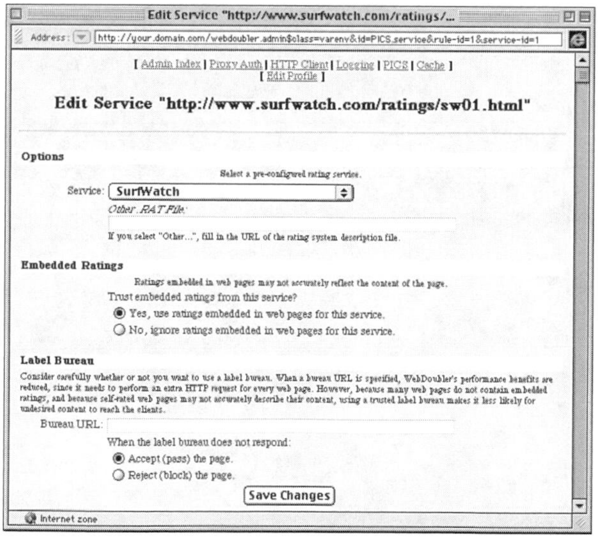

FIGURE 15.23
Click the New Service link to access this selection screen.

The first thing you can do is pick from a list of preconfigured rating services, including SurfWatch, SafeSurf, and several others. If you'd like, you can fill in the path to another, custom rating service. These services provide a ranking method for Web pages, as defined by the PICS standard. Your next decision will be whether you want to trust ratings that are embedded in Web pages. Because it's up to the Web page creator to appropriately embed the ratings, they might not accurately portray the contents of the page. If this is the case, you may want to choose the ignore ratings embedded in web pages option and opt for a label bureau instead.

Label bureaus offer a value-added service of providing their own ratings for Web pages. Each Web page a user requests is also looked up on the label bureau, which will provide rating information for that page and return it to the proxy. Based on the information returned by the label bureau, the page could be passed to the client or rejected. The drawback to this approach is that two requests have to be made for every page that's retrieved. This duplication could impact speed significantly on the network. As with any ratings, you're still at the mercy of the rankings of the label bureau, whether they have ranked the pages manually or have written software that examines a page and returns a rating based on what it finds. There will always be some discrepancy between what you feel should be filtered and what actually is.

Once you're finished defining a rating service, click the Save Changes button to return to our main PICS profile screen. Okay, now you've set up a service that will be used to rank your proxied pages. For my examples, I'm using the SurfWatch service. Now, let's see how we can customize what is actually filtered by the service. In the Filters section, you can define two different types of filters and create as many different filters as you'd like that will be used in the profile. The easiest type of filter to set up is a URL filter. This is a simple way of blocking access to a URL you know is bad or inappropriate for your network audience. To create a new URL filter, click the New URL Filter link. The filter creation screen, shown in Figure 15.24, should appear.

FIGURE 15.24

Create filters for URLs you don't want your users to access.

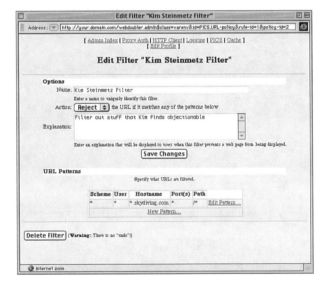

The first thing you're going to want to do is identify the filter, much as you did for the profile. If there are multiple administrators for the proxy server, it might be confusing to look at other people's filtering options if they have not provided reasonable comments along with them. For my setup, I've created a filter for a friend of mine, Kim Steinmetz. Kim is an avid skydiving fan, and, just as a practical joke, I'm going to filter out any URLs from skydiving.com that she might want to access. She probably wouldn't appreciate this much if I kept this filter around, but, for the sake of a reasonable (and temporary) example, it works. I've provided a name and explanation for the filter, as well as the action the proxy server will take (Reject) if it matches the filter to a Web page. I've already set up a pattern that will be used for identifying the skydiving.com Web pages by clicking on the New Pattern link in the URL Patterns area. My pattern setup is pretty simple, as you can see in Figure 15.25.

FIGURE 15.25

Use this screen to set up filters for individual users.

You can create more detailed patterns that operate only on certain users or on certain server ports—whatever is dictated by your needs.

That was pretty simple. Now let's take a look at setting up a label filter. We're going to need to set up a label filter before any of the rating services we've defined will be useful. After all, remember that PICS only defines a rating scale; it doesn't determine what is bad and what is good. That decision is left up to your judgment. Click the New Label Filter to create a new ratings label filter for your server, as shown in Figure 15.26. The initial filter display should be mainly self explanatory; like the URL filter, you have to identify the name of this filter and what it's going to do.

You must also tell the server under what conditions it should accept or reject a Web page. To develop the criteria for accepting or rejecting a page, we need to define tests that will be applied to each page based on the particular rating services we've defined. You create a new test by selecting the Test Service (the rating service) that you want to use, and then clicking the New Test… button. Depending on what services you've selected for your profile, the screen you see might look different from the one displayed in Figure 15.27, which is based on the SurfWatch rating system. PICS ratings are designed to be flexible and allow different rating systems to be developed. This is where you're going to see the variation that is offered by PICS.

FIGURE 15.26

If you like, you can create a new ratings label filter.

FIGURE 15.27

You can select criteria for filtering Web pages based on rated content.

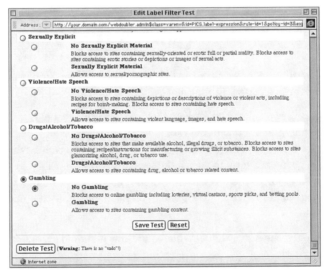

The *SurfWatch* ratings system allows you to create separate tests for sexually explicit, violent, drug-related, and gambling Web pages. Within each rating category is a true or false value. Depending on your PICS rating service, there could possibly be a scale of values to choose from, rather than just on or off. For example, you might be able to choose a level of violence that is allowed or allow violent information based on its news value. Because of the ability of the PICS system to have such a scale, you'll notice that at the top of the filter configuration screen, you can choose where the URLs rating must fall in order to be accepted. Because we're dealing with only yes or no answers here, I'm going to set the pop-up menu to read URL's rating must equal the selected value. I'm also going to choose the Gambling category and set the test so that No Gambling is allowed on the network. When I'm finished, I'll click the Save Test button. My test will now show up on the Edit Profile screen. You can continue to add as many URL and label filters as you'd like. That's all there is to it. Once you've completed your PICS setup, your proxy server should now be ready to use. Remember that if you'd like, you can go back to the Proxy Authentication module and set individual PICS profiles for each of your users.

That finishes our look at the MacOS-based proxy server solution. Unfortunately, once again, this solution is not viable for connecting several machines to the outside world. As Apple continues to upgrade the MacOS networking, hopefully proxy solutions will be developed that are similar to the Windows-based solution we're going to be looking at now.

Using Windows for Proxy Serving

The Windows platform has several different proxy servers that allow you to use a single machine with an Internet connection to bring the Internet to your entire intranet. Two popular proxy servers are WinProxy and WinGate. Both are excellent products and worthy of a look. I, personally, prefer the WinProxy program by Ositis Software for its ease of use and will be discussing its operation here. You may want to check out both products to find out which one works best for you. WinProxy is available in an unlimited connection version as well as a lite version, which is significantly cheaper but is limited to only three connections to the proxy server. You can download and evaluate WinProxy from `http://www.winproxy.com`.

If you'd like to check out WinGate, you can download an evaluation copy from `http://www.wingate.com/`.

The initial setup of WinProxy is extremely simple. Simply run the installer and sit back. If you have two Ethernet cards in your Windows machine, (one for the internal network and one for an Internet connection), you will be prompted to declare which card performs which function. If you have a dial-in connection for your Internet connection, the program will configure itself with a single internal network address. Once it has determined the specifics of your network configuration, WinProxy will take you through the steps of configuring any services you'd like to run through it. Because this is the easiest way to get the program up and running in a hurry, let's look at these steps. Within a few minutes, you should be able to connect your entire network to the world.

First, run the WinProxy program by clicking the Start menu, choosing Programs, clicking XXXXXX, and selecting WinProxy. The resulting wizard will prompt you to set up a mail server that your network is going to use, as shown in Figure 15.28.

If you have only internal mail service that doesn't connect to the Internet, then *do not* specify this server. The proxy's purpose is to provide access to servers outside your internal network. I'm configuring my server so that I have access to my work email machine, `postoffice.ag.ohio-state.edu`. This machine provides both my incoming and outgoing mail services, so I'll use it exclusively.

FIGURE 15.28

Configure your Internet mail servers in the WinProxy setup wizard.

The next step is to let the proxy server know if you're using dial-up networking as your connection to the Internet. You'll be prompted for this information whether you have multiple Ethernet cards or not. Because my configuration is going to be based on a dial-in account to the Internet, I'm going to tell WinProxy that I'm using Dial Up Networking, as shown in Figure 15.29.

FIGURE 15.29

Choose whether you're using Dial Up Networking to access the Internet.

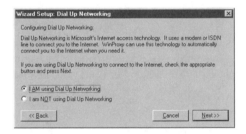

If you've chosen to use Dial Up Networking, as I have, your next step will be to tell WinProxy which Dial Up connection you plan to use, as shown in Figure 15.30. You also set a time limit for the connection to time out.

FIGURE 15.30

If you've chosen Dial Up Networking, your next step is to configure the service for WinProxy.

By allowing you to set a connection timeout, WinProxy will only stay connected to the network when you need network access. If a request is made for a network resource and the connection is currently offline, WinProxy will dial back into the Internet and re-establish the connection. If you have a time-limited Internet account or only have access through a long-distance line, this time-limiting capability should prove to be a godsend. The Web-caching part of the proxy will continue to operate, and if your users all use a specific Web site, it's entirely possible that they will be able to browse without any sort of active connection at all.

Once you've completed these simple steps, WinProxy will create and display a set of personalized instructions that tell you how to configure your internal network clients to take advantage of the proxy server. On my internal network, the computer running the proxy server has the address 192.168.0.245. The WinProxy server instructs me to configure my client applications as such:

> DNS Server—192.168.0.245
>
> HTTP proxy—192.168.0.245, port 80
>
> Security proxy—192.168.0.245, port 80
>
> SOCKS host—192.168.0.245, port 1080
>
> FTP proxy/firewall—192.168.0.245, port 21
>
> RealAudio—192.168.0.245, port 1090

This WinProxy status screen, shown in Figure 15.31 is nothing terribly exciting to look at, but it contains all the configuration information you need.

FIGURE 15.31

WinProxy displays connection status for the various services you've selected.

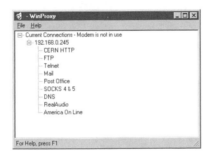

What Is SOCKS?

You've probably seen quite a few programs with *SOCKS* proxy configuration settings. SOCKS is a proxy server protocol that can handle many different transports all from a single configuration. If you're running a SOCKS proxy and your client application supports the SOCKS protocol, you don't need to do anything but set the same SOCKS settings (IP address and port) for each of the applications that need to run through the proxy. By keeping all configurations the same, SOCKS streamlines the process of using a proxy server. (By the way, the name is not exactly an acronym; it derives from *SOCK-et-S*, an internal development name that remained after release.)

The status screen displays a hierarchical list of clients using the proxy server and the services that they are accessing. After your initial configuration, the only IP address listed in the window should be the address of the proxy server itself, along with the services that you have configured it to provide. You should immediately be able to use your proxy server, assuming you have a working dial-up adapter configuration, or an active Internet connection via Ethernet. Nothing to it, right?

Before closing the books on WinProxy, which, for the services that it provides, is incredibly simple to configure and run, take a look at some of the advanced features that it offers. Under the surprisingly simple WinProxy monitoring Window lies a wealth of options, including some that are usually seen only when using NAT. To reach the advanced settings, choose Advanced Properties from the WinProxy File menu. Your screen should look like the one in Figure 15.32. If not, be sure that the General tab is currently selected.

FIGURE 15.32

WinProxy's Advanced Configuration dialog box lets you set a number of configuration options in its General tab.

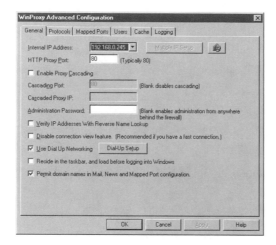

If you made any mistakes during the initial configuration process, this screen is where you can correct them. Take a look at some of the key features you might want to configure:

- Internal IP Address—The internal IP address can be reselected if you accidentally selected the outside address as opposed to your internal intranet address.

- CERN Proxy Port—The proxy port number that's used for your Web proxy. You'll need to change from the default (80) if there is a Web server running on the same machine as WinProxy.

- Proxy Cascading—The proxy cascading options are necessary to complete if your proxy server is behind yet another proxy server, in which case, your proxy will need to use the other proxy in order to communicate.

- Dial Up Networking—If you misconfigured your Dial Up Networking options during the initial installation, you can reconfigure the system here.

These are the most important settings that might affect the way your proxy server is behaving, or misbehaving. Now continue your look at the advanced settings by clicking the Protocols tab. You should see a dialog box much like the one shown in Figure 15.33.

FIGURE 15.33

In the Protocols tab, you determine which protocols you want the proxy to transmit.

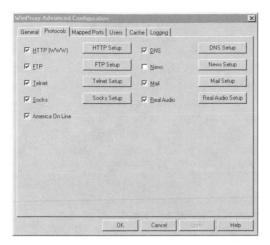

Here you can see all the protocols that have been configured to be transmitted through your proxy server. You might have noticed that there are a few here that you were not asked about during setup. If there are any services you would like to provide but have not yet configured, simply click the check box by the name of the service, and then click the setup button to the right of the service name. The configuration of individual services should be relatively straight-forward. For example, if I want to use the News (NNTP) protocol on my network, I simply click the News Setup... button. Then, in the resulting dialog box, I fill in the news server that I want to act as a proxy to. One item that you may want to change, even though it was configured during the setup phase, is mail. By default, the proxy does not handle IMAP requests and needs to have the IMAP server specified through its configuration screen.

Continuing right along, we come to one of the more interesting configuration options we can set up in WinProxy: mapped ports. Click the Mapped Ports tab to bring up the screen shown in Figure 15.34.

FIGURE 15.34

WinProxy lets you configure mapped ports to allow incoming connections to machines on your intranet.

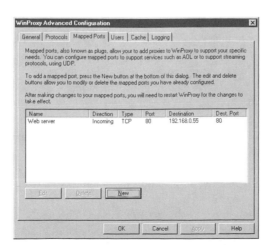

As you know, connections are made between ports. In the situation where there is only one true connection to the Internet, providing services to and from internal machines on your network can be a bit difficult. The problem is that an incoming connection only arrives at the machine with the direct Internet link. To allow incoming connections to talk to a computer on your internal network, you'll need to map a port on the directly connected machine. An incoming connection on that port will be mapped to an IP address on your internal network. This allows you to run servers on your internal network without needing them to have direct connections to the Internet. You can also set up an outgoing mapped port, which lets you set the destination address that will be contacted when you connect to a certain port on your proxy server. To set up either type of mapping, click the New button on the advanced configuration tab. The Edit Mapped Port dialog box, shown in Figure 15.35, appears.

FIGURE 15.35

Configure a new mapped port in this dialog box.

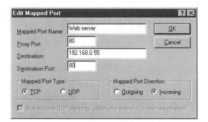

An example of this capability in use would be to allow you to run a name server on a machine on your internal network. To do this, you would give the mapped port a name, say "My Web Server." The Proxy port is the port on the proxy that the incoming traffic connects to, so you should set it to 80 to handle normal Web traffic. Next, you'll need a destination machine on your internal network that is running a Web server (Remember the Web servers that you set up in Chapter 12? Guess what, it's time to pull the OmniHTTPd server program you used back out!), put that machine's IP address in the Destination field, and port 80, once again, in the destination port field. Because the HTTP protocol uses TCP exclusively, you'll want to set the Mapped Port Type to TCP, and, because you're allowing incoming connections to this Web server, the Mapped Port Direction is Incoming.

The most important use for this feature is being able to configure your proxy server so that you can successfully play Internet-based games over it. (I'm only half kidding.) Most games work by having the client computer contact a central network game server; this isn't necessarily a dedicated machine, but in general at least one player's computer needs to act as a server for whatever game you might be playing. After the client makes an initial connection to the server and exchanges information, the remote server machine will attempt to open a connection to the client on a known TCP or UDP port. In the case of our network that's connected via a proxy server, we're going to need to know what that port is and map incoming connections on it so that they can reach the machine that's playing the game. The one drawback to this scheme is that only one computer on the network will be able to play a remotely hosted network game. If other machines want to play, they're going to need to have their own mappings, which obviously can't overlap with any other machines (incoming connections on a single port can't be sent to multiple internal computers). In the case of certain games, it might not even be possible to play them over a proxy server; Quake is a particular example that is a bit tricky to get working. When we look at NAT in the next chapter, you'll see why. Of course, there are many other programs that are just as tricky to get to work over a proxy server, but TCP/IP-based gaming applications are always a real challenge.

Another nice feature of this proxy server is the ability to allow different users to access different mail servers. To do this, you need to create users, or groups of users, in the Users portion of the advanced configuration. Click the Users tab to bring up the dialog box shown in Figure 15.36.

FIGURE 15.36
You can create user groups in WinProxy.

The main user list screen is self explanatory; you can create, edit, and delete users. To WinProxy, a user is an IP address. It does not mean an individual person, but rather an individual computer. On the MacOS, in WebDoubler, users were authenticated when they made use of the Web proxy. Because WinProxy handles a significantly greater amount of proxying, it cannot rely on an authentication system based on a singular protocol, thus the IP address definition of the user. Go ahead and set up a user account now. Click the New button to bring up the new user creation dialog box, as in Figure 15.37.

FIGURE 15.37
You define the new user in this dialog box.

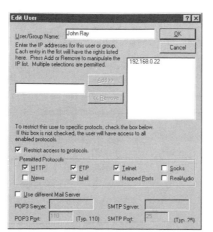

You'll need to set a user or group name (a group is simply a list of IP addresses), and then add as many IP addresses as necessary by using the Add and Remove buttons. You also have the ability to restrict the network services that the user has access to. If you select the Restrict access to protocols check box, you enable all the buttons in the Permitted Protocols section. You can then pick and choose the protocols that the IP address, or addresses, you're defining can use. Lastly, one of the really nifty features is the Use different Mail Server option. Depending on the IP address that the proxy server is being accessed by, it can proxy for multiple different email servers. If you do not maintain your own mail server and your users have their own accounts on various ISPs, this can be quite useful.

Things are winding down now with the configuration of WinProxy. You've seen many of the features that make it both powerful and extremely simple to use. There are still a few more things to look at, however. First, check out the Web caching abilities of WinProxy. Click the Cache tab to configure your cache settings, as shown in Figure 15.38.

FIGURE 15.38

Use the Cache tab to configure WinProxy's Web caching ability.

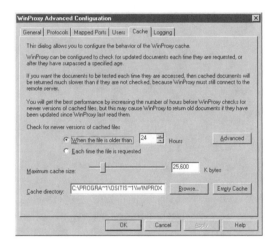

WinProxy does not use any terribly advanced algorithms to determine if a page in the Web cache is still good (or recent); rather, it gives you, the administrator, the option of setting an expiration time for each Web page. You may also tell it to check the site for a new version of a page each time the page is requested. The maximum allowable size of the cache file, as well as the directory that contains the cache are both specified here.

Finishing our look at WinProxy, we at last arrive at the Logging tab, where we can ask WinProxy to keep track of the connections that are made to and from the proxy server. See Figure 15.39.

WinProxy gives you two levels of logging capability: activity logging and detailed logging. Activity logging can also take place on any computer on your network, not just the proxy server. Included with WinProxy is a logging application, which listens for connections on port 8000 and writes log information received on that port to a file. You can put this application on a different computer and configure the activity logging to write the log file to that computer.

FIGURE 15.39

You can configure WinProxy to log connections made to the server.

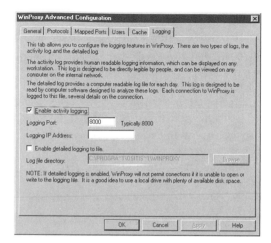

Activity logs are written in plain text and are meant to be read/analyzed manually. WinProxy also provides a detailing level of logging that is separate from the activity logging. The detailed level is meant to be used with log analysis software rather than read as a standalone document. It contains detailed information about each connection that is made to the proxy server.

That's it for WinProxy, a very complete, robust, and straightforward proxy application. You should be able to use it to create secure connections to the Internet from your internal intranet. You'll find that WinCache, the other Windows proxy routine I mentioned at the beginning of the section, works in a largely similar fashion. That leaves us with Linux to cover, so let's go ahead and take a look at the proxy capabilities we get with our free OS.

Using Linux for Proxy Serving

If you've been reading the rest of the book straight through, you're probably thinking, "Hey, this is Linux; it must have built-in proxy server support." Well, in this case, you're only partially right. Surprisingly enough, Linux has very little built-in proxy serving capabilities. The Apache Web server software that comes with Red Hat 5.x can act as a Web proxy, but other than that, you're going to have to look elsewhere for proxy solutions. I have not seen any proxy servers for Linux that approach the capabilities of WinProxy. If they exist, they aren't in widespread use. One possible explanation for this is that Linux has built-in NAT capabilities, so there is little reason for running a proxy server. Because we only have Web proxying to look at, let's go ahead and see how we can configure Apache to act as a proxy server.

Before we jump in, let's take a few moments to talk about your Linux configuration. Linux is not going to be the easiest computer to set up and maintain a dial-in connection with. If you're experienced with UNIX, then you aren't going to have a problem; however, for the first-time user, trying to configure Linux to dial into a network can be a bit confusing and frustrating. Red Hat 5.x now comes with software that enables you to graphically configure dial-in connections as you would on other operating systems, such as Windows or MacOS. Linux considers any connection to a network to be a network interface—much the same as Windows, which, when you're adding a dial-in connection to a network, requires you to add a dial-in adapter. For the purposes of using Linux as a proxy server and connection to the Internet for your network, I'm going to assume that you have two interfaces already configured on your Linux computer. This could be a dial-in interface and an Ethernet interface—or two Ethernet interfaces. I'm using a Linux machine with two Ethernet cards, one of which is connected directly to a cable modem, and the other is connected to my internal network. To get this working, you need to enable IP forwarding on your Linux machine and correctly configure your interfaces to use it. Red Hat Linux ships with the ability to perform IP forwarding, or move TCP/IP packets back and forth between your different network interfaces. If you've recompiled your kernel, this capability may have been removed from your system, in which case you're going to need to rebuild your *kernel* and compile it back in.

What Is a Kernel?

The *kernel* of an operating system is a small piece of executable code that handles all the basic interactions of the operating system with the hardware. Operations such as I/O (input/output), memory allocation, and so on are defined in the kernel. By building the rest of the operating system on top of the basic kernel, the OS itself is abstracted from the computing hardware. This is what gives Linux the capability to run on a huge range of computing platforms—from Intel processors, to PowerPCs, to even the tiny Palm Pilot PDA. Windows NT is also kernel based and is available in configurations for several different types of processors, the most widely used (and supported) being the Intel processor family and the DEC Alpha CPU.

I *highly* suggest that you do not attempt this exercise unless you're totally sure you know what you're doing, or are comfortable with re-installing the operating system if something goes wrong. On my system (and presumably yours), I can reconfigure and recompile the kernel with these commands:

```
>cd /usr/src/linux
>make config
```

Doing so should start the configuration process for the compilation of the kernel. Any settings that were previously used when compiling your current kernel are automatically used as the default value for all the configuration questions. Therefore, if you don't know the correct answer to one of the configuration questions, just use the default, and you should be fine. The questions you should be looking for, related to IP forwarding, are shown below. Because we're going to be looking at NAT, or IP Masquerading, under Linux in the next chapter, it would save us some time if we also compiled NAT support into the kernel at this time:

```
TCP/IP networking (CONFIG_INET) [Y/n/?] Y
IP: forwarding/gatewaying (CONFIG_IP_FORWARD) [Y/n/?] Y
IP: multicasting (CONFIG_IP_MULTICAST) [Y/n/?] Y
IP: masquerading (CONFIG_IP_MASQUERADE) [Y/n/?] Y
*
* Protocol-specific masquerading support will be built as modules.
*
IP: ipautofw masq support (CONFIG_IP_MASQUERADE_IPAUTOFW) [Y/n/?] Y
```

Once you've finished the configuration process, the script should tell you that it has finished and will ask you to run make dep; make clean to make sure that all the files are ready to start the kernel compilation process.

```
The linux kernel is now hopefully configured for your setup.
Check the top-level Makefile for additional configuration,
and do a 'make dep ; make clean' if you want to be sure all
the files are correctly re-made
```

With that in mind, the following series of commands *should* successfully recompile the kernel and kernel modules, and re-install the new modules on your system:

```
>make dep; make clean
>make zImage
>make modules
>make modules_install
```

This process could take the better part of an hour, depending on the speed of your computer and the number of modules that are configured to compile. Once completed, you'll be returned to a command prompt, but the new kernel will still not be installed. To install the new kernel, you're going to need to copy it from its freshly compiled location (usually /usr/src/linux/ arch/i386/boot/zImage) to the boot directory (usually /boot). If you would like to keep the old kernel around in case of trouble (a *very* good idea), you'll need to add an entry into the /etc/ lilo.conf file for the new kernel. Please read /usr/src/linux/README for detailed instructions on replacing your kernel file. Unfortunately, as Linux changes, so does the manner in which kernels are compiled and installed. Even if you've compiled a kernel before, be sure to read the README file on your Linux system to ensure the procedure hasn't changed.

A mistake in this part of the process can completely disrupt your ability to boot your computer. Always keep a backup of your old kernel around just in case.

What Can I Do to Protect Myself?

Compiling a new kernel can be a bit tricky, and, if there are problems, which usually *isn't* the case, your computer might now be able to boot. Before installing a new kernel, make sure you have a backup of the old one. The easiest way to do this is to use the /sbin/mkbootdisk command. This will create a disk that has a working version of your kernel and can boot your system in the event of an emergency.

To give you an example of the sort of mental anguish you can put yourself through at this stage, let me relate a story that happened only a few months ago when I was configuring our new departmental mail server and needed to recompile the kernel. I've rebuilt kernels more times than I care to think about—no problem. So, being a chance-taker, I went ahead and made some custom patches to the kernel code on our mail server (which was, at the time, serving around 600 email accounts). Because I was quite sure that I knew precisely how this was going to turn out, I deleted the original kernel source tree, deleted the old kernel, and waited for the new kernel to compile. Don't ever do this. Ever. It turned out that I had missed something during the patching process, and the kernel refused to compile. So, I'm left sitting in front of a machine that has *no* kernel file, that I can't build a kernel file for, and that if I shut off, or reboot, is never going to come back up. I felt quite stupid for a while. Luckily, I had made (on one of the days that I was thinking clearer) a backup disk of the original kernel, and, after half an hour of searching through piles of disks with no labels (that's another story altogether), I finally found it. The disk contained a custom version of the kernel with a variety of drivers that are not in the default Linux installation kernel. If I hadn't found the disk, my only hope would have been to re-download the original kernel source files and recompile the old version of the kernel… and pray that I got it right. I can't stress enough the need to be very cautious when you do this sort of thing, but enough of that—back to the topic at hand.

As I've mentioned, on my system I have two Ethernet cards; one is configured to talk to my cable modem, and the other is part of my internal network. There are three locations that all of this information is stored: /etc/sysconfig/network and two interface configuration files in /etc/sysconfig/network-scripts. Let's take a quick look at the way I have things set up. Your configuration may vary slightly but should be quite close. First, the /etc/sysconfig /network file:

```
NETWORKING=yes
FORWARD_IPV4=yes
HOSTNAME=pointy.poisontooth.com
GATEWAYDEV=eth0
GATEWAY=128.128.128.1
```

You can see that networking is enabled, IP Forwarding is enabled, the name of my Linux machine is pointy.poisontooth.com, and my first Ethernet card (called eth0 by the system) is used as my gateway to the Internet (it is the interface connected to the cable modem). You'll also notice that there is a gateway defined here. This is not a real gateway; if you have the IP address of a gateway for your Internet connection, whether dial-in, and so on, it should be placed here. My gateway is set by the cable modem providers DHCP server. The value here is simply a placeholder. Not much to that file, is there? Now let's take a quick look at the two files that make my network adapters work—ifcfg-eth0 and ifcfg-eth1—both in the /etc/sysconfig/network-scripts directory.

First, eth0 (ifcfg-eth0), my gateway device—the cable modem to the Internet:

```
DEVICE=eth0
ONBOOT=yes
BOOTPROTO=dhcp
BROADCAST=255.255.255.255
NETWORK=0.0.0.0
NETMASK=255.255.255.0
IPADDR=0.0.0.0
```

Once again, nothing too complicated here. Most of the configuration for this adapter happens automatically via the DHCP protocol. The file simply defines the device and tells the computer to initialize the interface when it boots (ONBOOT=yes). Because I don't specify the parameters manually, the line BOOTPROTO=dhcp tells the computer to send out a DHCP request on this interface and use the results to fill in the configuration details.

Second, eth1 (ifcfg-eth1), my Internal device, connects to the rest of my intranet:

```
DEVICE=eth1
ONBOOT=yes
BOOTPROTO=none
BROADCAST=192.168.255.255
NETWORK=192.168.0.0
NETMASK=255.255.0.0
IPADDR=192.168.0.1
```

Even simpler than the last configuration. Device eth1 is, once again, initialized on boot, and rather than using a boot protocol to configure the interface, it uses the settings in this file.

Be careful when editing the network-scripts interface files. Although I'm not entirely sure this problem still exists, I previously had a problem with editors creating backup configuration files in the directory. The backup files created some confusion with the software that reads the configuration and sets up the interface. It read the backup files as if they were the actual configuration files, and I ended up with a system that behaved much differently than I had anticipated. Just to be safe, be sure to clean up any backup files that might have been created; they are postfixed with a ~ character. A simple rm #~ should do the trick.

Believe it or not, that's really all there is to the network configuration aspect of using two network interfaces under Linux. The hardest part is the configuration and compilation of the kernel, which, once you've done it a few times (and made a few mistakes), will become second nature. If you've already set up the kernel with the options that I mentioned earlier and have successfully configured the system as I've shown here, you're actually ready to do NAT… but we're going to hold off on that for just a bit longer. Let's go ahead and get that Apache proxy server working now.

Remember that Apache keeps its configuration in three separate files, located in /etc/httpd/conf. To set up the proxy server, we're only going to need to edit one of the three files, so this shouldn't take long at all. The file you're going to need to configure is httpd.conf. Open the file and look for these lines; they'll be commented out in the stock Red Hat 5.x Apache configuration file using the # character:

```
ProxyRequests On

# To enable the cache as well, edit and uncomment the following lines:

CacheRoot /etc/httpd/proxy
CacheSize 15
CacheGcInterval 4
CacheMaxExpire 24
CacheLastModifiedFactor 0.1
CacheDefaultExpire 1
#NoCache a_domain.com another_domain.edu joes.garage_sale.com
```

Let's take a look at these configuration directives, their meanings, and a few others that might be useful for your proxy server:

- ProxyRequests On—This enables Apache to act as a proxy server. The Proxy operates on port 80 of your server, so you must configure your browsers appropriately.

- CacheRoot—Sets the path to the directory where Apache will store its cache information.

- CacheSize—The size of the cache in kilobytes. This is not an upper limit of the cache, as it can grow out of this limit. Periodically Apache will clean up the cache to bring it back within the CacheSize setting, however.

- CacheGcInterval—The number of hours (or a fraction of hours) that the server will run before checking and cleaning the cache file. Don't set this too high, or you might find that your disk space has filled up significantly higher than you expected.

- CacheMaxExpire—The maximum amount of time that can pass before a document is considered expired and will not be returned from the cache. If you access sites that change very frequently, you may want to make this number a bit smaller than 24 hours.

- CacheLastModifiedFactor—If a document does not have an expiration set for it, the proxy can calculate one based on the Last Modified date for the page. From the Apache documentation (`http://www.apache.org`), this is mathematically defined as

  ```
  expiry-period = time-since-last-modification * <factor>
  ```

  For example, if the document was last modified 10 hours ago and `<factor>` is `0.1`, then the expiry period will be set to `10*0.1 = 1 hour`.

- CacheDefaultExpire—The number of hours a document will be cached if no expiration date and so on can be retrieved.

- NoCache—List domains that you do not want to have cached here. I don't have any NoCache domains specified in my settings, but you might find that you need to use this for dynamic pages, such as stock quotes or news-sites.

Now, here are a few configuration options that are not included in the default httpd.conf file. You can use them in the file if you'd like. There are still more documented on the Apache site itself:

- NoProxy—Follow the NoProxy directive by a list of domain names or IP addresses separated by spaces. These could be servers on your local network that should not be contacted by the proxy server.

- ProxyBlock—Not nearly as configurable as the PICS-based filtering under WebDoubler on the Macintosh but still useful. The ProxyBlock command, followed by a list of words/ domains, will match block any requests that contain the inappropriate words or domain name.

Lastly, the Apache documentation also contains a directive that will let you limit the addresses that have access to your proxy server. This example is taken from the Apache Web site:

```
<Directory proxy:*>
order deny,allow
deny from [machines you'd like *not* to allow by IP address or name]
allow from [machines you'd like to allow by IP address or name]
</Directory>
```

Use the deny line to set up addresses or domains that you explicitly want access denied to. Vice versa for the allow line; here you can configure the machines that should be allowed to access the proxy server. This directive should be added to your access.conf file, rather than the httpd.conf file we had been looking at. To get things up and running without a reboot, just restart your Apache server process like this:

```
>/etc/rc.d/init.d/httpd restart
```

That's it for Apache and our quick look at using Linux as a proxy server. You have to do a bit more work to get a Linux proxy up and running, but the work you've completed here will let us bring the NAT server online very quickly in the next chapter.

You've done quite a bit in this chapter. You've had your first taste of connecting your network to the outside world. You set up three different proxy servers under three different operating systems. Without even knowing it, you even recompiled your Linux operating system and turned it into a full gateway/router. Now that we've seen what we can get from using a proxy, it's time to move on to NAT. If you've configured your proxy server and are completely happy with its performance, skip the next chapter. If you'd like to see another, potentially more versatile method of connecting to the Internet, then read on.

## CHAPTER 16

Using Proxy NAT Servers

by John Ray

In this chapter

Using the Mac OS as a NAT Server **338**

Using Windows as a NAT server **341**

Using Linux as a NAT Server **345**

Wrapping It Up **346**

You're Connected! **347**

By this time, you might have gathered that I am partial to using NAT to make my connections. The ability to have truly transparent Internet access without worrying about Web proxies, email proxies, and so forth is wonderful. When you are using NAT, your network pretty much becomes identical to any other Internet-connected network. The machine running NAT is identical to any other subnet router or gateway. A few differences come from only having a single IP address to represent an entire network but only in incoming connections. I initially worked with a few Windows-based proxy servers, but have moved all my connections to NAT servers—at home and at work.

Because NAT works at a lower level in the TCP/IP protocol than proxy servers, it actually needs to know less about the protocols that are being used on the network than a proxy server. What this means to you is that you will be spending less time configuring the system to use the different protocols you need, because they're just going to work. It's honestly that simple.

Keeping with the established format of this book, let's look at NAT products with the Mac OS. My favorite NAT server (from a graphical and price standpoint) runs under Mac OS so, no matter what platform you use, take a close look at the Mac OS NAT solutions—they're very nice and, from my experience, very stable. Also, although it will still be in development at press time, the upcoming Windows NT 5.0 offers an out-of-the-box NAT solution for your network. If you already have an NT-based system, you might want to read up on NT 5.0.

Using the Mac OS as a NAT Server

Remember the nice IP utility package that I mentioned in Chapter 3, "Exploring IP Addresses," for using ping, nslookup, and so on, for the Macintosh? The same company, Sustainable Softworks, also makes an excellent, reasonably priced, and simple to use NAT server. The product, IPNetRouter, is available for both PowerPC and 68K Macs (time to pull that old Quadra out of your closet!) at:

http://www.sustworks.com/

You can download, install, and use the full IPNetRouter package from this site, but you must purchase a serial number within three weeks to continue using the software.

IPNetRouter arrives as a StuffIt file that decompresses into a single executable file and several readme files. If you already have the PPP (or Apple Remote Access under System 8.5 or greater) control panel configured for a dial-in interface, you can immediately start IPNetRouter and use your Ethernet network interface for your internal network. IPNetRouter supports multiple simultaneously active network interfaces, which is unusual for most programs on the Mac. Before you actually begin using IPNetRouter, you're going to need to configure your TCP/IP control panel with two separate configurations: a dial-in configuration and an Ethernet configuration. Do this by selecting Configurations from the File menu. Name the PPP connection (or your dedicated Internet connection) as **IPNetRouter**. Then create a second TCP/IP configuration that has the IP address and subnet mask for the Ethernet card that will be serving your internal network. Be sure that the configuration for the internal network (*not* IPNetRouter) is active and that you have not set a router/gateway address for the internal network.

Start the IPNetRouter program now. You will see a screen similar to the one in Figure 16.1.

FIGURE 16.1

IPNetRouter presents this opening screen.

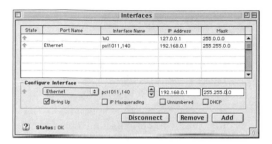

This program window is the main status display where most of your configuration takes place. Your current Ethernet interfaces are shown when you first launch IPNetRouter, including a loopback interface. Interfaces can be added to or removed from this screen by selecting the appropriate interface hardware from the pop-up menu then filling in the IP address and subnet mask. My Internet network will be run from the address 192.168.0.1, which is my Ethernet card. My Internet connection will come from my configured PPP interface, which I've added by selecting it in the Configure Interface section and clicking Add. If the Bring Up check box is selected, which it is by default, IPNetRouter immediately connects to the Internet. The status of each interface (active or inactive) is indicated by the State field. An up arrow means that everything is online and working. A down arrow indicates an inactive or down interface.

Now we will want to turn on IP masquerading for the PPP interface, because all the other interfaces are hiding behind it. Select the PPP interface in the Interfaces window and check the IP Masquerading box, then click the Add button. A Mask icon appears in the State field beside the PPP interface, as shown in Figure 16.2.

FIGURE 16.2

When you activate IP Masquerading you'll see a little domino mask appear by the PPP interface.

You'll probably want to configure your computer so that it automatically reconnects if disconnected, and automatically dials in to the network when there is packet activity on the wire. To do this, choose Gateway from the Window menu. The Gateway dialog box appears, as shown in Figure 16.3.

Part
IV

Ch

16

FIGURE 16.3

Use the Gateway dialog box to automatically reconnect if you are disconnected.

You have the option of toggling the Dial on Demand option, as well as *tickling* the PPP connection so that it will remain constantly connected by selecting the Remain Connected check box. If you are using a long distance connection or are paying for connect time, it would be in your best interest to not remain connected. If you are disconnected from the network and a machine on your internal network tries to access an outside resource, the user will have to wait a few seconds for a connection to be made, but the process will still be transparent. Do not disable IP forwarding, otherwise, your network will not be capable of sending or receiving any information.

What Is Tickling the Connection?

Don't worry; you can put away the feather. Sending packets on a regular interval is sometimes called tickling the connection. The remote computer receives the packets and does not disconnect your computer for inactivity.

When you are finished with this configuration dialog box, click Done. The last thing you might need to do is map incoming connections to a specific machine on your internal network. To do so, choose Port Mapping from the Window menu. A dialog box similar to the one in Figure 16.4 appears.

FIGURE 16.4

You map incoming connections to a specific machine by using this dialog box.

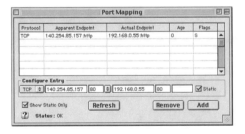

I've already included a sample mapping from my PPP connection (140.254.85.159) on port 80 to an internal Web server located at 192.168.0.55 on port 80. You'll need to use whatever IP addresses you've used for your own server. If you happened to set up a server on 192.168.0.55, you can follow the example exactly. Let's see what all the fields mean so that you can configure your own ports:

■ Protocol—You can map incoming connections using TCP,UDP,ICMP, and so on. Most traffic is generally TCP-based, but there are also UDP services that you might want to connect to your network, such as Quake, which uses UDP ports greater than 20,000

- Apparent Endpoint—The apparent address and port that the outside world connects to. This will always be the address of your PPP, cable-modem, or Internet connection. The port of the connection is also specified.

- Actual Endpoint—The actual internal address and port that will receive the mapped connection. You don't necessarily have to match addresses on a port-by-port basis. For example, if you had an internal network Web server running on port 80, you could run your outside-world server on port 90 and have incoming apparent connections mapped to an actual endpoint at port 90.

- Age—This is a status display and cannot be configured. The age is the number of 30-second intervals that have passed since the last time the mapping rule was used. In the case of a static mapping (which is what we're using), this display is unimportant.

- Static—If a mapping is set as static (like the example), it will always be in effect whenever you start IPNetRouter. Sometimes it is convenient to temporarily allow connections to internal machines. If you want to add a temporary mapping, deselect the Static check box. When the age of the temporary mapping exceeds 60, it is deleted from the port mappings. This lets you map a port for a specific connection, and then forget about it because it will remove itself 30 minutes after it stops being used.

Unfortunately, (and this is my pet peeve with many NAT programs), you cannot map a range of ports. I like being able to map a range because certain games (read Quake) require an entire port range to function properly. To use Quake with IPNetRouter, you would need to add far too many entries to make it worthwhile.

Overall, IPNetRouter is a very nice and quickly evolving NAT solution; the interface is clean and user-friendly. Even so, I need to mention a competing product that has a few extra features but comes at a significantly higher cost: Vicom Internet Gateway. You can visit their Web site at

http://www.vicomtech.com/

Vicom Internet Gateway is a wonderful NAT solution that offers two features which are extremely nice: mapping of port ranges and browsing control, which limits what internal users have access to—similar to the WebDoubler proxy server I mentioned in Chapter 15, "Using Proxy Servers." The Vicom Internet Gateway is priced significantly higher than the other NAT products we're reviewing, but is an excellent choice for schools or offices where additional control at the protocol level is desired.

Using Windows as a NAT server

Unfortunately, while the Windows platform has a variety of excellent proxy servers available, it boasts very few low-cost NAT alternatives. One NAT program that does exist is NAT32. NAT32 will run under Windows 95, 98, and NT. Although NAT32 is still a bit rough around the edges, it's easy to configure. You can download NAT32 from

http://www.nat32.com/

Part
IV

Ch
16

You'll need to unzip NAT32 to its own directory. There is currently no installation program, just the archived executable and a few support files. When you're ready to start using NAT32, double-click the Nat32 icon that appears in the Programs section of your Start menu. After collecting some basic information about you (your name and the registration number, if you have one), the NAT32 Options screen appears, as shown in Figure 16.5.

FIGURE 16.5

The first time you run it, NAT32 collects some basic configuration information.

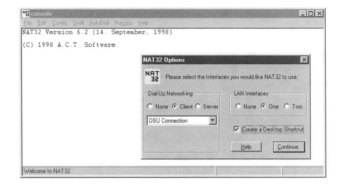

In this dialog box, you can choose the way that you want your network configured. I'm going to set up NAT for a dial-in network using my OSU Connection dial-up adapter profile. I only have one Ethernet interface on my computer, so the LAN Interfaces option is set appropriately. If you have multiple Ethernet cards and no dial-in networking, you would adjust the configuration radio buttons appropriately. If you'd like to create a shortcut for the configuration you are creating, click the Create a Desktop Shortcut button. When you are finished, click Continue.

If NAT32 has not run on your system previously, it will now need to modify your Windows SYSTEM.INI file. This takes a few seconds, after which you will need to reboot. After restarting the computer, run NAT32 again to continue.

Now you are prompted to configure your remaining network interfaces, as shown in Figure 16.6.

FIGURE 16.6

Just a few more configuration settings and NAT32 is ready to go.

I am configuring my Ethernet interface to have an IP address of 192.168.0.1 and a subnet mask of 255.255.0.0 from within the Network control panel. If you are unsure of how to configure your network addresses, refer to Chapter 5, "Configuring Client Workstations." The name server settings are pulled from the Microsoft TCP/IP configuration information that you set in the Network control panel, but you can change them here if you want. The gateway is any additional gateway for that subnet. Because we're dealing with two interfaces, one PPP and one Ethernet, the PPP interface will act as the gateway for the Ethernet interface. The software will handle this transparently for you, so you can leave the Gateway field blank. The Address Filter field lets you set an IP address that will be filtered (restricted) from being transmitted over this interface.

There are two other important options, especially if you are not using a dial-in connection. For my setup, the PPP connection is considered the primary interface. If you have two Ethernet interfaces, one connected to the Internet and another connected to your internal network, you will need to click the Primary Interface check box on the configuration screen of your Internet connection. If the interface you are configuring uses DHCP to get its IP address (as in the case of a cable modem), you might need to check the Use HDCP option.

As with the Mac's IPNetRouter software, there really isn't anything else to the NAT32 configuration. The NAT32 console window is usually minimized and can be expanded by clicking the NAT32 icon in the Windows System tray in the right-hand corner of the taskbar. The console itself, shown in Figure 16.7, is nothing very exciting to look at.

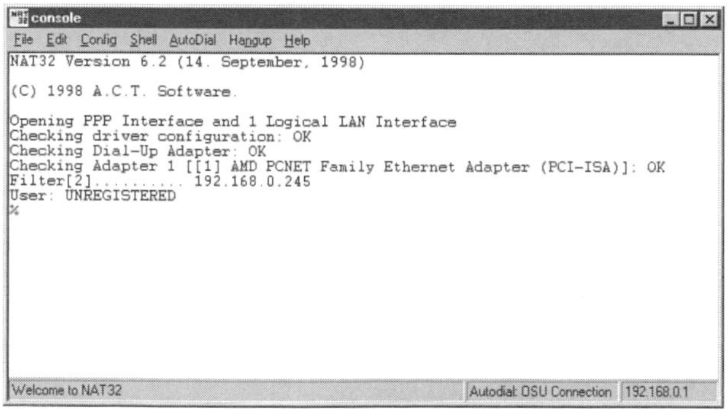

FIGURE 16.7

NAT32's console window displays connection information, albeit in a fairly prosaic fashion.

```
console
File Edit Config Shell AutoDial Hangup Help
NAT32 Version 6.2 (14. September, 1998)

(C) 1998 A.C.T. Software.

Opening PPP Interface and 1 Logical LAN Interface
Checking driver configuration: OK
Checking Dial-Up Adapter: OK
Checking Adapter 1 [[1] AMD PCNET Family Ethernet Adapter (PCI-ISA)]: OK
Filter[2]........... 192.168.0.245
User: UNREGISTERED
%
```
```
Welcome to NAT32                    Autodial: OSU Connection  192.168.0.1
```

From the NAT32 console, you can reconfigure your network interfaces by selecting the appropriate interface from the Config menu. You can also hang-up and dial in as well as enable or disable the auto-dial feature of NAT32, which allows it to dial in to the network when packet activity is sensed on the network.

Unfortunately, these steps are all that you can currently do with NAT32 without getting your hands a bit dirty. It is important that you provide the incoming connections with a path to the appropriate machine on your network. Luckily, that functionality does exist in NAT32; it just isn't pretty.

Part

IV

Ch

16

Let's say you want to run a Web server on an internal machine with the IP address 192.168.0.55. How do you map incoming connections on port 80 so that they are redirected to the appropriate computer?

You'll notice that there is a flashing % cursor in the NAT32 console window. Rather than just showing status messages, the console also enables you to configure NAT32 using command-line settings. The ppmap (permanent port map) function will let you map the port 80 address the way you want.

```
ppmap add tcp 80 192.168.0.55 80
```

Any incoming connections on port 80 are now mapped to port 80 on your Web server. If you later want to change this port mapping, you can use the ppmap delete function:

```
ppmap delete tcp 80
```

There are actually an incredible number of utilities that are built into the NAT32 package. To get an idea of the different functions you can access, type **help** at the command line. The Help screen in Figure 16.8 gives you an idea of the number of available commands. If you want more information about a specific command, you can type **help command name**, substituting the command you want for *command name* of course, for most of the listed commands. Or, you might actually want to type **help command name | more**, because many of the Help files are very long and take more than the available screen space to display.

FIGURE 16.8

NAT32's Help command lists the available commands and utilities.

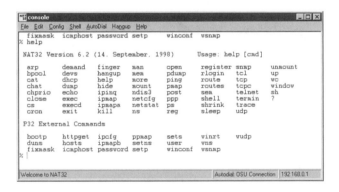

Although the user interface isn't pretty, the capability to ping, telnet, rlogin, and perform other network diagnostics from within the console is very useful. NAT32 provides the functionality of both the Macintosh IPNetRouter and IPNetMonitor packages rolled into one.

Unfortunately, there currently isn't a method available to map a range of ports to an internal host. The software does allow you to map all incoming UDP connections to your internal network, but doesn't provide a way of setting a port range, as you are about to do under Linux. Nonetheless, NAT32 is a powerful package that can quickly be configured to put your network online. Custom configuration takes a bit more than other packages, but the end result is entirely the same.

Using Linux as a NAT Server

Because of the little bit of extra effort put forth when configuring Apache as a proxy server in the last chapter, we can very quickly turn our two-card Linux computer into a NAT server. If you did not follow the instructions in Chapter 15 for using Linux as a proxy server, do so now; otherwise, the commands needed to enable NAT will probably not work. You might want to configure all these commands in a single shell script that can be run at startup, such as the /etc/rc.d/rc.local file. You might also include the commands in a script that you run to enable NAT when you need it.

Part

IV

Ch

16

The first command uses IPFWADM (IP forwarding administration) to disable all the packet forwarding between interfaces. This will give you a clean slate to build the NAT/IP masquerading rules on.

```
ipfwadm -F -p deny
```

Now that there is no packet forwarding taking place, add a second IPFWADM command to turn on IP masquerading. This allows any packets on your internal network be sent to any other network (by way of the NAT server).

```
ipfwadm -F -a m -S 192.168.0.0/16 -D 0.0.0.0/0
```

In case you're wondering, the /16 represents a 16-bit subnet mask of 255.255.0.0, which lets the forwarding software know what IP addresses are on the local network. Surprisingly enough, that's all there is to getting NAT running under Linux. You should now be able to use any computer on your internal network as if it was directly connected to the rest of the network. As with our other NAT solutions, however, it is nice to be able to map ports to specific internal machines and allow incoming connections. The Linux operating system actually includes several modules that map common services for you. I personally like to map the ports manually; that way I have complete control over what the server is doing, and I can quickly diagnose any problems that crop up—because undoubtedly I've created them. So, let's see how you can set up rules to forward incoming data to specific ports.

The command we're going to be using now is the IPAUTOFW (IP auto-forward) utility. It enables you to specify a protocol and port or ports that should be forwarded to an internal IP address. First of all, say we have an internal Web server at the address 192.160.0.55; the command that will forward all incoming tcp requests on port 80 is:

```
ipautofw -A -r tcp 80 -h 192.168.0.55
```

Sometimes you might want to forward a range of ports to an internal address. This is especially true in the case of a Quake server, where the initial connection to the server is used to decide a specific port number for the client, and then subsequent connections occur on other port numbers. From our other examples, you should now know that Quake uses the UDP and TCP protocols on port 20000 for the initial connection. After that, it uses a higher numbered port for the individual clients. I'm not entirely sure what the upper bound to the ports that Quake chooses is, but to be safe, you can map all available ports—up to 65,536. Here are the two rules

I have set that allow me to serve Quake games from an internal computer on the IP address 192.168.0.50:

```
ipautofw -A -r tcp 20000 65536 -h 192.168.0.50
ipautofw -A -r udp 20000 65536 -h 192.168.0.50
```

This is probably overkill; I believe that Quake only connects using TCP on port 20000, and then uses UDP for the subsequent connections. Because I don't have any other services that require TCP ports above 20000, I haven't had a need to change it. Incidentally, for all the gamers out there, this configuration also works very well for Quake 2.

You can continue to add other IP forwarding rules as you see fit. If you run POP servers or SMTP servers, you'll need to create rules for ports 25 and 110. The process is very simple, and you can actually run IPAUTOFW from a Linux command line to test the changes you've made on-the-fly.

Wrapping It Up

You now know how to set up a NAT server under three different platforms, but so far I've neglected to mention one very important piece of information: how to exactly configure your clients to use your NAT server. Presumably you have one of our three solutions configured with a connection to the Internet (via modem or other means), and an Ethernet card. We'll also presume that the Ethernet card is connected to a hub and you can communicate with the other computers on your local network. If not, you'd better skip back a few chapters and catch up! The final step in configuring your NAT-based network is to set the TCP/IP settings on the other computers so that they can use the network. All this amounts to is setting the gateway on the client computers to point to the address of the internal network interface on our computer running NAT. For the examples, this IP address has been 192.168.0.1. For a client computer on your internal network, a possible TCP/IP configuration would be:

IP address: 192.168.0.30

Subnet mask: 255.255.0.0

Router/Gateway: 192.168.0.1

Name server: Whatever the DNS of your ISP is

That's it! Configure your other computers in a similar manner, and you'll be experiencing the bliss of a well-connected intranet.

You're Connected!

I've discussed both proxies and NAT solutions to connecting to the Internet. These are both time-tested and relatively easy to manage connection methods that are used around the world everyday. NAT solutions have become increasingly popular in recent years as the processing power to handle modifying each packet has increased. There are devices available for sale that are essentially a black box with built-in modem (or multiple modems) and 10BASE-T hub. You connect your computers to the box and plug it into a phone line. After a few minutes of configuring the device to operate with your ISP, it will connect to the network and provide transparent NAT services to all the computers that are connected to it. There are several such devices on the market. One that I recently looked at is the WebRamp. We are currently using one of the WebRamp NAT solutions to connect a remote office to our dial-in network. The total amount of time to configure the device is under 10 minutes. More information on WebRamp is available at:

`http://www.rampnet.com/`

Another potential NAT solution is to pull an old 486 out of your closet and put it to use running NAT software. There is an excellent DOS packet-driver based NAT routing solution written by David Mischler. The software will run on any Intel system from the 286 on up. However, for the best performance, you should look at using at least a 486. Running under DOS, Mischler's IPRoute software requires only a floppy drive, and 640K of memory to operate. I ran my ISDN line through IPRoute for a year and a half using a 486-66 with only a 3.5[dp] floppy, no monitor, and no hard drive. It never once skipped a beat. If you'd like to find out more about IPRoute, head over to Dave Mischler's Web site at:

`http://www.mischler.com/`

If you have the spare equipment or can afford the cost of a basic used machine ($100 or less), this might be one of the most cost-effective connectivity solutions there is. I am currently using a Linux-based NAT solution because I also want serving capabilities from the machine itself. My 486 with 640K couldn't deliver in that respect.

Managing Your Network

Once your network has started to grow, you'll find a plethora of new problems that you face. Part 5 looks at the challenges presented in providing a "secure" network as well as some techniques for managing your network and users. Networks have a tendency to continue growing to fill all available space. Rather than fight with trying to find the resources to do everything yourself, take a look at some of the tools presented in Part 5—they just might save you some time.

17   Implementing Hardware Solutions 351

18   Using Security Techniques to Protect your Network and Data 361

19   Managing TCP/IP Network Resources 379

20   Configuring Networks with DHCP 393

21   Using SNMP and Other Diagnostic Tools to Monitor Your Network 411

22   Recognizing and Diagnosing Network Problems 437

Implementing Hardware Solutions

by John Ray

In this chapter

What is a Secure Network? **352**

Security in Stability **354**

Ways of Securing Your Network **354**

Security and Your Network **359**

Other Information Sources **360**

As you've followed the discussions and exercises in this book, you've used TCP/IP to accomplish a number of essential networking tasks. You have an intranet, and it is now connected—one way or another—to the Internet. If you have used a proxy or NAT server, you already have some security on your network. If you have paid for an entire subnet and each connection on your network is live on the Internet, then you are probably very open to attack. So, before you start getting scared let's take a look at what a secure network is, and what sort of steps you need to take to protect your investments.

What is a Secure Network?

Network security is a rather broad topic. Usually, when people think of a secure network they are thinking of a network that is unhackable. However, the topic of network security also includes the concept of secure data. As data is transmitted across the Internet, it is incredibly easy to compromise. Let's take a look at two examples of unsecure data. (I have already mentioned one of these types, but it's important to review because it covers both internal network security and the security of data that is being transmitted over the Internet.)

If you're like me, you probably use email daily. It has become a legitimate method of communication, even among people who don't consider themselves computer users. Not having an email address in this day and age is a definite disadvantage for anyone who is involved in business or research. There are usually company policies that dictate what is appropriate email to send over the company network. Nonetheless, we all send messages that are not related to work, or that might be a bit embarrassing if they were actually read by people other than those for whom they were intended. I'll be the first to admit that I have sent several email messages that—because of a bad day or an argument with someone at work—were sufficiently grumpy enough that they might have caused some tensions between myself and co-workers. So what's the problem? Say you send an off-color joke or two through email…maybe even send a few love letters to your significant other. No problem, right? Email is private, right? Actually, if you've followed the sessions in which you talked directly to an SMTP server, you probably already know that email isn't private.

Email can travel through multiple different servers to reach its destination. During its entire transmission, it is sent as plain text. This means that at any point during the transmission, the data can be intercepted and read. Surprisingly enough, this does not take a computer genius or a hacker to accomplish. It takes a piece of software called a *packet sniffer* and a connection to the network somewhere along the line your message will travel.

What Is a Packet Sniffer?

A packet sniffer is a piece of software which can be used to help diagnose network problems. It enables you to analyze and identify the types of packets that are being sent on the network. A common use of a packet sniffer is to identify the major sources of traffic on your network and the protocols that are using up the bandwidth. Steps can then be taken to reduce the traffic, or to determine why the traffic is being generated.

Packet sniffers, in the wrong hands, can be used to retrieve information from packets as they travel along the network. It is entirely possible to configure a packet sniffer to log all packets to or from port 25 (the SMTP port) to a file. If the snoop wants to grab email from the local network (that is, if one of your co-workers wants to spy on you), they can simply record all traffic to port 110 (the POP server port). Once the data is recorded, they can view it at their leisure. The data might be slightly garbled because of multiple different packets for different messages, but it's usually pretty easy to piece together messages.

As an experiment, I recently ran a packet sniffer on the local network in my building at work. There are roughly 45 network connections in the building, and within ten seconds of logging newsgroup traffic I saw several messages that, if I mentioned them here, would require this book to be sold in an adult bookstore. The total amount of time I spent setting up the packet sniffer was probably 30 seconds…I simply downloaded a precompiled sniffer and ran it.

So now you're probably thinking, "Well, the data isn't safe when it's being sent across the network, but the amount of time that it is on the line is only a few seconds (most email messages are transmitted to their destination within seconds). What chance is there that anyone is going to see the data during that time?" Once your message has reached its destination, it's safe, isn't it? Nope, not quite. As the message travels, the SMTP servers all see the entire text of the message. Do you trust your SMTP servers? Do you know the people who operate all the servers between your network and the destination? It takes only a few minutes to configure most SMTP servers to log all the data that they process.

If you're thinking that it's a bit far-fetched to worry about server operators, consider that there have been several instances in which big-name online services have, without the user's knowledge, read information from the client's hard drive and transferred it back to the remote server. If this sort of practice is carried out by large, trusted companies, is it that far-fetched for one of the thousands of server operators to have reasons—whether appropriate or inappropriate—for logging and reviewing mail information?

Take a few seconds to digest all that, and then let's think about the second example—transferring secure information over the Internet to a Web site. The most common secure transaction is the transfer of credit card information. As online commerce continues to grow, so does the number of people who transfer their credit card information over the network each day. The most obvious problem with this is that packets can be sniffed from the network, and credit card numbers can be discovered. Surprisingly enough, though, this is the stupid route for collecting and hacking credit card numbers. Why would a hacker spend their time trying to grab single numbers from the network when he can potentially have thousands of numbers, from a single source, all at once? Therefore, the obvious target of a credit card hacker is the destination of the packets that contain the credit card information.

When you order something online, what happens to the information you enter? Most likely it is stored somewhere. In a truly nightmarish situation, the information can be sent via email to a remote mailbox that holds all the purchasing information. More commonly, it is stored in some sort of database—perhaps a custom flat-file Perl database, or maybe a high-end SQL database. If you want to get a credit card number, do you try to grab one at a time as it comes into the

Part

V

Ch

17

database, or do you instead take the entire database? I know that I'd rather have the entire database—if I did such evil things, that is. So it now becomes the responsibility of your internal network (if you are hosting the site that is taking online orders) to be secure from outside attacks. It also falls to your database server or custom programming to be secure, and to not have any back doors. It's a tricky situation, and there is no easy answer as to how secure your network needs to be—or even if it is secure when you think it is.

There Really Is No Way for Me to Be Safe, Is There?

Before you get overly concerned by the contents of this chapter, I want to say that my point here is to demonstrate that security needs to be a concern on your network. The chances of your server being targeted and compromised is probably pretty small. You might never have a single break-in attempt; however, be aware of what can happen, and the ways in which people can take advantage of your network. Don't worry, it probably won't happen—but at least take some precautions to make your network less susceptible to attack.

Security in Stability

For some people, security is the capability of the network to perform critical tasks in a timely manner. For these people, a secure network is one that stays online and does what it's supposed to. For our purposes, however, there is more to security than just worrying about what's being sent over the network. This is a matter of protecting your machines from crashing attacks. Besides people out to steal your data, there are also those who are interested in breaking into your systems, using your resources, or just plain messing things up. Once again, in order to demonstrate the problems that this sort of insecurity can cause, I'll give an example. (I discussed this earlier in the book, but I'll now expand on its effect in my workplace.)

In 1997, an attack on the Windows 95 and NT machines in my workplace surfaced. This attack was called *winnuke*, and within a matter of days winnuke clients were available for every known version of UNIX, Mac OS, and even Windows machines themselves. Winnuke works by opening a connection to a networked Windows computer, then sends a single properly configured packet to the remote computer. The result under Windows 95 is that the computer *blue screens* (presents a fatal error) and, if recovered, disables all TCP/IP network access. Under Windows NT 4, you either get a solid system lock up or reboot the computer. In either case, the result is entirely unacceptable for a network that is providing any sort of service that needs to be reliable. In our case, Microsoft's Web servers crashed, hundreds of computers in classrooms crashed, and so on. It was a nightmare.

Without intentionally being cruel to Microsoft, I have an amusing story. The company provided fixes to the winnuke problem within one or two days of the initial discovery. The problem with the patch, however, was that it didn't completely solve the winnuke problem. The patch fixed all attacks that came from UNIX and Windows computers; however, because of the slightly different header information contained in the packets sent from Mac OS computers, they maintained the capability to crash Windows 95/NT machines at will. Needless to say, the entire situation was both embarrassing and a publicity nightmare for Microsoft. It took a few more days for a second patch—which completely fixed the situation—to be issued.

This situation didn't pass through my end of the woods unnoticed. The NT servers run by another department in my building were taken down for several weeks—and their administrator was out of the country and unreachable. Several buildings for which I am responsible might have had all their Windows-based computers crash within minutes of each other. Over 200 computers could have been brought to their knees within seconds…not a good situation at all. Checking the network with a packet sniffer revealed that someone had set up a program to run every day, right around noon, that was to winnuke the entire building subnet. It took a bit of tracking to find the responsible individual.

Meanwhile, what excuse can I give my users? The only solution to the winnuke problem is to install the appropriate patches on your computer. Imagine a network of hundreds of researchers and faculty members—all of whom are skilled in their fields, but not necessarily in computer operations. Trying to get each of them to install the patch to protect their system is impossible; furthermore, to be frank, to do it for them is well beyond my job description and the amount of available time I have. As a result, most of the machines are still unprotected, even after a year. I recently ran a test on my own department to see how many machines were still vulnerable. Of the machines that were tested, more than 65 percent could still be crashed with winnuke—not incredibly secure. So, besides worrying about your data, you also need to be aware of, and plan for, insecurities in the operating systems you intend to use.

Because it is a single-user system, Mac OS is either considered really secure or incredibly insecure—it entirely depends on the software that is running on the machine. As I mentioned in a previous chapter, programs that run under the current Mac OS have complete control over the machine. As such, they are written to provide their own security mechanisms rather than rely on mechanisms within the operating system itself. Several programs, including the WebSTAR Web server, are noted for their security. Hacking contests were held to test WebSTAR's security, and it did a remarkable job of remaining unhacked.

If you are using Mac OS as a primary platform, be sure to thoroughly research the software that is running on it. Apple has done a very nice job of providing updates for bugs in the software, but they took a very long time to provide protection against certain common TCP/IP attacks in their Open Transport software.

A rather unusual benefit of using the Mac OS as a server platform is that it is not a common server platform. Hackers attack machines to build their skills and go on hacking other machines. Hacking a Mac OS-based computer gains them little in hacking experience and does not give them access to the type of resources that can be uncovered on an NT or UNIX machine. It might sound a bit strange, but there really is security in obscurity.

Windows and Windows NT are the new kids on the block, and have been the subjects of many, if not most, of the recent attacks. Windows NT, in particular, is coming under special scrutiny by hackers specifically because of its claims to be a secure and superior operating system to UNIX. The more the operating system is hyped, the more people want to break into it. This is a natural growing process for any network operating system. UNIX has endured 20 years of scrutiny; now it is time for NT to do the same. Unfortunately, it is the early adopter of NT that pays for this on the job testing of NT. Once an exploit is discovered for the operating system, it is quickly shared throughout the Internet—high profile companies and organizations are targeted by hacker groups, attacks are launched, and computers are crashed. Here are a few of the exploits that have surfaced within the past few months:

- Email clients (Eudora and Outlook) can be tricked into accidentally executing attachments without the user's knowledge.

- Microsoft's dynamic Web page engine, Active Server Pages, can be tricked into returning program source code from the machine by adding a special extension to the URLs that were requested.

- A remote control program for Windows NT was released under the guise that it enables you to control an NT machine remotely. The program, in fact, is a rather clever work that uses Windows' insecurities to perform its remote control; it is a hacking tool disguised as a utility.

Microsoft is usually extremely fast in issuing fixes for bugs that are discovered, which is wonderful. The biggest problem is that the number of patches that come out for the Windows operating systems is sometimes difficult to keep up with. Make sure you have some sort of training for the clients on your network so that they know about security issues and keep their OS updated. Trying to maintain patches on more than a few computers quickly turns into a nightmare. It is better to give your users the knowledge to do things on their own rather than do it for them. Above all, keep track of known problems with the operating system (this applies to ANY operating system). There are many online resources which track known bugs and their fixes; one of my favorites is:

`http://www.rootshell.com/`

How Do I Keep Track of What Is Up to Date?

The best advice is to check the Web site of your OS provider on a regular basis. Microsoft posts Service Packs for NT several times a year. The service packs contain all the fixes for any known security holes and bugs. Similarly, on Red Hat Linux there is a steady stream of package upgrades that can be downloaded from the Red Hat Web site (www.redhat.com). Keeping up to date is your first line of defense.

So UNIX has had a few decades to have hackers pick it apart, so it must be secure, right? Nope. Linux, with its UNIX heritage, has inherited a large number of the problems of the common UNIX utilities—as well as a few bugs of its own. From a hacker's standpoint, UNIX makes an excellent platform for launching other attacks. Hacking is all about covering your trail as you go. Gaining login access to a UNIX computer buys a hacker a fully networked platform, often with a compiler, and the capability to hide his or her tracks.

Linux provides an incredible number of services that are installed through basic installation. This robustness is the basis for most of its insecurities. There is a constant stream of new sendmail bugs being discovered, for example, even though the software has been in active development for many years. Since the Linux kernel is relatively new, there are bugs that are discovered on a somewhat regular basis. Kernel-level bugs are generally a bad thing because disrupting operations at a kernel level usually results in serious system errors such as crashes or loss of network services.

Patching Linux exploits is usually much harder than running a Windows service pack. This might involve downloading patch files, applying them to kernel source code, and then recompiling and reinstalling the kernel. The Red Hat company places patches for exploits online, but even the Red Hat package manager (a system which makes installing software/updates very simple on a Linux machine) can't save you from recompiling the kernel in some instances. On the bright side, there have been very few crashing bugs that have affected Linux in the past year. Linux tends to stay online without much maintenance. If you shut down all the unnecessary services that are running on your Linux machines, you'll be less susceptible to attacks. The same goes for Windows 95, 98, and NT. The less you have running, the fewer doors that are left open for intrusion.

The bottom line here is to keep your operating system up to date. NT users in particular must pay close attention to bugs as they turn up in the operating system. The only way that your system can be secure from crashes, or from intrusion, is if you know everything that the hackers know so that you can stop them before they start.

Ways of Securing Your Network

Chapter 18, "Using Security Techniques to Protect Your Network and Data," takes a look at specific different techniques that can be used to protect your data and network. Before you move on, though, let's take a higher-level look at the techniques that will be discussed. There are two methods that are commonly used to protect data and networks: firewalls and data encryption.

Firewalls

A *firewall* is a rather colorful name for a simple traffic-blocking device. Firewalls operate by blocking traffic going into and out of a network. Since traffic is all based on a port number, firewalls enable you to pick who can transmit data, to what port they can transmit, and what sort of incoming connections are allowed on the network. A firewall sits between your intranet and the rest of the world. There can be several different firewalls on your network if, for some reason, you need to secure information from other parts of your organization.

FIGURE 17.1
Firewalls sit between two networks and allow only specific incoming or outgoing packets to pass. The server rejects any other packets.

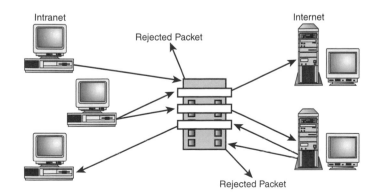

Firewalls come in two different forms—hardware based or software based. Both are really just very specialized routers or gateways. This probably seems relatively obvious because routers move data between different networks and so does a firewall. However, in the case of a firewall, it doesn't necessarily allow all the data to move between the ports. There are several different configurations of a firewall based on the different ways that data can be stopped at a point. The two different configurations you'll be looking at in Chapter 18 are *packet filtering* and *proxy* firewalls.

Packet Filtering Firewall

A *packet-filtering* firewall filters packets out of the network. Packets that match a specific rule are not passed between the two network interfaces on the firewall. In this configuration, some pieces of network traffic are allowed through, whereas others are stopped and discarded—this can work in either an incoming or outgoing direction.

Proxy Firewall   A more secure, but not as flexible, method of firewalling is to use a *proxy* firewall. This is the same as the proxy servers you've already seen, except in this case they are used to limit the amount of traffic between two networks rather than to provide connectivity to a smaller network. A proxy firewall does not allow any original packets from either side to pass through. Instead, it accepts requests for information and connections to be made, and, if approved, makes and maintains them on behalf of the requesting machine.

Other Types of Firewalls   If you choose to do further research on firewalls, you will undoubtedly come across information on two other types: the *Circuit-Level* firewall and the *Application Gateway*. A Circuit-Level firewall negotiates a connection between a machine on the internal network and one on the outside. If the connection is allowed, it can be made, and the firewall does not continue to check the packet flow between the two machines. An *Application Gateway* is simply a secure method of running certain applications. In order for applications to run successfully, they must authenticate themselves with an Application Gateway firewall. Once the authentication is completed, they can run normally.

A problem with firewalls is that they do not protect you from yourself. The assumption of the firewall network protection philosophy is that the attack on your network is going to come from the outside. If you have a large number of machines on your internal network, or are in a position where your internal network has a large number of unknown users (such as a library or classroom), then you might be vulnerable to attacks from the inside. On our campus network, there are multiple subnets running on a single network backbone, which means a potential of several hundred users all running on the same network—including public access workstations. Unless this network is physically broken somewhere and a firewall is installed, there is great risk of attack from the inside of the network. In such a case, a firewall provides no protection at all.

Data encryption

Well, you've read enough about protecting your network computers from the evils of the Internet (or intranet). But there is another protection method that is worth looking into if you are concerned about data being intercepted or read off of your networked computers: data encryption.

Data encryption is the process of taking data before or during transmission and encoding it into a format that is no longer human readable. The receiving computer applies decryption algorithms to the encrypted data and the original data is recovered. Most data encryption techniques in use now take quite a bit of processing power to crack, so people who want to get to your data are really going to have to work at it.

Data encryption techniques are generally effective, but often require an extra step to encode the data before sending. The next chapter looks at a common encryption technique that is used when sending email—but it is not supported by all email software. As a result, you often have to encrypt your messages, attach them to a plain text message, and then send the result. Unfortunately, it's easy to skip this extra step and not take the trouble to protect your data. If you employ a combination of firewalls and data encryption, you will have a very secure network.

Data Encryption and the US Government   If you choose data encryption as a method of securing your data, research your encryption techniques and make sure that they are legal in all the locations that you're going to be transferring data. The US government has a variety of highly controversial encryption export laws. It is illegal to export programs that use high levels of encryption just as it is illegal to export the source code to encrypt or decode.

The explosion of the Internet has brought to light this rather ludicrous law. Exporting encryption techniques is viewed as a breach of national security, yet the source code for many encryption techniques is easily accessible over the Internet. To keep people outside of the United States from downloading the information, there are often warnings such as "It is illegal to export this source code outside of the United States." Obviously, the information has made it into "enemy" hands, but it still remains illegal. If you choose an encryption method for your data that is only legal in the United States and then find that you need to communicate outside of the country, you're either going to have to break a federal law or send the data in some other format, or unencrypted. It's silly but, for the moment, that's the way things are.

Security and Your Network

Hopefully, you now have a few things to think about. Determine the type of security that you're going to need for your network. Decide if the data that you are sending is sensitive and needs to be protected. Pay close attention to newsgroups and bug-tracking Web sites to stay abreast of the current faults in whatever operating system you use. Probably the most useful advice that you can have is to make frequent backups of important data on your network. Power surges, crashed hard drives, and other physical problems can cause just as much trouble as any hackers on your network, and it is probably far more likely to happen.

Networks are created to facilitate the movement of information. No matter what you do, there is always a hole somewhere that someone can get through. We live in a day and age where teenagers from around the globe hack remote sites for days just so they can have the bragging rights to their friends. This comes with the territory, and either you're going to spend sleepless nights worried about your network security, or you are going to protect your data as best you can—and keep a backup stored someplace safe. In the case of the latter, knowing that you'd be capable of restoring your initial configuration even if a hacking catastrophe were to happen, is hopefully more than enough comfort to enable you to sleep at night.

Other Information Sources

Rootshell OS exploit archive

`http://www.rootshell.com/`

CERT Advisory center

`http://www.cert.org/`

3COM Information on Firewalls and Security

`http://www.3com.com/nsc/500619.html`

Using Security Techniques to Protect Your Network and Data

by John Ray

In this chapter

Data Encryption As a Security Measure   **366**

Security: The Final Word   **378**

Other Information Sources   **378**

Armed with a knowledge of what firewalls are and what data encryption is, you're ready to protect your network—but how do you do it? Do firewalls sound a bit confusing? Well, if you followed the chapter on setting up a proxy server for network connectivity, you already have the knowledge on how to set up a proxy-based firewall.

Think back to the configuration of the proxy server: What did it do? It acted as the connection point between your network and the rest of the world. The same thing goes for the NAT server. Both sit in between your network and the Internet (or more of your intranet). You have the ability to limit what traffic comes into and leaves your network based on the port number and originating/destination IP addresses. This is precisely the same job as a firewall. The biggest difference between what you've seen when using a proxy/NAT connection solution and a firewall is that the firewall must use two separate network interfaces to do its job. You can run NAT servers on a single card—in which case the card handles traffic for two different subnets—your internal subnet, and the external subnet, or Internet connection. This is not what you want to have happen when you're using a firewall, because packets from both networks travel across the same wire. The purpose of a firewall is to completely block network traffic you don't want; therefore, there must be a physical separation between the internal and external networks. Other than that, you've actually already seen the basic configuration of a firewall. Many of the NAT or proxy software packages advertise themselves as "routers" and "firewalls" because the purpose of the software is essentially the same: First and foremost, you're bridging two networks, and secondly, you're making decisions about the types of traffic that you want to allow on your network.

We won't be spending too much time on this topic, because most of it is going to be a rehash of the proxy and NAT chapters. Let's see how we can configure the software we've already looked at to act as a firewall, rather than just giving us connectivity to a different network.

Using a Mac OS Computer As a Firewall

The best package to illustrate packet-filtering based firewalling is Mac OS's IPNetRouter. IPNetRouter offers the most straightforward configuration and has a level of consistency in its interface that makes configuration and debugging mostly painless. Let's jump back to IPNetRouter now and see how we can use it and a Macintosh with two network cards to secure our network. To use IPNetRouter as *just* a firewall, you simply configure the application just as you would for NAT, except you don't need to enable IP. Other than that, the configuration is identical. Although this situation is a bit contrived, let's assume that I'm providing a firewall between my internal network and my PPP connection. Unfortunately, I don't have a second Ethernet card in my Mac, so let's just assume that my PPP connection is a second Ethernet card. There is no real difference in terms of configuration. (Remember, that's the beauty of the good old OSI network model; the Data Link Layer is separate from the TCP/IP protocol itself, so PPP truly is just as viable a network interface as an Ethernet card!) To access the IPNetRouter program, simply double-click the IPNetRouter icon or the icon for any configuration file that you may have created. The settings screen is shown by default. My configuration, so far, is shown in Figure 18.1.

FIGURE 18.1

Here's the IPNetRouter window showing my current configuration.

The next step in creating a filtering firewall is providing IP filtering services. For proxy servers, this is already an implicit feature. Proxy servers have a defined set of ports that can be used to transfer data. Incoming or outgoing data on other ports is simply not passed. When we configured WinProxy, remember that you had the option of telling the program what protocols you wanted to run on the network. Consider this as just a higher level of packet filtering. In IPNetMonitor, packet filtering is a very simple operation. Just select IP filtering from the Window menu. The main packet filtering screen is shown in Figure 18.2.

FIGURE 18.2

You configure packet filtering in this dialog box.

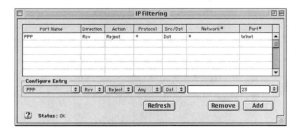

From here we can add up to 30 packet filtering rules to the system. Each of the pop-up menus corresponds with the field name above it. For my example, I've disabled all incoming Telnet connections to my network. To do this, I set up the following entry:

Port Name - PPP—I want to keep incoming connections that might arrive over the PPP connection.

Direction—I'll set this to "Rcv" or receive, because I'm worried about what is being received by this port, not what is being sent over it.

Action—I do not want any sort of connection to be established, so I'm going to choose "reject" to keep any packets matching my filter to not be forwarded to the Ethernet interface.

Protocol—Telnet operates using TCP, but, rather than specifying TCP explicitly, I'll set this option to Any. If you aren't sure if a protocol uses TCP, UDP, or ICMP, you can make sure your network is safe by choosing Any and blocking whatever protocol is being used.

Src/Dst—I have no idea where the source of Telnet connections is going to be, but I do know that I do not want its destination to be a machine on my network, so I'm going to choose "Dst" or destination.

Network#—There's no need for me to set a specific address that I want to block packets to, but I could if I wanted. Instead, I'll just leave this blank, and any IP addresses will be matched.

Port#—Last but not least (in fact, this is probably the most important setting), I need to set the port that I want to block. Telnet, as you know, is port 23, so that's what I'm blocking.

That's all there is to it. IPNetRouter, instead of just acting as a NAT server, is also configurable as a firewall. One thing you need to pay attention to, however, is by default, packets that aren't filtered out by the rule set will be passed. Be sure that you configure a complete rule set that takes all of your services into account. Don't assume that because you didn't set a filter to pass packets, they will automatically be blocked.

Using Windows As a Firewall

As I mentioned, the Windows proxy server can serve as an effective firewall. The configuration we've already set up will act as a firewall for your network. You have complete control over what protocols are running over your network, and you can even allow incoming access to different machines on your internal network by mapping ports. Figure 18.3 shows WinProxy's port mapping screen revisited.

FIGURE 18.3

The WinProxy software can be used to map out ports, forming an effective firewall.

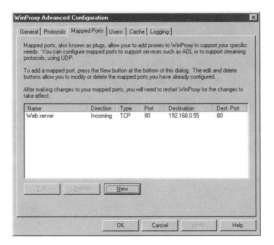

If you choose not to map any ports, you have effectively shut off the outside network from making any connections to your machines. The only harm that can come to your network is from the inside. The risks are primarily either from damage directly caused by individuals on your network, or by downloading viruses or other damaging binaries from the outside network. That was fast and painless, wasn't it? Proxy firewalls are probably the fastest to set up and the easiest to maintain. Because only one machine is actually exposed to network traffic, they are also very secure.

Using Linux As a Packet-Filtering Firewall

Like the Mac OS IPNetRouter, the software we've already looked at to set up our NAT configuration can also be used to quickly create an IP-filtering firewall. Given the machine configuration that we initially created for running the proxy server and that we later used for NAT, we can again add the additional functionality of packet filtering. This does not need to be used in conjunction with our NAT setup but can be used entirely separately to limit the packets that are sent between two Linux network interfaces. You'll probably want to create a shell script that will run these different commands either at startup or manually. You could also include them in the /etc/rc.d/rc.local file that is processed when Linux is booted. If you're running NAT services, you'll probably want to integrate these commands in with your NAT commands.

First, we'll use the ipfwadm (IP Forward Administration) tool to disallow any packets from being forwarded. This lets us build up a list of services we want to pass, rather than limiting the services we don't want transmitted.

```
ipfwadm -F -p deny
```

Okay, all packets are now being denied. Now, with only a few lines, we can allow packets to pass in and out of the firewall. Let's start by allowing connections to outside Web sites. We all need to browse, right?

```
ipfwadm -F -a accept -b -P tcp 192.168.0.* 80 -D 0.0.0.0/0
```

The ipfwadm utility is told to accept and forward TCP packets from our internal network (192.168.0.*) that are connecting to port 80 (the Web server port) and allow them to connect to any external IP address (0.0.0.0/0). You can create as many of these rules as you'd like. Another important setting might be name resolution. If you want to enable your entire internal network to speak to any outside name server, you could do this:

```
ipfwadm -F -a accept -b -P udp 192.168.0.* 53 -D 0.0.0.0/0
```

All traffic for port 53 using the UDP protocol is now allowed outside of the firewall. This should let us continue to use DNS lookups from the internal network.

Now, how about allowing outside connections to internal machines? For example, how about running an internal Web server and letting other people connect to it? Just as simple:

```
ipfwadm -F -a accept -b -P tcp -S 0.0.0.0/0 -D 192.168.0.99 80
```

Assuming you're running a nameserver on port 80 of the IP address 192.168.0.99, then all sources attempting to connect to this port will be forwarded.

That's all you need to do, and you've now secured your internal network behind a packet-filtering Linux-based firewall.

Other Firewalls

For our look into firewalls, I've assumed that you're using a network that has been developed using the techniques that we've discussed in the book. If you want to add a firewall to an existing network, you might want to look at hardware-based firewall solutions. Most dedicated

Part
V

Ch
18

routers and gateways can block traffic based on a port. Even some basic bridges offer packet-filtering capabilities. Using one of these devices eliminates the need for you to rely on one of your computer systems to do the work and on third-party software, which might be unsecure itself. The beauty of a hardware-based solution is that you can plug it in, spend a few minutes configuring it, and then forget about it except for occasional monitoring or auditing. The software-based configurations you see here rely on the security and stability of the operating systems they run under.

Data Encryption As a Security Measure

The two places you're most likely to find encryption in use on the Internet are in the two most common forms of communication, namely email and Web traffic. To handle transferring data over the Web, Netscape came up with the *SSL*, or *secure socket layer*, which we looked at briefly when covering the http protocol. Email is commonly protected with what is called *PGP*, or *Pretty Good Privacy*, which was created by Philip Zimmermann. No matter what the encryption technique, there is a common "handshaking" method used to pass information that is necessary for decoding the data.

For data to be stored in an unreadable format, it must be modified by some means. Obviously, if the same method is used by all network clients to encrypt the data, the idea of encryption becomes pointless. If the same algorithm is always applied, anyone can encrypt or decrypt any data. To make data secure, encryption engines make use of a *key* that is sometimes randomly generated, or picked by a user. This key is then used as part of the encryption process, and the encrypted data is then unique for that particular key. If the exact same data is encrypted but another key is used, the resulting datafile will be entirely different. For the data to be extracted into its original form, the key must be known by the receiving party. This key system is the basis for most of the encryption techniques currently used.

If you think about what I just said, you might notice a small problem—namely that the receiving party has to know the key that was used to encrypt the data. If you're distributing the data over the network, presumably you'd also want to distribute the key along with the data. Do you see the problem now? The key, which is what we need to retrieve the original information, is not encrypted. If you sent it along with the encrypted file, anyone could potentially grab the file and use the key to decrypt it. Not too safe. Because of this, we need to look at the idea of a *public key* and a *private key*.

The idea works basically like this: The public key and private key are related but cannot be used to derive either the public key from the private key, or vice versa. These keys are generated for you by the software, and both play an important role in the encryption process. The private key is exactly what it sounds like: private. You'll keep this key on your computer and not share it with anyone else; if it becomes compromised, your data is no longer safe. The public key, on the other hand, is what you distribute to the world. Most people using PGP include their public key in their message signatures. You can post it anywhere—on your Web page, on correspondence, wherever—it doesn't contain any information that can be used to decrypt your data. Now, with the two keys, the data encryption process works like this:

1. Someone wants to send you a private document, and they have your public key. They run their encryption software and feed it the file they want encoded and your public key. The resulting file is now secure. In fact, the person who encrypted it cannot decrypt it. They mail the file to you.

2. You receive the file and want to view it. You use your private key to decrypt the data. The encryption process works by encrypting the data with your public key in a way that makes it only decryptable using the private key.

3. If you want to respond to the send, you repeat the same process, only using their public key as the encryption key.

Separating the two keys so that the original key used for encrypting cannot be used to decrypt the data makes it possible to transmit encrypted data and keys over the network without having to worry about the keys being intercepted. Each person who needs to transmit data uses their private key and the public keys of the people they need to communicate with to encrypt outgoing data.

There are many different methods of actually encrypting the data that is transferred, but the public/private key system, and variations of it, is the mechanism behind the transferring of the data. In SSL, keys are generated and sent back and forth during a handshaking and authentication phase. There is no interaction, from the user's point of view, in terms of generating public and private keys. This all happens transparently and is not of any concern to the person who is sitting behind the computer. In the case of PGP, the keys are needed for more than a single connection and are thus visible and accessible by the user.

Part

V

Ch

18

Is That All There Is to Keys?

Okay, you caught me. There actually is a great deal of variation in the different methods that keys are transferred and used. The public/private key description should be looked on as a very high-level view of the mechanisms by which secure communications work. SSL, for example, has different levels of handshaking where the host computer sends keys back and forth to verify that it is who it claims to be, and the same goes for the client. There isn't necessarily a limit of two keys that are used. In PGP, there are two keys, but the private key is actually used to encode a third session key that is actually used to encode the main body of the information.

Generating keys is one thing, but encoding the data is something entirely different. The actual encryption process can (and is) carried out in many different ways. The goal of any encryption scheme is to find a method of sending the data such that it would be very difficult, and require far too much computing power, to make it worthwhile to anyone to try to have the key to decode it. There are several different encryption techniques in use today, such as *DES*, which was originally developed by the US government, and *RSA*, which is used in Web browsers, PGP, and other cryptology systems. Rather than trying to describe how these encryption standards work in my own words, here's an excerpt from the RSA Frequently Asked Questions list, hosted at:

`http://www.rsa.com/`

What you're about to read is highly mathematical and is provided just so you can get an idea of the amount of thought put into encryption techniques. Cereal-box decoder rings aren't going to cut it here:

From the RSA FAQ:

What Is RSA?

RSA is a public-key cryptosystem that offers both encryption and digital signatures (authentication). Ron Rivest, Adi Shamir, and Leonard Adleman developed RSA in 1977 [RSA78]; RSA stands for the first letter in each of its inventors' last names.

RSA works as follows: take two large primes, p and q, and compute their product $n = pq$; n is called the *modulus*. Choose a number, e, less than n and relatively prime to $(p\text{-}1)(q\text{-}1)$, which means e and $(p\text{-}1)(q\text{-}1)$ have no common factors except 1. Find another number d such that $(ed\text{ - }1)$ is divisible by $(p\text{-}1)(q\text{-}1)$. The values e and d are called the *public* and *private exponents*, respectively. The public key is the pair (n, e); the private key is (n, d). The factors p and q may be kept with the private key, or destroyed.

It is currently difficult to obtain the private key d from the public key (n, e). However if one could factor n into p and q, then one could obtain the private key d. Thus the security of RSA is based on the assumption that factoring is difficult. The discovery of an easy method of factoring would "break" RSA.

Here is how RSA can be used for encryption and digital signatures (in practice, the actual use is slightly different).

RSA Encryption   Suppose Alice wants to send a message m to Bob. Alice creates the ciphertext c by exponentiating: $c = me$ mod n, where e and n are Bob's public key. She sends c to Bob. To decrypt, Bob also exponentiates: $m = cd$ mod n; the relationship between e and d ensures that Bob correctly recovers m. Since only Bob knows d, only Bob can decrypt this message.

RSA Digital Signature   Suppose Alice wants to send a message m to Bob in such a way that Bob is assured the message is both authentic, has not been tampered with, and from Alice. Alice creates a digital signature s by exponentiating: $s = md$ mod n, where d and n are Alice's private key. She sends m and s to Bob. To verify the signature, Bob exponentiates and checks that the message m is recovered: $m = se$ mod n, where e and n are Alice's public key.

Thus encryption and authentication take place without any sharing of private keys: each person uses only another's public key or their own private key. Anyone can send an encrypted message or verify a signed message, but only someone in possession of the correct private key can decrypt or sign a message.

I've Heard of CAs, What Are They?

A CA or Certifying Authority is an entity that issues you a digital signature and is responsible for verifying that that signature is still valid. Obtaining an ID from a Certifying Authority provides peace of mind to people who communicate with you because it certifies that you're indeed who you say you are. A large provider of digital IDs is Verisign. You can visit their Web page for more information: http://www.verisign.com.

Luckily for all of us, the software that uses encryption techniques, such as RSA, is much easier to use than the encryption technique is to understand. Now let's see some PGP software that can be used to encrypt our data. Software is available for Windows, Mac OS, and UNIX machines, and is entirely free, so within a few minutes, you'll generate your own private and public key, and join the thousands of people who are already communicating securely. The biggest problem right now is that there are multiple distributions of PGP. A nice Mac OS and Windows 95/NT package can be downloaded from

```
http://www.nai.com/products/security/pgpfreeware.asp
```

MS-DOS and UNIX are downloadable from

```
http://web.mit.edu/network/pgp.html
```

Download the appropriate files for your operating system, unpack the utility, and we'll see how simple it is to actually encrypt information on your computer. The Mac OS and Windows versions of the PGPFreeware software are virtually identical aside from the user interface differences of the operating systems. Because of the similarity, there is no point in showing the same configuration for both systems. Instead, I'll point out any differences that may appear.

Using PGPFreeware on Mac OS and Windows

The PGPFreeware application installs two different utilities on your system: the PGPKey application and the PGPTools program. PGPTools is used to encrypt and sign different files, while the PGPKey program maintains a list of keys for people you will want to contact. The first thing you'll see upon running the PGPKey program is the Key Generation Wizard, shown in Figure 18.4. This will get you up and running very quickly with your own PGP key. First, you'll need to enter your full name and email address that will be stored with the key. The email address allows the PGP software to integrate itself into your email programs.

Next, choose the size of the keys you want to use, as shown in Figure 18.5. The larger the key size, the more secure your data will be, however, the longer it will take to encode. The default key size is 2,048 bits, which, from my experience, is quite fast on any Pentium or PowerPC based computer. Using large key sizes on a 486 may require a bit of patience.

FIGURE 18.4

PGP's Key Generation Wizard simplifies the encryption process.

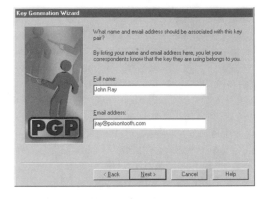

FIGURE 18.5

The next step is to choose the key size you want to employ.

If you'd like to set an expiration date for your key, you can do so in the next dialog box, shown in Figure 18.6. After the key expires, you won't be able to encrypt any further files. You may want to rotate your keys occasionally for security reasons, but there is little reason to do so.

FIGURE 18.6

You can choose to set an expiration date in this dialog box.

As an extra layer of security, the software will only allow you to sign documents if you have set a key-phrase (just a simple password) for yourself. This step, shown in Figure 18.7, keeps other people from impersonating you and signing secure documents using your key.

FIGURE 18.7

To sign documents, you need to supply a key phrase.

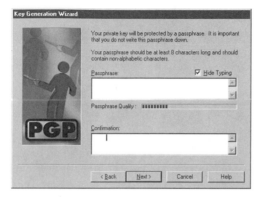

Last but not least, the software needs to generate a random number to use when forming the key. To do this, it will prompt you to move the mouse around the screen, type gibberish on the keyboard, or both, as shown in Figure 18.8. It uses your input to generate a random number and then the key.

FIGURE 18.8

By providing erratic mouse movement or keystrokes, you help the PGP program generate a random number.

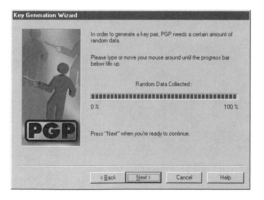

Finally, the PGP software generates your key. Depending on the speed of your machine, this could take a few minutes. Once completed, you have the option of sending the key to a key server. This is a very nice feature of this particular package, because the key server maintains a database of all registered keys. If you'd like to send a file to someone but you don't know the key, you can look them up on the server. If you'd rather not make your public key public, don't select the Send my key to root server now check box shown in Figure 18.9.

FIGURE 18.9

If you don't want to publicize your public key, make sure this check box is deselected.

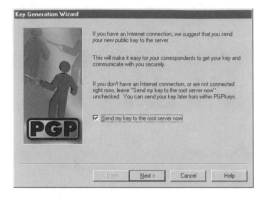

Congratulations! you now have your own PGP key, and it should be showing up in your PGPkeys window, as shown in Figure 18.10. The PGPKey window displays all the information about the keys that you have stored on your system, the size of the key, the level of "trust" you place on a particular key, expiration date, and so on. Play around in the PGPkeys window; you can expand individual keys to show more information about the individual and the key.

FIGURE 18.10

You now have your very own PGP key.

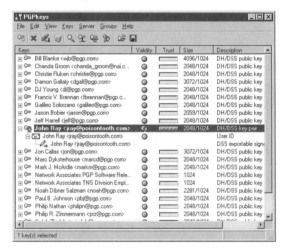

From the toolbar at the top of the PGPkeys window, you may delete keys, rerun the Key Generation Wizard, export and import key files, and, most importantly, search for other user's keys. Click the magnifying glass icon to display the search dialog box, shown in Figure 18.11.

You can search a key server for a particular user by entering in his or her user ID (most likely, a username from an email address), and clicking on the Search button. For example, if you wanted to search for me, just type **jray** into the search field and start the search. You'll see several jrays returned, one of which should be jray@poisontooth.com. If you'd like to add me to your stored list of keys, just drag my name from the search results over to your key window. You can now encrypt documents and send documents to me.

FIGURE 18.11

PGPkeys lets you search for a particular key.

So, how do you actually encrypt something? There are two ways. The straightforward way is to use the PGPTools program that came with the PGP software package. PGPTools, shown in Figure 18.12, provides several utilities, namely the ability to encrypt and decrypt data.

FIGURE 18.12

The PGPTools program provides actual encryption of data based on your key.

You'll also see options to sign the data. Doing so adds your signature to the encrypted file. Also included are two wipe utilities you can use to permanently erase files from your hard drive. PGPTools can also be activated by dragging and dropping files you want to encrypt or decrypt onto the PGPTools toolbar icons. Or you can use it by selecting the files you want to work with, and then right-clicking (or Control-Clicking, on the Macintosh) to bring up a PGP contextual menu that offers the same options as the toolbar. This, however, is the slow way of doing things. If you're like me, you want to be able to type a message and PGP encode it instantly, not worrying about clicking here and doing such-n-such. Don't worry! We can do that with PGPFreeware, too! When the PGP software is installing, it will integrate itself with the email software that's on your machine. This will allow you to quickly and easily use PGP without flipping back and forth to other programs.

Using Outlook Express and PGP on the Macintosh   For example, suppose you're using Outlook Express as your email client on a Macintosh. Installing PGP provides encryption routines to this client. Figure 18.13 shows the Outlook Express program window. Notice the "lock" menu icon at the center of the main menu bar.

To encrypt a message that I am sending, I simply type the message, and, when I'm done, I make sure my cursor is at the bottom of the message text. Next, I choose either Encrypt or Encrypt and Sign from the lock menu. Before the message can be encrypted, I'll need to choose the recipients who will be decoding it. A PGP Recipients dialog box appears, in which I can drag the appropriate names from the top pane to the bottom, as shown in Figure 18.14.

FIGURE 18.13

After you install PGP, you can encrypt email in your favorite client program.

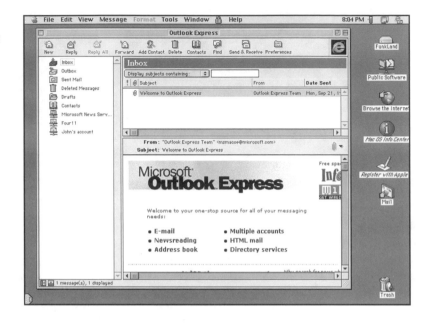

FIGURE 18.14

Choose the recipients who will be able to decode your message in this dialog box.

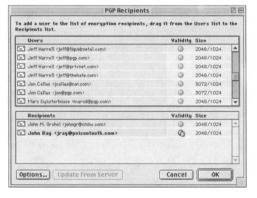

Once done, I click Okay, and the message will be encoded. Within a few seconds, my outgoing message will be rewritten as a PGP-encoded message and can be sent normally. An example of an encoded message appears in Figure 18.15. As you can see, my email message has been converted to gibberish.

Decoding an incoming PGP message works the same way. I simply select the encoded message and choose Decrypt/Verify from the lock menu. I'll be prompted for my key-password, which unlocks my private key and allows the software to decode the message.

FIGURE 18.15

After encoding, your message is no longer recognizable by human eyes.

Using PGP with Outlook Express on Windows   Using PGP under Outlook Express in the Windows platform is a tiny bit different than on the Macintosh—but in a good way! The PGP software installs a PGP menu in Outlook. From that menu, select Preferences and click the Email tab. As shown in Figure 18.16, you can set the PGP software to automatically encode and decode messages that are sent and received on your computer. No user interaction is required! That could hardly be any simpler.

Part

V

Ch

18

FIGURE 18.16

Under Windows, PGP adds a dialog box to Outlook Express that allows automatic encryption and decryption.

This level of integration with the software that *needs* to be secure is very nice. It makes PGP a utility that can be used on a regular basis, rather than something you have to pull out of some hidden directory and dust off every time you need to send something securely. Remember that you can also use PGP to encrypt local documents on your computer. There is no reason it has to be used with email—but it's certainly an excellent companion to electronic transmissions.

Using the UNIX-Based PGP on Linux

Unfortunately, because of variety of UNIX machines available and the different interfaces, you shouldn't expect a fancy interface like the ones available on the Mac OS and Windows computers. Instead, the Linux PGP is command-line driven but still gets the job done! Once you've retrieved and extracted the PGP archive from MIT, run the install script, `pgpinst`, which will install the PGP executables on your system.

First, we're going to need to generate a new key pair for ourselves. To do this, use the `pgpk` utility with the command line option `-g`.

```
pgpk -g

Pick your public/private keypair key size:
(Sizes are Diffie-Hellman/DSS; Read the user's guide for more information)
 1)    768/768  bits- Commercial grade, probably not currently breakable
 2)   1024/1024 bits- High commercial grade, secure for many years
 3)   2048/1024 bits- "Military" grade, secure for foreseeable future(default)
 4)   3072/1024 bits- Archival grade, slow, highest security
Choose 1, 2, 3 or 4, or enter desired number of Diffie-Hellman bits
(768 - 4096): 2048


You need a user ID for your public key.  The desired form for this
user ID is your FULL name, followed by your E-mail address enclosed in
<angle brackets>, if you have an E-mail address.  For example:
  Joe Smith <user@domain.com>
If you violate this standard, you will lose much of the benefits of
PGP 5.0's keyserver and email integration.

Enter a user ID for your public key: jray

Enter the validity period of your key in days from 0 - 999
0 is forever (and the default): 0

You need a pass phrase to protect your private key(s).
Your pass phrase can be any sentence or phrase and may have many
words, spaces, punctuation, or any other printable characters.
Enter pass phrase:
Enter again, for confirmation:
Enter pass phrase:
Collecting randomness for key...

We need to generate 407 random bits.  This is done by reading
/dev/random.  Depending on your system, you may be able
to speed this process by typing on your keyboard and/or moving your mouse.
   0 * -Enough, thank you.
*******  ................*******  .

Keypair created successfully.

If you wish to send this new key to a server, enter the URL of the server,
below.  If not, enter nothing.
```

Not too bad. Much like the configuration of the Mac and Windows Key generation, but not quite as flashy. Now, why don't we see if we can grab a public key to add to our keychain. I'm going to use a key server to add the public key of johngr@cmhc.com to my keychain.

```
pgpk -a hkp://keys.pgp.com/johngr@cmhc.com

Establishing connection
Sending request
Receiving data
Cleaning up
Complete.

Adding keys:

Key ring: 'hkp://keys.pgp.com/johngr@cmhc.com'
Type Bits KeyID     Created      Expires    Algorithm       Use
pub  1024 0xCCD70161 1997-07-21 ---------- DSS             Sign & Encrypt
sub  2048 0x0EB954FB 1997-07-21 ---------- Diffie-Hellman
uid  John M. Grohol <johngr@cmhc.com>

1 matching key found

Add these keys to your keyring? [Y/n] Y

Keys added successfully.
```

So far, so good. This isn't bad at all, is it? In fact, we're moving a bit faster than we did with those clunky graphics programs, aren't we? So we now know how to generate a key and retrieve keys for other users; how do we encrypt and sign a file? Once again, it's pretty simple! Just use the pgpe program (which is really calling the main pgp utility) to specify a recipient and the file we want to encrypt. For example, if I want to encrypt the file testfile for johngr@cmhc.com, I'd do it like this:

```
pgpe -r johngr@cmhc.com testfile

1024 bits, Key ID CCD70161, Created 1997-07-21
   "John M. Grohol <johngr@cmhc.com>"

Do you want to use the key with this name? [y/N] Y

Creating output file testfile.pgp
```

The output file, testfile.pgp, is encrypted and signed! So, with that under our belt, all we need to be able to do is decrypt a file that is sent to us. This time we're going to use pgpv. For this example, I'm decrypting a file called test2.pgp which has been sent to me.

```
pgpv test2.pgp

Message is encrypted.
Need a pass phrase to decrypt private key:
  2048 bits, Key ID B1072031, Created 1998-09-21
Enter pass phrase:
Pass phrase is good.
Opening file "test2" type binary.
```

Since Linux has the concept of "users," each user has his or her own PGP public and private key that is stored with each user's account information. Notice that I have not needed to identify myself or choose a specific key to decode/encode information. After the initial key generation has occurred, the rest of the operation is straightforward, and the appropriate key information is chosen for you. If you'd like to learn more about the capabilities of the Linux pgp package, view the man pages for pgp and pgpk.

Part
V

Ch
18

Security: The Final Word

There's more to network security than you've read about in the past two chapters. If you're concerned about security, which you should be if you have information that is private or irreplaceable, you should look for books related to your specific operating system. There are many books written on providing security for NT and UNIX, and you should not consider the information you've read so far to be a comprehensive picture of everything that can go wrong. With email viruses now being a reality, Word viruses running rampant, and so on, it's hard to say what's going to be discovered in the next month, year, or even week.

Other Information Sources

Firewall Vendor/Software resource `http://www.access.digex.net/~bdboyle/firewall.vendor.html`

Extensive Linux Firewall Information `http://sunsite.unc.edu/linux/HOWTO/Firewall-HOWTO.html`

RSA Encryption Information `http://www.rsa.com/`

## CHAPTER 19

Managing TCP/IP Network Resources

by John Ray

In this chapter

Where Things Go Wrong **380**

Hardware **380**

Software **384**

Users **390**

Somewhere in the Middle **392**

How big is your network? Ten users, 100 users, 10,000 users? If you're already looking at a network of 10,000 users, chances are you've got some sort of management procedure in place as it is. I'd like to take a little bit of space to talk about my experiences with the network that I administrate and some of the horror stories that have come up. Hopefully my experiences can help you make some decisions about your network before "bad things" happen. After all, it's better to learn from someone else's mistakes than your own! You'll also see some of the common solutions to these problems so you can take steps to prevent them before they occur.

Where Things Go Wrong

There are three areas that can cause trouble on your network. Here they are, along with an indication of what I'll talk about when I discuss each:

- Hardware
- Software
- Users

Unfortunately, these three areas cover *all* of the problems that can happen with a computer, regardless of whether it is on a network. The point is that there is no simple way of predicting where your network is going to break down or what part of it is going to cause you the most headaches. Rather than guess at this, let's look at each of these trouble spots, see what can go wrong on a typical network, and examine how the resources can better be managed to avoid problems.

Hardware

Obviously, this is a difficult area to guess what's going to go wrong. There are so many different hardware manufacturers and different types of computer equipment that, at times, it seems to be only the will of other worldly beings that keeps networks up and running. In Chapter 2, "Integrating TCP/IP and OSI Network Layers," I talked extensively about the different sorts of wiring used in networks and the problems that they can cause. I'm going to use some of this space to reiterate my thoughts on network wiring and configuration.

Thinnet

If I didn't convince you the first time, let me firmly restate my thoughts on thinnet, or coaxial cabling. It is purely evil. If you've chosen to wire your network using 10BASE-2, I suspect you have a very small network or you enjoy spending your time tracking down problems in the wiring. There is little to be gained by using 10BASE-2 and much to be lost. For small networks, it can be extremely convenient to run thinnet to each of the computers and have them instantly be networked. No need to buy any hubs to handle your connections—just add a piece of wire, and you're on the network!

If you're choosing to use thinnet, I urge you to buy the highest quality cables you can find—in particular, look for molded rubber attaching the BNC connector to the cable insulator. The rubber should help stiffen the "neck" of the connection, which is a common failure point in thinnet installations. Many of the buildings here on campus have old thinnet installations that were done using "crimp-on" BNC connectors. Their connections were created using a crimping tool that flattens a metal sleeve against the wire and holds the BNC connector in place. Unfortunately, this also weakens the area where the wire goes into the connector. After several years of use, inevitably the wire gets tugged, and over time strands of wire begin to break inside the connector. This can result in flaky network behavior or a completely dead network. Remember that one break on a thinnet line more or less spells doom for the entire network, so as soon as one of these connections fails, it's "lights-out" for everyone. To make matters worse, it isn't extremely easy to spot-check for these broken ends. I've seen BNC connectors where the wire is at a 90-degree angle to the connector, but it continues to work; yet other connections that look pristine are, in fact, broken. People connected to thinnet wiring often don't understand how gentle they need to treat the wire in order for it to work. If a person's computer is not where they'd like it to be on a desk, they pull on the computer until it is.

In one particularly bad case of this activity, a person needed to move their computer several feet away from its previous location. The computer itself was connected via thinnet to a colleague's machine in a locked office. For some reason, rather than running the thinnet through the wall between the two offices, they chose to run it underneath a connecting door. When I was finally called to look at the network (because it wasn't working), things had already gotten quite out of hand. The computer had been moved much further than the wire should have allowed. The connection was pulled out, and the person who had done all of this had tried to repair the connection by wrapping it all up in a huge ball of masking tape. To make matters worse, they said that they had heard a "loud bang" from the other room when they were moving their computer. I convinced someone to open the locked office, and, sure enough, the loud bang had been caused by them tugging at the wires enough to pull the other persons computer off their desk. By some miracle, the computer was still working, but I'm relatively certain that the owner, if they had been present, would have been extremely displeased.

If you choose to use thinnet, make it as inaccessible to user interaction as possible. Hide the wire as best you can, use wiring with connections designed to absorb some of the shock of being yanked or pulled, and provide enough slack wire for the user to be able to move the computer around within his or her area. After all, the wire's cheap; a few feet of slack will more than make up the expense in headache.

A second problem I've come across several times is the result of someone who knows almost enough to work on a network. By almost enough, I mean they know that for their computer to be on the network, they need to have wiring running to their computer and plugged into the back. Armed with this knowledge, they approach the situation in a rather logical manner: They use one of the "T" connections in the network to branch the thinnet into two segments, and then redirect the "new" cable into their offices and connect it to their devices. The biggest problem with this is that *sometimes* it actually works, but it's a toss-up as to whether it will work and what damage it may cause to the rest of the network. In any event, the network will not be stable, and there will be a high rate of transmission error in the line. Depending on how the person planned the wiring, it may be double terminated (each branch terminated), which would confuse matters all the more. I've seen cases where the engineers doing the wiring have thrown together branching solutions because it "mostly worked." This is little comfort when you're trying to track a problem, only to find that the wiring you're looking at shouldn't even exist. It's best to enforce a "no-touch" policy with your users. Most people don't intend to harm the network, but they do so inadvertently because they think that they might be able to solve a problem on their own, rather than ask for your assistance.

Lastly, the most common thinnet problem, at least for me, is the loss of termination. The most common causes for termination failure are (besides wires fraying and breaking) removal of the terminators themselves, and people who remove their computer from the network but leave the "T" attached to their computer. From a security standpoint, thinnet is extremely poor. Any user on your network can disrupt communications for everyone else. A single broken connection and hundreds of nodes may be affected. I still haven't quite determined *why* people feel a need to remove terminators from the network, or to disconnect network wires and not tell anyone. In the environment in which I work, there is simply no way I can keep track of who is doing what or where they're doing it. Computers change offices and are shuffled around each day. If a department calls and asks for my help, I happily give it to them. If they chose to rearrange network devices on their own, I inevitably get called in to pick up the pieces.

My advice, if you choose to use thinnet, is this: Do everything you can to educate your users on how delicate the network environment really is. People don't think that doing something to a wire in their private office can have substantial repercussions—but it can. Also, keep a very detailed map of all the wire that is laid for the network. When you're trying to find the repeater that the wire in office number 451 of 950 leads to, you'll be extremely glad that you did. Our network is slowly but surely moving to 10BASE-T, which has eliminated a significant percentage of the support calls I used to receive. Don't be afraid to mix network wiring; in some cases, it's perfectly acceptable to lay a thinnet backbone for the network, and then attach 10BASE-T hubs for the individual workgroups that will be on the network. Do whatever you feel comfortable setting up and maintaining—but beware of the consequences first!

Twisted Pair

Ahhhh… our good old friend, twisted pair. (Sounds like a heavy metal band, doesn't it?) Twisted-pair cabling is a much more manageable solution for your network. The number of headaches that can be saved by using twisted pair is unmeasureable. A single failure does not mean a failure for your entire network, and extending a cable for greater length does not involve splicing into the existing wiring and creating greater chances for failure.

Why Would I Splice a Cable in the First Place?

You can probably guess I was referring to thinnet cabling when I mentioned splicing. Buildings that have been wired in thinnet often have long strands that stretch for the length of a room without any connections. There are several classrooms on campus that have thinnet strung through them, but they were never intended to have outlets in place to accommodate network computer connections. With the growth of the Internet, it has been a necessity to have Internet access in the classrooms. To provide connection points, I've often had to cut the thinnet line and put BNC connections on each of the wires. Doing so disrupts network services for however long it takes to get the new connection in place. On a good day, I figure on 10 minutes or so. Besides the downtime, I've added a new failure point to the network, which is never a good thing.

There are only two problems I've encountered in several years of using twisted-pair equipment. The first problem is cables with RJ45 connectors (the "fat" phone-style connector typical of twisted-pair wiring) that have been molded incorrectly. Every now and then, I end up with a piece of cable that doesn't quite click into the Ethernet card. Rather than settling with a wire like this, get another piece; chances are you'll end up with a temperamental or otherwise faulty connection if you don't.

The second problem is not actually a problem but is something you need to be aware of. If the hub detects unusual activity on a port, it will partition it and remove it from the network. A malfunctioning Ethernet card caused a port of one of my hubs to be partitioned, and after replacing the card, the computer still didn't work. It took quite a bit of fussing before I realized that the computer and configuration was fine, but the line itself was dead. Usually all you need to do is press a button or cycle power to unpartition a port of the hub, but if you forget that this can happen, you might drive yourself nuts trying to find a problem that isn't even a problem. You might want to skim back over Chapter 2 where I discussed a few more wiring issues.

Overall, no matter what wiring choice you make, there are certain things I've found that have helped me immensely. Here are several tips that you should keep in mind:

- Keep a map of all the cables you've strung and the wire lengths.
- Label each of the wires according to the port of the hub or repeater that it connects to. If you have only a handful of computers, you might want to buy different colored 10BASE-T cable (it is often sold in multiple colors) to quickly differentiate what computer is connected where.
- If you're using thinnet, keep in mind that when diagnosing problems, you'll probably be following a strand of wire from station to station. Label each wire of a connection with the room the wiring is coming from and the next room that the wiring is going to.
- Leave enough wire for users to customize their work environment.
- If you can afford manageable hubs, buy them. Manageable hubs will let you monitor traffic on a per-machine or per-workgroup basis.

- Clearly state policies on connecting new computers to the network. Post them in a public area and explain to users *why* the policies are necessary.

- Don't be a superhuman. Don't think that a single person can administrate several buildings effectively. I've been stuck handling all the problems in eight different buildings, and it isn't fun; but, in my case, it was a matter of funding. Don't be afraid to hire administrators on a per-building or per-department basis; there will be plenty of work to keep them busy.

- Be patient! Things *will* go wrong. The more logically you can approach a problem, the faster it will be resolved.

Software

With hardware problems aside, we're left with software and user management issues. Let's tackle the software issues first. Software is significantly easier to mess up than you might think. The number of times you'll hear a user say, "I tried something, but then I'm sure I set everything back up the way you left it" is exceeded only by the number of times they'll say, "I didn't change anything, honest." There is some debate as to whether or not there actually is an evil gnome that perhaps sabotages network settings on a nightly basis. Considering that we see Santa Claus only once a year, he does have a bit of spare time to devote to such activities. Maybe instead of leaving coal in the stockings of naughty children, old Saint Nick now reconfigures their network software. I'm sure this is a rather unpopular view, but I tend to think that there is a much greater chance that it *is* the user—or at any rate "unofficial" software he or she installs—who is changing their own settings and breaking their own configurations. The primary service offered by my department is email and network connectivity. Given the basic services we offer, it's amazing the amount of bizarre configurations that people come up with.

TCP/IP Settings

I've had several people call me and say, "My computer isn't working...it just stopped a few hours ago." When I finally look at their computer, they have IP addresses configured for subnets that don't even exist on campus. If it isn't the IP address, it's nameservers that don't exist. And, of course, the standard response is "I swear it's always been like that." For whatever reason, things do end up getting changed. It's possible to lock these settings under most operating systems, but anyone interested in changing something will usually find a way to do it. A solution for managing your TCP/IP settings is DHCP. Chapter 4, "Controlling Network Traffic," covered the basics of DHCP, but talked mainly about DHCP as a method of assigning IP addresses. In practice, it can do much more than just assign an IP address. DHCP can be used to configure a wide range of TCP/IP options, such as

- IP Addresses
- Subnet Masks
- Gateways/Routers

- Name Servers
- WINS servers

This capability eliminates the need for you to provide settings on a machine-by-machine basis. If DHCP is used to configure the clients, they'll always end up with the correct settings. For users who have notebook computers that move in-between different subnets, it means you can truly just "plug and play" on whatever network you happen to be connected. In the next chapter, you're going to see how to set up a DHCP server. The biggest problem that people have with DHCP servers is they lose control over who has what addresses, and it becomes difficult to keep track of the users if they can't be traced back to a single IP address. In fact, I put off moving to DHCP for several years for these very same concerns. But the benefits far outweigh the costs. First of all, it's quite possible to set up a DHCP server where once a client has been assigned an IP address, they will keep it until the server administrator decides to reset the lease. When I first started looking at DHCP, we still had a mix of DOS packet drivers, MacTCP, and Windows 3.1 and 3.11 based computers. This mixture made using DHCP difficult, because DOS packet drivers rely on the network software itself to implement TCP/IP. If the software supported DHCP, it would run; if another package didn't support it, it would be unusable.

In the past few years, operating systems and TCP/IP implementations have progressed to the point where most of the problems with DHCP have disappeared. The problem, for instance, of not being able to track an individual user's computer is now less of a concern. Windows 95, 98, NT, and Mac OS 8.5x support the notion of client IDs, which are sent to the DHCP server. The client ID (usually the machine name) is associated with each lease stored on the server. It's much easier to identify a machine based on this string rather than its hardware address. Of course, it remains your responsibility to make sure that all your client computers have a unique identifier that will be sent to the DHCP server. I've used my DHCP logs to build a database associating hardware addresses to individual users. If someone changes his or her identifier, I can still figure out who the machine belongs to. In addition, Windows NT, and an upcoming version of the DHCP server distributed with Red Hat Linux, provide the capability to use the returned machine identifier to specify a hostname that can then be resolved by the machine's DNS server. The result is a system that assigns IP addresses dynamically and also resolves the hostnames of the machines dynamically. With this sort of configuration, you could potentially have a Web server that changes IP addresses but would always have the correct DNS entry (this is a rather extreme example and is just asking for trouble, but it should be possible). Because of the ability I have for tracking users, I've now deployed a DHCP server in my biggest trouble-spot building. This building, in particular, houses four departments and around 500 users (in two class C subnets). The largest department does not have a network administrator and has long been, to put it as politely as I can, a real pain. Rather than walk across campus to reconfigure someone's network settings, I'd much rather have them release an address and have their settings replaced with the correct values. It saves me time, and it saves them from having to place a support call and wait for me or someone else to arrive on-site and fix the problem.

Can I Use Static Addresses and Move to DHCP Later?

Yes, you can, but I wouldn't recommend it. The building I just described (with 500 users) had statically assigned addresses that have been tracked through an online IP database that I created. When it came time to move to DHCP, I needed to move all these users over to DHCP simultaneously. Luckily, because we're dealing with two class C subnets, I could do this one subnet at a time. Still, this meant 250 users needed to move at once, which is more than a handful. Without getting into too much detail, the process was a nightmare. The amount of error in the IP database was incredible. The "evil department," which made up 95 percent of this particular subnet, had not kept their room numbers up to date in the IP database. Many frustrating hours were spent trying to locate all the appropriate machines and move them to DHCP. In fact, of the 250 machines on this subnet, I've had to create static leases (which effectively don't let the DHCP server reassign an IP number) for around 80 of them, because I haven't been able to find them! If you're in the position of determining the future of a fast-growing network, implement DHCP now. You can do it later, but I promise it won't be fun.

Another big win for using DHCP is the elimination of the dreaded IP conflict error, shown in Figure 19.1 on a Mac OS-based system.

FIGURE 19.1

A Macintosh is experiencing a conflict with another device sharing the same IP address.

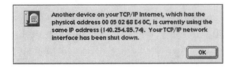

Another device on your TCP/IP Internet, which has the physical address 00 05 02 68 E4 0C, is currently using the same IP address (140.254.85.74). Your TCP/IP network interface has been shut down.

OK

In an organization with network policies as "open" as a university, IP conflicts are inevitable. Faculty and staff do what they want to with their computers, and support personnel do their best to keep on top of any changes. Let's take a quick look at the life of a typical computer on campus:

1. A computer arrives, replacing an old machine.
2. The new computer is configured with information from the old system.
3. The old system (retaining its configuration) is moved to a lab or to someone with an even older machine.
4. At some point, both computers are on at the same time, resulting in the IP conflict.
5. Repeat ad infinitum.

The trouble occurs in steps 2 and 3. Most computers are easy enough to configure that the owners pull the settings from their old machine and transfer them to the new computer. This is all very nice and, in fact, is precisely what I would hope they would do. Unfortunately, after configuring the new machine, most people forget to remove the configuration information from the old computer that they're passing on. The old system ends up going into a computer pool and is usually snatched up by some poor soul that is stuck using a 286. Delighted to have a new computer that he or she can finally surf the Net on, the new user plugs the computer into the network and, without doing anything, they're online! The problem is that they're online using the same old address that is now also assigned to someone's brand new 80 zillion MHz monster. If both machines try to talk on the network at the same time, boom, IP address conflict. Because of the way machines are allocated, it becomes next to impossible to determine where the old machine is. You can only hope that the person who calls and complains about the conflict is the person who *shouldn't* have the address. This is precisely the reason that keeping a static list of IP addresses is so hard. It's human nature to just plug things in and try them; if it works, why bother finding out if the settings are correct—it's working, isn't it? DHCP eliminates this problem completely. If both the new computer and the old computer are configured for DHCP, they'll both get separate addresses, and no one will end up with a conflict. The only minor difficulty is that you would still need the machine name to be defined correctly to identify who has what IP address. Given the situation in the environment where I work, this is not a really an issue. I have the choice of having conflicting addresses and no simple way of locating the conflict, or no conflicts and potentially misnamed computers. I choose the no conflicts route.

With so much *good* to say about DHCP, is there anything bad that's happened? Well, as I mentioned, you really should start using DHCP from the conception of your network. Doing so will save you the trouble of reconfiguring computers and trying to figure out where all your IP addresses have gone. One particularly annoying DHCP experience I've had is not really the fault of DHCP, but rather the overzealous nature of other users on the network. DHCP is a broadcast protocol. When a listening DHCP server sees a request on the wire, it responds with lease information. Being a broadcast, DHCP requests and responses are usually limited to a subnet and are blocked at bridges or routers. The catch is that there can only be one DHCP server per network. This might seem obvious, but consider my building with 500 people. There are multiple departments and multiple computer support people. If someone decides to set up their own server to serve DHCP for their office, they are effectively serving it for the entire network. This can have evil effects for both the person running the DHCP server and the users who are trying to use DHCP for their configuration. If there are multiple servers that are serving DHCP requests, the server that is "honored" is the one that responds the fastest. It becomes a toss-up as to whose server has issued a lease for a particular address. There might be instances of multiple leases for the same IP address if the two servers are assigning addresses from the same range. From the standpoint of the administrator, you find yourself looking at a machine with an IP address that it shouldn't have; you check your DHCP server, and there are no leases for it. The only consolation you might be able to grasp at is that somewhere on the network, someone else is probably scratching their heads and wondering about the exact same thing.

The biggest problem I've had with this so far is when someone decided to set up their own NT server to serve a Web page. NT is designed to make it simple to set up basic network services, which unfortunately often leads to people who have no business running certain services setting them up just because they can. This particular individual also turned on NT's DHCP server and configured it properly enough to work. But we already had a properly configured DHCP server running. The two machines both gave out leases, and when enough confusion occurred (machines with duplicate addresses, IP addresses that should have been static being assigned dynamically), I finally noticed what was going on. At that point it became a matter of tracking the person down and trying to resist using a sledgehammer to disable his DHCP service. For me, this is the biggest "gotcha" that exists with DHCP and with setting up network services in general. Never assume that what you're doing is isolated from everyone else. Keep track of the savvy users on your network and be sure to keep in touch with other people who might be setting up services.

To quickly add another little DHCP anecdote to the mix, let me mention the very first DHCP problem I ever encountered. About two years ago, a support person in another building put up the first DHCP server on Ag campus. It was mainly for testing purposes, but he started moving several of the traveling faculty to the system so they could plug their notebooks in when they were in their offices. Everything worked well for awhile, until he realized that all his leases were gone, and they were taken by devices that were not on his network. The original design of the network was that all the buildings had separate class C subnets assigned to them. Unfortunately, all the building subnets were bridged completely, so all the subnets could be used in any building. It turned out that the DHCP server was getting requests (and filling them) for a building that was located about a third of a mile from the server itself. Once again, be sure you know the topology of your network and the effect that your server can have on the network. If you start a DHCP server on your network, you might end up serving addresses to people across town—you just never know.

Application Settings

DHCP can handle setting up your TCP/IP settings, but can it do anything for other configuration options? Nope. There is an emerging standard that might prove useful for configuring network applications such as email. The *ACAP*, or *Application Configuration Access Protocol*, provides a network database that can hold configuration information for all the users on a network. As it stands now, what are the minimum pieces of information needed to configure an email client?

- Full Name
- Reply Address
- Username
- Password
- SMTP Server
- POP/IMAP Server

It isn't difficult to imagine that when you're trying to talk a user through setting up an email client over the phone, it's very possible that they'll mistype something or type something in the wrong field. They might not find out until later that the data is incorrect. The return address could be wrong, and replied-to mail could be bounced. If the SMTP or POP servers are wrong, the user might not be able to send or receive email, or both. Wouldn't it be nice to simply type in the name of a server, your employee ID, and have all the other settings filled in for you? This is precisely what ACAP does. Figure 19.2 shows the ACAP configuration screen from Eudora Pro v4.0.

FIGURE 19.2
The Eudora ACAP configuration screen enables automatic configuration.

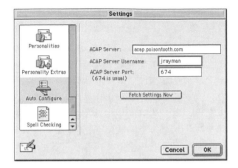

An ACAP server maintains a database of user information that can be easily retrieved with just a single passphrase and the hostname of the ACAP server. ACAP was designed to allow a large amount of configuration information to be stored—not just email client information. It's possible that ACAP support could be integrated into any program; the result would be a centralized preferences server that would allow you to sit down in front of any computer and automatically configure whatever program you want to run with your personal settings.

Unfortunately, ACAP is not a widely accepted protocol, but it's in the early stages of development. There are very few ACAP servers that are actually usable, so we aren't going to be looking at running any ACAP servers in this book. You might want to follow the progress that's made on the protocol because, if the protocol takes off, it could make life much easier for network administrators, and users who have to work on multiple workstations and need to take their settings with them. One of the commercially available servers is available from Qualcomm as part of their NT-based serving solutions. You can check out the Qualcomm server products at http://www.eudora.com/.

For Linux (and other UNIX) users, there is a freely developed server available from Carnegie Mellon University. I haven't taken the time to compile this myself under Linux, but, if you're adventurous, you might want to try http://andrew2.andrew.cmu.edu/cyrus/acap/.

I've been writing a limited ACAP server in Perl, but I'm really hoping that work on the CMU server and other freeware servers continues. I see a great amount of potential in ACAP, but, unless you use Eudora, you'll find it of little use with the current amount of commercial support.

Server-based configuration of IP addresses or application settings will undoubtedly prove to make your life as a network administrator significantly easier. It is easy, however, to be lazy once you have automated a process. Don't stop keeping track of computer systems if you install a DHCP server, and don't assume that because someone used an ACAP server that they won't have any problems with their configuration. Network automation tools supplement the network administrator; they do not replace him or her.

Part
V

Ch
19

Users

As your network grows, you'll probably find yourself creating address books that contain the names of many of the people on your network. This doesn't necessarily consume much time, but if you have a few hundred users, figure that each of them is doing the same thing. Rather than repeating the same activity at workstations across your network, wouldn't it be nice if a global contact list could be maintained for your entire network? This is precisely the purpose for Directory Services. Directory Services are lists of users and associated contact information, such as addresses and phone number/email information, including public keys for exchanging encrypted information. Directories are often organized in a hierarchical fashion based on the different departments within an organization. There is a variety of servers that can be used for accessing directory information; one of the most common directory access protocols is *finger*. Finger is a rather generic front-end that has typically been used on UNIX machines to return information about a particular user on that machine. However, it can also be added as a front-end to almost any directory service. OSU, for example, maintains a directory listing of all students and faculty. The directory is accessible via the finger and ph protocols, which are built into many email programs. For example, if I use finger to access my OSU ID, it will return the following:

```
finger =ray.30@osu.edu
Ray, John Emery

   Unique name at OSU = Ray.30
   Email addresses:
     Email forwarded to = jray@bigmac.ag.ohio-state.edu
     Published address  = Ray.30@osu.edu
   Current status = Currently employed
   Department (College) = Communications & Technolo (Food Agric & Env Sci Adm)
   Title = SYS DEV/EN
   Address:
     7879 Oasis Dr
     Greenwood        , Oh 43016
   Appointment:
     Osue-Comm & Technology (Osu Extension)
       216 Kottman Hall
                 2021 Coffey Rd
        Columbus       , Oh 43210
       (614) 292-1736
```

That's quite a bit of information! Please—no comments about my middle name. If you must say something, make sure it isn't loud enough for me to hear!

Finger and Ph are fine for returning text-based information from some sort of directory service. However, they are not very good at returning information in a form that is immediately usable inside an email client or information manager. One of the most common and widely accepted protocols for directory services is the *LDAP*, or *Lightweight Directory Access Protocol*. LDAP provides a standard front-end for accessing directory information. It can be employed as a front-end to other directory servers or as a standalone server. LDAP was initially designed to be a front-end to the *X.500* directory services, which is an aging directory access protocol that provides no TCP/IP access methods. LDAP works from within programs such as Eudora and

Outlook. Figure 19.3 shows LDAP directory services available from within Eudora Pro. LDAP directories can carry a variety of information with each user record, including photographs, sounds, and URLs.

FIGURE 19.3

Eudora Pro's LDAP directory services look like this under Windows.

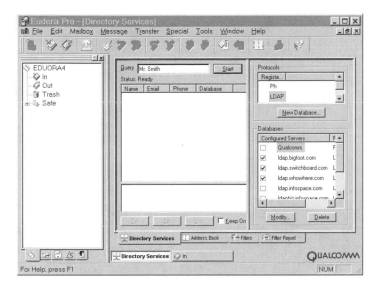

If a user is located in an LDAP directory, his or her information is displayed and can be imported directly into your email program. Directory services are extremely valuable in an information-sharing environment where email communications are of paramount importance. Software such as Microsoft Exchange for NT Server provides shared contact lists for its users, as well as shared directories and files. The email server software, CommuniGate Pro, that we explored is also planning on offering directory services based on the LDAP protocol. In addition, there are public LDAP servers you can access if you choose. A good resource for public directory services is "NameFlow-Paradise." If you're seeking further information on directory services or would like to access public directory servers, take a look here at http://www.dante.net/nameflow.html.

If you're interested in running an LDAP server yourself, the most popular LDAP implementation (UNIX only), which was written by the University of Michigan, is available for free from http://www.umich.edu/~dirsvcs/ldap/.

You can also find information about LDAP clients and other servers at the site. If you're running a network with only Mac OS and Windows-based clients, you should definitely look at the Microsoft Exchange Server. It's a relatively costly piece of software, but the collaborative features it provides are truly a godsend for managing user information, shared resources, and even scheduling. Other operating systems can use the Exchange through an Active Server Pages Web interface, but the full client (Outlook) is available only under Windows and Mac OS. Figure 19.4 shows a client connected to an Exchange server and the shared resources available.

Part

V

Ch

19

FIGURE 19.4

Microsoft Exchange
Server enables
extensive collaboration.

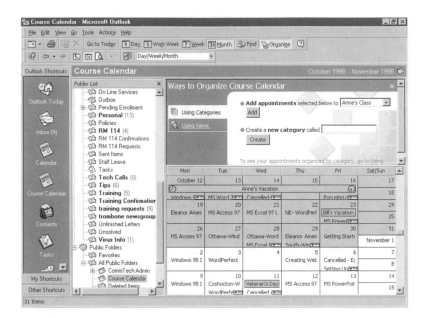

Somewhere in the Middle

Somewhere between managing hardware and software lies the SMTP protocol. I've already introduced you to the basic protocol itself and how it can be used to read and set information on network devices, but you have not yet seen it in action; don't worry, you'll get a chance in Chapter 21, "Using SNMP and Other Diagnostic Tools to Monitor Your Network." The Simple Network Management Protocol will be mainly useful for monitoring network hardware and traffic. Use SMTP, for example, to monitor the traffic moving into and out of your subnet. If there are huge leaps in the amount of packet activity, we can turn to other diagnostic methods to determine what is actually going on. SNMP is *not* going to enable you to actively manage user's network settings or application settings; it serves mainly as a monitoring tool. This does not mean that it is less useful than the other management solutions we've discussed; it's just different. Chapter 21 will look at several SNMP applications that might prove useful for diagnosing network problems.

How you choose to manage the resources that make up your network will be a personal choice. If you have a network that uses only a single operating system, you might not use any of the techniques we discussed. Each operating system has its own method of managing user information and accounts. In a cross-platform network, you shouldn't rely on any special capabilities in the operating system; you need to use true cross-platform standards such as these.

## CHAPTER 20

Configuring Networks with DHCP

by John Ray

In this chapter

Configuring Your Client for DHCP **394**

Serving DHCP Using Mac OS **398**

Serving DHCP Using Windows **402**

Serving DHCP Using Linux **408**

A very pleasing recent development in TCP/IP network software was the introduction of the *Dynamic Host Configuration Protocol (DHCP)*. DHCP can save you significant amounts of time maintaining your network configuration. It eliminates the need to create an IP database (it does that for you) and takes the responsibility of keeping the database up to date off your shoulders and places it on the DHCP server itself. If you currently manage a network of a few hundred computers that have statically assigned addresses, you're going to be overjoyed once you have DHCP up and running (which you will, by the end of this chapter!). You'll feel fulfilled and at peace with nature—or, at the very least, you'll have two or three fewer support calls coming in than you did before. Whatever the outcome, it can only be good! Before I look at DHCP server solutions, let's refresh our memories as to how to set up your client computers to send DHCP requests; it isn't going to do us much good to set up a DHCP server and not have any users, is it?

Configuring Your Client for DHCP

Configuring client computers for DHCP is usually easier than setting up static addresses. Because most of the information necessary to operate on the network comes from the server, you won't need to fill in any numbers of your own. Not a bad deal, huh? As before, let's go ahead and start with Mac OS-based clients.

Mac OS and DHCP

If you're going to be using DHCP on your Macintosh, I strongly recommend that you use System 8.5 or later. Previous versions of the system do not include all the nice features that are useful on a DHCP network—namely the capability of the client computer to identify itself to the DHCP server. On Windows networks, the computer typically will identify itself when it requests a lease. Rather than having to remember a string of hexadecimal characters from each computer's MAC (not Mac as in Macintosh) address, you can just look at the list of leases, pick out which one is identified as, say, John Ray's computer, and instantly know what's what. System 8.5 introduces this capability to the Macintosh DHCP client. From an administrative point of view, it's a wonderful feature to have. Don't be overly worried if you're stuck with an earlier version of the system, however; DHCP will still work.

To turn on DHCP on your Macintosh, choose TCP/IP from your Control Panel folder or menu. Figure 20.1 shows a Mac OS 8.5 TCP/IP configuration screen.

FIGURE 20.1

The Mac OS 8.5 TCP/IP configuration screen lets you activate DHCP services.

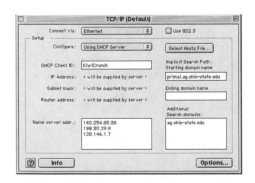

To have your Macintosh use DHCP to configure itself at startup, choose DHCP from the Configure pop-up menu. If you were set to Configure Manually previously, your fields should disappear and no longer be changeable. You can still specify DNS servers if you'd like, but this is optional, because the DHCP server also has the capability to set up name servers for its clients. Be sure to fill in the client identifier field with the name you want your computer to register under on the server. If you're using an older version of Mac OS, such as 8.0 or 8.1, your dialog box probably looks a lot like the one in Figure 20.2. In this case, you can only identify your lease on the server by the computer's hardware address.

FIGURE 20.2

Versions of Mac OS before 8.5 lack the capability to identify themselves to the DHCP server.

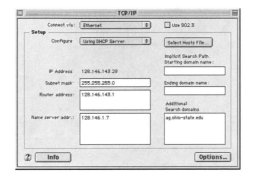

Once you've set your identifier, close the window and answer Yes to the Save Changes? prompt. Your computer is now setup and ready to use DHCP. If you have a DHCP server running, you should immediately be able to run a network application. The first packet activity on your computer will trigger Open Transport to send a DHCP request and configure your network accordingly. The TCP/IP control panel will display the configured IP address, and so on after it has successfully been granted a lease. This is shown in Figure 20.3.

FIGURE 20.3

A Mac OS system has successfully been granted a lease, and the TCP/IP control panel shows the results.

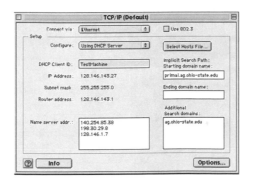

Part

V

Ch

20

That was a piece of cake, wasn't it? Okay, you've got the procedure down for the Macintosh, now how about Windows?

Windows 95/98 and DHCP

Like the Macintosh, Windows-based systems are also extremely simple to set up for DHCP. To configure Windows to be a client on a DHCP network, open the Network control panel. The first thing you'll need to do is set the name of the computer so that it will identify itself to the server. To do this, click the Identification tab in the Network window and fill in the Computer Name line. Figure 20.4 shows that my computer is named FuzzyKiwi. You might want to choose something a little more descriptive for your name!

FIGURE 20.4

Configure the name of the computer under the Identification tab of the Network control panel.

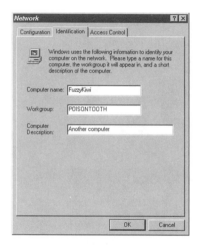

Next, you're going to need to tell Windows that you want it to use DHCP to configure its network information. To do so, choose the Configuration tab in the Network window, select the TCP/IP component that is installed for your network card, and then click Properties. Your display should now look similar to Figure 20.5.

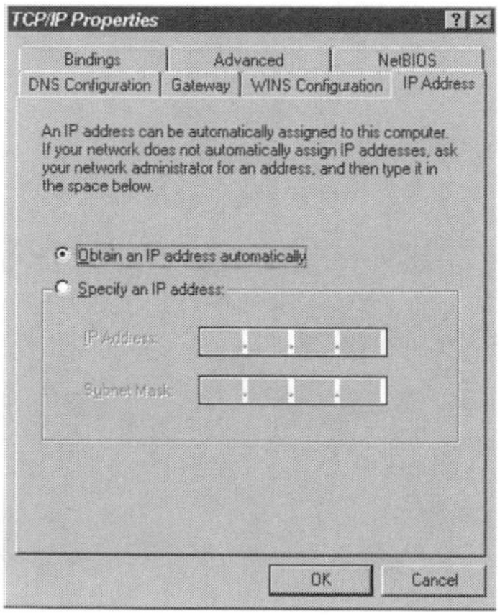

FIGURE 20.5

You'll enable DHCP in the TCP/IP configuration screen, shown here.

All you need to do to prepare your system to use DHCP is to click the Obtain an IP Address Automatically radio button on this screen. Once you've set your machine up for DHCP, you can click OK to save your changes and exit the control panel. Windows may then install a few files, and then ask you to reboot. Upon rebooting, your computer should automatically obtain a lease and configure itself for your TCP/IP network. If you want to see your IP address or request a new lease, you can use the winipcfg program to do just that. Click Start and then click Run and type **winipcfg** in the resulting dialog box. Within a few seconds, the dialog box shown in Figure 20.6 should appear.

FIGURE 20.6

If you feel more like a "tenant" than a "client," the winipcfg program lets you view your lease.

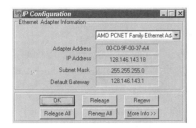

From this dialog box, you can release your lease (in other words, give up your IP address and renew your lease). If you click Release, your IP address should disappear from the window. Click Renew to get a new lease and restore your IP information. Once again, it takes only a few seconds to get a Windows DHCP client up and running on the network.

Linux and DHCP

Okay, you've breezed through those other two configurations, now how about Linux? Well, Linux is a bit more difficult to configure than Mac OS or Windows, but it's still pretty straight-forward. If you've successfully set up and configured Ethernet devices, you can have it reconfigure itself using DHCP with one simple setting. To do so, you're going to need to edit the configuration file for the interface you want configured using DHCP. Let's assume that your interface is eth0, which it should be if you have a single Ethernet card. If you're currently using the network card, you must first shut down the interface using the `ifdown` command:

```
>/etc/sysconfig/network-scripts/ifdown eth0
```

Once the command has completed, your Ethernet interface is returned to an unconfigured state, and you can set it up for DHCP. To do so, use your favorite editor to edit the interface configuration file that is appropriate for your card—in my case (and most cases), this is /etc/sysconfig/network-scripts/ifcfg-eth0.

The file probably looks something like this to begin with (using slightly different numbers):

```
DEVICE=eth0
IPADDR=140.254.85.38
NETMASK=255.255.255.0
NETWORK=140.254.85.0
BROADCAST=140.254.85.255
ONBOOT=yes
BOOTPROTO=none
```

Part
V

Ch

20

What you need to do is change the BOOTPROTO= line so that it equals DHCP, like this:

```
BOOTPROTO=DCHP
```

That's mostly it! Adding that option to the file will tell the computer to use DHCP whenever the interface is brought online. If you're using Red Hat Linux, be sure not to leave any backup files lying around after you edit the configuration. If you do, the Red Hat configuration software may try to initialize your interface twice, with two different configurations. Remove any backup files from the directory by typing

```
>rm /etc/sysconfig/network-scripts/*~
```

> **CAUTION**
>
> Be sure that you include the tilde (~) character to identify the telltale backup files. If you don't, you're going to erase everything in the network-scripts directory, which would be extremely bad!

When you're ready to bring your interface back online and lease an IP address, you can use the ifup command to bring it back online. Rebooting will also reinitialize the interfaces.

```
>/etc/sysconfig/network-scripts/ifup eth0
```

Okay! Now your clients are set up and ready to go with DHCP. You'd better get a DHCP server online fast, or the users aren't going to be able to do anything! DHCP servers are available for all our platforms, and in some cases are integrated with other connectivity software. I'm going to present the configuration and use of three standalone DHCP servers, but depending on your situation, an integrated solution might be better for you. For example, the software WinGate for Windows and Vicom Internet Gateway for Mac OS and Windows both offer integrated Internet connectivity and DHCP support. These are plug-and-play solutions that not only connect you to the Internet, but also connect you, and then configure all your computers automatically to access the network. The integration is a nice feature, but it also seems to come at an increased cost. You might find it more cost-effective to use separate server products for your network rather than using an all-in-one package. If you're interested in either of the integrated servers, check them out at

```
http://www.vicomsoft.com/   (Mac OS, Internet Gateway)
http://www.wingate.com/ -    (Windows, WinGate)
```

Of course, the Red Hat Linux OS already includes a DHCP server, so there's already an all-in-one solution available for free!

Serving DHCP Using Mac OS

Let's go ahead and start our exploration of DHCP servers by looking at Vicom's DHCP server for Mac OS. If you'd like to download a demo, it's available from Vicom's main Web site, which I mentioned a moment ago. Once you download the Vicom DHCP server, you should unstuff it and run the installer application. You cannot run the DHCP server on a system that isn't using

Open Transport. If you have an old SE/30, it makes a perfect DHCP server once you've upgraded it to System 7.5.5 and installed Open Transport. The installation process is simple: just run the installer, and then drag the DHCP server icon onto the drive you want to install it on. A few seconds later, the DHCP server and associated files will be installed. If you plan on using TCP/IP applications (other than the server itself) on the machine running the server, you need to make a change to your TCP/IP configuration. Open the TCP/IP control panel and click the Options… button in the lower-right corner of the dialog box. You must set your TCP/IP options so the TCP/IP is active and set to load only when needed. Your settings should look like those in Figure 20.7.

FIGURE 20.7

After you've installed Open Transport (or are running System 7.6 or later), set your TCP/IP options like this.

The DHCP Server will install Vicom's proprietary TCP/IP stack on your computer; you'll notice that your TCP/IP control panel settings look a bit different. Don't worry about this; the software configures itself and creates a new TCP/IP configuration named VICOM. If you need to switch back to your original settings, you can do so at any time, but the VICOM DHCP server will only function correctly under the VICOM configuration.

You can then go ahead and start the Vicom DHCP Server application by double-clicking its icon. The software will check your system, configure itself, and then ask you if you want to run TCP/IP applications on the server computer, as shown in Figure 20.8. If you do (which I assume you will), click the Restart button.

FIGURE 20.8

The DHCP server will configure itself to allow local applications to continue to run and then prompt you to restart.

Part
V

Ch
20

Once your computer has rebooted, restart the VICOM DHCP Server software. You should immediately be prompted to fill out the TCP/IP preferences for the server, as shown in Figure 20.9. Fill these out as you would the TCP/IP control panel settings. Then, when finished, click the OK button. If, for some reason, you don't see the DHCP preferences screen, you can access it at any time from within the server by choosing Preferences… from the Edit menu.

FIGURE 20.9

Once your computer restarts, you'll need to fill out the DHCP Server Preferences.

You should now see the main DHCP server status screen. Here you can quickly activate or deactivate the server with the On/Off toggle switch. You'll also see a graph of the amount of data transferred to and from the server, and the amount of CPU time the DHCP server is currently using. Figure 20.10 shows a typical non-busy server. Unless you're serving thousands of addresses, you'll probably never see too much activity on these graphs.

FIGURE 20.10

The DHCP Server status window shows a summary of network activity.

Before you can begin serving DHCP, you'll need to configure ranges of IP addresses that the server can use. This process is extremely simple. Just choose the DHCP Setup… option from the Network menu. You should see a configuration screen much like the one shown in Figure 20.11.

FIGURE 20.11

The DHCP Setup screen enables you to configure ranges of IP addresses.

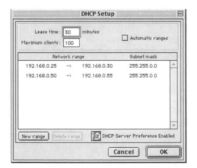

You'll also need to configure the lease time and the maximum number of clients that can use the server. The lease time is the maximum length of time that each DHCP client computer can request to lease a particular IP address. Some people set this value to several days or even weeks on a network that is relatively quiet and unchanging. On a network that is extremely dynamic, you might want to set this to a much lower number. By using a low number, such as 30 or 60 minutes, leases expire very quickly. The advantage to this is that IP addresses will not be stuck in limbo if a computer is taken off the network. They will expire within a few minutes, and then be available for another computer to use. In an exaggerated example, if you set a lease length of say a year, hooked up 10 computers temporarily to your network, and then disconnected them, you'd lose those IP addresses for a year. You could get them back by physically deleting the mapping in the DHCP server database. But, that's extra work, and you're trying to save yourself additional work by using DHCP in the first place, aren't you? The disadvantage to a short lease time, of course, is that it creates additional network traffic. The default renewal time is half the lease life. So, if you set the lease for 30 minutes, expect each client to request an extension to the lease every 15 minutes. What's best? You'll have to determine that as a network administrator, but that's why you're paid the big bucks!

Let's go ahead and configure a range of addresses that the DHCP server can use to assign to other computers on the network. If you click the Automatic ranges check box, the server will attempt to choose a range of addresses that it can use based on its own address. I'd rather do it myself, so I've disabled the Automatic ranges option in my configuration. To add a new range, click the New range button, and then fill in the starting address and ending address of the range you want to use. You'll also need to supply a subnet mask for each of the ranges you use. When you're done setting up your address ranges, click the OK button, and you're ready to start serving!

You can now go ahead and click the On/Off switch so that the VICOM DHCP Server starts. You should be able to identify that it is indeed running by the CPU meter and the fact that any measurable network traffic is displayed on the graph. Now, go ahead and see if it works! Hook up one of your appropriately configured client computers to the network and try running a TCP/IP-based application such as Netscape. If all has gone well, the software will set up an IP address for the client computer.

To view the addresses that are currently leased out, all you need to do is choose Show DHCP Clients from the File menu. You'll see a list of all the leases currently active, the hardware address of the computer that has the lease, the identifying name of the computer with the lease, and a real-time countdown to the end of each lease. There are currently two active leases on my test network: one for KimsParachute (remember my friend the skydiver?) and another for FuzzyKiwi. You can see these leases represented in Figure 20.12.

FIGURE 20.12.
The DHCP Client screen shows all the leases that are currently used on the server.

That's all there is to it. The VICOM DHCP server is a very straightforward and bare-bones approach to DHCP serving. There are some features that I'd like to see that don't seem to be present—most importantly, the capability to provide permanent leases. It's often easier to provide a static lease for a particular address than it is to define a series of ranges that work around an address. You'll see some additional features under the Windows and Linux servers, but, for a quick-and-easy DHCP server, you can't beat the VICOM product.

Serving DHCP Using Windows

The most common DHCP server for Windows is the Windows NT DHCP Server. But what if you want to run a DHCP server but you don't happen to have any NT servers running? Throughout this book, I've tried to provide networking solutions that do not require dedicated servers. I find that it is often the case that a company can come up with a spare 486 but can't afford to buy multiple dedicated servers. Putting old machines to work is a money-saver and is often easier to manage than running a full-blown server solution. The DHCP server you're going to be setting up now is ipLease by Billiter Consultants. If you'd like to try the software out, they offer a full-featured trial version with full product support by visiting their Web site at `http://www.billiter.com/`.

The ipLease software requires a bit of work to install and configure—not too much, but it isn't entirely automatic. First, create a new directory and place the ipLease software inside it. I'm going to install it into the directory C:\IPLEASE; feel free to use the same technique. Once you've gotten that far, open a command prompt by clicking Start, choosing Run, and typing **command** (or clicking the Programs group and launching an MS-DOS Prompt session). To finish the installation, type **cd C:\IPLEASE** to enter the directory you've created and **iplease -d** to decompress and install the software.

Now you're going to need to set the software up to serve leases. Be warned, this process is going to involve configuring a few .ini files by hand. The ipLease software provides an excellent front-end you can use to monitor the server. Currently, however, you'll need to do the configuration by hand. Don't worry; it'll only take a few minutes.

Once again, I'm going with the assumption that the server has been installed in the directory C:\IPLEASE; if you installed it somewhere else, you'll need to make sure that you're working within the appropriate directory structure.

To get the show on the road, open your IPLEASE directory, and then, once inside, switch to the SRV directory. This is where the actual server software resides. You'll see a sample configuration file that is named dhcpsvr.in0; copy or rename that file to dhcpsvr.ini.

Next, open the dhcpsvr.ini file in a text editor such as Notepad. You can do so by simply double-clicking the file once you've named it with the .ini extension. You'll now be setting up the information that the server needs to operate. The opened configuration file is shown in Figure 20.13.

First, you'll need to set an IP address that the server will use as its own. Use the address assigned to your computer already; you just need to tell ipLease what it is. About halfway through the configuration file, you should see a section that looks like this:

```
; ------------------------------------------------------------
; ServerIPAddr is the internet (TCP/IP) address of this server.
```

```
; If the machine on which the server will run is multi-homed
; (i.e.: uses more than one adapter to connect to an internet or
; internets), select the address on the network without a
; BOOTP relay agent, or the address on the network with the
; most DHCP client activity. (Or flip a coin.) If you run
; BOOTP relay agents on other networks, point them to
; the address you specify here.

; Use dotted decimal form and enter exactly one IP address.

ServerIPAddr=192.168.0.27
```

You need to change the ServerIPAddr line so that it's set to the IP address of your machine, as you can see on the very last line of the callout. I'm setting up this sample server on a machine with the address 192.168.0.27. Next, set the subnet address that ipLease will be serving. Because my network is using the class B subnet 192.168.0.0, I simply include that on the Subnetnum line:

```
; -----------------------------------------------------------------
; SubnetNum is the network number on which ServerIPAddr resides.
; This is NOT the subnet mask. It IS that mask AND'd with ServerIPAddr.

; Use dotted decimal form and enter exactly one network number.

SubnetNum=192.168.0.0
```

FIGURE 20.13

Edit the .ini file to configure the ipLease software.

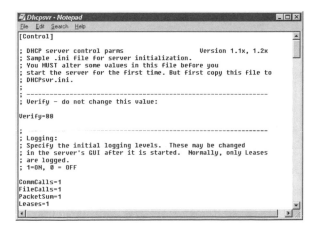

Okay, that's it for setting up the identifying information for the server. However, you'll still need to configure the information that's used to generate and grant leases. Move into the gen directory, located inside the main iplease directory. You should see a file named leases0.src. Copy or rename it to leases1.src and then open it in a text editor. Figure 20.14 shows the lease configuration file in the process of being edited.

FIGURE 20.14

The lease configuration information must also be edited by hand; it says so right at the top.

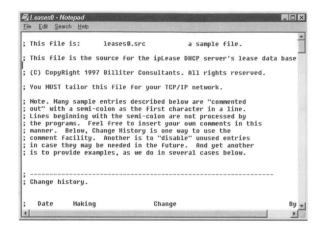

I'm going to paste in my configuration, and then explain what each line means, rather than build the configuration from scratch. I think you'll find that it's really rather simple but can be kind of ugly at first.

```
[Serverlocal]
AddressBase=192.168.0.0
SubnetMask=255.255.0.0
RangeInclude1=55 80
RangeInclude2=30 35
OptGroup=MinimalOpts

[MinimalOpts]
oAddrLeaseTime=3600
oDomainName=poisontooth.com
oRouter=192.168.0.1
oDNSServer=128.146.1.7
```

Before moving on, I'll explain what these settings represent.

AddressBase—The base address of your IP range. This does not necessarily mean that the IP address you specify will be used; it's simply a starting point for the server. I'm using 192.168.0.0.

SubnetMask—The subnet mask that will be assigned to all the DHCP clients. In my case, it's 255.255.0.0; set it to whatever is appropriate on your network.

Range Include—Defines ranges of addresses that can be used. For example, 55 80 enables the server to assign addresses from 192.168.0.55 to 192.168.0.80.

OptGroup—A subgroup within the .ini file that contains the options the server will use to configure the clients. The default configuration file has a minimum options file, which is what you see in the sample.

oAddrLeaseTime—The length of the lease in seconds. 3,600 seconds is an hour, so that should be fine for a dynamic network configuration.

oDomainName—The domain name that should be set in the client. Chances are you don't want to use the poisontooth.com domain name because it's mine!

oRouter—The default router for the network.

oDNSServer—DNS servers that the clients should be configured to use.

There are many other options that can also be configured, although a lot of them are not useful, except in extremely specific situations. Read through the documentation to see if anything could be applied on your network. For example:

oNetBiosNS—If you want to configure all your computers to use a specific NetBios Nameserver (a Windows WINS server), you could choose this option.

oTimeServer—Got a network timeserver running? The oTimeServer option will configure your clients to use the Timeserver if they're capable.

As I mentioned in the Mac OS DHCP section, it's often nice to define static addresses for use with DHCP. ipLease supports static leases, but they require special configuration information for each computer you want to have a static lease. For example, individual hosts such as this one can be added to your leases file:

```
[kamaandkim]
oClientID=0800078cb31bba
oHostName=kamaandkim
StaticIPAddress=192.168.0.99
oAddrLeaseTime=-1
```

This would define a static lease for a computer called KamaandKim, which would always receive the same IP address: 192.168.0.99.

Why Bother with Static Leases? Why not just exclude the addresses from the assignable range?

It's more consistent to provide static leases than it is to map certain addresses out from what can be assigned. It enables you to maintain a constant configuration for every machine on your network, yet still provide unchanging IP addresses for servers. It also gives you the ability to change the IP address for a given machine by changing it on the server. Even better, you can assign any of the other available options from your centralized server as well. This means that your WINS servers, DNS, and router settings, among others, can all be managed from your DHCP server.

Now that you have a lease configuration file defined, you're going to need to compile it into something that the server can use. To do this, you'll use the dhcpgen command-line program. Start up another DOS window and navigate so you're in the same directory as the leases1.src file, and then create the lease database by typing

```
>dhcpgen leases1
```

You'll see output resembling the following:

```
ipLease(TM) DHCP Gen Version 1.20 started at 10/11/1998 6:02:57 PM
CopyRight (C) 1997 Billiter Consultants. All rights reserved.
This version supports a maximum of 1024 leases.
```

Part

V

Ch

20

```
DHCP Gen serial 5640C8E14D9D95E2
Default lease time = 5432
HRDefaults option group created
AddressGroup ServerLocal created on network number 192.168.0.0
 with 60 addresses.
Now sorting the lease pool
Lease data base generation was successful.
60 addresses were created.
Of these, the count dedicated for static leases is 0.
```

Next, copy all the lease information files over to the server directory, and you should be ready to run. Enter the command

```
>copy leases1.* ..\SVR
```

If everything has been configured appropriately, you should be able to double-click the Dhcpsvr icon in the SVR directory, and the server should immediately start running using the parameters you've given it. The main status window is shown in Figure 20.15.

FIGURE 20.15

The DHCP server is up and running.

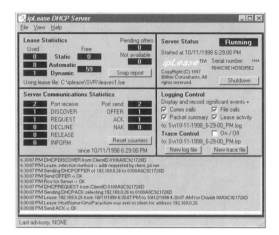

From the status window, you can watch as the server responds to DHCP requests and issues leases. You may want to re-read the section on DHCP if you're interested in what many of the details are referring to. For example, ipLease shows information at a low enough level that you can see the lease acknowledgments and broadcast requests as they come in. You have very little control over the server from this monitor window. If you want to shut down the server, you can do that, as well as enable and disable different levels of logging. (Remember, logging lets you monitor and intercept unauthorized usage, so it's best to keep it on.) The Lease Statistics portion of the screen gives you an overall picture of the number of computers using the DHCP server, and how many free addresses you have available. The bottom portion of the window displays the last few lines from the current log file. If you have full logging enabled, you're likely to see a wealth of information displayed here that documents the entire process of a computer requesting, accepting, and acknowledging acceptance of a lease.

If you'd like to take a look at detailed information about the leases that are currently active on your server, ipLease provides a very nice lease-viewing tool. Choose Leases from the View menu to show the lease database browsing tool. If you've already configured your clients to use DHCP, you may have leases that have been committed on the server. To view the first lease that has been made, click the Next Committed radio button, and then click the Find button. Figure 20.16 shows the lease information for KimsParachute—another Windows computer that just requested a lease from the server.

FIGURE 20.16

You can browse the leases at any time simply by choosing a menu command.

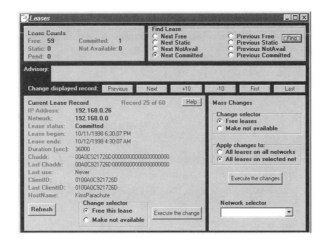

You can also use the radio buttons at the bottom of the screen to free a particular lease (which will enable other computers on the network to use that IP address) or mark a particular IP address as not available for leasing. If you choose to use one of these options, select the appropriate radio button, and then click Execute the change to apply your selection. You can also apply changes to the entire database using the Mass Changes control. You can, once again, free leases, or make them not available, based on a particular network or all the networks you're serving. Everything else should be straightforward; you can step through the database using the Change displayed record buttons or search for individual records based on the criteria in the Find Lease section.

The server, once configured, is very easy to run and can simply be minimized and run in the background on a machine on your network. It does not require a dedicated server and doesn't appear to use much CPU time at all. The ipLease program supports multiple networks and rather complex dynamic IP assignment configurations. If you have a particular DHCP need, ipLease will most likely be able to provide the solution. Read through the documentation that accompanies the program for information on how to set up far more complex configurations than what you've done here. If you don't have an NT server serving DHCP for your network, ipLease is the way to go.

Part
V

Ch
20

Serving DHCP Using Linux

Darn it if that Linux doesn't include everything! Red Hat 5.x includes a DHCP server along with the standard installation. The current versions of Red Hat include a beta version of a DHCP server developed by the Internet Software Consortium. The beta is stable, but you might want to check for updated versions. The ISC is planning on offering integrated DNS support and other new features in upcoming releases. The latest version is always a free download at ftp://ftp.isc.org/isc/dhcp.

There are two files that control the operation of the ICS DHCP server: the /etc/dhcpd.leases file, which contains all of the lease information, and the /etc/dhcpd.conf file, which holds the configuration information. In the standard installation, neither of these files is present, so the dhcpd server will not start. Go ahead and create both of these files now. You can do this by using the touch command, which updates the modification date on files or creates empty files if the filename supplied does not exist.

```
>touch /etc/dhcpd.leases
>touch /etc/dhcpd.conf
```

Now, you're going to need to set up the configuration file to assign addresses to your network. I'm currently using Linux to provide addresses to a building at work. Let's take a look at the configuration of that server. I'll explain the different options that can be used next.

```
>cat /etc/dhcpd.conf
shared-network KOTTMANHALL {
 subnet 128.146.142.0 netmask 255.255.255.0 {
 range 128.146.142.3 128.146.142.250;
 option routers 128.146.142.1;
 option domain-name-servers 140.254.85.38,128.146.1.7;
 option domain-name ag.ohio-state.edu;
 default-lease-time 12000;
 max-lease-time36000;
 }

        subnet 140.254.80.0 netmask 255.255.255.0 {
                range 140.254.80.3 140.254.80.10;
                option routers 140.254.80.1;
                option domain-name-servers 140.254.85.38,128.146.1.7;
                option domain-name ag.ohio-state.edu;
                default-lease-time 12000;
                max-lease-time  36000;
        }

}
```

The dhcpd configuration file is set up with sections and subsections that start and stop with the {} braces. This particular configuration file is relatively simple but different from our other two server examples because it spans two different subnets. Let's go through the options that are defined, starting at the top:

>sharednetwork—Defines a group of subnets within the configuration file. The building that this server operates in is called KOTTMANHALL, so I've named the Sharednetwork option appropriately.

subnet—Starts the definition of a subnet that will be used for address assignments. I have two different subnet sections defined in my configuration file: 128.146.142.0 and 140.254.80.0.

netmask—The netmask must follow the subnet declaration. Both of my subnets are class C subnets, so my netmask is 255.255.255.0.

range—Once a subnet has been defined, you specify options that are configured for that particular subnet. The first option I've set is the range of addresses that can be used. You can use the range option as many times as you'd like. Just put the starting address for assignment, followed by the last address that can be defined.

option routers—List the appropriate routers that need to be configured for the subnet after the option routers setting.

option domain-name-servers—Like the routers, just list the name servers you want used on your network.

option domain-name—Supply the domain name that the clients should be configured with. If your server is serving multiple subnets, you might want a different domain name for each subnet. Both of my particular subnets fall under the ag.ohio-state.edu domain.

default-lease-time—The default lease length, in seconds, that a client is given. This is not necessarily the length that the lease will be—just what the default setting is.

max-lease-time—The maximum length of time that a client can request for a lease.

Like the Windows-based server, there are many options that can be configured that are not used in my default configuration:

option netbios-name-server—This option, like its Windows counterpart, lets you set the NETBIOS name server on Windows-based computers. This is usually an NT machine running a WINS server.

option ntp-servers—Compare this, once again, to the Windows options. The ntp-servers option lets you configure a network time protocol server that can be used to set the clocks on your network devices.

To find out more about the available options, just check the appropriate man page: man dhcp-options. The online dhcpd documentation contains other information, including how to set up static leases (very similar to their Windows counterparts). Once you've set up a configuration file that fits your needs, go ahead and start the server. To do so, type the following:

```
>/etc/rc.d/init.d/dhcpd start
Starting dhcpd: dhcpd Internet Software Consortium DHCPD $Name: V2-BETA-1-
PATCHLEVEL-6 $
Copyright 1995, 1996, 1997, 1998 The Internet Software Consortium.
All rights reserved.
Listening on Socket/eth0/KOTTMANHALL
Sending on    Socket/eth0/KOTTMANHALL
```

If there are any errors in the configuration, dhcpd will not start and will list the lines in the configuration file that have caused the problem. As soon as the server is started, it should be ready to receive requests. The leases, as they're generated, are stored in the /etc/dhcpd.leases

Part

V

Ch

20

file you created earlier. My dhcp server currently serves several hundred addresses, so the leases file is pretty full. Here's a sample of what it currently holds:

```
>cat /etc/dhcpd.leases
lease 128.146.142.31 {
        starts 1 1998/10/12 03:40:54;
        ends 1 1998/10/12 03:40:53;
        hardware Ethernet 00:04:00:c8:ab:91;
        client-hostname RussBobSchelby;
}
lease 128.146.142.114 {
        starts 1 1998/10/12 03:41:04;
        ends 1 1998/10/12 07:01:04;
        hardware Ethernet 00:e0:b8:01:b4:38;
        client-hostname KimAnnStein;
}
lease 128.146.142.165 {
        starts 1 1998/10/12 03:44:06;
        ends 1 1998/10/12 07:04:06;
        hardware Ethernet 00:60:08:08:31:44;
        client-hostname MAbiado;
}
```

These are three leases that are currently included in my lease file. As you can see, each lease contains the start and end time of the lease, the hardware address of the computer with the lease, and the hostname (if any) of the computer that requested the lease.

Over time, the dhcpd.leases file grows to an enormous size (new leases are added to the end of the file; the old entries remain until a cleanup is performed). To clean up your leases file, just start and stop the server.

```
>/etc/rc.d/init.d/dhcpd stop
>/etc/rc.d/init.d/dhcpd start
```

I've been using the Linux DHCP server for the past several months, and it has been extremely maintenance free. Because the server is running under Linux and is completely text based, I can Telnet into the server and configure it, assign leases, delete leases, and so on, without walking over to the building that physically houses the server.

Whatever your DHCP server needs, you should be able to find a solution that works for you. The Mac OS-based server is extremely easy to configure and operate, but it lacks some of the higher-end features included in the Windows and Linux servers. If you're already using a Linux computer as your gateway to the Internet, you can simply enable the DHCP server and be up and running. I've been extremely pleased with the decision to move to DHCP and

Using SNMP and Other Diagnostic Tools to Monitor Your Network

by John Ray

In this chapter

Monitoring Your Network Using Mac OS **412**

Monitoring Your Network Using Windows **422**

Monitoring Your Network Using Linux **428**

Supplement, Don't Replace **435**

Your network is running smoothly, and it's growing every day. It's only natural that you might want some sort of ability to monitor what's going on. On a network composed of several subnets, it's almost a necessity. Rather than having to chase problems around, you can diagnose errors from your desktop or have your computer notify you if things go wrong.

The first things you're going to be looking at are Simple Network Management Protocol (SNMP) programs that you can use to monitor SNMP-capable devices on your network. There are thousands of SNMP devices, and it's difficult to know what's going to be in place on your network. Because of this, I'm going to be guiding you through a tour of SNMP as it applies to the network I use. Depending on your devices, you may be able to configure your equipment directly from the software itself. I generally use SNMP as a monitoring utility so I can get a graphical representation of what's going on with the network. SNMP software is not, however, a one-size-fits-all type of program. SNMP is a very open protocol and does not define the sort of way it can be used in the same way HTTP pretty much defines how a Web browser works. Because of this looseness, you'll rarely see SNMP software that's identical on different platforms. This is both a good and bad thing! It's easy to find a particular piece of SNMP software that you like, but that doesn't necessarily mean you're going to find something like it for your own machine. I'll be showing you three different SNMP packages that I've used. Each of the pieces of software is different from the other and has a different function on the network. If you've been reading only the how-to sections for your particular platform, I urge you to read the software descriptions for the other platforms; you might see something you like!

Besides SNMP, you'll also see a few diagnostic tools you can use to analyze what's taking place on your local subnet. With these tools, you can determine what protocols are making up the majority of your network traffic, find out what machines are sending or receiving specific types of traffic, and see the amount of bandwidth that's being used. Some of these tools, however, can also display the contents of packets on your network, which enables you to read user's passwords or other confidential information. Before you get any ideas, be sure to read Chapter 23, "Using and Administering Your Network Ethically," for a brief look at network ethics. Using software to spy on users is not cool, and in some cases may be illegal. It might be your network, but your users do have rights!

Monitoring Your Network Using Mac OS

I've been rather pleased with the selection of network monitoring software available for the Macintosh. Many times, the Mac is neglected for monitoring or connectivity type solutions because of the common use of Windows computers on networks. The first program you're going to see for the Mac OS is InterMapper from Dartmouth College. This is an extremely nicely designed piece of software that does precisely what the name implies: It allows you to map your network. The software is frequently updated and is constantly adding new features. It supports a variety of functions that help it stand out from other solutions, and it leverages the Mac OS environment by supporting the triggering of AppleScript programs based on events that happen to your network. This enables your computer to react to your network conditions and perform a wide variety of tasks without your interaction. If you've ever had something go wrong on your network while at a remote workstation and muttered, "If only I was at my desktop," this software comes close to letting you be there.

What Is AppleScript?

I'm assuming that if you're asking this question, you must not be familiar with the Mac OS. If you're a Mac user and you don't know, shame on you! AppleScript is one of the best-kept secrets of the Macintosh operating system. AppleScript is a scripting language that lets you control any AppleScript-capable application through a very English-like language. There are thousands of scriptable applications, and the scripting is made to be easy to use by even the most novice users. There are many scriptable network applications you can program. For example, if you had a Linux server, and SNMP InterMapper detected that the Web server was no longer running, it could trigger an AppleScript that logged into the Linux server and rebooted, or attempted to restart the server software. Better yet, you can compile AppleScripts and distribute them as standalone applications that run on any Mac OS computer. If you'd like more information, look for the AppleScript folder in the Apple Extras folder on your hard drive.

To download a demonstration version of the InterMapper software, visit its page on Dartmouth's Web site at `http://www.dartmouth.edu/netsoftware/intermapper/`.

InterMapper is a rather expensive application, so don't get too attached unless you can afford it. It does offer capabilities that are very useful and unique, however. The software should uncompress into a single application, which you can start immediately. Upon starting, the software will attempt to perform an auto-discovery on a particular address. This means that the SNMP information for a device will be examined, and if it contains routing information that points to other devices, they, in turn, will be discovered, and so on. Figure 21.1 shows the initial configuration dialog.

FIGURE 21.1

InterMapper begins by allowing you to select a starting device on the network.

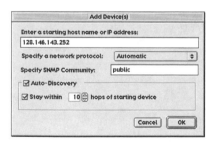

I'm starting InterMapper by pointing it at the bridge for my building. Auto-discovery is enabled, and the software is configured to find all SNMP devices within 10 hops of the device we just entered. Within a few seconds of entering the device IP, a graphic view of the devices that were located should be displayed. In my case, there are only two devices that are located: the router for Ag (or Agriculture) Campus and the bridge that I initially pointed the software at. Figure 21.2 shows the initial InterMapper display after running the discovery procedure. You can even drag the individual elements around to fit however you'd like to visualize the network.

Part

V

Ch

21

FIGURE 21.2

InterMapper has detected a few devices on my network and displays them graphically.

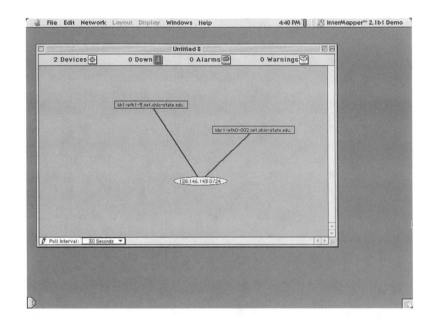

To find out more information about a particular device, simply double-click it to open an information window. In Figure 21.3, I've opened the SNMP information window for the building's bridge. You can see the device's status, location, and contact information.

FIGURE 21.3

SNMP status information is shown for the building bridge.

Everything you see in the mapping window is double clickable. For example, the network I've defined, 128.146.143.0, is actually comprised of two subnets that share the same wire. I can add in the second subnet for the building by double-clicking the network "bubble" and clicking the Add Subnet... button in the resulting dialog box. The information dialog for the network is shown in Figure 21.4.

FIGURE 21.4

You can double-click all the elements in the mapping display. Here, information for the subnet is displayed.

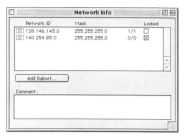

For devices that are not auto-discovered, go to the Network menu and select Add Device(s). This will enable you to add a large number of devices to your map that don't necessarily support SNMP. The dialog should look identical to the initial Add Device dialog that appears when you first start the program. Enter in an IP address that is on your network, and then choose the network protocol that the device is using. You have a wide variety of options, including Gopher, HTTP, IMAP, POP, AppleShareIP, and many other protocols. For example, I've added my AppleShare IP server to the network map. The information display for my server is shown in Figure 21.5.

FIGURE 21.5

Many devices can be added to the map, including AppleShare IP servers.

You can change the protocol information at any time by double-clicking to bring up the standard information display for an element and then editing the contents of the dialog box. Each protocol lets you set different criteria for how it determines that status of a device. For example, if I were to select the HTTP protocol, I can configure what Web pages request is sent to the server and what verifies a "good" response. This allows you to do more complex things than just check to see if a server is online; it lets you monitor specific resources and determine if they're functioning correctly. For applications in which you have mission-critical databases online, this ability is very useful.

But what good is the ability to determine the status of a network device if you can't act on its status? Fortunately, with InterMapper, you can set up Notifications that are triggered for certain network conditions. To create a notification, select the element you want to trigger a notification event, and then choose Attach Notification from the Network menu. Figure 21.6 shows some notifications that are attached to my network.

Part
V

Ch
21

FIGURE 21.6

You can ask InterMapper to notify you of changes in your network condition.

I've set up InterMapper to play a few sounds if my AppleShare IP server goes offline or comes online. I can set a delay before a notification takes place, as well as a repeat interval so I don't accidentally miss an event. I've also set up an email notification that will be triggered if different.ag.ohio-state.edu goes down. To add a new notification, click the Add User... button at the bottom of the notification window. Figure 21.7 shows the notification addition screen.

FIGURE 21.7

You can add a wide variety of different notifications and specify times during which notifications will be sent.

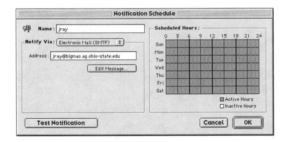

Notifications can come in the format of email, sounds, and even pages to your pager! The notification scheduling screen lets you configure a user that is responsible for receiving a notification, specific information for a particular notification (email address, pager number, and so on), as well as a notification schedule. If your server has scheduled downtime, for example, you probably don't want to be notified that it has gone offline during that time. You can turn on and off blocks of time by clicking in the notification-scheduling dialog box.

What determines if a device is offline? You can configure thresholds that will be used to notify you of problems. To do so, choose Device Threshold from the Network menu. If you're constantly being notified of down network devices, you might want to increase the number of lost packets that determine if a machine is offline. Figure 21.8 shows the threshold configuration dialog box.

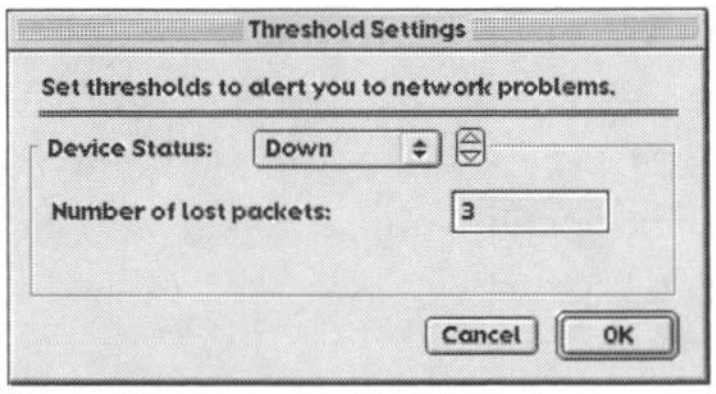

FIGURE 21.8

Threshold settings let you set the number of lost packets it takes before a network alert is issued.

Let's take another look at the mapping screen itself. Things are about to get really interesting. You may not have realized it, but the real fun hasn't even begun. Thus far, we've been concerned with laying out our network graphically, and we haven't actually done any monitoring. I've added another subnet to the graph and have enabled the actual network monitoring by clicking the small pencil in the lower-left corner of the graph window. My current graph is shown in Figure 21.9.

FIGURE 21.9

Network monitoring has begun!

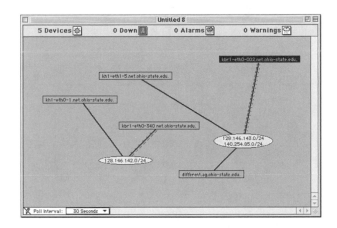

Things look pretty much the same in the graph, except you can probably see little dashed lines running between the subnets and the bridges for each of the subnets. If you're actually running the software, these lines are animated and, depending on the size of dashes, represent the amount of network traffic coming from and going to the individual subnets. The counters at the top of the window are now active as well. If there are down devices, they'll be indicated in the appropriate counter, as well as any pending alerts or warnings.

You can get detailed information about a traffic stream by clicking on it. In Figure 21.10, I've clicked on the stream of traffic between the bridge and my subnet.

FIGURE 21.10

Information about a stream of traffic is displayed when you click on it.

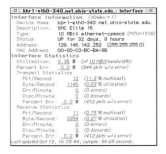

You can see that there are a variety of statistics available for the bridge. The Utilization of the network is at 2.56%—not very high, which is good. The amount of packets transmitted and received is also visible. You'll also notice that much of the numeric information is underlined

Part

V

Ch

21

like a hyperlink. That's because it *is* a link. Clicking on a statistic brings up a graph of the statistic, which will be drawn over time. You can map multiple statistics at a time; just click on multiple links. Figure 21.11 shows an outgoing traffic graph for the building. The graph was rather uninteresting to begin with, but I took it upon myself to generate a bit of traffic on the network and produced a few spikes for your viewing pleasure.

FIGURE 21.11

Network traffic and many other events can also be graphed.

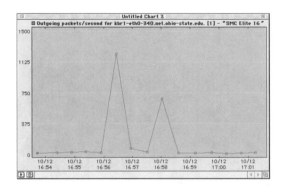

That pretty much covers the program! It's a very useful piece of software if you're willing to take the time to fully map your network devices. InterMapper even offers remote control through a built-in Telnet server. The interface is very consistent and intuitive. If you're a Mac user and have been intimidated by shoddy ports of network software to the Mac, don't hesitate to look at InterMapper. Developed on and for the Macintosh, it's a gem of a monitoring tool!

Now, let's turn our attention to a different network analysis tool for the Mac. I'll show you a far more complex product that does packet analysis for different types of protocols: Neon Software's NetMinder. This is a high-end packet sniffing package, which was created to replace the need to buy dedicated network diagnostic hardware. Besides capturing and displaying information about your network, NetMinder also diagnoses any problems it finds. You can download a demo of NetMinder from Neon Software at

http://www.neon.com/

Please pay close attention to the installation instructions. The current version of NetMinder requires you to install an included patch if you're using Mac OS 8.0, or install special Ethernet card drivers if you're using certain models of the Mac. If all is well, go ahead and start the NetMinder software.

Your screen will be a collection of several windows. Let's concentrate on the most important window first: the NetMinder Ethernet window. When you first start NetMinder, this window is blank. Let's make it look a bit interesting. Notice the button called Collect at the top of the window? Clicking that button will start the packet-collection process. You can see the packets collected, numbered, and analyzed in real-time as they come in. Figure 21.12 shows the NetMinder window after one minute of collection time on my network.

FIGURE 21.12

NetMinder collects and analyzes packets on your network.

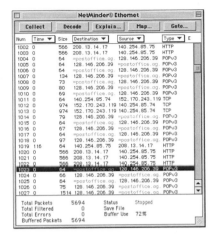

The listing displays the source and destination computers involved in a connection, as well as the protocol they're using to communicate. Each line is a separate packet, so you'll probably see several lines for each individual connection. In my example, you can see that there are quite a few POP3 connections to the machine postoffice.ag.ohio-state.edu. This is a semi-active mail server, so this amount of traffic is very typical. When you're finished collecting information, you can double-click an entry to show the full information that has been collected for the packet. Figure 21.13 shows a packet that was being set to the POP server. In the lower portion of the Window, you can see the contents of the packet—notice the POP command?

FIGURE 21.13

You can display information about each logged packet.

Part

V

Ch

21

You can see more information than just the contents of the packets. For example, choose the Trend Analysis selection from the Windows menu. Doing so will display a graph of packet traffic and bandwidth usage. Figure 21.14 shows a sample graph in the process of being generated.

FIGURE 21.14

NetMinder will graph your network traffic and bandwidth usage for you.

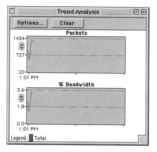

An interesting feature is the ability for NetMinder to actively warn you of problems that exist on your network. This feature can tip you off to impending trouble before you would normally find out the hard way. Choose the Packet Interference selection from the Windows menu. You can see in my example, Figure 21.15, that there is an address conflict. There is also a log of an attempt to talk to a computer using a protocol that is unsupported. Looking for this sort of activity may turn up attempts to hack computers on your network. Most hacking attempts start with a scan of your subnet to determine the services that are running on your network and where they're located. This activity should show up in the Packet Interference window.

FIGURE 21.15

NetMinder will show you any problems it detects on your network.

For an overall view of the activity on your network, there is a variety of different screens you can display to summarize collected information about your network. From the Analysis menu, you can choose Summary to display traffic statistics about your network. Figure 21.16 shows the summary for my network. Notice that my bandwidth usage is still less than 3 percent.

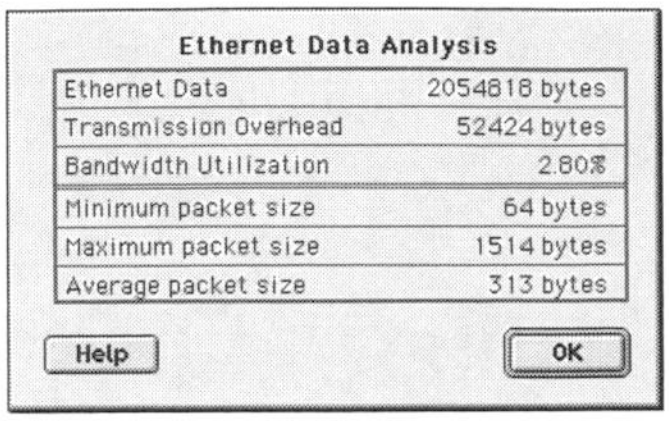

FIGURE 21.16

Want a quick summary of your network traffic? Click the Analysis menu and choose Summary.

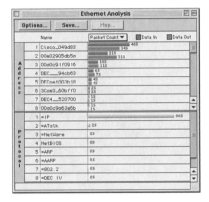

You can also choose Ethernet Analysis or TCP/IP Analysis to see a summary of the protocols being used on the network. The Ethernet analysis is, obviously, a summary of all the traffic that is moving on your Ethernet network. Figure 21.17 shows the Ethernet analysis for my network.

FIGURE 21.17

You can use NetMinder to view an analysis of all Ethernet traffic...

The TCP/IP analysis, as you might guess, limits the traffic analysis to only TCP/IP data. Figure 21.18 shows the TCP/IP traffic for my network. I'm generally only interested in TCP/IP data, but occasionally I look at Ethernet traffic to see what sort of activity our AppleShare server or NetWare servers are generating. In this case, the majority of traffic deals with my Web server.

FIGURE 21.18

...or limit the data to TCP/IP traffic only.

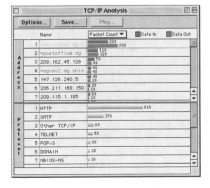

Part

V

Ch

21

There is far more that NetMinder can do to help you manage your network and diagnose problems. What you've seen here is merely a subset of the available features. Take a look at the demo; even with its limited capabilities, it can still reveal quite a bit about your network.

Monitoring Your Network Using Windows

The Mac OS programs you just saw are really nice, but they require that you tell them about most of your network. Let's take a look at a piece of software for the Windows platform that does some of the work for you. This program will not draw the fancy graphs of the NetMinder program, but it will let you browse a complete subnet at a time and will show all of the SNMP devices that are available on the network. The package is called IP Network Browser by Solar Winds. You can download a time-limited demo from

```
http://solarwinds.net/
```

Once you've downloaded the package, double-click the resulting icon to run the self-installing package. There is very little configuration that needs to take place, so you shouldn't have any problem there. When you're ready to browse your IP network, start the IP Network Browser software, which is installed in the SolarWinds program group under the Start menu.

The very first thing you'll see is a dialog box, shown in Figure 21.19, prompting you for the network you want to scan. You'll need to set the subnet mask by using the scroll bar located at the bottom of the window. I'm about to start a scan on my work subnet 140.254.85.0 with the subnet mask 255.255.255.0.

FIGURE 21.19

Select the subnet you want to scan by using the scroll bar.

When you're ready, click OK, and stand back. IP Network Browser will proceed to scan your entire subnet and display information about all the available machines. This is an excellent way to get a quick-and-dirty view of the devices on your network. I've let the scan run on my subnet, and now I have a window that lists my devices, shown in Figure 21.20.

If a particular IP address has a DNS entry, it will be resolved and displayed in the listing. The software also attempts to identify the type of device on the network and supplies an appropriate icon (if available) in the listing. Notice that this is a hierarchical listing; that is, there are certain devices that can be expanded to display further information. These are devices that the software has recognized as being SNMP devices. If you expand the listing for a particular device, you can see a wealth of configuration information that can tell you if a device is operating correctly, who owns the device, and other useful facts. Let's go ahead and take an expanded look at some of the devices on my network.

FIGURE 21.20

IP Network Browser is showing all the devices on my subnet.

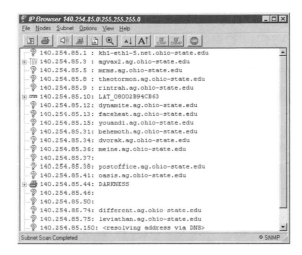

Figure 21.21 shows the first expanded view from my network. This is not a router or gateway—it's a computer! That's right! In case I haven't mentioned it before, it's possible to use SNMP to monitor and configure individual computer systems if they have the appropriate SNMP server software installed. The AgVAX has been our primary computer system on Ag campus for the past 10 years and will be decommissioned in the next 10 days (long before this book hits the stands), so showing it here is my tribute to the old war horse! May it rest in peace. In this view, I've expanded the TCP/IP network configuration display, which shows the two interfaces configured on the machine (the loopback interface, lo0, and the primary interface se0). Isn't that exciting? Well, no, not really. Let's take a look at something that's a bit more interesting.

FIGURE 21.21

IP Browser provides an expanded view of the now-defunct AgVAX computer.

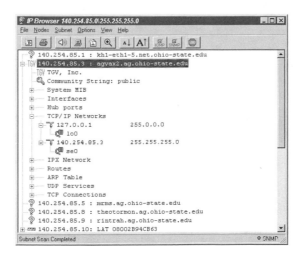

Take a look at Figure 21.22. Okay, once again, this isn't a "traditional" SNMP device either, but it isn't another computer. Instead, it's is a printer that is located in my office suite. In this example, you can see that there is a bit more information seen here. We've got the hardware address, device status, IP address, and operating state of the printer. If you were just moving into a network administration position, this would be very valuable information for learning about your network. Running IP Network Browser gives you a fast way to find out precisely what people have running on your network. There's still more that the program can reveal, however. Let's take a look at two more devices. First, and probably most interesting, check out a device on our network called a DECServer. Our DECServer provides dial-in support for our network. It is a tiny little box that supports 16 different modem lines and handles PPP and SLIP connections. It also lets you monitor the status of the connections via SNMP. Figure 21.23 shows the DECServer as displayed in IP Network Browser.

FIGURE 21.22

SNMP information for a printer is shown here.

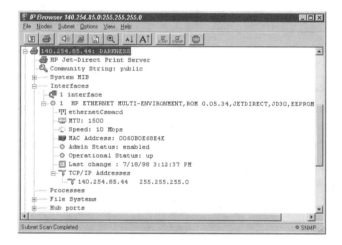

FIGURE 21.23

SNMP can also show information about terminal servers.

Notice the different interfaces that are displayed? The SNMP software shows the state of each of the different dial-in lines by representing them in different colors. I can expand any active interface to show the speed of the connection as well as the time at which the connection went active. The user shown on port 5 of the DECServer has been connected since 9:22 p.m. Keep in mind as you look at these screenshots that a single piece of software is displaying this information. It's not customized for the DECServer, or for my printer, or any of the other devices on the network. A similar piece of software on the Macintosh, for example, could potentially display the same information. If a software developer wanted to customize the software for a particular application, they could as well. An SNMP package for the DECServer could be developed that gave a real-time display of all the ports. The sky's the limit.

For our last display of SNMP prowess, I'm going to show you one of the same devices you saw displayed on the Macintosh: the bridge for my building.

In Figure 21.24, you can see the most information we've see so far for any device on the network. Network Browser displays the bridge location as well as contact information. You can also see that there are two interfaces, one for each side of the network (it is bridging things, after all!). There's also information about routing. The Next Hop is shown to be 128.146.143.1, which happens to be the primary router for Ag campus. Hopefully by now you understand just how much information can be carried using the SNMP protocol. You're still going to need to get up occasionally and actually physically *look* at devices on your network, but products such as IP Network Browser can eliminate the need to run different proprietary packages for each device on your network.

FIGURE 21.24

IP Network Browser now shows the building's bridge and contact information.

Okay, we've just completed our look at a single Windows SNMP monitoring package. There are many more SNMP tools available; I chose to look at this one because of its simple and friendly interface. Try running it on your network; you might find a few devices you weren't aware existed!

Now, it's time for a look at a different kind of network diagnostic tool: Ethload. Like the Mac OS NetMinder software, Ethload is a packet analysis tool. You might be surprised (if not startled) to learn that Ethload is a DOS-based program. There are Windows-based packet analysis tools, but I'm extremely partial to Ethload. I've been using Ethload faithfully for the past three years and have been delighted by its feature set and ease of use. Originally a freeware program, Ethload is now under active development and is distributed as shareware. You can download a copy from

`http://www.hec.be/~evyncke/`

The reason I *love* Ethload (and I'm serious about loving it; it's an excellent tool) is because it's DOS based. Not being a Win32 program enables Ethload to run on old hardware. I can slap a copy of Ethload onto an old 386 PC "luggable" and carry it over to a network that needs to be diagnosed. Once again, this is a program that can make old hardware useful. The problem is that in order to run Ethload, you're going to need to load a packet driver for your system. If you're unfamiliar with packet drivers, you'll probably want to contact the manufacturer of your Ethernet card for details on how to go about installing it.

What Is a Packet Driver?

A packet driver is the equivalent to the Network Adapter in Windows. It provides a low-level interface to the network card. It does not provide TCP/IP support or support for any other protocol. The software, which accesses the packet driver, must implement whatever protocols it intends to use.

Now, if you're interesting in using the product under Windows, that's also possible, but you're going to need to do a bit of work. To run the software, you need to install a Virtual Packet Driver for Windows. Doing so will provide the interface to the network card that the Ethload software expects. The program you want to install is called NDIS3PKT and is available in a free version from

`http://www.danlan.com/`

Read through the installation instructions for NDIS3PKT. You may need to refer to your Windows 95 manual and the Ethload documentation files for further information. Once NDIS3PKT is installed correctly, you'll be able to run Ethload in full-screen or windowed mode under Windows. The screenshots I've taken are not entirely representative of the full Ethload screen, mainly just the pertinent data. The actual software is very pretty and definitely worthy of a look, even if you're used to using Windows-only software.

Once Ethload is installed, you can start it by typing **ethload** from a DOS prompt. If you're running under Windows, you'll need to start the program with the -n option (by typing **ethload –n**).

The initial Ethload display is shown in Figure 21.25. Here you see a graph of network activity versus time, as well as a measurement of bandwidth usage, error rate, and other information that gives you a quick view of the current state of your network. Across the top of the screen are the options you can choose to navigate through the Ethload system.

FIGURE 21.25

The initial Ethload screen gives a clear picture of current network conditions.

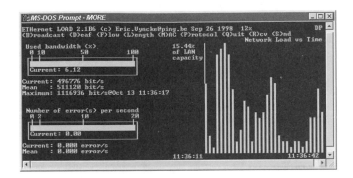

Pressing Esc will take you to the previous menu that you visited. Let's go ahead and see a few of the offerings that Ethload has in store for us. For example, type **s** or **r** to show the Ethernet addresses of the top senders or receivers, respectively, on your network. Figure 21.26 shows the top senders on my network.

FIGURE 21.26

Ethload can show the top traffic producing or receiving computers.

If you want to find out what protocols are being used on the network, type **p** to view the protocol information for your Ethernet network. Figure 21.27 shows an example of this screen. Remember, this is *Ethernet* traffic, not just TCP/IP traffic.

FIGURE 21.27

Ethload can show a variety of information about the protocols being used on your network, including Ethernet.

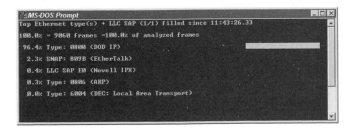

Part

V

Ch

21

If you're interested in TCP/IP traffic, you can navigate to the TCP/IP screen by typing **i**, followed by **t**. TCP/IP traffic is shown in order of use. You can see the amount of traffic that's being generated by Web servers, POP servers, and any other TCP/IP server that is running on your network. Figure 21.28 shows the TCP/IP protocols being used.

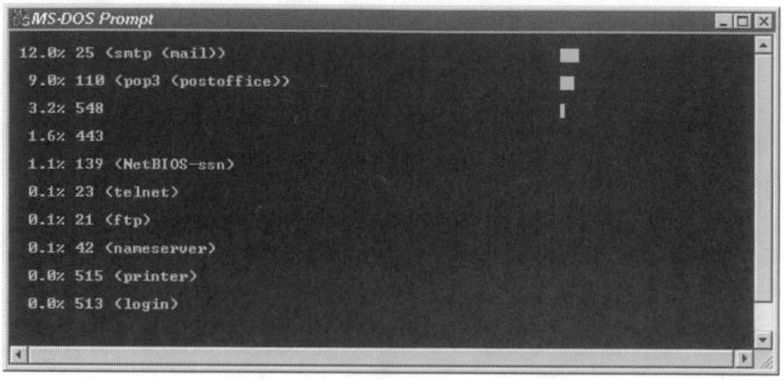

FIGURE 21.28

Protocols are listed in order of traffic; in this case, the majority of traffic is email related.

To see the actual connections taking place, type **c**. You'll see the source host and port followed by the destination machine and destination port, as shown in Figure 21.29. If you're experiencing unusually high traffic levels on your network, this display could help you figure out where the culprit is.

FIGURE 21.29

Connections, including their start and end points, are displayed when you type **c**.

Ethload has many more features than the ones you've seen here and is also a far more attractive program than what the screenshots here may indicate. I've used the software for several years and have not found anything even remotely similar that didn't cost several hundred dollars. The fact that it's DOS based may be a turn-off to some people, but, in fact, it enables it to run on a larger hardware base, and also makes it extremely fast and responsive. Check it out!

Monitoring Your Network Using Linux

Last but not least, we come to Linux. There are many SNMP programs that are available for UNIX systems, including Linux. Some are graphical, like the software we've seen for Windows and Mac OS; others are text based. Let's settle for a different type of application entirely—something that falls somewhere in the middle—a SNMP monitoring program that displays its information on a Web page. Doing so is going to require a little bit of configuration that is specific to my network devices, so you're not necessarily going to end up with anything like my setup. The software you'll be seeing here is called MRTG or Multi Router Traffic Grapher. Obviously, this is software with a single purpose: graphing router traffic! As I mentioned before, SNMP can be used in very specific applications, and this is one of them. The MRTG is used to display daily, monthly, and yearly data that is gathered and stored from a router on your network. Because the software stores all the data itself, it can generate graphs over extended periods of time. Most SNMP monitoring software does its job in the here-and-now. Whatever data is collected while the software is running is what you get. Best of all, like Linux, MRTG is freeware, so it won't cost you a thing. To use MRTG, however, you're going to need to install the GD graphics library first. GD is a graphics package that can be used as an extension to the Perl programming language to dynamically generate .GIF files and other graphics in real-time. You can pick up the current version of GD from

```
http://www.boutell.com/gd/
```

Once you have GD installed, you'll need to download MRTG, which is another free download, from

```
http://ee-staff.ethz.ch/~oetiker/webtools/mrtg/pub/
```

Both of these packages are going to come as a compressed source archive that you'll need to compile. Rather than give you a specific example of a compilation, I'd like to take a few minutes to give you an overview of what is normally required to install uncompiled software on your computer.

There are thousands of pieces of available UNIX software that can be used on your Linux computer, and all you need to do is compile them. Most software is distributed as a tar (or Tape Archive) file that has been compressed using gzip. You can recognize these types of files from the filename; usually a gzipped tar file will end in .tgz or .tar.gz. To decompress a gzipped file called `myfile.tar.gz`, run the gunzip program with it, like this:

```
>gunzip myfile.tar.gz
```

Once a file has been unzipped, you'll still need to expand the archive. This is a little different from the Windows and Mac platforms, in which generally the compression software also archives the files. Instead, you'll use tar to unarchive the file, which should now be named `myfile.tar` on your drive, like this:

```
>tar -xf myfile.tar
```

Okay, now you've decompressed and unarchived your software, so you're ready to start compiling. First, look inside the directory that the archive has expanded into. If you see a file called configure, the program most likely has the ability to automatically configure itself to your system. Just run ./configure to prepare the software for compilation.

Once configure has run, or if configure isn't included, you'll need to actually compile the software. Compilation is usually controlled via a file called a Makefile. The Makefile holds a series of rules that define what portions of the software need each other in order to work. You'll probably want to look through the Makefile and any README files that may have been included in the package. Often there are configuration details you'll need to change in the start of the Makefile. Once you're set up and ready to go, the rest is simple. Type **make**:

```
>make
```

Your computer should churn for awhile. Depending on the size of the software being installed and the speed of your computer, it may take minutes, or even hours, to compile a package. When the compilation is finished, typically there are Makefile rules defined for installing the package. To install all the files on your system, use the make command again, adding the install parameter:

```
>make install
```

That's usually all there is to it. Compiling software is a bit more time consuming than simply installing a pre-compiled package and being up and running in minutes, but it also opens the door to using many programs that are only distributed as source code.

In the case of MRTG, you're going to need to run make with a few slightly different options, and you'll need to install the software manually in a directory you create. Let's go ahead and compile MRTG now:

```
>make rateup
>make substitute
```

I'm going to be serving my MRTG Web pages from my main Web directory, /home/httpd/ html, so I'll need to copy all of the associated MRTG .GIF files there. (You might want to be a little less sloppy in your installation and create a separate directory for the MRTG images.)

```
>cp mrtg*gif /home/httpd/html
```

The remaining files should all be copied to the directory you want to run MRTG from. If you'd like to leave it in the same directory you've performed the compilation in, no problem. Whatever your choice, you're ready to run!

Now you're going to need to create a configuration file that tells MRTG about the router you want to monitor. I'm going to be monitoring the public router 128.146.143.252, which handles all incoming and outgoing traffic in my building. To set up the configuration file, just run the cfgmaker. I'm going to do that now:

```
>./cfgmaker public@128.146.143.252 > myconfig.cfg
```

There are several options you can set in the configuration file, but the cfgmaker should configure most of them for you. You'll need to manually edit the file, however, and include a line with the directory where MRTG will store the files that it generates; go ahead and edit your myconfig.cfg file and add a line that looks something like this (only appropriately configured for your system):

```
WorkDir: /home/httpd/html
```

Now you can go ahead and run mrtg on the configuration file that you've created.

```
>./mrtg myconfig.cfg
```

The first time you run MRTG, you'll probably see a variety of error messages as it looks for files that aren't present on the machine. You can safely ignore these messages, and subsequent executions of the program will not have errors. If everything ran as it should, you should now see several new files in the directory you specified with the WorkDir option. With any luck, there are some new HTML files in the directory that you can open up with your Web browser. Figures 21.30, 21.31, and 21.32 show MRTG after it has been run on a network for some time. The first figure shows the daily statistics, the second includes monthly and weekly data, and the third shows information gathered over an entire year.

FIGURE 21.30

MRTG can show daily information...

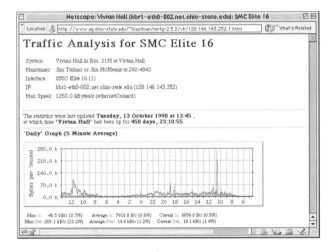

FIGURE 21.31

...as well as weekly and monthly statistics...

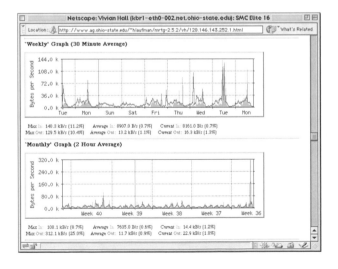

The pages also display various pieces of SNMP information about the device that's being queried, such as the location, contact information, and operating parameters. A maximum, average, and current traffic reading follows each graph as well. We typically have a computer that displays MRTG data in a Web browser continuously. Watching the graphs has tipped us off to several conditions on the network, including the operation of a pirate FTP site that sent traffic numbers to new heights.

Part
V

Ch
21

FIGURE 21.32

...and even yearly data!

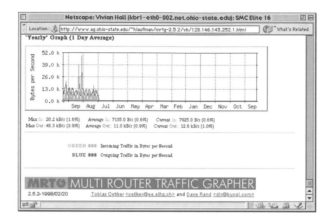

MRTG does not automatically continue to run after you start it. You'll need to create a "crontab" entry that will run the program at specific intervals and update the graph appropriately. For more information about crontab, type **man crontab** from a command prompt.

I'm going to create a crontab file (I'm calling mine "john.cron") that runs MRTG every 15 minutes. To do this, start a new file in emacs (or your favorite text editor), and add a line that looks like this (substitute the paths to MRTG as they appear on your system):

```
0,15,30,45 * * * * /bin/mrtg/mrtg /bin/mrtg/myconfig.cfg
```

Now, install it into your system-wide crontab file by using the `crontab` command:

```
>crontab john.cron
```

That's it! Your Linux box will poll whatever device you set up every 15 minutes and build the graphs over time. Because they're HTML based and your Linux box has a built-in Web server, you can monitor your network activity from anywhere you can run a Web server! But don't get any ideas about running your network from a local cyber cafe; chances are that won't go over very well with your fellow employees.

All right! That wasn't too bad; you compiled your first program on Linux, and everything worked fine, right? Usually there is very little trouble compiling well-written software on different UNIX-based platforms. The next package we're going to look at will also need to be compiled, but it requires even less work than MRTG did. It's called sniffit and can provide an easy way to look at network traffic on your wire. Sniffit is available from

```
http://reptile.rug.ac.be/~coder/sniffit/sniffit.html
```

The sniffit product is entirely text based, which means that you can access it from a remote terminal. I've used sniffit installations in buildings across campus to help other network administrators locate the source of network traffic and diagnose problems. The software itself can be used to log packet streams to and from hosts; this is bad. How you choose to use much of this software is up to you. Sniffit is a useful network tool but is also extremely useful for hackers. Don't be a hacker!

Download the latest version of sniffit from its home page and unarchive it as I discussed earlier (`gunzip sniffit.gz, tar -xf sniffit.tar`). The package is self configuring, so you can get things rolling pretty quickly by typing

```
>./configure
>make
```

Sniffit should be auto-configured for your Linux system and then compiled. The resulting application is a small binary file named sniffit; you may wish to copy it to your /sbin or /usr/sbin directory to maintain consistency with the rest of your network administration tools.

When you're ready to run sniffit, invoke it with the command line option -i. This puts sniffit into interactive mode, which is very easy to control. Otherwise, sniffit will execute a single function and then drop back to a command line. Not very exciting! Upon starting, sniffit will immediately begin displaying traffic on your network in the form of two columns: source IP and port, and destination IP and port. Figure 21.33 shows an active sniffit window.

FIGURE 21.33

Sniffit is monitoring network traffic.

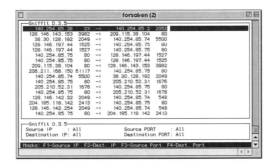

After running for a little while, you might want to see some of the statistics that sniffit has collected for your network. To do this, type **n** to bring up the stats window. In Figure 21.34, you can see this display, which is showing the number of packets per second being transmitted on the network, as well as the number of bytes per second.

FIGURE 21.34

Some simple network statistics are displayed by sniffit.

Part

V

Ch

21

The amount of data displayed in the Sniffit window can be a bit overwhelming (you can actually scroll up and down the list of connections by using your arrow keys). To limit the amount of information being shown, you can select a particular source or destination to be traced. To select a destination address, press F2 (or simply 2) and enter the address you want to monitor. Figure 21.35 shows network traffic that is bound for our primary Web server. Most of the traffic is headed to port 80, which is the httpd server.

FIGURE 21.35

Sniffit lets you specify a destination address to monitor.

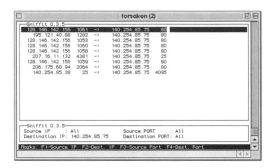

If you're more interested in what machines on your network are receiving *any* Web requests (rather than a particular machine), you can, instead, simply monitor traffic that's traveling to a specific port. Press F4 (or just 4) and enter the port you want to monitor. I've entered 80, and in Figure 21.36 you can see all the traffic that's headed to that port on all the machines on this network.

FIGURE 21.36

Rather than limiting the display by machine, you can also choose a specific port.

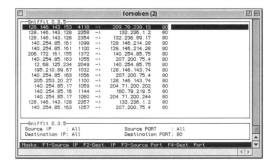

Lastly (and this is where sniffit can be abused), you can monitor any of the active connections that are displayed in a window. If you happen to notice a connection that has been around for some time and want to know what sort of data is being sent in the connection, use the arrow keys to highlight the connection in question, and then press Return to start monitoring the actual data being sent. For my example, shown in Figure 21.37, I've chosen a Web connection and have monitored it long enough to see the client sending information to the server about itself. Not too exciting in this case, but I'm sure you can see how this could be useful!

FIGURE 21.37
You can monitor the traffic that is sent over a specific connection.

Be sure to read the associated sniffit readme files, as they contain information about extended features of the software. As with the other applications we've looked at, there are other capabilities you might be interested in that didn't necessarily make it into the book. Also, be sure to search the Net for Linux and SNMP; you'll find a wealth of freely available SNMP software, in case the programs you've seen in this chapter are not to your liking.

Supplement, Don't Replace

We're at the end of the SNMP Monitoring chapter, and I'd like to take a few seconds to stress one very important point about networks. I'm sure I've said it before, and I don't doubt that I'll say it again: Do not place all of your faith in a piece of software! Network management tools can help reduce some of the load from the network administrator, but you cannot diagnose every problem that occurs by looking at your computer screen. Legwork will still be necessary, no matter how wonderful the software or how much automation is built in.

Recognizing and Diagnosing Network Problems

by John Ray

In this chapter

Diagnosing User Errors **439**

Diagnosing Configuration Errors **441**

Router Configuration Errors **446**

Subnet Mask Configuration Errors **446**

Diagnosing Software Errors **447**

Diagnosing Cabling Problems **448**

Netstat **449**

Diagnosing Network Hardware (Other Than Cabling) Problems **452**

The Right Way To Do Things **453**

This chapter looks at what you can do to diagnose problems with your network. Even before we get started, I'm going to tell you that this job won't be easy. If all you have to work with is a handful of software tools when you're troubleshooting your network, then you stand a better chance of finding your problem by guesswork alone. It's important for you to start the process knowing that you're going to have a tough time performing the diagnosis without the proper equipment. At the end of this chapter, you get to take a quick look at the right equipment for the job. However, given the price tag for an average wiring and protocol tester (the "right" test equipment—roughly $4,000), most network administrators spend years puzzling through network problems by the seat of their pants (and sometimes never finding their problems) before breaking down and buying a test set. In this chapter, I also rely heavily on UNIX-based tools. Because UNIX has been around much longer than either the Macintosh or Windows, the UNIX community has had to deal with network problems for longer; as a result, UNIX administrators have developed more tools. Although some UNIX tools do have Macintosh and Windows equivalents, if you're in charge of administrating a network, you might find it very useful to put together a pair of cheap Linux boxes that you can use for some parts of the diagnosis. (Not only would it make your diagnostics easier, it's a great use for old 386 machines!) Before getting into the details of how to diagnose problems, you need to familiarize yourself with where problems are likely to occur.

Network problems and apparent network problems have roughly five different general causes. Unfortunately, I have found that users often diagnose their problems incorrectly and frequently blame the machine or network when, in reality, the source of the problem is human error, and generally on the part of the user. On the other hand, it seems that when a user has a problem and spends hours trying to determine what he or she did wrong, it's actually a hardware or software problem and the frustrated user has been repeating the same operations on a machine that simply refuses to behave. Because of this tendency, and because none of the tools you use here can give an instant and definitive diagnosis of errors, it's best to keep the entire list of possible causes in mind and to examine it from the simplest to diagnose to the most complex. Here are the potential sources of network problems and apparent network problems—in order from quickest to check to the most difficult:

1. User errors
2. Configuration errors
3. Software errors
4. Network cabling problems
5. Network hardware (other than cabling) problems

These causes are listed in order of increasing difficulty of diagnosis, and it is the order in which you should consider any problem. Here's an example: Say you have a user who complains that the network isn't working. The first thing you should do is make certain that the user is typing the correct URL to his or her browser, rather than trying to determine whether one of your hubs is incorrectly handling the traffic. You're going to find and fix a lot of network problems much faster if you approach them from the order of increasing difficulty.

A Word to the Wise

Pay close attention to error messages and log files when trying to diagnose errors. Logs exist for a reason, and error messages are generally trying to tell you something. All too often administrators face the following scenario: A user complains, "The FTP server is down. I can't connect to it!" and calls in a technician to fix the problem. After an examination of the user's FTP connection log turns up a series of `Access Denied - Username or Password Incorrect` errors, a suitably careful retyping of his or her username and password usually clears up the network problem. It's the same story with HTTP servers. Often, users puzzle for hours, writing and rewriting and generally working themselves into a frenzy over a Web page they've written that will not load. If the Web page uses a CGI script, as often as not, a quick look in the log file gives a helpful suggestion; for example, `Script execution aborted - no execute permission` is frequently all the hint that's required to fix the problem. Additionally, it's crucial that you carefully document errors, log messages, any modifications you make to the system, and what changes in the response you have generated. Also, make backup copies of configuration files before you change anything. If you aren't taking careful notes and making backups as you go, you will end up tweaking your system right into a virtual corner from which you no longer remember how to extract it. All the more frustrating is when, just after discovering yourself to be firmly stuck in said corner, you find a footnote in your manual or a Web page on the Internet detailing the complete solution to your exact problem—in the state your machine was in only 15 minutes prior to the corner.

Finally, when trying to diagnose an error, it is always useful to find a consistent way to duplicate the error. An error that you can reproduce at will is much easier to find and fix than one that occurs intermittently. If you have the luck of most network administrators, however, machines in your general vicinity will usually work flawlessly and users will only experience their problems when you're not in the room.

Diagnosing User Errors

Start with the obvious: Is the user with the problem doing everything correctly? Strange as it may seem, sometimes a person manages to forget how to do something that he or she has done correctly every day for the past three years. Users come to me on a regular basis and ask, "Is there something wrong with the network or the Web server? I can't get to my home page!" Most of the time, they've simply managed to mistype their URL. Why they don't bookmark the URL so that they don't have to retype it every day, I do not know, but this problem is surprisingly common.

Beyond simple things like incorrectly typed URLs, here is a sampling of other problems that look similar to network errors but are simply human errors.

Did Someone Mistype a Hostname (Fully Qualified Domain Name)?

Not only can you get Host Not Found errors because of simple typos, but typos can also leave you with apparent missing pages and, in some cases, amazingly wrong pages. Although hostnames are frequently similar, they generally serve totally separate Web sites. (Always remember that the U.S. government uses .gov for its hostnames. Extensive embarrassment has been caused on at least one occasion by the mistaken substitution of a different top-level domain in the URL http://www.whitehouse.gov/. If you're adventurous enough to figure out the error, imagine the looks on a room full of potential investors' faces when this mistake was made during a "please won't you invest in our college" seminar.)

In addition to simply wrong (and potentially embarrassing) pages that can result from typos, a new variety of rather subversive and ethically quite questionable Web sites is popping up. These pages register domain names very similar to popular domains—names that are likely to result from typos of other domain names. They then mirror the contents of the correct Web site but with minor changes to suit whatever their agenda might be. If you're an online shopping mall with the URL http://www.shop_me_yeah.com/, you may very well find that you've been mirrored by a site named http://www.shop_me_yay.com/ or http://www.shop_me_yah.com/, which mirrors all your pages but shows the items with slightly higher prices. The phony site effectively represents itself to be your store, forwards to you any orders which it gets, and collects the difference between the elevated price and yours.

If a user reports that some minor thing on your site isn't the same as what you know it to be, before assuming that the user is a little touched, take a look at what he or she is seeing and make certain that your site isn't being mirrored.

Is the Case Correct?

UNIX is case sensitive and, frequently, URLs on PCs aren't. If someone has sent you a URL that looks like HTTP://WWW.POISONTOOTH.COM/MYPAGE.HTML and you keep getting Page Not Found errors, you might want to try http://www.poisontooth.com/mypage.html. You might also want to try other possible case combinations, as the author might have also made pages named http://www.poisontooth.com/Mypage.html or http://www.poisontooth.com/MyPage.html (and they'd all represent different pages on a UNIX server).

Is There a Space in the Name?

Macintosh and Windows platforms can have spaces in filenames. UNIX machines can have spaces in filenames as well, but if you want to use a filename with a space on a UNIX machine, you need to put it in quotes. From a Windows or Macintosh server, you might be able to access an URL like http://www.poisontooth.com/my secret directory/mypage.html, but because poisontooth.com is a Linux box, this URL will not work. As a matter of fact, this URL is impossible to access under some combinations of HTTP server and Web browser software. Some might let you access http://www.poisontooth.com/"my secret directory"/mypage.html, but this URL isn't guaranteed to work, either. In this case, the creation of a directory with spaces in the name is really the error—one frequently caused by Macintosh or Windows drag-and-drop Web site creation tools and users who just drop a chunk of their directory tree onto the Web. This problem can creep up and bite you with FTP, as well as with HTTP. Some FTP servers allow spaces in names, and some don't. Some are odd in that they allow spaces in names you're downloading, but won't accept spaces in names for upload. Your users can become quickly perplexed when documents they create on their PCs are refused when they try to upload them to the department's server. If you get the complaint, "I drag my documents onto the server icon, and only some of them show up on the server," you should suspect spaces in filenames. (Consider other odd characters as potential culprits, too—UNIX doesn't really appreciate much other than lower- and uppercase A–Z, numbers, dashes, underscores, and periods in filenames.)

There are plenty more opportunities for user typos and confusion resulting from user errors. Keep this type of error in mind whenever a user tells you that the network isn't working.

Diagnosing Configuration Errors

Although it is impossible to cover every potential configuration problem you might encounter, a handful of common configuration problems will cause similar problems in any TCP/IP program you are using.

Duplicate IP Addresses

If your machine gives you a startup error that says that you're duplicating an existing IP or that someone is duplicating your IP address (shown in Figure 22.1), you're either going to have to find another IP address or track down the person who's also using the same IP address.

FIGURE 22.1

This Windows machine has a duplicate IP address!

Resolving this type of issue is a task for your network administrator, who needs some software that can watch the network and correlate IP addresses with MAC (machine hardware physical) addresses and, ideally, a database of who has which MAC address on your subnet. The software in Chapter 21, "Using SNMP and Other Diagnostic Tools to Monitor Your Network," might be able to help you. Take a look! Of course, if you're using Dynamic Host Configuration Protocol (DHCP), then you may have a serious problem with your server. Check your leases file and make sure that an IP address hasn't been leased twice! Most likely you're going to find that one of your users has decided to become a network administrator for his or her own machine and has chosen an IP address that is also being served by your DHCP server.

Nameserver Configuration Errors

If you try to access a hostname and you get an Unknown Host or No Such Host or Domain Name error, there are three likely causes of the problem: (1) human error, as was discussed earlier, (2) the hostname simply doesn't exist, and (3) your nameserver isn't returning useful information regarding the name.

I'm Having ping Problems

When I try to ping biosci.ohio-state.edu, I get ping: unknown host biosci.ohio-state.edu *errors, but I can still send mail to someuser@biosci.ohio-state.edu. What's going on?*

Mail is, in many ways, a special case. You want your users to be able to send mail from their own machines, and as you saw earlier, the SMTP dialog sends out the mail as coming from username@usersmachine.subdomain.topdomain. Because mail comes addressed from a multitude of machines on a subnet and you don't want to have to run mail servers to receive replies on all those machines, there has to be a special way to handle mail. There must be a way of routing replies to a machine different from the one specified in the From: address. Nameserver MX records (Mail eXchanger records) handle this trick. If you look up the MX record for a hostname, you will see which machine actually is receiving mail for that hostname. To find out what's going on with biosci.ohio-state.edu, you can use the following code:

```
> nslookup
Default Server:  ns1.net.ohio-state.edu
Address:  128.146.1.7
> set querytype=MX
> biosci.ohio-state.edu
Server:  ns1.net.ohio-state.edu
Address:  128.146.1.7
biosci.ohio-state.edu   preference = 10,mail exchanger =
catbert.biosci.ohio-state.edu
catbert.biosci.ohio-state.edu   inet address = 140.254.12.236
```

What you see in the example is that a machine named catbert.biosci.ohio-state.edu actually handles the mail that is sent to biosci.ohio-state.edu. This is a very good thing, as biosci.ohio-state.edu isn't even a machine; it's just a domain name!

You can't do much about a hostname that doesn't exist—some hosts and domains pop up and go back down like a jack-in-the-box, so it shouldn't be too surprising when you hit a hostname that isn't there anymore. On occasion, whatever you're looking for might have changed its name to something similar, and you might be able to guess it. For example, if you're trying to access http://corona.biosci.ohio-state.edu/~genomes, you might have luck accessing http://www.biosci.ohio-state.edu/~genomes. In the early days of the World Wide Web, people set up Web servers on whatever machine they had handy and then renamed many of these machines to www.whatever when the Web started becoming more popular. If you absolutely must find a host, that is, you've convinced yourself that it's out there, but that you've either been given the wrong name or that the name has been changed, you can get a bit adventurous and do a little digging around with nslookup.

The process for trying to find a missing hostname is the same as the process for dealing with a broken nameserver, so we'll go over both here. Let's pretend you're trying to get to a Web page located at http://corona.biosci.ohio-state.edu/~genomes. This, in fact, used to be the URL for a database hosted here at Ohio State University College of Biological Sciences. The database still exists, but instead of being carried on a private machine from inside the college, it's been moved to the official college server. So you entered http://corona.biosci.ohio-state.edu/~genomes in our Web browser, and it said, No such host or domain name--check the URL and try again. Trying again hasn't done any good, and you really want to find this page…so what do you do?

First, remember when we mentioned Internic and how you can look up every registered domain through Internic? Well, let's start by assuming that your local nameserver might just be confused, and its name table might be out of date. Now you would go to Internic to find out where to get authoritative name information.

Guessing that the biosci.ohio-state.edu domain might still exist, even if corona.biosci.ohio-state.edu doesn't, let's try using whois to get a bit more information. Remember that if you don't have the appropriate software installed, you can use the Internic Web page to run whois.

```
> whois biosci.ohio-state.edu@internic.net
[internic.net]No match for "BIOSCI.OHIO-STATE.EDU".The InterNIC Registration
Services database contains ONLYnon-military and non-US Government Domains and
contacts.
Other associated whois servers:
   American Registry for Internet Numbers - whois.arin.net
   European IP Address Allocations        - whois.ripe.net
   Asia Pacific IP Address Allocations    - whois.apnic.net
   US Military                            - whois.nic.mil
   US Government                          - whois.nic.gov
```

Okay, so you've determined that biosci.ohio-state.edu isn't registered by itself…how about ohio-state.edu?

```
> whois ohio-state.edu@internic.net
[internic.net]
Registrant:Ohio State University (OHIO-STATE-DOM)    Academic Technology Services
1971 Neil Avenue - Room 406
   Columbus, OH 43210-1210


   Domain Name: OHIO-STATE.EDU

   Administrative Contact:
      Collins, Clifford A  (CAC5)  collins@NET.OHIO-STATE.EDU
      614-292-6180 (FAX) 614-292-7081
   Technical Contact:
      Steele, Greg E  (GS213)  steele@MPS.OHIO-STATE.EDU
      (614) 728-8100x203 (FAX) (614) 728-8110
   Zone Contact:
      Romig, Steven M  (SR27)  romig@NET.OHIO-STATE.EDU
      1-614-688-3412 (work) 1-614-263-7663 (ho (FAX) 614-292 614-263-7663 (FAX)
1-614-292-7081
```

```
Record last updated on 06-Jan-97.
Record created on 18-Aug-87.
Database last updated on 11-Oct-98 04:20:45 EDT.

Domain servers in listed order:

NS1.NET.OHIO-STATE.EDU        128.146.1.7
NS2.NET.OHIO-STATE.EDU        128.146.48.7
NCNOC.NCREN.NET               192.101.21.1
UUCP-GW-1.PA.DEC.COM          16.1.0.18 204.123.2.18
UUCP-GW-2.PA.DEC.COM          16.1.0.19
NS1.UCSD.EDU                  128.54.16.2


The InterNIC Registration Services database contains ONLY
non-military and non-US Government Domains and contacts.
Other associated whois servers:
   American Registry for Internet Numbers - whois.arin.net
   European IP Address Allocations        - whois.ripe.net
   Asia Pacific IP Address Allocations    - whois.apnic.net
   US Military                            - whois.nic.mil
   US Government                          - whois.nic.gov
```

Wow! That's a bit better. Now you know where to turn for authoritative information on the domain. Let's move and check whether OSU knows about corona.biosci.ohio-state.edu or whether that hostname really doesn't exist.

First, you can check nslookup to see whether OSU's nameservers know about corona. You should use OSU's primary nameserver to check this.

```
> nslookup
Default Server:  pantera.columbus.rr.comAddress:  204.210.252.250
      (that's not what you want, so change it now)> server 128.146.1.7
Default Server:  ns1.net.ohio-state.eduAddress:  128.146.1.7

      (that's more like it!)> set querytype=ANY
  (we want any info we can get!)
> corona.biosci.ohio-state.edu
Server:  ns1.net.ohio-state.edu
Address:  128.146.1.7
*** ns1.net.ohio-state.edu can't find    corona.biosci.ohio-state.edu: Non-
existent host/domain
```

Corona really doesn't seem to exist—where to now? Now you check for something that looks like corona might have been renamed to.

```
> ls biosci.ohio-state.edu
ls biosci.ohio-state.edu[ns1.net.ohio-state.edu] biosci.ohio-state.edu.
server = ns2.net.ohio-state.edu        biosci.ohio-state.edu.        server =
ns1.net.ohio-state.edu
 suzie                       140.254.12.99
 hannah                      140.254.14.21
 zeus                        140.254.12.81
 djc                         140.254.14.119
 duster                      128.146.250.16
 fiero                       140.254.52.40
  ...
```

```
zac                         140.254.14.67
rosalyn                     140.254.12.151
kek2                        140.254.12.103
vespa                       128.146.250.30
jimmac                      140.254.14.136
bosmina                     140.254.14.27
bigmac                      140.254.14.93
```

Nothing looks too promising here. I don't see www listed. Maybe we should go ahead, play a hunch, and see whether it exists.

```
> www.biosci.ohio-state.edu
Server:  ns1.net.ohio-state.edu
Address:  128.146.1.7www.biosci.ohio-state.edu        canonical name =
rosalyn.biosci.ohio-state.edu> exit
```

Ahh! So there's a possibility at least. If they had an old machine named corona and sent that name away, there's no reason to expect that www is a real machine either. From the information here, you see that www.biosci.ohio-state.edu is an alias (CNAME) to rosalyn.biosci.ohio-state.edu. So now you can try connecting to http://www.biosci.ohio-state.edu/~genomes/, or, if for some reason you still get the Host Not Found error, look back there at the list of machines for biosci.ohio-state.edu and find rosalyn. It happens to be 140.254.12.151, so try http://140.254.12.151/~genomes/; with luck, you will find what you're looking for. Figure 22.2 shows the fruits of your effort!

Remember, if your nameserver doesn't work when you try to get to a host, but other nameservers give proper information about this host, your nameserver is probably broken. In that case, you should try setting the nameserver in your TCP/IP configuration to a nameserver that actually gives the right answer.

FIGURE 22.2
Searching for a Web page pays off!

A different name server–related problem can be the cause of extremely slow network performance. If you're experiencing unusually slow connections or extremely long delays when trying to connect to remote machines, you should check to see whether your primary nameserver is working. Look in your TCP/IP connection settings to see what nameserver is listed first—this entry is usually the nameserver consulted first when your machine tries to look up a hostname. Try pinging this nameserver…or better yet, try using it to nslookup a name for you.

For example, let's say that you're trying to connect to www.poisontooth.com, and although the connections are getting through, they're taking much longer than they should. Check your nameserver configuration (see Chapter 5, "Configuring Client Workstations," for where this information is set on your system), and then use this nameserver for a nslookup query. If your primary nameserver was nisca.ohio-state.edu, you would issue the following commands:

```
>nslookup
Server:  ns2.net.ohio-state.eduAddress:  128.146.48.7
> server nisca.acs.ohio-state.edu
Default Server:  nisca.acs.ohio-state.eduAddress:  128.146.1.7
> www.poisontooth.com
Server:  nisca.acs.ohio-state.eduAddress:  128.146.1.7Non-authoritative answer:
Name:    poisontooth.dyn.ml.orgAddress:  140.254.85.38Aliases:
www.poisontooth.com
```

If nisca.acs.ohio-state.edu took a long time to return an answer to your query regarding www.poisontooth.com, this is probably the cause of your apparent network delays. Whenever you make a connection to a machine by name, the nameserver is consulted, and if it is under a heavy load, the nameserver may take a while to respond to you.

Another possible outcome of this test is that your primary nameserver (nisca in this example) never responds to your query. In this case, your primary nameserver is either down or failing. As a result, any connection you try to make ends up waiting for the primary nameserver to time out. After the primary times out, a secondary nameserver is consulted. If the secondary answers, you will experience another long delay while attempting to open connections. However, if your secondary nameserver is running properly (check it using the same nslookup test you just tried), you can speed things up again by simply setting your secondary (functional) nameserver as your primary nameserver. This step may require a reboot to take effect.

Router Configuration Errors

If you can contact machines on your local network, but can't access machines outside your subnet, chances are you're either missing a default route or that your default route is misconfigured. There's not much to diagnose here. Check your TCP/IP configuration (see Chapter 5) and make certain that the information agrees with the default router for your network. Remember that with most operating systems, you need to reboot to make any changed information active.

Subnet Mask Configuration Errors

A misconfigured subnet mask is the cause of a seemingly bizarre problem that confuses users to no end. However, when you understand the symptoms, it's an easy problem to diagnose. The most obvious symptom is that the user's machine can connect to most machines on the Internet in general, but can't seem to connect to machines on the local subnet to which it's attached. This problem usually comes to the network administrator's attention like this: A user offers the administrator a list of machines that he or she cannot connect to and asks whether the building network is down because he or she can connect to machines outside the building. When you hear that, you should immediately think subnet mask. Remember, if your subnet is a class C subnet, your subnet mask should be 255.255.255.0. If your subnet is anything else, you really should be asking your network administrator for some help because you're likely to make the administrator angry if you go fiddling around with these things without asking.

Diagnosing Software Errors

The potential for errors in your application software is great. An entire book on the subject would only begin to brush the surface of determining whether your particular application is experiencing a problem.

Realize that software authors have an enormous number of opportunities to accidentally introduce bugs. (A bug is, according to most programmers, simply an undocumented feature. Some bugs, however, would be undesired features, even if documented.) For example, your Web browser has literally millions of commands it must execute to display a Web page for you. All these commands must work together perfectly, and any errors can cause them to interact in incorrect and unpredictable fashions.

Even with the huge number of places that a piece of software can go wrong, you can perform several quick checks to at least get a feel for whether your software is a potential source of your problem.

- Do other machines on the same subnet (and especially other machines connected near the machine in question) experience the same problem? If you can duplicate your error on other machines, chances are it isn't that specific machine or its software.

- Do other similar applications on the machine experience the same problem? If Internet Explorer gets an error trying to access a Web page, try another version…or better yet, try Netscape. If all the browsers you can lay your hands on bring up identical errors, it's probably not the browser's fault.

- Do other general applications on the machine experience the same problem? If you're having name service problems with FTP, do other programs on your machine create similar troubles?

- Does ping or trace route find the host that your FTP client cannot? If all your software is experiencing the same problem, then you're probably looking at a system-level problem, rather than a problem with a specific application. However, this condition doesn't rule out an error at an operating system level. Thankfully, you're not likely to be the first person to find an operating system problem. Chances are pretty good that hundreds or thousands of people have probably run into the same thing before, and with the advent of the World Wide Web, they have a free forum in which to complain. If you suspect an operating system error, find a machine with which you can browse the Web and hit a search engine or two to see whether anyone has already found and fixed your problem. If you can't find anyone else complaining about your particular problem, you probably have some form of configuration problem rather than an actual program error.

■ Do you experience the same problem with any remote machine? If you're having trouble telnetting to one remote host, do you have the same trouble with all remote machines, or just with a particular machine? Maybe it's not your machine that's having a problem. If the problem occurs only with a particular group of remote machines, it probably relates to those machines as a group. It could be something like a routing problem or perhaps a problem with the name service providing for that subdomain. When checking remote machines to verify the existence of the problem, remember to check machines both in and outside your local subnet. Problems either entirely in your subnet or entirely outside your subnet are possibly configuration related (remember to check that subnet mask!), or they could possibly be router related.

Diagnosing Cabling Problems

To understand what to do, and what to look for when considering the potential for cabling problems, it is important to consider the potential sources of trouble with your wiring. Wiring generates network problems when it either introduces signals that shouldn't be there—via leaking them from outside or via the creation of internal reflections of the signal—or when it attenuates the signal that should be there to such an extent that the signal disappears. Noise signals can leak into cable two ways. The first is when the signal directly enters the cable because of contact with some noise-generating piece of equipment. That can include anything from electric motors, wiring, and computer equipment to just about anything that uses or carries electrical power—all such devices generate some amount of electrical noise. The second way noise signals can leak into a cable is by induction (the coupling of electric signals through space) from a sufficiently noisy, powerful source. Noise is generated internally to your network wiring when reflections are generated by impedance mismatches, missing terminators, or even sharp kinks in the cable.

Sharp Kinks! Are You Serious?

Yup—a sharp bend in a wire causes what is called "work hardening" at the bend. (Take a paperclip, straighten it out, and then put a sharp bend in the middle—be sure to make it as sharp a bend as possible. Now try to straighten it out again. Difficult, huh? That's because the section that you bent sharply is work hardened.) Work hardening causes a change in the crystal structure of the metal, which, in turn, causes an impedance discontinuity at the bend. Wiring destined for carrying high-bandwidth datastreams really does need to be treated rather gently.

Attenuation occurs when the signal must pass through a region of abnormally high impedance. This condition can be caused by breaks or near breaks in the electrical conductor (frequently caused by repeated bending of the cable), by corrosion of contacts, or by other contamination of contact surfaces.

Network problems related to wiring usually affect all the machines in direct electrical proximity to the problem. In the case of 10BASE-2 (thinnet coaxial cabling) networks, *direct proximity* generally means any machine on the same wiring segment. In the case of twisted pair networks, the problem might be localized to one branch of the network, or it might affect the entire subnet on which the problem segment is located. Using software to diagnose cabling problems is an iffy proposition at best. There are a few things to test first that might help you decide whether the problem is really a network problem before you start replacing every suspicious-looking piece of wire and connector in your network.

Part

V

Ch

22

Isn't There a Better Way to Do This?

Yes, there are two ways you can increase your chances at localizing the problem. First, and least likely, buy yourself a wiring and protocol tester—you'll save yourself so much grief that your sanity will thank me, even if your wallet won't. Second, put together a pair of Linux machines that you can wheel around your network and use as probe machines. You can insert them at two different points in your network, disconnect the rest of the network, and run diagnostics between the Linux boxes to check the integrity of the network segment between them. By strategically moving the Linux machines around your network, you can diagnose large portions of your network at once. It also helps you to localize the problem to specific segments much more quickly than is possible by the "test, examine, replace, repeat" routine that is necessary without either the right tool or without a pair of test machines.

Netstat

Issuing the command `netstat -i` on most TCP/IP-enabled servers returns significant information about the ongoing behavior of your network. Let's look at the information returned by running this command on one of the servers at OSU.

```
> netstat -i

Name  Mtu   Net/Dest     Address     Ipkts    Ierrs Opkts   Oerrs Collis Queue
le0   1500  140.254.12.0 catbert     1780278  26    741691  3     11333  0
lo0   1536  loopback     localhost   159077   0     159077  0     0      0
```

The information on the `le0` line tells describes the network. Specifically, it says that out of 1,780,278 input packets, 26 have had some sort of damage that made the contents unrecoverable. Out of 741,691 packets written to the network by this machine, there were three problems writing to the network, which weren't collisions. Both `Ierrs` and `Oerrs` should be very small numbers—26 input errors actually is quite a lot and suggests that something is wrong with this building's network. The fact that `Ierrs` is significantly larger than `Oerrs` indicates something relatively "remote" to this machine is likely to be the problem. In other words, something is corrupting data bound for this machine well before the data reaches the machine. If there were a problem with the network interface or with the cable directly connected to this computer, you would expect the machine to experience problems writing data at roughly the same rate as it experiences problems receiving data. A large number of collisions, 11,333 in this case, is to be expected. As you learned earlier, collisions are a part of TCP/IP network life. To determine whether you're having too many collisions, check the percentage of collisions to total output packets. In this case 11,333/741,691 = 1.5 percent—quite reasonable and indicative that this network is only moderately loaded. If your network shows 5 percent or more collisions, however, you should start to be worried. Collision rates increase rapidly above 5 percent or so because re-sent packets collide more frequently with other re-sent packets. A collision rate higher than 10 percent indicates a network that is seriously overloaded, and one that is quickly on the way to being unusable due to the volume of data being repeatedly re-sent. The figures returned by the previous form of netstat give information on the performance of the network since the network interface was brought up. Specify a time interval with netstat to get a more dynamic view of the network—and possibly to see problems that are generated as a result of running other commands that make use of the network. With a time interval of Z seconds specified, every Z seconds netstat reports data on the behavior it has observed in that time frame. On catbert, our previous sample machine, `netstat -i 5` returns the following data:

```
> netstat -i 5

       input   (le0)     output            input   (Total)    output
packets errs  packets errs  colls  packets errs  packets errs  colls
1787401 26     742979 3      11338  1946632 26     902210 3      11338
9       0      1       0     0      9       0      1      0      0
2       0      1       0     0      2       0      1      0      0
1168    0      4       0     0      1168    0      4      0      0
10      0      1       0     0      10      0      1      0      0
26      0      2       0     0      26      0      2      0      0
```

Each line of data (other than the first) is the data for the network behavior in the last 5 seconds. As you can see, on line 4 (time period 10 to 15 seconds) the machine shows a significant number of input packets: 1,168 packets input. This is due to running a packet-generating command on another machine on the network to stir things up a little.

Spray

Specifically, on a different machine on the same subnet, we ran

```
> spray catbert
sending 1162 packets of lnth 86 to catbert ...
in 10.4 seconds elapsed time,        624 packets (53.70%) dropped
Sent:   111 packets/sec, 9.4K bytes/sec
Rcvd:   51 packets/sec, 4.4K bytes/sec
```

Hmmm! Well, you can see where our 1,168 packets input came from (1,162 plus some additional random network traffic). The interesting thing though is the line that says 624 packets (53.70 %) dropped. There's something wrong here! We sent out 1,162 packets, catbert acknowledged getting what appears to be all of them, (netstat unfortunately doesn't report the echoed response packets as output packets) but only 538 of the packets made it back. Also interesting is the fact that the send rate is twice the receive rate (and just so you know, both of these rates are lousy. It's 11:00 p.m. in the evening, the building network is barely loaded, and we're getting transmission rates just over that of a good modem—wonderful network we're looking at here!). Let's try the same thing from another machine:

```
> spray catbert.biosci.ohio-state.edu

sending 1162 packets of lnth 86 to catbert.biosci.ohio-state.edu ...

in 0.7 seconds elapsed time,        no packets dropped       1706 packets/sec,
143.3K bytes/sec
```

Hey…that's more like it! Problem is, this command was run on a machine that's about a mile away from catbert—one in a different building on the other side of campus! We had no packets dropped (which is good), and we received a transmission rate that is roughly one-sixth of the maximum possible rate of our network (not bad for a campus the size of Ohio State). For me to get one-sixth of the available bandwidth between opposite ends of the campus is really quite good! So what do we learn from this exercise? We know that something is very, very wrong. Between two machines on the same network, we get slow transmission rates, and we lose quite a few packets. Spray reports packets dropped when the receiving machine can't keep up with the sending machine. But in this case, catbert can more than adequately deal with the network traffic (and demonstrates this capability both by dealing with data much faster when sent from a more distant machine and by registering all the incoming packets via netstat). Interestingly, we can tell that the data gets to catbert from both remote machines, but it seems to fail to return to one of them. This evidence actually indicates that, in the case of this "sick network," the problem is not with the wiring: Wiring problems are not usually direction dependent. Unfortunately, I can't walk you through finding and fixing the problem with this network, as it is one of those networks that drives its administrator and users nuts due to lack of proper diagnostic hardware. This is just another piece of evidence of the bizarre behavior of some networks and network hardware. If there had actually been a wiring problem, you would expect to see high Input and/or Output errors via netstat, and you're likely to see high packet loss via spray, in both directions. Also, the number of packets that spray shows as returning properly should roughly correlate to the number of packets that netstat shows as arriving at the target machine. Obviously, if 40 percent of the packets return according to spray, you should expect that roughly half of the lost packets got lost on the way to the target and half got lost on the way back. So, don't be surprised if netstat reports more packets arriving (but less than the total sent) at the target than spray reports arriving back at the test machine.

If you're experiencing a problem and suspect it's a cabling issue, you'd do well to start with a quick visual survey of your network wiring. Without a wiring tester, you're not going to be able to locate wiring faults by anything other than luck and guesswork. You'll get a quick introduction here to a few tools that can indicate whether your wiring might be having problems, but then you are on your own for finding the problem.

If you have 10BASE-2 cabling, find your terminators—50 percent of the time your network problems involve a terminator that evaporated. Also, check for corroded BNC connectors. Leaky plumbing and roofs, as well as overflowing sinks, have an annoying tendency to target network connectors.

Check to see whether an orphaned BNC "T" or barrel connector has come in contact with the metal chassis of some piece of equipment. The cases of many pieces of equipment are electrically noisy, and you can introduce significant electrical noise into your network if one of the metal shields on your BNC connectors comes in contact with any piece of equipment that is plugged into an AC power line.

Check to see whether a section of network cabling is wrapped around a wire that carries AC current. Although both coaxial cable and twisted pair are fairly good at rejecting electrical interference, they are not impervious. Many networks are implemented by dragging cabling around above dropped-ceiling tiles. In these installations, some network problems can frequently be eliminated by simply rearranging the path of the wire over the ceiling, eliminating or changing its contacts with the pre-existing power and lighting grid.

BNC Connectors Are Bad News

Wow, you might be saying, that's a whole lot of problems with BNC connectors. And you're probably wondering if they are really that bad?

Ummm—yes! Coaxial cable and BNC connectors are the bane of many a network administrator. Your ability to diagnose network problems is much better with twisted pair because you can conveniently pare off branches of the TP network until you isolate the problem, effectively walking right to the culprit machine or network segment in very few tries. TP experiences fewer failures as well because of the lack of exposed metal contacts and the relative robustness of the connection.

You'd be wise to check for the following culprits: twist-on BNC connectors that aren't twisted on and screw-together-to-clamp BNC connectors that have unscrewed. Other trouble spots are BNC connectors designed for thick-shielding wire installed on thin-shielding cable (these allow extra stress on the electrical components and frequently end up with the center conductor broken just inside the BNC connector) and, of course, the ever-missing terminators. If you have a twisted-pair network, you have fewer potential failure points and a much more easily diagnosed network topology. With the star topology of a TP network, you can simply go to your central hub and disconnect branches until the problem disappears. If you can isolate the problem to a particular branch, go to the hub on that branch (check to make certain it hasn't experienced any local rain showers lately) and start the routine again. With very few steps, you should be able to isolate your problem to a particular machine, piece of TP wiring, or hub. Replace whichever happens to be the case, and you're back in business!

Of course, if the problem disappears with the disconnection of any branch, or doesn't disappear even if you try disconnecting everything, you've probably proven that your network cabling isn't the problem.

Diagnosing Network Hardware (Other Than Cabling) Problems

Network hardware is particularly difficult to diagnose and is one area in which a protocol tester and a wiring tester are almost mandatory. The reason for the difficulty is that errors here can occur at less obvious layers of the network model. Routers can be damaging packet contents, gateways can be mistranslating protocols— both conditions are very difficult to diagnose without the ability to actually examine the integrity of packets and their contents conveniently across your entire network. Try rebooting or resetting your routers or smart switches (and checking your hardware to make certain that it's all still plugged in and hasn't been soaked recently by a leaking pipe). Beyond that, the only real suggestions that can be made at this level are to suspect network hardware when you have eliminated everything else. In the preceding netstat and spray examples, the problem may very well be hardware related. The building contains several antique (pre-1990!) repeaters and other assorted hardware that has never been well tested. Any one of these pieces of hardware could be selectively damaging packets as they are passed about the building. If the packets coming from outside the building don't have to pass through this piece of hardware, they won't be affected, but the packets passing through it internally will possibly be damaged. Pretty good theory, isn't it? But I wish I could find that flaky repeater!

The Right Way To Do Things

The proper way (and best way, if you value your sanity) to diagnose network problems is to get yourself a protocol analyzer and cable tester. These wonderful pieces of hardware can be hooked up to your network and can tell you, literally to the inch, the location of physical faults in your network. The better units can resolve multiple discrete physical faults that occur within a few inches of each other and give their distance along the network wiring from the test set to the nearest inch. Protocol analyzers can inject traffic of greatly varied types into your network. By injecting the traffic at one point and monitoring it at another, the analyzers can tell you what traffic is possibly being damaged, what traffic is passing through unimpeded, and what potential combinations of network traffic can cause the problem to manifest itself.

If you have a large network to administrate, access to a protocol analyzer and cable tester is invaluable in diagnosing and fixing network problems. I can't stress this point strongly enough. Software tools can begin to lead you in the direction of a problem after considerable testing and consideration, but in the end, you may never find the problem. With a protocol analyzer and a wiring tester (some come as combo units, some as separate pieces), you will be able to move across your network at almost a walking pace, tracking your way to the problem.

TCP/IP: Present and Future

Part 6 wraps up our look at TCP/IP by briefly discussing the do's and don'ts behind administrating a network. There are certain rules that you should follow to provide your users with an enjoyable computing experience. Some are common sense, others are learned from experience. Learn the ethics behind administrating a TCP/IP network today, than get a glimpse at what the future of TCP/IP holds.

23 Using and Administering Your Network Ethically 457

24 The Future of TCP/IP: IPng 467

Using and Administering Your Network Ethically

by John Ray

In this chapter

Bandwidth **458**

Information Sharing **461**

Information Privacy **465**

Don't Worry, We All Make Mistakes **466**

You've got yourself a network, or you're using a network, but are you being a good *netizen*? There are some rules to using networks that you may or may not be familiar with. Most of the rules are not enforced or even enforceable; it's up to your good conscience to do the right thing and contribute positively to the network community.

What Is a Netizen?

A *netizen* is an Internet term for *Network Citizen*. Much as the real world has citizens in a social structure, so does the network. You need to learn how to be a good netizen!

Perhaps the best place to start when discussing network ethics is to talk about what *not* to do rather than what *to* do. The network is a resource that must be managed; it cannot be taken for granted or exploited. So what are the parts of a network that can be misused? Let's divide the network up into three pieces:

- Bandwidth—This is the physical part of the network: how much data the network can carry. You have the ability to use it all, but shouldn't everyone have an equal share?

- Information Sharing—The primary purpose of a network is sharing information; what you choose to do with the information is another thing.

- Information Privacy—Network administrators have quite a bit of power at their hands and control information that might be very personal to users.

Now that we've got these three areas to focus on, let's look at them in detail. Much of this is my opinion and the general norms that are followed by the Internet community. You can certainly disagree with what I have to say, but don't jump headfirst into things. If your network is connected to the Internet, the consequences of your decisions might affect thousands of people. When you tick-off a few thousand people and have them start attacking your network and sending you hundreds of pieces of email, you'll quickly learn what you should and shouldn't do—but hopefully it won't get to that point.

Bandwidth

You use your network…you like it. You decide that you want to use it more…and more… Soon you start to notice that you don't have quite the same sort of speed that you used to have. You're using the network to its capacity. This might be fine for you, and you might be able to live with the decrease in speed, but what about the rest of the people on your network? It's easy to look at the latest and greatest network goodies and put them to use on your network, but are they really necessary, or are you using them for their gee-whiz value?

For example, the latest "cool thing" to do is create Web pages that are full of multimedia. We have radio stations streaming music, television networks streaming video, ActiveX and Java applications running everywhere. You've probably been to many Web pages, looked at the fancy graphics, and said, "Boy, this is pretty, but it sure takes a long time to load!" If you run your own server, you probably feel that you need to keep up with the latest trends in order to draw customers to our Web site. Don't be drawn into this trap! The best Web site delivers the most information in the most straightforward fashion without making the user wait. It's fun to look at the cool stuff, but it rarely makes it onto my bookmark list.

The first thing that most Web servers want to add is some sort of Webcam. Streaming video over the Web is very much in vogue these days; however, it also uses a significant amount of bandwidth. What might be fun for a few people could be slowing down the network for everyone. If you're using a large portion of your network's bandwidth for serving, you might want to look into something like switched Ethernet for your network. Using switches on your network will let you separate your Web (or other) traffic from the internal network traffic. This, in turn, would enable your internal workgroups to have full network bandwidth within their workgroup. Unfortunately, this does not solve the larger problem of a network where all the computers need to communicate to an outside network.

Know your network. Do not assume that the traffic you create is minimal. I have run simple backups to a networked tape drive that have spiked network bandwidth measurements and slowed down both web and email access. There was nothing exciting about the backups. It was just a remote copy of files between machines; however, it was enough to push network traffic beyond reasonable levels. If you don't know what services are running on your network, find out. Make sure you know what the requirements of the other users are before you determine what you're going to run.

Network bandwidth can be looked at like a limited resource. You can measure the amount of bandwidth certain types of traffic use and then determine how much will be needed for your applications. It isn't a situation where you can keep adding on forever; once you've used up your resources, you're going to need to buy a higher bandwidth connection or re-evaluate your needs. One of the biggest mistakes that can be made when creating a network is the assumption that network bandwidth usage is linear. Most software that measures bandwidth usage measures it on a scale from 1 to 100. It's impossible to actually achieve 100 percent bandwidth usage. Think of it as trying to achieve the speed of light. To achieve the speed of light, you need to expend energy to accelerate. Unfortunately, the closer you get to the speed of light, the more energy you need to expend. The end result is that to travel at the speed of light, you need to expend an infinite amount of energy. In the case of using network bandwidth, you need to fill the wire completely with a constant stream of packets. What happens as more and more machines contribute to the stream of packets? Collisions. The more collisions, the less data can be transmitted. So the closer to 100 percent usage, the more collisions, and the slower the bandwidth, usage increases. Trying to run network software with bandwidth usage over 60 percent is painful; anything over 75 percent, and your network is at a standstill. No data is moving anywhere because your collision rate has reached 100 percent.

Figure 23.1 shows the bandwidth usage of a typical network. On a particularly bad day, a printer was misconfigured in one of the buildings on campus. The printer proceeded to broadcast data so quickly that network usage reached new highs. At the time, all traffic was passed between all of the buildings on Ag Campus. The broadcast data literally froze computers across campus. Until the device causing the broadcast storm was located, my only advice to people was to disconnect their computers from the network.

FIGURE 23.1.

Bandwidth is typically measured as a percentage. Normal network usage should be relatively low.

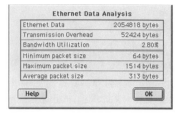

Ethernet Data Analysis	
Ethernet Data	2054818 bytes
Transmission Overhead	52424 bytes
Bandwidth Utilization	2.80%
Minimum packet size	64 bytes
Maximum packet size	1514 bytes
Average packet size	313 bytes

Help   OK

It's Not Really Impossible to Use 100 Percent of the Bandwidth, Is It?

In any reasonable network, yes, it is impossible for the very reasons I've discussed in the text. However, if a single machine is sending data over the network and no other computer is using the wire, then it should be theoretically possible to use 100 percent of the bandwidth. The data transfer would have to use a protocol with no error checking packets, which is also extremely unlikely—but, once again, possible.

On a typical network, the usage may never rise above 10 percent. Our buildings on campus show an average activity level of around 2 to 4 percent—or even less. This does not mean that the network is being under used. It's actually being used efficiently. Our Web servers average well over a million hits per month, and our graphic artists and publishers transfer many megabytes of files back and forth to the file servers each day. Yet, we still maintain very reasonable usage levels.

Low bandwidth usage makes it very easy to notice when things are going wrong with your network. Knowing what we know about our network at OSU, I can check for anomalies in the network traffic and seek out the cause. For example, we maintain 2 to 4 percent bandwidth usage with an occasional spike at around 15 percent. Interestingly enough, one would figure that activity spikes would occur during the "busy" portions of the day. Over the past several years, I've collected rather extensive statistics on our network and have determined that the most network activity occurs between 11:30 a.m. and 1:30 p.m.—approximately the same time people have lunch. My only guess is that during the lunch hour, people eat in front of their computers and surf the Net. Your results may vary, but I've been very impressed with the consistency of the results that I've found. At any rate, because of the known bandwidth usage on our network, I was able to identify that an account on a UNIX machine had been compromised and was being used as a pirate software storage site. After noticing usage spikes in the upper 50 percentile, I decided to trace what was causing all the traffic. I found that there were several outside machines that were talking to our main Web server on the FTP port. This led me to check the log files, which, in turn, revealed the account that had been compromised. A few calls to the owners of the account, a little bit of legwork, and a student found himself in a rather uncomfortable situation of his own creation. Keep a record of your own network activity because you might need it! It's very difficult to determine what is abnormal activity when you aren't entirely sure what normal activity is.

The point of all of this is that network bandwidth is a resource that must be managed like any other. You cannot simply add new applications running new protocols to your network without first seeing the effect they might have on your existing services.

Information Sharing

We live in the information age. We have access to the information super-highway. We're suffering from information overload. What does all of this mean? It means that with the advent of the computer network and the Internet in general, we now can access more information faster than ever before. This is wonderful! Personally, I've been able to find out about things that would have been very difficult without the Internet. I've shared information and ideas with people around the world, and I collaborate on programming projects with people I've never even met. If you're setting up a network, why are you doing it? To share information, of course! Whether you just want to surf the Web or publish scientific research, you're investing in information sharing.

In a perfect world, you'd be able to access the information you need and use it responsibly as you see fit. However, because of the global reaches of the Internet and the implications of the still young intellectual-property legislation, there are issues you must be aware of before you use or publish information across the network.

What Is Intellectual Property?

A program is a collection of bytes that sit on your floppy, CD-ROM, or hard drive. You own the physical device that's encoding the information, so you should own the program, right? Wrong. The software is the intellectual property of the publisher or programmer. Most likely (unless you've contracted for a program to be written), you only use a license to run the software. You are not allowed to copy it, share it, or modify it in any way.

What, exactly, do you have to worry about? *A lot.* Information that is obtained over the Internet is not necessarily "public domain" as you first might assume. You cannot just copy information from a Web page and use it as if it were your own. Text, Web graphics, and animations are all the intellectual property of the creator or the person who paid for their creation. As hard as it may be to believe, snagging a background graphic for your Web page could very well be stealing! To make matters even more complicated, linking to a graphic or Web page might also be against the law. This might sound a bit ludicrous, but, as you know, the Web was designed so that the physical location of data wasn't important. Using the URLs, you can link to images and data anywhere, from any other Web page. In the case of a Web graphic, it becomes a matter of how you're representing the graphic. You might not have "stolen" the graphic from someone's Web site, but you might be linking to it in a manner that is out of the context that the image was originally intended to be in. Sound complicated? It is.

Even more confusing, it may become troublesome to provide links to other people's Web pages themselves. Consider, for example, the Web search engines. Search engines rely on people visiting their Web sites and seeing the ads and extra features they have to offer. If you were to provide a quick-and-dirty form on your page that would enable a user to enter a search directly from your page, bypassing the main search engine homepage, this might constitute inappropriate use of someone else's resources. The laws (or lack thereof) governing the linking of information on the Internet are highly debated and are certainly likely to change rapidly in the upcoming months and years. The very scenario I've just described has recently played itself out in the development of Apple's new system software, Mac OS 8.5. System 8.5 includes a new find feature called Sherlock. Unlike previous find-file implementations, Sherlock extends its searching capabilities to the Internet and lets the user pick one or more prominent search engines to query when it looks for results. The results of the search are returned as a single list. This is great for the user but completely eliminates the need to ever visit a search engine page (am I the only one who never uses any of the extra stuff on the search engine pages?). Figure 23.2 shows the Sherlock feature in action.

FIGURE 23.2.

Sherlock lets you search the Internet without the hassle.

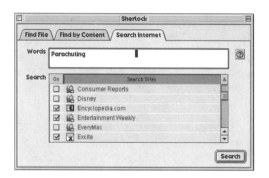

The Sherlock feature annoyed the search engine providers to the point where it seemed that the feature was in jeopardy of being scrapped. Apple negotiated with the search providers, and, apparently, their issues with the system were resolved. I'm not aware of the full details of the arrangements that were made, but considering that banners from the search engine pages are displayed along with the results, I could make a pretty good guess. Add to the mix new technologies such as Java, and the water gets even muddier. Java applications can be embedded on Web pages, can be linked to other Web pages, or downloaded to your hard drive. Just because a piece of software is available on a Web page doesn't mean it's free. A quick Save As… from within your Web browser, and you may have just committed software piracy.

Is It Safe to Do Anything?

Of course it is! Problems are caused by linking to pages inappropriately or by using graphics without the author's permission. How do you avoid these problems? Simple—just ask! Many Web sites contain guidelines about how to link to them, or contact information for the site authors. If you aren't sure if you should be using information, ask for permission. You might end up saving yourself worlds of grief.

If you're publishing data yourself, you should clearly post contact information for people who might like to use or reference your work. You might also want to consider becoming a part of the Open Content group, which defines a set of rules for using information from a particular site. The Open Content License (OCL) allows others to quote your work without asking permission. For more information about the OCL, check out their Web site at

http://www.opencontent.org/

If you publish on a daily basis, displaying the Open Content logo will probably save you considerable time answering email messages from people who want to use your information. The bottom-line: be careful, and always ask before you take. It's just common sense.

On the opposite end of information sharing, let's take a look at a very different problem: sharing too much information. The Internet has made it very easy to reach millions of people with your message. Unfortunately, what if the user isn't interested in receiving your message? If you're running a Web site, they simply don't bother going there. You might be tempted to buy email lists for the demographics you want to reach, and then use the lists to generate personalized email messages that you send out advertising products or services. If you do this, you've just become one of the lowest forms of Internet life: a spammer! Spamming is a very tempting thing to do. After all, you're reaching thousands of people, and if only a fraction of them read the message, it's still free advertising. For everyone else, however, you've just potentially wasted time and money. Think about it: You're sending out thousands of messages that thousands of people will have to download. If they're being charged for online usage, you're costing should reach a large number of people is best posted to a newsgroup or other public forum. Most spam messages are rather lengthy and are sent to a few thousand "harvested" email addresses at a time. This is eating up hundreds of megabytes of disk storage. If the email is targeted at the users of a specific ISP, it might fill the disk space of mail servers of the ISP. Not a good thing at all. You're not going to be making many friends if you take up spamming. In fact, spammers are one of the favorite targets of hackers. Once a spammer is identified and their servers are located, it's prime hunting season.

Another form of spamming is mailing-list spamming. Rather than collecting a list of email addresses, some people find open mailing lists (lists that anyone can post to) and send their advertisements to them instead. This is a quick and easy way to reach thousands of people without going through the trouble of collecting or buying email addresses. If you're a member of a mailing list, it's actually pretty easy to inadvertently spam the list. Posting off-topic information or replying to someone personally on the list is sometimes considered spam. Remember that whatever email you send will go to all of the people on the list. If you argue with someone on a list and it turns into a flame-fest, you're probably ticking off a whole group of people, not just the one you're arguing with.

What Is a Flame?

A *flame* is a "hot" piece of email. If you disagree strongly with what someone says, or just feel like throwing an insult their way, you flame them. Email lets everyone have an equal voice, so don't be surprised to see quiet people flaming up a storm. In some cases, flame wars can be quite fun, but in all cases, they should be kept away from mailing lists. I've sent a few flames by way of mailing lists before. Take my word for it—whatever you send will come back to you, tenfold.

If you choose to spam, may the Internet gods take pity on your soul. Respect the original goal of the Internet: to share information, not to force it down someone's throat. People like to exercise their power to make choices. You might want to set up a mailing list and give people the option of subscribing if they want to receive the information. This is another case of "just because you can do it, doesn't mean you should."

Lastly, I have a pet peeve I'd like to discuss: the use of non-standard standards on the Internet. It sccms that a common misconception is whatever you're using to create content on the Internet is the same thing that everyone else is using to both create and to look. HTML-based email clients are a great example. By default, OutLook Express uses HTML when it is sending email. Other email clients do this as well. Using HTML as an email format enables the user to include graphics, sounds, animations, and so on in their email. Anything that can be included on a Web page can be included in an email. The problem is, what if you aren't using an email client that includes the ability to view HTML? The answer is simple: You end up with a message that is filled with special HTML tags and characters and is rather difficult to read. It doesn't end there, however. Many people feel that word processors are a "standard" format on the Internet. It isn't uncommon for a message to be sent out on one of our mailing lists that is nothing but an attached WordPerfect or Microsoft Word document. I find this infuriating! Not only is a word processor a non-standard piece of software on my computer, but even if I did always have one installed, would it be the right one? Would it be the right version? Your guess is as good as mine.

Just a word of advice: If you must send styled text and graphics across the network, either make sure that everyone receiving the message is capable of displaying it in the format you've used or consider using the *PDF* or *Portable Document Format* developed by Adobe. The PDF format maintains fonts and graphics across Mac, Windows, and many UNIX platforms. To download a PDF viewer for your system or to find out more about the PDF format, browse over to Adobe's Web site at

`http://www.adobe.com/`

Remember, the backbone of the Internet is UNIX based. Those of us who sit in front of UNIX machines are used to being treated to fast, text-based applications. The flashy graphics and WordPerfect documents are meaningless to us! Try to respect and keep the original cross-platform spirit of the Internet alive. Even if the issue isn't one of being cross-platform, such as the case of using HTML in your email, it still is a matter of maintaining parity among platforms. I recently was called to look at a computer that was having email problems. It was running a rather old piece of email software called "nupop." It had literally been years since I had seen a nupop installation. Nupop is about as basic an email reader as you can get; it is DOS-character based and is not capable of handling attachments or any sort of styled text. Strangely enough, however, the person who was running this program was one of the largest contributors to our primary mailing list. He did not see any problem with his email client and actually resisted moving to a Windows-based product. This is precisely why you should never count on anyone having a particular product unless you've installed it yourself. People use software they like and need, and that doesn't necessarily match what you like or need.

Information Privacy

The last topic to discuss is information privacy. If you're managing your network, you're going to be storing information about your users. There's probably a darn good chance that the information is also private in nature. If you're running an email server, you have access to read all of your users' email (unless they know better and are using the PGP encryption technique discussed in Chapter 18, "Using Security Techniques to Protect Your Network and Data"). If you want to find out if your users are using email for work-related communication or if they're using it for personal messages, it would take a few seconds to scan through everyone's email and find out for yourself—but should you do it? I think the answer is pretty obvious. It's a decision that's based on your own views, but, if it were your email, I'm sure you wouldn't want other people reading through it. Even when people are having problems with their email, I do my best to look only at the messages necessary to solve the problem. There is a general misconception that email is "safe," at least once it reaches its destination. Unfortunately, the "final resting place" for email is probably when it's at its most vulnerable. Rather than "spy" on your users to make sure they're doing their jobs, define a network policy statement that explains what is considered appropriate and inappropriate use of the network. Allow leeway for some personal use of the network. If an employee is spending all day using his or her computer for personal correspondence, there is an obvious problem and the employee should be dealt with accordingly; no one, however, can claim that they are 100 percent innocent of never using company resources for personal business. I've said all along that the best way to get your users to treat the network with respect is to educate them about the capabilities of the network and your expectations for appropriate network use. Email is no different. I do my best to keep most of my personal email traffic limited to off-hours or lunch breaks, but I'm certainly guilty of having sent a few messages that I would feel a bit strange if someone other than the intended recipient had read. Treat your user's email with the same respect you would treat mail sent through the U.S. Postal Service. Opening "snail" mail that is not your own is a federal offense and a violation of privacy. Do not read or provide access to a user's email unless you're pretty certain that there has been a violation of your network use policies.

A second, more seductive practice might seem appealing instead: using packet sniffers and other diagnostic tools to watch your users. If you run a packet sniffer on your network, you can essentially watch anything that the users on your network are doing (email, Web sites, newsgroups, and so on), you can see all of the traffic as it goes by on the wire. I've spent some time doing this myself, because it's remarkably interesting to see both the amount of traffic and the way that people are using the network. Still, if you start actively logging the data and take the time to locate the sending machine for packets, you're still, in my opinion, invading the privacy of your users. Packet sniffers can be useful tools, but they also can be misused.

The bottom line? Respect your users. You can't expect everyone to completely ignore the outside world when they use your network. If you're providing access to the Internet, be prepared for your users to use the Internet. Email is a wonderful convenience, and it's assumed by most people to be a private happening. If you betray the trust of your users, you might find yourself in an awkward situation, and you'll likely be an unpopular figure around the office. If you feel that monitoring email activity is the only way to enforce the rules of the network, then, by all means, be sure to tell your users and supervisors of your intentions first!

Part

VI

Ch

23

Don't Worry, We All Make Mistakes

Don't worry too much if you happen to violate a few of the "network ethics" I've discussed in this chapter. There have been numerous times that I've made the mistake of misposting inappropriate material to a mailing list (just a flame or two). I've experimented with various programs and protocols that have been extremely costly in terms of the amount of network bandwidth that they use. It all goes with the territory. Use common sense, and everything will be okay!

## CHAPTER 24

The Future of TCP/IP: IPng

by John Ray

In this chapter

Enter IPv6 **469**

Addressing **469**

Simplified Headers **470**

Extensibility **472**

Security **473**

Quality of Service **473**

Transitioning to IPv6 **474**

Other Resources **475**

Wrapping It Up **475**

I'd like to say that you now know everything that there is to know about TCP/IP. Unfortunately, that wouldn't be true. In the past 20 chapters or so, you've scratched the surface of creating a useful and useable TCP/IP network from the ground up. You've looked at the hardware, protocols, and software that make it work. However, those topics are only a tiny subset of the big picture. As complete as I've tried to make this book, there is no single reference for TCP/IP, and there never will be. TCP/IP is an evolving standard that will continue to change and grow as long as computer networks remain a part of our lives. In fact, the very standard that we've looked at so far, IP version 4, is in the process of being replaced.

IPv4 is TCP/IP as we know it. From what we've talked about, you may not see any shortcomings in the protocol—but, like everything else in this world, it is subject to changes and evolution. The evolution of IPv4 is IP "The Next Generation" (literally) or *IPng*. IPng is also referred to as *IPv6*. In development since the early '90s, IPv6 became an RFC standard in January 1995, and it continues to be refined and developed.

What about IPv5; Did I Miss Something?

Version 5 of IP is assigned to RFC 1819, the Internet Stream Protocol. Version 5 not an upgrade of IPv4 and does not contain the evolutionary changes that are present in IPv6. Don't worry, you haven't slept through anything!

The main purpose of IPv6 is to overcome the largest limitation of the current implementation, namely, limited address space. IPv4 uses 32-bit IP addresses, typically represented by four 8-bit numbers separated by periods—the IP addresses that we've grown to know and love. If we could use all of the available 32-bit addresses, we would have a total of 2^{32} addresses, or almost 4,300,000,000 individual nodes that could be represented on the network. Remember that several ranges of addresses are reserved for private networks and that there is no guarantee that any given subnet is using 100 percent of its addresses. If you remember the discussion of subnets and subnet masks, then you'll remember that the need for "classless" addresses grew from the underutilization of the subnets and the need to simplify routing tables. Classless addresses were not a solution to the problem; they simply delayed the inevitable. The growth of the Internet and the rather reckless subnet assignment that occurred in its early days have led to a very serious problem.

We're running out of IP addresses.

The Internet was never intended to support the number of users that it currently has. There was never any question that 32 bits would be enough to represent the computers that made up the initial DARPA network. In addition to Internet connectivity, NAT and IP masquerading are also being used to help alleviate the address problem. Using a single IP address to represent potentially thousands of computers is certainly one way to get around the problem. Yet, once again, it is simply a stopgap solution.

Enter IPv6

IPv6, the solution that will save the day, offers several important features, but the leading push in its development was an increased address space. Instead of a 32-bit address, IPv6 introduces 128-bit addresses. With 128-bit addresses, an IPv6-based network cannot run out of addresses—2^{128} is an extremely large number. To utilize all the addresses that will be available in IPv6, you would literally need to be wading in computers wherever you walked. If we ever get to the point where a computer occupies every inch of the earth, our problems will be much bigger than not having enough IP addresses. A future world where toasters and reading lamps need IP addresses *might* pose a few problems for IPv6, but you'll probably need to own several hundred thousand toasters before you have to worry!

Addressing

When I started looking at IPv6, one of the first questions that crossed my mind was, What in the world do these puppies look like? Today's IP addresses are easy to look at—just a few numbers and periods. Off the top of my head, I can quote the IP addresses assigned to OSU's nameservers, my three primary Web servers at work, and a handful of other machines. Now, with IPv6, I'm going to be using a 128-bit address. If I represented the address in the same notation as the standard IPv4 address, it might look something like this:

```
128.146.143.123.243.231.233.112.211.121.001.201.250.071.124.12
```

Ack! That's just awful! Just the thought of trying to type something like that scares me—I'd hate to have use a monstrous scheme like that to address every machine on my network. Luckily for you and me, IPv6 is represented using a different format than the standard IPv4 notation. Instead of decimal numbers, IPv6 uses hexadecimal numbers, which allows a greater amount of data to be represented in a smaller space. If you're interested in trying a few decimal-to-hex (or vice versa) conversions on your own, take a look at this online JavaScript converter: at http://www.tw2.co.uk/webresources/hex.html.

Instead of the long, dotted-decimal format number that IPv4 uses, you'll be seeing addresses like this with IPv6:

```
FF03:A9:21:AC3:187:4B:321:32
```

Each segment is a 16-bit number separated by a colon (:). The huge number of addresses available in IPv6 means that there will probably be many zeros (0s) in the address. Taking this into account, IPv6 has a shortcut notation that makes it a bit easier to represent these addresses. The "::" characters can be substituted in for any long string of zeros. This shortcut can be used only once (otherwise, the number of zeros being represented by each instance would be unclear). Using "::," you can take an address that looks like

```
FF02:00:00:00:00:00:32A:32
```

and turn it into this:

```
FF02::32A:32
```

You'll be reading about the transition between IPv4 and IPv6 shortly, but while we're discussing the v6 addresses, let's take a look how IPv4 addresses can be represented using the v6 notation. Say, for example, I have the old v4 address 140.254.85.2 (which, by an astonishing coincidence, I do). If my network made the IPv6 transition and I kept using IPv4 devices on the network, my address would be represented on an IPv6 machine like this:

```
0:0:0:0:FFFF:140.254.85.2
```

If I take that one step further, I can use the double-colon shortcut to shorten the old address to

```
::FFFF:140.254.85.2
```

That's not bad at all. You should know what you're looking at if you happen to stumble across an IPv6 address. Chances are your computer system doesn't even support IPv6 yet, but it *is* coming—and it's best to be prepared.

So, besides the new addresses and expanded address space, what else does IPv6 offer? In the design of IPv6, several additions were made to leverage the knowledge that has been gained during the growth of the Internet. Remember that IPv4 was designed before anyone had any idea of what the Internet would become, what types of computers would be using it, and what they would be using it for. During the design of IPv6, the Internet Engineering Task Force (IETF) used these considerations to integrate new features into the IPv6 that would provide needed facilities for the Internet that are missing in the current IPv4 implementation. IPv6 provides a larger address space, as well as security, quality of service, extensibility, and simplified headers. I discuss some of those components in more detail in the following sections.

Simplified Headers

The IPv6 implementation uses 128-bit addresses, which means that, compared to version 4, IPv6 takes four times more space to represent an address. With both the source and destination addresses coded into the packet header, this additional space requirement alone equates to 256 bits, or 32 bytes, for IPv6, versus 64bits, or only 8 bytes for IPv4. This statistic might lead you to believe that IPv6 packets would have roughly four times the amount of overhead as IPv4. Luckily, IPv6 simplifies the header structure and gets rid of many of the fields in the IPv4 header. Figure 24.1 shows the header structure of the IPv4 packet—you might remember this figure from Chapter 2,"Integrating TCP/IP and OSI Network Layers." The following figure, Figure 24.2, shows the newly revised IPv6 header format.

FIGURE 24.1
The IPv4 packet header, as specified in RFC 0791.

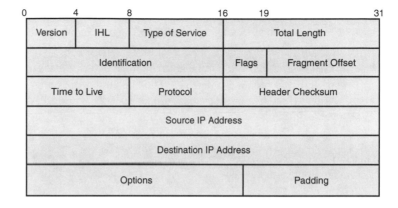

FIGURE 24.2
The IPv6 packet header is simplified from the v4 header, as defined in RFC 1752.

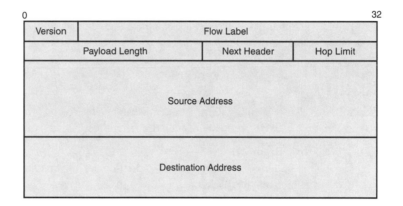

As you can see, the IPv6 header format is significantly cleaner. The designers made an effort to reduce the amount of overhead that would be caused by the extended addresses. The fields of the v6 header are described below. If you're interested in the header fields of the v4 implementation, turn back to Chapter 2 where I explain them in detail.

- Version—The Version field is just the version of IP that is being used. IPng is assigned the version number 6, so all IPv6 will simply encode 6 into this 4-bit field.

- Flow Label—Used by a machine to label a packet for special handling by routers and gateways. It can be used to specify a quality of service that is desired for the packet. This field is 28 bits long.

- Payload Length—The length of the data that is going to be contained in the packet following the header. This field is limited to 16 bits, which, in turn, limits that amount of data in a packet to 64K. If a packet needs to be longer, an extended header can be used, in which case, this value would be set to zero.

- Next Header—In a few minutes, you're going to be reading about the extensibility of IPv6. The 8-bit Next Header field identifies the type of header that can follow the IPv6 header.

- Hop Limit—The hop limit is similar to the time to live in that they both limit the amount of routing that a packet can undergo. The hop limit is decremented each time a packet is forwarded. If the hop limit reaches zero, the packet is discarded. Eight bits are used for this value, limiting the number of hops to 256.

- Source Address—The 128-bit IPv6 address of the computer that originally sent the packet.

- Destination Address—The 128-bit address of the computer or device that should be receiving the packet.

Nothing out of the ordinary in these fields, but the Next Header field probably tipped you off that there are other options to be investigated. IPv6 allows extended headers to follow the main IPv6 header. The extended headers can contain optional data and functionality. The next few sections look at some of the flexibility that these headers provide.

Extensibility

Different headers representing different options can be stacked on top of each other in the IPv6 specification. The currently defined headers that must be used in an IPv6 implementation are

- Hop-by-hop options—The hop-by-hop header defines information that must be examined by every router that the packet passes through in its travels. The hop-by-hop fields also specify a payload length that is greater than what can be represented in the 16 bits of the main IPv6 packet header.

- Routing header—The routing header specifies a path of devices that the packet must visit while it travels to its destination. Addresses are specified in a list in the header along with a strict or loose designation. *Strict routes* mean the packet must visit the nodes in order; *loose routes* do not guarantee any order.

- Fragment header—The fragment header sends a packet that is larger than the maximum transmission units that can be used on the network. The header contains information on the fragment order and an indication of the end of a fragmented packet. In IPv6 only the hosts create fragments, not the routers.

- Destination options—The destination options carry information that is used only by the computer that is receiving the data. Routers along the way do not examine this header.

- IP Authentication header—IPv4 currently sends only the original IP address along with each packet. This situation can lead to "IP Spoofing" where packets are sent with an address encoded that is not the address of the sending machine. IPv6 includes an optional authentication header that can include encrypted information about the sending machine. This information prevents outside machines from using spoofing to hijack a connection.

- IP Privacy header—IPv6 includes the capability to encrypt entire packets as they are transmitted over the network. This header contains information about the encryption that is applied to a packet. The sending and receiving computers perform encryption/decryption, eliminating the capability of packet sniffers to determine the contents of packets on the wire.

IPv6 also leaves itself open for other header options to be defined, and with each new option, it includes the capability to specify what a node should do with a packet that contains options that it doesn't understand. This feature allows IPv6 to continue to evolve and yet still work on networks that are not running the most recent version of the protocol.

Security

One of the most desired options available in IPv6 is security. IPv6 offers two native security options, which were briefly mentioned in the preceding section. IPv4 is wide open to IP spoofing, which has become an increasingly evil problem as IP-spoofing source code is now widespread on the Internet. I describe spoofing in a second, and you can visit the Rootshell security Web site (http://www.rootshell.com/) for more information.

With a bit of scarching, you should be able to find several examples of IP-based network attacks that incorporate IP spoofing. Spoofing itself isn't a means of attack; rather, it's a means of covering up an attack. Most of the current attack programs, including winnuke, have been updated to include IP spoofing, thus covering up the originating machine. If the IP address of an attack is spoofed, then the only way to determine the originating machine is to sniff the network where the packet originated. A recent DNS attack involved spoofing a neighboring DNS partner on a network, and because the partner is authenticated, the spoofing computer can place information on the DNS. This situation could potentially disrupt name resolution service by resolving hostnames to IP addresses that are not the correct addresses.

There are, of course, some techniques you can use to perform IP authentication—namely, having a machine attempt to contact and verify any instructions it may have received from a remote host. However, sophisticated hackers can even spoof some responses. The need for a standard way of authenticating packets has found its way into IPv6. The IPv6 authentication header can encode encrypted data that can identify the source of the packet. The second type of security, packet encryption, is already found in IPv4, but not in any truly standard format. SSL, for example, can encrypt data before it is sent. This encryption, however, must be implemented by the applications that are using it. Incorporating security on a packet basis into IPv6 enables applications to communicate securely without a need for customized security options.

Quality of Service

Unlike IPv4, packets can be labeled with a particular quality of service that enables routers and other traffic-control devices to react based on the settings in the flow field. Standard network operations receive a relatively low priority, which indicates that real-time service is not neces-

Part
VI

Ch
24

sary and that the packets can be delayed if network traffic levels are high. Other types of traffic, such as video feeds or live audio, might require higher priorities. This sort of traffic is referred to as *real-time* traffic because it must reach its destination within a certain time period. *Real time*, as a generic term, means that something must happen at once and cannot be delayed or interrupted. Real-time systems are extremely important for applications such as air-traffic control or (for a rather extreme example) control systems on board the space shuttle. Real-time networks simply extend the same concept to the network. The data transferred over a real-time network does not necessarily have to be audio or video; such applications are just common examples of what a real-time network might be useful for.

Transitioning to IPv6

The transition to IPv6 might seem relatively simple. Rewrite TCP/IP stacks for all of your client computers, and you should be all set, right? Well, not entirely. Each application that uses TCP/IP is going to have to be modified to understand the addresses of IPv6. DNS servers, for example, need to have a new record type defined to resolve the new addresses, and everything that deals with an IP address directly needs to understand the new format. In addition, routing and gateway hardware need to understand the new addressing formats and packet headers. Therefore, tens of thousands of applications and products need to be updated to understand IPv6. Compounding matters, the IETF estimates that the current IPv4 addresses won't run out until the year 2010. Although this deadline seems a bit close to me, it wasn't until the late '90s that anyone started to address the impending year 2000 problem. I suspect that the Internet will be pushed to the point of crisis and then experience a sudden shift to implement IPv6 as widely and quickly as possible.

Also, consider that IPv4 networks will still be in existence in some places after IPv6 has been implemented in others. Therefore, IPv4 cannot be completely removed for many years, if ever—so IPv4 and IPv6 need to coexist and operate in tandem for IPv6 to ever be completely accepted. To do so, either routers will need to be placed at IPv6 and IPv4 boundaries, or IPv6 will be tunneled over IPv4 by placing IPv4 headers onto the IPv6 packets. IPv6 was designed to make the transition as quick and painless as possible. Because of the amount of planning that went into IPv6, the transition is already happening on Internet backbones across the country. TCP/IP software is already in place or under development for all major operating systems and computers. It is simply a matter of time before your computer uses IPv6 to connect to the Internet.

Do I Need to Upgrade My Computer to IPv6 Right Now?

Luckily, the answer is no. With the advanced planning that went into IPv6, software and operating system developers have plenty of time to integrate the features of IPv6 into your system. You will probably receive IPv6 compatibility in a future operating system upgrade without even knowing it. Mac OS, Windows, and Linux are already advancing toward the IPv6 standard, so if you use a popular operating system, you won't be left out in the cold. The transition process is going to take several years. It will hardly be an overnight surprise when it happens to you.

IPv6 is a huge step forward for TCP/IP and a huge step for the future of the Internet. The extended security capabilities of IPv6 may eliminate the need for security measures like firewalls or software-based encryption such as PGP. The IPv6 standard is open and capable of being extended and provides enough address space to cover the planet in a blanket of computers. Unlike IPv4, IPv6 will probably have a very long and useful life. However, these thoughts are based on a protocol that isn't even in use yet. By the time IPv6 is widely implemented, the real picture might be very different.

Other Resources

The Internet Protocol v6 RFC 1752   `http://www.cis.ohio-state.edu/htbin/rfc/rfc1752.html`

The Internet Protocol v4 RFC 0791   `http://www.cis.ohio-state.edu/htbin/rfc/rfc0791.html`

Part
VI

Ch
24

Wrapping It Up

You've now reached the end of the book! You've seen how the TCP/IP protocol works, how to configure multiple different clients, and how to provide network services to and from those clients. If you've read every chapter, congratulations; you are now armed with the knowledge necessary to set up a fully functional TCP/IP network, manage it, and provide connectivity to the Internet. If you skipped material, I urge you to go back and take a look. I have discussed many programs that provide valuable services to your network. I sincerely hope that everyone who picked up a copy of this book found something of value. I enjoyed writing it and having a chance to vent some of my more frustrating (and sometimes amusing) networking experiences. There is far more information on TCP/IP than can be contained in any book. New RFC documents for developing protocols are added all the time. The Internet is growing, TCP/IP is growing, and I urge you to remain up-to-date on the current standards for TCP/IP and grow along with it.

Good luck!

The TCP/IP Protocol Suite

by John Ray

You have learned about the TCP/IP protocol suite by seeing the various protocols that comprise it broken down and explained. The information contained in this book is aimed at beginning-level users and provides a high-level view of the use and concepts behind TCP/IP. If you are interested in expanding your knowledge with information about this protocol suite, we have included the RFCs that describe the TCP/IP suite in depth. This is the information source upon which any TCP/IP implementation is based. Whether you are using a Macintosh, Windows, or Linux-based computer, these documents are what power your computer's ability to connect to the Internet and other TCP/IP networks now and in the future.

RFC 793	TCP
RFC 768	UDP
RFC 1340	IP
RFC 1883	IPv6
RFC 792	ICMP

Editor's note: The following appendix contains the complete RFC documents, unedited except for formatting.

RFC 793—TCP

RFC: 793
TRANSMISSION CONTROL PROTOCOL
DARPA INTERNET PROGRAM
PROTOCOL SPECIFICATION
September 1981
prepared for

Defense Advanced Research Projects Agency
Information Processing Techniques Office
1400 Wilson Boulevard
Arlington, Virginia 22209

by

Information Sciences Institute
University of Southern California
4676 Admiralty Way
Marina del Rey, California 90291

Table Of Contents

Preface

1.	Introduction	479
1.1	Motivation	480
1.2	Scope	481
1.3	About This Document	481
1.4	Interfaces	481
1.5	Operation	481
2.	Philosophy	483
2.1	Elements of the Internetwork System	483
2.2	Model of Operation	484
2.3	The Host Environment	485
2.4	Interfaces	485
2.5	Relation to Other Protocols	485
2.6	Reliable Communication	486
2.7	Connection Establishment and Clearing	486
2.8	Data Communication	488
2.9	Precedence and Security	488
2.10	Robustness Principle	488

3.   Functional Specification   489

3.1   Header Format   489

3.2   Terminology   492

3.3   Sequence Numbers   495

3.4   Establishing a connection   500

3.5   Closing a Connection   505

3.6   Precedence and Security   506

3.7   Data Communication   507

3.8   Interfaces   510

3.9   Event Processing   515

Glossary   529

References   535

Preface

This document describes the DoD Standard Transmission Control Protocol (TCP). There have been nine earlier editions of the ARPA TCP specification on which this standard is based, and the present text draws heavily from them. There have been many contributors to this work both in terms of concepts and in terms of text. This edition clarifies several details and removes the end-of-letter buffer-size adjustments, and redescribes the letter mechanism as a push function.

Jon Postel
Editor
RFC: 793
Replaces: RFC 761
IENs: 129, 124, 112, 81,
55, 44, 40, 27, 21, 5
TRANSMISSION CONTROL PROTOCOL
DARPA INTERNET PROGRAM
PROTOCOL SPECIFICATION

1. INTRODUCTION

The Transmission Control Protocol (TCP) is intended for use as a highly reliable host-to-host protocol between hosts in packet-switched computer communication networks, and in interconnected systems of such networks.

This document describes the functions to be performed by the Transmission Control Protocol, the program that implements it, and its interface to programs or users that require its services.

1.1. Motivation

Computer communication systems are playing an increasingly important role in military, government, and civilian environments. This document focuses its attention primarily on military computer communication requirements, especially robustness in the presence of communication unreliability and availability in the presence of congestion, but many of these problems are found in the civilian and government sector as well.

As strategic and tactical computer communication networks are developed and deployed, it is essential to provide means of interconnecting them and to provide standard interprocess communication protocols which can support a broad range of applications. In anticipation of the need for such standards, the Deputy Undersecretary of Defense for Research and Engineering has declared the Transmission Control Protocol (TCP) described herein to be a basis for DoD-wide inter-process communication protocol standardization.

TCP is a connection-oriented, end-to-end reliable protocol designed to fit into a layered hierarchy of protocols which support multi-network applications. The TCP provides for reliable inter-process communication between pairs of processes in host computers attached to distinct but interconnected computer communication networks. Very few assumptions are made as to the reliability of the communication protocols below the TCP layer. TCP assumes it can obtain a simple, potentially unreliable datagram service from the lower level protocols. In principle, the TCP should be able to operate above a wide spectrum of communication systems ranging from hard-wired connections to packet-switched or circuit-switched networks.

TCP is based on concepts first described by Cerf and Kahn in [1]. The TCP fits into a layered protocol architecture just above a basic Internet Protocol [2] which provides a way for the TCP to send and receive variable-length segments of information enclosed in internet datagram "envelopes". The internet datagram provides a means for addressing source and destination TCPs in different networks. The internet protocol also deals with any fragmentation or reassembly of the TCP segments required to achieve transport and delivery through multiple networks and interconnecting gateways. The internet protocol also carries information on the precedence, security classification and compartmentation of the TCP segments, so this information can be communicated end-to-end across multiple networks.

```
                    Protocol Layering

               +--------------------+
               |    higher-level     |
               +--------------------+
               |        TCP          |
               +--------------------+
               |  internet protocol  |
               +--------------------+
               |communication network|
               +--------------------+
                     Figure 1
```

Much of this document is written in the context of TCP implementations which are co-resident with higher level protocols in the host computer. Some computer systems will be connected to networks via front-end computers which house the TCP and internet protocol layers, as well as network specific software. The TCP specification describes an interface to the higher level protocols which appears to be implementable even for the front-end case, as long as a suitable host-to-front end protocol is implemented.

1.2. Scope

The TCP is intended to provide a reliable process-to-process communication service in a multinetwork environment. The TCP is intended to be a host-to-host protocol in common use in multiple networks.

1.3. About this Document

This document represents a specification of the behavior required of any TCP implementation, both in its interactions with higher level protocols and in its interactions with other TCPs. The rest of this section offers a very brief view of the protocol interfaces and operation. Section 2 summarizes the philosophical basis for the TCP design. Section 3 offers both a detailed description of the actions required of TCP when various events occur (arrival of new segments, user calls, errors, etc.) and the details of the formats of TCP segments.

1.4. Interfaces

The TCP interfaces on one side to user or application processes and on the other side to a lower level protocol such as Internet Protocol.

The interface between an application process and the TCP is illustrated in reasonable detail. This interface consists of a set of calls much like the calls an operating system provides to an application process for manipulating files. For example, there are calls to open and close connections and to send and receive data on established connections. It is also expected that the TCP can asynchronously communicate with application programs. Although considerable freedom is permitted to TCP implementors to design interfaces which are appropriate to a particular operating system environment, a minimum functionality is required at the TCP/user interface for any valid implementation.

The interface between TCP and lower level protocol is essentially unspecified except that it is assumed there is a mechanism whereby the two levels can asynchronously pass information to each other. Typically, one expects the lower level protocol to specify this interface. TCP is designed to work in a very general environment of interconnected networks. The lower level protocol which is assumed throughout this document is the Internet Protocol [2].

1.5. Operation

As noted above, the primary purpose of the TCP is to provide reliable, securable logical circuit or connection service between pairs of processes. To provide this service on top of a less reliable internet communication system requires facilities in the following areas:

Basic Data Transfer
Reliability

> Flow Control
>
> Multiplexing
>
> Connections
>
> Precedence and Security

The basic operation of the TCP in each of these areas is described in the following paragraphs.

Basic Data Transfer:

> The TCP is able to transfer a continuous stream of octets in each direction between its users by packaging some number of octets into segments for transmission through the internet system. In general, the TCPs decide when to block and forward data at their own convenience.
>
> Sometimes users need to be sure that all the data they have submitted to the TCP has been transmitted. For this purpose a push function is defined. To assure that data submitted to a TCP is actually transmitted the sending user indicates that it should be pushed through to the receiving user. A push causes the TCPs to promptly forward and deliver data up to that point to the receiver. The exact push point might not be visible to the receiving user and the push function does not supply a record boundary marker.

Reliability:

> The TCP must recover from data that is damaged, lost, duplicated, or delivered out of order by the internet communication system. This is achieved by assigning a sequence number to each octet transmitted, and requiring a positive acknowledgment (ACK) from the receiving TCP. If the ACK is not received within a timeout interval, the data is retransmitted. At the receiver, the sequence numbers are used to correctly order segments that may be received out of order and to eliminate duplicates. Damage is handled by adding a checksum to each segment transmitted, checking it at the receiver, and discarding damaged segments.
>
> As long as the TCPs continue to function properly and the internet system does not become completely partitioned, no transmission errors will affect the correct delivery of data. TCP recovers from internet communication system errors.

Flow Control:

> TCP provides a means for the receiver to govern the amount of data sent by the sender. This is achieved by returning a "window" with every ACK indicating a range of acceptable sequence numbers beyond the last segment successfully received. The window indicates an allowed number of octets that the sender may transmit before receiving further permission.

Multiplexing:

> To allow for many processes within a single Host to use TCP communication facilities simultaneously, the TCP provides a set of addresses or ports within each host. Concat-

enated with the network and host addresses from the internet communication layer, this forms a socket. A pair of sockets uniquely identifies each connection. That is, a socket may be simultaneously used in multiple connections.

The binding of ports to processes is handled independently by each Host. However, it proves useful to attach frequently used processes (e.g., a "logger" or timesharing service) to fixed sockets which are made known to the public. These services can then be accessed through the known addresses. Establishing and learning the port addresses of other processes may involve more dynamic mechanisms.

Connections:

The reliability and flow control mechanisms described above require that TCPs initialize and maintain certain status information for each data stream. The combination of this information, including sockets, sequence numbers, and window sizes, is called a connection. Each connection is uniquely specified by a pair of sockets identifying its two sides.

When two processes wish to communicate, their TCP's must first establish a connection (initialize the status information on each side). When their communication is complete, the connection is terminated or closed to free the resources for other uses.

Since connections must be established between unreliable hosts and over the unreliable internet communication system, a handshake mechanism with clock-based sequence numbers is used to avoid erroneous initialization of connections.

Precedence and Security:

The users of TCP may indicate the security and precedence of their communication. Provision is made for default values to be used when these features are not needed.

2. Philosophy

2.1. Elements of the Internetwork System

The internetwork environment consists of hosts connected to networks which are in turn interconnected via gateways. It is assumed here that the networks may be either local networks (e.g., the ETHERNET) or large networks (e.g., the ARPANET), but in any case are based on packet switching technology. The active agents that produce and consume messages are processes. Various levels of protocols in the networks, the gateways, and the hosts support an interprocess communication system that provides two-way data flow on logical connections between process ports.

The term packet is used generically here to mean the data of one transaction between a host and its network. The format of data blocks exchanged within the a network will generally not be of concern to us.

Hosts are computers attached to a network, and from the communication network's point of view, are the sources and destinations of packets. Processes are viewed as the active elements in host computers (in accordance with the fairly common definition of a process as a program in execution). Even terminals and files or other I/O devices are viewed as communicating with each other through the use of processes. Thus, all communication is viewed as inter-process communication.

Since a process may need to distinguish among several communication streams between itself and another process (or processes), we imagine that each process may have a number of ports through which it communicates with the ports of other processes.

2.2. Model of Operation

Processes transmit data by calling on the TCP and passing buffers of data as arguments. The TCP packages the data from these buffers into segments and calls on the internet module to transmit each segment to the destination TCP. The receiving TCP places the data from a segment into the receiving user's buffer and notifies the receiving user. The TCPs include control information in the segments which they use to ensure reliable ordered data transmission.

The model of internet communication is that there is an internet protocol module associated with each TCP which provides an interface to the local network. This internet module packages TCP segments inside internet datagrams and routes these datagrams to a destination internet module or intermediate gateway. To transmit the datagram through the local network, it is embedded in a local network packet.

The packet switches may perform further packaging, fragmentation, or other operations to achieve the delivery of the local packet to the destination internet module.

At a gateway between networks, the internet datagram is "unwrapped" from its local packet and examined to determine through which network the internet datagram should travel next. The internet datagram is then "wrapped" in a local packet suitable to the next network and routed to the next gateway, or to the final destination.

A gateway is permitted to break up an internet datagram into smaller internet datagram fragments if this is necessary for transmission through the next network. To do this, the gateway produces a set of internet datagrams; each carrying a fragment. Fragments may be further broken into smaller fragments at subsequent gateways. The internet datagram fragment format is designed so that the destination internet module can reassemble fragments into internet datagrams.

A destination internet module unwraps the segment from the datagram (after reassembling the datagram, if necessary) and passes it to the destination TCP.

This simple model of the operation glosses over many details. One important feature is the type of service. This provides information to the gateway (or internet module) to guide it in selecting the service parameters to be used in traversing the next network. Included in the type of service information is the precedence of the datagram. Datagrams may also carry security information to permit host and gateways that operate in multilevel secure environments to properly segregate datagrams for security considerations.

2.3. The Host Environment

The TCP is assumed to be a module in an operating system. The users access the TCP much like they would access the file system. The TCP may call on other operating system functions, for example, to manage data structures. The actual interface to the network is assumed to be controlled by a device driver module. The TCP does not call on the network device driver directly, but rather calls on the internet datagram protocol module which may in turn call on the device driver.

The mechanisms of TCP do not preclude implementation of the TCP in a front-end processor. However, in such an implementation, a host-to-front-end protocol must provide the functionality to support the type of TCP-user interface described in this document.

2.4. Interfaces

The TCP/user interface provides for calls made by the user on the TCP to OPEN or CLOSE a connection, to SEND or RECEIVE data, or to obtain STATUS about a connection. These calls are like other calls from user programs on the operating system, for example, the calls to open, read from, and close a file.

The TCP/internet interface provides calls to send and receive datagrams addressed to TCP modules in hosts anywhere in the internet system. These calls have parameters for passing the address, type of service, precedence, security, and other control information.

2.5. Relation to Other Protocols

The following diagram illustrates the place of the TCP in the protocol hierarchy:

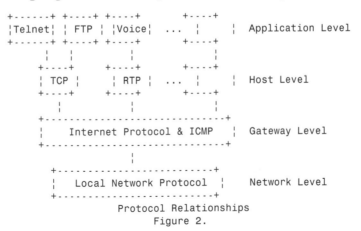

```
+------+ +----+ +----+         +----+
|Telnet| | FTP | |Voice|  ...  |    |    Application Level
+------+ +----+ +----+         +----+
   |       |      |               |
   |       |      |               |
 +----+      +----+           +----+
 | TCP |      | RTP |  ...  |    |    Host Level
 +----+      +----+           +----+
   |           |                 |
 +-------------------------------+
 |     Internet Protocol & ICMP   |    Gateway Level
 +-------------------------------+
                 |
     +-----------------------+
     |  Local Network Protocol  |    Network Level
     +-----------------------+
             Protocol Relationships
                  Figure 2.
```

It is expected that the TCP will be able to support higher level protocols efficiently. It should be easy to interface higher level protocols like the ARPANET Telnet or AUTODIN II THP to the TCP.

2.6. Reliable Communication

A stream of data sent on a TCP connection is delivered reliably and in order at the destination.

Transmission is made reliable via the use of sequence numbers and acknowledgments. Conceptually, each octet of data is assigned a sequence number. The sequence number of the first octet of data in a segment is transmitted with that segment and is called the segment sequence number. Segments also carry an acknowledgment number which is the sequence number of the next expected data octet of transmissions in the reverse direction. When the TCP transmits a segment containing data, it puts a copy on a retransmission queue and starts a timer; when the acknowledgment for that data is received, the segment is deleted from the queue. If the acknowledgment is not received before the timer runs out, the segment is retransmitted.

An acknowledgment by TCP does not guarantee that the data has been delivered to the end user, but only that the receiving TCP has taken the responsibility to do so.

To govern the flow of data between TCPs, a flow control mechanism is employed. The receiving TCP reports a "window" to the sending TCP. This window specifies the number of octets, starting with the acknowledgment number, that the receiving TCP is currently prepared to receive.

2.7. Connection Establishment and Clearing

To identify the separate data streams that a TCP may handle, the TCP provides a port identifier. Since port identifiers are selected independently by each TCP they might not be unique. To provide for unique addresses within each TCP, we concatenate an internet address identifying the TCP with a port identifier to create a socket which will be unique throughout all networks connected together.

A connection is fully specified by the pair of sockets at the ends. A local socket may participate in many connections to different foreign sockets. A connection can be used to carry data in both directions, that is, it is "full duplex".

TCPs are free to associate ports with processes however they choose. However, several basic concepts are necessary in any implementation. There must be well-known sockets which the TCP associates only with the "appropriate" processes by some means. We envision that processes may "own" ports, and that processes can initiate connections only on the ports they own. (Means for implementing ownership is a local issue, but we envision a Request Port user command, or a method of uniquely allocating a group of ports to a given process, e.g., by associating the high order bits of a port name with a given process.)

A connection is specified in the OPEN call by the local port and foreign socket arguments. In return, the TCP supplies a (short) local connection name by which the user refers to the connection in subsequent calls. There are several things that must be remembered about a connection. To store this information we imagine that there is a data structure called a Transmission Control Block (TCB). One implementation strategy would have the local connection name be a pointer to the TCB for this connection. The OPEN call also specifies whether the connection establishment is to be actively pursued, or to be passively waited for.

A passive OPEN request means that the process wants to accept incoming connection requests rather than attempting to initiate a connection. Often the process requesting a passive OPEN will accept a connection request from any caller. In this case a foreign socket of all zeros is used to denote an unspecified socket. Unspecified foreign sockets are allowed only on passive OPENs.

A service process that wished to provide services for unknown other processes would issue a passive OPEN request with an unspecified foreign socket. Then a connection could be made with any process that requested a connection to this local socket. It would help if this local socket were known to be associated with this service.

Well-known sockets are a convenient mechanism for a priori associating a socket address with a standard service. For instance, the "Telnet-Server" process is permanently assigned to a particular socket, and other sockets are reserved for File Transfer, Remote Job Entry, Text Generator, Echoer, and Sink processes (the last three being for test purposes). A socket address might be reserved for access to a "Look-Up" service which would return the specific socket at which a newly created service would be provided. The concept of a well-known socket is part of the TCP specification, but the assignment of sockets to services is outside this specification. (See [4].)

Processes can issue passive OPENs and wait for matching active OPENs from other processes and be informed by the TCP when connections have been established. Two processes which issue active OPENs to each other at the same time will be correctly connected. This flexibility is critical for the support of distributed computing in which components act asynchronously with respect to each other.

There are two principal cases for matching the sockets in the local passive OPENs and an foreign active OPENs. In the first case, the local passive OPENs has fully specified the foreign socket. In this case, the match must be exact. In the second case, the local passive OPENs has left the foreign socket unspecified. In this case, any foreign socket is acceptable as long as the local sockets match. Other possibilities include partially restricted matches.

If there are several pending passive OPENs (recorded in TCBs) with the same local socket, an foreign active OPEN will be matched to a TCB with the specific foreign socket in the foreign active OPEN, if such a TCB exists, before selecting a TCB with an unspecified foreign socket. The procedures to establish connections utilize the synchronize (SYN) control flag and involves an exchange of three messages. This exchange has been termed a three-way hand shake [3].

A connection is initiated by the rendezvous of an arriving segment containing a SYN and a waiting TCB entry each created by a user OPEN command. The matching of local and foreign sockets determines when a connection has been initiated. The connection becomes "established" when sequence numbers have been synchronized in both directions.

The clearing of a connection also involves the exchange of segments, in this case carrying the FIN control flag.

2.8. Data Communication

The data that flows on a connection may be thought of as a stream of octets. The sending user indicates in each SEND call whether the data in that call (and any preceeding calls) should be immediately pushed through to the receiving user by the setting of the PUSH flag.

A sending TCP is allowed to collect data from the sending user and to send that data in segments at its own convenience, until the push function is signaled, then it must send all unsent data. When a receiving TCP sees the PUSH flag, it must not wait for more data from the sending TCP before passing the data to the receiving process.

There is no necessary relationship between push functions and segment boundaries. The data in any particular segment may be the result of a single SEND call, in whole or part, or of multiple SEND calls.

The purpose of push function and the PUSH flag is to push data through from the sending user to the receiving user. It does not provide a record service.

There is a coupling between the push function and the use of buffers of data that cross the TCP/user interface. Each time a PUSH flag is associated with data placed into the receiving user's buffer, the buffer is returned to the user for processing even if the buffer is not filled. If data arrives that fills the user's buffer before a PUSH is seen, the data is passed to the user in buffer size units.

TCP also provides a means to communicate to the receiver of data that at some point further along in the data stream than the receiver is currently reading there is urgent data. TCP does not attempt to define what the user specifically does upon being notified of pending urgent data, but the general notion is that the receiving process will take action to process the urgent data quickly.

2.9. Precedence and Security

The TCP makes use of the internet protocol type of service field and security option to provide precedence and security on a per connection basis to TCP users. Not all TCP modules will necessarily function in a multilevel secure environment; some may be limited to unclassified use only, and others may operate at only one security level and compartment. Consequently, some TCP implementations and services to users may be limited to a subset of the multilevel secure case.

TCP modules which operate in a multilevel secure environment must properly mark outgoing segments with the security, compartment, and precedence. Such TCP modules must also provide to their users or higher level protocols such as Telnet or THP an interface to allow them to specify the desired security level, compartment, and precedence of connections.

2.10. Robustness Principle

TCP implementations will follow a general principle of robustness: be conservative in what you do, be liberal in what you accept from others.

3. Functional Specification

3.1. Header Format

TCP segments are sent as internet datagrams. The Internet Protocol header carries several information fields, including the source and destination host addresses [2]. A TCP header follows the internet header, supplying information specific to the TCP protocol. This division allows for the existence of host level protocols other than TCP.

TCP Header Format

```
    0                   1                   2                   3
    0 1 2 3 4 5 6 7 8 9 0 1 2 3 4 5 6 7 8 9 0 1 2 3 4 5 6 7 8 9 0 1
   +-+-+-+-+-+-+-+-+-+-+-+-+-+-+-+-+-+-+-+-+-+-+-+-+-+-+-+-+-+-+-+-+
   |          Source Port          |       Destination Port        |
   +-+-+-+-+-+-+-+-+-+-+-+-+-+-+-+-+-+-+-+-+-+-+-+-+-+-+-+-+-+-+-+-+
   |                        Sequence Number                        |
   +-+-+-+-+-+-+-+-+-+-+-+-+-+-+-+-+-+-+-+-+-+-+-+-+-+-+-+-+-+-+-+-+
   |                    Acknowledgment Number                      |
   +-+-+-+-+-+-+-+-+-+-+-+-+-+-+-+-+-+-+-+-+-+-+-+-+-+-+-+-+-+-+-+-+
   |  Data |           |U|A|P|R|S|F|                               |
   | Offset| Reserved  |R|C|S|S|Y|I|            Window             |
   |       |           |G|K|H|T|N|N|                               |
   +-+-+-+-+-+-+-+-+-+-+-+-+-+-+-+-+-+-+-+-+-+-+-+-+-+-+-+-+-+-+-+-+
   |           Checksum            |         Urgent Pointer        |
   +-+-+-+-+-+-+-+-+-+-+-+-+-+-+-+-+-+-+-+-+-+-+-+-+-+-+-+-+-+-+-+-+
   |                    Options                    |    Padding    |
   +-+-+-+-+-+-+-+-+-+-+-+-+-+-+-+-+-+-+-+-+-+-+-+-+-+-+-+-+-+-+-+-+
   |                             data                              |
   +-+-+-+-+-+-+-+-+-+-+-+-+-+-+-+-+-+-+-+-+-+-+-+-+-+-+-+-+-+-+-+-+
```

TCP Header Format

Note that one tick mark represents one bit position.

Figure 3.

Source Port: 16 bits

The source port number.

Destination Port: 16 bits

The destination port number.

Sequence Number: 32 bits

The sequence number of the first data octet in this segment (except when SYN is present). If SYN is present the sequence number is the initial sequence number (ISN) and the first data octet is ISN+1.

Acknowledgment Number: 32 bits

If the ACK control bit is set this field contains the value of the next sequence number the sender of the segment is expecting to receive. Once a connection is established this is always sent.

Data Offset: 4 bits

> The number of 32 bit words in the TCP Header. This indicates where the data begins. The TCP header (even one including options) is an integral number of 32 bits long.

Reserved: 6 bits

> Reserved for future use. Must be zero.

Control Bits: 6 bits (from left to right):

> URG: Urgent Pointer field significant
>
> ACK: Acknowledgment field significant
>
> PSH: Push Function
>
> RST: Reset the connection
>
> SYN: Synchronize sequence numbers
>
> FIN: No more data from sender

Window: 16 bits

> The number of data octets beginning with the one indicated in the acknowledgment field which the sender of this segment is willing to accept.

Checksum: 16 bits

> The checksum field is the 16 bit one's complement of the one's complement sum of all 16 bit words in the header and text. If a segment contains an odd number of header and text octets to be checksummed, the last octet is padded on the right with zeros to form a 16 bit word for checksum purposes. The pad is not transmitted as part of the segment. While computing the checksum, the checksum field itself is replaced with zeros.
>
> The checksum also covers a 96 bit pseudo header conceptually prefixed to the TCP header. This pseudo header contains the Source Address, the Destination Address, the Protocol, and TCP length.
>
> This gives the TCP protection against misrouted segments. This information is carried in the Internet Protocol and is transferred across the TCP/Network interface in the arguments or results of calls by the TCP on the IP.

```
+--------+--------+--------+--------+
|           Source Address          |
+--------+--------+--------+--------+
|         Destination Address       |
+--------+--------+--------+--------+
|  zero  |  PTCL  |    TCP Length    |
+--------+--------+--------+--------+
```

> The TCP Length is the TCP header length plus the data length in octets (this is not an explicitly transmitted quantity, but is computed), and it does not count the 12 octets of the pseudo header.

Urgent Pointer: 16 bits

> This field communicates the current value of the urgent pointer as a positive offset from the sequence number in this segment. The urgent pointer points to the sequence number of the octet following the urgent data. This field is only be interpreted in segments with the URG control bit set.

Options: variable

> Options may occupy space at the end of the TCP header and are a multiple of 8 bits in length. All options are included in the checksum. An option may begin on any octet boundary. There are two cases for the format of an option:
>
> Case 1: A single octet of option-kind.
>
> Case 2: An octet of option-kind, an octet of option-length, and the actual option-data octets.
>
> The option-length counts the two octets of option-kind and option-length as well as the option-data octets.
>
> Note that the list of options may be shorter than the data offset field might imply. The content of the header beyond the End-of-Option option must be header padding (i.e., zero).
>
> A TCP must implement all options.
>
> Currently defined options include (kind indicated in octal):

```
Kind      Length      Meaning
----      ------      ------
 0          -         End of option list.
 1          -         No-Operation.
 2          4         Maximum Segment Size.
```

Specific Option Definitions

End of Option List

```
+--------+
|00000000|
+--------+
  Kind=0
```

> This option code indicates the end of the option list. This might not coincide with the end of the TCP header according to the Data Offset field. This is used at the end of all options, not the end of each option, and need only be used if the end of the options would not otherwise coincide with the end of the TCP header.

No-Operation

```
+--------+
|00000001|
+--------+
  Kind=1
```

This option code may be used between options, for example, to align the beginning of a subsequent option on a word boundary. There is no guarantee that senders will use this option, so receivers must be prepared to process options even if they do not begin on a word boundary.

Maximum Segment Size

```
+--------+--------+--------+--------+
|00000010|00000100|   max seg size  |
+--------+--------+--------+--------+
 Kind=2    Length=4
```

Maximum Segment Size Option Data: 16 bits

If this option is present, then it communicates the maximum receive segment size at the TCP which sends this segment. This field must only be sent in the initial connection request (i.e., in segments with the SYN control bit set). If this option is not used, any segment size is allowed.

Padding: variable

The TCP header padding is used to ensure that the TCP header ends and data begins on a 32 bit boundary. The padding is composed of zeros.

3.2. Terminology

Before we can discuss very much about the operation of the TCP we need to introduce some detailed terminology. The maintenance of a TCP connection requires the remembering of several variables. We conceive of these variables being stored in a connection record called a Transmission Control Block or TCB. Among the variables stored in the TCB are the local and remote socket numbers, the security and precedence of the connection, pointers to the user's send and receive buffers, pointers to the retransmit queue and to the current segment. In addition several variables relating to the send and receive sequence numbers are stored in the TCB.

Send Sequence Variables

SND.UNA - send unacknowledged

SND.NXT - send next

SND.WND - send window

SND.UP - send urgent pointer

SND.WL1 - segment sequence number used for last window update

SND.WL2 - segment acknowledgment number used for last window update

ISS - initial send sequence number

Receive Sequence Variables

    RCV.NXT - receive next

    RCV.WND - receive window

    RCV.UP - receive urgent pointer

    IRS - initial receive sequence number

The following diagrams may help to relate some of these variables to the sequence space.

Send Sequence Space

```
        1           2           3           4
   - - - - - - - - -|- - - - - - - - - -|- - - - - - - - - -|- - - - - - - - -
            SND.UNA     SND.NXT     SND.UNA
                                    +SND.WND


   1 - old sequence numbers which have been acknowledged
   2 - sequence numbers of unacknowledged data
   3 - sequence numbers allowed for new data transmission
   4 - future sequence numbers which are not yet allowed

                    Send Sequence Space
```

The send window is the portion of the sequence space labeled 3 in figure 4.

Receive Sequence Space

```
          1           2           3
   - - - - - - - - -|- - - - - - - - - -|- - - - - - - - -
            RCV.NXT     RCV.NXT
                        +RCV.WND


   1 - old sequence numbers which have been acknowledged
   2 - sequence numbers allowed for new reception
   3 - future sequence numbers which are not yet allowed

                  Receive Sequence Space

                      Figure 5.
```

The receive window is the portion of the sequence space labeled 2 in figure 5.

There are also some variables used frequently in the discussion that take their values from the fields of the current segment.

Current Segment Variables

    SEG.SEQ - segment sequence number

    SEG.ACK - segment acknowledgment number

    SEG.LEN - segment length

    SEG.WND - segment window

    SEG.UP - segment urgent pointer

    SEG.PRC - segment precedence value

A connection progresses through a series of states during its lifetime. The states are: LISTEN, SYN-SENT, SYN-RECEIVED, ESTABLISHED, FIN-WAIT-1, FIN-WAIT-2, CLOSE-WAIT, CLOS-ING, LAST-ACK, TIME-WAIT, and the fictional state CLOSED. CLOSED is fictional because it represents the state when there is no TCB, and therefore, no connection. Briefly the meanings of the states are:

LISTEN - represents waiting for a connection request from any remote TCP and port.

SYN-SENT - represents waiting for a matching connection request after having sent a connection request.

SYN-RECEIVED - represents waiting for a confirming connection request acknowledgment after having both received and sent a connection request.

ESTABLISHED - represents an open connection, data received can be delivered to the user. The normal state for the data transfer phase of the connection.

FIN-WAIT-1 - represents waiting for a connection termination request from the remote TCP, or an acknowledgment of the connection termination request previously sent.

FIN-WAIT-2 - represents waiting for a connection termination request from the remote TCP.

CLOSE-WAIT - represents waiting for a connection termination request from the local user.

CLOSING - represents waiting for a connection termination request acknowledgment from the remote TCP.

LAST-ACK - represents waiting for an acknowledgment of the connection termination request previously sent to the remote TCP (which includes an acknowledgment of its connection termination request).

TIME-WAIT - represents waiting for enough time to pass to be sure the remote TCP received the acknowledgment of its connection termination request.

CLOSED - represents no connection state at all.

A TCP connection progresses from one state to another in response to events. The events are the user calls, OPEN, SEND, RECEIVE, CLOSE, ABORT, and STATUS; the incoming segments, particularly those containing the SYN, ACK, RST and FIN flags; and timeouts.

The state diagram in figure 6 illustrates only state changes, together with the causing events and resulting actions, but addresses neither error conditions nor actions which are not connected with state changes. In a later section, more detail is offered with respect to the reaction of the TCP to events.

N O T E   this diagram is only a summary and must not be taken as the total specification.

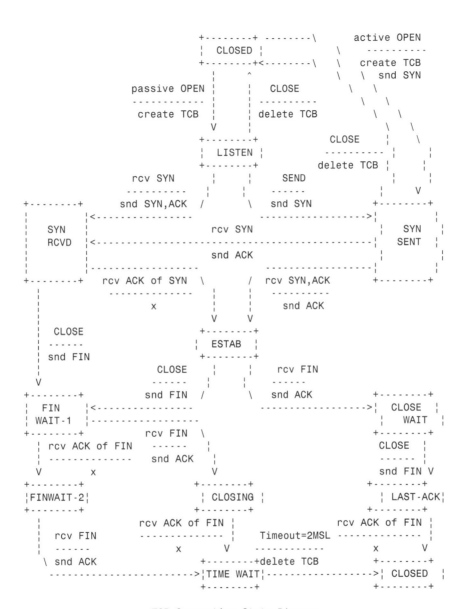

TCP Connection State Diagram
Figure 6.

3.3. Sequence Numbers

A fundamental notion in the design is that every octet of data sent over a TCP connection has a sequence number. Since every octet is sequenced, each of them can be acknowledged. The acknowledgment mechanism employed is cumulative so that an acknowledgment of sequence number X indicates that all octets up to but not including X have been received. This mechanism allows for straight-forward duplicate detection in the presence of retransmission. Numbering of octets within a segment is that the first data octet immediately following the header is the lowest numbered, and the following octets are numbered consecutively.

It is essential to remember that the actual sequence number space is finite, though very large. This space ranges from 0 to 2**32 - 1. Since the space is finite, all arithmetic dealing with sequence numbers must be performed modulo 2**32. This unsigned arithmetic preserves the relationship of sequence numbers as they cycle from 2**32 - 1 to 0 again. There are some subtleties to computer modulo arithmetic, so great care should be taken in programming the comparison of such values. The symbol "=<" means "less than or equal" (modulo 2**32).

The typical kinds of sequence number comparisons which the TCP must perform include:

(a) Determining that an acknowledgment refers to some sequence number sent but not yet acknowledged.

(b) Determining that all sequence numbers occupied by a segment have been acknowledged (e.g., to remove the segment from a retransmission queue).

(c) Determining that an incoming segment contains sequence numbers which are expected (i.e., that the segment "overlaps" the receive window).

In response to sending data the TCP will receive acknowledgments. The following comparisons are needed to process the acknowledgments.

SND.UNA = oldest unacknowledged sequence number

SND.NXT = next sequence number to be sent

SEG.ACK = acknowledgment from the receiving TCP (next sequence number expected by the receiving TCP)

SEG.SEQ = first sequence number of a segment

SEG.LEN = the number of octets occupied by the data in the segment (counting SYN and FIN)

SEG.SEQ+SEG.LEN-1 = last sequence number of a segment

A new acknowledgment (called an "acceptable ack"), is one for which the inequality below holds:

```
SND.UNA < SEG.ACK =< SND.NXT
```

A segment on the retransmission queue is fully acknowledged if the sum of its sequence number and length is less or equal than the acknowledgment value in the incoming segment.

When data is received the following comparisons are needed:

RCV.NXT = next sequence number expected on an incoming segments, and is the left or lower edge of the receive window

RCV.NXT+RCV.WND-1 = last sequence number expected on an incoming segment, and is the right or upper edge of the receive window

SEG.SEQ = first sequence number occupied by the incoming segment

SEG.SEQ+SEG.LEN-1 = last sequence number occupied by the incoming segment

A segment is judged to occupy a portion of valid receive sequence space if

```
RCV.NXT =< SEG.SEQ < RCV.NXT+RCV.WND
```

or

```
RCV.NXT =< SEG.SEQ+SEG.LEN-1 < RCV.NXT+RCV.WND
```

The first part of this test checks to see if the beginning of the segment falls in the window, the second part of the test checks to see if the end of the segment falls in the window; if the segment passes either part of the test it contains data in the window.

Actually, it is a little more complicated than this. Due to zero windows and zero length segments, we have four cases for the acceptability of an incoming segment:

```
Segment Receive  Test
Length  Window
------  ------   ----------------------------------------
   0       0     SEG.SEQ = RCV.NXT
   0      >0     RCV.NXT =< SEG.SEQ < RCV.NXT+RCV.WND
  >0       0     not acceptable
  >0      >0     RCV.NXT =< SEG.SEQ < RCV.NXT+RCV.WND
              or RCV.NXT =< SEG.SEQ+SEG.LEN-1 < RCV.NXT+RCV.WND
```

Note that when the receive window is zero no segments should be acceptable except ACK segments. Thus, it is be possible for a TCP to maintain a zero receive window while transmitting data and receiving ACKs. However, even when the receive window is zero, a TCP must process the RST and URG fields of all incoming segments.

We have taken advantage of the numbering scheme to protect certain control information as well. This is achieved by implicitly including some control flags in the sequence space so they can be retransmitted and acknowledged without confusion (i.e., one and only one copy of the control will be acted upon). Control information is not physically carried in the segment data space. Consequently, we must adopt rules for implicitly assigning sequence numbers to control. The SYN and FIN are the only controls requiring this protection, and these controls are used only at connection opening and closing. For sequence number purposes, the SYN is considered to occur before the first actual data octet of the segment in which it occurs, while the FIN is considered to occur after the last actual data octet in a segment in which it occurs. The segment length (SEG.LEN) includes both data and sequence space occupying controls. When a SYN is present then SEG.SEQ is the sequence number of the SYN.

Initial Sequence Number Selection   The protocol places no restriction on a particular connection being used over and over again. A connection is defined by a pair of sockets. New instances of a connection will be referred to as incarnations of the connection. The problem that arises from this is — "how does the TCP identify duplicate segments from previous incarnations of the connection?" This problem becomes apparent if the connection is being opened and closed in quick succession, or if the connection breaks with loss of memory and is then reestablished.

To avoid confusion we must prevent segments from one incarnation of a connection from being used while the same sequence numbers may still be present in the network from an earlier incarnation. We want to assure this, even if a TCP crashes and loses all knowledge of the sequence numbers it has been using. When new connections are created, an initial sequence number (ISN) generator is employed which selects a new 32 bit ISN. The generator is bound to a (possibly fictitious) 32 bit clock whose low order bit is incremented roughly every 4 microseconds. Thus, the ISN cycles approximately every 4.55 hours. Since we assume that segments will stay in the network no more than the Maximum Segment Lifetime (MSL) and that the MSL is less than 4.55 hours we can reasonably assume that ISN's will be unique.

For each connection there is a send sequence number and a receive sequence number. The initial send sequence number (ISS) is chosen by the data sending TCP, and the initial receive sequence number (IRS) is learned during the connection establishing procedure.

For a connection to be established or initialized, the two TCPs must synchronize on each other's initial sequence numbers. This is done in an exchange of connection establishing segments carrying a control bit called "SYN" (for synchronize) and the initial sequence numbers. As a shorthand, segments carrying the SYN bit are also called "SYNs". Hence, the solution requires a suitable mechanism for picking an initial sequence number and a slightly involved handshake to exchange the ISN's.

The synchronization requires each side to send it's own initial sequence number and to receive a confirmation of it in acknowledgment from the other side. Each side must also receive the other side's initial sequence number and send a confirming acknowledgment.

```
1) A --> B  SYN my sequence number is X
2) A <-- B  ACK your sequence number is X
3) A <-- B  SYN my sequence number is Y
4) A --> B  ACK your sequence number is Y
```

Because steps 2 and 3 can be combined in a single message this is called the three way (or three message) handshake.

A three way handshake is necessary because sequence numbers are not tied to a global clock in the network, and TCPs may have different mechanisms for picking the ISN's. The receiver of the first SYN has no way of knowing whether the segment was an old delayed one or not, unless it remembers the last sequence number used on the connection (which is not always possible), and so it must ask the sender to verify this SYN. The three way handshake and the advantages of a clock-driven scheme are discussed in [3].

Knowing When to Keep Quiet   To be sure that a TCP does not create a segment that carries a sequence number which may be duplicated by an old segment remaining in the network, the TCP must keep quiet for a maximum segment lifetime (MSL) before assigning any sequence numbers upon starting up or recovering from a crash in which memory of sequence numbers in use was lost. For this specification the MSL is taken to be 2 minutes. This is an engineering choice, and may be changed if experience indicates it is desirable to do so. Note that if a TCP is reinitialized in some sense, yet retains its memory of sequence numbers in use, then it need not wait at all; it must only be sure to use sequence numbers larger than those recently used.

The TCP Quiet Time Concept   This specification provides that hosts which "crash" without retaining any knowledge of the last sequence numbers transmitted on each active (i.e., not closed) connection shall delay emitting any TCP segments for at least the agreed Maximum Segment Lifetime (MSL) in the internet system of which the host is a part. In the paragraphs below, an explanation for this specification is given. TCP implementors may violate the "quiet time" restriction, but only at the risk of causing some old data to be accepted as new or new data rejected as old duplicated by some receivers in the internet system.

TCPs consume sequence number space each time a segment is formed and entered into the network output queue at a source host. The duplicate detection and sequencing algorithm in the TCP protocol relies on the unique binding of segment data to sequence space to the extent that sequence numbers will not cycle through all 2**32 values before the segment data bound to those sequence numbers has been delivered and acknowledged by the receiver and all duplicate copies of the segments have "drained" from the internet. Without such an assumption, two distinct TCP segments could conceivably be assigned the same or overlapping sequence numbers, causing confusion at the receiver as to which data is new and which is old. Remember that each segment is bound to as many consecutive sequence numbers as there are octets of data in the segment.

Under normal conditions, TCPs keep track of the next sequence number to emit and the oldest awaiting acknowledgment so as to avoid mistakenly using a sequence number over before its first use has been acknowledged. This alone does not guarantee that old duplicate data is drained from the net, so the sequence space has been made very large to reduce the probability that a wandering duplicate will cause trouble upon arrival. At 2 megabits/sec. it takes 4.5 hours to use up 2**32 octets of sequence space. Since the maximum segment lifetime in the net is not likely to exceed a few tens of seconds, this is deemed ample protection for foreseeable nets, even if data rates escalate to 10's of megabits/sec. At 100 megabits/sec, the cycle time is 5.4 minutes which may be a little short, but still within reason.

The basic duplicate detection and sequencing algorithm in TCP can be defeated, however, if a source TCP does not have any memory of the sequence numbers it last used on a given connection. For example, if the TCP were to start all connections with sequence number 0, then upon crashing and restarting, a TCP might re-form an earlier connection (possibly after half-open connection resolution) and emit packets with sequence numbers identical to or overlapping with packets still in the network which were emitted on an earlier incarnation of the same connection. In the absence of knowledge about the sequence numbers used on a particular connection, the TCP specification recommends that the source delay for MSL seconds before emitting segments on the connection, to allow time for segments from the earlier connection incarnation to drain from the system.

Even hosts which can remember the time of day and used it to select initial sequence number values are not immune from this problem (i.e., even if time of day is used to select an initial sequence number for each new connection incarnation).

Suppose, for example, that a connection is opened starting with sequence number S. Suppose that this connection is not used much and that eventually the initial sequence number function

(ISN(t)) takes on a value equal to the sequence number, say S1, of the last segment sent by this TCP on a particular connection. Now suppose, at this instant, the host crashes, recovers, and establishes a new incarnation of the connection. The initial sequence number chosen is S1 = ISN(t) — last used sequence number on old incarnation of connection! If the recovery occurs quickly enough, any old duplicates in the net bearing sequence numbers in the neighborhood of S1 may arrive and be treated as new packets by the receiver of the new incarnation of the connection.

The problem is that the recovering host may not know for how long it crashed nor does it know whether there are still old duplicates in the system from earlier connection incarnations.

One way to deal with this problem is to deliberately delay emitting segments for one MSL after recovery from a crash- this is the "quite time" specification. Hosts which prefer to avoid waiting are willing to risk possible confusion of old and new packets at a given destination may choose not to wait for the "quite time". Implementors may provide TCP users with the ability to select on a connection by connection basis whether to wait after a crash, or may informally implement the "quite time" for all connections. Obviously, even where a user selects to "wait," this is not necessary after the host has been "up" for at least MSL seconds.

To summarize: every segment emitted occupies one or more sequence numbers in the sequence space, the numbers occupied by a segment are "busy" or "in use" until MSL seconds have passed, upon crashing a block of space-time is occupied by the octets of the last emitted segment, if a new connection is started too soon and uses any of the sequence numbers in the space-time footprint of the last segment of the previous connection incarnation, there is a potential sequence number overlap area which could cause confusion at the receiver.

3.4. Establishing a connection

The "three-way handshake" is the procedure used to establish a connection. This procedure normally is initiated by one TCP and responded to by another TCP. The procedure also works if two TCP simultaneously initiate the procedure. When simultaneous attempt occurs, each TCP receives a "SYN" segment which carries no acknowledgment after it has sent a "SYN". Of course, the arrival of an old duplicate "SYN" segment can potentially make it appear, to the recipient, that a simultaneous connection initiation is in progress. Proper use of "reset" segments can disambiguate these cases.

Several examples of connection initiation follow. Although these examples do not show connection synchronization using data-carrying segments, this is perfectly legitimate, so long as the receiving TCP doesn't deliver the data to the user until it is clear the data is valid (i.e., the data must be buffered at the receiver until the connection reaches the ESTABLISHED state). The three-way handshake reduces the possibility of false connections. It is the implementation of a trade-off between memory and messages to provide information for this checking.

The simplest three-way handshake is shown in figure 7 below. The figures should be interpreted in the following way. Each line is numbered for reference purposes. Right arrows (—>)

indicate departure of a TCP segment from TCP A to TCP B, or arrival of a segment at B from A. Left arrows (<—), indicate the reverse. Ellipsis (...) indicates a segment which is still in the network (delayed). An "XXX" indicates a segment which is lost or rejected. Comments appear in parentheses. TCP states represent the state AFTER the departure or arrival of the segment (whose contents are shown in the center of each line). Segment contents are shown in abbreviated form, with sequence number, control flags, and ACK field. Other fields such as window, addresses, lengths, and text have been left out in the interest of clarity.

```
      TCP A                                                    TCP B
  1.  CLOSED                                                   LISTEN
  2.  SYN-SENT     --> <SEQ=100><CTL=SYN>              --> SYN-RECEIVED
  3.  ESTABLISHED <-- <SEQ=300><ACK=101><CTL=SYN,ACK> <-- SYN-RECEIVED
  4.  ESTABLISHED --> <SEQ=101><ACK=301><CTL=ACK>         --> ESTABLISHED
  5.  ESTABLISHED --> <SEQ=101><ACK=301><CTL=ACK><DATA> --> ESTABLISHED
```

Basic 3-Way Handshake for Connection Synchronization
Figure 7.

In line 2 of figure 7, TCP A begins by sending a SYN segment indicating that it will use sequence numbers starting with sequence number 100. In line 3, TCP B sends a SYN and acknowledges the SYN it received from TCP A. Note that the acknowledgment field indicates TCP B is now expecting to hear sequence 101, acknowledging the SYN which occupied sequence 100.

At line 4, TCP A responds with an empty segment containing an ACK for TCP B's SYN; and in line 5, TCP A sends some data. Note that the sequence number of the segment in line 5 is the same as in line 4 because the ACK does not occupy sequence number space (if it did, we would wind up ACKing ACK's!).

Simultaneous initiation is only slightly more complex, as is shown in figure 8. Each TCP cycles from CLOSED to SYN-SENT to SYN-RECEIVED to ESTABLISHED.

```
      TCP A                                                    TCP B
  1.  CLOSED                                                   CLOSED
  2.  SYN-SENT     --> <SEQ=100><CTL=SYN>              ...
  3.  SYN-RECEIVED <-- <SEQ=300><CTL=SYN>              <-- SYN-SENT
  4.              ... <SEQ=100><CTL=SYN>              --> SYN-RECEIVED
  5.  SYN-RECEIVED --> <SEQ=100><ACK=301><CTL=SYN,ACK> ...
  6.  ESTABLISHED <-- <SEQ=300><ACK=101><CTL=SYN,ACK> <-- SYN-RECEIVED
  7.              ... <SEQ=101><ACK=301><CTL=ACK>      --> ESTABLISHED
```

Simultaneous Connection Synchronization
Figure 8.

The principle reason for the three-way handshake is to prevent old duplicate connection initiations from causing confusion. To deal with this, a special control message, reset, has been devised. If the receiving TCP is in a non-synchronized state (i.e., SYN-SENT, SYN-RECEIVED), it returns to LISTEN on receiving an acceptable reset. If the TCP is in one of the synchronized states (ESTABLISHED, FIN-WAIT-1, FIN-WAIT-2, CLOSE-WAIT, CLOSING, LAST-ACK,

TIME-WAIT), it aborts the connection and informs its user. We discuss this latter case under "half-open" connections below.

```
TCP A                                             TCP B
  1.  CLOSED                                          LISTEN
  2.  SYN-SENT    --> <SEQ=100><CTL=SYN>              ...
  3.  (duplicate) ... <SEQ=90><CTL=SYN>           --> SYN-RECEIVED
  4.  SYN-SENT    <-- <SEQ=300><ACK=91><CTL=SYN,ACK>  <-- SYN-RECEIVED
  5.  SYN-SENT    --> <SEQ=91><CTL=RST>            --> LISTEN
  6.             ... <SEQ=100><CTL=SYN>            --> SYN-RECEIVED
  7.  SYN-SENT    <-- <SEQ=400><ACK=101><CTL=SYN,ACK>  <-- SYN-RECEIVED
  8.  ESTABLISHED --> <SEQ=101><ACK=401><CTL=ACK>     --> ESTABLISHED
```

Recovery from Old Duplicate SYN
Figure 9.

As a simple example of recovery from old duplicates, consider figure 9. At line 3, an old duplicate SYN arrives at TCP B. TCP B cannot tell that this is an old duplicate, so it responds normally (line 4). TCP A detects that the ACK field is incorrect and returns a RST (reset) with its SEQ field selected to make the segment believable. TCP B, on receiving the RST, returns to the LISTEN state. When the original SYN (pun intended) finally arrives at line 6, the synchronization proceeds normally. If the SYN at line 6 had arrived before the RST, a more complex exchange might have occurred with RST's sent in both directions.

Half-Open Connections and Other Anomalies   An established connection is said to be "half-open" if one of the TCPs has closed or aborted the connection at its end without the knowledge of the other, or if the two ends of the connection have become desynchronized owing to a crash that resulted in loss of memory. Such connections will automatically become reset if an attempt is made to send data in either direction. However, half-open connections are expected to be unusual, and the recovery procedure is mildly involved.

If at site A the connection no longer exists, then an attempt by the user at site B to send any data on it will result in the site B TCP receiving a reset control message. Such a message indicates to the site B TCP that something is wrong, and it is expected to abort the connection.

Assume that two user processes A and B are communicating with one another when a crash occurs causing loss of memory to A's TCP. Depending on the operating system supporting A's TCP, it is likely that some error recovery mechanism exists. When the TCP is up again, A is likely to start again from the beginning or from a recovery point. As a result, A will probably try to OPEN the connection again or try to SEND on the connection it believes open. In the latter case, it receives the error message "connection not open" from the local (A's) TCP. In an attempt to establish the connection, A's TCP will send a segment containing SYN. This scenario leads to the example shown in figure 10. After TCP A crashes, the user attempts to re-open the connection. TCP B, in the meantime, thinks the connection is open.

```
TCP A                                          TCP B
 1.  (CRASH)                                (send 300,receive 100)
 2.  CLOSED                                      ESTABLISHED
 3.  SYN-SENT --> <SEQ=400><CTL=SYN>           --> (??)
 4.  (!!)       <-- <SEQ=300><ACK=100><CTL=ACK>  <-- ESTABLISHED
 5.  SYN-SENT --> <SEQ=100><CTL=RST>           --> (Abort!!)
 6.  SYN-SENT                                    CLOSED
 7.  SYN-SENT --> <SEQ=400><CTL=SYN>           -->
```

Half-Open Connection Discovery
Figure 10.

When the SYN arrives at line 3, TCP B, being in a synchronized state, and the incoming segment outside the window, responds with an acknowledgment indicating what sequence it next expects to hear (ACK 100). TCP A sees that this segment does not acknowledge anything it sent and, being unsynchronized, sends a reset (RST) because it has detected a half-open connection. TCP B aborts at line 5. TCP A will continue to try to establish the connection; the problem is now reduced to the basic 3-way handshake of figure 7.

An interesting alternative case occurs when TCP A crashes and TCP B tries to send data on what it thinks is a synchronized connection. This is illustrated in figure 11. In this case, the data arriving at TCP A from TCP B (line 2) is unacceptable because no such connection exists, so TCP A sends a RST. The RST is acceptable so TCP B processes it and aborts the connection.

```
TCP A                                          TCP B
 1.  (CRASH)                                (send 300,receive 100)
 2.  (??)   <-- <SEQ=300><ACK=100><DATA=10><CTL=ACK>  <-- ESTABLISHED
 3.        --> <SEQ=100><CTL=RST>                     --> (ABORT!!)
```

Active Side Causes Half-Open Connection Discovery
Figure 11.

In figure 12, we find the two TCPs A and B with passive connections waiting for SYN. An old duplicate arriving at TCP B (line 2) stirs B into action. A SYN-ACK is returned (line 3) and causes TCP A to generate a RST (the ACK in line 3 is not acceptable). TCP B accepts the reset and returns to its passive LISTEN state.

```
     TCP A                                     TCP B
 1.  LISTEN                                     LISTEN
 2.       ... <SEQ=Z><CTL=SYN>                --> SYN-RECEIVED
 3.  (??) <-- <SEQ=X><ACK=Z+1><CTL=SYN,ACK>   <-- SYN-RECEIVED
 4.       --> <SEQ=Z+1><CTL=RST>              --> (return to LISTEN!)
 5.  LISTEN                                     LISTEN
```

Old Duplicate SYN Initiates a Reset on two Passive Sockets
Figure 12.

A variety of other cases are possible, all of which are accounted for by the following rules for RST generation and processing.

Reset Generation As a general rule, reset (RST) must be sent whenever a segment arrives which apparently is not intended for the current connection. A reset must not be sent if it is not clear that this is the case.

There are three groups of states:

1. If the connection does not exist (CLOSED) then a reset is sent in response to any incoming segment except another reset. In particular, SYNs addressed to a non-existent connection are rejected by this means.

    If the incoming segment has an ACK field, the reset takes its sequence number from the ACK field of the segment, otherwise the reset has sequence number zero and the ACK field is set to the sum of the sequence number and segment length of the incoming segment. The connection remains in the CLOSED state.

2. If the connection is in any non-synchronized state (LISTEN, SYN-SENT, SYN-RE-CEIVED), and the incoming segment acknowledges something not yet sent (the segment carries an unacceptable ACK), or if an incoming segment has a security level or compartment which does not exactly match the level and compartment requested for the connection, a reset is sent.

    If our SYN has not been acknowledged and the precedence level of the incoming segment is higher than the precedence level requested then either raise the local precedence level (if allowed by the user and the system) or send a reset; or if the precedence level of the incoming segment is lower than the precedence level requested then continue as if the precedence matched exactly (if the remote TCP cannot raise the precedence level to match ours this will be detected in the next segment it sends, and the connection will be terminated then). If our SYN has been acknowledged (perhaps in this incoming segment) the precedence level of the incoming segment must match the local precedence level exactly, if it does not a reset must be sent.

    If the incoming segment has an ACK field, the reset takes its sequence number from the ACK field of the segment, otherwise the reset has sequence number zero and the ACK field is set to the sum of the sequence number and segment length of the incoming segment. The connection remains in the same state.

3. If the connection is in a synchronized state (ESTABLISHED, FIN-WAIT-1, FIN-WAIT-2, CLOSE-WAIT, CLOSING, LAST-ACK, TIME-WAIT), any unacceptable segment (out of window sequence number or unacceptible acknowledgment number) must elicit only an empty acknowledgment segment containing the current send-sequence number and an acknowledgment indicating the next sequence number expected to be received, and the connection remains in the same state.

    If an incoming segment has a security level, or compartment, or precedence which does not exactly match the level, and compartment, and precedence requested for the connection,a reset is sent and connection goes to the CLOSED state. The reset takes its sequence number from the ACK field of the incoming segment.

Reset Processing In all states except SYN-SENT, all reset (RST) segments are validated by checking their SEQ-fields. A reset is valid if its sequence number is in the window. In the SYN-SENT state (a RST received in response to an initial SYN), the RST is acceptable if the ACK field acknowledges the SYN.

The receiver of a RST first validates it, then changes state. If the receiver was in the LISTEN state, it ignores it. If the receiver was in SYN-RECEIVED state and had previously been in the LISTEN state, then the receiver returns to the LISTEN state, otherwise the receiver aborts the connection and goes to the CLOSED state. If the receiver was in any other state, it aborts the connection and advises the user and goes to the CLOSED state.

3.5. Closing a Connection

CLOSE is an operation meaning "I have no more data to send." The notion of closing a full-duplex connection is subject to ambiguous interpretation, of course, since it may not be obvious how to treat the receiving side of the connection. We have chosen to treat CLOSE in a simplex fashion. The user who CLOSEs may continue to RECEIVE until he is told that the other side has CLOSED also. Thus, a program could initiate several SENDs followed by a CLOSE, and then continue to RECEIVE until signaled that a RECEIVE failed because the other side has CLOSED. We assume that the TCP will signal a user, even if no RECEIVEs are outstanding, that the other side has closed, so the user can terminate his side gracefully. A TCP will reliably deliver all buffers SENT before the connection was CLOSED so a user who expects no data in return need only wait to hear the connection was CLOSED successfully to know that all his data was received at the destination TCP. Users must keep reading connections they close for sending until the TCP says no more data.

There are essentially three cases:

1. The user initiates by telling the TCP to CLOSE the connection
2. The remote TCP initiates by sending a FIN control signal
3. Both users CLOSE simultaneously

Case 1: Local user initiates the close

In this case, a FIN segment can be constructed and placed on the outgoing segment queue. No further SENDs from the user will be accepted by the TCP, and it enters the FIN-WAIT-1 state. RECEIVEs are allowed in this state. All segments preceding and including FIN will be retransmitted until acknowledged. When the other TCP has both acknowledged the FIN and sent a FIN of its own, the first TCP can ACK this FIN. Note that a TCP receiving a FIN will ACK but not send its own FIN until its user has CLOSED the connection also.

Case 2: TCP receives a FIN from the network

If an unsolicited FIN arrives from the network, the receiving TCP can ACK it and tell the user that the connection is closing. The user will respond with a CLOSE, upon which the TCP can send a FIN to the other TCP after sending any remaining data. The TCP then waits until its own FIN is acknowledged whereupon it deletes the connection. If an ACK is not forthcoming, after the user timeout the connection is aborted and the user is told.

Case 3: both users close simultaneously

A simultaneous CLOSE by users at both ends of a connection causes FIN segments to be exchanged. When all segments preceding the FINs have been processed and acknowledged, each TCP can ACK the FIN it has received. Both will, upon receiving these ACKs, delete the connection.

```
      TCP A                                                    TCP B
1.    ESTABLISHED                                              ESTABLISHED
2.    (Close)
      FIN-WAIT-1  --> <SEQ=100><ACK=300><CTL=FIN,ACK>  --> CLOSE-WAIT
3.    FIN-WAIT-2  <-- <SEQ=300><ACK=101><CTL=ACK>       <-- CLOSE-WAIT
4.                                                           (Close)
      TIME-WAIT   <-- <SEQ=300><ACK=101><CTL=FIN,ACK>   <-- LAST-ACK
5.    TIME-WAIT   --> <SEQ=101><ACK=301><CTL=ACK>       --> CLOSED
6.    (2 MSL)
      CLOSED
```

                        Normal Close Sequence
                            Figure 13.

```
      TCP A                                                    TCP B
1.    ESTABLISHED                                              ESTABLISHED
2.    (Close)                                                  (Close)
      FIN-WAIT-1  --> <SEQ=100><ACK=300><CTL=FIN,ACK>  ... FIN-WAIT-1
                  <-- <SEQ=300><ACK=100><CTL=FIN,ACK>  <--
                  ... <SEQ=100><ACK=300><CTL=FIN,ACK>  -->
3.    CLOSING     --> <SEQ=101><ACK=301><CTL=ACK>      ... CLOSING
                  <-- <SEQ=301><ACK=101><CTL=ACK>      <--
                  ... <SEQ=101><ACK=301><CTL=ACK>      -->
4.    TIME-WAIT                                              TIME-WAIT
      (2 MSL)                                                (2 MSL)
      CLOSED                                                 CLOSED
```

                    Simultaneous Close Sequence
                          Figure 14.

3.6. Precedence and Security

The intent is that connection be allowed only between ports operating with exactly the same security and compartment values and at the higher of the precedence level requested by the two ports.

The precedence and security parameters used in TCP are exactly those defined in the Internet Protocol (IP) [2]. Throughout this TCP specification the term "security/compartment" is intended to indicate the security parameters used in IP including security, compartment, user group, and handling restriction.

A connection attempt with mismatched security/compartment values or a lower precedence value must be rejected by sending a reset. Rejecting a connection due to too low a precedence only occurs after an acknowledgment of the SYN has been received.

Note that TCP modules which operate only at the default value of precedence will still have to check the precedence of incoming segments and possibly raise the precedence level they use on the connection.

The security paramaters may be used even in a non-secure environment (the values would indicate unclassified data), thus hosts in non-secure environments must be prepared to receive the security parameters, though they need not send them.

3.7. Data Communication

Once the connection is established data is communicated by the exchange of segments. Because segments may be lost due to errors (checksum test failure), or network congestion, TCP uses retransmission (after a timeout) to ensure delivery of every segment. Duplicate segments may arrive due to network or TCP retransmission. As discussed in the section on sequence numbers the TCP performs certain tests on the sequence and acknowledgment numbers in the segments to verify their acceptability.

The sender of data keeps track of the next sequence number to use in the variable SND.NXT. The receiver of data keeps track of the next sequence number to expect in the variable RCV.NXT. The sender of data keeps track of the oldest unacknowledged sequence number in the variable SND.UNA. If the data flow is momentarily idle and all data sent has been acknowledged then the three variables will be equal.

When the sender creates a segment and transmits it the sender advances SND.NXT. When the receiver accepts a segment it advances RCV.NXT and sends an acknowledgment. When the data sender receives an acknowledgment it advances SND.UNA. The extent to which the values of these variables differ is a measure of the delay in the communication. The amount by which the variables are advanced is the length of the data in the segment. Note that once in the ESTABLISHED state all segments must carry current acknowledgment information.

The CLOSE user call implies a push function, as does the FIN control flag in an incoming segment.

Retransmission Timeout   Because of the variability of the networks that compose an internetwork system and the wide range of uses of TCP connections the retransmission timeout must be dynamically determined. One procedure for determining a retransmission time out is given here as an illustration.

An Example Retransmission Timeout Procedure

> Measure the elapsed time between sending a data octet with a particular sequence number and receiving an acknowledgment that covers that sequence number (segments sent do not have to match segments received). This measured elapsed time is the Round Trip Time (RTT). Next compute a Smoothed Round Trip Time (SRTT) as:
>
> SRTT = (ALPHA * SRTT) + ((1-ALPHA) * RTT)
>
> and based on this, compute the retransmission timeout (RTO) as:
>
> RTO = min[UBOUND,max[LBOUND,(BETA*SRTT)]]
>
> where UBOUND is an upper bound on the timeout (e.g., 1 minute), LBOUND is a lower bound on the timeout (e.g., 1 second), ALPHA is a smoothing factor (e.g., .8 to .9), and BETA is a delay variance factor (e.g., 1.3 to 2.0).

The Communication of Urgent Information   The objective of the TCP urgent mechanism is to allow the sending user to stimulate the receiving user to accept some urgent data and to permit the receiving TCP to indicate to the receiving user when all the currently known urgent data has been received by the user.

This mechanism permits a point in the data stream to be designated as the end of urgent information. Whenever this point is in advance of the receive sequence number (RCV.NXT) at the receiving TCP, that TCP must tell the user to go into "urgent mode"; when the receive sequence number catches up to the urgent pointer, the TCP must tell user to go into "normal mode". If the urgent pointer is updated while the user is in "urgent mode", the update will be invisible to the user.

The method employs a urgent field which is carried in all segments transmitted. The URG control flag indicates that the urgent field is meaningful and must be added to the segment sequence number to yield the urgent pointer. The absence of this flag indicates that there is no urgent data outstanding.

To send an urgent indication the user must also send at least one data octet. If the sending user also indicates a push, timely delivery of the urgent information to the destination process is enhanced.

Managing the Window   The window sent in each segment indicates the range of sequence numbers the sender of the window (the data receiver) is currently prepared to accept. There is an assumption that this is related to the currently available data buffer space available for this connection.

Indicating a large window encourages transmissions. If more data arrives than can be accepted, it will be discarded. This will result in excessive retransmissions, adding unnecessarily to the load on the network and the TCPs. Indicating a small window may restrict the transmission of data to the point of introducing a round trip delay between each new segment transmitted.

The mechanisms provided allow a TCP to advertise a large window and to subsequently advertise a much smaller window without having accepted that much data. This, so called "shrinking the window," is strongly discouraged. The robustness principle dictates that TCPs will not shrink the window themselves, but will be prepared for such behavior on the part of other TCPs.

The sending TCP must be prepared to accept from the user and send at least one octet of new data even if the send window is zero. The sending TCP must regularly retransmit to the receiving TCP even when the window is zero. Two minutes is recommended for the retransmission interval when the window is zero. This retransmission is essential to guarantee that when either TCP has a zero window the re-opening of the window will be reliably reported to the other.

When the receiving TCP has a zero window and a segment arrives it must still send an acknowledgment showing its next expected sequence number and current window (zero).

The sending TCP packages the data to be transmitted into segments which fit the current window, and may repackage segments on the retransmission queue. Such repackaging is not required, but may be helpful.

In a connection with a one-way data flow, the window information will be carried in acknowledgment segments that all have the same sequence number so there will be no way to reorder them if they arrive out of order. This is not a serious problem, but it will allow the window information to be on occasion temporarily based on old reports from the data receiver. A refinement to avoid this problem is to act on the window information from segments that carry the highest acknowledgment number (that is segments with acknowledgment number equal or greater than the highest previously received).

The window management procedure has significant influence on the communication performance. The following comments are suggestions to implementers.

Window Management Suggestions   Allocating a very small window causes data to be transmitted in many small segments when better performance is achieved using fewer large segments.

One suggestion for avoiding small windows is for the receiver to defer updating a window until the additional allocation is at least X percent of the maximum allocation possible for the connection (where X might be 20 to 40).

Another suggestion is for the sender to avoid sending small segments by waiting until the window is large enough before sending data. If the the user signals a push function then the data must be sent even if it is a small segment.

Note that the acknowledgments should not be delayed or unnecessary retransmissions will result. One strategy would be to send an acknowledgment when a small segment arrives (with out updating the window information), and then to send another acknowledgment with new window information when the window is larger.

The segment sent to probe a zero window may also begin a break up of transmitted data into smaller and smaller segments. If a segment containing a single data octet sent to probe a zero window is accepted, it consumes one octet of the window now available. If the sending TCP simply sends as much as it can whenever the window is non zero, the transmitted data will be broken into alternating big and small segments. As time goes on, occasional pauses in the receiver making window allocation available will result in breaking the big segments into a small and not quite so big pair. And after a while the data transmission will be in mostly small segments.

The suggestion here is that the TCP implementations need to actively attempt to combine small window allocations into larger windows, since the mechanisms for managing the window tend to lead to many small windows in the simplest minded implementations.

3.8. Interfaces

There are of course two interfaces of concern: the user/TCP interface and the TCP/lower-level interface. We have a fairly elaborate model of the user/TCP interface, but the interface to the lower level protocol module is left unspecified here, since it will be specified in detail by the specification of the lowel level protocol. For the case that the lower level is IP we note some of the parameter values that TCPs might use.

User/TCP Interface   The following functional description of user commands to the TCP is, at best, fictional, since every operating system will have different facilities. Consequently, we must warn readers that different TCP implementations may have different user interfaces. However, all TCPs must provide a certain minimum set of services to guarantee that all TCP implementations can support the same protocol hierarchy. This section specifies the functional interfaces required of all TCP implementations.

TCP User Commands   The following sections functionally characterize a USER/TCP interface. The notation used is similar to most procedure or function calls in high level languages, but this usage is not meant to rule out trap type service calls (e.g., SVCs, UUOs, EMTs).

The user commands described below specify the basic functions the TCP must perform to support interprocess communication. Individual implementations must define their own exact format, and may provide combinations or subsets of the basic functions in single calls. In particular, some implementations may wish to automatically OPEN a connection on the first SEND or RECEIVE issued by the user for a given connection.

In providing interprocess communication facilities, the TCP must not only accept commands, but must also return information to the processes it serves. The latter consists of:

a. general information about a connection (e.g., interrupts, remote close, binding of unspecified foreign socket).

b. replies to specific user commands indicating success or various types of failure.

Open

Format: OPEN (local port, foreign socket, active/passive [, timeout] [, precedence] [, security/compartment] [, options]) -> local connection name

We assume that the local TCP is aware of the identity of the processes it serves and will check the authority of the process to use the connection specified. Depending upon the implementation of the TCP, the local network and TCP identifiers for the source address will either be supplied by the TCP or the lower level protocol (e.g., IP). These considerations are the result of concern about security, to the extent that no TCP be able to masquerade as another one, and so on. Similarly, no process can masquerade as another without the collusion of the TCP.

If the active/passive flag is set to passive, then this is a call to LISTEN for an incoming connection. A passive open may have either a fully specified foreign socket to wait for a particular connection or an unspecified foreign socket to wait for any call. A fully specified passive call can be made active by the subsequent execution of a SEND.

A transmission control block (TCB) is created and partially filled in with data from the OPEN command parameters.

On an active OPEN command, the TCP will begin the procedure to synchronize (i.e., establish) the connection at once.

The timeout, if present, permits the caller to set up a timeout for all data submitted to TCP. If data is not successfully delivered to the destination within the timeout period, the TCP will abort the connection. The present global default is five minutes.

The TCP or some component of the operating system will verify the users authority to open a connection with the specified precedence or security/compartment. The absence of precedence or security/compartment specification in the OPEN call indicates the default values must be used.

TCP will accept incoming requests as matching only if the security/compartment information is exactly the same and only if the precedence is equal to or higher than the precedence requested in the OPEN call.

The precedence for the connection is the higher of the values requested in the OPEN call and received from the incoming request, and fixed at that value for the life of the connection.Implementers may want to give the user control of this precedence negotiation. For example, the user might be allowed to specify that the precedence must be exactly matched, or that any attempt to raise the precedence be confirmed by the user.

A local connection name will be returned to the user by the TCP. The local connection name can then be used as a short hand term for the connection defined by the <local socket, foreign socket> pair.

Send

Format: SEND (local connection name, buffer address, byte count, PUSH flag, URGENT flag [,timeout])

This call causes the data contained in the indicated user buffer to be sent on the indicated connection. If the connection has not been opened, the SEND is considered an error. Some implementations may allow users to SEND first; in which case, an automatic OPEN would be done. If the calling process is not authorized to use this connection, an error is returned.

If the PUSH flag is set, the data must be transmitted promptly to the receiver, and the PUSH bit will be set in the last TCP segment created from the buffer. If the PUSH flag is not set, the data may be combined with data from subsequent SENDs for transmission efficiency.

If the URGENT flag is set, segments sent to the destination TCP will have the urgent pointer set. The receiving TCP will signal the urgent condition to the receiving process if the urgent pointer indicates that data preceding the urgent pointer has not been consumed by the receiving process. The purpose of urgent is to stimulate the receiver to process the urgent data and to indicate to the receiver when all the currently known urgent data has been received. The number of times the sending user's TCP signals urgent will not necessarily be equal to the number of times the receiving user will be notified of the presence of urgent data.

If no foreign socket was specified in the OPEN, but the connection is established (e.g., because a LISTENing connection has become specific due to a foreign segment arriving for the local socket), then the designated buffer is sent to the implied foreign socket. Users who make use of OPEN with an unspecified foreign socket can make use of SEND without ever explicitly knowing the foreign socket address.

However, if a SEND is attempted before the foreign socket becomes specified, an error will be returned. Users can use the STATUS call to determine the status of the connection. In some implementations the TCP may notify the user when an unspecified socket is bound.

If a timeout is specified, the current user timeout for this connection is changed to the new one.

In the simplest implementation, SEND would not return control to the sending process until either the transmission was complete or the timeout had been exceeded. However, this simple method is both subject to deadlocks (for example, both sides of the connection might try to do SENDs before doing any RECEIVEs) and offers poor performance, so it is not recommended. A more sophisticated implementation would return immediately to allow the process to run concurrently with network I/O, and, furthermore, to allow multiple SENDs to be in progress. Multiple SENDs are served in first come, first served order, so the TCP will queue those it cannot service immediately.

We have implicitly assumed an asynchronous user interface in which a SEND later elicits some kind of SIGNAL or pseudo-interrupt from the serving TCP. An alternative is to return a response immediately. For instance, SENDs might return immediate local acknowledgment, even if the segment sent had not been acknowledged by the distant TCP. We could optimistically assume eventual success. If we are wrong, the connection will close anyway due to the timeout. In implementations of this kind (synchronous), there will still be some asynchronous signals, but these will deal with the connection itself, and not with specific segments or buffers.

In order for the process to distinguish among error or success indications for different SENDs, it might be appropriate for the buffer address to be returned along with the coded response to the SEND request. TCP-to-user signals are discussed below, indicating the information which should be returned to the calling process.

Receive

Format: RECEIVE (local connection name, buffer address, byte count) -> byte count, urgent flag, push flag

This command allocates a receiving buffer associated with the specified connection. If no OPEN precedes this command or the calling process is not authorized to use this connection, an error is returned.

In the simplest implementation, control would not return to the calling program until either the buffer was filled, or some error occurred, but this scheme is highly subject to deadlocks. A more sophisticated implementation would permit several RECEIVEs to be outstanding at once. These would be filled as segments arrive. This strategy permits increased throughput at the cost of a more elaborate scheme (possibly asynchronous) to notify the calling program that a PUSH has been seen or a buffer filled.

If enough data arrive to fill the buffer before a PUSH is seen, the PUSH flag will not be set in the response to the RECEIVE. The buffer will be filled with as much data as it can hold. If a PUSH is seen before the buffer is filled the buffer will be returned partially filled and PUSH indicated.

If there is urgent data the user will have been informed as soon as it arrived via a TCP-to-user signal. The receiving user should thus be in "urgent mode". If the URGENT flag is on, additional urgent data remains. If the URGENT flag is off, this call to RECEIVE has returned all the urgent data, and the user may now leave "urgent mode". Note that data following the urgent pointer (non-urgent data) cannot be delivered to the user in the same buffer with preceeding urgent data unless the boundary is clearly marked for the user.

To distinguish among several outstanding RECEIVEs and to take care of the case that a buffer is not completely filled, the return code is accompanied by both a buffer pointer and a byte count indicating the actual length of the data received.

Alternative implementations of RECEIVE might have the TCP allocate buffer storage, or the TCP might share a ring buffer with the user.

Close

Format: CLOSE (local connection name)

This command causes the connection specified to be closed. If the connection is not open or the calling process is not authorized to use this connection, an error is returned. Closing connections is intended to be a graceful operation in the sense that outstanding SENDs will be transmitted (and retransmitted), as flow control permits, until all have been serviced. Thus, it should be acceptable to make several SEND calls, followed by a CLOSE, and expect all the data to be sent to the destination. It should also be clear that users should continue to RECEIVE on CLOSING connections, since the other side may be trying to transmit the last of its data. Thus, CLOSE means "I have no more to send" but does not mean "I will not receive any more." It may happen (if the user level protocol is not well thought out) that the closing side is unable to get rid of all its data before timing out. In this event, CLOSE turns into ABORT, and the closing TCP gives up.

The user may CLOSE the connection at any time on his own initiative, or in response to various prompts from the TCP (e.g., remote close executed, transmission timeout exceeded, destination inaccessible).

Because closing a connection requires communication with the foreign TCP, connections may remain in the closing state for a short time. Attempts to reopen the connection before the TCP replies to the CLOSE command will result in error responses.

Close also implies push function.

Status

Format: STATUS (local connection name) -> status data

This is an implementation dependent user command and could be excluded without adverse effect. Information returned would typically come from the TCB associated with the connection.

This command returns a data block containing the following information:

> local socket,
>
> foreign socket,
>
> local connection name,
>
> receive window,
>
> send window,
>
> connection state,
>
> number of buffers awaiting acknowledgment,
>
> number of buffers pending receipt,
>
> urgent state,
>
> precedence,
>
> security/compartment,
>
> and transmission timeout.

Depending on the state of the connection, or on the implementation itself, some of this information may not be available or meaningful. If the calling process is not authorized to use this connection, an error is returned. This prevents unauthorized processes from gaining information about a connection.

Abort

Format: ABORT (local connection name)

This command causes all pending SENDs and RECEIVES to be aborted, the TCB to be removed, and a special RESET message to be sent to the TCP on the other side of the connection. Depending on the implementation, users may receive abort indications for each outstanding SEND or RECEIVE, or may simply receive an ABORT-acknowledgment.

TCP-to-User Messages   It is assumed that the operating system environment provides a means for the TCP to asynchronously signal the user program. When the TCP does signal a user program, certain information is passed to the user. Often in the specification the information will be an error message. In other cases there will be information relating to the completion of processing a SEND or RECEIVE or other user call.

The following information is provided:

Local Connection Name	Always
Response String	Always
Buffer Address	Send & Receive
Byte count (counts bytes received)	Receive
Push flag	Receive
Urgent flag	Receive

TCP/Lower-Level Interface   The TCP calls on a lower level protocol module to actually send and receive information over a network. One case is that of the ARPA internetwork system where the lower level module is the Internet Protocol (IP) [2].

If the lower level protocol is IP it provides arguments for a type of service and for a time to live. TCP uses the following settings for these parameters:

Type of Service = Precedence: routine, Delay: normal, Throughput: normal, Reliability: normal; or 00000000.

Time to Live = one minute, or 00111100.

Note that the assumed maximum segment lifetime is two minutes. Here we explicitly ask that a segment be destroyed if it cannot be delivered by the internet system within one minute.

If the lower level is IP (or other protocol that provides this feature) and source routing is used, the interface must allow the route information to be communicated. This is especially important so that the source and destination addresses used in the TCP checksum be the originating source and ultimate destination. It is also important to preserve the return route to answer connection requests.

Any lower level protocol will have to provide the source address, destination address, and protocol fields, and some way to determine the "TCP length", both to provide the functional equivlent service of IP and to be used in the TCP checksum.

3.9. Event Processing

The processing depicted in this section is an example of one possible implementation. Other implementations may have slightly different processing sequences, but they should differ from those in this section only in detail, not in substance.

The activity of the TCP can be characterized as responding to events. The events that occur can be cast into three categories: user calls, arriving segments, and timeouts. This section describes the processing the TCP does in response to each of the events. In many cases the processing required depends on the state of the connection.

Events that occur:

> User Calls
>
>> OPEN
>>
>> SEND
>>
>> RECEIVE
>>
>> CLOSE
>>
>> ABORT
>>
>> STATUS
>
> Arriving Segments
>
>> SEGMENT ARRIVES
>
> Timeouts
>
>> USER TIMEOUT
>>
>> RETRANSMISSION TIMEOUT
>>
>> TIME-WAIT TIMEOUT

The model of the TCP/user interface is that user commands receive an immediate return and possibly a delayed response via an event or pseudo interrupt. In the following descriptions, the term "signal" means cause a delayed response.

Error responses are given as character strings. For example, user commands referencing connections that do not exist receive "error: connection not open".

Please note in the following that all arithmetic on sequence numbers, acknowledgment numbers, windows, et cetera, is modulo $2**32$ the size of the sequence number space. Also note that "=<" means less than or equal to (modulo $2**32$).

A natural way to think about processing incoming segments is to imagine that they are first tested for proper sequence number (i.e., that their contents lie in the range of the expected "receive window" in the sequence number space) and then that they are generally queued and processed in sequence number order.

When a segment overlaps other already received segments we reconstruct the segment to contain just the new data, and adjust the header fields to be consistent.

N O T E Note that if no state change is mentioned the TCP stays in the same state.

OPEN Call

> CLOSED STATE (i.e., TCB does not exist)
>
> Create a new transmission control block (TCB) to hold connection state information. Fill in local socket identifier, foreign socket, precedence, security/compartment, and user timeout information. Note that some parts of the foreign socket may be unspecified in a

passive OPEN and are to be filled in by the parameters of the incoming SYN segment. Verify the security and precedence requested are allowed for this user, if not return "error: precedence not allowed" or "error: security/compartment not allowed." If passive enter the LISTEN state and return. If active and the foreign socket is unspecified, return "error: foreign socket unspecified"; if active and the foreign socket is specified, issue a SYN segment. An initial send sequence number (ISS) is selected. A SYN segment of the form <SEQ=ISS><CTL=SYN> is sent. Set SND.UNA to ISS, SND.NXT to ISS+1, enter SYN-SENT state, and return.

If the caller does not have access to the local socket specified, return "error: connection illegal for this process". If there is no room to create a new connection, return "error: insufficient resources".

LISTEN STATE

If active and the foreign socket is specified, then change the connection from passive to active, select an ISS. Send a SYN segment, set SND.UNA to ISS, SND.NXT to ISS+1. Enter SYN-SENT state. Data associated with SEND may be sent with SYN segment or queued for transmission after entering ESTABLISHED state. The urgent bit if requested in the command must be sent with the data segments sent as a result of this command. If there is no room to queue the request, respond with "error: insufficient resources". If Foreign socket was not specified, then return "error: foreign socket unspecified".

SYN-SENT STATE

SYN-RECEIVED STATE

ESTABLISHED STATE

FIN-WAIT-1 STATE

FIN-WAIT-2 STATE

CLOSE-WAIT STATE

CLOSING STATE

LAST-ACK STATE

TIME-WAIT STATE

Return "error: connection already exists".

SEND Call

CLOSED STATE (i.e., TCB does not exist)

If the user does not have access to such a connection, then return "error: connection illegal for this process".

Otherwise, return "error: connection does not exist".

LISTEN STATE

If the foreign socket is specified, then change the connection from passive to active, select an ISS. Send a SYN segment, set SND.UNA to ISS, SND.NXT to ISS+1. Enter SYN-SENT state. Data associated with SEND may be sent with SYN segment or queued for transmission after entering ESTABLISHED state. The urgent bit if requested in the command must be sent with the data segments sent as a result of this command. If there is no room to queue the request, respond with "error: insufficient resources". If Foreign socket was not specified, then return "error: foreign socket unspecified".

SYN-SENT STATE

SYN-RECEIVED STATE

Queue the data for transmission after entering ESTABLISHED state. If no space to queue, respond with "error: insufficient resources".

ESTABLISHED STATE

CLOSE-WAIT STATE

Segmentize the buffer and send it with a piggybacked acknowledgment (acknowledgment value = RCV.NXT). If there is insufficient space to remember this buffer, simply return "error: insufficient resources".

If the urgent flag is set, then SND.UP <- SND.NXT-1 and set the urgent pointer in the outgoing segments.

FIN-WAIT-1 STATE

FIN-WAIT-2 STATE

CLOSING STATE

LAST-ACK STATE

TIME-WAIT STATE

Return "error: connection closing" and do not service request.

RECEIVE Call

CLOSED STATE (i.e., TCB does not exist)

If the user does not have access to such a connection, return "error: connection illegal for this process".

Otherwise return "error: connection does not exist".

LISTEN STATE

SYN-SENT STATE

SYN-RECEIVED STATE

Queue for processing after entering ESTABLISHED state. If there is no room to queue this request, respond with "error: insufficient resources".

ESTABLISHED STATE

FIN-WAIT-1 STATE

FIN-WAIT-2 STATE

If insufficient incoming segments are queued to satisfy the request, queue the request. If there is no queue space to remember the RECEIVE, respond with "error: insufficient resources".

Reassemble queued incoming segments into receive buffer and return to user. Mark "push seen" (PUSH) if this is the case.

If RCV.UP is in advance of the data currently being passed to the user notify the user of the presence of urgent data.

When the TCP takes responsibility for delivering data to the user that fact must be communicated to the sender via an acknowledgment. The formation of such an acknowledgment is described below in the discussion of processing an incoming segment.

CLOSE-WAIT STATE

Since the remote side has already sent FIN, RECEIVEs must be satisfied by text already on hand, but not yet delivered to the user. If no text is awaiting delivery, the RECEIVE will get a "error: connection closing" response. Otherwise, any remaining text can be used to satisfy the RECEIVE.

CLOSING STATE

LAST-ACK STATE

TIME-WAIT STATE

Return "error: connection closing".

CLOSE Call

CLOSED STATE (i.e., TCB does not exist)

If the user does not have access to such a connection, return "error: connection illegal for this process".

Otherwise, return "error: connection does not exist".

LISTEN STATE

Any outstanding RECEIVEs are returned with "error: closing" responses. Delete TCB, enter CLOSED state, and return.

SYN-SENT STATE

Delete the TCB and return "error: closing" responses to any queued SENDs, or RECEIVEs.

SYN-RECEIVED STATE

If no SENDs have been issued and there is no pending data to send, then form a FIN segment and send it, and enter FIN-WAIT-1 state; otherwise queue for processing after entering ESTABLISHED state.

ESTABLISHED STATE

Queue this until all preceding SENDs have been segmentized, then form a FIN segment and send it. In any case, enter FIN-WAIT-1 state.

FIN-WAIT-1 STATE

FIN-WAIT-2 STATE

Strictly speaking, this is an error and should receive a "error: connection closing" response. An "ok" response would be acceptable, too, as long as a second FIN is not emitted (the first FIN may be retransmitted though).

CLOSE-WAIT STATE

Queue this request until all preceding SENDs have been segmentized; then send a FIN segment, enter CLOSING state.

CLOSING STATE

LAST-ACK STATE

TIME-WAIT STATE

Respond with "error: connection closing".

ABORT Call

CLOSED STATE (i.e., TCB does not exist)

If the user should not have access to such a connection, return "error: connection illegal for this process".

Otherwise return "error: connection does not exist".

LISTEN STATE

Any outstanding RECEIVEs should be returned with "error: connection reset" responses. Delete TCB, enter CLOSED state, and return.

SYN-SENT STATE

All queued SENDs and RECEIVEs should be given "connection reset" notification, delete the TCB, enter CLOSED state, and return.

SYN-RECEIVED STATE

ESTABLISHED STATE

FIN-WAIT-1 STATE

FIN-WAIT-2 STATE

CLOSE-WAIT STATE

Send a reset segment:

```
<SEQ=SND.NXT><CTL=RST>
```

All queued SENDs and RECEIVEs should be given "connection reset" notification; all segments queued for transmission (except for the RST formed above) or retransmission should be flushed, delete the TCB, enter CLOSED state, and return.

CLOSING STATE

LAST-ACK STATE

TIME-WAIT STATE

Respond with "ok" and delete the TCB, enter CLOSED state, and return.

STATUS Call

CLOSED STATE (i.e., TCB does not exist)

If the user should not have access to such a connection, return "error: connection illegal for this process".

Otherwise return "error: connection does not exist".

LISTEN STATE

Return "state = LISTEN", and the TCB pointer.

SYN-SENT STATE

Return "state = SYN-SENT", and the TCB pointer.

SYN-RECEIVED STATE

Return "state = SYN-RECEIVED", and the TCB pointer.

ESTABLISHED STATE

Return "state = ESTABLISHED", and the TCB pointer.

FIN-WAIT-1 STATE

Return "state = FIN-WAIT-1", and the TCB pointer.

FIN-WAIT-2 STATE

Return "state = FIN-WAIT-2", and the TCB pointer.

CLOSE-WAIT STATE

Return "state = CLOSE-WAIT", and the TCB pointer.

CLOSING STATE

Return "state = CLOSING", and the TCB pointer.

LAST-ACK STATE

Return "state = LAST-ACK", and the TCB pointer.

TIME-WAIT STATE

Return "state = TIME-WAIT", and the TCB pointer.

SEGMENT ARRIVES

If the state is CLOSED (i.e., TCB does not exist) then all data in the incoming segment is discarded. An incoming segment containing a RST is discarded. An incoming segment not containing a RST causes a RST to be sent in response. The acknowledgment and sequence field values are selected to make the reset sequence acceptable to the TCP that sent the offending segment.

If the ACK bit is off, sequence number zero is used,

```
<SEQ=0><ACK=SEG.SEQ+SEG.LEN><CTL=RST,ACK>
```

If the ACK bit is on,

```
<SEQ=SEG.ACK><CTL=RST>
```

Return.

If the state is LISTEN then

first check for an RST

An incoming RST should be ignored. Return.

second check for an ACK

Any acknowledgment is bad if it arrives on a connection still in the LISTEN state. An acceptable reset segment should be formed for any arriving ACK-bearing segment. The RST should be formatted as follows:

```
<SEQ=SEG.ACK><CTL=RST>
```

Return.

third check for a SYN

If the SYN bit is set, check the security. If the security/compartment on the incoming segment does not exactly match the security/compartment in the TCB then send a reset and return.

```
<SEQ=SEG.ACK><CTL=RST>
```

If the SEG.PRC is greater than the TCB.PRC then if allowed by the user and the system set TCB.PRC<-SEG.PRC, if not allowed send a reset and return.

```
<SEQ=SEG.ACK><CTL=RST>
```

If the SEG.PRC is less than the TCB.PRC then continue.

Set RCV.NXT to SEG.SEQ+1, IRS is set to SEG.SEQ and any other control or text should be queued for processing later. ISS should be selected and a SYN segment sent of the form:

```
<SEQ=ISS><ACK=RCV.NXT><CTL=SYN,ACK>
```

SND.NXT is set to ISS+1 and SND.UNA to ISS. The connection state should be changed to SYN-RECEIVED. Note that any other incoming control or data (combined with SYN) will be processed in the SYN-RECEIVED state, but processing of SYN and ACK should not be repeated. If the listen was not fully specified (i.e., the foreign socket was not fully specified), then the unspecified fields should be filled in now.

fourth other text or control

Any other control or text-bearing segment (not containing SYN) must have an ACK and thus would be discarded by the ACK processing. An incoming RST segment could not be valid, since it could not have been sent in response to anything sent by this incarnation of the connection. So you are unlikely to get here, but if you do, drop the segment, and return.

If the state is SYN-SENT then

first check the ACK bit

If the ACK bit is set

If SEG.ACK =< ISS, or SEG.ACK > SND.NXT, send a reset (unless the RST bit is set, if so drop the segment and return)

```
<SEQ=SEG.ACK><CTL=RST>
```

and discard the segment. Return.

If SND.UNA =< SEG.ACK =< SND.NXT then the ACK is acceptable.

second check the RST bit

If the RST bit is set

If the ACK was acceptable then signal the user "error: connection reset", drop the segment, enter CLOSED state, delete TCB, and return. Otherwise (no ACK) drop the segment and return.

third check the security and precedence

If the security/compartment in the segment does not exactly match the security/compartment in the TCB, send a reset

If there is an ACK

```
<SEQ=SEG.ACK><CTL=RST>
```

Otherwise

```
<SEQ=0><ACK=SEG.SEQ+SEG.LEN><CTL=RST,ACK>
```

If there is an ACK

The precedence in the segment must match the precedence in the TCB, if not, send a reset

```
<SEQ=SEG.ACK><CTL=RST>
```

If there is no ACK

If the precedence in the segment is higher than the precedence in the TCB then if allowed by the user and the system raise the precedence in the TCB to that in the segment, if not allowed to raise the prec then send a reset.

```
<SEQ=0><ACK=SEG.SEQ+SEG.LEN><CTL=RST,ACK>
```

If the precedence in the segment is lower than the precedence in the TCB continue.

If a reset was sent, discard the segment and return.

fourth check the SYN bit

This step should be reached only if the ACK is ok, or there is no ACK, and it the segment did not contain a RST.

If the SYN bit is on and the security/compartment and precedence are acceptable then, RCV.NXT is set to SEG.SEQ+1, IRS is set to SEG.SEQ. SND.UNA should be advanced to equal SEG.ACK (if there is an ACK), and any segments on the retransmission queue which are thereby acknowledged should be removed.

If SND.UNA > ISS (our SYN has been ACKed), change the connection state to ESTABLISHED, form an ACK segment

```
<SEQ=SND.NXT><ACK=RCV.NXT><CTL=ACK>
```

and send it. Data or controls which were queued for transmission may be included. If there are other controls or text in the segment then continue processing at the sixth step below where the URG bit is checked, otherwise return.

Otherwise enter SYN-RECEIVED, form a SYN,ACK segment

```
<SEQ=ISS><ACK=RCV.NXT><CTL=SYN,ACK>
```

and send it. If there are other controls or text in the segment, queue them for processing after the ESTABLISHED state has been reached, return.

fifth, if neither of the SYN or RST bits is set then drop the segment and return.

Otherwise,

first check sequence number

SYN-RECEIVED STATE

ESTABLISHED STATE

FIN-WAIT-1 STATE

FIN-WAIT-2 STATE

CLOSE-WAIT STATE

CLOSING STATE

LAST-ACK STATE

TIME-WAIT STATE

Segments are processed in sequence. Initial tests on arrival are used to discard old duplicates, but further processing is done in SEG.SEQ order. If a segment's contents straddle the boundary between old and new, only the new parts should be processed.

There are four cases for the acceptability test for an incoming segment:

```
Segment Receive  Test
Length  Window
------  ------   -----------------------------------------
  0       0      SEG.SEQ = RCV.NXT
  0      >0      RCV.NXT =< SEG.SEQ < RCV.NXT+RCV.WND
 >0       0      not acceptable
 >0      >0      RCV.NXT =< SEG.SEQ < RCV.NXT+RCV.WND
                 or RCV.NXT =< SEG.SEQ+SEG.LEN-1 < RCV.NXT+RCV.WND
```

If the RCV.WND is zero, no segments will be acceptable, but special allowance should be made to accept valid ACKs, URGs and RSTs.

If an incoming segment is not acceptable, an acknowledgment should be sent in reply (unless the RST bit is set, if so drop the segment and return):

```
<SEQ=SND.NXT><ACK=RCV.NXT><CTL=ACK>
```

After sending the acknowledgment, drop the unacceptable segment and return.

In the following it is assumed that the segment is the idealized segment that begins at RCV.NXT and does not exceed the window. One could tailor actual segments to fit this assumption by trimming off any portions that lie outside the window (including SYN and FIN), and only processing further if the segment then begins at RCV.NXT. Segments with higher begining sequence numbers may be held for later processing.

second check the RST bit,

SYN-RECEIVED STATE

If the RST bit is set

If this connection was initiated with a passive OPEN (i.e., came from the LISTEN state), then return this connection to LISTEN state and return. The user need not be informed. If this connection was initiated with an active OPEN (i.e., came from SYN-SENT state) then the connection was refused, signal the user "connection refused". In either case, all segments on the retransmission queue should be removed. And in the active OPEN case, enter the CLOSED state and delete the TCB, and return.

ESTABLISHED

FIN-WAIT-1

FIN-WAIT-2

CLOSE-WAIT

If the RST bit is set then, any outstanding RECEIVEs and SEND should receive "reset" responses. All segment queues should be flushed. Users should also receive an unsolicited general "connection reset" signal. Enter the CLOSED state, delete the TCB, and return.

CLOSING STATE

LAST-ACK STATE

TIME-WAIT

If the RST bit is set then, enter the CLOSED state, delete the TCB, and return.

third check security and precedence

SYN-RECEIVED

If the security/compartment and precedence in the segment do not exactly match the security/compartment and precedence in the TCB then send a reset, and return.

ESTABLISHED STATE

If the security/compartment and precedence in the segment do not exactly match the security/compartment and precedence in the TCB then send a reset, any outstanding RECEIVEs and SEND should receive "reset" responses. All segment queues should be flushed. Users should also receive an unsolicited general "connection reset" signal. Enter the CLOSED state, delete the TCB, and return.

N O T E   Note this check is placed following the sequence check to prevent a segment from an old connection between these ports with a different security or precedence from causing an abort of the current connection.

fourth, check the SYN bit,

SYN-RECEIVED

ESTABLISHED STATE

FIN-WAIT STATE-1

FIN-WAIT STATE-2

CLOSE-WAIT STATE

CLOSING STATE

LAST-ACK STATE

TIME-WAIT STATE

If the SYN is in the window it is an error, send a reset, any outstanding RECEIVEs and SEND should receive "reset" responses, all segment queues should be flushed, the user should also receive an unsolicited general "connection reset" signal, enter the CLOSED state, delete the TCB, and return.

If the SYN is not in the window this step would not be reached and an ack would have been sent in the first step (sequence number check).

fifth check the ACK field,

if the ACK bit is off drop the segment and return

if the ACK bit is on

SYN-RECEIVED STATE

If SND.UNA =< SEG.ACK =< SND.NXT then enter ESTABLISHED state and continue processing.

If the segment acknowledgment is not acceptable, form a reset segment,

```
<SEQ=SEG.ACK><CTL=RST>
```

and send it.

ESTABLISHED STATE

If SND.UNA < SEG.ACK =< SND.NXT then, set SND.UNA <- SEG.ACK. Any segments on the retransmission queue which are thereby entirely acknowledged are removed. Users should receive positive acknowledgments for buffers which have been SENT and fully acknowledged (i.e., SEND buffer should be returned with "ok" response). If the ACK is a duplicate (SEG.ACK < SND.UNA), it can be ignored. If the ACK acks something not yet sent (SEG.ACK > SND.NXT) then send an ACK, drop the segment, and return.

If SND.UNA < SEG.ACK =< SND.NXT, the send window should be updated. If (SND.WL1 < SEG.SEQ or (SND.WL1 = SEG.SEQ and SND.WL2 =< SEG.ACK)), set SND.WND <- SEG.WND, set SND.WL1 <- SEG.SEQ, and set SND.WL2 <- SEG.ACK.

N O T E Note that SND.WND is an offset from SND.UNA, that SND.WL1 records the sequence number of the last segment used to update SND.WND, and that SND.WL2 records the acknowledgment number of the last segment used to update SND.WND. The check here prevents using old segments to update the window.

FIN-WAIT-1 STATE

In addition to the processing for the ESTABLISHED state, if our FIN is now acknowledged then enter FIN-WAIT-2 and continue processing in that state.

FIN-WAIT-2 STATE

In addition to the processing for the ESTABLISHED state, if the retransmission queue is empty, the user's CLOSE can be acknowledged ("ok") but do not delete the TCB.

CLOSE-WAIT STATE

Do the same processing as for the ESTABLISHED state.

CLOSING STATE

In addition to the processing for the ESTABLISHED state, if the ACK acknowledges our FIN then enter the TIME-WAIT state, otherwise ignore the segment.

LAST-ACK STATE

The only thing that can arrive in this state is an acknowledgment of our FIN. If our FIN is now acknowledged, delete the TCB, enter the CLOSED state, and return.

TIME-WAIT STATE

The only thing that can arrive in this state is a retransmission of the remote FIN. Acknowledge it, and restart the 2 MSL timeout.

sixth, check the URG bit,

ESTABLISHED STATE

FIN-WAIT-1 STATE

FIN-WAIT-2 STATE

If the URG bit is set, RCV.UP <- max(RCV.UP,SEG.UP), and signal the user that the remote side has urgent data if the urgent pointer (RCV.UP) is in advance of the data consumed. If the user has already been signaled (or is still in the "urgent mode") for this continuous sequence of urgent data, do not signal the user again.

CLOSE-WAIT STATE

CLOSING STATE

LAST-ACK STATE

TIME-WAIT

This should not occur, since a FIN has been received from the remote side. Ignore the URG.

seventh, process the segment text,

ESTABLISHED STATE

FIN-WAIT-1 STATE

FIN-WAIT-2 STATE

Once in the ESTABLISHED state, it is possible to deliver segment text to user RECEIVE buffers. Text from segments can be moved into buffers until either the buffer is full or the segment is empty. If the segment empties and carries an PUSH flag, then the user is informed, when the buffer is returned, that a PUSH has been received.

When the TCP takes responsibility for delivering the data to the user it must also acknowledge the receipt of the data.

Once the TCP takes responsibility for the data it advances RCV.NXT over the data accepted, and adjusts RCV.WND as apporopriate to the current buffer availability. The total of RCV.NXT and RCV.WND should not be reduced.

Please note the window management suggestions in section 3.7.

Send an acknowledgment of the form:

```
<SEQ=SND.NXT><ACK=RCV.NXT><CTL=ACK>
```

This acknowledgment should be piggybacked on a segment being transmitted if possible without incurring undue delay.

CLOSE-WAIT STATE

CLOSING STATE

LAST-ACK STATE

TIME-WAIT STATE

This should not occur, since a FIN has been received from the remote side. Ignore the segment text.

eighth, check the FIN bit,

Do not process the FIN if the state is CLOSED, LISTEN or SYN-SENT since the SEG.SEQ cannot be validated; drop the segment and return.

If the FIN bit is set, signal the user "connection closing" and return any pending RECEIVEs with same message, advance RCV.NXT over the FIN, and send an acknowledgment for the FIN. Note that FIN implies PUSH for any segment text not yet delivered to the user.

SYN-RECEIVED STATE

ESTABLISHED STATE

Enter the CLOSE-WAIT state.

FIN-WAIT-1 STATE

If our FIN has been ACKed (perhaps in this segment), then

enter TIME-WAIT, start the time-wait timer, turn off the other timers; otherwise enter the CLOSING state.

FIN-WAIT-2 STATE

Enter the TIME-WAIT state. Start the time-wait timer, turn off the other timers.

CLOSE-WAIT STATE

Remain in the CLOSE-WAIT state.

CLOSING STATE

Remain in the CLOSING state.

LAST-ACK STATE

Remain in the LAST-ACK state.

TIME-WAIT STATE

Remain in the TIME-WAIT state. Restart the 2 MSL time-wait timeout.

and return.

USER TIMEOUT

For any state if the user timeout expires, flush all queues, signal the user "error: connection aborted due to user timeout" in general and for any outstanding calls, delete the TCB, enter the CLOSED state and return.

RETRANSMISSION TIMEOUT

For any state if the retransmission timeout expires on a segment in the retransmission queue, send the segment at the front of the retransmission queue again, reinitialize the retransmission timer, and return.

TIME-WAIT TIMEOUT

If the time-wait timeout expires on a connection delete the TCB, enter the CLOSED state and return.

Glossary

1822

BBN Report 1822, "The Specification of the Interconnection of a Host and an IMP". The specification of interface between a host and the ARPANET.

ACK

A control bit (acknowledge) occupying no sequence space, which indicates that the acknowledgment field of this segment specifies the next sequence number the sender of this segment is expecting to receive, hence acknowledging receipt of all previous sequence numbers.

ARPANET message

The unit of transmission between a host and an IMP in the ARPANET. The maximum size is about 1012 octets (8096 bits).

ARPANET packet

> A unit of transmission used internally in the ARPANET between IMPs. The maximum size is about 126 octets (1008 bits).

connection

> A logical communication path identified by a pair of sockets.

datagram

> A message sent in a packet switched computer communications network.

Destination Address

> The destination address, usually the network and host identifiers.

FIN

> A control bit (finis) occupying one sequence number, which indicates that the sender will send no more data or control occupying sequence space.

fragment

> A portion of a logical unit of data, in particular an internet fragment is a portion of an internet datagram.

FTP

> A file transfer protocol.

header

> Control information at the beginning of a message, segment, fragment, packet or block of data.

host

> A computer. In particular a source or destination of messages from the point of view of the communication network.

Identification

> An Internet Protocol field. This identifying value assigned by the sender aids in assembling the fragments of a datagram.

IMP

> The Interface Message Processor, the packet switch of the ARPANET.

internet address

> A source or destination address specific to the host level.

internet datagram

> The unit of data exchanged between an internet module and the higher level protocol together with the internet header.

internet fragment

A portion of the data of an internet datagram with an internet header.

IP

Internet Protocol.

IRS

The Initial Receive Sequence number. The first sequence number used by the sender on a connection.

ISN

The Initial Sequence Number. The first sequence number used on a connection, (either ISS or IRS). Selected on a clock based procedure.

ISS

The Initial Send Sequence number. The first sequence number used by the sender on a connection.

leader

Control information at the beginning of a message or block of data. In particular, in the ARPANET, the control information on an ARPANET message at the host-IMP interface.

left sequence

This is the next sequence number to be acknowledged by the data receiving TCP (or the lowest currently unacknowledged sequence number) and is sometimes referred to as the left edge of the send window.

local packet

The unit of transmission within a local network.

module

An implementation, usually in software, of a protocol or other procedure.

MSL

Maximum Segment Lifetime, the time a TCP segment can exist in the internetwork system. Arbitrarily defined to be 2 minutes.

octet

An eight bit byte.

Options

An Option field may contain several options, and each option may be several octets in length. The options are used primarily in testing situations; for example, to carry timestamps. Both the Internet Protocol and TCP provide for options fields.

packet

> A package of data with a header which may or may not be logically complete. More often a physical packaging than a logical packaging of data.

port

> The portion of a socket that specifies which logical input or output channel of a process is associated with the data.

process

> A program in execution. A source or destination of data from the point of view of the TCP or other host-to-host protocol.

PUSH

> A control bit occupying no sequence space, indicating that this segment contains data that must be pushed through to the receiving user.

RCV.NXT

> receive next sequence number

RCV.UP

> receive urgent pointer

RCV.WND

> receive window

receive next sequence number

> This is the next sequence number the local TCP is expecting to receive.

receive window

> This represents the sequence numbers the local (receiving) TCP is willing to receive. Thus, the local TCP considers that segments overlapping the range RCV.NXT to RCV.NXT + RCV.WND - 1 carry acceptable data or control. Segments containing sequence numbers entirely outside of this range are considered duplicates and discarded.

RST

> A control bit (reset), occupying no sequence space, indicating that the receiver should delete the connection without further interaction. The receiver can determine, based on the sequence number and acknowledgment fields of the incoming segment, whether it should honor the reset command or ignore it. In no case does receipt of a segment containing RST give rise to a RST in response.

RTP

> Real Time Protocol: A host-to-host protocol for communication of time critical information.

SEG.ACK

>segment acknowledgment

SEG.LEN

>segment length

SEG.PRC

>segment precedence value

SEG.SEQ

>segment sequence

SEG.UP

>segment urgent pointer field

SEG.WND

>segment window field

segment

>A logical unit of data, in particular a TCP segment is the unit of data transfered between a pair of TCP modules.

segment acknowledgment

>The sequence number in the acknowledgment field of the arriving segment.

segment length

>The amount of sequence number space occupied by a segment, including any controls which occupy sequence space.

segment sequence

>The number in the sequence field of the arriving segment.

send sequence

>This is the next sequence number the local (sending) TCP will use on the connection. It is initially selected from an initial sequence number curve (ISN) and is incremented for each octet of data or sequenced control transmitted.

send window

>This represents the sequence numbers which the remote (receiving) TCP is willing to receive. It is the value of the window field specified in segments from the remote (data receiving) TCP. The range of new sequence numbers which may be emitted by a TCP lies between SND.NXT and SND.UNA + SND.WND - 1. (Retransmissions of sequence numbers between SND.UNA and SND.NXT are expected, of course.)

SND.NXT

> send sequence

SND.UNA

> left sequence

SND.UP

> send urgent pointer

SND.WL1

> segment sequence number at last window update

SND.WL2

> segment acknowledgment number at last window update

SND.WND

> send window

socket

> An address which specifically includes a port identifier, that is, the concatenation of an Internet Address with a TCP port.

Source Address

> The source address, usually the network and host identifiers.

SYN

> A control bit in the incoming segment, occupying one sequence number, used at the initiation of a connection, to indicate where the sequence numbering will start.

TCB

> Transmission control block, the data structure that records the state of a connection.

TCB.PRC

> The precedence of the connection.

TCP

> Transmission Control Protocol: A host-to-host protocol for reliable communication in internetwork environments.

App
A

TOS

> Type of Service, an Internet Protocol field.

Type of Service

> An Internet Protocol field which indicates the type of service for this internet fragment.

URG

> A control bit (urgent), occupying no sequence space, used to indicate that the receiving user should be notified to do urgent processing as long as there is data to be consumed with sequence numbers less than the value indicated in the urgent pointer.

urgent pointer

> A control field meaningful only when the URG bit is on. This field communicates the value of the urgent pointer which indicates the data octet associated with the sending user's urgent call.

References

[1] Cerf, V., and R. Kahn, "A Protocol for Packet Network Intercommunication", IEEE Transactions on Communications, Vol. COM-22, No. 5, pp 637-648, May 1974.

[2] Postel, J. (ed.), "Internet Protocol - DARPA Internet Program Protocol Specification", RFC 791, USC/Information Sciences Institute, September 1981.

[3] Dalal, Y. and C. Sunshine, "Connection Management in Transport Protocols", Computer Networks, Vol. 2, No. 6, pp. 454-473, December 1978.

[4] Postel, J., "Assigned Numbers", RFC 790, USC/Information Sciences Institute, September 1981.

RFC 768—UDP

RFC 768 J. Postel

ISI

28 August 1980

User Datagram Protocol

Introduction

This User Datagram Protocol (UDP) is defined to make available a datagram mode of packet-switched computer communication in the environment of an interconnected set of computer networks. This protocol assumes that the Internet Protocol (IP) [1] is used as the underlying protocol.

This protocol provides a procedure for application programs to send messages to other programs with a minimum of protocol mechanism. The protocol is transaction oriented, and delivery and duplicate protection are not guaranteed. Applications requiring ordered reliable delivery of streams of data should use the Transmission Control Protocol (TCP) [2].

Format

```
 0      7 8     15 16    23 24     31
+--------+--------+--------+--------+
|        Source   |     Destination |
|         Port    |        Port     |
+--------+--------+--------+--------+
|                 |                 |
|        Length   |     Checksum    |
+--------+--------+--------+--------+
|
|         data octets ...
+---------------- ...

      User Datagram Header Format
```

Fields

Source Port is an optional field, when meaningful, it indicates the port of the sending process, and may be assumed to be the port to which a reply should be addressed in the absence of any other information. If not used, a value of zero is inserted.

Destination Port has a meaning within the context of a particular internet destination address.

Length is the length in octets of this user datagram including this header and the data. (This means the minimum value of the length is eight.)

Checksum is the 16-bit one's complement of the one's complement sum of a pseudo header of information from the IP header, the UDP header, and the data, padded with zero octets at the end (if necessary) to make a multiple of two octets.

The pseudo header conceptually prefixed to the UDP header contains the source address, the destination address, the protocol, and the UDP length. This information gives protection against misrouted datagrams.

This checksum procedure is the same as is used in TCP.

```
 0      7 8     15 16    23 24    31
+--------+--------+--------+--------+
|             source address       |
+--------+--------+--------+--------+
|          destination address     |
+--------+--------+--------+--------+
|  zero  |protocol|   UDP length    |
+--------+--------+--------+--------+
```

If the computed checksum is zero, it is transmitted as all ones (the equivalent in one's complement arithmetic). An all zero transmitted checksum value means that the transmitter generated no checksum (for debugging or for higher level protocols that don't care).

User Interface

A user interface should allow

- the creation of new receive ports,
- receive operations on the receive ports that return the data octets and an indication of source port and source address,
- and an operation that allows a datagram to be sent, specifying the data, source and destination ports and addresses to be sent.

IP Interface

The UDP module must be able to determine the source and destination internet addresses and the protocol field from the internet header. One possible UDP/IP interface would return the whole internet datagram including all of the internet header in response to a receive operation. Such an interface would also allow the UDP to pass a full internet datagram complete with header to the IP to send. The IP would verify certain fields for consistency and compute the internet header checksum.

Protocol Application

The major uses of this protocol is the Internet Name Server [3], and the Trivial File Transfer [4].

Protocol Number

This is protocol 17 (21 octal) when used in the Internet Protocol. Other protocol numbers are listed in [5].

References

[1] Postel, J., "Internet Protocol," RFC 760, USC/Information Sciences Institute, January 1980.

[2] Postel, J., "Transmission Control Protocol," RFC 761, USC/Information Sciences Institute, January 1980.

[3] Postel, J., "Internet Name Server," USC/Information Sciences Institute, IEN 116, August 1979.

[4] Sollins, K., "The TFTP Protocol," Massachusetts Institute of Technology, IEN 133, January 1980.

[5] Postel, J., "Assigned Numbers," USC/Information Sciences Institute, RFC 762, January 1980.

RFC 1340—IP

Network Working Group   J. Reynolds
Request for Comments: 1340   J. Postel
Obsoletes RFCs: ISI
1060, 1010, 990, 960,   July 1992

943, 923, 900, 870, 820, 790, 776, 770,

762, 758,755, 750, 739,

604, 503, 433, 349

Obsoletes IENs: 127, 117, 93

Assigned Numbers

Status of this Memo

This memo is a status report on the parameters (i.e., numbers and keywords) used in protocols in the Internet community. Distribution of this memo is unlimited.

Table of Contents

INTRODUCTION

Data Notations

Special Addresses

VERSION NUMBERS

PROTOCOL NUMBERS

WELL KNOWN PORT NUMBERS

REGISTERED PORT NUMBERS

INTERNET MULTICAST ADDRESSES

IANA ETHERNET ADDRESS BLOCK

IP TOS PARAMETERS

IP TIME TO LIVE PARAMETER

DOMAIN SYSTEM PARAMETERS

BOOTP PARAMETERS

NETWORK MANAGEMENT PARAMETERS

MILNET LOGICAL ADDRESSES

MILNET LINK NUMBERS

MILNET X.25 ADDRESS MAPPINGS

IEEE 802 NUMBERS OF INTEREST

ETHERNET NUMBERS OF INTEREST

ETHERNET VENDOR ADDRESS COMPONENTS

ETHERNET MULTICAST ADDRESSES

XNS PROTOCOL TYPES

PROTOCOL/TYPE FIELD ASSIGNMENTS

PRONET 80 TYPE NUMBERS

POINT-TO-POINT PROTOCOL FIELD ASSIGNMENTS

ADDRESS RESOLUTION PROTOCOL PARAMETERS

REVERSE ADDRESS RESOLUTION PROTOCOL OPERATION CODES

DYNAMIC REVERSE ARP

INVERSE ADDRESS RESOULUTION PROTOCOL

X.25 TYPE NUMBERS

PUBLIC DATA NETWORK NUMBERS

TELNET OPTIONS

MAIL ENCRYPTION TYPES

MIME TYPES

CHARACTER SETS

MACHINE NAMES

SYSTEM NAMES

PROTOCOL AND SERVICE NAMES

TERMINAL TYPE NAMES

DOCUMENTS

PEOPLE

Security Considerations

Authors' Addresses

Introduction

This Network Working Group Request for Comments documents the currently assigned values from several series of numbers used in network protocol implementations. This RFC will be updated periodically, and in any case current information can be obtained from the Internet Assigned Numbers Authority (IANA). If you are developing a protocol or application that will require the use of a link, socket, port, protocol, etc., please contact the IANA to receive a number assignment.

Joyce K. Reynolds
Internet Assigned Numbers Authority
USC - Information Sciences Institute
4676 Admiralty Way
Marina del Rey, California 90292-6695
Phone: (310) 822-1511
Electronic mail: IANA@ISI.EDU

Most of the protocols mentioned here are documented in the RFC series of notes. Some of the items listed are undocumented. Further information on protocols can be found in the memo "IAB Official Protocol Standards" [62].

In the entries below, the name and mailbox of the responsible individual is indicated. The bracketed entry, e.g., [nn,iii], at the right hand margin of the page indicates a reference for the listed protocol, where the number ("nn") cites the document and the letters ("iii") cites the person. Whenever possible, the letters are a NIC Ident as used in the WhoIs (NICNAME) service.

Data Notations

The convention in the documentation of Internet Protocols is to express numbers in decimal and to picture data in "big-endian" order [21]. That is, fields are described left to right, with the most significant octet on the left and the least significant octet on the right.

The order of transmission of the header and data described in this document is resolved to the octet level. Whenever a diagram shows a group of octets, the order of transmission of those octets is the normal order in which they are read in English. For example, in the following diagram the octets are transmitted in the order they are numbered.

```
 0                   1                   2                   3
 0 1 2 3 4 5 6 7 8 9 0 1 2 3 4 5 6 7 8 9 0 1 2 3 4 5 6 7 8 9 0 1
+-+-+-+-+-+-+-+-+-+-+-+-+-+-+-+-+-+-+-+-+-+-+-+-+-+-+-+-+-+-+-+-+
|       1       |       2       |       3       |       4       |
+-+-+-+-+-+-+-+-+-+-+-+-+-+-+-+-+-+-+-+-+-+-+-+-+-+-+-+-+-+-+-+-+
|       5       |       6       |       7       |       8       |
+-+-+-+-+-+-+-+-+-+-+-+-+-+-+-+-+-+-+-+-+-+-+-+-+-+-+-+-+-+-+-+-+
|       9       |      10       |      11       |      12       |
+-+-+-+-+-+-+-+-+-+-+-+-+-+-+-+-+-+-+-+-+-+-+-+-+-+-+-+-+-+-+-+-+
```

Transmission Order of Bytes

Whenever an octet represents a numeric quantity the left most bit in the diagram is the high order or most significant bit. That is, the bit labeled 0 is the most significant bit. For example, the following diagram represents the value 170 (decimal).

```
 0 1 2 3 4 5 6 7
+-+-+-+-+-+-+-+-+
|1 0 1 0 1 0 1 0|
+-+-+-+-+-+-+-+-+
Significance of Bits
```

Similarly, whenever a multi-octet field represents a numeric quantity the left most bit of the whole field is the most significant bit. When a multi-octet quantity is transmitted the most significant octet is transmitted first.

Special Addresses:

There are five classes of IP addresses: Class A through Class E [119]. Of these, Class E addresses are reserved for experimental use. A gateway which is not participating in these experiments must ignore all datagrams with a Class E destination IP address. ICMP Destination Unreachable or ICMP Redirect messages must not result from receiving such datagrams.

There are certain special cases for IP addresses [11]. These special cases can be concisely summarized using the earlier notation for an IP address:

IP-address ::= { <Network-number>, <Host-number> }

or

IP-address ::= { <Network-number>, <Subnet-number>, <Host-number> }

if we also use the notation "-1" to mean the field contains all 1 bits. Some common special cases are as follows:

(a) {0, 0}

This host on this network. Can only be used as a source address (see note later).

(b) {0, <Host-number>}

Specified host on this network. Can only be used as a source address.

(c) { -1, -1}

Limited broadcast. Can only be used as a destination address, and a datagram with this address must never be forwarded outside the (sub-)net of the source.

(d) {<Network-number>, -1}

Directed broadcast to specified network. Can only be used as a destination address.

(e) {<Network-number>, <Subnet-number>, -1}

Directed broadcast to specified subnet. Can only be used as a destination address.

(f) {<Network-number>, -1, -1}

Directed broadcast to all subnets of specified subnetted network. Can only be used as a destination address.

(g) {127, <any>}

Internal host loopback address. Should never appear outside a host.

Version Numbers

In the Internet Protocol (IP) [45,105] there is a field to identify the version of the internetwork general protocol. This field is 4 bits in size.

```
Assigned Internet Version Numbers
Decimal Keyword     Version            References
------ ------       ------             ---------
    0                Reserved          [JBP]
  1-3                Unassigned        [JBP]
    4     IP         Internet Protocol [105,JBP]
    5     ST         ST Datagram Mode  [49,JWF]
 6-14                Unassigned        [JBP]
   15                Reserved          [JBP]
```

Protocol Numbers

In the Internet Protocol (IP) [45,105] there is a field, called Protocol, to identify the the next level protocol. This is an 8 bit field.

Assigned Internet Protocol Numbers

```
Decimal       Keyword       Protocol                      References
- - - - -     - - - - -     - - - - - - -                 - - - - - - - - -
   0                        Reserved                      [JBP]
   1          ICMP          Internet Control Message      [97,JBP]
   2          IGMP          Internet Group Management     [43,JBP]
   3          GGP           Gateway-to-Gateway            [60,MB]
   4          IP            IP in IP (encasulation)       [JBP]
   5          ST            Stream                        [49,JWF]
   6          TCP           Transmission Control          [106,JBP]
   7          UCL           UCL                           [PK]
   8          EGP           Exterior Gateway Protocol     [123,DLM1]
   9          IGP           any private interior gateway  [JBP]
  10          BBN-RCC-MON   BBN RCC Monitoring            [SGC]
  11          NVP-II        Network Voice Protocol        [22,SC3]
  12          PUP           PUP                           [8,XEROX]
  13          ARGUS         ARGUS                         [RWS4]
  14          EMCON         EMCON                         [BN7]
  15          XNET          Cross Net Debugger            [56,JFH2]
  16          CHAOS         Chaos                         [NC3]
  17          UDP           User Datagram                 [104,JBP]
  18          MUX           Multiplexing                  [23,JBP]
  19          DCN-MEAS      DCN Measurement Subsystems    [DLM1]
  20          HMP           Host Monitoring               [59,RH6]
  21          PRM           Packet Radio Measurement      [ZSU]
  22          XNS-IDP       XEROX NS IDP                  [133,XEROX]
  23          TRUNK-1       Trunk-1                       [BWB6]
  24          TRUNK-2       Trunk-2                       [BWB6]
  25          LEAF-1        Leaf-1                        [BWB6]
  26          LEAF-2        Leaf-2                        [BWB6]
  27          RDP           Reliable Data Protocol        [138,RH6]
  28          IRTP          Internet Reliable Transaction [79,TXM]
  29          ISO-TP4       ISO Transport Protocol Class 4 [63,RC77]
  30          NETBLT        Bulk Data Transfer Protocol   [20,DDC1]
  31          MFE-NSP       MFE Network Services Protocol [124,BCH2]
  32          MERIT-INP     MERIT Internodal Protocol     [HWB]
  33          SEP           Sequential Exchange Protocol  [JC120]
  34          3PC           Third Party Connect Protocol  [SAF3]
  35          IDPR          Inter-Domain Policy           [MXS1]
                            Routing Protocol
  36          XTP           XTP                           [GXC]
  37          DDP           Datagram Delivery Protocol    [WXC]
  38          IDPR-CMTP     IDPR Control Message          [MXS1]
                            Transport Proto
  39          TP++          TP++ Transport Protocol       [DXF]
  40          IL            IL Transport Protocol         [DXP2]
  41-60                     Unassigned                    [JBP]
  61                        any host internal protocol    [JBP]
  62          CFTP          CFTP                          [50,HCF2]
```

63		any local network	[JBP]
64	SAT-EXPAK	SATNET and Backroom EXPAK	[SHB]
65	KRYPTOLAN	Kryptolan	[PXL1]
66	RVD	MIT Remote Virtual Disk Protocol	[MBG]
67	IPPC	Internet Pluribus Packet Core	[SHB]
68		any distributed file system	[JBP]
69	SAT-MON	SATNET Monitoring	[SHB]
70	VISA	VISA Protocol	[GXT1]
71	IPCV	Internet Packet Core Utility	[SHB]
72	CPNX	Computer Protocol Network Executive	[DXM2]
73	CPHB	Computer Protocol Heart Beat	[DXM2]
74	WSN	Wang Span Network	[VXD]
75	PVP	Packet Video Protocol	[SC3]
76	BR-SAT-MON	Backroom SATNET Monitoring	[SHB]
77	SUN-ND	SUN ND PROTOCOL-Temporary	[WM3]
78	WB-MON	WIDEBAND Monitoring	[SHB]
79	WB-EXPAK	WIDEBAND EXPAK	[SHB]
80	ISO-IP	ISO Internet Protocol	[MTR]
81	VMTP	VMTP	[DRC3]
82	SECURE-VMTP	SECURE-VMTP	[DRC3]
83	VINES	VINES	[BXH]
84	TTP	TTP	[JXS]
85	NSFNET-IGP	NSFNET-IGP	[HWB]
86	DGP	Dissimilar Gateway Protocol	[74,ML109]
87	TCF	TCF	[GAL5]
88	IGRP	IGRP	[18,GXS]
89	OSPFIGP	OSPFIGP	[83,JTM4]
90	Sprite-RPC	Sprite RPC Protocol	[143,BXW]
91	LARP	Locus Address Resolution Protocol	[BXH]
92	MTP	Multicast Transport Protocol	[SXA]
93	AX.25	AX.25 Frames	[BK29]
94	IPIP	IP-within-IP Encapsulation Protocol	[JXI1]
95	MICP	Mobile Internetworking Control Pro.	[JXI1]
96	AES-SP3-D	AES Security Protocol 3-D	[HXH]
97	ETHERIP	Ethernet-within-IP Encapsulation	[RXH1]
98	ENCAP	Encapsulation Header	[148,RXB3]
99-254		Unassigned	[JBP]
255		Reserved	[JBP]

Well Known Port Numbers

The Well Known Ports are controlled and assigned by the IANA and on most systems can only be used by system (or root) processes or by programs executed by privileged users.

Ports are used in the TCP [45,106] to name the ends of logical connections which carry long term conversations. For the purpose of providing services to unknown callers, a service contact port is defined. This list specifies the port used by the server process as its contact port. The contact port is sometimes called the "well-known port".

To the extent possible, these same port assignments are used with the UDP [46,104].

The assigned ports use a small portion of the possible port numbers. For many years the assigned ports were in the range 0-255. Recently, the range for assigned ports managed by the IANA has been expanded to the range 0-1023.

```
Port Assignments:
   Keyword        Decimal    Description              References
   - - - - - -    - - - - -   - - - - - - - - - -     - - - - - - - - - -
                  0/tcp       Reserved                 [JBP]
                  0/udp       Reserved                 [JBP]
   tcpmux         1/tcp       TCP Port Service Multiplexer   [MKL]
   tcpmux         1/udp       TCP Port Service Multiplexer   [MKL]
   compressnet    2/tcp       Management Utility       [BV15]
   compressnet    2/udp       Management Utility       [BV15]
   compressnet    3/tcp       Compression Process      [BV15]
   compressnet    3/udp       Compression Process      [BV15]
                  4/tcp       Unassigned               [JBP]
                  4/udp       Unassigned               [JBP]
   rje            5/tcp       Remote Job Entry         [12,JBP]
   rje            5/udp       Remote Job Entry         [12,JBP]
                  6/tcp       Unassigned               [JBP]
                  6/udp       Unassigned               [JBP]
   echo           7/tcp       Echo                     [95,JBP]
   echo           7/udp       Echo                     [95,JBP]
                  8/tcp       Unassigned               [JBP]
                  8/udp       Unassigned               [JBP]
   discard        9/tcp       Discard                  [94,JBP]
   discard        9/udp       Discard                  [94,JBP]
                  10/tcp      Unassigned               [JBP]
                  10/udp      Unassigned               [JBP]
   systat         11/tcp      Active Users             [89,JBP]
   systat         11/udp      Active Users             [89,JBP]
                  12/tcp      Unassigned               [JBP]
                  12/udp      Unassigned               [JBP]
   daytime        13/tcp      Daytime                  [93,JBP]
   daytime        13/udp      Daytime                  [93,JBP]
                  14/tcp      Unassigned               [JBP]
                  14/udp      Unassigned               [JBP]
                  15/tcp      Unassigned [was netstat] [JBP]
                  15/udp      Unassigned               [JBP]
                  16/tcp      Unassigned               [JBP]
                  16/udp      Unassigned               [JBP]
   qotd           17/tcp      Quote of the Day         [100,JBP]
   qotd           17/udp      Quote of the Day         [100,JBP]
   msp            18/tcp      Message Send Protocol    [RXN]
   msp            18/udp      Message Send Protocol    [RXN]
   chargen        19/tcp      Character Generator      [92,JBP]
   chargen        19/udp      Character Generator      [92,JBP]
   ftp-data       20/tcp      File Transfer [Default Data]   [96,JBP]
   ftp-data       20/udp      File Transfer [Default Data]   [96,JBP]
   ftp            21/tcp      File Transfer [Control]  [96,JBP]
   ftp            21/udp      File Transfer [Control]  [96,JBP]
                  22/tcp      Unassigned               [JBP]
                  22/udp      Unassigned               [JBP]
```

```
telnet      23/tcp    Telnet                           [112,JBP]
telnet      23/udp    Telnet                           [112,JBP]
            24/tcp    any private mail system          [RA11]
            24/udp    any private mail system          [RA11]
smtp        25/tcp    Simple Mail Transfer             [102,JBP]
smtp        25/udp    Simple Mail Transfer             [102,JBP]
            26/tcp    Unassigned                       [JBP]
            26/udp    Unassigned                       [JBP]
nsw-fe      27/tcp    NSW User System FE               [24,RHT]
nsw-fe      27/udp    NSW User System FE               [24,RHT]
            28/tcp    Unassigned                       [JBP]
            28/udp    Unassigned                       [JBP]
msg-icp     29/tcp    MSG ICP                          [85,RHT]
msg-icp     29/udp    MSG ICP                          [85,RHT]
            30/tcp    Unassigned                       [JBP]
            30/udp    Unassigned                       [JBP]
msg-auth    31/tcp    MSG Authentication               [85,RHT]
msg-auth    31/udp    MSG Authentication               [85,RHT]
            32/tcp    Unassigned                       [JBP]
            32/udp    Unassigned                       [JBP]
dsp         33/tcp    Display Support Protocol         [EXC]
dsp         33/udp    Display Support Protocol         [EXC]
            34/tcp    Unassigned                       [JBP]
            34/udp    Unassigned                       [JBP]
            35/tcp    any private printer server       [JBP]
            35/udp    any private printer server       [JBP]
            36/tcp    Unassigned                       [JBP]
            36/udp    Unassigned                       [JBP]
time        37/tcp    Time                             [108,JBP]
time        37/udp    Time                             [108,JBP]
            38/tcp    Unassigned                       [JBP]
            38/udp    Unassigned                       [JBP]
rlp         39/tcp    Resource Location    Protocol    [MA]
rlp         39/udp    Resource Location    Protocol    [MA]
            40/tcp    Unassigned                       [JBP]
            40/udp    Unassigned                       [JBP]
graphics    41/tcp    Graphics                         [129,JBP]
graphics    41/udp    Graphics                         [129,JBP]
nameserver  42/tcp    Host Name    Server              [99,JBP]
nameserver  42/udp    Host Name    Server              [99,JBP]
nicname     43/tcp    Who Is                           [55,ANM2]
nicname     43/udp    Who Is                           [55,ANM2]
mpm-flags   44/tcp    MPM FLAGS    Protocol            [JBP]
mpm-flags   44/udp    MPM FLAGS    Protocol            [JBP]
mpm         45/tcp    Message Processing               [98,JBP]
                      Module [recv]
mpm         45/udp    Message Processing               [98,JBP]
                      Module [recv]
mpm-snd     46/tcp    MPM [default send]               [98,JBP]
mpm-snd     46/udp    MPM [default send]               [98,JBP]
ni-ftp      47/tcp    NI FTP                           [134,SK8]
ni-ftp      47/udp    NI FTP                           [134,SK8]
            48/tcp    Unassigned                       [JBP]
            48/udp    Unassigned                       [JBP]
login       49/tcp    Login Host Protocol              [PHD1]
```

```
login          49/udp    Login Host Protocol          [PHD1]
re-mail-ck     50/tcp    Remote Mail Checking         [171,SXD1]
                         Protocol
re-mail-ck     50/udp    Remote Mail Checking         [171,SXD1]
                         Protocol
la-maint       51/tcp    IMP Logical Address          [76,AGM]
                         Maintenance
la-maint       51/udp    IMP Logical Address          [76,AGM]
                         Maintenance
xns-time       52/tcp    XNS Time Protocol            [SXA]
xns-time       52/udp    XNS Time Protocol            [SXA]
domain         53/tcp    Domain Name Server           [81,95,PM1]
domain         53/udp    Domain Name Server           [81,95,PM1]
xns-ch         54/tcp    XNS Clearinghouse            [SXA]
xns-ch         54/udp    XNS Clearinghouse            [SXA]
isi-gl         55/tcp    ISI Graphics Language        [7,RB9]
isi-gl         55/udp    ISI Graphics Language        [7,RB9]
xns-auth       56/tcp    XNS Authentication           [SXA]
xns-auth       56/udp    XNS Authentication           [SXA]
               57/tcp    any private terminal access  [JBP]
               57/udp    any private terminal access  [JBP]
xns-mail       58/tcp    XNS Mail                     [SXA]
xns-mail       58/udp    XNS Mail                     [SXA]
               59/tcp    any private file service     [JBP]
               59/udp    any private file service     [JBP]
               60/tcp    Unassigned                   [JBP]
               60/udp    Unassigned                   [JBP]
ni-mail        61/tcp    NI MAIL                      [5,SK8]
ni-mail        61/udp    NI MAIL                      [5,SK8]
acas           62/tcp    ACA Services                 [EXW]
acas           62/udp    ACA Services                 [EXW]
via-ftp        63/tcp    VIA Systems - FTP            [DXD]
via-ftp        63/udp    VIA Systems - FTP            [DXD]
covia          64/tcp    Communications               [TXD]
                         Integrator (CI)
covia          64/udp    Communications               [TXD]
                         Integrator (CI)
tacacs-ds      65/tcp    TACACS-Database Service      [3,KH43]
tacacs-ds      65/udp    TACACS-Database Service      [3,KH43]
sql*net        66/tcp    Oracle SQL*NET               [JFH2]
sql*net        66/udp    Oracle SQL*NET               [JFH2]
bootps         67/tcp    Bootstrap   Protocol Server  [36,WJC2]
bootps         67/udp    Bootstrap   Protocol Server  [36,WJC2]
bootpc         68/tcp    Bootstrap   Protocol Client  [36,WJC2]
bootpc         68/udp    Bootstrap   Protocol Client  [36,WJC2]
tftp           69/tcp    Trivial File Transfer        [126,DDC1]
tftp           69/udp    Trivial File Transfer        [126,DDC1]
gopher         70/tcp    Gopher                       [MXC1]
gopher         70/udp    Gopher                       [MXC1]
netrjs-1       71/tcp    Remote Job Service           [10,RTB3]
netrjs-1       71/udp    Remote Job Service           [10,RTB3]
netrjs-2       72/tcp    Remote Job Service           [10,RTB3]
netrjs-2       72/udp    Remote Job Service           [10,RTB3]
netrjs-3       73/tcp    Remote Job Service           [10,RTB3]
netrjs-3       73/udp    Remote Job Service           [10,RTB3]
```

netrjs-4	74/tcp	Remote Job Service	[10,RTB3]
netrjs-4	74/udp	Remote Job Service	[10,RTB3]
	75/tcp	any private dial out service	[JBP]
	75/udp	any private dial out service	[JBP]
	76/tcp	Unassigned	[JBP]
	76/udp	Unassigned	[JBP]
	77/tcp	any private RJE service	[JBP]
	77/udp	any private RJE service	[JBP]
vettcp	78/tcp	vettcp	[CXL1]
vettcp	78/udp	vettcp	[CXL1]
finger	79/tcp	Finger	[52,KLH]
finger	79/udp	Finger	[52,KLH]
www	80/tcp	World Wide Web HTTP	[TXL]
www	80/udp	World Wide Web HTTP	[TXL]
hosts2-ns	81/tcp	HOSTS2 Name Server	[EAK1]
hosts2-ns	81/udp	HOSTS2 Name Server	[EAK1]
xfer	82/tcp	XFER Utility	[TXS2]
xfer	82/udp	XFER Utility	[TXS2]
mit-ml-dev	83/tcp	MIT ML Device	[DXR3]
mit-ml-dev	83/udp	MIT ML Device	[DXR3]
ctf	84/tcp	Common Trace Facility	[HXT]
ctf	84/udp	Common Trace Facility	[HXT]
mit-ml-dev	85/tcp	MIT ML Device	[DXR3]
mit-ml-dev	85/udp	MIT ML Device	[DXR3]
mfcobol	86/tcp	Micro Focus Cobol	[SXE]
mfcobol	86/udp	Micro Focus Cobol	[SXE]
	87/tcp	any private terminal link	[JBP]
	87/udp	any private terminal link	[JBP]
kerberos	88/tcp	Kerberos	[BCN]
kerberos	88/udp	Kerberos	[BCN]
su-mit-tg	89/tcp	SU/MIT Telnet Gateway	[MRC]
su-mit-tg	89/udp	SU/MIT Telnet Gateway	[MRC]
dnsix	90/tcp	DNSIX Securit Attribute Token Map	[CXW1]
dnsix	90/udp	DNSIX Securit Attribute Token Map	[CXW1]
mit-dov	91/tcp	MIT Dover Spooler	[EBM]
mit-dov	91/udp	MIT Dover Spooler	[EBM]
npp	92/tcp	Network Printing Protocol	[LXM]
npp	92/udp	Network Printing Protocol	[LXM]
dcp	93/tcp	Device Control Protocol	[DT15]
dcp	93/udp	Device Control Protocol	[DT15]
objcall	94/tcp	Tivoli Object Dispatcher	[TXB1]
objcall	94/udp	Tivoli Object Dispatcher	[TXB1]
supdup	95/tcp	SUPDUP	[27,MRC]
supdup	95/udp	SUPDUP	[27,MRC]
dixie	96/tcp	DIXIE Protocol Specification	[TXH1]
dixie	96/udp	DIXIE Protocol Specification	[TXH1]
swift-rvf	97/tcp	Swift Remote Vitural File Protocol	[MXR]
swift-rvf	97/udp	Swift Remote Vitural File Protocol	[MXR]
tacnews	98/tcp	TAC News	[ANM2]
tacnews	98/udp	TAC News	[ANM2]
metagram	99/tcp	Metagram Relay	[GEOF]

metagram	99/udp	Metagram Relay	[GEOF]
newacct	100/tcp	[unauthorized use]	
hostname	101/tcp	NIC Host Name Server	[54,ANM2]
hostname	101/udp	NIC Host Name Server	[54,ANM2]
iso-tsap	102/tcp	ISO-TSAP	[16,MTR]
iso-tsap	102/udp	ISO-TSAP	[16,MTR]
gppitnp	103/tcp	Genesis Point-to-Point Trans Net	[PXM1]
gppitnp	103/udp	Genesis Point-to-Point Trans Net	[PXM1]
acr-nema	104/tcp	ACR-NEMA Digital Imag. & Comm. 300	[PXM1]
acr-nema	104/udp	ACR-NEMA Digital Imag. & Comm. 300	[PXM1]
csnet-ns	105/tcp	Mailbox Name Nameserver	[127,MS56]
csnet-ns	105/udp	Mailbox Name Nameserver	[127,MS56]
3com-tsmux	106/tcp	3COM-TSMUX	[JXS5]
3com-tsmux	106/udp	3COM-TSMUX	[JXS5]
rtelnet	107/tcp	Remote Telnet Service	[101,JBP]
rtelnet	107/udp	Remote Telnet Service	[101,JBP]
snagas	108/tcp	SNA Gateway Access Server	[KXM]
snagas	108/udp	SNA Gateway Access Server	[KXM]
pop2	109/tcp	Post Office Protocol - Version 2	[14,JKR1]
pop2	109/udp	Post Office Protocol - Version 2	[14,JKR1]
pop3	110/tcp	Post Office Protocol - Version 3	[122,MTR]
pop3	110/udp	Post Office Protocol - Version 3	[122,MTR]
sunrpc	111/tcp	SUN Remote Procedure Call	[DXG]
sunrpc	111/udp	SUN Remote Procedure Call	[DXG]
mcidas	112/tcp	McIDAS Data Transmission Protocol	[GXD]
mcidas	112/udp	McIDAS Data Transmission Protocol	[GXD]
auth	113/tcp	Authentication Service	[130,MCSJ]
auth	113/udp	Authentication Service	[130,MCSJ]
audionews	114/tcp	Audio News Multicast	[MXF2]
audionews	114/udp	Audio News Multicast	[MXF2]
sftp	115/tcp	Simple File Transfer Protocol	[73,MKL1]
sftp	115/udp	Simple File Transfer Protocol	[73,MKL1]
ansanotify	116/tcp	ANSA REX Notify	[NXH]
ansanotify	116/udp	ANSA REX Notify	[NXH]
uucp-path	117/tcp	UUCP Path Service	[44,MAE]
uucp-path	117/udp	UUCP Path Service	[44,MAE]
sqlserv	118/tcp	SQL Services	[LXB3]
sqlserv	118/udp	SQL Services	[LXB3]
nntp	119/tcp	Network News Transfer Protocol	[65,PL4]
nntp	119/udp	Network News Transfer Protocol	[65,PL4]
cfdptkt	120/tcp	CFDPTKT	[JXO3]

cfdptkt	120/udp	CFDPTKT	[JXO3]
erpc	121/tcp	Encore Expedited Remote Pro.Call	[132,JXO]
erpc	121/udp	Encore Expedited Remote Pro.Call	[132,JXO]
smakynet	122/tcp	SMAKYNET	[MXO]
smakynet	122/udp	SMAKYNET	[MXO]
ntp	123/tcp	Network Time Protocol	[80,DLM1]
ntp	123/udp	Network Time Protocol	[80,DLM1]
ansatrader	124/tcp	ANSA REX Trader	[NXH]
ansatrader	124/udp	ANSA REX Trader	[NXH]
locus-map	125/tcp	Locus PC-Interface Net Map Ser	[137,EP53]
locus-map	125/udp	Locus PC-Interface Net Map Ser	[137,EP53]
unitary	126/tcp	Unisys Unitary Login	[FEIL]
unitary	126/udp	Unisys Unitary Login	[FEIL]
locus-con	127/tcp	Locus PC-Interface Conn Server	[137,EP53]
locus-con	127/udp	Locus PC-Interface Conn Server	[137,EP53]
gss-xlicen	128/tcp	GSS X License Verification	[JXL]
gss-xlicen	128/udp	GSS X License Verification	[JXL]
pwdgen	129/tcp	Password Generator Protocol	[141,FJW]
pwdgen	129/udp	Password Generator Protocol	[141,FJW]
cisco-fna	130/tcp	cisco FNATIVE	[WXB]
cisco-fna	130/udp	cisco FNATIVE	[WXB]
cisco-tna	131/tcp	cisco TNATIVE	[WXB]
cisco-tna	131/udp	cisco TNATIVE	[WXB]
cisco-sys	132/tcp	cisco SYSMAINT	[WXB]
cisco-sys	132/udp	cisco SYSMAINT	[WXB]
statsrv	133/tcp	Statistics Service	[DLM1]
statsrv	133/udp	Statistics Service	[DLM1]
ingres-net	134/tcp	INGRES-NET Service	[MXB]
ingres-net	134/udp	INGRES-NET Service	[MXB]
loc-srv	135/tcp	Location Service	[JXP]
loc-srv	135/udp	Location Service	[JXP]
profile	136/tcp	PROFILE Naming System	[LLP]
profile	136/udp	PROFILE Naming System	[LLP]
netbios-ns	137/tcp	NETBIOS Name Service	[JBP]
netbios-ns	137/udp	NETBIOS Name Service	[JBP]
netbios-dgm	138/tcp	NETBIOS Datagram Service	[JBP]
netbios-dgm	138/udp	NETBIOS Datagram Service	[JBP]
netbios-ssn	139/tcp	NETBIOS Session Service	[JBP]
netbios-ssn	139/udp	NETBIOS Session Service	[JBP]
emfis-data	140/tcp	EMFIS Data Service	[GB7]
emfis-data	140/udp	EMFIS Data Service	[GB7]
emfis-cntl	141/tcp	EMFIS Control Service	[GB7]
emfis-cntl	141/udp	EMFIS Control Service	[GB7]
bl-idm	142/tcp	Britton-Lee IDM	[SXS1]
bl-idm	142/udp	Britton-Lee IDM	[SXS1]
imap2	143/tcp	Interim Mail Access Protocol v2	[MRC]
imap2	143/udp	Interim Mail Access Protocol v2	[MRC]

news	144/tcp	NewS	[JAG]
news	144/udp	NewS	[JAG]
uaac	145/tcp	UAAC Protocol	[DAG4]
uaac	145/udp	UAAC Protocol	[DAG4]
iso-tp0	146/tcp	ISO-IP0	[86,MTR]
iso-tp0	146/udp	ISO-IP0	[86,MTR]
iso-ip	147/tcp	ISO-IP	[MTR]
iso-ip	147/udp	ISO-IP	[MTR]
cronus	148/tcp	CRONUS-SUPPORT	[135,JXB]
cronus	148/udp	CRONUS-SUPPORT	[135,JXB]
aed-512	149/tcp	AED 512 Emulation Service	[AXB]
aed-512	149/udp	AED 512 Emulation Service	[AXB]
sql-net	150/tcp	SQL-NET	[MXP]
sql-net	150/udp	SQL-NET	[MXP]
hems	151/tcp	HEMS	[87,CXT]
hems	151/udp	HEMS	[87,CXT]
bftp	152/tcp	Background File Transfer Program	[AD14]
bftp	152/udp	Background File Transfer Program	[AD14]
sgmp	153/tcp	SGMP	[37,MS9]
sgmp	153/udp	SGMP	[37,MS9]
netsc-prod	154/tcp	NETSC	[SH37]
netsc-prod	154/udp	NETSC	[SH37]
netsc-dev	155/tcp	NETSC	[SH37]
netsc-dev	155/udp	NETSC	[SH37]
sqlsrv	156/tcp	SQL Service	[CMR]
sqlsrv	156/udp	SQL Service	[CMR]
knet-cmp	157/tcp	KNET/VM Command/Message Protocol	[77,GSM11]
knet-cmp	157/udp	KNET/VM Command/Message Protocol	[77,GSM11]
pcmail-srv	158/tcp	PCMail Server	[19,MXL]
pcmail-srv	158/udp	PCMail Server	[19,MXL]
nss-routing	159/tcp	NSS-Routing	[JXR]
nss-routing	159/udp	NSS-Routing	[JXR]
sgmp-traps	160/tcp	SGMP-TRAPS	[37,MS9]
sgmp-traps	160/udp	SGMP-TRAPS	[37,MS9]
snmp	161/tcp	SNMP	[15,MTR]
snmp	161/udp	SNMP	[15,MTR]
snmptrap	162/tcp	SNMPTRAP	[15,MTR]
snmptrap	162/udp	SNMPTRAP	[15,MTR]
cmip-man	163/tcp	CMIP/TCP Manager	[4,AXB1]
cmip-man	163/udp	CMIP/TCP Manager	[4,AXB1]
cmip-agent	164/tcp	CMIP/TCP Agent	[4,AXB1]
smip-agent	164/udp	CMIP/TCP Agent	[4,AXB1]
xns-courier	165/tcp	Xerox	[144,SXA]
xns-courier	165/udp	Xerox	[144,SXA]
s-net	166/tcp	Sirius Systems	[BXL]
s-net	166/udp	Sirius Systems	[BXL]
namp	167/tcp	NAMP	[MS9]
namp	167/udp	NAMP	[MS9]
rsvd	168/tcp	RSVD	[NT12]
rsvd	168/udp	RSVD	[NT12]
send	169/tcp	SEND	[WDW11]

send	169/udp	SEND	[WDW11]
print-srv	170/tcp	Network PostScript	[BKR]
print-srv	170/udp	Network PostScript	[BKR]
multiplex	171/tcp	Network Innovations Multiplex	[KXD]
multiplex	171/udp	Network Innovations Multiplex	[KXD]
cl/1	172/tcp	Network Innovations CL/1	[KXD]
cl/1	172/udp	Network Innovations CL/1	[KXD]
xyplex-mux	173/tcp	Xyplex	[BXS]
xyplex-mux	173/udp	Xyplex	[BXS]
mailq	174/tcp	MAILQ	[RXZ]
mailq	174/udp	MAILQ	[RXZ]
vmnet	175/tcp	VMNET	[CXT]
vmnet	175/udp	VMNET	[CXT]
genrad-mux	176/tcp	GENRAD-MUX	[RXT]
genrad-mux	176/udp	GENRAD-MUX	[RXT]
xdmcp	177/tcp	X Display Manager Control Protocol	[RWS4]
xdmcp	177/udp	X Display Manager Control Protocol	[RWS4]
nextstep	178/tcp	NextStep Window Server	[LXH]
NextStep	178/udp	NextStep Window Server	[LXH]
bgp	179/tcp	Border Gateway Protocol	[KSL]
bgp	179/udp	Border Gateway Protocol	[KSL]
ris	180/tcp	Intergraph	[DXB]
ris	180/udp	Intergraph	[DXB]
unify	181/tcp	Unify	[VXS]
unify	181/udp	Unify	[VXS]
audit	182/tcp	Unisys Audit SITP	[GXG]
audit	182/udp	Unisys Audit SITP	[GXG]
ocbinder	183/tcp	OCBinder	[JXO1]
ocbinder	183/udp	OCBinder	[JXO1]
ocserver	184/tcp	OCServer	[JXO1]
ocserver	184/udp	OCServer	[JXO1]
remote-kis	185/tcp	Remote-KIS	[RXD1]
remote-kis	185/udp	Remote-KIS	[RXD1]
kis	186/tcp	KIS Protocol	[RXD1]
kis	186/udp	KIS Protocol	[RXD1]
aci	187/tcp	Application Communication Interface	[RXC1]
aci	187/udp	Application Communication Interface	[RXC1]
mumps	188/tcp	Plus Five's MUMPS	[HS23]
mumps	188/udp	Plus Five's MUMPS	[HS23]
qft	189/tcp	Queued File Transport	[WXS]
qft	189/udp	Queued File Transport	[WXS]
gacp	190/tcp	Gateway Access Control Protocol	[PCW]
cacp	190/udp	Gateway Access Control Protocol	[PCW]
prospero	191/tcp	Prospero	[BCN]
prospero	191/udp	Prospero	[BCN]
osu-nms	192/tcp	OSU Network Monitoring System	[DXK]

osu-nms	192/udp	OSU Network Monitoring System	[DXK]
srmp	193/tcp	Spider Remote Monitoring Protocol	[TXS]
srmp	193/udp	Spider Remote Monitoring Protocol	[TXS]
irc	194/tcp	Internet Relay Chat Protocol	[JXO2]
irc	194/udp	Internet Relay Chat Protocol	[JXO2]
dn6-nlm-aud	195/tcp	DNSIX Network Level Module Audit	[LL69]
dn6-nlm-aud	195/udp	DNSIX Network Level Module Audit	[LL69]
dn6-smm-red	196/tcp	DNSIX Session Mgt Module Audit Redir	[LL69]
dn6-smm-red	196/udp	DNSIX Session Mgt Module Audit Redir	[LL69]
dls	197/tcp	Directory Location Service	[SXB]
dls	197/udp	Directory Location Service	[SXB]
dls-mon	198/tcp	Directory Location Service Monitor	[SXB]
dls-mon	198/udp	Directory Location Service Monitor	[SXB]
smux	199/tcp	SMUX	[MTR]
smux	199/udp	SMUX	[MTR]
src	200/tcp	IBM System Resource Controller	[GXM]
src	200/udp	IBM System Resource Controller	[GXM]
at-rtmp	201/tcp	AppleTalk Routing Maintenance	[RXC]
at-rtmp	201/udp	AppleTalk Routing Maintenance	[RXC]
at-nbp	202/tcp	AppleTalk Name Binding	[RXC]
at-nbp	202/udp	AppleTalk Name Binding	[RXC]
at-3	203/tcp	AppleTalk Unused	[RXC]
at-3	203/udp	AppleTalk Unused	[RXC]
at-echo	204/tcp	AppleTalk Echo	[RXC]
at-echo	204/udp	AppleTalk Echo	[RXC]
at-5	205/tcp	AppleTalk Unused	[RXC]
at-5	205/udp	AppleTalk Unused	[RXC]
at-zis	206/tcp	AppleTalk Zone Information	[RXC]
at-zis	206/udp	AppleTalk Zone Information	[RXC]
at-7	207/tcp	AppleTalk Unused	[RXC]
at-7	207/udp	AppleTalk Unused	[RXC]
at-8	208/tcp	AppleTalk Unused	[RXC]
at-8	208/udp	AppleTalk Unused	[RXC]
tam	209/tcp	Trivial Authenticated Mail Protocol	[DXB1]
tam	209/udp	Trivial Authenticated Mail Protocol	[DXB1]
z39.50	210/tcp	ANSI Z39.50	[MXN]
z39.50	210/udp	ANSI Z39.50	[MXN]
914c/g	211/tcp	Texas Instruments 914C/G Terminal	[BXH1]
914c/g	211/udp	Texas Instruments	[BXH1]

```
                              914C/G Terminal
anet         212/tcp    ATEXSSTR                        [JXT]
anet         212/udp    ATEXSSTR                        [JXT]
ipx          213/tcp    IPX                             [DP666]
ipx          213/udp    IPX                             [DP666]
vmpwscs      214/tcp    VM PWSCS                        [DXS]
vmpwscs      214/udp    VM PWSCS                        [DXS]
softpc       215/tcp    Insignia Solutions              [MXT]
softpc       215/udp    Insignia Solutions              [MXT]
atls         216/tcp    Access Technology License       [LXD]
                        Server
atls         216/udp    Access Technology License       [LXD]
                        Server
dbase        217/tcp    dBASE Unix                      [DXG1]
dbase        217/udp    dBASE Unix                      [DXG1]
mpp          218/tcp    Netix Message Posting           [STY]
                        Protocol
mpp          218/udp    Netix Message Posting           [STY]
                        Protocol
uarps        219/tcp    Unisys ARPs                     [AXM1]
uarps        219/udp    Unisys ARPs                     [AXM1]
imap3        220/tcp    Interactive Mail Access         [JXR2]
                        Protocol v3
imap3        220/udp    Interactive Mail Access         [JXR2]
                        Protocol v3
fln-spx      221/tcp    Berkeley rlogind with           [KXA]
                        SPX auth
fln-spx      221/udp    Berkeley rlogind with           [KXA]
                        SPX auth
fsh-spx      222/tcp    Berkeley rshd with SPX auth     [KXA]
fsh-spx      222/udp    Berkeley rshd with SPX auth     [KXA]
cdc          223/tcp    Certificate Distribution        [KXA]
                        Center
cdc          223/udp    Certificate Distribution        [KXA]
                        Center

             224-241    Reserved                        [JBP]

sur-meas     243/tcp    Survey Measurement              [6,DDC1]
sur-meas     243/udp    Survey Measurement              [6,DDC1]
link         245/tcp    LINK                            [1,RDB2]
link         245/udp    LINK                            [1,RDB2]
dsp3270      246/tcp    Display Systems Protocol        [39,WJS1]
dsp3270      246/udp    Display Systems Protocol        [39,WJS1]

             247-255    Reserved                        [JBP]

pawserv      345/tcp    Perf Analysis Workbench
pawserv      345/udp    Perf Analysis Workbench
zserv        346/tcp    Zebra server
zserv        346/udp    Zebra server
fatserv      347/tcp    Fatmen Server
fatserv      347/udp    Fatmen Server
clearcase    371/tcp    Clearcase                       [DXL1]
clearcase    371/udp    Clearcase                       [DXL1]
```

```
ulistserv    372/tcp    Unix Listserv                     [AXK]
ulistserv    372/udp    Unix Listserv                     [AXK]
legent-1     373/tcp    Legent Corporation                [KXB]
legent-1     373/udp    Legent Corporation                [KXB]
legent-2     374/tcp    Legent Corporation                [KXB]
legent-2     374/udp    Legent Corporation                [KXB]
exec         512/tcp    remote process execution;
                        authentication performed using
                        passwords and UNIX loppgin names
biff         512/udp    used by mail system to notify users
                        of new mail received; currently
                        receives messages    only from
                        processes    on the same machine
login        513/tcp    remote login a la telnet;
                        automatic authentication performed
                        based on priviledged port numbers
                        and distributed data bases which
                        identify "authentication domains"
who          513/udp    maintains    data bases showing who's
                        logged in to machines on a local
                        net and the load average of the
                        machine
cmd          514/tcp    like exec, but automatic
                        authentication is    performed as for
                        login server
syslog       514/udp
printer      515/tcp    spooler
printer      515/udp    spooler
talk         517/tcp    like tenex link, but across
                        machine unfortunately, doesn't
                        use link protocol (this is actually
                        just a rendezvous port from which a
                        tcp connection is established)
talk         517/udp    like tenex link, but across
                        machine - unfortunately, doesn't
                        use link protocol (this is actually
                        just a rendezvous port from which a
                        tcp connection is established)
ntalk        518/tcp
ntalk        518/udp
utime        519/tcp    unixtime
utime        519/udp    unixtime
efs          520/tcp    extended file name server
router       520/udp    local routing process (on    site);
                        uses variant of Xerox NS routing
                        information protocol
timed        525/tcp    timeserver
timed        525/udp    timeserver
tempo        526/tcp    newdate
tempo        526/udp    newdate
courier      530/tcp    rpc
courier      530/udp    rpc
conference   531/tcp    chat
conference   531/udp    chat
netnews      532/tcp    readnews
```

netnews	532/udp	readnews	
netwall	533/tcp	for emergency broadcasts	
netwall	533/udp	for emergency broadcasts	
uucp	540/tcp	uucpd	
uucp	540/udp	uucpd	
klogin	543/tcp		
klogin	543/udp		
kshell	544/tcp	krcmd	
kshell	544/udp	krcmd	
new-rwho	550/tcp	new-who	
new-rwho	550/udp	new-who	
dsf	555/tcp		
dsf	555/udp		
remotefs	556/tcp	rfs server	
remotefs	556/udp	rfs server	
rmonitor	560/tcp	rmonitord	
rmonitor	560/udp	rmonitord	
monitor	561/tcp		
monitor	561/udp		
chshell	562/tcp	chcmd	
chshell	562/udp	chcmd	
9pfs	564/tcp	plan 9 file service	
9pfs	564/udp	plan 9 file service	
whoami	565/tcp	whoami	
whoami	565/udp	whoami	
meter	570/tcp	demon	
meter	570/udp	demon	
meter	571/tcp	udemon	
meter	571/udp	udemon	
ipcserver	600/tcp	Sun IPC server	
ipcserver	600/udp	Sun IPC server	
nqs	607/tcp	nqs	
nqs	607/udp	nqs	
mdqs	666/tcp		
mdqs	666/udp		
elcsd	704/tcp	errlog copy/server daemon	
elcsd	704/udp	errlog copy/server daemon	
netcp	740/tcp	NETscout Control Protocol	[AXS2]
netcp	740/udp	NETscout Control Protocol	[AXS2]
netgw	741/tcp	netGW	[OXK]
netgw	741/udp	netGW	[OXK]
netrcs	742/tcp	Network based Rev. Cont. Sys.	[GXC2]
netrcs	742/udp	Network based Rev. Cont. Sys.	[GXC2]
flexlm	744/tcp	Flexible License Manager	[MXC2]
flexlm	744/udp	Flexible License Manager	[MXC2]
fujitsu-dev	747/tcp	Fujitsu Device Control	
fujitsu-dev	747/udp	Fujitsu Device Control	
ris-cm	748/tcp	Russell Info Sci Calendar Manager	
ris-cm	748/udp	Russell Info Sci Calendar Manager	
kerberos-adm	749/tcp	kerberos administration	
kerberos-adm	749/udp	kerberos administration	

```
rfile            750/tcp
loadav           750/udp
pump             751/tcp
pump             751/udp
qrh              752/tcp
qrh              752/udp
rrh              753/tcp
rrh              753/udp
tell             754/tcp        send
tell             754/udp        send
nlogin           758/tcp
nlogin           758/udp
con              759/tcp
con              759/udp
ns               760/tcp
ns               760/udp
rxe              761/tcp
rxe              761/udp
quotad           762/tcp
quotad           762/udp
cycleserv        763/tcp
cycleserv        763/udp
omserv           764/tcp
omserv           764/udp
webster          765/tcp
webster          765/udp
phonebook        767/tcp        phone
phonebook        767/udp        phone
vid              769/tcp
vid              769/udp
cadlock          770/tcp
cadlock          770/udp
rtip             771/tcp
rtip             771/udp
cycleserv2       772/tcp
cycleserv2       772/udp
submit           773/tcp
notify           773/udp
rpasswd          774/tcp
acmaint_dbd      774/udp
entomb           775/tcp
acmaint_         775/udp
   transd
wpages           776/tcp
wpages           776/udp
wpgs             780/tcp
wpgs             780/udp
hp-              781/tcp        hp performance data collector
   collector
hp-              781/udp        hp performance data collector
   collector
hp-managed-      782/tcp        hp performance data managed node
   node
hp-managed-      782/udp        hp performance data managed node
   node
```

```
hp-alarm-    783/tcp    hp performance data alarm manager
   mgr
hp-alarm-    783/udp    hp performance data alarm manager
   mgr
mdbs_daemon 800/tcp
mdbs_daemon 800/udp
device       801/tcp
device       801/udp
xtreelic     996/tcp    XTREE License Server
xtreelic     996/udp    XTREE License Server
maitrd       997/tcp
maitrd       997/udp
busboy       998/tcp
puparp       998/udp
garcon       999/tcp
applix       999/udp    Applix ac
puprouter    999/tcp
puprouter    999/udp
cadlock      1000/tcp
ock          1000/udp
```

Registered Port Numbers

The Registered Ports are not controlled by the IANA and on most systems can be used by ordinary user processes or programs executed by ordinary users.

Ports are used in the TCP [45,106] to name the ends of logical connections which carry long term conversations. For the purpose of providing services to unknown callers, a service contact port is defined. This list specifies the port used by the server process as its contact port. While the IANA can not control uses of these ports it does register or list uses of these ports as a convienence to the community.

To the extent possible, these same port assignments are used with the UDP [46,104].

The Registered Ports are in the range 1024-65535.

```
Port Assignments:
   Keyword          Decimal    Description                   References
   ------           ------     -----------                   ----------
   blackjack        1025/tcp   network blackjack
   blackjack        1025/udp   network blackjack
   hermes           1248/tcp
   hermes           1248/udp
   bbn-mmc          1347/tcp   multi media conferencing
   bbn-mmc          1347/udp   multi media conferencing
   bbn-mmx          1348/tcp   multi media conferencing
   bbn-mmx          1348/udp   multi media conferencing
   sbook            1349/tcp   Registration Network Protocol [SXS4]
   sbook            1349/udp   Registration Network Protocol [SXS4]
   editbench        1350/tcp   Registration Network Protocol [SXS4]
   editbench        1350/udp   Registration Network Protocol [SXS4]
   equationbuilder  1351/tcp   Digital Tool Works (MIT)      [TXT1]
   equationbuilder  1351/udp   Digital Tool Works (MIT)      [TXT1]
   lotusnote        1352/tcp   Lotus Note                    [GXP1]
```

```
lotusnote       1352/udp    Lotus Note                  [GXP1]
ingreslock      1524/tcp    ingres
ingreslock      1524/udp    ingres
orasrv          1525/tcp    oracle
orasrv          1525/udp    oracle
prospero-np     1525/tcp    prospero non-privileged
prospero-np     1525/udp    prospero non-privileged
tlisrv          1527/tcp    oracle
tlisrv          1527/udp    oracle
coauthor        1529/tcp    oracle
coauthor        1529/udp    oracle
issd            1600/tcp
issd            1600/udp
nkd             1650/tcp
nkd             1650/udp
callbook        2000/tcp
callbook        2000/udp
dc              2001/tcp
wizard          2001/udp    curry
globe           2002/tcp
globe           2002/udp
mailbox         2004/tcp
emce            2004/udp    CCWS mm conf
berknet         2005/tcp
oracle          2005/udp
invokator       2006/tcp
raid-cc         2006/udp    raid
dectalk         2007/tcp
raid-am         2007/udp
conf            2008/tcp
terminaldb      2008/udp
news            2009/tcp
whosockami      2009/udp
search          2010/tcp
pipe_server     2010/udp
raid-cc         2011/tcp    raid
servserv        2011/udp
ttyinfo         2012/tcp
raid-ac         2012/udp
raid-am         2013/tcp
raid-cd         2013/udp
troff           2014/tcp
raid-sf         2014/udp
cypress         2015/tcp
raid-cs         2015/udp
bootserver      2016/tcp
bootserver      2016/udp
cypress-stat    2017/tcp
bootclient      2017/udp
terminaldb      2018/tcp
rellpack        2018/udp
whosockami      2019/tcp
about           2019/udp
xinupageserver  2020/tcp
xinupageserver  2020/udp
```

```
servexec        2021/tcp
xinuexpansion1  2021/udp
down            2022/tcp
xinuexpansion2  2022/udp
xinuexpansion3  2023/tcp
xinuexpansion3  2023/udp
xinuexpansion4  2024/tcp
xinuexpansion4  2024/udp
ellpack         2025/tcp
xribs           2025/udp
scrabble        2026/tcp
scrabble        2026/udp
shadowserver    2027/tcp
shadowserver    2027/udp
submitserver    2028/tcp
submitserver    2028/udp
device2         2030/tcp
device2         2030/udp
blackboard      2032/tcp
blackboard      2032/udp
glogger         2033/tcp
glogger         2033/udp
scoremgr        2034/tcp
scoremgr        2034/udp
imsldoc         2035/tcp
imsldoc         2035/udp
objectmanager   2038/tcp
objectmanager   2038/udp
lam             2040/tcp
lam             2040/udp
interbase       2041/tcp
interbase       2041/udp
isis            2042/tcp
isis            2042/udp
isis-bcast      2043/tcp
isis-bcast      2043/udp
rimsl           2044/tcp
rimsl           2044/udp
cdfunc          2045/tcp
cdfunc          2045/udp
sdfunc          2046/tcp
sdfunc          2046/udp
dls             2047/tcp
dls             2047/udp
dls-monitor     2048/tcp
dls-monitor     2048/udp
shilp           2049/tcp
shilp           2049/udp
www-dev         2784/tcp    world wide web - development
www-dev         2784/udp    world wide web - development
NSWS            3049/tcp
NSWS            3049/ddddp
rfa             4672/tcp    remote file access server
rfa             4672/udp    remote file access server
commplex-main   5000/tcp
```

```
commplex-main      5000/udp
commplex-link      5001/tcp
commplex-link      5001/udp
rfe                5002/tcp   radio free ethernet
rfe                5002/udp   radio free ethernet
rmonitor_secure    5145/tcp
rmonitor_secure    5145/udp
padl2sim           5236/tcp
padl2sim           5236/udp
sub-process        6111/tcp   HP SoftBench Sub-Process Control
sub-process        6111/udp   HP SoftBench Sub-Process Control
xdsxdm             6558/udp
xdsxdm             6558/tcp
afs3-fileserver    7000/tcp   file server itself
afs3-fileserver    7000/udp   file server itself
afs3-callback      7001/tcp   callbacks to cache managers
afs3-callback      7001/udp   callbacks to cache managers
afs3-prserver      7002/tcp   users & groups database
afs3-prserver      7002/udp   users & groups database
afs3-vlserver      7003/tcp   volume location database
afs3-vlserver      7003/udp   volume location database
afs3-kaserver      7004/tcp   AFS/Kerberos authentication service
afs3-kaserver      7004/udp   AFS/Kerberos authentication service
afs3-volser        7005/tcp   volume managment server
afs3-volser        7005/udp   volume managment server
afs3-errors        7006/tcp   error interpretation service
afs3-errors        7006/udp   error interpretation service
afs3-bos           7007/tcp   basic overseer process
afs3-bos           7007/udp   basic overseer process
afs3-update        7008/tcp   server-to-server updater
afs3-update        7008/udp   server-to-server updater
afs3-rmtsys        7009/tcp   remote cache manager service
afs3-rmtsys        7009/udp   remote cache manager service
man                9535/tcp
man                9535/udp
isode-dua          17007/tcp
isode-dua          17007/udp
```

Internet Multicast Addresses

Host Extensions for IP Multicasting (RFC-1112) [43] specifies the extensions required of a host implementation of the Internet Protocol (IP) to support multicasting. Current addresses are listed below.

```
224.0.0.0     Reserved                                [43,JBP]
224.0.0.1     All Systems on this Subnet              [43,JBP]
224.0.0.2     All Routers on this Subnet              [JBP]
224.0.0.3     Unassigned                              [JBP]
224.0.0.4     DVMRP Routers                           [140,JBP]
224.0.0.5     OSPFIGP OSPFIGP All Routers             [83,JXM1]
224.0.0.6     OSPFIGP OSPFIGP Designated Routers      [83,JXM1]
224.0.0.7     ST Routers                              [KS14]
224.0.0.8     ST Hosts                                [KS14]
224.0.0.9     RIP2 Routers                            [GSM11]
224.0.0.10-   Unassigned                              [JBP]
```

```
224.0.0.255

224.0.1.0      VMTP Managers Group              [17,DRC3]
224.0.1.1      NTP Network Time Protocol        [80,DLM1]
224.0.1.2      SGI-Dogfight                     [AXC]
224.0.1.3      Rwhod                            [SXD]
224.0.1.4      VNP                              [DRC3]
224.0.1.5      Artificial Horizons - Aviator    [BXF]
224.0.1.6      NSS - Name Service Server        [BXS2]
224.0.1.7      AUDIONEWS - Audio News Multicast  [MXF2]
224.0.1.8      SUN NIS+ Information Service     [CXM3]
224.0.1.9      MTP Multicast Transport Protocol  [SXA]
224.0.1.10-    Unassigned                       [JBP]
224.0.1.255

224.0.2.1      "rwho" Group (BSD) (unofficial)  [JBP]
224.0.2.2      SUN RPC PMAPPROC_CALLIT          [BXE1]

224.0.3.0-     RFE Generic Service              [DXS3]
224.0.3.255
224.0.4.0-     RFE Individual Conferences       [DXS3]
224.0.4.255

224.1.0.0-     ST Multicast Groups              [KS14]
224.1.255.255
224.2.0.0-     Multimedia Conference Calls      [SC3]
224.2.255.255
232.x.x.x      VMTP transient    groups         [17,DRC3]
```

These addresses are listed in the Domain Name Service under MCAST.NET and 224.IN-ADDR.ARPA.

Note that when used on an Ethernet or IEEE 802 network, the 23 low-order bits of the IP Multicast address are placed in the low-order 23 bits of the Ethernet or IEEE 802 net multicast address

Iana Ethernet Address Block

The IANA owns an Ethernet address block which may be used for multicast address asignments or other special purposes.

The address block in IEEE binary is (which is in bit transmission order):

```
0000 0000 0000 0000 0111 1010
```

In the normal Internet dotted decimal notation this is 0.0.94 since the bytes are transmitted higher order first and bits within bytes are transmitted lower order first (see "Data Notation" in the Introduction).

IEEE   CSMA/CD and Token Bus bit transmission order: 00 00 5E

IEEE   Token Ring bit transmission order: 00 00 7A

Appearance on the wire (bits transmitted from left to right):

```
0                          23                          47
|                          |                           |
1000 0000 0000 0000 0111 1010 xxxx xxx0 xxxx xxxx xxxx xxxx
|                                    |
Multicast Bit                       0 = Internet Multicast
                                    1 = Assigned by IANA for
                                        other uses
```

Appearance in memory (bits transmitted right-to-left within octets, octets transmitted left-to-right):

```
0                          23                          47
|                          |                           |
0000 0001 0000 0000 0101 1110 0xxx xxxx xxxx xxxx xxxx xxxx
           |                   |
           Multicast Bit       0 = Internet Multicast
                               1 = Assigned by IANA for other
                                   uses
```

The latter representation corresponds to the Internet standard bit-order, and is the format that most programmers have to deal with.

Using this representation, the range of Internet Multicast addresses is:

```
01-00-5E-00-00-00  to  01-00-5E-7F-FF-FF  in hex, or
1.0.94.0.0.0  to  1.0.94.127.255.255  in dotted decimal
```

IP TOS Parameters

This documents the default Type-of-Service values that are currently recommended for the most important Internet protocols.

There are four assigned TOS values: low delay, high throughput, high reliability, and low cost; in each case, the TOS value is used to indicate "better". Only one TOS value or property can be requested in any one IP datagram.

Generally, protocols which are involved in direct interaction with a human should select low delay, while data transfers which may involve large blocks of data are need high throughput. Finally, high reliability is most important for datagram-based Internet management functions.

Application protocols not included in these tables should be able to make appropriate choice of low delay (8 decimal, 1000 binary) or high throughput (4 decimail, 0100 binary).

The following are recommended values for TOS:

Type-of-Service	Value	
Protocol	**TOS Value**	
TELNET (1)	1000	(minimize delay)
FTP		

continues

continued

Type-of-Service	Value	
Protocol	**TOS Value**	
Control	1000	(minimize delay)
Data (2)	0100	(maximize throughput)
TFTP	1000	(minimize delay)
SMTP (3)		
Command phase	1000	(minimize delay)
DATA phase	0100	(maximize throughput)
Domain Name Service		
UDP Query	1000	(minimize delay)
TCP Query	0000	
Zone Transfer	0100	(maximize throughput)
NNTP	0001	(minimize monetary cost)
ICMP		
Errors	0000	
Requests	0000 (4)	
Responses	<same as request> (4)	
Any IGP	0010	(maximize reliability)
EGP	0000	
SNMP	0010	(maximize reliability)
BOOTP	0000	

Notes:

1. Includes all interactive user protocols (e.g., rlogin).
2. Includes all bulk data transfer protocols (e.g., rcp).
3. If the implementation does not support changing the TOS during the lifetime of the connection, then the recommended TOS on opening the connection is the default TOS (0000).

4. Although ICMP request messages are normally sent with the default TOS, there are sometimes good reasons why they would be sent with some other TOS value. An ICMP response always uses the same TOS value as was used in the corresponding ICMP request message.

An application may (at the request of the user) substitute 0001 (minimize monetary cost) for any of the above values.

IP TIME TO LIVE PARAMETER

The current recommended default time to live (TTL) for the Internet Protocol (IP) [45,105] is 64.

DOMAIN SYSTEM PARAMETERS

The Internet Domain Naming System (DOMAIN) includes several parameters. These are documented in RFC-1034, [81] and RFC-1035 [82]. The CLASS parameter is listed here. The per CLASS parameters are defined in separate RFCs as indicated.

Domain System Parameters:

Decimal	Name	References
0	Reserved	[PM1]
1	Internet (IN)	[81,PM1]
2	Unassigned	[PM1]
3	Chaos (CH)	[PM1]
4	Hessoid (HS)	[PM1]
5-65534	Unassigned	[PM1]
65535	Reserved	[PM1]

In the Internet (IN) class the following TYPEs and QTYPEs are defined:

TYPE	value and	meaning	
A	1	a host address	[82]
NS	2	an authoritative name server	[82]
MD	3	a mail destination (Obsolete - use MX)	[82]
MF	4	a mail forwarder (Obsolete - use MX)	[82]

continues

continued

TYPE	value and	meaning	
CNAME	5	the canonical name for an alias	[82]
SOA	6	marks the start of a zone of authority	[82]
MB	7	a mailbox domain name (EXPERIMENTAL)	[82]
MG	8	a mail group member (EXPERIMENTAL)	[82]
MR	9	a mail rename domain name (EXPERIMENTAL)	[82]
NULL	10	a null RR (EXPERIMENTAL)	[82]
WKS	11	a well known service description	[82]
PTR	12	a domain name pointer	[82]
HINFO	13	host information	[82]
MINFO	14	mailbox or mail list information	[82]
MX	15	mail exchange	[82]
TXT	16	text strings	[82]
RP	17	for Responsible Person	[172]
AFSDB	18	for AFS Data Base location	[172]
X25	19	for X.25 PSDN address	[172]
ISDN	20	for ISDN address	[172]
RT	21	for Route Through	[172]
NSAP	22	for NSAP address, NSAP style A record	[174]
NSAP-PTR	23	for domain name pointer, NSAP style	[174]
AXFR	252	transfer of an entire zone	[82]
MAILB	253	mailbox-related RRs (MB, MG or MR)	[82]
MAILA	254	mail agent RRs (Obsolete - see MX)	[82]
*	255	A request for all records	[82]

BOOTP PARAMETERS

The Bootstrap Protocol (BOOTP) RFC-951 [36] describes an IP/UDP bootstrap protocol (BOOTP) which allows a diskless client machine to discover its own IP address, the address of a server host, and the name of a file to be loaded into memory and executed. The BOOTP Vendor Information Extensions RFC-1084 [117] describes an addition to the Bootstrap Protocol (BOOTP).

Vendor Extensions are listed below:

Tag Name	Data Length	Meaning
0 Pad	0	None
1 Subnet Mask	4	Subnet Mask Value
2 Time Zone	4	Time Offset in Seconds from UTC
3 Gateways	N	N/4 Gateway addresses
4 Time Server	N	N/4 Timeserver addresses
5 Name Server	N	N/4 IEN-116 Server addresses
6 Domain Server	N	N/4 DNS Server addresses
7 Log Server	N	N/4 Logging Server addresses
8 Quotes Server	N	N/4 Quotes Server addresses
9 LPR Server	N	N/4 Printer Server addresses
10 Impress Server	N	N/4 Impress Server addresses
11 RLP Server	N	N/4 RLP Server addresses
12 Hostname	N	Hostname string
13 Boot File Size	2	Size of boot file in 512 byte checks
14 Merit Dump File		Client to dump and name the file to dump it to
15-127 Unassigned		
128-154 Reserved		
255 End	0	None

NETWORK MANAGEMENT PARAMETERS

For the management of hosts and gateways on the Internet a data structure for the information has been defined. This data structure should be used with any of several possible management protocols, such as the "Simple Network Management Protocol" (SNMP) RFC-1157 [15], or the "Common Management Information Protocol over TCP" (CMOT) [142].

The data structure is the "Structure and Indentification of Management Information for TCP/IP-based Internets" (SMI) RFC-1155 [120], and the "Management Information Base for Network Management of TCP/IP-based Internets" (MIB-II) [121].

The SMI includes the provision for panrameters or codes to indicate experimental or private data structures. These parameter assignments are listed here.

The older "Simple Gateway Monitoring Protocol" (SGMP) RFC-1028 [37] also defined a data structure. The parameter assignments used with SGMP are included here for hist orical completeness.

The network management object identifiers are under the iso (1), org (3), dod (6), internet (1), or 1.3.6.1, branch of the name space.

SMI Network Management Directory Codes:

Prefix: 1.3.6.1.1.

Decimal	Name	Description	References
all	Reserved	Reserved for future use	[IANA]

SMI Network Management MGMT Codes:

Prefix: 1.3.6.1.2.

Decimal	Name	Description	References
0	Reserved		[IANA]
1	MIB		[149,KZM]

Prefix: 1.3.6.1.2.1. (mib-2)

Decimal	Name	Description	References
0	Reserved	Reserved	[IANA]
1	system	System	[150,KZM]
2	interfaces	Interfaces	[150,KZM]
3	at	Address Translation	[150,KZM]
4	ip	Internet Protocol	[150,KZM]
5	icmp	Internet Control Message	[150,KZM]
6	tcp	Transmission Control Protocol	[150,KZM]
7	udp	User Datagram Protocol	[150,KZM]
8	egp	Exterior Gateway Protocol	[150,KZM]
9	cmot	CMIP over TCP	[150,KZM]
10	transmission	Transmission	[150,KZM]
11	snmp	Simple Network Management	[150,KZM]
12	GenericIF	Generic Interface Extensions	[151,163,KZM]

Decimal	Name	Description	References
13	Appletalk	Appletalk Networking	[152,SXW]
14	ospf	Open Shortest Path First	[153,FB77]
15	bgp	Border Gateway Protocol	[154,SW159]
16	rmon	Remote Network Monitoring	[155,SXW]
17	bridge	Bridge Objects	[156,EXD]
18	DecnetP4	Decnet Phase	4
19	Character	Character Streams	[165,BS221]
20	snmp	Parties SNMP Parties	[177,KZM]
21	snmp	Secrets SNMP Secrets	[177,KZM]

Prefix: 1.3.6.1.2.1.10 (transmission)

Decimal	Name	Description
7	IEEE802.3 CSMACD—like Objects	[157,JXC]
8	IEEE802.4 Token Bus-like Objects	[158,163,KZM]
9	IEEE802.5 Token Ring-like Objects	[159,163,KZM]
15	FDDI FDDI Objects	[160,JDC20]
18	DS1 T1 Carrier Objects	[161,163,FB77]
30	DS3 DS3 Interface Objects	[162,163,TXC]
31	SIP SMDS Interface Objects	[164,TXC]
32	FRAME-RELAY Frame Relay Objects	[168,CXB]
33	RS-232 RS-232 Objects	[166,BS221]
34	Parallel Parallel Printer Objects	[167,BS221]

SMI Network Management Experimental Codes:

Prefix: 1.3.6.1.3.

Decimal	Name	Description	References
0	Reserved	[JKR1]	
1	CLNS	ISO CLNS Objects	[GS2]
* 2	T1-Carrier	T1 Carrier Objects	[FB77]
* 3	IEEE802.3	Ethernet-like Objects	[JXC]

continues

continued

Decimal	Name	Description	References
* 4	IEEE802.5	Token Ring-like Objects	[EXD]
* 5	DECNet-PHIV	DECNet Phase IV	[JXS2]
* 6	Interface	Generic Interface Objects	[KZM]
* 7	IEEE802.4	Token Bus-like Objects	[KZM]
* 8	FDDI	FDDI Objects	[JDC20]
9	LANMGR-1	LAN Manager V1 Objects	[JXG1]
10	LANMGR-TRAPS	LAN Manager Trap Objects	[JXG1]
11	Views	SNMP View Objects	[CXD]
12	SNMP-AUTH	SNMP Authentication Objects	[KZM]
* 13	BGP	Border Gateway Protocol	[SW159]
* 14	Bridge	Bridge MIB	[FB77]
* 15	DS3	DS3 Interface Type	[TXC]
* 16	SIP	SMDS Interface Protocol	[TXC]
* 17	Appletalk	Appletalk Networking	[SXW]
18	PPP	PPP Objects	[FJK2]
* 19	Character	MIB Character MIB	[BS221]
* 20	RS-232 MIB	RS-232 MIB	[BS221]
* 21	Parallel MIB	Parallel MIB	[BS221]
22	atsign-proxy	Proxy viaCommunity	[RXF]
* 23	OSPF	OSPF MIB	[FB77]
24	Alert-Man	Alert-Man	[LS8]
25	FDDI-Synoptics	FDDI-Synoptics	[DXP1]
* 26	Frame Relay	Frame Relay MIB	[CXB]
* 27	rmon	Remote Network Management MIB	[SXW]
28	IDPR	IDPR MIB	[RAW44]
29	HUBMIB	IEEE 802.3 Hub MIB	[DXM5]
30	IPFWDTBLMIB	IP Forwarding Table MIB	[FB77]
31	LATM MIB		[TXC]
32	SONET MIB		[TXC]
33	IDENT		[MTR]
34	MIME-MHS		[MTR]

* = obsoleted

SMI Network Management Private Enterprise Codes:

Prefix: 1.3.6.1.4.1.

Decimal	Name	References
0	Reserved	[JKR1]
1	Proteon	[JS28]
2	IBM	[VXC]
3	CMU	[SXW]
4	Unix	[KXS]
5	ACC	[AB20]
6	TWG	[KZM]
7	CAYMAN	[BP52]
8	PSI	[MS9]
9	cisco	[GXS]
10	NSC	[GS123]
11	HP	[RDXS]
12	Epilogue	[KA4]
13	U of Tennessee	[JDC20]
14	BBN	[RH6]
15	Xylogics, Inc.	[JRL3]
16	Timeplex	[LXB1]
17	Canstar	[SXP]
18	Wellfleet	[JCB1]
19	TRW	[HXL]
20	MIT	[JR35]
21	EON	[MXW]
22	Spartacus	[YXK]
23	Excelan	[RXB]
24	Spider Systems	[VXW]
25	NSFNET	[HWB]
26	Hughes LAN Systems	[KZM]

continues

continued

Decimal	Name	References
27	Intergraph	[GS91]
28	Interlan	[BXT]
29	Vitalink Communications	[FXB]
30	Ulana	[BXA]
31	NSWC	[SRN1]
32	Santa Cruz Operation	[KR35]
33	Xyplex	[BXS]
34	Cray	[HXE]
35	Bell Northern Research	[GXW]
36	DEC	[RXB1]
37	Touch	[BXB]
38	Network Research Corp.	[BXV]
39	Baylor College of Medicine	[SB98]
40	NMFECC-LLNL	[SXH]
41	SRI	[DW181]
42	Sun Microsystems	[DXY]
43	3Com	[TB6]
44	CMC	[DXP]
45	SynOptics	[DXP1]
46	Cheyenne Software	[RXH]
47	Prime Computer	[MXS]
48	MCNC/North Carolina Data Network	[KXW]
49	Chipcom	[JXC]
50	Optical Data Systems	[JXF]
51	gated	[JXH]
52	Cabletron Systems	[RXD]
53	Apollo Computers	[JXB]
54	DeskTalk Systems, Inc.	[DXK]
55	SSDS	[RXS]

Decimal	Name	References
56	Castle Rock Computing	[JXS1]
57	MIPS Computer Systems	[CXM]
58	TGV, Inc.	[KAA]
59	Silicon Graphics, Inc.	[RXJ]
60	University of British Columbia	[DXM354]
61	Merit	[BXN]
62	FiberCom	[EXR]
63	Apple Computer Inc	[JXH1]
64	Gandalf	[HXK]
65	Dartmouth	[PXK]
66	David Systems	[KXD1]
67	Reuter	[BXZ]
68	Cornell	[DC126]
69	LMS	[MLS34]
70	Locus Computing Corp.	[AXS]
71	NASA	[SS92]
72	Retix	[AXM]
73	Boeing	[JXG]
74	AT&T	[RXB2]
75	Ungermann-Bass	[DXM]
76	Digital Analysis Corp.	[SXK]
77	LAN Manager	[DXK]
78	Netlabs	[JB478]
79	ICL	[JXI]
80	Auspex Systems	[BXE]
81	Lannet Company	[EXR]
82	Network Computing Devices	[DM280]
83	Raycom Systems	[BXW1]
84	Pirelli Focom Ltd.	[SXL]
85	Datability Software Systems	[LXF]

continues

continued

Decimal	Name	References
86	Network Application Technology	[YXW]
87	LINK (Lokales Informatik-Netz Karlsruhe)	[GXS]
88	NYU	[BJR2]
89	RND	[RXN]
90	InterCon Systems Corporation	[AW90]
91	LearningTree Systems	[JXG2]
92	Webster Computer Corporation	[RXE]
93	Frontier Technologies Corporation	[PXA]
94	Nokia Data Communications	[DXE]
95	Allen-Bradely Company	[BXK]
96	CERN	[JXR]
97	Sigma Network Systems, Inc.	[KXV]
98	Emerging Technologies, Inc.	[DXB2]
99	SNMP Research	[JDC20]
100	Ohio State University	[SXA1]
101	Ultra Network Technologies	[JXD]
102	Microcom	[AXF]
103	Martin Marietta Astronautic Group	[DR137]
104	Micro Technology	[MXE]
105	Process Software Corporation	[BV15]
106	Data General Corporation	[JXK]
107	Bull Company	[AXB]
108	Emulex Corporation	[JXF1]
109	Warwick University Computing Services	[IXD]
110	Network General Corporation	[JXD1]
111	Oracle	[JPH17]
112	Control Data Corporation	[NXR]
113	Hughes Aircraft Company	[KZM]
114	Synernetics, Inc.	[JXP1]
115	Mitre	[BM60]

Decimal	Name	References
116	Hitachi, Ltd.	[HXU]
117	Telebit	[MXL2]
118	Salomon Technology Services	[PXM]
119	NEC Corporation	[YXA]
120	Fibermux	[KH157]
121	FTP Software Inc.	[SXK1]
122	Sony	[TXH]
123	Newbridge Networks Corporation	[JXW]
124	Racal-Milgo Information Systems	[MXR]
125	CR SYSTEMS	[SXS2]
126	DSET Corporation	[DXS]
127	Computone	[BXV]
128	Tektronix, Inc.	[DT167]
129	Interactive Systems Corporation	[SXA2]
130	Banyan Systems Inc.	[DXT]
131	Sintrom Datanet Limited	[SXW]
132	Bell Canada	[MXF]
133	Crosscomm Corporation	[RXS1]
134	Rice University	[CXF]
135	T3Plus Networking, Inc.	[HXF]
136	Concurrent Computer Corporation	[JRL3]
137	Basser	[PXO]
138	Luxcom	[RXB]
139	Artel	[JXZ]
140	Independence Technologies, Inc. (ITI)	[GXB]
141	Frontier Software Development	[NXP]
142	Digital Computer Limited	[OXF]
143	Eyring, Inc.	[RH227]
144	Case Communications	[PXK]
145	Penril DataComm, Inc.	[KXH1]

continues

continued

Decimal	Name	References
146	American Airlines	[BXK1]
147	Sequent Computer Systems	[SXH1]
148	Bellcore	[KXT]
149	Konkord Communications	[KXJ]
150	University of Washington	[CXW]
151	Develcon	[SXM]
152	Solarix Systems	[PXA1]
153	Unifi Communications Corp.	[YXH]
154	Roadnet	[DXS]
155	Network Systems Corp.	[NXE]
156	ENE (European Network Engineering)	[PXC]
157	Dansk Data Elektronik A/S	[PXH]
158	Morning Star Technologies	[KXF]
159	Dupont EOP	[OXR]
160	Legato Systems, Inc.	[JXK1]
161	Motorola SPS	[VXE]
162	European Space Agency (ESA)	[EXX]
163	BIM	[BXL2]
164	Rad Data Communications Ltd.	[OXI]
165	Intellicom	[PXS]
166	Shiva Corporation	[NXL]
167	Fujikura America	[DXR]
168	Xlnt Designs INC (XDI)	[MA108]
169	Tandem Computers	[RXD3]
170	BICC	[DXB3]
171	D-Link Systems, Inc.	[HXN]
172	AMP, Inc.	[RXD4]
173	Netlink	[MXZ]
174	C. Itoh Electronics	[LXD1]
175	Sumitomo Electric Industries (SEI)	[KXT1]

App

A

Decimal	Name	References
176	DHL Systems, Inc.	[DXG2]
177	Network Equipment Technologies	[MXT1]
178	APTEC Computer Systems	[LXB]
179	Schneider & Koch & Co., Datensysteme GmbH	[TXR1]
180	Hill Air Force Base	[RXW]
181	ADC Kentrox	[BXK2]
182	Japan Radio Co.	[NXK]
183	Versitron	[MXH]
184	Telecommunication Systems	[HXL1]
185	Interphase	[GXW1]
186	Toshiba Corporation	[MXA]
187	Clearpoint Research Corp.	[FJK2]
188	Ascom Gfeller Ltd.	[AXS1]
189	Fujitsu America	[CXL]
190	NetCom Solutions, Inc.	[DXC]
191	NCR	[CXK]
192	Dr. Materna GmbH	[TXB]
193	Ericsson Business Communications	[GXN]
194	Metaphor Computer Systems	[PXR]
195	Patriot Partners	[PXR]
196	The Software Group Limited (TSG)	[RP211]
197	Kalpana, Inc.	[AXB3]
198	University of Waterloo	[RXW1]
199	CCL/ITRI	[MXC]
200	Coeur Postel	[PXK2]
201	Mitsubish Cable Industries, Ltd.	[MXH1]
202	SMC	[LXS]
203	Crescendo Communication, Inc.	[PXJ]
204	Goodall Software Engineering	[DG223]

continues

continued

Decimal	Name	References
205	Intecom	[BXP]
206	Victoria University of Wellington	[JXS3]
207	Allied Telesis, Inc.	[SXH2]
208	Dowty Network Systems A/S	[HXE1]
209	Protools	[GXA]
210	Nippon Telegraph and Telephone Corp.	[TXS1]
211	Fujitsu Limited	[IXH]
212	Network Peripherals Inc.	[CXC]
213	Netronix, Inc.	[JXR3]
214	University of Wisconsin - Madison	[DW328]
215	NetWorth, Inc.	[CXS]
216	Tandberg Data A/S	[HXH]
217	Technically Elite Concepts, Inc.	[RXD5]
218	Labtam Australia Pty. Ltd.	[MXP1]
219	Republic Telcom Systems, Inc.	[SXH3]
220	ADI Systems, Inc.	[PXL]
221	Microwave Bypass Systems, Inc.	[TXA]
222	Pyramid Technology Corp.	[RXR]
223	Unisys_Corp	[LXB2]
224	LANOPTICS LTD. Israel	[IXD1]
225	NKK Corporation	[JXY]
226	MTrade UK Ltd.	[PXD]
227	Acals	[PXC1]
228	ASTEC, Inc.	[HXF1]
229	Delmarva Power	[JXS4]
230	Telematics International, Inc.	[KXS1]
231	Siemens Nixdorf Informations Syteme AG	[GXK]
232	Compaq	[SXB]
233	NetManage, Inc.	[WXD]
234	NCSU Computing Center	[DXJ]

Decimal	Name	References
235	Empirical Tools and Technologies	[KA4]
236	Samsung Group	[HXP]
237	Takaoka Electric Mfg. Co., Ltd.	[HXH2]
238	Netrix Systems Corporation	[EXM]
239	WINDATA	[BXR]
240	RC International A/S	[CXD1]
241	Netexp Research	[HXB]
242	Internode Systems Pty Ltd	[SXH4]
243	netCS Informationstechnik GmbH	[OXK]
244	Lantronix	[RXL]
245	Avatar Consultants	[KH157]
246	Furukawa Electoric Co. Ltd.	[SXF]
247	AEG Electrcom	[RXN2]
248	Richard Hirschmann GmbH & Co.	[HXN1]
249	G2R Inc.	[KXH]
250	University of Michigan	[TXH1]
251	Netcomm, Ltd.	[WXS2]
252	Sable Technology Corporation	[RXT]
253	Xerox	[EXR3]
254	Conware Computer Consulting GmbH	[MXS2]
255	Compatible Systems Corp.	[JG423]
256	Scitec Communications Systems Ltd.	[SXL1]
257	Transarc Corporation	[PXB]
258	Matsushita Electric Industrial Co., Ltd.	[NXM]
259	ACCTON Technology	[DXR1]
260	Star-Tek, Inc.	[CXM1]
261	Codenoll Tech. Corp.	[DXW]
262	Formation, Inc.	[CXM2]
263	Seiko Instruments, Inc. (SII)	[YXW1]
264	RCE (Reseaux de Communication d'Entreprise	[EXB S.A.)

continues

continued

Decimal	Name	References
265	Xenocom, Inc.	[SXW2]
266	AEG KABEL	[HXT1]
267	Systech Computer Corporation	[BXP1]
268	Visual	[BXO]
269	SDD (Scandinavian Airlines Data Denmark A/S)	[PXF]
270	Zenith Electronics Corporation	[DXL]
271	TELECOM FINLAND	[PXJ1]
272	BinTec Computersystems	[MXS3]
273	EUnet Germany	[MXS4]
274	PictureTel Corporation	[OXJ]
275	Michigan State University	[LXW]
276	GTE Telecom Incorporated	[LXO]
277	Cascade Communications Corp.	[CS1]
278	Hitachi Cable, Ltd.	[TXA1]
279	Olivetti	[MXF1]
280	Vitacom Corporation	[PXR1]
281	INMOS	[GXH]
282	AIC Systems Laboratories Ltd.	[GXM1]
283	Cameo Communications, Inc.	[AXB4]
284	Diab Data AB	[MXL1]
285	Olicom A/S	[LXP]
286	Digital-Kienzle Computersystems	[HXD]
287	CSELT(Centro Studi E Laboratori Telecomunicazioni)	[PXC2]
288	Electronic Data Systems	[MXH2]
289	McData Corporation	[GXL]
290	Harris Computer Systems Division (HCSD)	[DXR2]
291	Technology Dynamics, Inc.	[CXS1]
292	DATAHOUSE Information Systems Ltd.	[KXL]

Decimal	Name	References
293	DSIR Network Group	[TXP]
294	Texas Instruments	[BXS1]
295	PlainTree Systems Inc.	[PXC3]
296	Hedemann Software Development	[SXH5]
297	Fuji Xerox Co., Ltd.	[HXK1]
298	Asante Technology	[HXM]
299	Stanford University	[BXM]
300	Digital Link	[JXT1]
301	Raylan Corporation	[MXL2]
302	Datacraft	[AXL]
303	Hughes	[KZM]
304	Farallon Computing, Inc.	[SXS3]
305	GE Information Services	[SXB2]
306	Gambit Computer Communications	[ZXS]
307	Livingston Enterprises, Inc.	[SXW3]
308	Star Technologies	[JXM1]
309	Micronics Computers Inc.	[DXC1]
310	Basis, Inc.	[HXS]
311	Microsoft	[JXB1]
312	US West Advance Technologies	[DXH]
313	University College London	[SXC]
314	Eastman Kodak Company	[WXC1]
315	Network Resources Corporation	[KXW1]
316	Atlas Telecom	[BXK2]
317	Bridgeway	[UXV]
318	American Power Conversion Corp.	[PXY]
319	DOE Atmospheric Radiation Measurement Project	[PXK3]
320	VerSteeg CodeWorks	[BXV]
321	Verilink Corp	[BXV]

continues

continued

Decimal	Name	References
322	Sybus Corportation	[MXB2]
323	Tekelec	[BXG]
324	NASA Ames Research Center	[NXC]
325	Simon Fraser University	[RXU]
326	Fore Systems, Inc.	[EXC1]
327	Centrum Communications, Inc.	[VXL]
328	NeXT Computer, Inc.	[LXL]
329	Netcore, Inc.	[SXM1]
330	Northwest Digital Systems	[BXD]
331	Andrew Corporation	[TXT]
332	DigiBoard	[DXK2]
333	Computer Network Technology Corp.	[BXM1]
334	Lotus Development Corp.	[BXF1]
335	MICOM Communication Corporation	[DXB4]
336	ASCII Corporation	[TXO]
337	PUREDATA Research/USA	[BXF2]
338	NTT DATA	[YXK1]
339	Empros Systems International	[DXT1]
340	Kendall Square Research (KSR)	[DXH1]
341	Martin Marietta Energy Systems	[GXH1]
342	Network Innovations	[PXG]
343	Intel Corporation	[CXT1]
344	Proxar	[CXH]
345	Epson Research Center	[RXS2]
346	Fibernet	[GXS1]
347	Box Hill Systems Corporation	[TXJ]
348	American Express Travel Related Services	[JXC1]
349	Compu-Shack	[TXV]
350	Parallan Computer, Inc.	[CXD2]
351	Stratacom	[CXI]

Decimal	Name	References
352	Open Networks Engineering, Inc.	[RXB4]
353	ATM Forum	[KZM]
354	SSD Management, Inc.	[BXR1]
355	Automated Network Management, Inc.	[CXV]
356	Magnalink Communications Corporation	[DXK3]
357	TIL Systems, Ltd.	[GXM2]
358	Skyline Technology, Inc.	[DXW1]
359	Nu-Mega Technologies, Inc.	[DXS4]
360	Morgan Stanley & Co. Inc.	[VXK]
361	Integrated Business Network	[MXB3]
362	L & N Technologies, Ltd.	[SXL2]
363	Cincinnati Bell Information Systems, Inc.	[DXM4]
364	OSCOM International	[FXF]
365	MICROGNOSIS	[PXA2]
366	Datapoint Corporation	[LZ15]
367	RICOH Co. Ltd.	[TXW]
368	Axis Communications AB	[MG277]
369	Pacer Software	[WXT]
370	Axon Networks Inc.	[RXI]
371	Brixton Systems, Inc.	[PXE]
372	GSI	[PXB1]
373	Tatung Co., Ltd.	[CXC1]
374	DIS Research LTD	[RXC2]
375	Quotron Systems, Inc.	[RXS3]
376	Dassault Electronique	[OXC]
377	Corollary, Inc.	[JXG3]
378	SEEL, Ltd.	[KXR]
379	Lexcel	[MXE]
380	W.J. Parducci & Associates, Inc.	[WXP]
381	OST	[AXP1]

continues

continued

Decimal	Name	References
382	Megadata Pty Ltd.	[AXM2]
383	LLNL Livermore Computer Center	[DXN]
384	Dynatech Communications	[GXW2]
385	Symplex Communications Corp.	[CXA]
386	Tribe Computer Works	[KXF1]
387	Taligent, Inc.	[LXA]
388	Symbol Technology, Inc.	[JXC2]
389	Lancert	[MXH3]
390	Alantec	[PXV]
391	Ridgeback Solutions	[EXG]
392	Metrix, Inc.	[DXV]
393	Excutive Systems/XTree Company	[DXC2]
394	NRL Communication Systems Branch	[RXR1]
395	I.D.E. Corporation	[RXS4]
396	Matsushita Electric Works, Ltd.	[CXH1]
397	MegaPAC	[IXG]
398	Pilkington Communication Systems	[DXA]
440	Amnet, Inc.	[RM1]
441	Chase Research	[KXG]
442	PEER Networks	[TS566]
443	Gateway Communications, Inc.	[EXF]
444	Peregrine Systems	[EXO]
445	Daewoo Telecom	[SXO]
446	Norwegian Telecom Research	[PXY1]
447	WilTel	[AXP]
448	Ericsson-Camtec	[SXP1]
449	Codex	[TXM1]
450	Basis	[HXS]
451	AGE Logic	[SXL3]

Decimal	Name	References
452	INDE Electronics	[GXD1]
453	ISODE Consortium	[SH284]
454	J.I. Case	[MXO1]
455	Trillium Digital Systems	[CXC2]
456	Bacchus Inc.	[EXG]
457	MCC	[DR48]
458	Stratus Computer	[KXC]
459	Quotron	[RXS3]
460	Beame & Whiteside	[CXB1]
461	Cellular Technical Servuces	[GXH2]

SGMP Vendor Specific Codes: [obsoletc]

Prefix: 1,255,

Decimal	Name	References
0	Reserved	[JKR1]
1	Proteon	[JS18]
2	IBM	[JXR]
3	CMU	[SXW]
4	Unix	[MS9]
5	ACC	[AB20]
6	TWG	[MTR]
7	CAYMAN	[BP52]
8	NYSERNET	[MS9]
9	cisco	[GS2]
10	BBN	[RH6]
11	Unassigned	[JKR1]
12	MIT	[JR35]
13-254	Unassigned	[JKR1]
255	Reserved	[JKR1]

MILNET LOGICAL ADDRESSES

The MILNET facility for "logical addressing" is described in RFC-878 [57] and RFC-1005 [109]. A portion of the possible logical addresses are reserved for standard uses.

There are 49,152 possible logical host addresses. Of these, 256 are reserved for assignment to well-known functions. Assignments for well-known functions are made by the IANA. Assignments for other logical host addresses are made by the NIC.

Logical Address Assignments:

Decimal	Description	References
0	Reserved	[JBP]
1	The BBN Core Gateways	[MB]
2-254	Unassigned	[JBP]
255	Reserved	[JBP]

MILNET LINK NUMBERS

The word "link" here refers to a field in the original MILNET Host/IMP interface leader. The link was originally defined as an 8-bit field. Later specifications defined this field as the "message-id" with a length of 12 bits. The name link now refers to the high order 8 bits of this 12-bit message-id field. The Host/IMP interface is defined in BBN Report 1822 [2].

The low-order 4 bits of the message-id field are called the sub-link.

Unless explicitly specified otherwise for a particular protocol, there is no sender to receiver significance to the sub-link. The sender may use the sub-link in any way he chooses (it is returned in the RFNM by the destination IMP), the receiver should ignore the sub-link.

Link	Assignments:	
Decimal	**Description**	**References**
0-63	BBNCC Monitoring	[MB]
64-149	Unassigned	[JBP]
150	Xerox NS IDP	[133,XEROX]
151	Unassigned	[JBP]
152	PARC Universal Protocol	[8,XEROX]
153	TIP Status Reporting	[JGH]
154	TIP Accounting	[JGH]
155	Internet Protocol [regular]	[105,JBP]

Decimal	Description	References
156-158	Internet Protocol [experimental]	[105,JBP]
159	Figleaf Link	[JBW1]
160	Blacker Local Network Protocol	[DM28]
161-194	Unassigned	[JBP]
195	ISO-IP	[64,RXM]
196-247	Experimental Protocols	[JBP]
248-255	Network Maintenance	[JGH]

MILNET X.25 ADDRESS MAPPINGS

All MILNET hosts are assigned addresses by the Defense Data Network (DDN). The address of a MILNET host may be obtained from the Network Information Center (NIC), represented as an ASCII text string in what is called "host table format". This section describes the process by which MILNET X.25 addresses may be derived from addresses in the NIC host table format.

A NIC host table address consists of the ASCII text string representations of four decimal numbers separated by periods, corresponding to the four octeted of a thirty-two bit Internet address. The four decimal numbers are referred to in this section as "n", "h' "l", and "i". Thus, a host table address may be represented as: "n.h.l.i". Each of these four numbers will have either one, two, or three decimal digits and will never have a value greater than 255.

For example, in the host table, address: "10.2.0.124", n=10, h=2, l=0, and i=124. To convert a host table address to a MILNET X.25 address:

1. If h < 64, the host table address corresponds to the X.25 physical address:

   ZZZZ F IIIHHZZ (SS)

   where:

   ZZZZ = 0000 as required

   F = 0 because the address is a physical address; III is a three decimal digit respresentation of "i", right-adjusted and padded with leading zeros if required; HH is a two decimal digit representation of "h", right-adjusted and padded with leading zeros if required;

   ZZ = 00 and

   (SS) is optional

   In the example given above, the host table address 10.2.0.124 corresponds to the X.25 physical address 000001240200.

2. If h > 64 or h =   64, the   host table address corresponds to the X.25 logical address ZZZZ F RRRRRZZ (SS)

   where:

   ZZZZ = 0000 as required

   F = 1 because the address is a logical address; RRRRR is a five decimal digit representation of the result "r" of the calculation r = h * 256 + i (Note that the decimal representation of "r" will always require five digits); ZZ = 00 and (SS)   is optional

Thus, the host table address 10.83.0.207 corresponds to the X.25 logical address 000012145500.

In both cases, the "n" and "l" fields of the   host table address are not used.

IEEE 802 NUMBERS OF INTEREST

Some of the networks of all classes are IEEE 802 Networks. These systems may use a Link Service Access Point (LSAP) field in much the same way the MILNET uses the "link" field. Further, there is an extension of the LSAP header called the Sub-Network Access Protocol (SNAP).

The IEEE likes to describe numbers in binary in bit transmission order, which is the opposite of the big-endian order used throughout the Internet protocol documentation.

Assignments:

Link Service Access Point	Description	References
IEEE Internet		
binary binary	decimal	
00000000 00000000	0 Null LSAP	[IEEE]
01000000 00000010	2 Indiv LLC Sublayer Mgt	[IEEE]
11000000 00000011	3 Group LLC Sublayer Mgt	[IEEE]
00100000 00000100	4 SNA Path Control	[IEEE]
01100000 00000110	6 Reserved (DOD IP)	[104,JBP]
01110000 00001110	14 PROWAY-LAN	[IEEE]
01110010 01001110	78 EIA-RS 511	[IEEE]
01111010 01011110	94 ISI IP	[JBP]
01110001 10001110	142 PROWAY-LAN	[IEEE]
01010101 10101010	170 SNAP	[IEEE]
01111111 11111110	254 ISO CLNS IS 8473	[64,JXJ]
11111111 11111111	255 Global DSAP	[IEEE]

These numbers (and others) are assigned by the IEEE Standards Office.

The address is: IEEE Standards Office, 345 East 47th Street, New York, N.Y. 10017, Attn: Vince Condello. Phone: (212) 705-7092.

At an ad hoc special session on "IEEE 802 Networks and ARP", held during the TCP Vendors Workshop (August 1986), an approach to a consistent way to send DoD-IP datagrams and other IP related protocols (such as the Address Resolution Protocol (ARP)) on 802 networks was developed, using the SNAP extension (see RFC-1042 [90]).

ETHERNET NUMBERS OF INTEREST

Many of the networks of all classes are Ethernets (10Mb) or Experimental Ethernets (3Mb). These systems use a message "type" field in much the same way the ARPANET uses the "link" field.

If you need an Ethernet type, contact the Xerox Corporation, Xerox Systems Institute, 475 Oakmead Parkway, Sunnyvale, CA 94086, Attn: Ms. Fonda Pallone, (415) 813-7164.

The following list is contributed unverified information from various sources.

Assignments:

Ethernet	Exp. Ethernet	Description	References
decimal Hex	decimal	octal	
000 0000-05DC	-	IEEE802.3 Length Field	[XEROX]
257 0101-01FF	-	Experimental	[XEROX]
512 0200	512 1000	XEROX PUP (see 0A00)	[8,XEROX]
513 0201	-	PUP Addr Trans (see 0A01)	[XEROX]
1536 0600	1536 3000	XEROX NS IDP	[133,XEROX]
2048 0800	513 1001	DOD IP	[105,JBP]
2049 0801	-	X.75 Internet	[XEROX]
2050 0802	-	NBS Internet	[XEROX]
2051 0803	-	ECMA Internet	[XEROX]
2052 0804	-	Chaosnet	[XEROX]
2053 0805	-	X.25 Level 3	[XEROX]
2054 0806	-	ARP	[88,JBP]
2055 0807	-	XNS Compatability	[XEROX]
2076 081C	-	Symbolics Private	[DCP1]
2184 0888-088A	-	Xyplex	[XEROX]

continues

continues

Ethernet	Exp. Ethernet	Description	References
2304 0900	-	Ungermann-Bass net debugr	[XEROX]
2560 0A00	-	Xerox IEEE802.3 PUP	[XEROX]
2561 0A01	-	PUP Addr Trans	[XEROX]
2989 0BAD	-	Banyan Systems	[XEROX]
4096 1000	-	Berkeley Trailer nego	[XEROX]
4097 1001-100F	-	Berkeley Trailer encap/IP	[XEROX]
5632 1600	-	Valid Systems	[XEROX]
16962 4242	-	PCS Basic Block Protocol	[XEROX]
21000 5208	-	BBN Simnet	[XEROX]
24576 6000	-	DEC Unassigned (Exp.)	[XEROX]
24577 6001	-	DEC MOP Dump/Load	[XEROX]
24578 6002	-	DEC MOP Remote Console	[XEROX]
24579 6003	-	DEC DECNET Phase IV Route	[XEROX]
24580 6004	-	DEC LAT	[XEROX]
24581 6005	-	DEC Diagnostic Protocol	[XEROX]
24582 6006	-	DEC Customer Protocol	[XEROX]
24583 6007	-	DEC LAVC, SCA	[XEROX]
24584 6008-6009	-	DEC Unassigned	[XEROX]
24586 6010-6014	-	3Com Corporation	[XEROX]
28672 7000	-	Ungermann-Bass download	[XEROX]
28674 7002	-	Ungermann-Bass dia/loop	[XEROX]
28704 7020-7029	-	LRT	[XEROX]
28720 7030	-	Proteon	[XEROX]
28724 7034	-	Cabletron	[XEROX]
32771 8003	-	Cronus VLN	[131,DT15]
32772 8004	-	Cronus Direct	[131,DT15]
32773 8005	-	HP Probe	[XEROX]
32774 8006	-	Nestar	[XEROX]

Ethernet	Exp. Ethernet	Description	References
32776 8008	-	AT&T	[XEROX]
32784 8010	-	Excelan	[XEROX]
32787 8013	-	SGI diagnostics	[AXC]
32788 8014	-	SGI network games	[AXC]
32789 8015	-	SGI reserved	[AXC]
32790 8016	-	SGI bounce server	[AXC]
32793 8019	-	Apollo Computers	[XEROX]
32815 802E	-	Tymshare	[XEROX]
32816 802F	-	Tigan, Inc.	[XEROX]
32821 8035	-	Reverse ARP	[48,JXM]
32822 8036	-	Aeonic Systems	[XEROX]
32824 8038	-	DEC LANBridge	[XEROX]
32825 8039-803C	-	DEC Unassigned	[XEROX]
32829 803D	-	DEC Ethernet Encryption	[XEROX]
32830 803E	-	DEC Unassigned	[XEROX]
32831 803F	-	DEC LAN Traffic Monitor	[XEROX]
32832 8040-8042	-	DEC Unassigned	[XEROX]
32836 8044	-	Planning Research Corp.	[XEROX]
32838 8046	-	AT&T	[XEROX]
32839 8047	-	AT&T	[XEROX]
32841 8049	-	ExperData	[XEROX]
32859 805B	-	Stanford V Kernel exp.	[XEROX]
32860 805C	-	Stanford V Kernel prod.	[XEROX]
32861 805D	-	Evans & Sutherland	[XEROX]
32864 8060	-	Little Machines	[XEROX]
32866 8062	-	Counterpoint Computers	[XEROX]
32869 8065-8066	-	Univ. of Mass. @ Amherst	[XEROX]
32871 8067	-	Veeco Integrated Auto.	[XEROX]
32872 8068	-	General Dynamics	[XEROX]

continues

continues

Ethernet	Exp. Ethernet	Description	References
32873 8069	-	AT&T	[XEROX]
32874 806A	-	Autophon	[XEROX]
32876 806C	-	ComDesign	[XEROX]
32877 806D	-	Computgraphic Corp.	[XEROX]
32878 806E-8077	-	Landmark Graphics Corp.	[XEROX]
32890 807A	-	Matra	[XEROX]
32891 807B	-	Dansk Data Elektronik	[XEROX]
32892 807C	-	Merit Internodal	[HWB]
32893 807D-807F	-	Vitalink Communications	[XEROX]
32896 8080	-	Vitalink TransLAN III	[XEROX]
32897 8081-8083	-	Counterpoint Computers	[XEROX]
32923 809B	-	Appletalk	[XEROX]
32924 809C-809E	-	Datability	[XEROX]
32927 809F	-	Spider Systems Ltd.	[XEROX]
32931 80A3	-	Nixdorf Computers	[XEROX]
32932 80A4-80B3	-	Siemens Gammasonics Inc.	[XEROX]
32960 80C0-80C3	-	DCA Data Exchange Cluster	[XEROX]
32966 80C6	-	Pacer Software	[XEROX]
32967 80C7	-	Applitek Corporation	[XEROX]
32968 80C8-80CC	-	Intergraph Corporation	[XEROX]
32973 80CD-80CE	-	Harris Corporation	[XEROX]
32974 80CF-80D2	-	Taylor Instrument	[XEROX]
32979 80D3-80D4	-	Rosemount Corporation	[XEROX]
32981 80D5	-	IBM SNA Service on Ether	[XEROX]
32989 80DD	-	Varian Associates	[XEROX]
32990 80DE-80DF	-	Integrated Solutions TRFS	[XEROX]
32992 80E0-80E3	-	Allen-Bradley	[XEROX]
32996 80E4-80F0	-	Datability	[XEROX]

Ethernet	Exp. Ethernet	Description	References
33010 80F2	-	Retix	[XEROX]
33011 80F3	-	AppleTalk AARP (Kinetics)	[XEROX]
33012 80F4-80F5	-	Kinetics	[XEROX]
33015 80F7	-	Apollo Computer	[XEROX]
33023 80FF-8103	-	Wellfleet Communications	[XEROX]
33031 8107-8109	-	Symbolics Private	[XEROX]
33072 8130	-	Waterloo Microsystems	[XEROX]
33073 8131	-	VG Laboratory Systems	[XEROX]
33079 8137-8138	-	Novell, Inc.	[XEROX]
33081 8139-813D	-	KTI	[XEROX]
33100 814C	-	SNMP	[JKR1]
36864 9000	-	Loopback	[XEROX]
36865 9001	-	3Com (Bridge) XNS Sys Mgmt	[XEROX]
36866 9002	-	3Com (Bridge) TCP-IP Sys	[XEROX]
36867 9003	-	3Com (Bridge) loop detect	[XEROX]
65280 FF00	-	BBN VITAL-LanBridge cache	[XEROX]

The standard for transmission of IP datagrams over Ethernets and Experimental Ethernets is specified in RFC-894 [61] and RFC-895 [91] respectively.

NOTE Ethernet 48-bit address blocks are assigned by the IEEE.
IEEE Standards Office, 345 East 47th Street, New York, N.Y. 10017, Attn: Vince Condello.
Phone: (212) 705-7092. ▪

ETHERNET VENDOR ADDRESS COMPONENTS

Ethernet hardware addresses are 48 bits, expressed as 12 hexadecimal digits (0-9, plus A-F, capitalized). These 12 hex digits consist of the first/left 6 digits (which should match the vendor of the Ethernet interface within the station) and the last/right 6 digits which specify the interface serial number for that interface vendor.

Ethernet addresses might be written unhyphenated (e.g., 123456789ABC), or with one hyphen (e.g., 123456-789ABC), but should be written hyphenated by octets (e.g., 12-34-56-78-9A-BC).

These addresses are physical station addresses, not multicast nor broadcast, so the second hex digit (reading from the left) will be even, not odd.

At present, it is not clear how the IEEE assigns Ethernet block addresses. Whether in blocks of 2**24 or 2**25, and whether multicasts are assigned with that block or separately. A portion of the vendor block address is reportedly assigned serially, with the other portion intentionally assigned randomly. If there is a global algorithm for which addresses are designated to be physical (in a chipset) versus logical (assigned in software), or globally-assigned versus locally-assigned addresses, some of the known addresses do not follow the scheme (e.g., AA0003; 02xxxx).

00000C Cisco

00000F NeXT

000010 Sytek

00001D Cabletron

000020 DIAB (Data Intdustrier AB)

000022 Visual Technology

00002A TRW

00005A S & Koch

00005E IANA

000065 Network General

00006B MIPS

000077 MIPS

00007A Ardent

000089 Cayman Systems Gatorbox

000093 Proteon

00009F Ameristar Technology

0000A2 Wellfleet

0000A3 Network Application Technology

0000A6 Network General (internal assignment, not for products)

0000A7 NCD X-terminals

0000A9 Network Systems

0000AA Xerox Xerox machines

0000B3 CIMLinc

0000B7 Dove Fastnet

0000BC Allen-Bradley

0000C0 Western Digital

0000C6 HP Intelligent Networks Operation (formerly Eon Systems)

0000C8 Altos

0000C9 Emulex Terminal Servers

0000D7 Dartmouth College (NED Router)

0000D8 3Com? Novell? PS/2

0000DD Gould

0000DE Unigraph

0000E2 Acer Counterpoint

0000EF Alantec

0000FD High Level Hardvare (Orion, UK)

000102 BBN BBN internal usage (not registered)

001700 Kabel

00802D Xylogics, Inc. Annex terminal servers

00808C Frontier Software Development

0080C2 IEEE 802.1 Committee

0080D3 Shiva

00AA00 Intel

00DD00 Ungermann-Bass

00DD01 Ungermann-Bass

020701 Racal InterLan

020406 BBN BBN internal usage (not registered)

026086 Satelcom MegaPac (UK)

02608C 3Com IBM PC; Imagen; Valid; Cisco

02CF1F CMC Masscomp; Silicon Graphics; Prime EXL

080002 3Com (Formerly Bridge)

080003 ACC (Advanced Computer Communications)

080005 Symbolics Symbolics LISP machines

080008 BBN

080009 Hewlett-Packard

08000A Nestar Systems

08000B Unisys

080011 Tektronix, Inc.

080014 Excelan BBN Butterfly, Masscomp, Silicon Graphics

080017 NSC

08001A Data General

08001B Data General

08001E Apollo

080020 Sun Sun machines

080022 NBI

080025 CDC

080026 Norsk Data (Nord)

080027 PCS Computer Systems GmbH

080028 TI Explorer

08002B DEC

08002E Metaphor

08002F Prime Computer Prime 50-Series LHC300

080036 Intergraph CAE stations

080037 Fujitsu-Xerox

080038 Bull

080039 Spider Systems

080041 DCA Digital Comm. Assoc.

080045 ???? (maybe Xylogics, but they claim not to know this number)

080046 Sony

080047 Sequent

080049 Univation

08004C Encore

08004E BICC

080056 Stanford University

080058 ??? DECsystem-20

08005A IBM

080067 Comdesign

080068 Ridge

080069 Silicon Graphics

08006E Excelan

080075 DDE (Danish Data Elektronik A/S)

08007C Vitalink TransLAN III

080080 XIOS

080086 Imagen/QMS

080087 Xyplex terminal servers

080089 Kinetics AppleTalk-Ethernet interface

08008B Pyramid

08008D XyVision XyVision machines

080090 Retix Inc Bridges

484453 HDS ???

800010 AT&T

AA0000 DEC obsolete

AA0001 DEC obsolete

AA0002 DEC obsolete

AA0003 DEC Global physical address for some DEC machines

AA0004 DEC Local logical address for systems running DECNET

ETHERNET MULTICAST ADDRESSES

Ethernet Address	Type Field Usage	
Multicast Addresses:		
01-00-5E-00-00-00- 01-00-5E-7F-FF-FF	0800	Internet Multicast (RFC-1112) [43]
01-00-5E-80-00-00- 01-00-5E-FF-FF-FF	????	Internet reserved by IANA
01-80-C2-00-00-00	-802-	Spanning tree (for bridges)
09-00-02-04-00-01?	8080?	Vitalink printer
09-00-02-04-00-02?	8080?	Vitalink management
09-00-09-00-00-01	8005	HP Probe
09-00-09-00-00-01	-802-	HP Probe
09-00-09-00-00-04	8005?	HP DTC
09-00-1E-00-00-00	8019?	Apollo DOMAIN
09-00-2B-00-00-00	6009?	DEC MUMPS?
09-00-2B-00-00-01	8039?	DEC DSM/DTP?
09-00-2B-00-00-02	803B?	DEC VAXELN?
09-00-2B-00-00-03	8038	DEC Lanbridge Traffic Monitor (LTM)
09-00-2B-00-00-04	????	DEC MAP End System Hello
09-00-2B-00-00-05	????	DEC MAP Intermediate System Hello
09-00-2B-00-00-06	803D?	DEC CSMA/CD Encryption?
09-00-2B-00-00-07	8040?	DEC NetBios Emulator?

continues

continued

Ethernet	Type	
09-00-2B-00-00-0F	6004	DEC Local Area Transport (LAT)
09-00-2B-00-00-1x	????	DEC Experimental
09-00-2B-01-00-00	8038	DEC LanBridge Copy packets (All bridges)
09-00-2B-01-00-01	8038	DEC LanBridge Hello packets (All local bridges) 1 packet per second, sent by the designated LanBridge
09-00-2B-02-00-00	????	DEC DNA Lev. 2 Routing Layer routers?
09-00-2B-02-01-00	803C?	DEC DNA Naming Service Advertisement?
09-00-2B-02-01-01	803C?	DEC DNA Naming Service Solicitation?
09-00-2B-02-01-02	803E?	DEC DNA Time Service?
09-00-2B-03-xx-xx	????	DEC default filtering by bridges?
09-00-2B-04-00-00	8041?	DEC Local Area Sys. Transport (LAST)?
09-00-2B-23-00-00	803A?	DEC Argonaut Console?
09-00-4E-00-00-02?	8137?	Novell IPX
09-00-56-00-00-00-	????	Stanford reserved
09-00-56-FE-FF-FF		
09-00-56-FF-00-00-	805C	Stanford V Kernel, version 6.0
09-00-56-FF-FF-FF		
09-00-77-00-00-01	????	Retix spanning tree bridges
09-00-7C-02-00-05	8080?	Vitalink diagnostics
09-00-7C-05-00-01	8080?	Vitalink gateway?
0D-1E-15-BA-DD-06	????	HP
AB-00-00-01-00-00	6001	DEC Maintenance Operation Protocol (MOP) Dump/Load Assistance
AB-00-00-02-00-00	6002	DEC Maintenance Operation Protocol (MOP) Remote Console 1 System ID packet every 8-10 minutes, by every: DEC LanBridge DEC DEUNA interface DEC DELUA interface DEC DEQNA interface (in a certain mode)
AB-00-00-03-00-00	6003	DECNET Phase IV end node Hello packets 1 packet every 15 seconds, sent by each DECNET host

Ethernet	Type	
AB-00-00-04-00-00	6003	DECNET Phase IV Router Hello packets 1 packet every 15 seconds, sent by the DECNET router
AB-00-00-05-00-00 AB-00-03-FF-FF-FF	????	Reserved DEC through
AB-00-03-00-00-00	6004	DEC Local Area Transport (LAT) - old
AB-00-04-00-xx-xx	????	Reserved DEC customer private use
AB-00-04-01-xx-yy	6007	DEC Local Area VAX Cluster groups Sys. Communication Architecture (SCA)
CF-00-00-00-00-00	9000	Ethernet Configuration Test protocol (Loopback) Broadcast Address:
FF-FF-FF-FF-FF-FF	0600	XNS packets, Hello or gateway search? 6 packets every 15 seconds, per XNS station
FF-FF-FF-FF-FF-FF	0800	IP (e.g. RWHOD via UDP) as needed
FF-FF-FF-FF-FF-FF	0804	CHAOS
FF-FF-FF-FF-FF-FF	0806	ARP (for IP and CHAOS) as needed
FF-FF-FF-FF-FF-FF	0BAD	Banyan
FF-FF-FF-FF-FF-FF	1600	VALID packets, Hello or gateway search? 1 packets every 30 seconds, per VALID station
FF-FF-FF-FF-FF-FF	8035	Reverse ARP
FF-FF-FF-FF-FF-FF	807C	Merit Internodal (INP)
FF-FF-FF-FF-FF-FF	809B	EtherTalk

XNS PROTOCOL TYPES

Assigned well-known socket numbers

Routing Information	1
Echo	2
Router Error	3
Experimental	40-77

Assigned internet packet types

Routing Information	1
Echo	2

Error	3
Packet Exchange	4
Sequenced Packet	5
PUP	12
DoD IP	13
Experimental	20-37

PROTOCOL/TYPE FIELD ASSIGNMENTS

Below are two tables describing the arrangement of protocol fields or type field assignments so that one could send NS Datagrams on the MILNET or Internet Datagrams on 10Mb Ethernet, and also protocol and type fields so one could encapsulate each kind of Datagram in the other.

```
  \        upper¦ DoD IP   ¦ PUP      ¦ NS IP  ¦
  lower \  ¦       ¦          ¦         ¦
  - - - - - - - - - - - -¦- - - - - - -¦- - - - - - - -¦- - - - - - -¦
          ¦ Type   ¦ Type     ¦ Type    ¦
  3Mb Ethernet ¦ 1001   ¦ 1000     ¦ 3000   ¦
          ¦ octal  ¦ octal    ¦ octal   ¦
  - - - - - - - - - - - -¦- - - - - - -¦- - - - - - - -¦- - - - - - -¦
          ¦ Type   ¦ Type     ¦ Type    ¦
  10 Mb Ethernet¦ 0800  ¦ 0200     ¦ 0600   ¦
          ¦ hex    ¦ hex      ¦ hex     ¦
  - - - - - - - - - - - -¦- - - - - - -¦- - - - - - - -¦- - - - - - -¦
          ¦ Link   ¦ Link     ¦ Link    ¦
  MILNET      ¦ 155   ¦ 152      ¦ 150    ¦
          ¦ decimal¦ decimal  ¦ decimal ¦
  - - - - - - - - - - - -¦- - - - - - -¦- - - - - - - -¦- - - - - - -¦


  \        upper¦ DoD IP   ¦ PUP      ¦ NS IP  ¦
  lower \  ¦       ¦          ¦         ¦
  - - - - - - - - - - - -¦- - - - - - -¦- - - - - - - -¦- - - - - - -¦
          ¦       ¦Protocol¦Protocol¦
  DoD IP     ¦ X    ¦ 12       ¦ 22     ¦
          ¦       ¦ decimal¦ decimal ¦
  - - - - - - - - - - - -¦- - - - - - -¦- - - - - - - -¦- - - - - - -¦
          ¦       ¦          ¦         ¦
  PUP       ¦ ?    ¦ X       ¦ ?      ¦
          ¦       ¦          ¦         ¦
  - - - - - - - - - - - -¦- - - - - - -¦- - - - - - - -¦- - - - - - -¦
          ¦ Type   ¦ Type     ¦         ¦
  NS IP      ¦ 13    ¦ 12       ¦ X      ¦
          ¦ decimal¦ decimal  ¦         ¦
  - - - - - - - - - - - -¦- - - - - - -¦- - - - - - - -¦- - - - - - -¦
```

PRONET 80 TYPE NUMBERS

Below is the current list of PRONET 80 Type Numbers. Note: a protocol that is on this list does not necessarily mean that there is any implementation of it on ProNET.

Of these, protocols 1, 14, and 20 are the only ones that have ever been seen in ARP packets.

For reference, the header is (one byte/line):

| destination hardware | address |

source hardware address

data	link header version (2)
data	link header protocol number
data	link header reserved (0)
data	link header reserved (0)

Some protocols have been known to tuck stuff in the reserved fields.

Those who need a protocol number on ProNET-10/80 should contact John Shriver (jas@proteon.com).

1. IP
2. IP with trailing headers
3. Address Resolution Protocol
4. Proteon HDLC
5. VAX Debugging Protocol (MIT)
10. Novell NetWare (IPX and pre-IPX) (old format, 3 byte trailer)
11. Vianetix
12. PUP
13. Watstar protocol (University of Waterloo)
14. XNS
15. Diganostics
16. Echo protocol (link level)
17. Banyan Vines
20. DECnet (DEUNA Emulation)
21. Chaosnet
23. IEEE 802.2 or ISO   8802/2 Data Link
24. Reverse Address Resolution Protocol
29. TokenVIEW-10
31. AppleTalk LAP Data Packet
33. Cornell Boot Server Location Protocol
34. Novell NetWare IPX (new format, no trailer, new XOR checksum)

POINT-TO-POINT PROTOCOL FIELD   ASSIGNMENTS

PPP DLL PROTOCOL NUMBERS

The Point-to-Point Protocol (PPP) Data Link Layer [146,147,175] contains a 16 bit Protocol field to identify the the encapsulated protocol. The Protocol field is consistent with the ISO 3309 (HDLC) extension mechanism for Address fields. All Protocols MUST be assigned such that the least significant bit of the most significant octet equals "0", and the least significant bit of the least significant octet equals "1".

Assigned PPP DLL Protocol Numbers

Value (in hex) Protocol Name

0001	to 001f reserved (transparency inefficient)
0021	Internet Protocol
0023	OSI Network Layer
0025	Xerox NS IDP
0027	DECnet Phase IV
0029	Appletalk
002b	Novell IPX
002d	Van Jacobson Compressed TCP/IP
002f	Van Jacobson Uncompressed TCP/IP
0031	Bridging PDU
0033	Stream Protocol (ST-II)
0035	Banyan Vines
0037	reserved (until 1993)
00ff	reserved (compression inefficient)
0201	802.1d Hello Packets
0231	Luxcom
0233	Sigma Network Systems
8021	Internet Protocol Control Protocol
8023	OSI Network Layer Control Protocol
8025	Xerox NS IDP Control Protocol
8027	DECnet Phase IV Control Protocol
8029	Appletalk Control Protocol

802b	Novell IPX Control Protocol
802d	Reserved
802f	Reserved
8031	Bridging NCP
8033	Stream Protocol Control Protocol
8035	Banyan Vines Control Protocol
8037	reserved till 1993
80ff	reserved (compression inefficient
c021	Link Control Protocol
c023	Password Authentication Protocol
c025	Link Quality Report
c223	Challenge Handshake Authentication Protocol

Protocol field values in the "0—" to "3—" range identify the network-layer protocol of specific datagrams, and values in the "8— -" to "b—" range identify datagrams belonging to the associated Network Control Protocol (NCP), if any.

It is recommended that values in the "02—" to "1e—" and "—01" to "—1f" ranges not be assigned, as they are compression inefficient.

Protocol field values in the "4—" to "7—" range are used for protocols with low volume traffic which have no associated NCP.

Protocol field values in the "c—" to "e—" range identify datagrams as Control Protocols (such as LCP).

PPP LCP AND IPCP CODES

The Point-to-Point Protocol (PPP) Link Control Protocol (LCP) [146] and Internet Protocol Control Protocol (IPCP) [147] contain an 8 bit Code field which identifies the type of packet. These Codes are assigned as follows:

Code	Packet Type
1	Configure-Request
2	Configure-Ack
3	Configure-Nak
4	Configure-Reject
5	Terminate-Request

continued

Code	Packet Type
6	Terminate-Ack
7	Code-Reject
8	* Protocol-Reject
9	* Echo-Request
10	* Echo-Reply
11	* Discard-Request
12	* RESERVED

* LCP Only

PPP LCP CONFIGURATION OPTION TYPES

The Point-to-Point Protocol (PPP) Link Control Protocol (LCP) specifies a number of Configuration Options [146] which are distinguished by an 8 bit Type field. These Types are assigned as follows:

Type	Configuration Option
1	Maximum-Receive-Unit
2	Async-Control-Character-Map
3	Authentication-Protocol
4	Quality-Protocol
5	Magic-Number
6	RESERVED
7	Protocol-Field-Compression
8	Address-and-Control-Field-Compression
9	FCS-Alternatives

PPP IPCP CONFIGURATION OPTION TYPES

The Point-to-Point Protocol (PPP) Internet Protocol Control Protocol (IPCP) specifies a number of Configuration Options [147] which are distinguished by an 8 bit Type field. These Types are assigned as follows:

Type	Configuration Option
1	IP-Addresses (deprecated)
2	IP-Compression-Protocol
3	IP-Address

PPP BRIDGING CONFIGURATION OPTION TYPES

The Point-to-Point Protocol (PPP) Extensions for Bridging specifies a number of Configuration Options [176] which are distinguished by an 8 bit Type field. These Types are assigned as follows:

Type	Configuration Option
1	Remote Ring Identification
2	Line Identification
3	MAC Type Selection
4	Tinygram Compression
5	LAN Identification

PPP BRIDGING MAC TYPES

The Point-to-Point Protocol (PPP) Extensions for Bridging [176] contains an 8 bit MAC Type field which identifies the MAC encapsulated. These Types are assigned as follows:

Type	MAC
0	Reserved
1	IEEE 802.3/Ethernet
2	IEEE 802.4
3	IEEE 802.5
4	FDDI

ADDRESS RESOLUTION PROTOCOL PARAMETERS

The Address Resolution Protocol (ARP) specified in RFC-826 [88] has several parameters. The assigned values for these parameters are listed here.

Assignments:

Operation Code (op)

    1 REQUEST

    2 REPLY

Hardware Type (hrd)

Type Description	References
1 Ethernet (10Mb)	[JBP]
2 Experimental Ethernet (3Mb)	[JBP]
3 Amateur Radio AX.25	[PXK]
4 Proteon ProNET Token Ring	[JBP]
5 Chaos	[GXP]
6 IEEE 802 Networks	[JBP]
7 ARCNET	[JBP]
8 Hyperchannel	[JBP]
9 Lanstar	[TU]
10 Autonet Short Address	[MXB1]
11 LocalTalk	[JKR1]
12 LocalNet (IBM PCNet or SYTEK LocalNET)	[JXM]
13 Ultra link	[RXD2]
14 SMDS	[GXC1]
15 Frame Relay	[AGM]
16 Asynchronous Transmission Mode (ATM)	[JXB2]

Protocol Type (pro)

Use the same codes as listed in the section called "Ethernet Numbers of Interest" (all hardware types use this code set for the protocol type).

REVERSE ADDRESS RESOLUTION PROTOCOL OPERATION CODES

The Reverse Address Resolution Protocol (RARP) specified in RFC-903 [48] has the following operation codes:

Assignments:

Operation Code (op)

> 3 request Reverse
>
> 4 reply Reverse

DYNAMIC REVERSE ARP

Assignments:

Operation Code (op)

> 5 DRARP-Request
>
> 6 DRARP-Reply
>
> 7 DRARP-Error

For further information, contact: David Brownell (suneast!helium!db@Sun.COM).

INVERSE ADDRESS RESOULUTION PROTOCOL

The Inverse Address Resolution Protocol (IARP) specified in RFC-1293 [173] has the following operation codes:

Assignments:

Operation Code (op)

> 8 InARP-Request
>
> 9 InARP-Reply

X.25 TYPE NUMBERS

CCITT defines the high order two bits of the first octet of call user data as follows:

> 00 - Used for other CCITT recomendations (such as X.29)
>
> 01 - Reserved for use by "national" administrative authorities
>
> 10 - Reserved for use by international administrative authoorities
>
> 11 - Reserved for arbitrary use between consenting DTEs

Call User	Data (hex) Protocol	Reference
01	PAD	[GS2]
C5	Blacker front-end descr dev	[AGM]
CC	IP	[69,AGM]*
CD	ISO-IP	[AGM]
DD	Network Monitoring	[AGM]

*NOTE: ISO SC6/WG2 approved assignment in   ISO 9577 (January 1990).

PUBLIC DATA NETWORK NUMBERS

One of the Internet Class A Networks is the international system of Public Data Networks. This section lists the mapping between the Internet Addresses and the Public Data Network Addresses (X.121).

Assignments:

Internet	Public Data Net	Description	References
014.000.000.000	Reserved		[JBP]
014.000.000.001	3110-317-00035	00 PURDUE-TN	[TN]
014.000.000.002	3110-608-00027	00 UWISC-TN	[TN]
014.000.000.003	3110-302-00024	00 UDEL-TN	[TN]
014.000.000.004	2342-192-00149	23 UCL-VTEST	[PK]
014.000.000.005	2342-192-00300	23 UCL-TG	[PK]
014.000.000.006	2342-192-00300	25 UK-SATNET	[PK]
014.000.000.007	3110-608-00024	00 UWISC-IBM	[MS56]
014.000.000.008	3110-213-00045	00 RAND-TN	[MO2]
014.000.000.009	2342-192-00300	23 UCL-CS	[PK]
014.000.000.010	3110-617-00025	00 BBN-VAN-GW	[JD21]
014.000.000.011	2405-015-50300	00 CHALMERS	[UXB]
014.000.000.012	3110-713-00165	00 RICE	[PAM6]
014.000.000.013	3110-415-00261	00 DECWRL	[PAM6]
014.000.000.014	3110-408-00051	00 IBM-SJ	[SXA3]
014.000.000.015	2041-117-01000	00 SHAPE	[JFW]
014.000.000.016	2628-153-90075	00 DFVLR4-X25	[GB7]
014.000.000.017	3110-213-00032	00 ISI-VAN-GW	[JD21]
014.000.000.018	2624-522-80900	52 FGAN-SIEMENS-X25	[GB7]
014.000.000.019	2041-170-10000	00 SHAPE-X25	[JFW]
014.000.000.020	5052-737-20000	50 UQNET	[AXH]
014.000.000.021	3020-801-00057	50 DMC-CRC1	[VXT]
014.000.000.022	2624-522-80329	02 FGAN-FGANFFMVAX-X25	[GB7]
014.000.000.023	2624-589-00908	01 ECRC-X25	[PXD]
014.000.000.024	2342-905-24242	83 UK-MOD-RSRE	[JXE2]

Internet	Public Data Net	Description	References
014.000.000.025	2342-905-24242	82 UK-VAN-RSRE	[AXM]
014.000.000.026	2624-522-80329	05 DFVLRSUN-X25	[GB7]
014.000.000.027	2624-457-11015	90 SELETFMSUN-X25	[BXD]
014.000.000.028	3110-408-00146	00 CDC-SVL	[RAM57]
014.000.000.029	2222-551-04400	00 SUN-CNUCE	[ABB2]
014.000.000.030	2222-551-04500	00 ICNUCEVM-CNUCE	[ABB2]
014.000.000.031	2222-551-04600	00 SPARE-CNUCE	[ABB2]
014.000.000.032	2222-551-04700	00 ICNUCEVX-CNUCE	[ABB2]
014.000.000.033	2222-551-04524	00 CISCO-CNUCE	[ABB2]
014.000.000.034	2342-313-00260	90 SPIDER-GW	[AD67]
014.000.000.035	2342-313-00260	91 SPIDER-EXP	[AD67]
014.000.000.036	2342-225-00101	22 PRAXIS-X25A	[TXR]
014.000.000.037	2342-225-00101	23 PRAXIS-X25B	[TXR]
014.000.000.038	2403-712-30250	00 DIAB-TABY-GW	[FXB]
014.000.000.039	2403-715-30100	00 DIAB-LKP-GW	[FXB]
014.000.000.040	2401-881-24038	00 DIAB-TABY1-GW	[FXB]
014.000.000.041	2041-170-10060	00 STC	[TC27]
014.000.000.042	2222-551-00652	60 CNUCE	[TC27]
014.000.000.043	2422-510-05900	00 Tollpost-Globe AS	[OXG]
014.000.000.044	2422-670-08900	00 Tollpost-Globe AS	[OXG]
014.000.000.045	2422-516-01000	00 Tollpost-Globe AS	[OXG]
014.000.000.046	2422-450-00800	00 Tollpost-Globe AS	[OXG]
014.000.000.047	2422-610-00200	00 Tollpost-Globe AS	[OXG]
014.000.000.048	2422-310-00300	00 Tollpost-Globe AS	[OXG]
014.000.000.049	2422-470-08800	00 Tollpost-Globe AS	[OXG]
014.000.000.050	2422-210-04600	00 Tollpost-Globe AS	[OXG]
014.000.000.051	2422-130-28900	00 Tollpost-Globe AS	[OXG]
014.000.000.052	2422-310-27200	00 Tollpost-Globe AS	[OXG]
014.000.000.053	2422-250-05800	00 Tollpost-Globe AS	[OXG]
014.000.000.054	2422-634-05900	00 Tollpost-Globe AS	[OXG]

continues

continued

Internet	Public Data Net	Description	References
014.000.000.055	2422-670-08800	00 Tollpost-Globe AS	[OXG]
014.000.000.056	2422-430-07400	00 Tollpost-Globe AS	[OXG]
014.000.000.057	2422-674-07800	00 Tollpost-Globe AS	[OXG]
014.000.000.058	2422-230-16900	00 Tollpost-Globe AS	[OXG]
014.000.000.059	2422-518-02900	00 Tollpost-Globe AS	[OXG]
014.000.000.060	2422-370-03100	00 Tollpost-Globe AS	[OXG]
014.000.000.061	2422-516-03400	00 Tollpost-Globe AS	[OXG]
014.000.000.062	2422-616-04400	00 Tollpost-Globe AS	[OXG]
014.000.000.063	2422-650-23500	00 Tollpost-Globe AS	[OXG]
014.000.000.064	2422-330-02500	00 Tollpost-Globe AS	[OXG]
014.000.000.065	2422-350-01900	00 Tollpost-Globe AS	[OXG]
014.000.000.066	2422-410-00700	00 Tollpost-Globe AS	[OXG]
014.000.000.067	2422-539-06200	00 Tollpost-Globe AS	[OXG]
014.000.000.068	2422-630-07200	00 Tollpost-Globe AS	[OXG]
014.000.000.069	2422-470-12300	00 Tollpost-Globe AS	[OXG]
014.000.000.070	2422-470-13000	00 Tollpost-Globe AS	[OXG]
014.000.000.071	2422-170-04600	00 Tollpost-Globe AS	[OXG]
014.000.000.072	2422-516-04300	00 Tollpost-Globe AS	[OXG]
014.000.000.073	2422-530-00700	00 Tollpost-Globe AS	[OXG]
014.000.000.074	2422-650-18800	00 Tollpost-Globe AS	[OXG]
014.000.000.075	2422-450-24500	00 Tollpost-Globe AS	[OXG]
014.000.000.076	2062-243-15631	00 DPT-BXL-DDC	[LZ15]
014.000.000.077	2062-243-15651	00 DPT-BXL-DDC2	[LZ15]
014.000.000.078	3110-312-00431	00 DPT-CHI	[LZ15]
014.000.000.079	3110-512-00135	00 DPT-SAT-ENG	[LZ15]
014.000.000.080	2080-941-90550	00 DPT-PAR	[LZ15]
014.000.000.081	4545-511-30600	00 DPT-PBSC	[LZ15]
014.000.000.082	4545-513-30900	00 DPT-HONGKONG	[LZ15]
014.000.000.083	4872-203-55000	00 UECI-TAIPEI	[LZ15]
014.000.000.084	2624-551-10400	20 DPT-HANOVR	[LZ15]

Internet	Public Data Net	Description	References
014.000.000.085	2624-569-00401	99 DPT-FNKFRT	[LZ15]
014.000.000.086	3110-512-00134	00 DPT-SAT-SUPT	[LZ15]
014.000.000.087	4602-3010-0103	20 DU-X25A	[JK64]
014.000.000.088	4602-3010-0103	21 FDU-X25B	[JK64]
014.000.000.089	2422-150-33700	00 Tollpost-Globe AS	[OXG]
014.000.000.090	2422-271-07100	00 Tollpost-Globe AS	[OXG]
014.000.000.091	2422-516-00100	00 Tollpost-Globe AS	[OXG]
014.000.000.092	2422-650-18800	00 Norsk Informas.	[OXG]
014.000.000.093	2422-250-30400	00 Tollpost-Globe AS	[OXG]
014.000.000.094-014.255.255.254		Unassigned	[JBP]
014.255.255.255	Reserved		[JBP]

The standard for transmission of IP datagrams over the Public Data Network is specified in RFC-877 [69].

TELNET OPTIONS

The Telnet Protocol has a number of options that may be negotiated. These options are listed here. "IAB Official Protocol Standards" [62] provides more detailed information.

Options	Name	References
0	Binary Transmission	[110,JBP]
1	Echo	[111,JBP]
2	Reconnection	[42,JBP]
3	Suppress Go Ahead	[114,JBP]
4	Approx Message Size Negotiation	[133,JBP]
5	Status	[113,JBP]
6	Timing Mark	[115,JBP]
7	Remote Controlled Trans and Echo	[107,JBP]
8	Output Line Width	[40,JBP]
9	Output Page Size	[41,JBP]
10	Output Carriage-Return Disposition	[28,JBP]
11	Output Horizontal Tab Stops	[32,JBP]

continues

Options	Name	References
12	Output Horizontal Tab Disposition	[31,JBP]
13	Output Formfeed Disposition	[29,JBP]
14	Output Vertical Tabstops	[34,JBP]
15	Output Vertical Tab Disposition	[33,JBP]
16	Output Linefeed Disposition	[30,JBP]
17	Extended ASCII	[136,JBP]
18	Logout	[25,MRC]
19	Byte Macro	[35,JBP]
20	Data Entry Terminal	[145,38,JBP]
22	SUPDUP	[26,27,MRC]
22	SUPDUP Output	[51,MRC]
23	Send Location	[68,EAK1]
24	Terminal Type	[128,MS56]
25	End of Record	[103,JBP]
26	TACACS User Identification	[1,BA4]
27	Output Marking	[125,SXS]
28	Terminal Location Number	[84,RN6]
29	Telnet 3270 Regime	[116,JXR]
30	X.3 PAD	[70,SL70]
31	Negotiate About Window Size	[139,DW183]
32	Terminal Speed	[57,CLH3]
33	Remote Flow Control	[58,CLH3]
34	Linemode	[9,DB14]
35	X Display Location	[75,GM23]
36	Environment Option	[DB14]
37	Authentication Option	[DB14]
38	Encryption Option	[DB14]
255	Extended-Options-List	[109,JBP]

MAIL ENCRYPTION TYPES

RFC-822 specifies that Encryption Types for mail may be assigned. There are currently no RFC-822 encryption types assigned. Please use instead the Mail Privacy procedures defined in [71,72,66].

MIME TYPES

RFC-1341 [169] specifies that Content Types, Content Subtypes, Character Sets, Access Types, and Conversion values for MIME mail will be assigned and listed by the IANA.

Content Types and Subtypes

Type	Subtype	Description	Reference
text	plain		[169,NSB]
richtext			
multipart	mixed		[169,NSB]
alternative			
digest			
parallel			
message	rfc822		[169,NSB]
partial			
external-body			
application	octet-stream		[169,NSB]
postscript			
oda			
image	jpeg		[169,NSB]
gif			
audio	basic		[169,NSB]
video	mpeg		[169,NSB]

Character Sets

Type	Description	Reference
US-ASCII	the default character set	[169,NSB]
ISO-8859-1	see ISO_8859-1:1987 below	[169,NSB]

continues

continued

Type	Description	Reference
ISO-8859-2	see ISO_8859-2:1987 below	[169,NSB]
ISO-8859-3	see ISO_8859-3:1988 below	[169,NSB]
ISO-8859-4	see ISO_8859-4:1988 below	[169,NSB]
ISO-8859-5	see ISO_8859-5:1988 below	[169,NSB]
ISO-8859-6	see ISO_8859-6:1987 below	[169,NSB]
ISO-8859-7	see ISO_8859-7:1987 below	[169,NSB]
ISO-8859-8	see ISO_8859-8:1988 below	[169,NSB]
ISO-8859-9	see ISO_8859-9:1989 below	[169,NSB]

Access Types

Type	Description	Reference
FTP		[169,NSB]
ANON-FTP		[169,NSB]
TFTP		[169,NSB]
AFS		[169,NSB]
LOCAL-FILE		[169,NSB]
MAIL-SERVER		[169,NSB]

Conversion Values

Conversion values or Content Transfer Encodings.

Type	Description	Reference
7BIT		[169,NSB]
8BIT		[169,NSB]
BASE64		[169,NSB]
BINARY		[169,NSB]
QUOTED-PRINTABLE		[169,NSB]

CHARACTER SETS

Character Set	Reference
ISO_646.basic:1983	[170,KXS2]
INVARIANT	[170,KXS2]
ISO_646.irv:1983	[170,KXS2]
BS_4730	[170,KXS2]
ANSI_X3.4-1968	[170,KXS2]
NATS-SEFI	[170,KXS2]
NATS-SEFI-ADD	[170,KXS2]
NATS-DANO	[170,KXS2]
NATS-DANO-ADD	[170,KXS2]
SEN_850200_B	[170,KXS2]
SEN_850200_C	[170,KXS2]
JIS_C6220-1969-jp	[170,KXS2]
JIS_C6220-1969-ro	[170,KXS2]
IT	[170,KXS2]
PT	[170,KXS2]
ES	[170,KXS2]
greek7-old	[170,KXS2]
latin-greek	[170,KXS2]
DIN_66003	[170,KXS2]
NF_Z_62-010_(1973)	[170,KXS2]
Latin-greek-1	[170,KXS2]
ISO_5427	[170,KXS2]
JIS_C6226-1978	[170,KXS2]
BS_viewdata	[170,KXS2]
INIS	[170,KXS2]
INIS-8	[170,KXS2]
INIS-cyrillic	[170,KXS2]
ISO_5427:1981	[170,KXS2]

continued

Character Set	Reference
ISO_5428:1980	[170,KXS2]
GB_1988-80	[170,KXS2]
GB_2312-80	[170,KXS2]
NS_4551-1	[170,KXS2]
NS_4551-2	[170,KXS2]
NF_Z_62-010	[170,KXS2]
videotex-suppl	[170,KXS2]
PT2	[170,KXS2]
ES2	[170,KXS2]
MSZ_7795.3	[170,KXS2]
JIS_C6226-1983	[170,KXS2]
greek7	[170,KXS2]
ASMO_449	[170,KXS2]
iso-ir-90	[170,KXS2]
JIS_C6229-1984-a	[170,KXS2]
JIS_C6229-1984-b	[170,KXS2]
JIS_C6229-1984-b-add	[170,KXS2]
JIS_C6229-1984-hand	[170,KXS2]
JIS_C6229-1984-hand-add	[170,KXS2]
JIS_C6229-1984-kana	[170,KXS2]
ISO_2033-1983	[170,KXS2]
ANSI_X3.110-1983	[170,KXS2]
ISO_8859-1:1987	[170,KXS2]
ISO_8859-2:1987	[170,KXS2]
T.61-7bit	[170,KXS2]
T.61-8bit	[170,KXS2]
ISO_8859-3:1988	[170,KXS2]
ISO_8859-4:1988	[170,KXS2]
ECMA-cyrillic	[170,KXS2]
CSA_Z243.4-1985-1	[170,KXS2]

Character Set	Reference
CSA_Z243.4-1985-2	[170,KXS2]
CSA_Z243.4-1985-gr	[170,KXS2]
ISO_8859-7:1987	[170,KXS2]
ISO_8859-6:1987	[170,KXS2]
T.101-G2	[170,KXS2]
ISO_8859-8:1988	[170,KXS2]
CSN_369103	[170,KXS2]
JUS_I.B1.002	[170,KXS2]
ISO_6937-2-add	[170,KXS2]
IEC_P27-1	[170,KXS2]
ISO_8859-5:1988	[170,KXS2]
JUS_I.B1.003-serb	[170,KXS2]
JUS_I.B1.003-mac	[170,KXS2]
ISO_8859-9:1989	[170,KXS2]
KS_C_5601-1987	[170,KXS2]
greek-ccitt	[170,KXS2]
NC_NC00-10:81	[170,KXS2]
ISO_6937-2-25	[170,KXS2]
GOST_19768-74	[170,KXS2]
ISO_8859-supp	[170,KXS2]
ISO_10367-box	[170,KXS2]
latin6	[170,KXS2]
latin-lap	[170,KXS2]
JIS_X0212-1990	[170,KXS2]
DS_2089	[170,KXS2]
us-dk	[170,KXS2]
dk-us	[170,KXS2]
JIS_X0201	[170,KXS2]
KSC5636	[170,KXS2]
DEC-MCS	[170,KXS2]

App

A

continues

continued

Character Set	Reference
hp-roman8	[170,KXS2]
macintosh	[170,KXS2]
IBM037	[170,KXS2]
IBM038	[170,KXS2]
IBM273	[170,KXS2]
IBM274	[170,KXS2]
IBM275	[170,KXS2]
IBM277	[170,KXS2]
IBM278	[170,KXS2]
IBM280	[170,KXS2]
IBM281	[170,KXS2]
IBM284	[170,KXS2]
IBM285	[170,KXS2]
IBM290	[170,KXS2]
IBM297	[170,KXS2]
IBM420	[170,KXS2]
IBM423	[170,KXS2]
IBM424	[170,KXS2]
IBM437	[170,KXS2]
IBM500	[170,KXS2]
IBM850	[170,KXS2]
IBM851	[170,KXS2]
IBM852	[170,KXS2]
IBM855	[170,KXS2]
IBM857	[170,KXS2]
IBM860	[170,KXS2]
IBM861	[170,KXS2]
IBM862	[170,KXS2]
IBM863	[170,KXS2]

Character Set	Reference
IBM864	[170,KXS2]
IBM865	[170,KXS2]
IBM868	[170,KXS2]
IBM869	[170,KXS2]
IBM870	[170,KXS2]
IBM871	[170,KXS2]
IBM880	[170,KXS2]
IBM891	[170,KXS2]
IBM903	[170,KXS2]
IBM904	[170,KXS2]
IBM905	[170,KXS2]
IBM918	[170,KXS2]
IBM1026	[170,KXS2]
EBCDIC-AT-DE	[170,KXS2]
EBCDIC-AT-DE-A	[170,KXS2]
EBCDIC-CA-FR	[170,KXS2]
EBCDIC-DK-NO	[170,KXS2]
EBCDIC-DK-NO-A	[170,KXS2]
EBCDIC-FI-SE	[170,KXS2]
EBCDIC-FI-SE-A	[170,KXS2]
EBCDIC-FR	[170,KXS2]
EBCDIC-IT	[170,KXS2]
EBCDIC-PT	[170,KXS2]
EBCDIC-ES	[170,KXS2]
EBCDIC-ES-A	[170,KXS2]
EBCDIC-ES-S	[170,KXS2]
EBCDIC-UK	[170,KXS2]
EBCDIC-US	[170,KXS2]

MACHINE NAMES

These are the Official Machine Names as they appear in the Domain Name System HINFO records and the NIC Host Table. Their use is described in RFC-952 [53].

A machine name or CPU type may be up to 40 characters taken from the set of uppercase letters, digits, and the two punctuation characters hyphen and slash. It must start with a letter, and end with a letter or digit.

ALTO	DEC-1080
ALTOS-6800	DEC-1090
AMDAHL-V7	DEC-1090B
APOLLO	DEC-1090T
ATARI-104ST	DEC-2020T
ATT-3B1	DEC-2040
ATT-3B2	DEC-2040T
ATT-3B20	DEC-2050T
ATT-7300	DEC-2060
BBN-C/60	DEC-2060T
BURROUGHS-B/29	DEC-2065
BURROUGHS-B/4800	DEC-FALCON
BUTTERFLY	DEC-KS10
C/30	DEC-VAX-11730
C/70	DORADO
CADLINC	DPS8/70M
CADR	ELXSI-6400
CDC-170	EVEREX-386
CDC-170/750	FOONLY-F2
CDC-173	FOONLY-F3
CELERITY-1200	FOONLY-F4
CLUB-386	GOULD
COMPAQ-386/20	GOULD-6050
COMTEN-3690	GOULD-6080
CP8040	GOULD-9050
CRAY-1	GOULD-9080

CRAY-X/MP	H-316
CRAY-2	H-60/68
CTIWS-117	H-68
DANDELION	H-68/80
DEC-10	H-89
DEC-1050	HONEYWELL-DPS-6
DEC-1077	HONEYWELL-DPS-8/70
HP3000	ONYX-Z8000
HP3000/64	PDP-11
IBM-158	PDP-11/3
IBM-360/67	PDP-11/23
IBM-370/3033	PDP-11/24
IBM-3081	PDP-11/34
IBM-3084QX	PDP-11/40
IBM-3101	PDP-11/44
IBM-4331	PDP-11/45
IBM-4341	PDP-11/50
IBM-4361	PDP-11/70
IBM-4381	PDP-11/73
IBM-4956	PE-7/32
IBM-6152	PE-3205
IBM-PC	PERQ
IBM-PC/AT	PLEXUS-P/60
IBM-PC/RT	PLI
IBM-PC/XT	PLURIBUS
IBM-SERIES/1	PRIME-2350
IMAGEN	PRIME-2450
IMAGEN-8/300	PRIME-2755
IMSAI	PRIME-9655
INTEGRATED-SOLUTIONS	PRIME-9755
INTEGRATED-SOLUTIONS-68K	PRIME-9955II

INTEGRATED-SOLUTIONS-CREATOR	PRIME-2250
INTEGRATED-SOLUTIONS-CREATOR-8	PRIME-2655
INTEL-386	PRIME-9955
INTEL-IPSC	PRIME-9950
IS-1	PRIME-9650
IS-68010	PRIME-9750
LMI	PRIME-2250
LSI-11	PRIME-750
LSI-11/2	PRIME-850
LSI-11/23	PRIME-550II
LSI-11/73	PYRAMID-90
M68000	PYRAMID-90MX
MAC-II	PYRAMID-90X
MASSCOMP	RIDGE
MC500	RIDGE-32
MC68000	RIDGE-32C
MICROPORT	ROLM-1666
MICROVAX	S1-MKIIA
MICROVAX-I	SMI
MV/8000	SEQUENT-BALANCE-8000
NAS3-5	SIEMENS
NCR-COMTEN-3690	SILICON-GRAPHICS
NEXT/N1000-316	SILICON-GRAPHICS-IRIS
NOW	SGI-IRIS-2400
SGI-IRIS-2500	SUN-3/50
SGI-IRIS-3010	SUN-3/60
SGI-IRIS-3020	SUN-3/75
SGI-IRIS-3030	SUN-3/80
SGI-IRIS-3110	SUN-3/110
SGI-IRIS-3115	SUN-3/140
SGI-IRIS-3120	SUN-3/150

SGI-IRIS-3130	SUN-3/160
SGI-IRIS-4D/20	SUN-3/180
SGI-IRIS-4D/20G	SUN-3/200
SGI-IRIS-4D/25	SUN-3/260
SGI-IRIS-4D/25G	SUN-3/280
SGI-IRIS-4D/25S	SUN-3/470
SGI-IRIS-4D/50	SUN-3/480
SGI-IRIS-4D/50G	SUN-4/60
SGI-IRIS-4D/50GT	SUN-4/110
SGI-IRIS-4D/60	SUN-4/150
SGI-IRIS-4D/60G	SUN-4/200
SGI-IRIS-4D/60T	SUN-4/260
SGI-IRIS-4D/60GT	SUN-4/280
SGI-IRIS-4D/70	SUN-4/330
SGI-IRIS-4D/70G	SUN-4/370
SGI-IRIS-4D/70GT	SUN-4/390
SGI-IRIS-4D/80GT	SUN-50
SGI-IRIS-4D/80S	SUN-100
SGI-IRIS-4D/120GTX	SUN-120
SGI-IRIS-4D/120S	SUN-130
SGI-IRIS-4D/210GTX	SUN-150
SGI-IRIS-4D/210S	SUN-170
SGI-IRIS-4D/220GTX	SUN-386i/250
SGI-IRIS-4D/220S	SUN-68000
SGI-IRIS-4D/240GTX	SYMBOLICS-3600
SGI-IRIS-4D/240S	SYMBOLICS-3670
SGI-IRIS-4D/280GTX	SYMMETRIC-375
SGI-IRIS-4D/280S	SYMULT
SGI-IRIS-CS/12	TANDEM-TXP
SGI-IRIS-4SERVER-8	TANDY-6000
SPERRY-DCP/10	TEK-6130

SUN	TI-EXPLORER
SUN-2	TP-4000
SUN-2/50	TRS-80
SUN-2/100	UNIVAC-1100
SUN-2/120	UNIVAC-1100/60
SUN-2/130	UNIVAC-1100/62
SUN-2/140	UNIVAC-1100/63
SUN-2/150	UNIVAC-1100/64
SUN-2/160	UNIVAC-1100/70
SUN-2/170	UNIVAC-1160
UNKNOWN	
VAX-11/725	
VAX-11/730	
VAX-11/750	
VAX-11/780	
VAX-11/785	
VAX-11/790	
VAX-11/8600	
VAX-8600	
WANG-PC002	
WANG-VS100	
WANG-VS400	
WYSE-386	
XEROX-1108	
XEROX-8010	
ZENITH-148	

SYSTEM NAMES

These are the Official System Names as they appear in the Domain Name System HINFO records and the NIC Host Table. Their use is described in RFC-952 [53].

A system name may be up to 40 characters taken from the set of upper-case letters, digits, and the three punctuation characters hyphen, period, and slash. It must start with a letter, and end with a letter or digit.

AEGIS	LISP	SUN OS 3.5
APOLLO	LISPM	SUN OS 4.0
AIX/370	LOCUS	SWIFT
AIX-PS/2	MACOS	TAC
BS-2000	MINOS	TANDEM
CEDAR	MOS	TENEX
CGW	MPE5	TOPS10
CHORUS	MSDOS	TOPS20
CHRYSALIS	MULTICS	TOS
CMOS	MUSIC	TP3010
CMS	MUSIC/SP	TRSDOS
COS	MVS	ULTRIX
CPIX	MVS/SP	UNIX
CTOS	NEXUS	UNIX-BSD
CTSS	NMS	UNIX-V1AT
DCN	NONSTOP	UNIX-V
DDNOS	NOS-2	UNIX-V.1
DOMAIN	NTOS	UNIX-V.2
DOS	OS/DDP	UNIX-V.3
EDX	OS/2	UNIX-PC
ELF	OS4	UNKNOWN
EMBOS	OS86	UT2D
EMMOS	OSX	V
EPOS	PCDOS	VM
FOONEX	PERQ/OS	VM/370
FUZZ	PLI	VM/CMS
GCOS	PSDOS/MIT	VM/SP
GPOS	PRIMOS	VMS
HDOS	RMX/RDOS	VMS/EUNICE

IMAGEN	ROS	VRTX
INTERCOM	RSX11M	WAITS
IMPRESS	RTE-A	WANG
INTERLISP	SATOPS	WIN32
IOS	SCO-XENIX/386	X11R3
IRIX	SCS	XDE
ISI-68020	SIMP	XENIX
ITS	SUN	

PROTOCOL AND SERVICE NAMES

These are the Official Protocol Names as they appear in the Domain Name System WKS records and the NIC Host Table. Their use is described in RFC-952 [53].

A protocol or service may be up to 40 characters taken from the set of uppercase letters, digits, and the punctuation character hyphen. It must start with a letter, and end with a letter or digit.

ARGUS	ARGUS Protocol
ARP	Address Resolution Protocol
AUTH	Authentication Service
BBN-RCC-MON	BBN RCC Monitoring
BL-IDM	Britton Lee Intelligent Database Machine
BOOTP	Bootstrap Protocol
BOOTPC	Bootstrap Protocol Client
BOOTPS	Bootstrap Protocol Server
BR-SAT-MON	Backroom SATNET Monitoring
CFTP	CFTP
CHAOS	CHAOS Protocol
CHARGEN	Character Generator Protocol
CISCO-FNA	CISCO FNATIVE
CISCO-TNA	CISCO TNATIVE
CISCO-SYS	CISCO SYSMAINT
CLOCK	DCNET Time Server Protocol
CMOT	Common Mgmnt Info Scr and Prot over TCP/IP

COOKIE-JAR	Authentication Scheme
CSNET-NS	CSNET Mailbox Nameserver Protocol
DAYTIME	Daytime Protocol
DCN-MEAS	DCN Measurement Subsystems Protocol
DCP	Device Control Protocol
DGP	Dissimilar Gateway Protocol
DISCARD	Discard Protocol
DMF-MAIL	Digest Message Format for Mail
DOMAIN	Domain Name System
ECHO	Echo Protocol
EGP	Exterior Gateway Protocol
EHF-MAIL	Encoding Header Field for Mail
EMCON	Emission Control Protocol
EMFIS-CNTL	EMFIS Control Service
EMFIS-DATA	EMFIS Data Service
FINGER	Finger Protocol
FTP	File Transfer Protocol
FTP-DATA	File Transfer Protocol Data
GGP	Gateway Gateway Protocol
GRAPHICS	Graphics Protocol
HMP	Host Monitoring Protocol
HOST2-NS	Host2 Name Server
HOSTNAME	Hostname Protocol
ICMP	Internet Control Message Protocol
IGMP	Internet Group Management Protocol
IGP	Interior Gateway Protocol
IMAP2	Interim Mail Access Protocol version 2
INGRES-NET	INGRES-NET Service
IP	Internet Protocol
IPCU	Internet Packet Core Utility
IPPC	Internet Pluribus Packet Core

IP-ARC	Internet Protocol on ARCNET
IP-ARPA	Internet Protocol on ARPANET
IP-CMPRS	Compressing TCP/IP Headers
IP-DC	Internet Protocol on DC Networks
IP-DVMRP	Distance Vector Multicast Routing Protocol
IP-E	Internet Protocol on Ethernet Networks
IP-EE	Internet Protocol on Exp. Ethernet Nets
IP-FDDI	Transmission of IP over FDDI
IP-HC	Internet Protocol on Hyperchannnel
IP-IEEE	Internet Protocol on IEEE 802
IP-IPX	Transmission of 802.2 over IPX Networks
IP-MTU	IP MTU Discovery Options
IP-NETBIOS	Internet Protocol over NetBIOS Networks
IP-SLIP	Transmission of IP over Serial Lines
IP-WB	Internet Protocol on Wideband Network
IP-X25	Internet Protocol on X.25 Networks
IRTP	Internet Reliable Transaction Protocol
ISI-GL	ISI Graphics Language Protocol
ISO-TP4	ISO Transport Protocol Class 4
ISO-TSAP	ISO TSAP
LA-MAINT	IMP Logical Address Maintenance
LARP	Locus Address Resoultion Protocol
LDP	Loader Debugger Protocol
LEAF-1	Leaf-1 Protocol
LEAF-2	Leaf-2 Protocol
LINK	Link Protocol
LOC-SRV	Location Service
LOGIN	Login Host Protocol
MAIL	Format of Electronic Mail Messages
MERIT-INP	MERIT Internodal Protocol
METAGRAM	Mctagram Relay

MIB	Management Information Base
MIT-ML-DEV	MIT ML Device
MFE-NSP	MFE Network Services Protocol
MIT-SUBNET	MIT Subnet Support
MIT-DOV	MIT Dover Spooler
MPM	Internet Message Protocol (Multimedia Mail)
MPM-FLAGS	MPM Flags Protocol
MPM-SND	MPM Send Protocol
MSG-AUTH	MSG Authentication Protocol
MSG-ICP	MSG ICP Protocol
MUX	Multiplexing Protocol
NAMESERVER	Host Name Server
NETBIOS-DGM	NETBIOS Datagram Service
NETBIOS-NS	NETBIOS Name Service
NETBIOS-SSN	NETBIOS Session Service
NETBLT	Bulk Data Transfer Protocol
NETED	Network Standard Text Editor
NETRJS	Remote Job Service
NI-FTP	NI File Transfer Protocol
NI-MAIL	NI Mail Protocol
NICNAME	Who Is Protocol
NFILE	A File Access Protocol
NNTP	Network News Transfer Protocol
NSW-FE	NSW User System Front End
NTP	Network Time Protocol
NVP-II	Network Voice Protocol
OSPF	Open Shortest Path First Interior GW Protocol
PCMAIL	Pcmail Transport Protocol
POP2	Post Office Protocol - Version 2
POP3	Post Office Protocol - Version 3
PPP	Point-to-Point Protocol

PRM	Packet Radio Measurement
PUP	PUP Protocol
PWDGEN	Password Generator Protocol
QUOTE	Quote of the Day Protocol
RARP	A Reverse Address Resolution Protocol
RATP	Reliable Asynchronous Transfer Protocol
RE-MAIL-CK	Remote Mail Checking Protocol
RDP	Reliable Data Protocol
RIP	Routing Information Protocol
RJE	Remote Job Entry
RLP	Resource Location Protocol
RTELNET	Remote Telnet Service
RVD	Remote Virtual Disk Protocol
SAT-EXPAK	Satnet and Backroom EXPAK
SAT-MON	SATNET Monitoring
SEP	Sequential Exchange Protocol
SFTP	Simple File Transfer Protocol
SGMP	Simple Gateway Monitoring Protocol
SNMP	Simple Network Management Protocol
SMI	Structure of Management Information
SMTP	Simple Mail Transfer Protocol
SQLSRV	SQL Service
ST	Stream Protocol
STATSRV	Statistics Service
SU-MIT-TG	SU/MIT Telnet Gateway Protocol
SUN-RPC	SUN Remote Procedure Call
SUPDUP	SUPDUP Protocol
SUR-MEAS	Survey Measurement
SWIFT-RVF	Remote Virtual File Protocol
TACACS-DS	TACACS-Database Service
TACNEWS	TAC News

TCP	Transmission Control Protocol
TCP-ACO	TCP Alternate Checksum Option
TELNET	Telnet Protocol
TFTP	Trivial File Transfer Protocol
THINWIRE	Thinwire Protocol
TIME	Time Server Protocol
TP-TCP	ISO Transport Service on top of the TCP
TRUNK-1	Trunk-1 Protocol
TRUNK-2	Trunk-2 Protocol
UCL	University College London Protocol
UDP	User Datagram Protocol
NNTP	Network News Transfer Protocol
USERS	Active Users Protocol
UUCP-PATH	UUCP Path Service
VIA-FTP	VIA Systems-File Transfer Protocol
VISA	VISA Protocol
VMTP	Versatile Message Transaction Protocol
WB-EXPAK	Wideband EXPAK
WB-MON	Wideband Monitoring
XNET	Cross Net Debugger
XNS-IDP	Xerox NS IDP

TERMINAL TYPE NAMES

These are the Official Terminal Type Names. Their use is described in RFC-930 [128]. The maximum length of a name is 40 characters.

A terminal names may be up to 40 characters taken from the set of upper-case letters, digits, and the two punctuation characters hyphen and slash. It must start with a letter, and end with a letter or digit.

ADDS-CONSUL-980	DATAMEDIA-1521
ADDS-REGENT-100	DATAMEDIA-2500
ADDS-REGENT-20	DATAMEDIA-3025
ADDS-REGENT-200	DATAMEDIA-3025A

ADDS-REGENT-25	DATAMEDIA-3045
ADDS-REGENT-40	DATAMEDIA-3045A
ADDS-REGENT-60	DATAMEDIA-DT80/1
ADDS-VIEWPOINT	DATAPOINT-2200
ADDS-VIEWPOINT-60	DATAPOINT-3000
AED-512	DATAPOINT-3300
AMPEX-DIALOGUE-210	DATAPOINT-3360
AMPEX-DIALOGUE-80	DEC-DECWRITER-I
AMPEX-210	DEC-DECWRITER-II
AMPEX-230	DEC-GIGI
ANDERSON-JACOBSON-510	DEC-GT40
ANDERSON-JACOBSON-630	DEC-GT40A
ANDERSON-JACOBSON-832	DEC-GT42
ANDERSON-JACOBSON-841	DEC-LA120
ANN-ARBOR-AMBASSADOR	DEC-LA30
ANSI	DEC-LA36
ARDS	DEC-LA38
BITGRAPH	DEC-VT05
BUSSIPLEXER	DEC-VT100
CALCOMP-565	DEC-VT101
CDC-456	DEC-VT102
CDI-1030	DEC-VT125
CDI-1203	DEC-VT131
C-ITOH-101	DEC-VT132
C-ITOH-50	DEC-VT200
C-ITOH-80	DEC-VT220
CLNZ	DEC-VT240
COMPUCOLOR-II	DEC-VT241
CONCEPT-100	DEC-VT300
CONCEPT-104	DEC-VT320
CONCEPT-108	DEC-VT340

DATA-100	DEC-VT50
DATA-GENERAL-6053	DEC-VT50H
DATAGRAPHIX-132A	DEC-VT52
DATAMEDIA-1520	DEC-VT55
DEC-VT61	HP-2626
DEC-VT62	HP-2626A
DELTA-DATA-5000	HP-2626P
DELTA-DATA-NIH-7000	HP-2627
DELTA-TELTERM-2	HP-2640
DIABLO-1620	HP-2640A
DIABLO-1640	HP-2640B
DIGILOG-333	HP-2645
DTC-300S	HP-2645A
DTC-382	HP-2648
EDT-1200	HP-2648A
EXECUPORT-4000	HP-2649
EXECUPORT-4080	HP-2649A
FACIT-TWIST-4440	IBM-1050
FREEDOM-100	IBM-2741
FREEDOM-110	IBM-3101
FREEDOM-200	IBM-3101-10
GENERAL-TERMINAL-100A	IBM-3151
GENERAL-TERMINAL-101	IBM-3179-2
GIPSI-TX-M	IBM-3180-2
GIPSI-TX-ME	IBM-3196-A1
GIPSI-TX-C4	IBM-3275-2
GIPSI-TX-C8	IBM-3276-2
GSI	IBM-3276-3
HAZELTINE-1420	IBM-3276-4
HAZELTINE-1500	IBM-3277-2
HAZELTINE-1510	IBM-3278-2

HAZELTINE-1520	IBM-3278-3
HAZELTINE-1552	IBM-3278-4
HAZELTINE-2000	IBM-3278-5
HAZELTINE-ESPRIT	IBM-3279-2
HITACHI-5601	IBM-3279-3
HITACHI-5603	IBM-3477-FC
HITACHI-5603E	IBM-3477-FG
HITACHI-5603EA	IBM-5081
HITACHI-560X	IBM-5151
HITACHI-560XE	IBM-5154
HITACHI-560XEA	IBM-5251-11
HITACHI-560PR	IBM-5291-1
HITACHI-HOAP1	IBM-5292-2
HITACHI-HOAP2	IBM-5555-B01
HITACHI-HOAP3	IBM-5555-C01
HITACHI-HOAP4	IBM-6153
HP-2392	IBM-6154
HP-2621	IBM-6155
HP-2621A	IBM-AED
HP-2621P	IBM-3278-2-E
HP-2623	IBM-3278-3-E
IBM-3278-4-E	TEC
IBM-3278-5-E	TEKTRONIX-4006
IBM-3279-2-E	TEKTRONIX-4010
IBM-3279-3-E	TEKTRONIX-4012
IMLAC	TEKTRONIX-4013
INFOTON-100	TEKTRONIX-4014
INFOTON-400	TEKTRONIX-4023
INFOTONKAS	TEKTRONIX-4024
ISC-8001	TEKTRONIX-4025
LSI-ADM-1	TEKTRONIX-4027

LSI-ADM-11	TEKTRONIX-4105
LSI-ADM-12	TEKTRONIX-4107
LSI-ADM-2	TEKTRONIX-4110
LSI-ADM-20	TEKTRONIX-4112
LSI-ADM-22	TEKTRONIX-4113
LSI-ADM-220	TEKTRONIX-4114
LSI-ADM-3	TEKTRONIX-4115
LSI-ADM-31	TEKTRONIX-4125
LSI-ADM-3A	TEKTRONIX-4404
LSI-ADM-42	TELERAY-1061
LSI-ADM-5	TELERAY-3700
MEMOREX-1240	TELERAY-3800
MICROBEE	TELETEC-DATASCREEN
MICROTERM-ACT-IV	TELETERM-1030
MICROTERM-ACT-V	TELETYPE-33
MICROTERM-ERGO-301	TELETYPE-35
MICROTERM-MIME-1	TELETYPE-37
MICROTERM-MIME-2	TELETYPE-38
MICROTERM-ACT-5A	TELETYPE-40
MICROTERM-TWIST	TELETYPE-43
NEC-5520	TELEVIDEO-910
NETRONICS	TELEVIDEO-912
NETWORK-VIRTUAL-TERMINAL	TELEVIDEO-920
OMRON-8025AG	TELEVIDEO-920B
PERKIN-ELMER-550	TELEVIDEO-920C
PERKIN-ELMER-1100	TELEVIDEO-925
PERKIN-ELMER-1200	TELEVIDEO-955
PERQ	TELEVIDEO-950
PLASMA-PANEL	TELEVIDEO-970
QUME-SPRINT-5	TELEVIDEO-975
QUME-101	TERMINET-1200

QUME-102	TERMINET-300
SOROC	TI-700
SOROC-120	TI-733
SOUTHWEST-TECHNICAL-PRODUCTS-CT82	TI-735
SUN	TI-743
SUPERBEE	TI-745
SUPERBEE-III-M	TI-800
TYCOM	
UNIVAC-DCT-500	
VIDEO-SYSTEMS-1200	
VIDEO-SYSTEMS-5000	
VOLKER-CRAIG-303	
VOLKER-CRAIG-303A	
VOLKER-CRAIG-404	
VISUAL-200	
VISUAL-55	
WYSE-30	
WYSE-50	
WYSE-60	
WYSE-75	
WYSE-85	
XEROX-1720	
XTERM	
ZENITH-H19	
ZENITH-Z29	
ZENTEC-30	

DOCUMENTS

1. Anderson, B., "TACACS User Identification Telnet Option", RFC-927, BBN, December 1984.
2. BBN, "Specifications for the Interconnection of a Host and an IMP", Report 1822, Bolt Beranek and Newman, Cambridge, Massachusetts, revised, December 1981.

3. BBN, "User Manual for TAC User Database Tool", Bolt Beranek and Newman, September 1984.

4. Ben-Artzi, Amatzia, "Network Management for TCP/IP Network: An Overview", 3Com, May 1988.

5. Bennett, C., "A Simple NIFTP-Based Mail System", IEN 169, University College, London, January 1981.

6. Bhushan, A., "A Report on the Survey Project", RFC-530, NIC 17375, June 1973.

7. Bisbey, R., D. Hollingworth, and B. Britt, "Graphics Language (version 2.1)", ISI/TM-80-18, Information Sciences Institute, July 1980.

8. Boggs, D., J. Shoch, E. Taft, and R. Metcalfe, "PUP: An Internetwork Architecture", XEROX Palo Alto Research Center, CSL-79-10, July 1979; also in IEEE Transactions on Communication, Volume COM-28, Number 4, April 1980.

9. Borman, D., Editor, "Telnet Linemode Option", RFC 1116, Cray Research, Inc., August 1989.

10. Braden, R., "NETRJS Protocol", RFC-740, NIC 42423, Information Sciences Institute, November 1977.

11. Braden, R., and J. Postel, "Requirements for Internet Gateways", RFC-1009, Obsoletes RFC-985, Information Sciences Institute, June 1987.

12. Bressler, B., "Remote Job Entry Protocol", RFC-407, NIC 12112, October 1972.

13. Bressler, R., "Inter-Entity Communication — An Experiment", RFC-441, NIC 13773, January 1973.

14. Butler, M., J. Postel, D. Chase, J. Goldberger, and J. K. Reynolds, "Post Office Protocol - Version 2", RFC-937, Information Sciences Institute, February 1985.

15. Case, J., M. Fedor, M. Schoffstall, and J. Davin, "A Simple Network Management Protocol", RFC-1157, (Obsoletes RFC-1067, RFC-1098), SNMP Research, Performance Systems International, Performance Systems International, MIT Laboratory for Computer Science, May 1990.

16. Cass, D., and M. Rose, "ISO Transport Services on Top of the TCP", RFC-983, NTRC, April 1986.

17. Cheriton, D., "VMTP: Versatile Message Transaction Protocol Specification", RFC-1045, pgs 103 & 104, Stanford University, February 1988.

18. Cisco Systems, "Gateway Server Reference Manual", Manual Revision B, January 10, 1988.

19. Clark, D., "PCMAIL: A Distributed Mail System for Personal Computers", RFC-984, MIT, May 1986.

20. Clark, D., M. Lambert, and L. Zhang, "NETBLT: A Bulk Data Transfer Protocol", RFC-969, MIT Laboratory for Computer Science, December 1985.

21. Cohen, D., "On Holy Wars and a Plea for Peace", IEEE Computer Magazine, October 1981.

22. Cohen, D., "Specifications for the Network Voice Protocol", RFC-741, ISI/RR 7539, Information Sciences Institute, March 1976.

23. Cohen, D. and J. Postel, "Multiplexing Protocol", IEN 90, Information Sciences Institute, May 1979.

24. COMPASS, "Semi-Annual Technical Report", CADD-7603-0411, Massachusetts Computer Associates, 4 March 1976. Also as, "National Software Works, Status Report No. 1," RADC-TR-76-276, Volume 1, September 1976. And COMPASS. "Second Semi-Annual Report," CADD-7608-1611, Massachusetts Computer Associates, August 1976.

25. Crispin, M., "Telnet Logout Option", Stanford University-AI, RFC-727, April 1977.

26. Crispin, M., "Telnet SUPDUP Option", Stanford University-AI, RFC-736, October 1977.

27. Crispin, M., "SUPDUP Protocol", RFC-734, NIC 41953, October 1977.

28. Crocker, D., "Telnet Output Carriage-Return Disposition Option", RFC-652, October 1974.

29. Crocker, D., "Telnet Output Formfeed Disposition Option", RFC-655, October 1974.

30. Crocker, D., "Telnet Output Linefeed Disposition", RFC-658, October 1974.

31. Crocker, D., "Telnet Output Horizontal Tab Disposition Option", RFC-654, October 1974.

32. Crocker, D., "Telnet Output Horizontal Tabstops Option", RFC-653, October 1974.

33. Crocker, D., "Telnet Output Vertical Tab Disposition Option", RFC-657, October 1974.

34. Crocker, D., "Telnet Output Vertical Tabstops Option", RFC-656, October 1974.

35. Crocker, D. and R. Gumpertz, "Revised Telnet Byte Marco Option", RFC-735, November 1977.

36. Croft, B., and J. Gilmore, "BOOTSTRAP Protocol (BOOTP)", RFC-951, Stanford and SUN Microsytems, September 1985.

37. Davin, J., J. Case, M. Fedor, and M. Schoffstall, "A Simple Gateway Monitoring Protocol", RFC-1028, November 1987.

38. Day, J., "Telnet Data Entry Terminal Option", RFC-732, September 1977.

39. DCA, "3270 Display System Protocol", #1981-08.

40. DDN Protocol Handbook, "Telnet Output Line Width Option", NIC 50005, December 1985.

41. DDN Protocol Handbook, "Telnet Output Page Size Option", NIC 50005, December 1985.

42. DDN Protocol Handbook, "Telnet Reconnection Option", NIC 50005, December 1985.

43. Deering, S., "Host Extensions for IP Multicasting", RFC-1112, Obsoletes RFC-988, RFC-1054, Stanford University, August 1989.

44. Elvy, M., and R. Nedved, "Network Mail Path Service", RFC-915, Harvard and CMU, July 1986.

45. Feinler, E., editor, "DDN Protocol Handbook", Network Information Center, SRI International, December 1985.

46. Feinler, E., editor, "Internet Protocol Transition Workbook", Network Information Center, SRI International, March 1982.

47. Feinler, E. and J. Postel, eds., "ARPANET Protocol Handbook", NIC 7104, for the Defense Communications Agency by SRI International, Menlo Park, California, Revised January 1978.

48. Finlayson, R., T. Mann, J. Mogul, and M. Theimer, "A Reverse Address Resolution Protocol", RFC-903, Stanford University, June 1984.

49. Forgie, J., "ST - A Proposed Internet Stream Protocol", IEN 119, MIT Lincoln Laboratory, September 1979.

50. Forsdick, H., "CFTP", Network Message, Bolt Beranek and Newman, January 1982.

51. Greenberg, B., "Telnet SUPDUP-OUTPUT Option", RFC-749, MIT-Multics, September 1978.

52. Harrenstien, K., "Name/Finger", RFC-742, NIC 42758, SRI International, December 1977.

53. Harrenstien, K., M. Stahl, and E. Feinler, "DOD Internet Host Table Specification", RFC-952, Obsoletes RFC-810, October 1985.

54. Harrenstien, K., V. White, and E. Feinler, "Hostnames Server", RFC-811, SRI International, March 1982.

55. Harrenstien, K., and V. White, "Nicname/Whois", RFC-812, SRI International, March 1982.

56. Haverty, J., "XNET Formats for Internet Protocol Version 4", IEN 158, October 1980.

57. Hedrick, C., "Telnet Terminal Speed Option", RFC-1079, Rutgers University, December 1988.

58. Hedrick, C., "Telnet Remote Flow Control Option", RFC-1080, Rutgers University, December 1988.

59. Hinden, R., "A Host Monitoring Protocol", RFC-869, Bolt Beranek and Newman, December 1983.

60. Hinden, R., and A. Sheltzer, "The DARPA Internet Gateway", RFC-823, September 1982.

61. Hornig, C., "A Standard for the Transmission of IP Datagrams over Ethernet Networks, RFC-894, Symbolics, April 1984.

62. Internet Activities Board, J. Postel, Editor, "IAB Official Protocol Standards", RFC-1280, Internet Activities March 1992.

63. International Standards Organization, "ISO Transport Protocol Specification - ISO DP 8073", RFC-905, April 1984.

64. International Standards Organization, "Protocol for Providing the Connectionless-Mode Network Services", RFC-926, ISO, December 1984.

65. Kantor, B., and P. Lapsley, "Network News Transfer Protocol", RFC-977, UC San Diego & UC Berkeley, February 1986.

66. Kent, S., and J. Linn, "Privacy Enhancement for Internet Electronic Mail: Part II — Certificate-Based Key Management", BBNCC and DEC, August 1989.

67. Khanna, A., and A. Malis, "The ARPANET AHIP-E Host Access Protocol (Enhanced AHIP)", RFC-1005, BBN Communications Corporation, May 1987.

68. Killian, E., "Telnet Send-Location Option", RFC-779, April 1981.

69. Korb, J., "A Standard for the Transmission of IP Datagrams Over Public Data Networks", RFC-877, Purdue University, September 1983.

70. Levy, S., and T. Jacobson, "Telnet X.3 PAD Option", RFC-1053, Minnesota Supercomputer Center, April 1988.

71. Linn, J., "Privacy Enhancement for Internet Electronic Mail: Part I: Message Encipherment and Authentication Procedures", RFC-1113, Obsoletes RFC-989 and RFC-1040, DEC, August 1989.

72. Linn, J., "Privacy Enhancement for Internet Electronic Mail: Part III — Algorithms, Modes, and Identifiers", RFC-1115, DEC, August 1989.

73. Lottor, M., "Simple File Transfer Protocol", RFC-913, MIT, September 1984.

74. M/A-COM Government Systems, "Dissimilar Gateway Protocol Specification, Draft Version", Contract no. CS901145, November 16, 1987.

75. Marcy, G., "Telnet X Display Location Option", RFC-1096, Carnegie Mellon University, March 1989.

76. Malis, A., "Logical Addressing Implementation Specification", BBN Report 5256, pp 31-36, May 1983.

77. Malkin, G., "KNET/VM Command Message Protocol Functional Overview", Spartacus, Inc., January 4, 1988.

78. Metcalfe, R. M. and D. R. Boggs, "Ethernet: Distributed Packet Switching for Local Computer Networks", Communications of the ACM, 19 (7), pp 395-402, July 1976.

79. Miller, T., "Internet Reliable Transaction Protocol", RFC-938, ACC, February 1985.

80. Mills, D., "Network Time Protocol (Version 1), Specification and Implementation", RFC-1059, University of Delaware, July 1988.

81. Mockapetris, P., "Domain Names - Concepts and Facilities", RFC-1034, Obsoletes RFCs 882, 883, and 973, Information Sciences Institute, November 1987.

82. Mockapetris, P., "Domain Names - Implementation and Specification", RFC-1035, Obsoletes RFCs 882, 883, and 973, Information Sciences Institute, November 1987.

83. Moy, J., "The OSPF Specification", RFC 1131, Proteon, October 1989.

84. Nedved, R., "Telnet Terminal Location Number Option", RFC-946, Carnegie-Mellon University, May 1985.

85. NSW Protocol Committee, "MSG: The Interprocess Communication Facility for the National Software Works", CADD-7612-2411, Massachusetts Computer Associates, BBN 3237, Bolt Beranek and Newman, Revised December 1976.

86. Onions, J., and M. Rose, "ISO-TP0 bridge between TCP and X.25", RFC-1086, Nottingham, TWG, December 1988.

87. Partridge, C. and G. Trewitt, The High-Level Entity Management System (HEMS), RFCs 1021, 1022, 1023, and 1024, BBN/NNSC, Stanford, October, 1987.

88. Plummer, D., "An Ethernet Address Resolution Protocol or Converting Network Protocol Addresses to 48-bit Ethernet Addresses for Transmission on Ethernet Hardware", RFC-826, MIT-LCS, November 1982.

89. Postel, J., "Active Users", RFC-866, Information Sciences Institute, May 1983.

90. Postel, J., and J. Reynolds, "A Standard for the Transmission of IP Datagrams over IEEE 802 Networks", RFC-1042, USC/Information Sciences Institute, February 1988.

91. Postel, J., "A Standard for the Transmission of IP Datagrams over Experimental Ethernet Networks, RFC-895, Information Sciences Institute, April 1984.

92. Postel, J., "Character Generator Protocol", RFC-864, Information Sciences Institute, May 1983.

93. Postel, J., "Daytime Protocol", RFC-867, Information Sciences Institute, May 1983.

94. Postel, J., "Discard Protocol", RFC-863, Information Sciences Institute, May 1983.

95. Postel, J., "Echo Protocol", RFC-862, Information Sciences Institute, May 1983.

96. Postel, J. and J. Reynolds, "File Transfer Protocol", RFC-959, Information Sciences Institute, October 1985.

97. Postel, J., "Internet Control Message Protocol - DARPA Internet Program Protocol Specification", RFC-792, Information Sciences Institute, September 1981.

98. Postel, J., "Internet Message Protocol", RFC-759, IEN 113, Information Sciences Institute, August 1980.

99. Postel, J., "Name Server", IEN 116, Information Sciences Institute, August 1979.

100. Postel, J., "Quote of the Day Protocol", RFC-865, Information Sciences Institute, May 1983.

101. Postel, J., "Remote Telnet Service", RFC-818, Information Sciences Institute, November 1982.

102. Postel, J., "Simple Mail Transfer Protocol", RFC-821, Information Sciences Institute, August 1982.

103. Postel, J., "Telnet End of Record Option", RFC-885, Information Sciences Institute, December 1983.

104. Postel, J., "User Datagram Protocol", RFC-768 Information Sciences Institute, August 1980.

105. Postel, J., ed., "Internet Protocol - DARPA Internet Program Protocol Specification", RFC-791, Information Sciences Institute, September 1981.

106. Postel, J., ed., "Transmission Control Protocol - DARPA Internet Program Protocol Specification", RFC-793, Information Sciences Institute, September 1981.

107. Postel, J. and D. Crocker, "Remote Controlled Transmission and Echoing Telnet Option", RFC-726, March 1977.

108. Postel, J., and K. Harrenstien, "Time Protocol", RFC-868, Information Sciences Institute, May 1983.

109. Postel, J. and J. Reynolds, "Telnet Extended Options - List Option", RFC-861, Information Sciences Institute, May 1983.

110. Postel, J. and J. Reynolds, "Telnet Binary Transmission", RFC-856, Information Sciences Institute, May 1983.

111. Postel, J. and J. Reynolds, "Telnet Echo Option", RFC-857, Information Sciences Institute, May 1983.

112. Postel, J., and J. Reynolds, "Telnet Protocol Specification", RFC-854, Information Sciences Institute, May 1983.

113. Postel, J. and J. Reynolds, "Telnet Status Option", RFC-859, Information Sciences Institute, May 1983.

114. Postel, J. and J. Reynolds, "Telnet Suppress Go Ahead Option", RFC-858, Information Sciences Institute, May 1983.

115. Postel, J. and J. Reynolds, "Telnet Timing Mark Option", RFC-860, Information Sciences Institute, May 1983.

116. Rekhter, J., "Telnet 3270 Regime Option", RFC-1041, IBM, January 1988.

117. Reynolds, J., "BOOTP Vendor Information Extensions", RFC 1084, Information Sciences Institute, December 1988.

118. Reynolds, J. and J. Postel, "Official Internet Protocols", RFC-1011, USC/Information Sciences Institute, May 1987. NOTE: This document is replaced by "IAB Official Protocol Standards" 62. ..

119. Romano, S., M. Stahl, and M. Recker, "Internet Numbers", RFC-1166, SRI-NIC, May 1990.

120. Rose, M., and K. McCloghrie, "Structure and Identification of Management Information for TCP/IP-based internets", RFC-1155, Performance Systems International, Hughes LAN Systems, May 1990.

121. McCloghrie, K., and M. Rose, "Management Information Base for Network Management of TCP/IP-based internets: MIB-II", RFC-1213, Hughes LAN Systems, Performance Systems International, March 1991.

122. Rose, M., "Post Office Protocol - Version 3", RFC 1225, PSI, May 1991.

123. Seamonson, L. J., and E. C. Rosen, "STUB" Exterior Gateway Protocol", RFC-888, BBN Communications Corporation, January 1984.

124. Shuttleworth, B., "A Documentary of MFENet, a National Computer Network", UCRL-52317, Lawrence Livermore Labs, Livermore, California, June 1977.

125. Silverman, S., "Output Marking Telnet Option", RFC-933, MITRE, January 1985.

126. Sollins, K., "The TFTP Protocol (Revision 2)", RFC-783, MIT/LCS, June 1981.

127. Solomon, M., L. Landweber, and D. Neuhengen, "The CSNET Name Server", Computer Networks, v.6, n.3, pp. 161-172, July 1982.

128. Solomon, M., and E. Wimmers, "Telnet Terminal Type Option", RFC-930, Supercedes RFC-884, University of Wisconsin, Madison, January 1985.

129. Sproull, R., and E. Thomas, "A Networks Graphics Protocol", NIC 24308, August 1974.

130. St. Johns, M., "Authentication Service", RFC-931, TPSC, January 1985.

131. Tappan, D., "The CRONUS Virtual Local Network", RFC-824, Bolt Beranek and Newman, August 1982.

132. Taylor, J., "ERPC Functional Specification", Version 1.04, HYDRA Computer Systems, Inc., July 1984.

133. "The Ethernet, A Local Area Network: Data Link Layer and Physical Layer Specification", AA-K759B-TK, Digital Equipment Corporation, Maynard, MA. Also as: "The Ethernet - A Local Area Network", Version 1.0, Digital Equipment Corporation, Intel Corporation, Xerox Corporation, September 1980. And: "The Ethernet, A Local Area Network: Data Link Layer and Physical Layer Specifications", Digital, Intel and Xerox, November 1982. And: XEROX, "The Ethernet, A Local Area Network: Data Link Layer and Physical Layer Specification", X3T51/80-50, Xerox Corporation, Stamford, CT., October 1980.

134. The High Level Protocol Group, "A Network Independent File Transfer Protocol", INWG Protocol Note 86, December 1977.

135. Thomas, Bob, "The Interhost Protocol to Support CRONUS/DIAMOND Interprocess Communication", BBN, September 1983.

136. Tovar, "Telnet Extended ASCII Option", RFC-698, Stanford University-AI, July 1975.

137. Uttal, J., J. Rothschild, and C. Kline, "Transparent Integration of UNIX and MS-DOS", Locus Computing Corporation.

138. Velten, D., R. Hinden, and J. Sax, "Reliable Data Protocol", RFC-908, BBN Communications Corporation, July 1984.

139. Waitzman, D., "Telnet Window Size Option", RFC-1073, BBN STC, October, 1988.

140. Waitzman, D., C. Partridge, and S. Deering "Distance Vector Multicast Routing Protocol", RFC-1075, BBN STC and Stanford University, November 1988.

141. Wancho, F., "Password Generator Protocol", RFC-972, WSMR, January 1986.

142. Warrier, U., and L. Besaw, "The Common Management Information Services and Protocol over TCP/IP (CMOT)", RFC-1095, Unisys Corp. and Hewlett-Packard, April 1989.

143. Welch, B., "The Sprite Remote Procedure Call System", Technical Report, UCB/Computer Science Dept., 86/302, University of California at Berkeley, June 1986.

144. Xerox, "Courier: The Remote Procedure Protocol", XSIS 038112, December 1981.

145. Yasuda, A., and T. Thompson, "TELNET Data Entry Terminal Option DODIIS Implementation", RFC 1043, DIA, February 1988.

146. Simpson, W., "The Point-to-Point Protocol (PPP) for the Transmission of Multi-Protocol Datagrams Over Point-to-Point Links", RFC 1331, Daydreamer, May 1992.

147. McGregor, G., "The (PPP) Internet Protocol Control Protocol (IPCP)", RFC 1332, Merit, May 1992.

148. Woodburn, W., and D. Mills, " A Scheme for an Internet Encapsulation Protocol: Version 1", RFC 1241, SAIC, University of Delaware, July 1991.

149. McCloghrie, K., and M. Rose, "Management Information Base for Network Management of TCP/IP-based internets", Hughes LAN Systems, Performance Systems International, May 1990.

150. McCloghrie, K., and M. Rose, "Management Information Base for Network Management of TCP/IP-based internets: MIB-II", RFC 1213, Hughes LAN Systems, Performance Systems International, March 1991.

151. McCloghrie, K., Editor, "Extensions to the Generic-Interface MIB", RFC 1229, Hughes LAN Systems, May 1991.

152. Waldbusser, S., Editor, "AppleTalk Management Information Base", RFC 1243, Carnegie Mellon University, July 1991.

153. Baker, F., and R. Coltun, "OSPF Version 2 Management Information Base", RFC 1253, ACC, Computer Science Center, August 1991.

154. Willis, S, and J. Burruss, "Definitions of Managed Objects for the Border Gateway Protocol (Version 3)", RFC 1269, Wellfleet Communications Inc., October 1991.

155. Waldbusser, S., "Remote Network Monitoring Management Information Base", RFC 1271, Carnegie Mellon University, November 1991.

156. Decker, E., Langille, P., Rijsinghani, A., and K. McCloghrie, "Definitions of Managed Objects for Bridges", RFC 1286, cisco Systems, Inc., DEC, Hughes LAN Systems, Inc., December 1991.

157. Cook, J., Editor, Definitions of Managed Objects for the Ethernet-like Interface Types", RFC 1284, Chipcom Corporation, December 1991.

158. McCloghrie, K., and R. Fox, "IEEE 802.4 Token Bus MIB", RFC 1230, Hughes LAN Systems, Inc., Synoptics, Inc., May 1991.

159. McCloghrie, K., Fox, R., and E. Decker, "IEEE 802.5 Token Ring MIB", RFC 1231, Hughes LAN Systems, Inc., Synoptics, Inc., cisco Systems, Inc., May 1991.

160. Case, J., "FDDI Management Information Base", RFC 1285, SNMP Research, Incorporated, January 1992.

161. Baker, F., and C. Kolb, Editors, "Definitions of Managed Objects for the DS1 Interface Type", RFC 1232, ACC, Performance Systems International, Inc., May 1991.

162. Cox, T., and K. Tesink, Editors, "Definitions of Managed Objects for the DS3 Interface Type", RFC 1233, Bell Communications Research, May 1991.

163. Reynolds, J., "Reassignment of Experimental MIBs to Standard MIBs", RFC 1239, ISI, June 1991.

164. Cox, T., and K. Tesnik, Editors, "Definitions of Managed Objects for the SIP Interface Type", RFC 1304, Bell Communications Research, February 1992.

165. Stewart, B., Editor, "Definitions of Managed Objects for Character Stream Devices", RFC 1316, Xyplex, Inc., April 1992.

166. Stewart, B., Editor, "Definitions of Managed Objects for RS-232-like Hardware Devices", RFC 1317, Xyplex, Inc., April 1992.

167. Stewart, B., Editor, "Definitions of Managed Objects for Parallel-printer-like Hardware Devices", RFC 1318, Xyplex, Inc., April 1992.

168. Brown, C., Baker, F., and C. Carvalho, "Management Information Base for Frame Relay DTEs", RFC 1315, Wellfleet Communications, Inc., Advanced Computer Communications, April 1992.

169. Borenstein, N., and N. Freed, "MIME (Multipurpose Internet Mail Extensions): Mechanisms for Specifying and Describing the Format of Internet Message Bodies", RFC 1341, Bellcore, Innosoft, June 1992.

170. Simonsen, K., "Character Mnemonics & Character Sets", RFC 1345, Rationel Almen Planlaegning, June 1992.

171. Dorner, S., and P. Resnick, "Remote Mail Checking Protocol", RFC 1339, U. of Illinois at Urbana-Champaign, June 1992.

172. Everhart, C., Mamakos, L., Ullmann, R., and P. Mockapetris, Editors, "New DNS RR Definitions", RFC 1183, Transarc, University of Maryland, Prime Computer, ISI, October 1990.

173. Bradley, T., and C. Brown, "Inverse Address Resolution Protocol", RFC 1293, Wellfleet Communications, Inc., January 1992.

174. Manning, B. "DNS NSAP RRs", RFC 1348, Rice University, July 1992.

175. Simpson, W., "PPP Link Quality Monitoring", RFC 1333, Daydreamer, May 1992.

176. Baker, F., Editor, "Point-to-Point Protocol Extensions for Bridging", RFC 1220, ACC, April 1991.

177. McCloghrie, K., Davin, J., and J. Galvin, "Definitions of Managed Objects for Administration of SNMP Parties", RFC 1353, Hughes LAN Systems, Inc., MIT Laboratory for Computer Science, Trusted Information Systems, Inc., July 1992.

PEOPLE

[AB20] Art Berggreen ACC art@SALT.ACC.COM

[ABB2] A. Blasco Bonito CNUCE blasco@ICNUCEVM.CNUCE.CNR.IT

[AD14] Annette DeSchon ISI DESCHON@ISI.EDU

[AGM] Andy Malis BBN Malis@BBN.COM

[AKH5] Arthur Hartwig UQNET munnari!wombat.decnet.uq.oz.au!ccarthur@UUNET.UU.NET

[ANM2] April N. Marine SRI april@nisc.sri.com

[AW90] Amanda Walker Intercon AMANDA@INTERCON.COM

[AXB] Albert G. Broscius UPENN broscius@DSL.CIS.UPENN.EDU

[AXB1] Amatzia Ben-Artzi —none—

[AXB2] Andre Baux Bull baux@ec.bull.fr

[AXB3] Anil Bhavnani Kalpana, Inc. —none—

[AXB4] Alan Brind Cameo Communications, Inc. —none—

[AXC] Andrew Cherenson SGI arc@SGI.COM

[AXC1] Anthony Chung Sytek sytek!syteka!anthony@HPLABS.HP.COM

[AXF] Annmarie Freitas Microcom —none—

[AXH] Arthur Harvey DEC harvey@gah.enet.dec.com

[AXK] Anastasios Kotsikonas Boston University tasos@cs.bu.edu

[AXL] Alan Lloyd Datacraft alan@datacraft.oz

[AXM] Alex Martin Retix —none—

[AXM1] Ashok Marwaha Unisys —none—

[AXM2] Andrew McRae Megadata Pty Ltd. andrew@megadata.mega.oz.au

[AXP] Anil Prasad WilTel wiltel!aprasad@uunet.UU.NET

[AXP1] A. Pele OST —none—

[AXS] Arthur Salazar Locus lcc.arthur@SEAS.UCLA.EDU

[AXS1] Andrew Smith Ascom andrew@hasler.ascom.ch

[AXS2] Anil Singhal Frontier —none—

[BA4] Brian Anderson BBN baanders@CCQ.BBN.COM

[BCH2] Barry Howard LLNL Howard@NMFECC.LLNL.GOV

[BCN] B. Clifford Neuman ISI bcn@isi.edu

[BD70] Bernd Doleschal SEL Doleschal@A.ISI.EDU

[BH144] Bridget Halsey Banyan bah@BANYAN.BANYAN.COM

[BJR2] Bill Russell NYU russell@cmcl2.NYU.EDU

[BK29] Brian Kantor UCSD brian@UCSD.EDU

[BKR] Brian Reid DEC reid@DECWRL.DEC.COM

[BM60] Bede McCall Mitre bede@mitre.org

[BP52] Brad Parker CAYMAN brad@cayman.Cayman.COM

[BS221] Bob Stewart Xyplex STEWART@XYPLEX.COM

[BV15] Bernie Volz PSC VOLZ@PROCESS.COM

[BWB6] Barry Boehm DARPA boehm@DARPA.MIL

[BXA] Bill Anderson MITRE wda@MITRE-BEDFORD.ORG

[BXB] Brad Benson Touch —none—

[BXD] Brian Dockter Northwest Digital Systems —none—

[BXE] Brian A. Ehrmantraut Auspex Systems bae@auspex.com

[BXE1] Brendan Eich SGI brendan@illyria.wpd.sgi.com

[BXF] Bruce Factor Artificial Horizons, Inc. ahi!bigapple!bruce@uunet.UU.NET

[BXF1] Bill Flanagan Lotus Development Corp. bflanagan@lotus.com

[BXF2] Bob Friesenhahn PUREDATA Research/USA pdrusa!bob@uunet.UU.NET

[BXG] Bob Grady Tekelec —none—

[BXH] Brian Horn Locus —none—

[BXH1] Bill Harrell TI —none—

[BXK] Bill King Allen-Bradley Co. abvax!calvin.icd.ab.com!wrk@uunet.UU.NET

[BXK1] Bill Keatley American Airlines —none—

[BXK2] Bruce Kropp ADC Kentrox ktxc8!bruce@uunet.UU.NET

[BXL] Brian Lloyd SIRIUS —none—

[BXL1] Brian Lloyd Telebit brian@robin.telebit.com

[BXL2] Bernard Lemercier BIM bl@sunbim.be

[BXM] RL "Bob" Morgan Stanford University morgan@jessica.stanford.edu

[BXM1] Bob Meierhofer Computer Network Technology Corp. —none—

[BXN] Bill Norton Merit wbn@MERIT.EDU

[BXO] Brian O'Shea Visual bos@visual.com

[BXP] Brad Parke Intecom —none—

[BXP1] Brian Petry Systech Computer Corporation systech!bpetry@uunet.UU.NET

[BXR] Bob Rosenbaum WINDATA —none—

[BXR1] Bill Rose SSD Management, Inc. —none—

[BXS] Bill Simpson ACS bsimpson@vela.acs.oakland.edu

[BXS1] Blair Sanders Texas Instruments Blair_Sanders@mcimail.com

[BXS2] Bill Schilit Xerox PARC schilit@parc.xerox.com [BXT] Bruce Taber Interlan tabcr@europa.InterLan.COM

[BXV] Bill Versteeg NCR bvs@NCR.COM

[BXW] Brent Welch Sprite brent%sprite.berkeley.edu@GINGER.BERKELEY.EDU

[BXW1] Bruce Willins Raycom —none—

[BXZ] Bob Zaniolo Reuter —none—

[CLH3] Charles Hedrick RUTGERS HEDRICK@ARAMIS.RUTGERS.EDU

[CMR] Craig Rogers ISI Rogers@ISI.EDU

[CS1] Chikong Shue Cascade Communications Corp. alpo!chi@uunet.uu.net

[CWL] Charles W. Lynn, Jr. BBN CLYNN@BBN.COM

[CXA] Cyrus Azar Symplex Communications Corp. —none—

[CXB] Caralyn Brown Wellfleet cbrown%wellfleet.com@talcott.harvard.edu

[CXB1] Carl Beame Beame & Whiteside beame@ns.bws.com

[CXC] Creighton Chong Network Peripherals Inc. cchong@fastnet.com

[CXC1] Chih-Yi Chen Tatung Co., Ltd. TCCISM1%TWNTTIT.BITNET@pucc.Princeton.EDU

[CXC2] Chuck Chriss Trillium Digital Systems 76675.1372@compuserve.com

[CXD] Chuck Davin MIT jrd@ptt.lcs.mit.edu

[CXD1] Carl H. Dreyer RC International A/S chd@rci.dk

[CXD2] Charles Dulin Parallan Computer, Inc. —none—

[CXF] Catherine Foulston RICE cathyf@rice.edu

[CXH] Ching-Fa Hwang Proxar cfh@proxar.com

[CXH1] Claude Huss Matsushita Tokyo Research Labs claude@trc.mew.mei.co.jp

[CXI1] Clyde Iwamoto Stratacom cki@strata.com

[CXL] Chung Lam Fujitsu —none—

[CXL1] Christopher Leong DEC leong@kolmod.mlo.dec.com

[CXM] Charles Marker II MIPS marker@MIPS.COM

[CXM1] Carl Madison Star-Tek, Inc. carl@startek.com

[CXM2] Carl Marcinik Formation, Inc. —none—

[CXM3] Chuck McManis Sun Chuck.McManis@Eng.Sun.COM

[CXR] Cheryl Krupczak NCR clefor@secola.columbia.ncr.com

[CXS] Craig Scott NetWorth, Inc. —none—

[CXS1] Chip Standifer Technology Dynamics, Inc. TDYNAMICS@MCIMAIL.COM

[CXT] Christopher Tengi Princeton tengi@Princeton.EDU

[CXT1] Chris Thomas Intel Corporation —none—

[CXV] Carl Vanderbeek Automated Network Management, Inc. —none—

[CXW] Christopher Wheeler UW cwheeler@cac.washignton.edu

[CXW1] Charles Watt SecureWare watt@sware.com

[DAG4] David A. Gomberg MITRE gomberg@GATEWAY.MITRE.ORG

[DB14] Dave Borman Cray dab@CRAY.COM

[DC126] Dick Cogger Cornell rhx@CORNELLC.CIT.CORNELL.EDU

[DCP1] David Plummer MIT DCP@SCRC-QUABBIN.ARPA

[DDC1] David Clark MIT ddc@LCS.MIT.EDU

[DG223] Doug Goodall Goodall Software goodall!doug@uunet.uu.net

[DJK13] David Kaufman DeskTalk —none—

[DLM1] David Mills LINKABIT Mills@HUEY.UDEL.EDU

[DM28] Dennis Morris DCA Morrisd@IMO-UVAX.DCA.MIL

[DM280] Dave Mackie NCD lupine!djm@UUNET.UU.NET

[DM354] Don McWilliam UBC mcwillm@CC.UBC.CA

[DP4Q] Drew Perkins InterStream Drew.Perkins@ANDREW.CMU.EDU

[DP666] Don Provan Novell donp@xlnvax.novell.com

[DR48] Doug Rosenthal MCC rosenthal@mcc.com

[DR137] David Rageth Martin Marietta DAVE@MMC.COM

[DRC3] Dave Cheriton STANFORD cheriton@PESCADERO.STANFORD.EDU

[DT15] Daniel Tappan BBN Tappan@BBN.COM

[DT167] Dennis Thomas Tektronics dennist@tektronix.TEK.COM

[DW181] David Wolfe SRI ctabka@TSCA.ISTC.SRI.COM

[DW183] David Waitzman BBN dwaitzman@BBN.COM

[DW238] Dave Windorski UWisc DAVID.WINDORSKI@MAIL.ADMIN.WISC.EDU

[DXA] Dave Atkinson Kinmel Park —none—

[DXB] Dave Buehmann Intergraph ingr!daveb@UUNET.UU.NET

[DXB1] Dan Bernstein NYU brnstnd@stealth.acf.nyu.edu

[DXB2] Dennis E. Baasch Emerging Technologies, Inc. etinc!dennis@uu.psi.com

[DXB3] David A. Brown BICC fzbicdb@uk.ac.ucl

[DXB4] Donna Beatty MICOM Communication Corporation SYSAD@prime.micom.com

[DXC] Dale Cabell NetCom —none—

[DXC1] Darren Croke Micronics Computers Inc. dc@micronics.com

[DXC2] Dale Cabell XTree cabell@smtp.xtree.com

[DXD] Dennis J.W. Dube VIA SYSTEMS —none—

[DXE] Douglas Egan Nokia —none—

[DXF] Dave Feldmeier Bellcore dcf@thumper.bellcore.com

[DXG] David Goldberg SMI sun!dg@UCBARPA.BERKELEY.EDU

[DXG1] Don Gibson Aston-Tate sequent!aero!twinsun!ashtate.A-T.COM!dong@uunet.UU.NET

[DXG2] David B. Gurevich DHL Systems dgurevic@rhubarb.ssf-sys.dhl.com

[DXH] Donna Hopkins US West Advance Technologies dmhopki@uswat.uswest.com

[DXH1] Dave Hudson Kendall Square Research (KSR) tdh@uunet.UU.NET

[DXJ] David Joyner NCSU Computing Center david@unity.ncsu.edu

[DXK] Doug Karl OSU KARL-D@OSU-20.IRCC.OHIO-STATE.EDU

[DXK1] Dwain Kinghorn Microsoft microsoft!dwaink@cs.washington.edu

[DXK2] Dror Kessler DigiBoard dror@digibd.com

[DXK3] David E. Kaufman Magnalink Communications Corporation —none—

[DXL] David Lin Zenith —none—

[DXL1] Dave LeBlang Atria Software leglang@atria.com

[DXM] Didier Moretti Ungermann-Bass —none—

[DXM2] David Mittnacht Computer Protocol —none—

[DXM3] Danny Mitzel Hughes dmitzel@whitney.hac.com

[DXM4] Deron Meranda Cincinnati Bell Info. Systems, Inc. bem56094@ucunix.san.uc.EDU

[DXM5] Donna McMaster SynOptics mcmaster@synoptics.com

[DXN] Danny Nessett LLNL Livermore Computer Center nessett@ocfmail.ocf.llnl.gov

[DXP] Dave Preston CMC —none—

[DXP1] David Perkins Synoptics dperkins@synoptics.com

[DXP2] Dave Presotto AT&T presotto@reseach.att.com

[DXR] Debbie Reed Fujikura —none—

[DXR1] Don Rooney ACCTON —none—

[DXR2] David Rhein HCSD davidr@ssd.csd.harris.com

[DXR3] David Reed MIT-LCS —none—

[DXS] Dan Shia DSET dset!shia@uunet.UU.NET

[DXS1] Daisy Shen IBM —none—

[DXS2] Dale Shelton Roadnet —none—

[DXS3] Daniel Steinber SUN Daniel.Steinberg@Eng.Sun.COM

[DXS4] Dirk Smith Nu-Mega Technologies, Inc. —none—

[DXT] Deepak Taneja Banyan Deepak=Tancja%Eng%Banyan@Thing.banyan.com

[DXT1] David Taylor Empros Systems International dtaylor@ems.cdc.com

[DXV] D. Venkatrangan Metrix venkat@metrix.com

[DXW] Dan Willie Codenoll Tech. Corp. —none—

[DXW1] Don Weir Skyline Technology, Inc. —none—

[DY26] Dennis Yaro SUN yaro@SUN.COM

[EAK4] Earl Killian LLL EAK@MORDOR.S1.GOV

[EBM] Eliot Moss MIT EBM@XX.LCS.MIT.EDU

[EP53] Eric Peterson Locus lcc.eric@SEAS.UCLA.EDU

[EXB] Etienne Baudras-Chardigny RCE —none—

[EXC] Ed Cain DCA cain@edn-unix.dca.mil

[EXC1] Eric Cooper Fore Systems, Inc. ecc@fore.com

[EXD] Eric Decker cisco cire@cisco.com

[EXF] Ed Fudurich Gateway Communications, Inc. —none—

[EXG] Errol Ginsberg Ridgeback Solutions bacchus!zulu!errol@uu2.psi.com

[EXM] Eldon S. Mast Netrix Systems Corporation esm@netrix.com

[EXO] Eric Olinger Peregrine Systems eric@peregrine.com

[EXR] Eric Rubin FiberCom err@FIBERCOM.COM

[EXR1] Efrat Ramati Lannet Co. —none—

[EXR2] Edwards E. Reed Xerox ipcontact.cin_ops@xerox.com

[EXW] E. Wald DEC ewald@via.enet.dec.com

[EXX] Eduardo ESA EDUATO%ESOC.BITNET@CUNYVM.CUNY.EDU

[FB77] Fred Baker ACC fbaker@acc.com

[FEIL] Unisys feil@kronos.nisd.cam.unisys.com

[FJW] Frank J. Wancho WSMR WANCHO@WSMR-SIMTEL20.ARMY.MIL

[FXB1] Felix Burton DIAB FB@DIAB.SE

[FXF] Farhad Fozdar OSCOM International f_fozdar@fennel.cc.uwa.edu.au

[GAL5] Guillermo A. Loyola IBM LOYOLA@IBM.COM

[GB7] Gerd Beling FGAN GBELING@ISI.EDU

[GEOF] Geoff Goodfellow OSD Geoff@FERNWOOD.MPK.CA.US

[GM23] Glenn Marcy CMU Glenn.Marcy@A.CS.CMU.EDU

[GS2] Greg Satz cisco satz@CISCO.COM

[GS91] Guy Streeter Intergraph guy@guy.bll.ingr.com

[GS123] Geof Stone NSC geof@NETWORK.COM

[GSM11] Gary S. Malkin Xylogics GMALKIN@XYLOGICS.COM

[GXA] Glen Arp Protools —none—

[GXB] Gerard Berthet Independence Technologies gerard@indetech.com

[GXC] Greg Chesson SGI Greg@SGI.COM

[GXC1] George Clapp Bellcore meritec!clapp@bellcore.bellcore.com

[GXC2] Gordon C. Galligher gorpong@ping.chi.il.us

[GXD] Glenn Davis Unidata davis@unidata.ucar.edu

[GXD1] Gordon Day INDE Electronics gday@cs.ubc.ca

[GXG] Gil Greenbaum Unisys gcole@nisd.cam.unisys.com

[GXH] Graham Hudspith INMOS gwh@inmos.co.uk

[GXH1] Gary Haney Martin Marietta Energy Systems haneyg@ornl.gov

[GXH2] Greg Hummel Cellular Technical Servuces —none—

[GXK] Gunther Kroenert Siemens Nixdorf Informationssyteme AG —none—

[GXL] Glenn Levitt McData Corporation gpl0363@mcmail.mcdata.com

[GXM] Gerald McBrearty IBM —none—

[GXM1] Glenn Mansfield AIC Systems Laboratories Ltd. glenn@aic.co.jp

[GXM2] Garry McCracken TIL Systems, Ltd. —none—

[GXN] Gunnar Nilsson Ericsson —none—

[GXP] Gill Pratt MIT gill%mit-ccc@MC.LCS.MIT.EDU

[GXP1] Greg Pflaum IRIS iris.com!Greg_Pflaum@uunet.uu.net

[GXS] Guenther Schreiner LINK snmp-admin@ira.uka.de

[GXS1] George Sandoval Fibernet —none—

[GXT] Glenn Trewitt STANFORD trewitt@AMADEUS.STANFORD.EDU

[GXT1] Gene Tsudik USC tsudik@USC.EDU

[GXW] Glenn Waters Bell Northern gwaters@BNR.CA

[GXW1] Gil Widdowson Interphase —none—

[GXW2] Graham Welling Dynatech Communications s8000!gcw@uunet.uu.net

[HCF2] Harry Forsdick BBN Forsdick@BBN.COM

[HS23] Hokey Stenn Plus5 hokey@PLUS5.COM

[HWB] Hans-Werner Braun MICHIGAN HWB@MCR.UMICH.EDU

[HXB] Henk Boetzkes Netexp Research —none—

[HXD] Hans Jurgen Dorr Digital-Kienzle Computersystems —none—

[HXE] Hunaid Engineer Cray hunaid@OPUS.CRAY.COM

[HXE1] Hartvig Ekner Dowty Network Systems A/S hj@dowtyns.dk

[HXF] Harley Frazee T3Plus harley@io.t3plus.com

[HXF1] Hiroshi Fujii ASTEC, Inc. fujii@astec.co.jp

[HXH] Harald Hoeg Tandberg Data A/S haho%huldra.uucp@nac.no

[HXH1] Howard C. Herbert AES —none—

[HXH2] Hidekazu Hagiwara Takaoka Electric Mfg. Co., Ltd. hagiwara@takaoka.takaoka-electric.co.jp

[HXK] Henry Kaijak Gandalf —none—

[HXK1] Hiroshi Kume Fuji Xerox Co., Ltd. Kume%KSPB%Fuji_Xerox@tcpgw.netg.ksp.fujixerox.co.jp

[HXL] Henry Lee TRW henry@trwind.ind.trw.com

[HXL1] Hugh Lockhart Telecommunication Systems —none—

[HXM] Hsiang Ming Ma Asante Technology —none—

[HXN] Henry P. Nagai D-Link —none—

[HXN1] Heinz Nisi Richard Hirschmann GmbH & Co. mia@intsun.rus.uni-stuttgart.de

[HXP] Hong K. Paik Samsung paik@samsung.com

[HXS] Heidi Stettner Basis, Inc. heidi@mtxinu.COM

[HXT] Hugh Thomas DEC thomas@oils.enet.dec.com

[HXT1] Hubert Theissen AEG KABEL —none—

[HXU] Hirotaka Usuda Hitachi —none—

[IEEE] Vince Condello IEEE —none—

[IXD] Ian Dickinson WUCS vato@cu.warwick.ac.uk

[IXD1] Israel Drori LANOPTICS LTD. Israel raanan@techunix.technion.ac.il

[IXG] Ian George MegaPAC —none—

[IXH] Ippei Hayashi Fujitsu Limited hayashi@sysrap.cs.fujitsu.co.jp

[JAG] James Gosling SUN JAG@SUN.COM

[JB478] Jonathan Biggar Netlabs jon@netlabs.com

[JBP] Jon Postel ISI Postel@ISI.EDU

[JBW1] Joseph Walters, Jr. BBN JWalters@BBN.COM

[JCB1] John Burruss BBN JBurruss@VAX.BBN.COM

[JCM48] Jeff Mogul DEC mogul@DECWRL.DEC.COM

[JD21] Jonathan Dreyer BBN Dreyer@CCV.BBN.COM

[JDC20] Jeffrey Case UTK case@UTKUX1.UTK.EDU

[JFH2] Jack Haverty Oracle Corporation jhaverty@ORACLE.COM

[JFW] Jon F. Wilkes STC Wilkes@CCINT1.RSRE.MOD.UK

[JGH] Jim Herman BBN Herman@CCJ.BBN.COM

[JG423] John Gawf Compatible Systems Corporation gawf@compatible.com

[JJB25] John Bowe BBN jbowe@PINEAPPLE.BBN.COM

[JPH17] John Hanley Oracle jhanley@oracle.com

[JKR1] Joyce K. Reynolds ISI JKRey@ISI.EDU

[JR35] Jon Rochlis MIT jon@ATHENA.MIT.EDU

[JRL3] John R. LoVerso CCUR loverso@westford.ccur.com

[JS28] John A. Shriver Proteon jas@PROTEON.COM

[JTM4] John Moy Proteon jmoy@PROTEON.COM

[JWF] Jim Forgie MIT/LL FORGIE@XN.LL.MIT.EDU

[JXB] Jeffrey Buffun Apollo jbuffum@APOLLO.COM

[JXB1] John M. Ballard Microsoft jballard@microsoft.com

[JXB2] John Burnett ATM —none—

[JXC] John Cook Chipcom cook@chipcom.com

[JXC1] Jeff Carton American Express Travel Rel. Ser. jcarton@amex-trs.com

[JXC2] Joseph Chen Symbol Technology, Inc. —none—

[JXD] Julie Dmytryk Ultra Julie_Dmytryk.MKT@usun.ultra.com

[JXD1] James Davidson NGC ngc!james@uunet.UU.NET

[JXE2] Jeanne Evans UKMOD JME%RSRE.MOD.UK@CS.UCL.AC.UK

[JXF] Josh Fielk Optical Data Systems —none—

[JXF1] Jeff Freeman Emulex —none—

[JXG] Jerry Geisler Boeing —none—

[JXG1] Jim Greuel HP jimg%hpcndpc@hplabs.hp.com

[JXG2] Jeremy Greene LearningTree taipan!greene@uunet.UU.NET

[JXG3] James L. Gula Corollary, Inc. gula@corollary.com

[JXH] Jeffrey C. Honig Cornell jch@gated.cornell.edu

[JXH1] Jim Hayes Apple Hayes@APPLE.COM

[JXI] Jon Infante ICL —none—

[JXI1] John Ioannidis Columbia ji@close.cs.columbia.edu

[JXK] Joanna Karwowska DGC karwowska@dg-rtp.dg.com

[JXK1] Jon Kepecs Legato kepecs@Legato.COM

[JXL] John Light GSS johnl@gssc.gss.com

[JXM] Joseph Murdock Network Resources Corporation —none—

[JXM1] Jim Miner Star Technologies miner@star.com

[JXO] Jack O'Neil ENCORE —none—

[JXO1] Jerrilynn Okamura Ontologic —none—

[JXO2] Jarkko Oikarinen Tolsun jto@TOLSUN.OULU.FI

[JXO3] John Ioannidis Columbia ji@close.cs.columbia.edu

[JXP] Joe Pato Apollo apollo!pato@EDDIE.MIT.EDU

[JXP1] Jas Parmar Synernetics jas@synnet.com

[JXP2] John Pickens 3Com jrp@3Com.com

[JXR] Jacob Rekhter IBM Yakov@IBM.COM

[JXR1] Jens T. Rasmussen CERN jenst%cernvax.cern.ch@CUNYVM.CUNY.EDU

[JXR2] James Rice Stanford RICE@SUMEX-AIM.STANFORD.EDU

[JXR3] Jacques Roth Netronix, Inc. —none—

[JXS] Jim Stevens Rockwell Stevens@ISI.EDU

[JXS1] John Sancho CastleRock —none—

[JXS2] Jon Saperia DEC saperia@tcpjon.enet.dec.com

[JXS3] Jonathan Stone Victoria University jonathan@isor.vuw.ac.nz

[JXS4] John K. Scoggin, Jr. Delmarva Power scoggin@delmarva.com

[JXS5] Jeremy Siegel 3COM jzs@NSD.3Com.COM

[JXT] Jim Taylor Kodak taylor@heart.epps.kodak.com

[JXT1] Jimmy Tu Digital Link jimmy@dl.com

[JXW] James Watt NNC —none—

[JXY] J. Yoshida NKK Corp. —none—

[JXZ] Jon Ziegler Artel Ziegler@Artel.com

[KAA] Ken Adelman TGV, Inc. Adelman@TGV.COM

[KA4] Karl Auerbach Empirical Tools and Technologies karl@empirical.com

[KH43] Kathy Huber BBN khuber@bbn.com

[KH157] Kory Hamzeh Fibermux ames!avatar.com!kory@harvard.harvard.edu

[KLH] Ken Harrenstien SRI KLH@nisc.sri.com

[KR35] Keith Reynolds SCO keithr@SCO.COM

[KSL] Kirk Lougheed cisco LOUGHEED@MATHOM.CISCO.COM

[KXA] Kannan Alagappan DEC kannan@sejour.enet.dec.comp

[KXB] Keith Boyce Legent —none—

[KXC] Ken Chapman Stratus Computer Ken_Chapman@vos.stratus.com

[KXD] Kevin DeVault NI —none—

[KXD1] Kathryn de Graaf David Systems degraaf@davidsys.com

[KXF] Karl Fox MST karl@MorningStar.Com

[KXF1] Ken Fujimoto Tribe Computer Works fuji@tribe.com

[KXG] Kevin Gage Chase Research

[KXH] Khalid Hireche G2R Inc. —none—

[KXH1] Keith Hogan Penril keith%penril@uunet.uu.net

[KXJ] Ken Jones KonKord konkord!ksj@uunet.uu.net

[KXL] Kim Le DATAHOUSE Information Systems Ltd. —none—

[KXM] Kevin Murphy DEC murphy@sevens.lkg.dec.com

[KXR] Ken Ritchie SEEL —none—

[KXS] Keith Sklower Berkeley sklower@okeeffe.berkeley.edu

[KXS1] Kevin Smith Telematics International, Inc. —none—

[KXS2] Keld Simonsen RAP Keld.Simonsen@dkuug.dk

[KXT] Kaj Tesink Bellcore kaj@nvuxr.cc.bellcore.com

[KXT1] Kent Tsuno SEI tsuno@sumitomo.com

[KXV] Ken Virgile Sigma Net. Sys. signet!ken@xylogics.COM

[KXW] Ken Whitfield MCNC ken@MCNC.ORG

[KXW1] Kathy Weninger Network Resources Corporation —none—

[KZM] Keith McCloghrie HLS KZM@HLS.COM

[LL69] Lawrence Lebahn DIA DIA3@PAXRV-NES.NAVY.MIL

[LLP] Larry Peterson ARIZONA llp@ARIZONA.EDU

[LS8] Louis Steinberg Rutgers lou@ARAMIS.RUTGERS.EDU

[LXA] Lorenzo Aguilar Taligent lorenzo@taligent.com

[LXB] Larry Burton APTEC Computer Systems ssds!larryb@uunet.UU.NET

[LXB1] Laura Bridge Timeplex laura@uunet.UU.NET

[LXB2] Lawrence Brown Unisys —none—

[LXB3] Larry Barnes DEC barnes@broke.enet.dec.com

[LXD] Larry DeLuca AT henrik@EDDIE.MIT.EDU

[LXD1] Larry Davis C. Itoh Electronics —none—

[LXE] Len Edmondson SUN len@TOPS.SUN.COM

[LXF] Larry Fischer DSS lfischer@dss.com

[LXH] Leo Hourvitz NeXt leo@NEXT.COM

[LXL] Lennart Lovstrand NeXT Computer, Inc. Lennart_Lovstrand@NeXT.COM

[LXM] Louis Mamakos UMD louie@sayshell.umd.edu

[LXO] Larry Osterman GTE Telecom larryo@gtetele.com

[LXP] Lars Povlsen Olicom A/S krus@olicom.dk

[LXS] Lance Sprung SMC —none—

[LXW] Lih-Er Wey MSU WEYLE@msu.edu

[LZ15] Lee Ziegenhals Datapoint lcz@sat.datapoint.com

[MA] Mike Accetta CMU MIKE.ACCETTA@CMU-CS-A.EDU

[MA108] Mike Anello XDI mike@xlnt.com

[MAR10] Mark A. Rosenstein MIT mar@ATHENA.MIT.EDU

[MB] Michael Brescia BBN Brescia@CCV.BBN.COM

[MBG] Michael Greenwald SYMBOLICS Greenwald@SCRC-STONY-BROOK.SYMBOLICS.COM

[MCSJ] Mike StJohns TPSC stjohns@UMD5.UMD.EDU

[ME38] Marc A. Elvy Marble ELVY@CARRARA.MARBLE.COM

[MG277] Martin Gren Axis Communications AB martin@axis.se

[MKL] Mark Lottor SRI MKL@nisc.sri.com

[ML109] Mike Little MACOM little@MACOM4.ARPA

[MLS34] L. Michael Sabo TMAC Sabo@DOCKMASTER.NCSC.MIL

[MO2] Michael O'Brien AEROSPACE obrien@AEROSPACE.AERO.ORG

[MRC] Mark Crispin Simtel MRC@WSMR-SIMTEL20.ARMY.MIL

[MS9] Marty Schoffstahl Nysernet schoff@NISC.NYSER.NET

[MS56] Marvin Solomon WISC solomon@CS.WISC.EDU

[MTR] Marshall T. Rose PSI mrose@PSI.COM

[MXA] Mike Asagami Toshiba toshiba@mothra.nts.uci.edu

[MXB] Mike Berrow Relational Technology —none—

[MXB1] Mike Burrows DEC burrows@SRC.DEC.COM

[MXB2] Mark T. Dauscher Sybus Corportation mdauscher@sybus.com

[MXB3] Michael Bell Integrated Business Network —none—

[MXC] Ming-Perng Chen CCL/ITRI
N100CMP0%TWNITRI1.BITNET@CUNYVM.CUNY.EDU

[MXC1] Mark McCahill UMN mpm@boombox.micro.umn.edu

[MXC2] Matt Christiano Olivettti globes@matt@oliveb.atc.olivetti.com

[MXE] Mike Erlinger Lexel mike@lexcel.com

[MXF] Mark Fabbi Bell Canada markf@gpu.utcs.utoronto.ca

[MXF1] Marco Framba Olivetti framba@orc.olivetti.com

[MXF2] Martin Forssen Chalmers maf@dtek.chalmers.se

[MXH] Matt Harris Versitron —none—

[MXH1] Masahiko Hori Mitsubishi Cable Industries, Ltd. —none—

[MXH2] Mark Holobach Electronic Data Systems holobach@tis.eds.com

[MXH3] Mark Hankin Lancert —none—

[MXL] Mark L. Lambert MIT markl@PTT.LCS.MIT.EDU

[MXL1] Mats Lindstrom Diab Data AB mli@diab.se

[MXL2] Mark S. Lewis Telebit mlewis@telebit.com

[MXN] Mark Needleman UCDLA mhnur%uccmvsa.bitnet@cornell.cit.cornell.edu

[MXL2] Mark Lenney Raylan Corporation —none—

[MXO] Mike O'Dowd EPFL odowd@ltisun8.epfl.ch

[MXO1] Mike Oswald J.I. Case mike@helios.uwsp.edu

[MXP] Martin Picard Oracle —none—

[MXP1] Michael Podhorodecki Labtam Australia Pty. Ltd. michael@labtam.oz.au

[MXR] Maurice R. Turcotte RMIS mailrus!uflorida!rm1!dnmrt%rmatl@uunet.UU.NET

[MXS] Mike Spina Prime WIZARD%enr.prime.com@RELAY.CS.NET

[MXS1] Martha Steenstrup BBN MSteenst@BBN.COM

[MXS2] Michael Sapich CCCBS sapich@conware.de

[MXS3] Marc Sheldon BinTec ms@BinTec.DE

[MXS4] Marc Sheldon EUnet Germany ms@Germany.EU.net

[MXT] Martyn Thomas Insignia Solutions —none—

[MXT1] Mark Tom NET marktom@tom.net.com

[MXW] Michael Waters EON —none—

[MXZ] Mauro Zallocco Netlink —none—

[NC3] J. Noel Chiappa MIT JNC@XX.LCS.MIT.EDU

[NT12] Neil Todd IST mcvax!ist.co.uk!neil@UUNET.UU.NET

[NXC] Nick Cuccia NASA Ames Research Center cuccia@nas.nasa.gov

[NXE] Nadya K. El-Afandi NSC nadya@khara.network.com

[NXH] Nicola J. Howarth ANSA njh@ansa.co.uk

[NXK] Nagayuki Kojima Japan Radio Co. nkojima@lab.nihonmusen.co.jp

[NXL] Nik Langrind Shiva Corp. nik@Shiva.COM

[NXM] Nob Mizuno Matsushita Electric Industrial Co., Ltd. mizuno@isl.mei.co.jp

[NXP] Narendra Popat FSD —none—

[NXR] Nelluri L. Reddy CDC reddy@uc.msc.umn.edu

[OXC] Olivier J. Caleff Dassault caleff@dassault-elec.fr

[OXF] Osamu Fujiki DCL —none—

[OXG] Oyvind Gjerstad Tollpost-Globe AS ogj%tglobe2.UUCP@nac.no

[OXI] Oft Israel Rad —none—

[OXJ] Oliver Jones PictureTel Corporation oj@pictel.com

[OXK] Oliver Korfmacher netCS Informationstechnik GmbH okorf@bunt.netcs.com

[OXR] Oscar Rodriguez Dupont —none—

[PAM6] Paul McNabb RICE pam@PURDUE.EDU

[PCW] C. Philip Wood LANL cpw@LANL.GOV

[PD39] Pete Delaney ECRC pete%crcvax.uucp%germany.csnet@RELAY.CS.NET

[PHD1] Pieter Ditmars BBN pditmars@BBN.COM

[PK] Peter Kirstein UCL Kirstein@NSS.CS.UCL.AC.UK

[PL4] Phil Lapsley BERKELEY phil@UCBARPA.BERKELEY.EDU

[PM1] Paul Mockapetris ISI PVM@ISI.EDU

[PXA] Prakash Ambegaonkar FTC —none—

[PXA1] Paul Afshar Solarix Systems paul@solar1.portal.com

[PXA2] Paul Andon MICROGNOSIS pandon@micrognosis.co.uk

[PXB] Pat Barron Transarc Corporation Pat_Barron@TRANSARC.COM

[PXB1] Pascal Bataille GSI pascal.bataille@gsi.fr

[PXC] Peter Cox ENE —none—

[PXC1] Patrick Cheng TRW pcheng@dill.ind.trw.com

[PXC2] Paolo Coppo CSELT coppo@cz8700.cselt.stet.it

[PXC3] Paul Chefurka PlainTree Systems Inc. chefurka@plntree.UUCP

[PXD] Peter Delchiappo MTrade UK Ltd. —none—

[PXE] Peter S. Easton Brixton Systems, Inc. easton@brixton.com

[PXF] Per Futtrup SDD (Scandinavian Airlines Data Denmark A/S) —none—

[PXG] Pete Grillo Network Innovations pl0143@mail.psi.net

[PXH] Per Bech Hansen DDE pbh@dde.dk

[PXJ] Prem Jain Crescendo prem@cres.com

[PXJ1] Petri Jokela Telecom Finland —none—

[PXK] Philip Koch Dartmouth Philip.Koch@DARTMOUTH.EDU

[PXK1] Peter Kumik Case Comm. —none—

[PXK2] Professor Kynikos Special Consultant —none—

[PXK3] Paul Krystosek DOE Atmospheric Radiation Measurement Project krystosk@eid.anl.gov

[PXL] Paul Liu ADI Systems, Inc. —none—

[PXL1] Reter de Laval SECTRA pdl@sectra.se

[PXM] Paul Maurer II STS —none—

[PXM1] Patrick McNamee GE —none—

[PXO] Paul O'Donnell Basser paulod@cs.su.oz.au

[PXR] Paul Rodwick Metaphor —none—

[PXR1] Parag Rastogi Vitacom Corporation parag@cup.portal.com

[PXS] Paul Singh Intellicom —none—

[PXV] Paul V. Fries Alantec pvf@alantec.com

[PXY] Peter C. Yoest American Power Conversion Corp. apc!yoest@uunet.uu.net

[PXY1] Paul Hoff Norwegian Telecom Research paalh@brage.nta.no

[RA11] Rick Adams UUNET rick@UUNET.UU.NET

[RAM57] Rex Mann CDC —none—

[RAW44] Robert A. Woodburn Sparta WOODY@SPARTA.COM

[RDXS] R. Dwight Schettler HP rds%hpcndm@HPLABS.HP.COM

[RH6] Robert Hinden BBN Hinden@CCV.BBN.COM

[RH227] Ron Holt Eyring, Inc. ron@Eyring.COM

[RHT] Robert Thomas BBN BThomas@F.BBN.COM

[RM1] Richard Mak Amnet, Inc. mak@amnet.COM

[RN6] Rudy Nedved CMU Rudy.Nedved@CMU-CS-A.EDU

[RP211] Ragnar Paulson TSG tsgfred!ragnar@uunet.UU.NET

[RTB3] Bob Braden ISI Braden@ISI.EDU

[RWS4] Robert W. Scheifler ARGUS RWS@XX.LCS.MIT.EDU

[RXB] Ramesh Babu Luxcom krbabu@btr.com

[RXB1] Ron Bhanukitsiri DEC rbhank@DECVAX.DEC.COM

[RXB2] Rich Bantel AT&T rgb@mtung.att.com

[RXB3] Robert Woodburn SAIC woody@cseic.saic.com

[RXB4] Russ Blaesing Open Networks Engineering, Inc. rrb@one.com

[RXC] Rob Chandhok CMU chandhok@gnome.cs.cmu.edu

[RXC1] Rick Carlos TI rick.ticipa.csc.ti.com

[RXC2] Ray Compton DIS Research LTD rayc@command.com

[RXD] Roger Dev Cabletron —none—

[RXD1] Ralph Droms NRI rdroms@NRI.RESTON.VA.US

[RXD2] Rajiv Dhingra Ultranet rajiv@ULTRA.COM

[RXD3] Rex Davis Tandem —none—

[RXD4] Rick Downs AMP —none—

[RXD5] Russell S. Dietz Technically Elite Concepts, Inc. Russell_Dietz@Mcimail.com

[RXE] Robert R. Elz Webster Computer kre@munnari.oz.au

[RXF] Richard Fox Synoptics rfox@synoptics.com

[RXH] Reijane Huai Cheyenne sibal@CSD2.NYU.EDU

[RXH1] Russ Housley Xerox Russ_Housley.McLean_CSD@xerox.com

[RXI] Robin Iddon Axon Networks Inc. axon@cix.clink.co.uk

[RXJ] Ronald Jacoby SGI rj@SGI.COM

[RXL] Rich Lyman Lantronix rich@alecto.gordian.com

[RXM] Robert Myhill BBN Myhill@CCS.BBN.COM

[RXN] Rina Nethaniel RND —none—

[RXN1] Russ Nelson Clarkson nelson@clutx.clarkson.edu

[RXN2] R. Nurnberg AEG Electrcom —none—

[RXR] Richard Rein Pyramid Technology Corp. rein@pyramid.com

[RXR1] R. K. Nair NRL nair@itd.nrl.navy.mil

[RXS] Ron Strich SSDS —none—

[RXS1] Reuben Sivan Crosscomm crossc!rsivan@uunet.UU.NET

[RXS2] Richard Schneider Epson Research Center rschneid@epson.com

[RXS3] Richard P. Stubbs Quotron Systems, Inc. richard@atd.quotron.com

[RXS4] Rob Spade I.D.E. Corporation —none—

[RXT] Ron Thornton GenRad thornton@qm7501.genrad.com

[RXT1] Rodney Thayer Sable —none—

[RXU] Robert Urquhart Simon Fraser University quipu@sfu.ca

[RXW] Russell G. Wilson Hill AFB rwilson@oodis01.af.mil

[RXW1] R. J. White Univ. of Waterloo snmp-tech@watmath.waterloo.edu

[RXZ] Rayan Zachariassen Toronto rayan@AI.TORONTO.EDU

[SAF3] Stuart A. Friedberg UWISC stuart@CS.WISC.EDU

[SB98] Stan Barber BCM SOB@BCM.TMC.EDU

[SC3] Steve Casner ISI Casner@ISI.EDU

[SGC] Steve Chipman BBN Chipman@F.BBN.COM

[SH284] Steve Hardcastle-Kille ISODE Consortium S.Kille@isode.com

[SHB] Steven Blumenthal BBN BLUMENTHAL@VAX.BBN.COM

[SH37] Sergio Heker JVNC heker@JVNCC.CSC.ORG

[SL70] Stuart Levy UMN slevy@UC.MSC.UMN.EDU

[SMB] Scott Bellew Purdue smb@cs.purdue.edu

[SRN1] Stephen Northcutt NSWC SNORTHC@RELAY-NSWC.NAVY.MIL

[SS92] Steve Schoch NASA SCHOCH@AMES.ARC.NASA.GOV

[STY] Shannon Yeh Netix yeh@netix.com

[SW159] Steven Willis Wellfleet swillis@WELLFLEET.COM

[SXA] Susie Armstrong XEROX Armstrong.wbst128@XEROX.COM

[SXA1] Shamim Ahmed OSU ahmed@nisca.ircc.ohio-state.edu

[SXA2] Steve Alexander ISC stevea@i88.isc.com

[SXA3] Sten Andler IBM —none—

[SXB] Steve Briggs Compaq steveb@se.hou.compaq.com

[SXB2] Steve Bush GEIS sfb@ncoast.org

[SXC] Shaw C. Chuang University College London S.Chuang@cs.ucl.ac.uk

[SXD] Steve Deering Stanford deering@PECASERO.STANFORD.EDU

[SXD1] Steve Dorner U. of Illinois s-dorner@UIUC.EDU

[SXE] Simon Edwards Micro Focus UK —none—

[SXF] Shoji Fukutomi Furukawa Electoric Co. Ltd.
kddlab!polo.furukawa.co.jp!fuku@uunet.UU.NET

[SXH] Steven Hunter LLNL hunter@CCC.MFECC.LLNL.GOV

[SXH1] Scott Hahn Sequent sdh@sequent.com

[SXH2] Scott Holley Allied Telesis, Inc. SCOTT_CLINTON_HOLLEY@cup.portal.com

[SXH3] Steve Harris Republic Telcom Systems, Inc. rtsc!harris@boulder.Colorado.edu

[SXH4] Simon Hackett Internode Systems Pty Ltd simon@ucs.adelaide.edu.au

[SXH5] Stefan Hedemann Hedemann Software Development 100015.2504@compuserve.com

[SXK] Skip Koppenhaver DAC stubby!skip@uunet.UU.NET

[SXK1] Stev Knowles FTP stev@vax.ftp.com

[SXL] Sam Lau Pirelli/Focom —none—

[SXL1] Stephen Lewis Scitec —none—

[SXL2] Steve Loring L & N Technologies, Ltd. —none—

[SXL3] Syd Logan AGE Logic syd@age.com

[SXM] Sheri Mayhew Develcon zaphod!sherim@herald.usask.ca

[SXM1] Skip Morton Netcore, Inc. —none—

[SXO] SeeYoung Oh Daewoo Telecom oco@scorpio.dwt.co.kr

[SXP] Sanand Patel Canstar sanand@HUB.TORONTO.EDU

[SXP1] Satish Popat Ericsson-Camtec —none—

[SXS] Steve Silverman MITRE Blankert@MITRE-GATEWAY.ORG

[SXS1] Susie Snitzer Britton-Lee —none—

[SXS2] Soren H. Sorensen CR SYSTEMS —none—

[SXS3] Steven Sweeney Farallon Computing, Inc. —none—

[SXS4] Simson L. Garfinkel NeXt simsong@next.cambridge.ma.us

[SXW] Steve Waldbusser CMU sw01+@andrew.cmu.edu

[SXW1] Simon van Winkelen SDL —none—

[SXW2] Sean Welch Xenocom, Inc. welch@raven.ulowell.edu

[SXW3] Steve Willens Livingston Enterprises, Inc. steve@livingston.com

[TC27] Thomas Calderwood BBN TCALDERW@BBN.COM

[TN] Thomas Narten Purdue narten@PURDUE.EDU

[TS566] Timon Sloane PeerNet peernet!timon@uunet.UU.NET

[TU] Tom Unger UMich tom@CITI.UMICH.EDU

[TXA] Tad Artis Microwave Bypass Systems, Inc. —none—

[TXA1] Takahiro Asai Hitachi Cable, Ltd. —none—

[TXB] Torsten Beyer Dr. Materna GmbH tb@Materna.de

[TXB1] Tom Bereiter Tiviloi —none—

[TXC] Tracy Cox Bellcore tacox@sabre.bellcore.com

[TXD] "Tundra" Tim Daneliuk Covia tundraix!tundra@clout.chi.il.us

[TXH] Takashi Hagiwara Sony Hagiwara@Sm.Sony.Co.Jp

[TXH1] Tim Howes UMich Tim.Howes@terminator.cc.umich.edu

[TXJ] Tim Jones Box Hill Systems Corporation tim@boxhill.com

[TXL] Tim Berners-Lee CERN timbl@nxoc01.cern.ch

[TXM] Trudy Miller ACC Trudy@ACC.COM

[TXM1] Thomas McGinty Codex —none—

[TXO] Toshiharu Ohno ASCII Corporation tony-o@ascii.co.jp

[TXP] Tony van der Peet DSIR Network Group srghtvp@grv.dsir.govt.nz

[TXR] Tim Rylance Praxis praxis!tkr@UUNET.UU.NET

[TXR1] Thomas Ruf Schneider & Koch tom@rsp.de

[TXS] Ted J. Socolofsky Spider Teds@SPIDER.CO.UK

[TXS1] Toshiharu Sugawara NTTC sugawara%wink.ntt.jp@RELAY.CS.NET

[TXS2] Thomas M. Smith GE Aerospace tmsmith@esc.syr.ge.com

[TXT] Ted Tran Andrew Corporation —none—

[TXT1] Terrence J. Talbot BU lexcube!tjt@bu.edu

[TXV] Tomas Vocetka Compu-Shack OPLER%CSEARN.bitnet@CUNYVM.CUNY.EDU

[TXW] Toshio Watanabe RICOH Co. Ltd. watanabe@godzilla.rsc.spdd.ricoh.co.jp

[UB3] Ulf Bilting CHALMERS bilting@PURDUE.EDU

[UXV] Umberto Vizcaino Bridgeway —none—

[UW2] Unni Warrier Netlabs unni@NETLABS.COM

[VJ] Van Jacobson LBL van@CSAM.LBL.GOV

[VXC] Vik Chandra IBM vc@ralvm6.vnet.ibm.com

[VXD] Victor Dafoulas Wang Labs —none—

[VXE] Vince Enriquez Motorola enriquez@sps.mot.com

[VXK] Victor Kazdoba Morgan Stanley & Co. Inc. vsk@katana.is.morgan.com

[VXL] Vince Liu Centrum Communications, Inc. —none—

[VXS] Vinod Singh Unify —none—

[VXT] V. Taylor CANADA vktaylor@NCS.DND.CA

[WDW11] William D. Wisner wisner@HAYES.FAI.ALASKA.EDU

[WJC2] Bill Croft STANFORD Croft@SUMEX-AIM.STANFORD.EDU

[WJS1] Weldon J. Showalter DCA Gamma@MINTAKA.DCA.MIL

[WLB8] William L. Biagi Advintech CSS002.BLBIAGI@ADVINTECH-MVS.ARPA

[WM3] William Melohn SUN Melohn@SUN.COM

[WXC] Wesley Craig UMICH Wesley.Craig@terminator.cc.umich.edu

[WXC1] W. James Colosky Eastman Kodak Company wjc@tornado.kodak.com

[WXD] William Dunn NetManage, Inc. netmanage@cup.portal.com

[WXP] W.J. Parducci & Associates, Inc. Bill Parducci 70262.1267@compuserve.com

[WXS] Wayne Schroeder SDSC schroeder@SDS.SDSC.EDU

[WXS2] W.R. Maynard-Smith Netcomm, Ltd. —none—

[WXT] Wayne Tackabury Pacer Software wft@pacersoft.com

[VXW] Val Wilson Spider val@spider.co.uk

[YXA] Yoshiyuki Akiyama NEC kddlab!ccs.mt.nec.co.jp!y-akiyam@uunet.uu.net

[YXH] Yigal Hochberg Unifi yigal@unifi.com

[YXK] Yoav Kluger Spartacus ykluger@HAWK.ULOWELL.EDU

[YXK1] Yasuhiro Kohata NTT DATA kohata@rd.nttdata.jp

[YXW] Y.C. Wang Network Application Technology —none—

[YXW1] Yasuyoshi Watanabe Seiko Instruments, Inc. (SII) —none—

[XEROX] Fonda Pallone Xerox —none—

[ZSU] Zaw-Sing Su SRI ZSu@TSCA.ISTC.SRI.COM

[ZXS] Zohar Seigal Gambit Computer —none—

Security Considerations

Security issues are not discussed in this memo.

Authors' Addresses

Joyce K. Reynolds
Information Sciences Institute
University of Southern California
4676 Admiralty Way
Marina del Rey, CA 90292
Phone: (310) 822-1511
Email: JKREY@ISI.EDU

Jon Postel
Information Sciences Institute
University of Southern California
4676 Admiralty Way
Marina del Rey, CA 90292
Phone: (310) 822-1511
Email: POSTEL@ISI.EDU

RFC 1883–IPv6

Network Working Group   S.Deering, Xerox PARC

Request for Comments: 1883   R. Hinden, Ipsilon Networks

Category: Standards Track   December 1995

App

A

Internet Protocol, Version 6 (IPv6)

Specification

Status of this Memo

This document specifies an Internet standards track protocol for the Internet community, and requests discussion and suggestions for improvements. Please refer to the current edition of the "Internet Official Protocol Standards" (STD 1) for the standardization state and status of this protocol. Distribution of this memo is unlimited.

Abstract   This document specifies version 6 of the Internet Protocol (IPv6), also sometimes referred to as IP Next Generation or IPng.

Table of Contents

1. Introduction
2. Terminology
3. IPv6 Header Format
4. IPv6 Extension Headers
   4.1 Extension Header Order
   4.2 Options
   4.3 Hop-by-Hop Options Header
   4.4 Routing Header
   4.5 Fragment Header
   4.6 Destination Options Header
   4.7 No Next Header5
5. Packet Size Issues
6. Flow Labels
7. Priority
8. Upper-Layer Protocol Issues
   8.1 Upper-Layer Checksums
   8.2 Maximum Packet Lifetime
   8.3 Maximum Upper-Layer Payload Size

Appendix A. Formatting Guidelines for Options

Security Considerations

Acknowledgments

Authors' Addresses

References

1. Introduction

IP version 6 (IPv6) is a new version of the Internet Protocol, designed as a successor to IP version 4 (IPv4) [RFC-791]. The changes from IPv4 to IPv6 fall primarily into the following categories:

Expanded Addressing Capabilities   IPv6 increases the IP address size from 32 bits to 128 bits, to support more levels of addressing hierarchy, a much greater number of addressable nodes, and simpler auto-configuration of addresses. The scalability of multicast routing is improved by adding a "scope" field to multicast addresses. And a new type of address called an "anycast address" is defined, used to send a packet to any one of a group of nodes.

Header Format Simplification   Some IPv4 header fields have been dropped or made optional, to reduce the common-case processing cost of packet handling and to limit the bandwidth cost of the IPv6 header.

Improved Support for Extensions and Options   Changes in the way IP header options are encoded allows for more efficient forwarding, less stringent limits on the length of options, and greater flexibility for introducing new options in the future.

Flow Labeling Capability   A new capability is added to enable the labeling of packets belonging to particular traffic "flows" for which the sender requests special handling, such as non-default quality of service or "real-time" service.

Authentication and Privacy Capabilities   Extensions to support authentication, data integrity, and (optional) data confidentiality are specified for IPv6.

This document specifies the basic IPv6 header and the initially-defined IPv6 extension headers and options. It also discusses packet size issues, the semantics of flow labels and priority, and the effects of IPv6 on upper-layer protocols. The format and semantics of IPv6 addresses are specified separately in [RFC-1884]. The IPv6 version of ICMP, which all IPv6 implementations are required to include, is specified in [RFC-1885].

2. Terminology

node - a device that implements IPv6.

router - a node that forwards IPv6 packets not explicitly addressed to itself. [See Note below].

host - any node that is not a router. [See Note below].

upper layer - a protocol layer immediately above IPv6. Examples are transport protocols such as TCP and UDP, control protocols such as ICMP, routing protocols such as OSPF, and internet or lower-layer protocols being "tunneled" over (i.e., encapsulated in) IPv6 such as IPX, AppleTalk, or IPv6 itself.

link - a communication facility or medium over which nodes can communicate at the link layer, i.e., the layer immediately below IPv6. Examples are Ethernets (simple or bridged); PPP links; X.25, Frame Relay, or ATM networks; and internet (or higher) layer "tunnels", such as tunnels over IPv4 or IPv6 itself.

neighbors - nodes attached to the same link.

interface - a node's attachment to a link.

address - an IPv6-layer identifier for an interface or a set of interfaces.

packet - an IPv6 header plus payload.

link MTU - the maximum transmission unit, i.e., maximum packet size in octets, that can be conveyed in one piece over a link.

path MTU - the minimum link MTU of all the links in a path between a source node and a destination node.

N O T E Note it is possible, though unusual, for a device with multiple interfaces to be configured to forward non-self-destined packets arriving from some set (fewer than all) of its interfaces, and to discard non-self-destined packets arriving from its other interfaces. Such a device must obey the protocol requirements for routers when receiving packets from, and interacting with neighbors over, the former (forwarding) interfaces. It must obey the protocol requirements for hosts when receiving packets from, and interacting with neighbors over, the latter (non-forwarding) interfaces.

3. IPv6 Header Format

```
+-+-+-+-+-+-+-+-+-+-+-+-+-+-+-+-+-+-+-+-+-+-+-+-+-+-+-+-+-+-+-+-+
|Version| Prio. |                   Flow Label                  |
+-+-+-+-+-+-+-+-+-+-+-+-+-+-+-+-+-+-+-+-+-+-+-+-+-+-+-+-+-+-+-+-+
|         Payload Length        |  Next Header  |   Hop Limit   |
+-+-+-+-+-+-+-+-+-+-+-+-+-+-+-+-+-+-+-+-+-+-+-+-+-+-+-+-+-+-+-+-+
|                                                               |
+                                                               +
|                                                               |
+                                                               +
|                         Source Address                        |
+                                                               +
|                                                               |
+                                                               +
|                                                               |
+-+-+-+-+-+-+-+-+-+-+-+-+-+-+-+-+-+-+-+-+-+-+-+-+-+-+-+-+-+-+-+-+
|                                                               |
+                                                               +
|                                                               |
+                                                               +
|                      Destination Address                      |
+                                                               +
|                                                               |
+                                                               +
|                                                               |
+-+-+-+-+-+-+-+-+-+-+-+-+-+-+-+-+-+-+-+-+-+-+-+-+-+-+-+-+-+-+-+-+
```

Version 4-bit Internet Protocol version number = 6.

Prio. 4-bit priority value. See section 7.

Flow Label 24-bit flow label. See section 6.

Payload Length 16-bit unsigned integer. Length of payload, i.e., the rest of the packet following the IPv6 header, in octets. If zero, indicates that the payload length is carried in a Jumbo Payload hop-by-hop option. Next Header 8-bit selector. Identifies the type of header immediately following the IPv6 header. Uses the same values as the IPv4 Protocol field [RFC-1700 et seq.].

Hop Limit 8-bit unsigned integer. Decremented by 1 by each node that forwards the packet. The packet is discarded if Hop Limit is decremented to zero.Source Address 128-bit address of the originator of the packet. See [RFC-1884].

Destination Address 128-bit address of the intended recipient of the packet (possibly not the ultimate recipient, if a Routing header is present). See [RFC-1884] and section 4.4.

4. IPv6 Extension Headers

In IPv6, optional internet-layer information is encoded in separate headers that may be placed between the IPv6 header and the upper-layer header in a packet. There are a small number of such extension headers, each identified by a distinct Next Header value. As illustrated in these examples, an IPv6 packet may carry zero, one, or more extension headers, each identified by the Next Header field of the preceding header:

```
+--------------+------------------------
|  IPv6 header | TCP header + data
|              |
| Next Header =|
|    TCP       |
+--------------+------------------------


+--------------+----------------+-------------------------
|  IPv6 header | Routing header | TCP header + data
|              |                |
| Next Header =| Next Header =  |
|    Routing   |     TCP        |
+--------------+----------------+-------------------------


+--------------+----------------+----------------+----------------
|  IPv6 header | Routing header | Fragment header | fragment of TCP
|              |                |                 | header + data
| Next Header =| Next Header =  | Next Header =   |
|    Routing   |    Fragment    |     TCP         |
+--------------+----------------+----------------+----------------
```

With one exception, extension headers are not examined or processed by any node along a packet's delivery path, until the packet reaches the node (or each of the set of nodes, in the case of multicast) identified in the Destination Address field of the IPv6 header. There, normal demultiplexing on the Next Header field of the IPv6 header invokes the module to process the first extension header, or the upper-layer header if no extension header is present. The contents and semantics of each extension header determine whether or not to proceed to the next header. Therefore, extension headers must be processed strictly in the order they appear in the packet; a receiver must not, for example, scan through a packet looking for a particular kind of extension header and process that header prior to processing all preceding ones.

The exception referred to in the preceding paragraph is the Hop-by-Hop Options header, which carries information that must be examined and processed by every node along a packet's delivery path, including the source and destination nodes. The Hop-by-Hop Options header, when present, must immediately follow the IPv6 header. Its presence is indicated by the value zero in the Next Header field of the IPv6 header.

If, as a result of processing a header, a node is required to proceed to the next header but the Next Header value in the current header is unrecognized by the node, it should discard the packet and send an ICMP Parameter Problem message to the source of the packet, with an ICMP Code value of 2 ("unrecognized Next Header type encountered") and the ICMP Pointer field containing the offset of the unrecognized value within the original packet. The same action should be taken if a node encounters a Next Header value of zero in any header other than an IPv6 header.

Each extension header is an integer multiple of 8 octets long, in order to retain 8-octet alignment for subsequent headers. Multi-octet fields within each extension header are aligned on their natural boundaries, i.e., fields of width n octets are placed at an integer multiple of n octets from the start of the header, for $n = 1, 2, 4$, or 8.

A full implementation of IPv6 includes implementation of the following extension headers:

Hop-by-Hop Options

Routing (Type 0)

Fragment

Destination Options

Authentication

Encapsulating Security Payload

The first four are specified in this document; the last two are specified in [RFC-1826] and [RFC-1827], respectively.

4.1 Extension Header Order   When more than one extension header is used in the same packet, it is recommended that those headers appear in the following order:

IPv6 header

Hop-by-Hop Options header

Destination Options header (note 1)

Routing header

Fragment header

Authentication header (note 2)

Encapsulating Security Payload header (note 2)

Destination Options header (note 3)

upper-layer header

note 1: for options to be processed by the first destination that appears in the IPv6 Destination Address field plus subsequent destinations listed in the Routing header.

note 2: additional recommendations regarding the relative order of the Authentication and Encapsulating Security Payload headers are given in [RFC-1827].

note 3: for options to be processed only by the final destination of the packet.

Each extension header should occur at most once, except for the Destination Options header which should occur at most twice (once before a Routing header and once before the upper-layer header).

If the upper-layer header is another IPv6 header (in the case of IPv6 being tunneled over or encapsulated in IPv6), it may be followed by its own extensions headers, which are separately subject to the same ordering recommendations.

If and when other extension headers are defined, their ordering constraints relative to the above listed headers must be specified.

IPv6 nodes must accept and attempt to process extension headers in any order and occurring any number of times in the same packet, except for the Hop-by-Hop Options header which is restricted to appear immediately after an IPv6 header only. Nonetheless, it is strongly advised that sources of IPv6 packets adhere to the above recommended order until and unless subsequent specifications revise that recommendation.

4.2 Options   Two of the currently-defined extension headers — the Hop-by-Hop Options header and the Destination Options header — carry a variable number of type-length-value (TLV) encoded "options", of the following format:

```
+-+-+-+-+-+-+-+-+-+-+-+-+-+-+-+-+-  - - - - - - -
¦  Option Type  ¦ Opt Data Len ¦  Option Data
+-+-+-+-+-+-+-+-+-+-+-+-+-+-+-+-+-  - - - - - - -
```

Option Type 8-bit identifier of the type of option.

Opt Data Len 8-bit unsigned integer. Length of the Option Data field of this option, in octets.

Option Data Variable-length field. Option-Type-specific data.

The sequence of options within a header must be processed strictly in the order they appear in the header; a receiver must not, for example, scan through the header looking for a particular kind of option and process that option prior to processing all preceding ones.

The Option Type identifiers are internally encoded such that their highest-order two bits specify the action that must be taken if the processing IPv6 node does not recognize the Option Type:

00 - skip over this option and continue processing the header.

01 - discard the packet.

10 - discard the packet and, regardless of whether or not the packets's Destination Address was a multicast address, send an ICMP Parameter Problem, Code 2, message to the packet's Source Address, pointing to the unrecognized Option Type.

11 - discard the packet and, only if the packet's Destination Address was not a multicast address, send an ICMP Parameter Problem, Code 2, message to the packet's Source Address, pointing to the unrecognized Option Type.

The third-highest-order bit of the Option Type specifies whether or not the Option Data of that option can change en-route to the packet's final destination. When an Authentication header is present in the packet, for any option whose data may change en-route, its entire Option Data field must be treated as zero-valued octets when computing or verifying the packet's authenticating value.

> 0 - Option Data does not change en-route

> 1 - Option Data may change en-route

Individual options may have specific alignment requirements, to ensure that multi-octet values within Option Data fields fall on natural boundaries. The alignment requirement of an option is specified using the notation xn+y, meaning the Option Type must appear at an integer multiple of x octets from the start of the header, plus y octets. For example:

> 2n means any 2-octet offset from the start of the header.

> 8n+2 means any 8-octet offset from the start of the header, plus 2 octets.

There are two padding options which are used when necessary to align subsequent options and to pad out the containing header to a multiple of 8 octets in length. These padding options must be recognized by all IPv6 implementations:

Pad1 option (alignment requirement: none)

```
+-+-+-+-+-+-+-+-+
|       0       |
+-+-+-+-+-+-+-+-+
```

N O T E The format of the Pad1 option is a special case — it does not have length and value fields. ▪

The Pad1 option is used to insert one octet of padding into the Options area of a header. If more than one octet of padding is required, the PadN option, described next, should be used, rather than multiple Pad1 options.

PadN option (alignment requirement: none)

```
+-+-+-+-+-+-+-+-+-+-+-+-+-+-+-+-+- - - - - - - -
|       1       |  Opt Data Len |  Option Data
+-+-+-+-+-+-+-+-+-+-+-+-+-+-+-+-+- - - - - - - -
```

The PadN option is used to insert two or more octets of padding into the Options area of a header. For N octets of padding, the Opt Data Len field contains the value N-2, and the Option Data consists of N-2 zero-valued octets.

Appendix A contains formatting guidelines for designing new options.

4.3 Hop-by-Hop Options Header The Hop-by-Hop Options header is used to carry optional information that must be examined by every node along a packet's delivery path. The Hop-by-Hop Options header is identified by a Next Header value of 0 in the IPv6 header, and has the following format:

```
+-+-+-+-+-+-+-+-+-+-+-+-+-+-+-+-+-+-+-+-+-+-+-+-+-+-+-+-+-+-+-+-+
|   Next Header  |  Hdr Ext Len  |                              |
+-+-+-+-+-+-+-+-+-+-+-+-+-+-+-+-+                              +
|                                                              |
.                                                              .
.                            Options                           .
.                                                              .
|                                                              |
+-+-+-+-+-+-+-+-+-+-+-+-+-+-+-+-+-+-+-+-+-+-+-+-+-+-+-+-+-+-+-+-+
```

Next Header 8-bit selector. Identifies the type of header immediately following the Hop-by-Hop Options header. Uses the same values as the IPv4 Protocol field [RFC-1700 et seq.].

Hdr Ext Len 8-bit unsigned integer. Length of the Hop-by-Hop Options header in 8-octet units, not including the first 8 octets.

Options Variable-length field, of length such that the complete Hop-by-Hop Options header is an integer multiple of 8 octets long. Contains one or more TLV-encoded options, as described in section 4.2.

In addition to the Pad1 and PadN options specified in section 4.2, the following hop-by-hop option is defined:

Jumbo Payload option (alignment requirement: $4n + 2$)

```
                                  +-+-+-+-+-+-+-+-+-+-+-+-+-+-+-+-+
                                  |      194      |Opt Data Len=4 |
      +-+-+-+-+-+-+-+-+-+-+-+-+-+-+-+-+-+-+-+-+-+-+-+-+-+-+-+-+-+-+
      |                     Jumbo Payload Length                  |
      +-+-+-+-+-+-+-+-+-+-+-+-+-+-+-+-+-+-+-+-+-+-+-+-+-+-+-+-+-+-+
```

The Jumbo Payload option is used to send IPv6 packets with payloads longer than 65,535 octets. The Jumbo Payload Length is the length of the packet in octets, excluding the IPv6 header but including the Hop-by-Hop Options header; it must be greater than 65,535. If a packet is received with a Jumbo Payload option containing a Jumbo Payload Length less than or equal to 65,535, an ICMP Parameter Problem message, Code 0, should be sent to the packet's source, pointing to the high-order octet of the invalid Jumbo Payload Length field.

The Payload Length field in the IPv6 header must be set to zero in every packet that carries the Jumbo Payload option. If a packet is received with a valid Jumbo Payload option present and a non-zero IPv6 Payload Length field, an ICMP Parameter Problem message, Code 0, should be sent to the packet's source, pointing to the Option Type field of the Jumbo Payload option.

The Jumbo Payload option must not be used in a packet that carries a Fragment header. If a Fragment header is encountered in a packet that contains a valid Jumbo Payload option, an ICMP Parameter Problem message, Code 0, should be sent to the packet's source, pointing to the first octet of the Fragment header.

An implementation that does not support the Jumbo Payload option cannot have interfaces to links whose link MTU is greater than 65,575 (40 octets of IPv6 header plus 65,535 octets of payload).

4.4 Routing Header   The Routing header is used by an IPv6 source to list one or more intermediate nodes to be "visited" on the way to a packet's destination. This function is very similar to IPv4's Source Route options. The Routing header is identified by a Next Header value of 43 in the immediately preceding header, and has the following format:

```
+-+-+-+-+-+-+-+-+-+-+-+-+-+-+-+-+-+-+-+-+-+-+-+-+-+-+-+-+-+-+-+-+
¦  Next Header  ¦  Hdr Ext Len  ¦  Routing Type ¦ Segments Left ¦
+-+-+-+-+-+-+-+-+-+-+-+-+-+-+-+-+-+-+-+-+-+-+-+-+-+-+-+-+-+-+-+-+
¦                                                               ¦
.                                                               .
.                       type-specific data                     .
.                                                               .
¦                                                               ¦
+-+-+-+-+-+-+-+-+-+-+-+-+-+-+-+-+-+-+-+-+-+-+-+-+-+-+-+-+-+-+-+-+
```

Next Header 8-bit selector. Identifies the type of header immediately following the Routing header. Uses the same values as the IPv4 Protocol field [RFC-1700 et seq.].

Hdr Ext Len 8-bit unsigned integer. Length of the Routing header in 8-octet units, not including the first 8 octets.

Routing Type 8-bit identifier of a particular Routing header variant.

Segments Left 8-bit unsigned integer. Number of route segments remaining, i.e., number of explicitly listed intermediate nodes still to be visited before reaching the final destination.

type-specific data Variable-length field, of format determined by the Routing Type, and of length such that the complete Routing header is an integer multiple of 8 octets long.

If, while processing a received packet, a node encounters a Routing header with an unrecognized Routing Type value, the required behavior of the node depends on the value of the Segments Left field, as follows:

If Segments Left is zero, the node must ignore the Routing header and proceed to process the next header in the packet, whose type is identified by the Next Header field in the Routing header.

If Segments Left is non-zero, the node must discard the packet and send an ICMP Parameter Problem, Code 0, message to the packet's Source Address, pointing to the unrecognized Routing Type.

The Type 0 Routing header has the following format:

```
+-+-+-+-+-+-+-+-+-+-+-+-+-+-+-+-+-+-+-+-+-+-+-+-+-+-+-+-+-+-+-+-+
¦  Next Header  ¦  Hdr Ext Len  ¦ Routing Type=0¦ Segments Left ¦
+-+-+-+-+-+-+-+-+-+-+-+-+-+-+-+-+-+-+-+-+-+-+-+-+-+-+-+-+-+-+-+-+
¦   Reserved    ¦               Strict/Loose Bit Map            ¦
+-+-+-+-+-+-+-+-+-+-+-+-+-+-+-+-+-+-+-+-+-+-+-+-+-+-+-+-+-+-+-+-+
¦                                                               ¦
+                                                               +
¦                                                               ¦
+                         Address[1]                            +
¦                                                               ¦
+                                                               +
¦                                                               ¦
```

Next Header 8-bit selector. Identifies the type of header immediately following the Routing header. Uses the same values as the IPv4 Protocol field [RFC-1700 et seq.].

Hdr Ext Len 8-bit unsigned integer. Length of the Routing header in 8-octet units, not including the first 8 octets. For the Type 0 Routing header, Hdr Ext Len is equal to two times the number of addresses in the header, and must be an even number less than or equal to 46.

Routing Type 0.

Segments Left 8-bit unsigned integer. Number of route segments remaining, i.e., number of explicitly listed intermediate nodes still to be visited before reaching the final destination. Maximum legal value = 23.

Reserved 8-bit reserved field. Initialized to zero for transmission; ignored on reception.

Strict/Loose Bit Map 24-bit bit-map, numbered 0 to 23, left-to-right. Indicates, for each segment of the route, whether or not the next destination address must be a neighbor of the preceding address: 1 means strict (must be a neighbor), 0 means loose (need not be a neighbor).

Address[1..n] Vector of 128-bit addresses, numbered 1 to n.

Multicast addresses must not appear in a Routing header of Type 0, or in the IPv6 Destination Address field of a packet carrying a Routing header of Type 0.

If bit number 0 of the Strict/Loose Bit Map has value 1, the Destination Address field of the IPv6 header in the original packet must identify a neighbor of the originating node. If bit number 0 has value 0, the originator may use any legal, non-multicast address as the initial Destination Address.

Bits numbered greater than n, where n is the number of addresses in the Routing header, must be set to 0 by the originator and ignored by receivers.

A Routing header is not examined or processed until it reaches the node identified in the Destination Address field of the IPv6 header. In that node, dispatching on the Next Header field of the immediately preceding header causes the Routing header module to be invoked, which, in the case of Routing Type 0, performs the following algorithm:

```
if Segments Left = 0 {
   proceed to process the next header in the packet, whose type is
   identified by the Next Header field in the Routing header
}
else if Hdr Ext Len is odd or greater than 46 {
      send an ICMP Parameter Problem, Code 0, message to the Source
      Address, pointing to the Hdr Ext Len field, and discard the
      packet
}
else {
   compute n, the number of addresses in the Routing header, by
   dividing Hdr Ext Len by 2

   if Segments Left is greater than n {
      send an ICMP Parameter Problem, Code 0, message to the Source
      Address, pointing to the Segments Left field, and discard the
      packet
   }
   else {
      decrement Segments Left by 1;
      compute i, the index of the next address to be visited in
      the address vector, by subtracting Segments Left from n

      if Address [i] or the IPv6 Destination Address is multicast {
         discard the packet
      }
      else {
         swap the IPv6 Destination Address and Address[i]

         if bit i of the Strict/Loose Bit map has value 1 and the
         new Destination Address is not the address of a neighbor
         of this node {
            send an ICMP Destination Unreachable -- Not a Neighbor
            message to the Source Address and discard the packet
         }
         else if the IPv6 Hop Limit is less than or equal to 1 {
            send an ICMP Time Exceeded -- Hop Limit Exceeded in
            Transit message to the Source Address and discard the
            packet
         }
         else {
            decrement the Hop Limit by 1

            resubmit the packet to the IPv6 module for transmission
            to the new destination
         }
      }
   }
}
```

As an example of the effects of the above algorithm, consider the case of a source node S sending a packet to destination node D, using a Routing header to cause the packet to be routed via intermediate nodes I1, I2, and I3. The values of the relevant IPv6 header and Routing header fields on each segment of the delivery path would be as follows:

As the packet travels from S to I1:

Source Address = S Hdr Ext Len = 6

Destination Address = I1 Segments Left = 3

Address[1] = I2 (if bit 0 of the Bit Map is 1, Address[2] = I3 S and I1 must be neighbors; Address[3] = D this is checked by S)

As the packet travels from I1 to I2:

Source Address = S Hdr Ext Len = 6

Destination Address = I2 Segments Left = 2

Address[1] = I1 (if bit 1 of the Bit Map is 1, Address[2] = I3 I1 and I2 must be neighbors; Address[3] = D this is checked by I1)

As the packet travels from I2 to I3:

Source Address = S Hdr Ext Len = 6

Destination Address = I3 Segments Left = 1

Address[1] = I1 (if bit 2 of the Bit Map is 1, Address[2] = I2 I2 and I3 must be neighbors; Address[3] = D this is checked by I2)

As the packet travels from I3 to D:

Source Address = S Hdr Ext Len = 6

Destination Address = D Segments Left = 0

Address[1] = I1 (if bit 3 of the Bit Map is 1, Address[2] = I2 I3 and D must be neighbors; Address[3] = I3 this is checked by I3)

4.5 Fragment Header   The Fragment header is used by an IPv6 source to send packets larger than would fit in the path MTU to their destinations. (Note: unlike IPv4, fragmentation in IPv6 is performed only by source nodes, not by routers along a packet's delivery path — see section 5.) The Fragment header is identified by a Next Header value of 44 in the immediately preceding header, and has the following format:

```
+-+-+-+-+-+-+-+-+-+-+-+-+-+-+-+-+-+-+-+-+-+-+-+-+-+-+-+-+-+-+-+-+
|  Next Header  |    Reserved   |      Fragment Offset    |Res|M|
+-+-+-+-+-+-+-+-+-+-+-+-+-+-+-+-+-+-+-+-+-+-+-+-+-+-+-+-+-+-+-+-+
|                         Identification                       |
+-+-+-+-+-+-+-+-+-+-+-+-+-+-+-+-+-+-+-+-+-+-+-+-+-+-+-+-+-+-+-+-+
```

Next Header 8-bit selector. Identifies the initial header type of the Fragmentable Part of the original packet (defined below). Uses the same values as the IPv4 Protocol field [RFC-1700 et seq.].

Reserved 8-bit reserved field. Initialized to zero for transmission; ignored on reception.

Fragment Offset 13-bit unsigned integer. The offset, in 8-octet units, of the data following this header, relative to the start of the Fragmentable Part of the original packet.

Res 2-bit reserved field. Initialized to zero for transmission; ignored on reception.

M flag 1 = more fragments; 0 = last fragment.

Identification 32 bits. See description below.

In order to send a packet that is too large to fit in the MTU of the path to its destination, a source node may divide the packet into fragments and send each fragment as a separate packet, to be reassembled at the receiver.

For every packet that is to be fragmented, the source node generates an Identification value. The Identification must be different than that of any other fragmented packet sent recently* with the same Source Address and Destination Address. If a Routing header is present, the Destination Address of concern is that of the final destination.

* "recently" means within the maximum likely lifetime of a packet, including transit time from source to destination and time spent awaiting reassembly with other fragments of the same packet. However, it is not required that a source node know the maximum packet lifetime. Rather, it is assumed that the requirement can be met by maintaining the Identification value as a simple, 32-bit, "wrap-around" counter, incremented each time a packet must be fragmented. It is an implementation choice whether to maintain a single counter for the node or multiple counters, e.g., one for each of the node's possible source addresses, or one for each active (source address, destination address) combination.

The initial, large, unfragmented packet is referred to as the "original packet", and it is considered to consist of two parts, as illustrated:

original packet:

```
+------------------+---------------------//---------------------+
|  Unfragmentable  |              Fragmentable                  |
|       Part       |                 Part                       |
+------------------+---------------------//---------------------+
```

The Unfragmentable Part consists of the IPv6 header plus any extension headers that must be processed by nodes en route to the destination, that is, all headers up to and including the Routing header if present, else the Hop-by-Hop Options header if present, else no extension headers.

The Fragmentable Part consists of the rest of the packet, that is, any extension headers that need be processed only by the final destination node(s), plus the upper-layer header and data.

The Fragmentable Part of the original packet is divided into fragments, each, except possibly the last ("rightmost") one, being an integer multiple of 8 octets long. The fragments are transmitted in separate "fragment packets" as illustrated:

original packet:

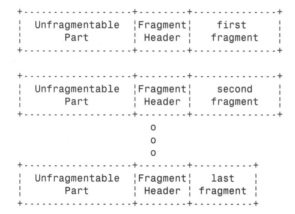

fragment packets:

Each fragment packet is composed of:

1. The Unfragmentable Part of the original packet, with the Payload Length of the original IPv6 header changed to contain the length of this fragment packet only (excluding the length of the IPv6 header itself), and the Next Header field of the last header of the Unfragmentable Part changed to 44.

2. A Fragment header containing:

   The Next Header value that identifies the first header of the Fragmentable Part of the original packet. A Fragment Offset containing the offset of the fragment, in 8-octet units, relative to the start of the Fragmentable Part of the original packet. The Fragment Offset of the first ("leftmost") fragment is 0.

   An M flag value of 0 if the fragment is the last ("rightmost") one, else an M flag value of 1.

   The Identification value generated for the original packet.

3. The fragment itself.

The lengths of the fragments must be chosen such that the resulting fragment packets fit within the MTU of the path to the packets' destination(s).

At the destination, fragment packets are reassembled into their original, unfragmented form, as illustrated:

reassembled original packet:

```
+-----------------+---------------------//----------------------+
¦ Unfragmentable  ¦              Fragmentable                    ¦
¦     Part        ¦                  Part                        ¦
+-----------------+---------------------//----------------------+
```

The following rules govern reassembly:

An original packet is reassembled only from fragment packets that have the same Source Address, Destination Address, and Fragment Identification.

The Unfragmentable Part of the reassembled packet consists of all headers up to, but not including, the Fragment header of the first fragment packet (that is, the packet whose Fragment Offset is zero), with the following two changes:

The Next Header field of the last header of the Unfragmentable Part is obtained from the Next Header field of the first fragment's Fragment header.

The Payload Length of the reassembled packet is computed from the length of the Unfragmentable Part and the length and offset of the last fragment. For example, a formula for computing the Payload Length of the reassembled original packet is:

```
PL.orig = PL.first - FL.first - 8 + (8 * FO.last) + FL.last
```

where

PL.orig = Payload Length field of reassembled packet.

PL.first = Payload Length field of first fragment packet.

FL.first = length of fragment following Fragment header of first fragment packet.

FO.last = Fragment Offset field of Fragment header of last fragment packet.

FL.last = length of fragment following Fragment header of last fragment packet.

The Fragmentable Part of the reassembled packet is constructed from the fragments following the Fragment headers in each of the fragment packets. The length of each fragment is computed by subtracting from the packet's Payload Length the length of the headers between the IPv6 header and fragment itself; its relative position in Fragmentable Part is computed from its Fragment Offset value.

The Fragment header is not present in the final, reassembled packet.

The following error conditions may arise when reassembling fragmented packets:

If insufficient fragments are received to complete reassembly of a packet within 60 seconds of the reception of the first-arriving fragment of that packet, reassembly of that packet must be abandoned and all the fragments that have been received for that packet must be discarded.

If the first fragment (i.e., the one with a Fragment Offset of zero) has been received, an ICMP Time Exceeded — Fragment Reassembly Time Exceeded message should be sent to the source of that fragment.

If the length of a fragment, as derived from the fragment packet's Payload Length field, is not a multiple of 8 octets and the M flag of that fragment is 1, then that fragment must be discarded and an ICMP Parameter Problem, Code 0, message should be sent to the source of the fragment, pointing to the Payload Length field of the fragment packet.

If the length and offset of a fragment are such that the Payload Length of the packet reassembled from that fragment would exceed 65,535 octets, then that fragment must be discarded and an ICMP Parameter Problem, Code 0, message should be sent to the source of the fragment, pointing to the Fragment Offset field of the fragment packet.

The following conditions are not expected to occur, but are not considered errors if they do:

The number and content of the headers preceding the Fragment header of different fragments of the same original packet may differ. Whatever headers are present, preceding the Fragment header in each fragment packet, are processed when the packets arrive, prior to queueing the fragments for reassembly. Only those headers in the Offset zero fragment packet are retained in the reassembled packet.

The Next Header values in the Fragment headers of different fragments of the same original packet may differ. Only the value from the Offset zero fragment packet is used for reassembly.

(e)4.6 Destination Options Header

The Destination Options header is used to carry optional information that need be examined only by a packet's destination node(s). The Destination Options header is identified by a Next Header value of 60 in the immediately preceding header, and has the following format:

```
+-+-+-+-+-+-+-+-+-+-+-+-+-+-+-+-+-+-+-+-+-+-+-+-+-+-+-+-+-+-+-+-+
|   Next Header  |  Hdr Ext Len  |                              |
+-+-+-+-+-+-+-+-+-+-+-+-+-+-+-+-+                              +
|                                                              |
.                                                              .
.                            Options                           .
.                                                              .
|                                                              |
+-+-+-+-+-+-+-+-+-+-+-+-+-+-+-+-+-+-+-+-+-+-+-+-+-+-+-+-+-+-+-+-+
```

Next Header 8-bit selector. Identifies the type of header immediately following the Destination Options header. Uses the same values as the IPv4 Protocol field [RFC-1700 et seq.].

Hdr Ext Len 8-bit unsigned integer. Length of the Destination Options header in 8-octet units, not including the first 8 octets.

Options Variable-length field, of length such that the complete Destination Options header is an integer multiple of 8 octets long. Contains one or more TLV-encoded options, as described in section 4.2.

The only destination options defined in this document are the Pad1 and PadN options specified in section 4.2.

Note that there are two possible ways to encode optional destination information in an IPv6 packet: either as an option in the Destination Options header, or as a separate extension header. The Fragment header and the Authentication header are examples of the latter approach. Which approach can be used depends on what action is desired of a destination node that does not understand the optional information:

- if the desired action is for the destination node to discard the packet and, only if the packet's Destination Address is not a multicast address, send an ICMP Unrecognized Type message to the packet's Source Address, then the information may be encoded either as a separate header or as an option in the

  Destination Options header whose Option Type has the value 11 in its highest-order two bits. The choice may depend on such factors as which takes fewer octets, or which yields better alignment or more efficient parsing.

- if any other action is desired, the information must be encoded as an option in the Destination Options header whose Option Type has the value 00, 01, or 10 in its highest-order two bits, specifying the desired action (see section 4.2).

4.7 No Next Header   The value 59 in the Next Header field of an IPv6 header or any extension header indicates that there is nothing following that header. If the Payload Length field of the IPv6 header indicates the presence of octets past the end of a header whose Next Header field contains 59, those octets must be ignored, and passed on unchanged if the packet is forwarded.

5. Packet Size Issues

IPv6 requires that every link in the internet have an MTU of 576 octets or greater. On any link that cannot convey a 576-octet packet in one piece, link-specific fragmentation and reassembly must be provided at a layer below IPv6.

From each link to which a node is directly attached, the node must be able to accept packets as large as that link's MTU. Links that have a configurable MTU (for example, PPP links [RFC-1661]) must be configured to have an MTU of at least 576 octets; it is recommended that a larger MTU be configured, to accommodate possible encapsulations (i.e., tunneling) without incurring fragmentation.

It is strongly recommended that IPv6 nodes implement Path MTU Discovery [RFC-1191], in order to discover and take advantage of paths with MTU greater than 576 octets. However, a minimal IPv6 implementation (e.g., in a boot ROM) may simply restrict itself to sending packets no larger than 576 octets, and omit implementation of Path MTU Discovery.

In order to send a packet larger than a path's MTU, a node may use the IPv6 Fragment header to fragment the packet at the source and have it reassembled at the destination(s). However, the use of such fragmentation is discouraged in any application that is able to adjust its packets to fit the measured path MTU (i.e., down to 576 octets).

A node must be able to accept a fragmented packet that, after reassembly, is as large as 1500 octets, including the IPv6 header. A node is permitted to accept fragmented packets that reassemble to more than 1500 octets. However, a node must not send fragments that reassemble to a size greater than 1500 octets unless it has explicit knowledge that the destination(s) can reassemble a packet of that size.

In response to an IPv6 packet that is sent to an IPv4 destination (i.e., a packet that undergoes translation from IPv6 to IPv4), the originating IPv6 node may receive an ICMP Packet Too Big message reporting a Next-Hop MTU less than 576. In that case, the IPv6 node is not required to reduce the size of subsequent packets to less than 576, but must include a Fragment header in those packets so that the IPv6-to-IPv4 translating router can obtain a suitable Identification value to use in resulting IPv4 fragments. Note that this means the payload may have to be reduced to 528 octets (576 minus 40 for the IPv6 header and 8 for the Fragment header), and smaller still if additional extension headers are used.

N O T E   Path MTU Discovery must be performed even in cases where a host "thinks" a destination is attached to the same link as itself. ■

N O T E   Unlike IPv4, it is unnecessary in IPv6 to set a "Don't Fragment" flag in the packet header in order to perform Path MTU Discovery; that is an implicit attribute of every IPv6 packet. Also, those parts of the RFC-1191 procedures that involve use of a table of MTU "plateaus" do not apply to IPv6, because the IPv6 version of the "Datagram Too Big" message always identifies the exact MTU to be used. ■

6. Flow Labels

The 24-bit Flow Label field in the IPv6 header may be used by a source to label those packets for which it requests special handling by the IPv6 routers, such as non-default quality of service or "real-time" service. This aspect of IPv6 is, at the time of writing, still experimental and subject to change as the requirements for flow support in the Internet become clearer. Hosts or routers that do not support the functions of the Flow Label field are required to set the field to zero when originating a packet, pass the field on unchanged when forwarding a packet, and ignore the field when receiving a packet.

A flow is a sequence of packets sent from a particular source to a particular (unicast or multicast) destination for which the source desires special handling by the intervening routers. The nature of that special handling might be conveyed to the routers by a control protocol, such as a resource reservation protocol, or by information within the flow's packets themselves, e.g., in a hop-by-hop option. The details of such control protocols or options are beyond the scope of this document.

There may be multiple active flows from a source to a destination, as well as traffic that is not associated with any flow. A flow is uniquely identified by the combination of a source address and a non-zero flow label. Packets that do not belong to a flow carry a flow label of zero.

A flow label is assigned to a flow by the flow's source node. New flow labels must be chosen (pseudo-)randomly and uniformly from the range 1 to FFFFFF hex. The purpose of the random allocation is to make any set of bits within the Flow Label field suitable for use as a hash key by routers, for looking up the state associated with the flow.

All packets belonging to the same flow must be sent with the same source address, destination address, priority, and flow label. If any of those packets includes a Hop-by-Hop Options header, then they all must be originated with the same Hop-by-Hop Options header contents (excluding the Next Header field of the Hop-by-Hop Options header). If any of those packets includes a Routing header, then they all must be originated with the same contents in all extension headers up to and including the Routing header (excluding the Next Header field in the Routing header). The routers or destinations are permitted, but not required, to verify that these conditions are satisfied. If a violation is detected, it should be reported to the source by an ICMP Parameter Problem message, Code 0, pointing to the high-order octet of the Flow Label field (i.e., offset 1 within the IPv6 packet).

Routers are free to "opportunistically" set up flow-handling state for any flow, even when no explicit flow establishment information has been provided to them via a control protocol, a hop-by-hop option, or other means. For example, upon receiving a packet from a particular source with an unknown, non-zero flow label, a router may process its IPv6 header and any necessary extension headers as if the flow label were zero. That processing would include determining the next-hop interface, and possibly other actions, such as updating a hop-by-hop option, advancing the pointer and addresses in a Routing header, or deciding on how to queue the packet based on its Priority field. The router may then choose to "remember" the results of those processing steps and cache that information, using the source address plus the flow label as the cache key. Subsequent packets with the same source address and flow label may then be handled by referring to the cached information rather than examining all those fields that, according to the requirements of the previous paragraph, can be assumed unchanged from the first packet seen in the flow.

Cached flow-handling state that is set up opportunistically, as discussed in the preceding paragraph, must be discarded no more than 6 seconds after it is established, regardless of whether or not packets of the same flow continue to arrive. If another packet with the same source address and flow label arrives after the cached state has been discarded, the packet undergoes full, normal processing (as if its flow label were zero), which may result in the re-creation of cached flow state for that flow.

The lifetime of flow-handling state that is set up explicitly, for example by a control protocol or a hop-by-hop option, must be specified as part of the specification of the explicit set-up mechanism; it may exceed 6 seconds.

A source must not re-use a flow label for a new flow within the lifetime of any flow-handling state that might have been established for the prior use of that flow label. Since flow-handling state with a lifetime of 6 seconds may be established opportunistically for any flow, the minimum interval between the last packet of one flow and the first packet of a new flow using the same flow label is 6 seconds. Flow labels used for explicitly set-up flows with longer flow-state lifetimes must remain unused for those longer lifetimes before being re-used for new flows.

When a node stops and restarts (e.g., as a result of a "crash"), it must be careful not to use a flow label that it might have used for an earlier flow whose lifetime may not have expired yet. This may be accomplished by recording flow label usage on stable storage so that it can be remembered across crashes, or by refraining from using any flow labels until the maximum lifetime of any possible previously established flows has expired (at least 6 seconds; more if explicit flow set-up mechanisms with longer lifetimes might have been used). If the minimum time for rebooting the node is known (often more than 6 seconds), that time can be deducted from the necessary waiting period before starting to allocate flow labels.

There is no requirement that all, or even most, packets belong to flows, i.e., carry non-zero flow labels. This observation is placed here to remind protocol designers and implementors not to assume otherwise. For example, it would be unwise to design a router whose performance would be adequate only if most packets belonged to flows, or to design a header compression scheme that only worked on packets that belonged to flows.

7. Priority

The 4-bit Priority field in the IPv6 header enables a source to identify the desired delivery priority of its packets, relative to other packets from the same source. The Priority values are divided into two ranges: Values 0 through 7 are used to specify the priority of traffic for which the source is providing congestion control, i.e., traffic that "backs off" in response to congestion, such as TCP traffic. Values 8 through 15 are used to specify the priority of traffic that does not back off in response to congestion, e.g., "real-time" packets being sent at a constant rate.

For congestion-controlled traffic, the following Priority values are recommended for particular application categories:

> 0 - uncharacterized traffic
>
> 1 - "filler" traffic (e.g., netnews)
>
> 2 - unattended data transfer (e.g., email)
>
> 3 - (reserved)
>
> 4 - attended bulk transfer (e.g., FTP, NFS)
>
> 5 - (reserved)
>
> 6 - interactive traffic (e.g., telnet, X)
>
> 7 - internet control traffic (e.g., routing protocols, SNMP)

For non-congestion-controlled traffic, the lowest Priority value (8) should be used for those packets that the sender is most willing to have discarded under conditions of congestion (e.g., high-fidelity video traffic), and the highest value (15) should be used for those packets that the sender is least willing to have discarded (e.g., low-fidelity audio traffic). There is no relative ordering implied between the congestion-controlled priorities and the non-congestion-controlled priorities.

8. Upper-Layer Protocol Issues

8.1 Upper-Layer Checksums Any transport or other upper-layer protocol that includes the addresses from the IP header in its checksum computation must be modified for use over IPv6, to include the 128-bit IPv6 addresses instead of 32-bit IPv4 addresses. In particular, the following illustration shows the TCP and UDP "pseudo-header" for IPv6:

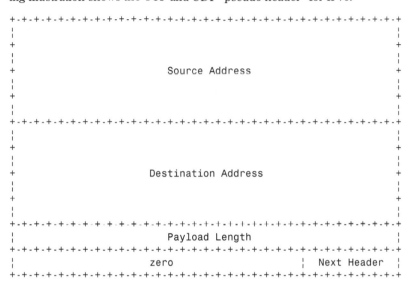

- If the packet contains a Routing header, the Destination Address used in the pseudo-header is that of the final destination. At the originating node, that address will be in the last element of the Routing header; at the recipient(s), that address will be in the Destination Address field of the IPv6 header.
- The Next Header value in the pseudo-header identifies the upper-layer protocol (e.g., 6 for TCP, or 17 for UDP). It will differ from the Next Header value in the IPv6 header if there are extension headers between the IPv6 header and the upper-layer header.
- The Payload Length used in the pseudo-header is the length of the upper-layer packet, including the upper-layer header. It will be less than the Payload Length in the IPv6 header (or in the Jumbo Payload option) if there are extension headers between the IPv6 header and the upper-layer header.
- Unlike IPv4, when UDP packets are originated by an IPv6 node, the UDP checksum is not optional. That is, whenever originating a UDP packet, an IPv6 node must compute a UDP checksum over the packet and the pseudo-header, and, if that computation yields a result of zero, it must be changed to hex FFFF for placement in the UDP header. IPv6 receivers must discard UDP packets containing a zero checksum, and should log the error.

The IPv6 version of ICMP [RFC-1885] includes the above pseudo-header in its checksum computation; this is a change from the IPv4 version of ICMP, which does not include a pseudo-header in its checksum. The reason for the change is to protect ICMP from misdelivery or corruption of those fields of the IPv6 header on which it depends, which, unlike IPv4, are not covered by an internet-layer checksum. The Next Header field in the pseudo-header for ICMP contains the value 58, which identifies the IPv6 version of ICMP.

8.2 Maximum Packet Lifetime   Unlike IPv4, IPv6 nodes are not required to enforce maximum packet lifetime. That is the reason the IPv4 "Time to Live" field was renamed "Hop Limit" in IPv6. In practice, very few, if any, IPv4 implementations conform to the requirement that they limit packet lifetime, so this is not a change in practice. Any upper-layer protocol that relies on the internet layer (whether IPv4 or IPv6) to limit packet lifetime ought to be upgraded to provide its own mechanisms for detecting and discarding obsolete packets.

8.3 Maximum Upper-Layer Payload Size   When computing the maximum payload size available for upper-layer data, an upper-layer protocol must take into account the larger size of the IPv6 header relative to the IPv4 header. For example, in IPv4, TCP's MSS option is computed as the maximum packet size (a default value or a value learned through Path MTU Discovery) minus 40 octets (20 octets for the minimum-length IPv4 header and 20 octets for the minimum-length TCP header). When using TCP over IPv6, the MSS must be computed as the maximum packet size minus 60 octets, because the minimum-length IPv6 header (i.e., an IPv6 header with no extension headers) is 20 octets longer than a minimum-length IPv4 header.

Appendix A. Formatting Guidelines for Options

This appendix gives some advice on how to lay out the fields when designing new options to be used in the Hop-by-Hop Options header or the Destination Options header, as described in section 4.2. These guidelines are based on the following assumptions:

- One desirable feature is that any multi-octet fields within the Option Data area of an option be aligned on their natural boundaries, i.e., fields of width n octets should be placed at an integer multiple of n octets from the start of the Hop-by- Hop or Destination Options header, for n = 1, 2, 4, or 8.

- Another desirable feature is that the Hop-by-Hop or Destination Options header take up as little space as possible, subject to the requirement that the header be an integer multiple of 8 octets long.

- It may be assumed that, when either of the option-bearing headers are present, they carry a very small number of options, usually only one.

These assumptions suggest the following approach to laying out the fields of an option: order the fields from smallest to largest, with no interior padding, then derive the alignment requirement for the entire option based on the alignment requirement of the largest field (up to a maximum alignment of 8 octets). This approach is illustrated in the following examples:

Example 1   If an option X required two data fields, one of length 8 octets and one of length 4 octets, it would be laid out as follows:

```
                                  +-+-+-+-+-+-+-+-+-+-+-+-+-+-+-+-+
                                  ¦ Option Type=X ¦Opt Data Len=12¦
 +-+-+-+-+-+-+-+-+-+-+-+-+-+-+-+-+-+-+-+-+-+-+-+-+-+-+-+-+-+-+-+-+
 ¦                        4-octet field                          ¦
 +-+-+-+-+-+-+-+-+-+-+-+-+-+-+-+-+-+-+-+-+-+-+-+-+-+-+-+-+-+-+-+-+
 ¦                                                               ¦
 +                        8-octet field                         +
 ¦                                                               ¦
 +-+-+-+-+-+-+-+-+-+-+-+-+-+-+-+-+-+-+-+-+-+-+-+-+-+-+-+-+-+-+-+-+
```

Its alignment requirement is 8n+2, to ensure that the 8-octet field starts at a multiple-of-8 offset from the start of the enclosing header. A complete Hop-by-Hop or Destination Options header containing this one option would look as follows:

```
 +-+-+-+-+-+-+-+-+-+-+-+-+-+-+-+-+-+-+-+-+-+-+-+-+-+-+-+-+-+-+-+-+
 ¦   Next Header  ¦ Hdr Ext Len=1 ¦ Option Type=X ¦Opt Data Len=12¦
 +-+-+-+-+-+-+-+-+-+-+-+-+-+-+-+-+-+-+-+-+-+-+-+-+-+-+-+-+-+-+-+-+
 ¦                        4-octet field                          ¦
 +-+-+-+-+-+-+-+-+-+-+-+-+-+-+-+-+-+-+-+-+-+-+-+-+-+-+-+-+-+-+-+-+
 ¦                                                               ¦
 +                        8-octet field                         +
 ¦                                                               ¦
 +-+-+-+-+-+-+-+-+-+-+-+-+-+-+-+-+-+-+-+-+-+-+-+-+-+-+-+-+-+-+-+-+
```

Example 2   If an option Y required three data fields, one of length 4 octets, one of length 2 octets, and one of length 1 octet, it would be laid out as follows:

```
                                            +-+-+-+-+-+-+-+-+
                                            ¦ Option Type=Y ¦
 +-+-+-+-+-+-+-+-+-+-+-+-+-+-+-+-+-+-+-+-+-+-+-+-+-+-+-+-+-+-+-+-+
 ¦Opt Data Len=7 ¦ 1-octet field ¦        2-octet field          ¦
 +-+-+-+-+-+-+-+-+-+-+-+-+-+-+-+-+-+-+-+-+-+-+-+-+-+-+-+-+-+-+-+-+
 ¦                        4-octet field                          ¦
 +-+-+-+-+-+-+-+-+-+-+-+-+-+-+-+-+-+-+-+-+-+-+-+-+-+-+-+-+-+-+-+-+
```

Its alignment requirement is 4n+3, to ensure that the 4-octet field starts at a multiple-of-4 offset from the start of the enclosing header. A complete Hop-by-Hop or Destination Options header containing this one option would look as follows:

```
 +-+-+-+-+-+-+-+-+-+-+-+-+-+-+-+-+-+-+-+-+-+-+-+-+-+-+-+-+-+-+-+-+
 ¦   Next Header  ¦ Hdr Ext Len=1 ¦ Pad1 Option=0 ¦ Option Type=Y ¦
 +-+-+-+-+-+-+-+-+-+-+-+-+-+-+-+-+-+-+-+-+-+-+-+-+-+-+-+-+-+-+-+-+
 ¦Opt Data Len=7 ¦ 1-octet field ¦        2-octet field          ¦
 +-+-+-+-+-+-+-+-+-+-+-+-+-+-+-+-+-+-+-+-+-+-+-+-+-+-+-+-+-+-+-+-+
 ¦                        4-octet field                          ¦
 +-+-+-+-+-+-+-+-+-+-+-+-+-+-+-+-+-+-+-+-+-+-+-+-+-+-+-+-+-+-+-+-+
 ¦ PadN Option=1 ¦Opt Data Len=2 ¦       0       ¦       0       ¦
 +-+-+-+-+-+-+-+-+-+-+-+-+-+-+-+-+-+-+-+-+-+-+-+-+-+-+-+-+-+-+-+-+
```

Example 3   A Hop-by-Hop or Destination Options header containing both options X and Y from Examples 1 and 2 would have one of the two following formats, depending on which option appeared first:

```
+-+-+-+-+-+-+-+-+-+-+-+-+-+-+-+-+-+-+-+-+-+-+-+-+-+-+-+-+-+-+-+-+
¦ Next Header  ¦ Hdr Ext Len=3 ¦ Option Type=X ¦Opt Data Len=12¦
+-+-+-+-+-+-+-+-+-+-+-+-+-+-+-+-+-+-+-+-+-+-+-+-+-+-+-+-+-+-+-+-+
¦                        4-octet field                         ¦
+-+-+-+-+-+-+-+-+-+-+-+-+-+-+-+-+-+-+-+-+-+-+-+-+-+-+-+-+-+-+-+-+
¦                                                              ¦
+                        8-octet field                        +
¦                                                              ¦
+-+-+-+-+-+-+-+-+-+-+-+-+-+-+-+-+-+-+-+-+-+-+-+-+-+-+-+-+-+-+-+-+
¦ PadN Option=1 ¦Opt Data Len=1 ¦       0       ¦ Option Type=Y ¦
+-+-+-+-+-+-+-+-+-+-+-+-+-+-+-+-+-+-+-+-+-+-+-+-+-+-+-+-+-+-+-+-+
¦Opt Data Len=7 ¦ 1-octet field ¦        2-octet field          ¦
+-+-+-+-+-+-+-+-+-+-+-+-+-+-+-+-+-+-+-+-+-+-+-+-+-+-+-+-+-+-+-+-+
¦                        4-octet field                         ¦
+-+-+-+-+-+-+-+-+-+-+-+-+-+-+-+-+-+-+-+-+-+-+-+-+-+-+-+-+-+-+-+-+
¦ PadN Option=1 ¦Opt Data Len=2 ¦       0       ¦       0       ¦
+-+-+-+-+-+-+-+-+-+-+-+-+-+-+-+-+-+-+-+-+-+-+-+-+-+-+-+-+-+-+-+-+


+-+-+-+-+-+-+-+-+-+-+-+-+-+-+-+-+-+-+-+-+-+-+-+-+-+-+-+-+-+-+-+-+
¦ Next Header  ¦ Hdr Ext Len=3 ¦ Pad1 Option=0 ¦ Option Type=Y ¦
+-+-+-+-+-+-+-+-+-+-+-+-+-+-+-+-+-+-+-+-+-+-+-+-+-+-+-+-+-+-+-+-+
¦Opt Data Len=7 ¦ 1-octet field ¦        2-octet field          ¦
+-+-+-+-+-+-+-+-+-+-+-+-+-+-+-+-+-+-+-+-+-+-+-+-+-+-+-+-+-+-+-+-+
¦                        4-octet field                         ¦
+-+-+-+-+-+-+-+-+-+-+-+-+-+-+-+-+-+-+-+-+-+-+-+-+-+-+-+-+-+-+-+-+
¦ PadN Option=1 ¦Opt Data Len=4 ¦       0       ¦       0       ¦
+-+-+-+-+-+-+-+-+-+-+-+-+-+-+-+-+-+-+-+-+-+-+-+-+-+-+-+-+-+-+-+-+
¦       0       ¦       0       ¦ Option Type=X ¦Opt Data Len=12¦
+-+-+-+-+-+-+-+-+-+-+-+-+-+-+-+-+-+-+-+-+-+-+-+-+-+-+-+-+-+-+-+-+
¦                        4-octet field                         ¦
+-+-+-+-+-+-+-+-+-+-+-+-+-+-+-+-+-+-+-+-+-+-+-+-+-+-+-+-+-+-+-+-+
¦                                                              ¦
+                        8-octet field                        +
¦                                                              ¦
+-+-+-+-+-+-+-+-+-+-+-+-+-+-+-+-+-+-+-+-+-+-+-+-+-+-+-+-+-+-+-+-+
```

Security Considerations

This document specifies that the IP Authentication Header [RFC-1826] and the IP Encapsulating Security Payload [RFC-1827] be used with IPv6, in conformance with the Security Architecture for the Internet Protocol [RFC-1825].

Acknowledgments

The authors gratefully acknowledge the many helpful suggestions of the members of the IPng working group, the End-to-End Protocols research group, and the Internet Community At Large.

Authors' Addresses

Stephen E. Deering
Xerox Palo Alto Research Center
3333 Coyote Hill Road
Palo Alto, CA 94304
USA
Phone: +1 415 812 4839
Fax: +1 415 812 4471
EMail: deering@parc.xerox.com

Robert M. Hinden
Ipsilon Networks, Inc.
2191 E. Bayshore Road, Suite 100
Palo Alto, CA 94303
USA
Phone: +1 415 846 4604
Fax: +1 415 855 1414
EMail: hinden@ipsilon.com

References

[RFC-1825] Atkinson, R., "Security Architecture for the Internet Protocol", RFC 1825, Naval Research Laboratory, August 1995.

[RFC-1826] Atkinson, R., "IP Authentication Header", RFC 1826, Naval Research Laboratory, August 1995.

[RFC-1827] Atkinson, R., "IP Encapsulating Security Protocol (ESP)", RFC 1827, Naval Research Laboratory, August 1995.

[RFC-1885] Conta, A., and S. Deering, "Internet Control Message Protocol (ICMPv6) for the Internet Protocol Version 6 (IPv6) Specification", RFC 1885, Digital Equipment Corporation, Xerox PARC, December 1995.

[RFC-1884] Hinden, R., and S. Deering, Editors, "IP Version 6 Addressing Architecture", RFC 1884, Ipsilon Networks, Xerox PARC, December 1995.

[RFC-1191] Mogul, J., and S. Deering, "Path MTU Discovery", RFC 1191, DECWRL, Stanford University, November 1990.

[RFC-791] Postel, J., "Internet Protocol", STD 5, RFC 791, USC/Information Sciences Institute, September 1981.

[RFC-1700] Reynolds, J., and J. Postel, "Assigned Numbers", STD 2, RFC 1700, USC/Information Sciences Institute, October 1994.

[RFC-1661] Simpson, W., Editor, "The Point-to-Point Protocol (PPP)", STD 51, RFC 1661, Daydreamer, July 1994.

RFC 792—ICMP

rfc792

Network Working Group J. Postel

Request for Comments: 792 ISI September 1981

Updates: RFCs 777, 760

Updates: IENs 109, 128

INTERNET CONTROL MESSAGE PROTOCOL

DARPA INTERNET PROGRAM

PROTOCOL SPECIFICATION

Introduction

The Internet Protocol (IP) [1] is used for host-to-host datagram service in a system of interconnected networks called the Catenet [2]. The network connecting devices are called Gateways. These gateways communicate between themselves for control purposes via a Gateway to Gateway Protocol (GGP) [3,4]. Occasionally a gateway or destination host will communicate with a source host, for example, to report an error in datagram processing. For such purposes this protocol, the Internet Control Message Protocol (ICMP), is used. ICMP, uses the basic support of IP as if it were a higher level protocol, however, ICMP is actually an integral part of IP, and must be implemented by every IP module.

ICMP messages are sent in several situations: for example, when a datagram cannot reach its destination, when the gateway does not have the buffering capacity to forward a datagram, and when the gateway can direct the host to send traffic on a shorter route.

The Internet Protocol is not designed to be absolutely reliable. The purpose of these control messages is to provide feedback about problems in the communication environment, not to make IP reliable. There are still no guarantees that a datagram will be delivered or a control message will be returned. Some datagrams may still be undelivered without any report of their loss. The higher level protocols that use IP must implement their own reliability procedures if reliable communication is required.

The ICMP messages typically report errors in the processing of datagrams. To avoid the infinite regress of messages about messages etc., no ICMP messages are sent about ICMP messages. Also ICMP messages are only sent about errors in handling fragment zero of fragemented datagrams. (Fragment zero has the fragment offset equal zero).

Message Formats

ICMP messages are sent using the basic IP header. The first octet of the data portion of the datagram is a ICMP type field; the value of this field determines the format of the remaining data. Any field labeled "unused" is reserved for later extensions and must be zero when sent, but receivers should not use these fields (except to include them in the checksum). Unless otherwise noted under the individual format descriptions, the values of the internet header fields are as follows:

Version

4

IHL

Internet header length in 32-bit words.

Type of Service

0

Total Length

Length of internet header and data in octets.

Identification, Flags, Fragment Offset

Used in fragmentation, see [1].

Time to Live

Time to live in seconds; as this field is decremented at each machine in which the datagram is processed, the value in this field should be at least as great as the number of gateways which this datagram will traverse.

Protocol

ICMP = 1

Header Checksum

The 16 bit one's complement of the one's complement sum of all 16 bit words in the header. For computing the checksum, the checksum field should be zero. This checksum may be replaced in the future.

Source Address

The address of the gateway or host that composes the ICMP message. Unless otherwise noted, this can be any of a gateway's addresses.

Destination Address

The address of the gateway or host to which the message should be sent.

Destination Unreachable Message

```
0                   1                   2                   3
0 1 2 3 4 5 6 7 8 9 0 1 2 3 4 5 6 7 8 9 0 1 2 3 4 5 6 7 8 9 0 1
+-+-+-+-+-+-+-+-+-+-+-+-+-+-+-+-+-+-+-+-+-+-+-+-+-+-+-+-+-+-+-+-+
|     Type      |     Code      |          Checksum             |
+-+-+-+-+-+-+-+-+-+-+-+-+-+-+-+-+-+-+-+-+-+-+-+-+-+-+-+-+-+-+-+-+
|                             unused                            |
+-+-+-+-+-+-+-+-+-+-+-+-+-+-+-+-+-+-+-+-+-+-+-+-+-+-+-+-+-+-+-+-+
|      Internet Header + 64 bits of Original Data Datagram      |
+-+-+-+-+-+-+-+-+-+-+-+-+-+-+-+-+-+-+-+-+-+-+-+-+-+-+-+-+-+-+-+-+
```

IP Fields: Destination Address

> The source network and address from the original datagram's data.

ICMP Fields: Type

> 3

Code

> 0 = net unreachable;
>
> 1 = host unreachable;
>
> 2 = protocol unreachable;
>
> 3 = port unreachable;
>
> 4 = fragmentation needed and DF set;
>
> 5 = source route failed.

Checksum

> The checksum is the 16-bit ones's complement of the one's complement sum of the ICMP message starting with the ICMP Type. For computing the checksum , the checksum field should be zero. This checksum may be replaced in the future.

Internet Header + 64 bits of Data Datagram

> The internet header plus the first 64 bits of the original datagram's data. This data is used by the host to match the message to the appropriate process. If a higher level protocol uses port numbers, they are assumed to be in the first 64 data bits of the original datagram's data.

Description

> If, according to the information in the gateway's routing tables, the network specified in the internet destination field of a datagram is unreachable, e.g., the distance to the network is infinity, the gateway may send a destination unreachable message to the internet source host of the datagram. In addition, in some networks, the gateway may be able to determine if the internet destination host is unreachable. Gateways in these networks may send destination unreachable messages to the source host when the destination host is unreachable.

If, in the destination host, the IP module cannot deliver the datagram because the indicated protocol module or process port is not active, the destination host may send a destination unreachable message to the source host.

Another case is when a datagram must be fragmented to be forwarded by a gateway yet the Don't Fragment flag is on. In this case the gateway must discard the datagram and may return a destination unreachable message.

Codes 0, 1, 4, and 5 may be received from a gateway. Codes 2 and 3 may be received from a host.

Time Exceeded Message

```
 0                   1                   2                   3
 0 1 2 3 4 5 6 7 8 9 0 1 2 3 4 5 6 7 8 9 0 1 2 3 4 5 6 7 8 9 0 1
+-+-+-+-+-+-+-+-+-+-+-+-+-+-+-+-+-+-+-+-+-+-+-+-+-+-+-+-+-+-+-+-+
|     Type      |     Code      |           Checksum            |
+-+-+-+-+-+-+-+-+-+-+-+-+-+-+-+-+-+-+-+-+-+-+-+-+-+-+-+-+-+-+-+-+
|                            unused                             |
+-+-+-+-+-+-+-+-+-+-+-+-+-+-+-+-+-+-+-+-+-+-+-+-+-+-+-+-+-+-+-+-+
|      Internet Header + 64 bits of Original Data Datagram      |
+-+-+-+-+-+-+-+-+-+-+-+-+-+-+-+-+-+-+-+-+-+-+-+-+-+-+-+-+-+-+-+-+
```

IP Fields: Destination Address

The source network and address from the original datagram's data.

ICMP Fields: Type

11

Code

0 = time to live exceeded in transit;

1 = fragment reassembly time exceeded.

Checksum

The checksum is the 16-bit ones's complement of the one's complement sum of the ICMP message starting with the ICMP Type. For computing the checksum , the checksum field should be zero. This checksum may be replaced in the future.

Internet Header + 64 bits of Data Datagram

The internet header plus the first 64 bits of the original datagram's data. This data is used by the host to match the message to the appropriate process. If a higher level protocol uses port numbers, they are assumed to be in the first 64 data bits of the original datagram's data.

Description

If the gateway processing a datagram finds the time to live field is zero it must discard the datagram. The gateway may also notify the source host via the time exceeded message.

If a host reassembling a fragmented datagram cannot complete the reassembly due to missing fragments within its time limit it discards the datagram, and it may send a time exceeded message.

If fragment zero is not available then no time exceeded need be sent at all.

Code 0 may be received from a gateway. Code 1 may be received from a host.

Parameter Problem Message

```
 0                   1                   2                   3
 0 1 2 3 4 5 6 7 8 9 0 1 2 3 4 5 6 7 8 9 0 1 2 3 4 5 6 7 8 9 0 1
+-+-+-+-+-+-+-+-+-+-+-+-+-+-+-+-+-+-+-+-+-+-+-+-+-+-+-+-+-+-+-+-+
|     Type      |     Code      |           Checksum            |
+-+-+-+-+-+-+-+-+-+-+-+-+-+-+-+-+-+-+-+-+-+-+-+-+-+-+-+-+-+-+-+-+
|    Pointer    |                   unused                      |
+-+-+-+-+-+-+-+-+-+-+-+-+-+-+-+-+-+-+-+-+-+-+-+-+-+-+-+-+-+-+-+-+
|      Internet Header + 64 bits of Original Data Datagram      |
+-+-+-+-+-+-+-+-+-+-+-+-+-+-+-+-+-+-+-+-+-+-+-+-+-+-+-+-+-+-+-+-+
```

IP Fields: Destination Address

The source network and address from the original datagram's data.

ICMP Fields: Type

12

Code

0 = pointer indicates the error.

Checksum

The checksum is the 16-bit ones's complement of the one's complement sum of the ICMP message starting with the ICMP Type. For computing the checksum , the checksum field should be zero. This checksum may be replaced in the future.

Pointer

If code = 0, identifies the octet where an error was detected.

Internet Header + 64 bits of Data Datagram

The internet header plus the first 64 bits of the original datagram's data. This data is used by the host to match the message to the appropriate process. If a higher level protocol uses port numbers, they are assumed to be in the first 64 data bits of the original datagram's data.

Description

If the gateway or host processing a datagram finds a problem with the header parameters such that it cannot complete processing the datagram it must discard the datagram. One potential source of such a problem is with incorrect arguments in an option. The gateway or host may also notify the source host via the parameter problem message.

This message is only sent if the error caused the datagram to be discarded.

The pointer identifies the octet of the original datagram's header where the error was detected (it may be in the middle of an option). For example, 1 indicates something is wrong with the Type of Service, and (if there are options present) 20 indicates something is wrong with the type code of the first option.

Code 0 may be received from a gateway or a host.

Source Quench Message

IP Fields: Destination Address

The source network and address of the original datagram's data.

ICMP Fields:

Type

4

Code

0

Checksum

The checksum is the 16-bit ones's complement of the one's complement sum of the ICMP message starting with the ICMP Type. For computing the checksum , the checksum field should be zero. This checksum may be replaced in the future.

Internet Header + 64 bits of Data Datagram

The internet header plus the first 64 bits of the original datagram's data. This data is used by the host to match the message to the appropriate process. If a higher level protocol uses port numbers, they are assumed to be in the first 64 data bits of the original datagram's data.

Description

A gateway may discard internet datagrams if it does not have the buffer space needed to queue the datagrams for output to the next network on the route to the destination network. If a gateway discards a datagram, it may send a source quench message to the internet source host of the datagram. A destination host may also send a source quench message if datagrams arrive too fast to be processed. The source quench message is a request to the host to cut back the rate at which it is sending traffic to the internet destination. The gateway may send a source quench message for every message that it discards. On receipt of a source quench message, the source host should cut back the rate at which it is sending traffic to the specified destination until it no longer receives source quench messages from the gateway. The source host can then gradually increase the rate at which it sends traffic to the destination until it again receives source quench messages.

The gateway or host may send the source quench message when it approaches its capacity limit rather than waiting until the capacity is exceeded. This means that the data datagram which triggered the source quench message may be delivered.

Code 0 may be received from a gateway or a host.

Redirect Message

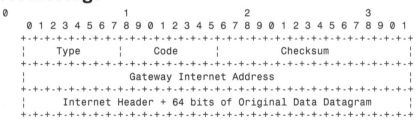

IP Fields: Destination Address

The source network and address of the original datagram's data.

ICMP Fields:

Type

5

Code

0 = Redirect datagrams for the Network.

1 = Redirect datagrams for the Host.

2 = Redirect datagrams for the Type of Service and Network.

3 = Redirect datagrams for the Type of Service and Host.

Checksum

The checksum is the 16-bit ones's complement of the one's complement sum of the ICMP message starting with the ICMP Type. For computing the checksum , the checksum field should be zero. This checksum may be replaced in the future.

Gateway Internet Address

Address of the gateway to which traffic for the network specified in the internet destination network field of the original datagram's data should be sent.

Internet Header + 64 bits of Data Datagram

The internet header plus the first 64 bits of the original datagram's data. This data is used by the host to match the message to the appropriate process. If a higher level protocol uses port numbers, they are assumed to be in the first 64 data bits of the original datagram's data.

Description

The gateway sends a redirect message to a host in the following situation. A gateway, G1, receives an internet datagram from a host on a network to which the gateway is attached. The gateway, G1, checks its routing table and obtains the address of the next gateway, G2, on the route to the datagram's internet destination network, X. If G2 and the host identified by the internet source address of the datagram are on the same network, a redirect message is sent to the host. The redirect message advises the host to send its traffic for network X directly to gateway G2 as this is a shorter path to the destination. The gateway forwards the original datagram's data to its internet destination.

For datagrams with the IP source route options and the gateway address in the destination address field, a redirect message is not sent even if there is a better route to the ultimate destination than the next address in the source route.

Codes 0, 1, 2, and 3 may be received from a gateway.

Echo or Echo Reply Message

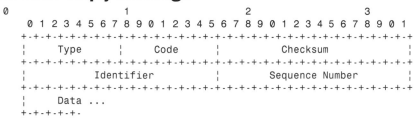

IP Fields:

Addresses

The address of the source in an echo message will be the destination of the echo reply message. To form an echo reply message, the source and destination addresses are simply reversed, the type code changed to 0, and the checksum recomputed.

IP Fields:

Type

8 for echo message;

0 for echo reply message.

Code

0

Checksum

The checksum is the 16-bit ones's complement of the one's complement sum of the ICMP message starting with the ICMP Type. For computing the checksum , the checksum field should be zero. If the total length is odd, the received data is padded with one octet of zeros for computing the checksum. This checksum may be replaced in the future.

Identifier

If code = 0, an identifier to aid in matching echos and replies, may be zero.

Sequence Number

If code = 0, a sequence number to aid in matching echos and replies, may be zero.

Description

The data received in the echo message must be returned in the echo reply message.

The identifier and sequence number may be used by the echo sender to aid in matching the replies with the echo requests. For example, the identifier might be used like a port in TCP or UDP to identify a session, and the sequence number might be incremented on each echo request sent. The echoer returns these same values in the echo reply.

Code 0 may be received from a gateway or a host.

Timestamp or Timestamp Reply Message

```
0                   1                   2                   3
0 1 2 3 4 5 6 7 8 9 0 1 2 3 4 5 6 7 8 9 0 1 2 3 4 5 6 7 8 9 0 1
+-+-+-+-+-+-+-+-+-+-+-+-+-+-+-+-+-+-+-+-+-+-+-+-+-+-+-+-+-+-+-+-+
|     Type      |     Code      |           Checksum            |
+-+-+-+-+-+-+-+-+-+-+-+-+-+-+-+-+-+-+-+-+-+-+-+-+-+-+-+-+-+-+-+-+
|           Identifier          |        Sequence Number        |
+-+-+-+-+-+-+-+-+-+-+-+-+-+-+-+-+-+-+-+-+-+-+-+-+-+-+-+-+-+-+-+-+
|     Originate Timestamp                                       |
+-+-+-+-+-+-+-+-+-+-+-+-+-+-+-+-+-+-+-+-+-+-+-+-+-+-+-+-+-+-+-+-+
|     Receive Timestamp                                         |
+-+-+-+-+-+-+-+-+-+-+-+-+-+-+-+-+-+-+-+-+-+-+-+-+-+-+-+-+-+-+-+-+
|     Transmit Timestamp                                        |
+-+-+-+-+-+-+-+-+-+-+-+-+-+-+-+-+-+-+-+-+-+-+-+-+-+-+-+-+-+-+-+-+
```

IP Fields:

Addresses

The address of the source in a timestamp message will be the destination of the timestamp reply message. To form a timestamp reply message, the source and destination addresses are simply reversed, the type code changed to 14, and the checksum recomputed.

IP Fields:

Type

13 for timestamp message;

14 for timestamp reply message.

Code

0

Checksum

The checksum is the 16-bit ones's complement of the one's complement sum of the ICMP message starting with the ICMP Type. For computing the checksum , the checksum field should be zero. This checksum may be replaced in the future.

Identifier

If code = 0, an identifier to aid in matching timestamp and replies, may be zero.

Sequence Number

If code = 0, a sequence number to aid in matching timestamp and replies, may be zero.

Description

The data received (a timestamp) in the message is returned in the reply together with an additional timestamp. The timestamp is 32 bits of milliseconds since midnight UT. One use of these timestamps is described by Mills [5].

The Originate Timestamp is the time the sender last touched the message before sending it, the Receive Timestamp is the time the echoer first touched it on receipt, and the Transmit Timestamp is the time the echoer last touched the message on sending it.

If the time is not available in miliseconds or cannot be provided with respect to midnight UT then any time can be inserted in a timestamp provided the high order bit of the timestamp is also set to indicate this non-standard value.

The identifier and sequence number may be used by the echo sender to aid in matching the replies with the requests. For example, the identifier might be used like a port in TCP or UDP to identify a session, and the sequence number might be incremented on each request sent. The destination returns these same values in the reply.

Code 0 may be received from a gateway or a host.

Information Request or Information Reply Message

```
 0                   1                   2                   3
 0 1 2 3 4 5 6 7 8 9 0 1 2 3 4 5 6 7 8 9 0 1 2 3 4 5 6 7 8 9 0 1
+-+-+-+-+-+-+-+-+-+-+-+-+-+-+-+-+-+-+-+-+-+-+-+-+-+-+-+-+-+-+-+-+
|     Type      |     Code      |           Checksum            |
+-+-+-+-+-+-+-+-+-+-+-+-+-+-+-+-+-+-+-+-+-+-+-+-+-+-+-+-+-+-+-+-+
|           Identifier          |        Sequence Number        |
+-+-+-+-+-+-+-+-+-+-+-+-+-+-+-+-+-+-+-+-+-+-+-+-+-+-+-+-+-+-+-+-+
```

IP Fields:

Addresses

> The address of the source in a information request message will be the destination of the information reply message. To form a information reply message, the source and destination addresses are simply reversed, the type code changed to 16, and the checksum recomputed.

IP Fields:

Type

> 15 for information request message;
>
> 16 for information reply message.

Code

> 0

Checksum

> The checksum is the 16-bit ones's complement of the one's complement sum of the ICMP message starting with the ICMP Type. For computing the checksum , the checksum field should be zero. This checksum may be replaced in the future.

Identifier

> If code = 0, an identifier to aid in matching request and replies, may be zero.

Sequence Number

> If code = 0, a sequence number to aid in matching request and replies, may be zero.

Description

> This message may be sent with the source network in the IP header source and destination address fields zero (which means "this" network). The replying IP module should send the reply with the addresses fully specified. This message is a way for a host to find out the number of the network it is on.
>
> The identifier and sequence number may be used by the echo sender to aid in matching the replies with the requests. For example, the identifier might be used like a port in TCP or UDP to identify a session, and the sequence number might be incremented on each request sent. The destination returns these same values in the reply.
>
> Code 0 may be received from a gateway or a host.

Summary of Message Types

0 Echo Reply

3 Destination Unreachable

4 Source Quench

5 Redirect

8 Echo

11 Time Exceeded

12 Parameter Problem

13 Timestamp

14 Timestamp Reply

15 Information Request

16 Information Reply

References

[1] Postel, J. (ed.), "Internet Protocol - DARPA Internet Program Protocol Specification," RFC 791, USC/Information Sciences Institute, September 1981.

[2] Cerf, V., "The Catenet Model for Internetworking," IEN 48, Information Processing Techniques Office, Defense Advanced Research Projects Agency, July 1978.

[3] Strazisar, V., "Gateway Routing: An Implementation Specification", IEN 30, Bolt Beranek and Newman, April 1979.

[4] Strazisar, V., "How to Build a Gateway", IEN 109, Bolt Beranek and Newman, August 1979.

[5] Mills, D., "DCNET Internet Clock Service," RFC 778, COMSAT Laboratories, April 1981.

Using TCP/IP Remotely

by John Ray

You've almost certainly used PPP to connect to the Internet from home. Have you ever wondered exactly how this process works? RFC 1661 will give you the details behind the most popular dial-in method to the Internet. If you're a veteran to accessing the network remotely, check out RFC 1055, which discusses SLIP—the Serial Line Internet Protocol. It's interesting to compare the simplicity of the SLIP protocol in RFC 1055 to the relatively complex and comprehensive PPP.

RFC 1055	SLIP
RFC 1661	PPP

Editor's note: The following appendix contains the complete RFC documents, unedited except for formatting.

A NONSTANDARD FOR TRANSMISSION OF IP DATAGRAMS OVER SERIAL LINES: SLIP

INTRODUCTION

The TCP/IP protocol family runs over a variety of network media: IEEE 802.3 (ethernet) and 802.5 (token ring) LAN's, X.25 lines, satellite links, and serial lines. There are standard encapsulations for IP packets defined for many of these networks, but there is no standard for serial lines. SLIP, Serial Line IP, is a currently a de facto standard, commonly used for point-to-point serial connections running TCP/IP. It is not an Internet standard. Distribution of this memo is unlimited.

HISTORY

SLIP has its origins in the 3COM UNET TCP/IP implementation from the early 1980's. It is merely a packet framing protocol: SLIP defines a sequence of characters that frame IP packets on a serial line, and nothing more. It provides no addressing, packet type identification, error detection/correction or compression mechanisms. Because the protocol does so little, though, it is usually very easy to implement.

Around 1984, Rick Adams implemented SLIP for 4.2 Berkeley Unix and Sun Microsystems workstations and released it to the world. It quickly caught on as an easy reliable way to connect TCP/IP hosts and routers with serial lines.

SLIP is commonly used on dedicated serial links and sometimes for dialup purposes, and is usually used with line speeds between 1200bps and 19.2Kbps. It is useful for allowing mixes of hosts and routers to communicate with one another (host-host, host-router and router-router are all common SLIP network configurations).

AVAILABILITY

SLIP is available for most Berkeley UNIX-based systems. It is included in the standard 4.3BSD release from Berkeley. SLIP is available for Ultrix, Sun UNIX and most other Berkeley-derived UNIX systems. Some terminal concentrators and IBM PC implementations also support it.

SLIP for Berkeley UNIX is available via anonymous FTP from uunet.uu.net in pub/sl.shar.Z. Be sure to transfer the file in binary mode and then run it through the UNIX uncompress program. Take the resulting file and use it as a shell script for the UNIX /bin/sh (for instance, /bin/sh sl.shar).

PROTOCOL

The SLIP protocol defines two special characters: END and ESC. END is octal 300 (decimal 192) and ESC is octal 333 (decimal 219) not to be confused with the ASCII ESCape character; for the purposes of this discussion, ESC will indicate the SLIP ESC character. To send a packet, a SLIP host simply starts sending the data in the packet. If a data byte is the same code as END character, a two byte sequence of ESC and octal 334 (decimal 220) is sent instead. If it the same as an ESC character, an two byte sequence of ESC and octal 335 (decimal 221) is sent instead. When the last byte in the packet has been sent, an END character is then transmitted.

Phil Karn suggests a simple change to the algorithm, which is to begin as well as end packets with an END character. This will flush any erroneous bytes which have been caused by line noise. In the normal case, the receiver will simply see two back-to-back END characters, which will generate a bad IP packet. If the SLIP implementation does not throw away the zero-length IP packet, the IP implementation certainly will. If there was line noise, the data received due to it will be discarded without affecting the following packet.

Because there is no 'standard' SLIP specification, there is no real defined maximum packet size for SLIP. It is probably best to accept the maximum packet size used by the Berkeley UNIX SLIP drivers: 1006 bytes including the IP and transport protocol headers (not including the framing characters). Therefore any new SLIP implementations should be prepared to accept 1006 byte datagrams and should not send more than 1006 bytes in a datagram.

DEFICIENCIES

There are several features that many users would like SLIP to provide which it doesn't. In all fairness, SLIP is just a very simple protocol designed quite a long time ago when these problems were not really important issues. The following are commonly perceived shortcomings in the existing SLIP protocol: - addressing: both computers in a SLIP link need to know each other's IP addresses for routing purposes. Also, when using SLIP for hosts to dial-up a router, the addressing scheme may be quite dynamic and the router may need to inform the dialing host of the host's IP address. SLIP currently provides no mechanism for hosts to communicate addressing information over a SLIP connection. - type identification: SLIP has no type field. Thus, only one protocol can be run over a SLIP connection, so in a configuration of two DEC computers running both TCP/IP and DECnet, there is no hope of having TCP/IP and DECnet share one serial line between them while using SLIP. While SLIP is "Serial Line IP", if a serial line connects two multi-protocol computers, those computers should be able to use more than one protocol over the line. - error detection/correction: noisy phone lines will corrupt packets in transit. Because the line speed is probably quite low (likely 2400 baud), retransmitting a packet is very expensive. Error detection is not absolutely necessary at the SLIP level because any IP application should detect damaged packets (IP header and UDP and TCP checksums should suffice), although some common applications like NFS usually ignore the checksum and depend on the network media to detect damaged packets. Because it takes so long to re-transmit a packet which was corrupted by line noise, it would be efficient if SLIP could provide some sort of simple error correction mechanism of its own. - compression: because dial-in lines are so slow (usually 2400bps), packet compression would cause large improvements in packet throughput. Usually, streams of packets in a single TCP connection have few changed fields in the IP and TCP headers, so a simple compression algorithms might just send the changed parts of the headers instead of the complete headers.

Some work is being done by various groups to design and implement a successor to SLIP which will address some or all of these problems.

SLIP DRIVERS

The following C language functions send and receive SLIP packets. They depend on two functions, send_char() and recv_char(), which send and receive a single character over the serial line.

/* SLIP special character codes

```
*/
#define END     0300    /* indicates end of packet */
#define ESC     0333    /* indicates byte stuffing */
#define ESC_END   0334    /* ESC ESC_END means END data byte */
#define ESC_ESC   0335    /* ESC ESC_ESC means ESC data byte */
    /* SEND_PACKET: sends a packet of length "len", starting at
     * location "p".
     */
  void send_packet(p, len)
        char *p;
        int len; {

    /* send an initial END character to flush out any data that may
     * have accumulated in the receiver due to line noise
     */
      send_char(END);

    /* for each byte in the packet, send the appropriate character
     * sequence
     */
        while(len--) {
                switch(*p) {
                /* if it's the same code as an END character, we send a
                 * special two character code so as not to make the
                 * receiver think we sent an END
                 */
                case END:
                        send_char(ESC);
                        send_char(ESC_END);
                        break;

                /* if it's the same code as an ESC character,
                 * we send a special two character code so as not
                 * to make the receiver think we sent an ESC
                 */
                case ESC:
                        send_char(ESC);
                        send_char(ESC_ESC);
                        break;


                /* otherwise, we just send the character
                 */
```

```
                          default:
                                  send_char(*p);
                                  }

                          p++;
                          }

                  /* tell the receiver that we're done sending the packet
                   */
                  send_char(END);
                  }

/* RECV_PACKET: receives a packet into the buffer located at "p".
 *      If more than len bytes are received, the packet will
 *      be truncated.
 *      Returns the number of bytes stored in the buffer.
 */
int recv_packet(p, len)
        char *p;
        int len; {
        char c;
        int received = 0;

        /* sit in a loop reading bytes until we put together
         * a whole packet.
         * Make sure not to copy them into the packet if we
         * run out of room.
         */
        while(1) {
                /* get a character to process
                 */
                c = recv_char();

                /* handle bytestuffing if necessary
                 */
                switch(c) {

                /* if it's an END character then we're done with
                 * the packet
                 */
                case END:
                        /* a minor optimization: if there is no
                         * data in the packet, ignore it. This is
                         * meant to avoid bothering IP with all
                         * the empty packets generated by the
                         * duplicate END characters which are in
                         * turn sent to try to detect line noise.
                         */
                        if(received)
                                return received;
                        else
                                break;
```

continues

Continued

```
      /* if it's the same code as an ESC character, wait
       * and get another character and then figure out
       * what to store in the packet based on that.
       */
      case ESC:
              c = recv_char();

              /* if "c" is not one of these two, then we
               * have a protocol violation.  The best bet
               * seems to be to leave the byte alone and
               * just stuff it into the packet
               */
              switch(c) {
              case ESC_END:
                      c = END;
                      break;
              case ESC_ESC:
                      c = ESC;
                      break;
                      }

      /* here we fall into the default handler and let
       * it store the character for us
       */
      default:
              if(received < len)
                      p[received++] = c;
              }
      }
}
```

Network Working Group   W. Simpson, Editor
Request for Comments: 1661   Daydreamer
STD: 51   July 1994
Obsoletes: 1548
Category: Standards Track

The Point-to-Point Protocol (PPP)

Status of this Memo

This document specifies an Internet standards track protocol for the Internet community, and requests discussion and suggestions for improvements. Please refer to the current edition of the "Internet Official Protocol Standards" (STD 1) for the standardization state and status of this protocol. Distribution of this memo is unlimited.

Abstract

The Point-to-Point Protocol (PPP) provides a standard method for transporting multi-protocol datagrams over point-to-point links. PPP is comprised of three main components:

1. A method for encapsulating multi-protocol datagrams.
2. A Link Control Protocol (LCP) for establishing, configuring, and testing the data-link connection.
3. A family of Network Control Protocols (NCPs) for establishing and configuring different network-layer protocols.

This document defines the PPP organization and methodology, and the PPP encapsulation, together with an extensible option negotiation mechanism which is able to negotiate a rich assortment of configuration parameters and provides additional management functions. The PPP Link Control Protocol (LCP) is described in terms of this mechanism.

App

B

Table of Contents

1.	Introduction	715
1.1	Specification of Requirements	716
1.2	Terminology	717
2.	PPP Encapsulation	717
3.	PPP Link Operation	719
3.1	Overview	719
3.2	Phase Diagram	719
3.3	Link Dead (physical-layer not ready)	720
3.4	Link Establishment Phase	720
3.5	Authentication Phase	720
3.6	Network-Layer Protocol Phase	721
3.7	Link Termination Phase	722
4.	The Option Negotiation Automaton	722
4.1	State Transition Table	723
4.2	States	725
4.3	Events	727
4.4	Actions	731
4.5	Loop Avoidance	733
4.6	Counters and Timers	733
5.	LCP Packet Formats	734
5.1	Configure-Request	736
5.2	Configure-Ack	737
5.3	Configure-Nak	738
5.4	Configure-Reject	739
5.5	Terminate-Request and Terminate-Ack	740
5.6	Code-Reject	741
5.7	Protocol-Reject	742
5.8	Echo-Request and Echo-Reply	743
5.9	Discard-Request	745
6.	LCP Configuration Options	746
6.1	Maximum-Receive-Unit (MRU)	747
6.2	Authentication-Protocol	748
6.3	Quality-Protocol	749

6.4   Magic-Number   751

6.5   Protocol-Field-Compression (PFC)   753

6.6   Address-and-Control-Field-Compression (ACFC)   754

SECURITY CONSIDERATIONS   755

REFERENCES   755

ACKNOWLEDGEMENTS   755

CHAIR'S ADDRESS   756

EDITOR'S ADDRESS   756

App
B

1. Introduction

The Point-to-Point Protocol is designed for simple links which transport packets between two peers. These links provide full-duplex simultaneous bi-directional operation, and are assumed to deliver packets in order. It is intended that PPP provide a common solution for easy connection of a wide variety of hosts, bridges and routers

[1].

Encapsulation

The PPP encapsulation provides for multiplexing of different network-layer protocols simultaneously over the same link. The PPP encapsulation has been carefully designed to retain compatibility with most commonly used supporting hardware.

Only 8 additional octets are necessary to form the encapsulation when used within the default HDLC-like framing. In environments where bandwidth is at a premium, the encapsulation and framing may be shortened to 2 or 4 octets.

To support high speed implementations, the default encapsulation uses only simple fields, only one of which needs to be examined for demultiplexing. The default header and information fields fall on 32-bit boundaries, and the trailer may be padded to an arbitrary boundary.

Link Control Protocol

In order to be sufficiently versatile to be portable to a wide variety of environments, PPP provides a Link Control Protocol (LCP). The LCP is used to automatically agree upon the encapsulation format options, handle varying limits on sizes of packets, detect a looped-back link and other common misconfiguration errors, and terminate the link. Other optional facilities provided are authentication of the identity of its peer on the link, and determination when a link is functioning properly and when it is failing.

Network Control Protocols

Point-to-Point links tend to exacerbate many problems with the current family of network protocols. For instance, assignment and management of IP addresses, which is a problem even in LAN environments, is especially difficult over circuit-switched point-to-point links (such as dial-up modem servers). These problems are handled by a family of Network Control Protocols (NCPs), which each manage the specific needs required by their respective network-layer protocols. These NCPs are defined in companion documents.

Configuration

It is intended that PPP links be easy to configure. By design, the standard defaults handle all common configurations. The implementor can specify improvements to the default configuration, which are automatically communicated to the peer without operator intervention. Finally, the operator may explicitly configure options for the link which enable the link to operate in environments where it would otherwise be impossible.

This self-configuration is implemented through an extensible option negotiation mechanism, wherein each end of the link describes to the other its capabilities and requirements. Although the option negotiation mechanism described in this document is specified in terms of the Link Control Protocol (LCP), the same facilities are designed to be used by other control protocols, especially the family of NCPs.

1.1. Specification of Requirements

In this document, several words are used to signify the requirements of the specification. These words are often capitalized.

MUST This word, or the adjective "required", means that the definition is an absolute requirement of the specification.

MUST NOT This phrase means that the definition is an absolute prohibition of the specification.

SHOULD This word, or the adjective "recommended", means that there may exist valid reasons in particular circumstances to ignore this item, but the full implications must be understood and carefully weighed before choosing a different course.

MAY This word, or the adjective "optional", means that this item is one of an allowed set of alternatives. An implementation which does not include this option MUST be prepared to interoperate with another implementation which does include the option.

1.2. Terminology

This document frequently uses the following terms:

datagram The unit of transmission in the network layer (such as IP). A datagram may be encapsulated in one or more packets passed to the data link layer.

frame The unit of transmission at the data link layer. A frame may include a header and/or a trailer, along with some number of units of data.

packet The basic unit of encapsulation, which is passed across the interface between the network layer and the data link layer. A packet is usually mapped to a frame; the exceptions are when data link layer fragmentation is being performed, or when multiple packets are incorporated into a single frame.

peer The other end of the point-to-point link.

silently discard The implementation discards the packet without further processing. The implementation SHOULD provide the capability of logging the error, including the contents of the silently discarded packet, and SHOULD record the event in a statistics counter.

2. PPP Encapsulation

The PPP encapsulation is used to disambiguate multiprotocol datagrams. This encapsulation requires framing to indicate the beginning and end of the encapsulation. Methods of providing framing are specified in companion documents.

A summary of the PPP encapsulation is shown below. The fields are transmitted from left to right.

```
+----------+------------+--------+
| Protocol | Information | Padding |
| 8/16 bits|     *       |    *    |
+----------+------------+--------+
```

Protocol Field

The Protocol field is one or two octets, and its value identifies the datagram encapsulated in the Information field of the packet. The field is transmitted and received most significant octet first.

The structure of this field is consistent with the ISO 3309 extension mechanism for address fields. All Protocols MUST be odd; the least significant bit of the least significant octet MUST equal "1". Also, all Protocols MUST be assigned such that the least significant bit of the most significant octet equals "0". Frames received which don't comply with these rules MUST be treated as having an unrecognized Protocol.

Protocol field values in the "0***" to "3***" range identify the network-layer protocol of specific packets, and values in the "8***" to "b***" range identify packets belonging to the associated Network Control Protocols (NCPs), if any.

Protocol field values in the "4***" to "7***" range are used for protocols with low volume traffic which have no associated NCP. Protocol field values in the "c***" to "f***" range identify packets as link-layer Control Protocols (such as LCP).

Up-to-date values of the Protocol field are specified in the most recent "Assigned Numbers" RFC [2]. This specification reserves the following values:

Value (in hex)	Protocol Name
0001	Padding Protocol
0003 to 001f	reserved (transparency inefficient)
007d	reserved (Control Escape)
00cf	reserved (PPP NLPID)
00ff	reserved (compression inefficient)
8001 to 801f	unused
807d	unused
80cf	unused
80ff	unused
c021	Link Control Protocol
c023	Password Authentication Protocol
c025	Link Quality Report
c223	Challenge Handshake Authentication Protocol

Developers of new protocols MUST obtain a number from the Internet Assigned Numbers Authority (IANA), at IANA@isi.edu.

Information Field

The Information field is zero or more octets. The Information field contains the datagram for the protocol specified in the Protocol field.

The maximum length for the Information field, including Padding, but not including the Protocol field, is termed the Maximum Receive Unit (MRU), which defaults to 1500 octets. By negotiation, consenting PPP implementations may use other values for the MRU.

Padding

On transmission, the Information field MAY be padded with an arbitrary number of octets up to the MRU. It is the responsibility of each protocol to distinguish padding octets from real information.

3. PPP Link Operation

3.1. Overview

In order to establish communications over a point-to-point link, each end of the PPP link MUST first send LCP packets to configure and test the data link. After the link has been established, the peer MAY be authenticated.

Then, PPP MUST send NCP packets to choose and configure one or more network-layer protocols. Once each of the chosen network-layer protocols has been configured, datagrams from each network-layer protocol can be sent over the link.

The link will remain configured for communications until explicit LCP or NCP packets close the link down, or until some external event occurs (an inactivity timer expires or network administrator intervention).

3.2. Phase Diagram

In the process of configuring, maintaining and terminating the point-to-point link, the PPP link goes through several distinct phases which are specified in the following simplified state diagram:

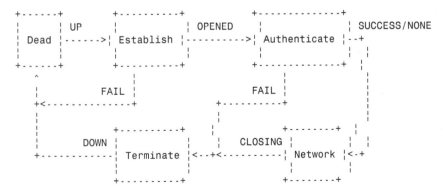

Not all transitions are specified in this diagram. The following semantics MUST be followed.

3.3. Link Dead (physical-layer not ready)

The link necessarily begins and ends with this phase. When an external event (such as carrier detection or network administrator configuration) indicates that the physical-layer is ready to be used, PPP will proceed to the Link Establishment phase.

During this phase, the LCP automaton (described later) will be in the Initial or Starting states. The transition to the Link Establishment phase will signal an Up event to the LCP automaton.

Implementation Note:

Typically, a link will return to this phase automatically after the disconnection of a modem. In the case of a hard-wired link, this phase may be extremely short — merely long enough to detect the presence of the device.

3.4. Link Establishment Phase

The Link Control Protocol (LCP) is used to establish the connection through an exchange of Configure packets. This exchange is complete, and the LCP Opened state entered, once a Configure-Ack packet (described later) has been both sent and received.

All Configuration Options are assumed to be at default values unless altered by the configuration exchange. See the chapter on LCP Configuration Options for further discussion.

It is important to note that only Configuration Options which are independent of particular network-layer protocols are configured by LCP. Configuration of individual network-layer protocols is handled by separate Network Control Protocols (NCPs) during the Network-Layer Protocol phase.

Any non-LCP packets received during this phase MUST be silently discarded.

The receipt of the LCP Configure-Request causes a return to the Link Establishment phase from the Network-Layer Protocol phase or Authentication phase.

3.5. Authentication Phase

On some links it may be desirable to require a peer to authenticate itself before allowing network-layer protocol packets to be exchanged.

By default, authentication is not mandatory. If an implementation desires that the peer authenticate with some specific authentication protocol, then it MUST request the use of that authentication protocol during Link Establishment phase.

Authentication SHOULD take place as soon as possible after link establishment. However, link quality determination MAY occur concurrently. An implementation MUST NOT allow the exchange of link quality determination packets to delay authentication indefinitely.

Advancement from the Authentication phase to the Network-Layer Protocol phase MUST NOT occur until authentication has completed. If authentication fails, the authenticator SHOULD proceed instead to the Link Termination phase.

Only Link Control Protocol, authentication protocol, and link quality monitoring packets are allowed during this phase. All other packets received during this phase MUST be silently discarded.

Implementation Notes:

An implementation SHOULD NOT fail authentication simply due to timeout or lack of response. The authentication SHOULD allow some method of retransmission, and proceed to the Link Termination phase only after a number of authentication attempts has been exceeded.

The implementation responsible for commencing Link Termination phase is the implementation which has refused authentication to its peer.

3.6. Network-Layer Protocol Phase

Once PPP has finished the previous phases, each network-layer protocol (such as IP, IPX, or AppleTalk) MUST be separately configured by the appropriate Network Control Protocol (NCP).

Each NCP MAY be Opened and Closed at any time.

Implementation Note:

Because an implementation may initially use a significant amount of time for link quality determination, implementations SHOULD avoid fixed timeouts when waiting for their peers to configure a NCP.

After a NCP has reached the Opened state, PPP will carry the corresponding network-layer protocol packets. Any supported network-layer protocol packets received when the corresponding NCP is not in the Opened state MUST be silently discarded.

Implementation Note:

While LCP is in the Opened state, any protocol packet which is unsupported by the implementation MUST be returned in a Protocol- Reject (described later). Only protocols which are supported are silently discarded.

During this phase, link traffic consists of any possible combination of LCP, NCP, and network-layer protocol packets.

3.7. Link Termination Phase

PPP can terminate the link at any time. This might happen because of the loss of carrier, authentication failure, link quality failure, the expiration of an idle-period timer, or the administrative closing of the link.

LCP is used to close the link through an exchange of Terminate packets. When the link is closing, PPP informs the network-layer protocols so that they may take appropriate action.

After the exchange of Terminate packets, the implementation SHOULD signal the physical-layer to disconnect in order to enforce the termination of the link, particularly in the case of an authentication failure. The sender of the Terminate-Request SHOULD disconnect after receiving a Terminate-Ack, or after the Restart counter expires. The receiver of a Terminate-Request SHOULD wait for the peer to disconnect, and MUST NOT disconnect until at least one Restart time has passed after sending a Terminate-Ack. PPP SHOULD proceed to the Link Dead phase.

Any non-LCP packets received during this phase MUST be silently discarded.

Implementation Note:

The closing of the link by LCP is sufficient. There is no need for each NCP to send a flurry of Terminate packets. Conversely, the fact that one NCP has Closed is not sufficient reason to cause the termination of the PPP link, even if that NCP was the only NCP currently in the Opened state.

4. The Option Negotiation Automaton

The finite-state automaton is defined by events, actions and state transitions. Events include reception of external commands such as Open and Close, expiration of the Restart timer, and reception of packets from a peer. Actions include the starting of the Restart timer and transmission of packets to the peer.

Some types of packets — Configure-Naks and Configure-Rejects, or Code-Rejects and Protocol-Rejects, or Echo-Requests, Echo-Replies and Discard-Requests — are not differentiated in the automaton descriptions. As will be described later, these packets do indeed serve different functions. However, they always cause the same transitions.

Events	Actions
Up	= lower layer is Up tlu = This-Layer-Up
Down = lower layer is Down	tld = This-Layer-Down
Open = administrative Open	tls = This-Layer-Started
Close= administrative Close	tlf = This-Layer-Finished
TO+	= Timeout with counter > 0 irc = Initialize-Restart-Count

Events	Actions
TO-	= Timeout with counter expired
	zrc = Zero-Restart-Count
RCR+ = Receive-Configure-Request (Good)	scr = Send-Configure-Request
RCR- = Receive-Configure-Request (Bad)	
RCA	= Receive-Configure-Ack
	sca = Send-Configure-Ack
RCN	= Receive-Configure-Nak/Rej
	scn = Send-Configure-Nak/Rej
RTR	= Receive-Terminate-Request
	str = Send-Terminate-Request
RTA	= Receive-Terminate-Ack
	sta = Send-Terminate-Ack
RUC	= Receive-Unknown-Code
	scj = Send-Code-Reject
RXJ+	= Receive-Code-Reject (permitted)
	or Receive-Protocol-Reject
RXJ-	= Receive-Code-Reject (catastrophic)
	or Receive-Protocol-Reject
RXR	= Receive-Echo-Request or Receive-Echo-Reply
	or Receive-Discard-Request ser = Send-Echo-Reply

App

B

4.1. State Transition Table

The complete state transition table follows. States are indicated horizontally, and events are read vertically. State transitions and actions are represented in the form action/new-state. Multiple actions are separated by commas, and may continue on succeeding lines as space requires; multiple actions may be implemented in any convenient order. The state may be followed by a letter, which indicates an explanatory footnote. The dash ('-') indicates an illegal transition.

```
       | State
       |   0         1         2        3         4         5
Events | Initial  Starting  Closed   Stopped   Closing   Stopping
-------+----------------------------------------------------------
Up     |   2      irc,scr/6    -        -         -         -
Down   |   -         -         0      tls/1       0         1
Open   | tls/1       1      irc,scr/6  3r        5r        5r
Close  |   0       tlf/0       2        2         4         4
       |
```

```
TO+ |    -         -         -         -        str/4     str/5
TO- |    -         -         -         -        tlf/2     tlf/3

RCR+|    -         -       sta/2  irc,scr,sca/8   4         5
RCR-|    -         -       sta/2  irc,scr,scn/6   4         5
RCA |    -         -       sta/2     sta/3        4         5
RCN |    -         -       sta/2     sta/3        4         5

RTR |    -         -       sta/2     sta/3      sta/4     sta/5
RTA |    -         -         2         3        tlf/2     tlf/3

RUC |    -         -       scj/2     scj/3      scj/4     scj/5
RXJ+|    -         -         2         3          4         5
RXJ-|    -         -       tlf/2     tlf/3      tlf/2     tlf/3

RXR |    -         -         2         3          4         5
      State
        6         7         8         9
Events| Req-Sent  Ack-Rcvd  Ack-Sent  Opened
------+-------------------------------------------
Up   |    -         -         -         -
Down |    1         1         1       tld/1
Open |    6         7         8        9r
Close|irc,str/4 irc,str/4 irc,str/4 tld,irc,str/4

TO+  |  scr/6     scr/6     scr/8        -
TO-  | tlf/3p    tlf/3p    tlf/3p        -

RCR+ |  sca/8   sca,tlu/9   sca/8   tld,scr,sca/8
RCR- |  scn/6     scn/7     scn/6   tld,scr,scn/6
RCA  |  irc/7    scr/6x   irc,tlu/9  tld,scr/6x
RCN  |irc,scr/6  scr/6x   irc,scr/8  tld,scr/6x

RTR  |  sta/6     sta/6     sta/6  tld,zrc,sta/5
RTA  |    6         6         8      tld,scr/6

RUC  |  scj/6     scj/7     scj/8     scj/9
RXJ+ |    6         6         8         9
RXJ- |  tlf/3     tlf/3     tlf/3  tld,irc,str/5

RXR  |    6         7         8       ser/9
```

The states in which the Restart timer is running are identifiable by the presence of TO events. Only the Send-Configure-Request, Send-Terminate-Request and Zero-Restart-Count actions start or re-start the Restart timer. The Restart timer is stopped when transitioning from any state where the timer is running to a state where the timer is not running.

The events and actions are defined according to a message passing architecture, rather than a signalling architecture. If an action is desired to control specific signals (such as DTR), additional actions are likely to be required.

[p]	Passive option; see Stopped state discussion.
[r]	Restart option; see Open event discussion.
[x]	Crossed connection; see RCA event discussion.

4.2. States

Following is a more detailed description of each automaton state.

Initial

In the Initial state, the lower layer is unavailable (Down), and no Open has occurred. The Restart timer is not running in the Initial state.

Starting

The Starting state is the Open counterpart to the Initial state. An administrative Open has been initiated, but the lower layer is still unavailable (Down). The Restart timer is not running in the Starting state.

When the lower layer becomes available (Up), a Configure-Request is sent.

Closed

In the Closed state, the link is available (Up), but no Open has occurred. The Restart timer is not running in the Closed state.

Upon reception of Configure-Request packets, a Terminate-Ack is sent. Terminate-Acks are silently discarded to avoid creating a loop.

Stopped

The Stopped state is the Open counterpart to the Closed state. It is entered when the automaton is waiting for a Down event after the This-Layer-Finished action, or after sending a Terminate-Ack. The Restart timer is not running in the Stopped state.

Upon reception of Configure-Request packets, an appropriate response is sent. Upon reception of other packets, a Terminate- Ack is sent. Terminate-Acks are silently discarded to avoid creating a loop.

Rationale:

The Stopped state is a junction state for link termination, link configuration failure, and other automaton failure modes. These potentially separate states have been combined.

There is a race condition between the Down event response (from the This-Layer-Finished action) and the Receive-Configure- Request event. When a Configure-Request arrives before the Down event, the Down event will supercede by returning the automaton to the Starting state. This prevents attack by repetition.

Implementation Option:

After the peer fails to respond to Configure-Requests, an implementation MAY wait passively for the peer to send Configure-Requests. In this case, the This-Layer-Finished action is not used for the TO- event in states Req-Sent, Ack- Rcvd and Ack-Sent.

This option is useful for dedicated circuits, or circuits which have no status signals available, but SHOULD NOT be used for switched circuits.

Closing

In the Closing state, an attempt is made to terminate the connection. A Terminate-Request has been sent and the Restart timer is running, but a Terminate-Ack has not yet been received.

Upon reception of a Terminate-Ack, the Closed state is entered. Upon the expiration of the Restart timer, a new Terminate-Request is transmitted, and the Restart timer is restarted. After the Restart timer has expired Max-Terminate times, the Closed state is entered.

Stopping

The Stopping state is the Open counterpart to the Closing state. A Terminate-Request has been sent and the Restart timer is running, but a Terminate-Ack has not yet been received.

Rationale:

The Stopping state provides a well defined opportunity to terminate a link before allowing new traffic. After the link has terminated, a new configuration may occur via the Stopped or Starting states.

Request-Sent

In the Request-Sent state an attempt is made to configure the connection. A Configure-Request has been sent and the Restart timer is running, but a Configure-Ack has not yet been received nor has one been sent.

Ack-Received

In the Ack-Received state, a Configure-Request has been sent and a Configure-Ack has been received. The Restart timer is still running, since a Configure-Ack has not yet been sent.

Ack-Sent

In the Ack-Sent state, a Configure-Request and a Configure-Ack have both been sent, but a Configure-Ack has not yet been received. The Restart timer is running, since a Configure-Ack has not yet been received.

Opened

In the Opened state, a Configure-Ack has been both sent and received. The Restart timer is not running.

When entering the Opened state, the implementation SHOULD signal the upper layers that it is now Up. Conversely, when leaving the Opened state, the implementation SHOULD signal the upper layers that it is now Down.

4.3. Events

Transitions and actions in the automaton are caused by events.

Up

This event occurs when a lower layer indicates that it is ready to carry packets.

Typically, this event is used by a modem handling or calling process, or by some other coupling of the PPP link to the physical media, to signal LCP that the link is entering Link Establishment phase.

It also can be used by LCP to signal each NCP that the link is entering Network-Layer Protocol phase. That is, the This-Layer-Up action from LCP triggers the Up event in the NCP.

Down

This event occurs when a lower layer indicates that it is no longer ready to carry packets.

Typically, this event is used by a modem handling or calling process, or by some other coupling of the PPP link to the physical media, to signal LCP that the link is entering Link Dead phase.

It also can be used by LCP to signal each NCP that the link is leaving Network-Layer Protocol phase. That is, the This-Layer-Down action from LCP triggers the Down event in the NCP.

Open

This event indicates that the link is administratively available for traffic; that is, the network administrator (human or program) has indicated that the link is allowed to be Opened. When this event occurs, and the link is not in the Opened state, the automaton attempts to send configuration packets to the peer.

If the automaton is not able to begin configuration (the lower layer is Down, or a previous Close event has not completed), the establishment of the link is automatically delayed.

When a Terminate-Request is received, or other events occur which cause the link to become unavailable, the automaton will progress to a state where the link is ready to re-open. No additional administrative intervention is necessary.

Implementation Option:

Experience has shown that users will execute an additional Open command when they want to renegotiate the link. This might indicate that new values are to be negotiated.

Since this is not the meaning of the Open event, it is suggested that when an Open user command is executed in the Opened, Closing, Stopping, or Stopped states, the implementation issue a Down event, immediately followed by an Up event. Care must be taken that an intervening Down event cannot occur from another source.

The Down followed by an Up will cause an orderly renegotiation of the link, by progressing through the Starting to the Request-Sent state. This will cause the renegotiation of the link, without any harmful side effects.

Close

This event indicates that the link is not available for traffic; that is, the network administrator (human or program) has indicated that the link is not allowed to be Opened. When this event occurs, and the link is not in the Closed state, the automaton attempts to terminate the connection. Futher attempts to re-configure the link are denied until a new Open event occurs.

Implementation Note:

When authentication fails, the link SHOULD be terminated, to prevent attack by repetition and denial of service to other users. Since the link is administratively available (by definition), this can be accomplished by simulating a Close event to the LCP, immediately followed by an Open event. Care must be taken that an intervening Close event cannot occur from another source.

The Close followed by an Open will cause an orderly termination of the link, by progressing through the Closing to the Stopping state, and the This-Layer-Finished action can disconnect the link. The automaton waits in the Stopped or Starting states for the next connection attempt.

Timeout (TO+,TO-)

This event indicates the expiration of the Restart timer. The Restart timer is used to time responses to Configure-Request and Terminate-Request packets.

The TO+ event indicates that the Restart counter continues to be greater than zero, which triggers the corresponding Configure-Request or Terminate-Request packet to be retransmitted.

The TO- event indicates that the Restart counter is not greater than zero, and no more packets need to be retransmitted.

Receive-Configure-Request (RCR+,RCR-)

This event occurs when a Configure-Request packet is received from the peer. The Configure-Request packet indicates the desire to open a connection and may specify Configuration Options. The Configure-Request packet is more fully described in a later section.

The RCR+ event indicates that the Configure-Request was acceptable, and triggers the transmission of a corresponding Configure-Ack.

The RCR- event indicates that the Configure-Request was unacceptable, and triggers the transmission of a corresponding Configure-Nak or Configure-Reject.

Implementation Note:

These events may occur on a connection which is already in the Opened state. The implementation MUST be prepared to immediately renegotiate the Configuration Options.

Receive-Configure-Ack (RCA)

This event occurs when a valid Configure-Ack packet is received from the peer. The Configure-Ack packet is a positive response to a Configure-Request packet. An out of sequence or otherwise invalid packet is silently discarded.

Implementation Note:

Since the correct packet has already been received before reaching the Ack-Rcvd or Opened states, it is extremely unlikely that another such packet will arrive. As specified, all invalid Ack/Nak/Rej packets are silently discarded, and do not affect the transitions of the automaton.

However, it is not impossible that a correctly formed packet will arrive through a coincidentally-timed cross-connection. It is more likely to be the result of an implementation error. At the very least, this occurance SHOULD be logged.

Receive-Configure-Nak/Rej (RCN)

This event occurs when a valid Configure-Nak or Configure-Reject packet is received from the peer. The Configure-Nak and Configure-Reject packets are negative responses to a Configure- Request packet. An out of sequence or otherwise invalid packet is silently discarded.

Implementation Note:

Although the Configure-Nak and Configure-Reject cause the same state transition in the automaton, these packets have significantly different effects on the Configuration Options sent in the resulting Configure-Request packet.

Receive-Terminate-Request (RTR)

This event occurs when a Terminate-Request packet is received. The Terminate-Request packet indicates the desire of the peer to close the connection.

Implementation Note:

This event is not identical to the Close event (see above), and does not override the Open commands of the local network administrator. The implementation MUST be prepared to receive a new Configure-Request without network administrator intervention.

Receive-Terminate-Ack (RTA)

This event occurs when a Terminate-Ack packet is received from the peer. The Terminate-Ack packet is usually a response to a Terminate-Request packet. The Terminate-Ack packet may also indicate that the peer is in Closed or Stopped states, and serves to re-synchronize the link configuration.

Receive-Unknown-Code (RUC)

This event occurs when an un-interpretable packet is received from the peer. A Code-Reject packet is sent in response.

Receive-Code-Reject, Receive-Protocol-Reject (RXJ+,RXJ-)

This event occurs when a Code-Reject or a Protocol-Reject packet is received from the peer.

The RXJ+ event arises when the rejected value is acceptable, such as a Code-Reject of an extended code, or a Protocol-Reject of a NCP. These are within the scope of normal operation. The implementation MUST stop sending the offending packet type.

The RXJ- event arises when the rejected value is catastrophic, such as a Code-Reject of Configure-Request, or a Protocol-Reject of LCP! This event communicates an unrecoverable error that terminates the connection.

Receive-Echo-Request, Receive-Echo-Reply, Receive-Discard-Request (RXR)

This event occurs when an Echo-Request, Echo-Reply or Discard- Request packet is received from the peer. The Echo-Reply packet is a response to an Echo-Request packet. There is no reply to an Echo-Reply or Discard-Request packet.

4.4. Actions

Actions in the automaton are caused by events and typically indicate the transmission of packets and/or the starting or stopping of the Restart timer.

Illegal-Event (-)

This indicates an event that cannot occur in a properly implemented automaton. The implementation has an internal error, which should be reported and logged. No transition is taken, and the implementation SHOULD NOT reset or freeze.

This-Layer-Up (tlu)

This action indicates to the upper layers that the automaton is entering the Opened state.

Typically, this action is used by the LCP to signal the Up event to a NCP, Authentication Protocol, or Link Quality Protocol, or MAY be used by a NCP to indicate that the link is available for its network layer traffic.

This-Layer-Down (tld)

This action indicates to the upper layers that the automaton is leaving the Opened state.

Typically, this action is used by the LCP to signal the Down event to a NCP, Authentication Protocol, or Link Quality Protocol, or MAY be used by a NCP to indicate that the link is no longer available for its network layer traffic.

This-Layer-Started (tls)

This action indicates to the lower layers that the automaton is entering the Starting state, and the lower layer is needed for the link. The lower layer SHOULD respond with an Up event when the lower layer is available.

This results of this action are highly implementation dependent.

This-Layer-Finished (tlf)

This action indicates to the lower layers that the automaton is entering the Initial, Closed or Stopped states, and the lower layer is no longer needed for the link. The lower layer SHOULD respond with a Down event when the lower layer has terminated.

Typically, this action MAY be used by the LCP to advance to the Link Dead phase, or MAY be used by a NCP to indicate to the LCP that the link may terminate when there are no other NCPs open.

This results of this action are highly implementation dependent.

Initialize-Restart-Count (irc)

This action sets the Restart counter to the appropriate value (Max-Terminate or Max-Configure). The counter is decremented for each transmission, including the first.

Implementation Note:

In addition to setting the Restart counter, the implementation MUST set the timeout period to the initial value when Restart timer backoff is used.

Zero-Restart-Count (zrc)

This action sets the Restart counter to zero.

Implementation Note:

This action enables the FSA to pause before proceeding to the desired final state, allowing traffic to be processed by the peer. In addition to zeroing the Restart counter, the implementation MUST set the timeout period to an appropriate value.

Send-Configure-Request (scr)

A Configure-Request packet is transmitted. This indicates the desire to open a connection with a specified set of Configuration Options. The Restart timer is started when the Configure-Request packet is transmitted, to guard against packet loss. The Restart counter is decremented each time a Configure-Request is sent.

Send-Configure-Ack (sca)

A Configure-Ack packet is transmitted. This acknowledges the reception of a Configure-Request packet with an acceptable set of Configuration Options.

Send-Configure-Nak (scn)

A Configure-Nak or Configure-Reject packet is transmitted, as appropriate. This negative response reports the reception of a Configure-Request packet with an unacceptable set of Configuration Options.

Configure-Nak packets are used to refuse a Configuration Option value, and to suggest a new, acceptable value. Configure-Reject packets are used to refuse all negotiation about a Configuration Option, typically because it is not recognized or implemented. The use of Configure-Nak versus Configure-Reject is more fully described in the chapter on LCP Packet Formats.

Send-Terminate-Request (str)

A Terminate-Request packet is transmitted. This indicates the desire to close a connection. The Restart timer is started when the Terminate-Request packet is transmitted, to guard against packet loss. The Restart counter is decremented each time a Terminate-Request is sent.

Send-Terminate-Ack (sta)

A Terminate-Ack packet is transmitted. This acknowledges the reception of a Terminate-Request packet or otherwise serves to synchronize the automatons.

Send-Code-Reject (scj)

A Code-Reject packet is transmitted. This indicates the reception of an unknown type of packet.

Send-Echo-Reply (ser)

An Echo-Reply packet is transmitted. This acknowledges the reception of an Echo-Request packet.

4.5. Loop Avoidance

The protocol makes a reasonable attempt at avoiding Configuration Option negotiation loops. However, the protocol does NOT guarantee that loops will not happen. As with any negotiation, it is possible to configure two PPP implementations with conflicting policies that will never converge. It is also possible to configure policies which do converge, but which take significant time to do so. Implementors should keep this in mind and SHOULD implement loop detection mechanisms or higher level timeouts.

4.6. Counters and Timers

Restart Timer

There is one special timer used by the automaton. The Restart timer is used to time transmissions of Configure-Request and Terminate-Request packets. Expiration of the Restart timer causes a Timeout event, and retransmission of the corresponding Configure-Request or Terminate-Request packet. The Restart timer MUST be configurable, but SHOULD default to three (3) seconds.

Implementation Note:

The Restart timer SHOULD be based on the speed of the link. The default value is designed for low speed (2,400 to 9,600 bps), high switching latency links (typical telephone lines). Higher speed links, or links with low switching latency, SHOULD have correspondingly faster retransmission times.

Instead of a constant value, the Restart timer MAY begin at an initial small value and increase to the configured final value. Each successive value less than the final value SHOULD be at least twice the previous value. The initial value SHOULD be large enough to account for the size of the packets, twice the round trip time for transmission at the link speed, and at least an additional 100 milliseconds to allow the peer to process the packets before responding. Some circuits add another 200 milliseconds of satellite delay. Round trip times for modems operating at 14,400 bps have been measured in the range of 160 to more than 600 milliseconds.

Max-Terminate

There is one required restart counter for Terminate-Requests. Max-Terminate indicates the number of Terminate-Request packets sent without receiving a Terminate-Ack before assuming that the peer is unable to respond. Max-Terminate MUST be configurable, but SHOULD default to two (2) transmissions.

Max-Configure

A similar counter is recommended for Configure-Requests. Max-Configure indicates the number of Configure-Request packets sent without receiving a valid Configure-Ack, Configure-Nak or Configure-Reject before assuming that the peer is unable to respond. Max-Configure MUST be configurable, but SHOULD default to ten (10) transmissions.

Max-Failure

A related counter is recommended for Configure-Nak. Max-Failure indicates the number of Configure-Nak packets sent without sending a Configure-Ack before assuming that configuration is not converging. Any further Configure-Nak packets for peer requested options are converted to Configure-Reject packets, and locally desired options are no longer appended. Max-Failure MUST be configurable, but SHOULD default to five (5) transmissions.

5. LCP Packet Formats

There are three classes of LCP packets:

1. Link Configuration packets used to establish and configure a link (Configure-Request, Configure-Ack, Configure-Nak and Configure-Reject).

2. Link Termination packets used to terminate a link (Terminate-Request and Terminate-Ack).

3. Link Maintenance packets used to manage and debug a link (Code-Reject, Protocol-Reject, Echo-Request, Echo-Reply, and Discard-Request).

In the interest of simplicity, there is no version field in the LCP packet. A correctly functioning LCP implementation will always respond to unknown Protocols and Codes with an easily recognizable LCP packet, thus providing a deterministic fallback mechanism for implementations of other versions.

Regardless of which Configuration Options are enabled, all LCP Link Configuration, Link Termination, and Code-Reject packets (codes 1 through 7) are always sent as if no Configuration Options were negotiated. In particular, each Configuration Option specifies a default value. This ensures that such LCP packets are always recognizable, even when one end of the link mistakenly believes the link to be open.

App

B

Exactly one LCP packet is encapsulated in the PPP Information field, where the PPP Protocol field indicates type hex c021 (Link Control Protocol).

A summary of the Link Control Protocol packet format is shown below. The fields are transmitted from left to right.

```
 0                   1                   2                   3
 0 1 2 3 4 5 6 7 8 9 0 1 2 3 4 5 6 7 8 9 0 1 2 3 4 5 6 7 8 9 0 1
+-+-+-+-+-+-+-+-+-+-+-+-+-+-+-+-+-+-+-+-+-+-+-+-+-+-+-+-+-+-+-+-+
|     Code      |   Identifier  |            Length             |
+-+-+-+-+-+-+-+-+-+-+-+-+-+-+-+-+-+-+-+-+-+-+-+-+-+-+-+-+-+-+-+-+
|    Data ...
+-+-+-+-+-+
```

Code

The Code field is one octet, and identifies the kind of LCP packet. When a packet is received with an unknown Code field, a Code-Reject packet is transmitted.

Up-to-date values of the LCP Code field are specified in the most recent "Assigned Numbers" RFC [2]. This document concerns the following values:

1	Configure-Request
2	Configure-Ack
3	Configure-Nak
4	Configure-Reject
5	Terminate-Request
6	Terminate-Ack
7	Code-Reject

8	Protocol-Reject
9	Echo-Request
10	Echo-Reply
11	Discard-Request

Identifier

The Identifier field is one octet, and aids in matching requests and replies. When a packet is received with an invalid Identifier field, the packet is silently discarded without affecting the automaton.

Length

The Length field is two octets, and indicates the length of the LCP packet, including the Code, Identifier, Length and Data fields. The Length MUST NOT exceed the MRU of the link.

Octets outside the range of the Length field are treated as padding and are ignored on reception. When a packet is received with an invalid Length field, the packet is silently discarded without affecting the automaton.

Data

The Data field is zero or more octets, as indicated by the Length field. The format of the Data field is determined by the Code field.

5.1. Configure-Request

Description

An implementation wishing to open a connection MUST transmit a Configure-Request. The Options field is filled with any desired changes to the link defaults. Configuration Options SHOULD NOT be included with default values.

Upon reception of a Configure-Request, an appropriate reply MUST be transmitted.

A summary of the Configure-Request packet format is shown below. The fields are transmitted from left to right.

```
 0                   1                   2                   3
 0 1 2 3 4 5 6 7 8 9 0 1 2 3 4 5 6 7 8 9 0 1 2 3 4 5 6 7 8 9 0 1
+-+-+-+-+-+-+-+-+-+-+-+-+-+-+-+-+-+-+-+-+-+-+-+-+-+-+-+-+-+-+-+-+
|     Code      |  Identifier   |            Length             |
+-+-+-+-+-+-+-+-+-+-+-+-+-+-+-+-+-+-+-+-+-+-+-+-+-+-+-+-+-+-+-+-+
| Options ...
+-+-+-+-+
```

Code

1 for Configure-Request.

Identifier

The Identifier field MUST be changed whenever the contents of the Options field changes, and whenever a valid reply has been received for a previous request. For retransmissions, the Identifier MAY remain unchanged.

Options

The options field is variable in length, and contains the list of zero or more Configuration Options that the sender desires to negotiate. All Configuration Options are always negotiated simultaneously. The format of Configuration Options is further described in a later chapter.

5.2. Configure-Ack

Description

If every Configuration Option received in a Configure-Request is recognizable and all values are acceptable, then the implementation MUST transmit a Configure-Ack. The acknowledged Configuration Options MUST NOT be reordered or modified in any way.

On reception of a Configure-Ack, the Identifier field MUST match that of the last transmitted Configure-Request. Additionally, the Configuration Options in a Configure-Ack MUST exactly match those of the last transmitted Configure-Request. Invalid packets are silently discarded.

A summary of the Configure-Ack packet format is shown below. The fields are transmitted from left to right.

```
 0                   1                   2                   3
 0 1 2 3 4 5 6 7 8 9 0 1 2 3 4 5 6 7 8 9 0 1 2 3 4 5 6 7 8 9 0 1
+-+-+-+-+-+-+-+-+-+-+-+-+-+-+-+-+-+-+-+-+-+-+-+-+-+-+-+-+-+-+-+-+
¦     Code      ¦   Identifier  ¦            Length             ¦
+-+-+-+-+-+-+-+-+-+-+-+-+-+-+-+-+-+-+-+-+-+-+-+-+-+-+-+-+-+-+-+-+
¦ Options ...
+-+-+-+-+
```

Code

2 for Configure-Ack.

Identifier

The Identifier field is a copy of the Identifier field of the Configure-Request which caused this Configure-Ack.

Options

The Options field is variable in length, and contains the list of zero or more Configuration Options that the sender is acknowledging. All Configuration Options are always acknowledged simultaneously.

5.3. Configure-Nak

Description

If every instance of the received Configuration Options is recognizable, but some values are not acceptable, then the implementation MUST transmit a Configure-Nak. The Options field is filled with only the unacceptable Configuration Options from the Configure-Request. All acceptable Configuration Options are filtered out of the Configure-Nak, but otherwise the Configuration Options from the Configure-Request MUST NOT be reordered.

Options which have no value fields (boolean options) MUST use the Configure-Reject reply instead.

Each Configuration Option which is allowed only a single instance MUST be modified to a value acceptable to the Configure-Nak sender. The default value MAY be used, when this differs from the requested value.

When a particular type of Configuration Option can be listed more than once with different values, the Configure-Nak MUST include a list of all values for that option which are acceptable to the Configure-Nak sender. This includes acceptable values that were present in the Configure-Request.

Finally, an implementation may be configured to request the negotiation of a specific Configuration Option. If that option is not listed, then that option MAY be appended to the list of Nak'd Configuration Options, in order to prompt the peer to include that option in its next Configure-Request packet. Any value fields for the option MUST indicate values acceptable to the Configure-Nak sender.

On reception of a Configure-Nak, the Identifier field MUST match that of the last transmitted Configure-Request. Invalid packets are silently discarded.

Reception of a valid Configure-Nak indicates that when a new Configure-Request is sent, the Configuration Options MAY be modified as specified in the Configure-Nak. When multiple instances of a Configuration Option are present, the peer SHOULD select a single value to include in its next Configure-Request packet.

Some Configuration Options have a variable length. Since the Nak'd Option has been modified by the peer, the implementation MUST be able to handle an Option length which is different from the original Configure-Request.

A summary of the Configure-Nak packet format is shown below. The fields are transmitted from left to right.

```
 0                   1                   2                   3
 0 1 2 3 4 5 6 7 8 9 0 1 2 3 4 5 6 7 8 9 0 1 2 3 4 5 6 7 8 9 0 1
+-+-+-+-+-+-+-+-+-+-+-+-+-+-+-+-+-+-+-+-+-+-+-+-+-+-+-+-+-+-+-+-+
|     Code      |  Identifier   |            Length             |
+-+-+-+-+-+-+-+-+-+-+-+-+-+-+-+-+-+-+-+-+-+-+-+-+-+-+-+-+-+-+-+-+
|  Options ...
+-+-+-+-+-+
```

Code

3 for Configure-Nak.

Identifier

The Identifier field is a copy of the Identifier field of the Configure-Request which caused this Configure-Nak.

Options

The Options field is variable in length, and contains the list of zero or more Configuration Options that the sender is Nak'ing. All Configuration Options are always Nak'd simultaneously.

5.4. Configure-Reject

Description

If some Configuration Options received in a Configure-Request are not recognizable or are not acceptable for negotiation (as configured by a network administrator), then the implementation MUST transmit a Configure-Reject. The Options field is filled with only the unacceptable

Configuration Options from the Configure-Request. All recognizable and negotiable Configuration Options are filtered out of the Configure-Reject, but otherwise the Configuration Options MUST NOT be reordered or modified in any way.

On reception of a Configure-Reject, the Identifier field MUST match that of the last transmitted Configure-Request. Additionally, the Configuration Options in a Configure-Reject MUST be a proper subset of those in the last transmitted Configure-Request. Invalid packets are silently discarded.

Reception of a valid Configure-Reject indicates that when a new Configure-Request is sent, it MUST NOT include any of the Configuration Options listed in the Configure-Reject.

A summary of the Configure-Reject packet format is shown below. The fields are transmitted from left to right.

```
 0                   1                   2                   3
 0 1 2 3 4 5 6 7 8 9 0 1 2 3 4 5 6 7 8 9 0 1 2 3 4 5 6 7 8 9 0 1
+-+-+-+-+-+-+-+-+-+-+-+-+-+-+-+-+-+-+-+-+-+-+-+-+-+-+-+-+-+-+-+-+
|     Code      |  Identifier   |            Length             |
+-+-+-+-+-+-+-+-+-+-+-+-+-+-+-+-+-+-+-+-+-+-+-+-+-+-+-+-+-+-+-+-+
| Options ...
+-+-+-+-+-+
```

Code

4 for Configure-Reject.

Identifier

The Identifier field is a copy of the Identifier field of the Configure-Request which caused this Configure-Reject.

Options

The Options field is variable in length, and contains the list of zero or more Configuration Options that the sender is rejecting. All Configuration Options are always rejected simultaneously.

5.5. Terminate-Request and Terminate-Ack

Description

LCP includes Terminate-Request and Terminate-Ack Codes in order to provide a mechanism for closing a connection.

An implementation wishing to close a connection SHOULD transmit a Terminate-Request. Terminate-Request packets SHOULD continue to be sent until Terminate-Ack is received, the lower layer indicates that it has gone down, or a sufficiently large number have been transmitted such that the peer is down with reasonable certainty.

Upon reception of a Terminate-Request, a Terminate-Ack MUST be transmitted.

Reception of an unelicited Terminate-Ack indicates that the peer is in the Closed or Stopped states, or is otherwise in need of re-negotiation.

A summary of the Terminate-Request and Terminate-Ack packet formats is shown below. The fields are transmitted from left to right.

App

B

```
 0                   1                   2                   3
 0 1 2 3 4 5 6 7 8 9 0 1 2 3 4 5 6 7 8 9 0 1 2 3 4 5 6 7 8 9 0 1
+-+-+-+-+-+-+-+-+-+-+-+-+-+-+-+-+-+-+-+-+-+-+-+-+-+-+-+-+-+-+-+-+
|     Code      |  Identifier   |            Length             |
+-+-+-+-+-+-+-+-+-+-+-+-+-+-+-+-+-+-+-+-+-+-+-+-+-+-+-+-+-+-+-+-+
|    Data ...
+-+-+-+-+
```

Code

5 for Terminate-Request;

6 for Terminate-Ack.

Identifier

On transmission, the Identifier field MUST be changed whenever the content of the Data field changes, and whenever a valid reply has been received for a previous request. For retransmissions, the Identifier MAY remain unchanged.

On reception, the Identifier field of the Terminate-Request is copied into the Identifier field of the Terminate-Ack packet.

Data

The Data field is zero or more octets, and contains uninterpreted data for use by the sender. The data may consist of any binary value. The end of the field is indicated by the Length.

5.6. Code-Reject

Description

Reception of a LCP packet with an unknown Code indicates that the peer is operating with a different version. This MUST be reported back to the sender of the unknown Code by transmitting a Code-Reject.

Upon reception of the Code-Reject of a code which is fundamental to this version of the protocol, the implementation SHOULD report the problem and drop the connection, since it is unlikely that the situation can be rectified automatically.

A summary of the Code-Reject packet format is shown below. The fields are transmitted from left to right.

```
 0                   1                   2                   3
 0 1 2 3 4 5 6 7 8 9 0 1 2 3 4 5 6 7 8 9 0 1 2 3 4 5 6 7 8 9 0 1
+-+-+-+-+-+-+-+-+-+-+-+-+-+-+-+-+-+-+-+-+-+-+-+-+-+-+-+-+-+-+-+-+
|     Code      |   Identifier  |            Length             |
+-+-+-+-+-+-+-+-+-+-+-+-+-+-+-+-+-+-+-+-+-+-+-+-+-+-+-+-+-+-+-+-+
| Rejected-Packet ...
+-+-+-+-+-+-+-+-+
```

Code

7 for Code-Reject.

Identifier

The Identifier field MUST be changed for each Code-Reject sent.

Rejected-Packet

The Rejected-Packet field contains a copy of the LCP packet which is being rejected. It begins with the Information field, and does not include any Data Link Layer headers nor an FCS. The Rejected-Packet MUST be truncated to comply with the peer's established MRU.

5.7. Protocol-Reject

Description

Reception of a PPP packet with an unknown Protocol field indicates that the peer is attempting to use a protocol which is unsupported. This usually occurs when the peer attempts to configure a new protocol. If the LCP automaton is in the Opened state, then this MUST be reported back to the peer by transmitting a Protocol-Reject.

Upon reception of a Protocol-Reject, the implementation MUST stop sending packets of the indicated protocol at the earliest opportunity.

Protocol-Reject packets can only be sent in the LCP Opened state. Protocol-Reject packets received in any state other than the LCP Opened state SHOULD be silently discarded.

A summary of the Protocol-Reject packet format is shown below. The fields are transmitted from left to right.

```
 0                   1                   2                   3
 0 1 2 3 4 5 6 7 8 9 0 1 2 3 4 5 6 7 8 9 0 1 2 3 4 5 6 7 8 9 0 1
+-+-+-+-+-+-+-+-+-+-+-+-+-+-+-+-+-+-+-+-+-+-+-+-+-+-+-+-+-+-+-+-+
|     Code      |   Identifier  |            Length             |
+-+-+-+-+-+-+-+-+-+-+-+-+-+-+-+-+-+-+-+-+-+-+-+-+-+-+-+-+-+-+-+-+
|        Rejected-Protocol       |      Rejected-Information ...
+-+-+-+-+-+-+-+-+-+-+-+-+-+-+-+-+-+-+-+-+-+-+-+-+-+-+
```

Code

8 for Protocol-Reject.

Identifier

The Identifier field MUST be changed for each Protocol-Reject sent.

Rejected-Protocol

The Rejected-Protocol field is two octets, and contains the PPP Protocol field of the packet which is being rejected.

Rejected-Information

The Rejected-Information field contains a copy of the packet which is being rejected. It begins with the Information field, and does not include any Data Link Layer headers nor an FCS. The Rejected-Information MUST be truncated to comply with the peer's established MRU.

5.8. Echo-Request and Echo-Reply

Description

LCP includes Echo-Request and Echo-Reply Codes in order to provide a Data Link Layer loopback mechanism for use in exercising both directions of the link. This is useful as an aid in debugging, link quality determination, performance testing, and for numerous other functions.

Upon reception of an Echo-Request in the LCP Opened state, an Echo-Reply MUST be transmitted.

Echo-Request and Echo-Reply packets MUST only be sent in the LCP Opened state. Echo-Request and Echo-Reply packets received in any state other than the LCP Opened state SHOULD be silently discarded.

A summary of the Echo-Request and Echo-Reply packet formats is shown below. The fields are transmitted from left to right.

```
 0                   1                   2                   3
 0 1 2 3 4 5 6 7 8 9 0 1 2 3 4 5 6 7 8 9 0 1 2 3 4 5 6 7 8 9 0 1
+-+-+-+-+-+-+-+-+-+-+-+-+-+-+-+-+-+-+-+-+-+-+-+-+-+-+-+-+-+-+-+-+
|     Code      |  Identifier   |            Length             |
+-+-+-+-+-+-+-+-+-+-+-+-+-+-+-+-+-+-+-+-+-+-+-+-+-+-+-+-+-+-+-+-+
|                          Magic-Number                         |
+-+-+-+-+-+-+-+-+-+-+-+-+-+-+-+-+-+-+-+-+-+-+-+-+-+-+-+-+-+-+-+-+
|    Data ...
+-+-+-+-+-+
```

Code

9 for Echo-Request;

10 for Echo-Reply.

Identifier

On transmission, the Identifier field MUST be changed whenever the content of the Data field changes, and whenever a valid reply has been received for a previous request. For retransmissions, the Identifier MAY remain unchanged.

On reception, the Identifier field of the Echo-Request is copied into the Identifier field of the Echo-Reply packet.

Magic-Number

The Magic-Number field is four octets, and aids in detecting links which are in the looped-back condition. Until the Magic-Number Configuration Option has been successfully negotiated, the Magic-Number MUST be transmitted as zero. See the Magic-Number Configuration Option for further explanation.

Data

The Data field is zero or more octets, and contains uninterpreted data for use by the sender. The data may consist of any binary value. The end of the field is indicated by the Length.

5.9. Discard-Request

Description

LCP includes a Discard-Request Code in order to provide a Data Link Layer sink mechanism for use in exercising the local to remote direction of the link. This is useful as an aid in debugging, performance testing, and for numerous other functions.

Discard-Request packets MUST only be sent in the LCP Opened state. On reception, the receiver MUST silently discard any Discard-Request that it receives.

A summary of the Discard-Request packet format is shown below. The fields are transmitted from left to right.

```
 0                   1                   2                   3
 0 1 2 3 4 5 6 7 8 9 0 1 2 3 4 5 6 7 8 9 0 1 2 3 4 5 6 7 8 9 0 1
+-+-+-+-+-+-+-+-+-+-+-+-+-+-+-+-+-+-+-+-+-+-+-+-+-+-+-+-+-+-+-+-+
|     Code      |   Identifier  |            Length             |
+-+-+-+-+-+-+-+-+-+-+-+-+-+-+-+-+-+-+-+-+-+-+-+-+-+-+-+-+-+-+-+-+
|                         Magic-Number                          |
+-+-+-+-+-+-+-+-+-+-+-+-+-+-+-+-+-+-+-+-+-+-+-+-+-+-+-+-+-+-+-+-+
|    Data ...
+-+-+-+-+-+
```

Code

11 for Discard-Request.

Identifier

The Identifier field MUST be changed for each Discard-Request sent.

Magic-Number

The Magic-Number field is four octets, and aids in detecting links which are in the looped-back condition. Until the Magic-Number Configuration Option has been successfully negotiated, the Magic-Number MUST be transmitted as zero. See the Magic-Number Configuration Option for further explanation.

Data

The Data field is zero or more octets, and contains uninterpreted data for use by the sender. The data may consist of any binary value. The end of the field is indicated by the Length.

6. LCP Configuration Options

LCP Configuration Options allow negotiation of modifications to the default characteristics of a point-to-point link. If a Configuration Option is not included in a Configure-Request packet, the default value for that Configuration Option is assumed.

Some Configuration Options MAY be listed more than once. The effect of this is Configuration Option specific, and is specified by each such Configuration Option description. (None of the Configuration Options in this specification can be listed more than once.)

The end of the list of Configuration Options is indicated by the Length field of the LCP packet.

Unless otherwise specified, all Configuration Options apply in a half-duplex fashion; typically, in the receive direction of the link from the point of view of the Configure-Request sender.

Design Philosophy

The options indicate additional capabilities or requirements of the implementation that is requesting the option. An implementation which does not understand any option SHOULD interoperate with one which implements every option.

A default is specified for each option which allows the link to correctly function without negotiation of the option, although perhaps with less than optimal performance.

Except where explicitly specified, acknowledgement of an option does not require the peer to take any additional action other than the default.

It is not necessary to send the default values for the options in a Configure-Request.

A summary of the Configuration Option format is shown below. The fields are transmitted from left to right.

```
 0                   1
 0 1 2 3 4 5 6 7 8 9 0 1 2 3 4 5 6 7 8 9
+-+-+-+-+-+-+-+-+-+-+-+-+-+-+-+-+-+-+-+-+
|     Type      |    Length     |    Data ...
+-+-+-+-+-+-+-+-+-+-+-+-+-+-+-+-+-+-+-+-+
```

Type

The Type field is one octet, and indicates the type of Configuration Option. Up-to-date values of the LCP Option Type field are specified in the most recent "Assigned Numbers" RFC [2]. This document concerns the following values:

0	RESERVED
1	Maximum-Receive-Unit
3	Authentication-Protocol
4	Quality-Protocol
5	Magic-Number

7	Protocol-Field-Compression
8	Address-and-Control-Field-Compression

Length

The Length field is one octet, and indicates the length of this Configuration Option including the Type, Length and Data fields.

If a negotiable Configuration Option is received in a Configure-Request, but with an invalid or unrecognized Length, a Configure-Nak SHOULD be transmitted which includes the desired Configuration Option with an appropriate Length and Data.

Data

The Data field is zero or more octets, and contains information specific to the Configuration Option. The format and length of the Data field is determined by the Type and Length fields.

When the Data field is indicated by the Length to extend beyond the end of the Information field, the entire packet is silently discarded without affecting the automaton.

6.1. Maximum-Receive-Unit (MRU)

Description

This Configuration Option may be sent to inform the peer that the implementation can receive larger packets, or to request that the peer send smaller packets.

The default value is 1500 octets. If smaller packets are requested, an implementation MUST still be able to receive the full 1500 octet information field in case link synchronization is lost.

Implementation Note:

This option is used to indicate an implementation capability. The peer is not required to maximize the use of the capacity. For example, when a MRU is indicated which is 2048 octets, the peer is not required to send any packet with 2048 octets. The peer need not Configure-Nak to indicate that it will only send smaller packets, since the implementation will always require support for at least 1500 octets.

A summary of the Maximum-Receive-Unit Configuration Option format is shown below. The fields are transmitted from left to right.

Type

1

Length

4

Maximum-Receive-Unit

The Maximum-Receive-Unit field is two octets, and specifies the maximum number of octets in the Information and Padding fields. It does not include the framing, Protocol field, FCS, nor any transparency bits or bytes.

6.2. Authentication-Protocol

Description

On some links it may be desirable to require a peer to authenticate itself before allowing network-layer protocol packets to be exchanged.

This Configuration Option provides a method to negotiate the use of a specific protocol for authentication. By default, authentication is not required.

An implementation MUST NOT include multiple Authentication-Protocol Configuration Options in its Configure-Request packets. Instead, it SHOULD attempt to configure the most desirable protocol first. If that protocol is Configure-Nak'd, then the implementation SHOULD attempt the next most desirable protocol in the next Configure-Request.

The implementation sending the Configure-Request is indicating that it expects authentication from its peer. If an implementation sends a Configure-Ack, then it is agreeing to authenticate with the specified protocol. An implementation receiving a Configure-Ack SHOULD expect the peer to authenticate with the acknowledged protocol.

There is no requirement that authentication be full-duplex or that the same protocol be used in both directions. It is perfectly acceptable for different protocols to be used in each direction. This will, of course, depend on the specific protocols negotiated.

A summary of the Authentication-Protocol Configuration Option format is shown below. The fields are transmitted from left to right.

```
 0                   1                   2                   3
 0 1 2 3 4 5 6 7 8 9 0 1 2 3 4 5 6 7 8 9 0 1 2 3 4 5 6 7 8 9 0 1
+-+-+-+-+-+-+-+-+-+-+-+-+-+-+-+-+-+-+-+-+-+-+-+-+-+-+-+-+-+-+-+-+
|     Type      |    Length     |    Authentication-Protocol    |
+-+-+-+-+-+-+-+-+-+-+-+-+-+-+-+-+-+-+-+-+-+-+-+-+-+-+-+-+-+-+-+-+
|     Data ...
+-+-+-+-+-+
```

Type

3

Length

>= 4

Authentication-Protocol

The Authentication-Protocol field is two octets, and indicates the authentication protocol desired. Values for this field are always the same as the PPP Protocol field values for that same authentication protocol.

Up-to-date values of the Authentication-Protocol field are specified in the most recent "Assigned Numbers" RFC [2]. Current values are assigned as follows:

Value (in hex)	Protocol
c023	Password Authentication Protocol
c223	Challenge Handshake Authentication Protocol

Data

The Data field is zero or more octets, and contains additional data as determined by the particular protocol.

6.3. Quality-Protocol

Description

On some links it may be desirable to determine when, and how often, the link is dropping data. This process is called link quality monitoring.

This Configuration Option provides a method to negotiate the use of a specific protocol for link quality monitoring. By default, link quality monitoring is disabled.

The implementation sending the Configure-Request is indicating that it expects to receive monitoring information from its peer. If an implementation sends a Configure-Ack, then it is agreeing to send the specified protocol. An implementation receiving a Configure-Ack SHOULD expect the peer to send the acknowledged protocol.

There is no requirement that quality monitoring be full-duplex or that the same protocol be used in both directions. It is perfectly acceptable for different protocols to be used in each direction. This will, of course, depend on the specific protocols negotiated.

A summary of the Quality-Protocol Configuration Option format is shown below. The fields are transmitted from left to right.

```
 0                   1                   2                   3
 0 1 2 3 4 5 6 7 8 9 0 1 2 3 4 5 6 7 8 9 0 1 2 3 4 5 6 7 8 9 0 1
+-+-+-+-+-+-+-+-+-+-+-+-+-+-+-+-+-+-+-+-+-+-+-+-+-+-+-+-+-+-+-+-+
|     Type      |    Length     |         Quality-Protocol      |
+-+-+-+-+-+-+-+-+-+-+-+-+-+-+-+-+-+-+-+-+-+-+-+-+-+-+-+-+-+-+-+-+
|     Data ...
+-+-+-+-+-+
```

Type

4

Length

>= 4

Quality-Protocol

The Quality-Protocol field is two octets, and indicates the link quality monitoring protocol desired. Values for this field are always the same as the PPP Protocol field values for that same monitoring protocol.

Up-to-date values of the Quality-Protocol field are specified in the most recent "Assigned Numbers" RFC [2]. Current values are assigned as follows:

Value (in hex)	Protocol
c025	Link Quality Report

Data

The Data field is zero or more octets, and contains additional data as determined by the particular protocol.

6.4. Magic-Number

Description

This Configuration Option provides a method to detect looped-back links and other Data Link Layer anomalies. This Configuration Option MAY be required by some other Configuration Options such as the Quality-Protocol Configuration Option. By default, the Magic-Number is not negotiated, and zero is inserted where a Magic-Number might otherwise be used.

Before this Configuration Option is requested, an implementation MUST choose its Magic-Number. It is recommended that the Magic-Number be chosen in the most random manner possible in order to guarantee with very high probability that an implementation will arrive at a unique number. A good way to choose a unique random number is to start with a unique seed. Suggested sources of uniqueness include machine serial numbers, other network hardware addresses, time-of-day clocks, etc. Particularly good random number seeds are precise measurements of the inter-arrival time of physical events such as packet reception on other connected networks, server response time, or the typing rate of a human user. It is also suggested that as many sources as possible be used simultaneously.

When a Configure-Request is received with a Magic-Number Configuration Option, the received Magic-Number is compared with the Magic-Number of the last Configure-Request sent to the peer. If the two Magic-Numbers are different, then the link is not looped-back, and the Magic-Number SHOULD be acknowledged. If the two Magic-Numbers are equal, then it is possible, but not certain, that the link is looped-back and that this Configure-Request is actually the one last sent. To determine this, a Configure-Nak MUST be sent specifying a different Magic-Number value. A new Configure-Request SHOULD NOT be sent to the peer until normal processing would cause it to be sent (that is, until a Configure-Nak is received or the Restart timer runs out).

Reception of a Configure-Nak with a Magic-Number different from that of the last Configure-Nak sent to the peer proves that a link is not looped-back, and indicates a unique Magic-Number. If the Magic-Number is equal to the one sent in the last Configure-Nak, the possibility of a looped-back link is increased, and a new Magic-Number MUST be chosen. In either case, a new Configure-Request SHOULD be sent with the new Magic-Number.

If the link is indeed looped-back, this sequence (transmit Configure-Request, receive Configure-Request, transmit Configure-Nak, receive Configure-Nak) will repeat over and over again. If the link is not looped-back, this sequence might occur a few times, but it is extremely unlikely to occur repeatedly. More likely, the Magic-Numbers chosen at either end will quickly diverge, terminating the sequence. The following table shows the probability of collisions assuming that both ends of the link select Magic-Numbers with a perfectly uniform distribution:

Number of Collisions	Probability
1	$1/2^{**}32 = 2.3$ E-10
2	$1/2^{**}32^{**}2 = 5.4$ E-20
3	$1/2^{**}32^{**}3 = 1.3$ E-29

Good sources of uniqueness or randomness are required for this divergence to occur. If a good source of uniqueness cannot be found, it is recommended that this Configuration Option not be enabled; Configure-Requests with the option SHOULD NOT be transmitted and any Magic-Number Configuration Options which the peer sends SHOULD be either acknowledged or rejected. In this case, looped-back links cannot be reliably detected by the implementation, although they may still be detectable by the peer.

If an implementation does transmit a Configure-Request with a Magic-Number Configuration Option, then it MUST NOT respond with a Configure-Reject when it receives a Configure-Request with a Magic-Number Configuration Option. That is, if an implementation desires to use Magic Numbers, then it MUST also allow its peer to do so. If an implementation does receive a Configure-Reject in response to a Configure-Request, it can only mean that the link is not looped-back, and that its peer will not be using Magic- Numbers. In this case, an implementation SHOULD act as if the negotiation had been successful (as if it had instead received a Configure-Ack).

The Magic-Number also may be used to detect looped-back links during normal operation, as well as during Configuration Option negotiation. All LCP Echo-Request, Echo-Reply, and Discard- Request packets have a Magic-Number field. If Magic-Number has been successfully negotiated, an implementation MUST transmit these packets with the Magic-Number field set to its negotiated Magic-Number.

The Magic-Number field of these packets SHOULD be inspected on reception. All received Magic-Number fields MUST be equal to either zero or the peer's unique Magic-Number, depending on whether or not the peer negotiated a Magic-Number.

Reception of a Magic-Number field equal to the negotiated local Magic-Number indicates a looped-back link. Reception of a Magic- Number other than the negotiated local Magic-Number, the peer's negotiated Magic-Number, or zero if the peer didn't negotiate one, indicates a link which has been (mis)configured for communications with a different peer.

Procedures for recovery from either case are unspecified, and may vary from implementation to implementation. A somewhat pessimistic procedure is to assume a LCP Down event. A further Open event will begin the process of re-establishing the link, which can't complete until the looped-back condition is terminated, and Magic-Numbers are successfully negotiated. A more optimistic procedure (in the case of a looped-back link) is to begin transmitting LCP Echo-Request packets until an appropriate Echo-Reply is received, indicating a termination of the looped- back condition.

A summary of the Magic-Number Configuration Option format is shown below. The fields are transmitted from left to right.

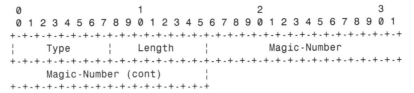

Type

5

Length

6

Magic-Number

The Magic-Number field is four octets, and indicates a number which is very likely to be unique to one end of the link. A Magic-Number of zero is illegal and MUST always be Nak'd, if it is not Rejected outright.

6.5. Protocol-Field-Compression (PFC)

Description

This Configuration Option provides a method to negotiate the compression of the PPP Protocol field. By default, all implementations MUST transmit packets with two octet PPP Protocol fields.

PPP Protocol field numbers are chosen such that some values may be compressed into a single octet form which is clearly distinguishable from the two octet form. This Configuration Option is sent to inform the peer that the implementation can receive such single octet Protocol fields.

As previously mentioned, the Protocol field uses an extension mechanism consistent with the ISO 3309 extension mechanism for the Address field; the Least Significant Bit (LSB) of each octet is used to indicate extension of the Protocol field. A binary "0" as the LSB indicates that the Protocol field continues with the following octet. The presence of a binary "1" as the LSB marks the last octet of the Protocol field. Notice that any number of "0" octets may be prepended to the field, and will still indicate the same value (consider the two binary representations for 3, 00000011 and 00000000 00000011).

When using low speed links, it is desirable to conserve bandwidth by sending as little redundant data as possible. The Protocol- Field-Compression Configuration Option allows a trade-off between implementation simplicity and bandwidth efficiency. If successfully negotiated, the ISO 3309 extension mechanism may be used to compress the Protocol field to one octet instead of two. The large majority of packets are compressible since data protocols are typically assigned with Protocol field values less than 256.

Compressed Protocol fields MUST NOT be transmitted unless this Configuration Option has been negotiated. When negotiated, PPP implementations MUST accept PPP packets with either double-octet or single-octet Protocol fields, and MUST NOT distinguish between them.

The Protocol field is never compressed when sending any LCP packet. This rule guarantees unambiguous recognition of LCP packets.

When a Protocol field is compressed, the Data Link Layer FCS field is calculated on the compressed frame, not the original uncompressed frame.

A summary of the Protocol-Field-Compression Configuration Option format is shown below. The fields are transmitted from left to right.

```
 0                   1
 0 1 2 3 4 5 6 7 8 9 0 1 2 3 4 5
+-+-+-+-+-+-+-+-+-+-+-+-+-+-+-+-+
|      Type      |     Length    |
+-+-+-+-+-+-+-+-+-+-+-+-+-+-+-+-+
```

Type

7

Length

2

6.6. Address-and-Control-Field-Compression (ACFC)

Description

This Configuration Option provides a method to negotiate the compression of the Data Link Layer Address and Control fields. By default, all implementations MUST transmit frames with Address and Control fields appropriate to the link framing.

Since these fields usually have constant values for point-to-point links, they are easily compressed. This Configuration Option is sent to inform the peer that the implementation can receive compressed Address and Control fields.

If a compressed frame is received when Address-and-Control-Field- Compression has not been negotiated, the implementation MAY silently discard the frame.

The Address and Control fields MUST NOT be compressed when sending any LCP packet. This rule guarantees unambiguous recognition of LCP packets.

When the Address and Control fields are compressed, the Data Link Layer FCS field is calculated on the compressed frame, not the original uncompressed frame.

A summary of the Address-and-Control-Field-Compression configuration option format is shown below. The fields are transmitted from left to right.

```
 0                   1
 0 1 2 3 4 5 6 7 8 9 0 1 2 3 4 5
+-+-+-+-+-+-+-+-+-+-+-+-+-+-+-+-+
|      Type       |     Length    |
+-+-+-+-+-+-+-+-+-+-+-+-+-+-+-+-+
```

Type

8

Length

2

Security Considerations

Security issues are briefly discussed in sections concerning the Authentication Phase, the Close event, and the Authentication-Protocol Configuration Option.

References

[1] Perkins, D., "Requirements for an Internet Standard Point-to-Point Protocol", RFC 1547, Carnegie Mellon University, December 1993.

[2] Reynolds, J., and Postel, J., "Assigned Numbers", STD 2, RFC 1340, USC/Information Sciences Institute, July 1992.

Acknowledgements

This document is the product of the Point-to-Point Protocol Working Group of the Internet Engineering Task Force (IETF). Comments should be submitted to the ietf-ppp@merit.edu mailing list.

Much of the text in this document is taken from the working group requirements [1]; and RFCs 1171 & 1172, by Drew Perkins while at Carnegie Mellon University, and by Russ Hobby of the University of California at Davis.

William Simpson was principally responsible for introducing consistent terminology and philosophy, and the re-design of the phase and negotiation state machines.

Many people spent significant time helping to develop the Point-to- Point Protocol. The complete list of people is too numerous to list, but the following people deserve special thanks: Rick Adams, Ken Adelman, Fred Baker, Mike Ballard, Craig Fox, Karl Fox, Phill Gross, Kory Hamzeh, former WG chair Russ Hobby, David Kaufman, former WG chair Steve Knowles, Mark Lewis, former WG chair Brian Lloyd, John LoVerso, Bill Melohn, Mike Patton, former WG chair Drew Perkins, Greg Satz, John Shriver, Vernon Schryver, and Asher Waldfogel.

Special thanks to Morning Star Technologies for providing computing resources and network access support for writing this specification.

Chair's Address

The working group can be contacted via the current chair:

> Fred Baker
> Advanced Computer Communications
> 315 Bollay Drive
> Santa Barbara, California 93117
> fbaker@acc.com

Editor's Address

Questions about this memo can also be directed to:

> William Allen Simpson
> Daydreamer
> Computer Systems Consulting Services
> 1384 Fontaine
> Madison Heights, Michigan 48071
>
> Bill.Simpson@um.cc.umich.edu
> bsimpson@MorningStar.com

Glossary

10BASE-2—See Thinnet.

10BASE-T—See Twisted Pair.

ACAP—Application Configuration Access Protocol. Enables applications to automatically configure themselves to a certain set of preferences given only a username and an ACAP server.

ADSL—Asymmetric Digital Subscriber Line. A very high-speed network service that approaches T1 speeds at a very low cost.

Apache—A very popular free Web server that is available on many different platforms.

Appleshare IP—Appleís high-end server software. Provides email, Web, FTP, and file serving support.

Application Layer—The seventh, and last, layer in the OSI model. This layer is made up of the applications that use TCP/IP, such as Web browsers.

AUI Port—A port on an Ethernet card that allows a device to connect to the old standard "thicknet" network.

Backdoor—A secret entrance into a computer system that is frequently exploited by computer hackers.

Backoff Algorithm—Process that involves waiting a number of microseconds to retransmit. Used in Ethernet to deal with collisions.

Blue Screen—The sign of a crashed Windows computer. The Blue Screen of Death indicates a problem has occurred and usually provides you with an error message code.

BNC—Another name for coaxial Ethernet cable, based on the circular style connectors.

Bridges—Low-level network devices that "bridge" traffic between two different networks.

Broadcast Storm—Broadcast data gone awry often caused by a malfunctioning machine that is sending out data extremely quickly. This can disrupt normal network operations very easily.

Broadcasting—Sending data over the network in a way that can be received by a large number of hosts.

Browse Master—The computer that maintains the list of browseable NetBIOS names for a Windows network.

Bus Topology—Network system where all nodes share a common wire.

Cable Modems—Hardware that connects to a cable television system that in the best cases is very much like ADSL, but in the worst cases has very lopsided data transmission. Currently there are several standards of cable modems, some that perform well, others that work poorly.

Cache—A cache stores data that is accessed frequently so that it can be retrieved more quickly.

Checksum—A method of summing data values and transmitting them with the data to ensure accurate transmission. The receiving computer performs the same calculations and compares its value to the received checksum. If the numbers match, the data has been received successfully.

Class A, B, C—An old method of defining a subnet mask.

Collision—Created when two packets of information overlap and become unreadable.

Cookies—Files that are stored on your local computer from a remote Web server. Used to keep information that can identify you to the server at a later date.

CRC—Cyclical Redundancy Check. Portion of a data frame that helps to check for data transmission errors.

Cross-Over Port—A specially wired port on a hub that can be used to link two hubs together.

Daemon—A common term used to refer to a piece of server software.

Data Encryption—Modifying data to make it unusable in its "encrypted" form. RSA and DES are types of data encryption.

Data Link Layer—Second layer in the OSI model and handles low-level communications between pieces of network hardware.

DHCP—Dynamic Host Configuration Protocol. Enables auto-configuration of IP addresses on remote computers.

DNS Server—Domain Name Service Server. Provides name resolution service for a network.

EOL—End of Line. A character that represents the end of a line of text. Unfortunately, this is hardly ever the same between different operating systems. This makes sharing text files troublesome.

Ethernet—The primary standard in TCP/IP network communication.

Ethernet Card—Connects nodes to a network, usually using Thinnet or Twisted Pair.

EtherTalk—Appleís Ethernet-based network file and printer sharing standard.

File Permissions—Rights and restrictions assigned to files in multiuser systems to protect files from users who should not have access to them.

Finger—A simple protocol used for retrieving directory information.

Firewall—A network device that stops traffic from entering or leaving a subnet.

Flame—A piece of hostile email.

FQDN—See Fully Qualified Domain Name.

Fragmentation—When packets are segmented to travel over certain types of networks.

Frame—A unit of data transmitted over the network.

FTP—File Transfer Protocol. A low-level and extremely fast method of transferring files over TCP/IP networks.

Fully Qualified Domain Name—The user-friendly, complete version of an IP address on the Internet. This is the actual serverís name; for example: `www.poisontooth.com`.

Gateway—Network hardware or software that provides a connection between two different networks.

Gopher—A protocol similar in concept to HTTP, but not as fancy.

Hardware—The computer, network cable, satellite dish, or any other devices you use when linking two or more computers.

Hardware Address—A unique, 48-bit address for each Ethernet device, assigned by the manufacturer.

Hop—When data moves between two different networks, it has made a "hop."

Hostname—The user-friendly version of an IP address. This is the actual serverís name; for example, "server7" is a hostname.

HTTP—Hypertext Transfer Protocol. Enables styled text, graphics, and other forms of media to be transmitted over the Internet.

Hub—Network hardware that acts as a central connection point to provide network access for several computers.

ICMP—See Internet Control Message Protocol.

IMAP—Internet Message Access Protocol. A new protocol that, unlike POP3, maintains a list of messages on a server and provides a standard method of accessing them.

Internet Control Message Protocol (ICMP)—Implemented as part of the TCP/IP suite, the ICMP is used to return status information about devices on the network.

Internet Engineering Task Force—The body that defines and refines Internet standards. Comprised of members from around the world.

InterNIC—The organization responsible for maintaining domain name registration information.

IP Address—The unique identifying address for a computer on a TCP/IP network.

IP Forwarding—The process of moving packets from one network interface to another.

IPng—Internet Protocol "The Next Generation." Defines a new Transport Layer for TCP/IP. IPng includes 128-bit addresses and several other enhancements.

IPv6—See IPng.

IRC—Internet Relay Chat. A real-time chat protocol widely used on the Internet.

ISDN—Integrated Services Digital Network. A digital phone line that enables speeds slightly faster than an analog connection.

ISO—International Standards Organization. Composed of members from over 75 countries who work together to compile and maintain engineering standards from around the world.

Kernel—The basic unit of many operating systems, including Linux and Windows NT. Contains only the core information to interface with the computerís hardware.

LDAP—Lightweight Directory Access Protocol. A very popular directory access method that is "TCP/IP friendly" and allows integrated address books in any LDAP-compatible application.

Lease—DHCP servers "lease" IP addresses to their clients. An individual IP address assigned by such a server is often referred to as a lease.

LMHOSTS—Windows or Linux Samba files that contain the IP addresses of NetBIOS hosts.

Localhost—A standard hostname that refers to the machine that it is used on; that is, it points back to itself.

MAC Address—Media Access Control address. See Hardware Address.

Mailing Lists—Distributes email sent to a single list address to subscribers of the list.

MBONE—A Multicast Backbone, often used for transmitting video and audio.

Multihoming—Using multiple network interfaces on a single computer.

Multiplexing—Running multiple TCP/IP connections simultaneously.

NAT—Network Address Translation. A very fast and useful method of connecting a group of network computers to the Internet through a single connection.

NetBIOS—A transport that enables Windows file sharing to be used over TCP/IP.

Netizen—An Internet term for Network Citizen. Much as the real world has citizens in a social structure, so does the network.

netstat—A utility that displays the current state of network connections for a computer.

Network Layer—The third layer in the OSI model, it defines a standard for communicating between different Data Link Layers.

NIC—Network Interface Card. Connects your computer to a network.

NNTP—Network News Transfer Protocol. Used for reading and writing to newsgroups.

Nodes—Any device that is connected to a network, usually referring to a computer.

NTP—Network Time Protocol. A protocol capable of setting device clocks to match a centralized time server.

ODBC—Open Database Connectivity. A standard that allows different operating systems and different pieces of software to access a database server and retrieve the same information.

Open Transport—The current Macintosh networking standard. Replaces the old MacTCP driver.

OSI—The Open Systems Interconnect network model provides an abstract view of how a network functions, from the wiring that connects the computers to the programs we use to communicate. Seven layers form the key components of the OSI model; they are the Physical, Data Link, Network, Transport, Session, Presentation, and Application Layers.

Packet—A unit of data transmitted over the network.

Packet Sniffer—A hardware or software device that grabs packets off of a network line and lets you examine them.

Partitioning—The "cutting-off" of a port on a hub due to unusual network activity.

PDF—Portable Document Format. A standard format for storing text and graphics that is viewable across a wide variety of platforms.

PGP—Pretty Good Privacy. An encryption standard that is typically used for sending private email.

Physical Layer—First layer in the OSI model, provides the physical connections between machines.

PICS—Platform for Internet Content Selection. Defines a standard for rating content.

ping—A common utility that sends ICMP packets to a remote computer to check its status.

POP—Post Office Protocol. A widely used protocol for retrieving email from a central server. POP is sometimes referred to as *POP3*, which simply refers to version 3 of the POP protocol.

Port—A virtual connection point that TCP/IP services can connect to. For example, a Web server (HTTP) operates on port 80.

PPP—Point to Point Protocol; flexible, widely supported transport protocol. Most often used to dial into TCP/IP networks.

Presentation Layer—The sixth layer in the OSI model; it defines vocabularies, or protocols, that applications use to communicate.

Private Key—Used to decrypt messages that have been sent using public key encryption.

Proxy Server—A proxy server isolates computers from the outside network. It places requests on their behalf with other servers.

Public Key—A key that is used to encrypt messages that you are sending to someone. The messages can be unlocked only by the corresponding Private Key.

Real-time—A term indicating that something must happen within a certain length of time. A real-time network guarantees delivery of data within a certain time after packet transmission.

Repeater—Identical to a hub, but generally referring to a device that provides hub-like services using Thinnet wiring.

Request for Comments (RFC)—Documents that define network standards.

RFC—See Request for Comments.

RIP—Router Information Protocol, used for exchanging routing information between devices.

RJ45—The "phone-style" connector that is used on Twisted Pair Ethernet cabling.

Router—A piece of network hardware that moves network traffic toward its final destination.

Samba—Implements SMB sharing for Linux and other UNIX-based computers.

Service—The Microsoft term for a "daemon." See also Daemon.

Session Layer—The fifth layer in the OSI model, works with the transport layer to provide point-to-point communications.

SLIP—Serial Line Internet Protocol, defines a method of providing TCP/IP support over serial lines.

Smart Hubs—A hub that offers more than "plug and play" operating. Often including the ability to remotely disable, enable, and monitor individual ports.

SMB—Simple Message Block Protocol. The standard for Windows file sharing.

SMTP—Simple Mail Transport Protocol. The protocol that is used to send email over the Internet.

SNMP—Simple Network Management Protocol. Provides a standard by which different network devices can be monitored and controlled.

Sockets—The start and endpoint of a TCP/IP connection. Each machine involved in TCP/IP traffic must communicate over a socket.

SOCKS—A standard proxy-firewall configuration that is widely supported by many software packages.

Spam—Any unwanted email. Usually sent in bulk by "spammers" using an unprotected SMTP server.

Spanning Tree—An algorithm for determining if loops exist in a structure.

Spoofing—Impersonating an IP address by modifying a packet before sending it. A common hacking practice.

SSL—Secure Sockets Layer. The standard for secure Web communications.

Star Topology—Network configuration utilizing hubs and twisted pair wiring. Often laid out in a configuration that resembles a star.

Step Down Hub—A hub that slows down data transmission for a slower network to communicate with a faster network.

Subnet—An individual network, usually separated from a larger network by a bridge.

Subnet Mask—Resembling an IP address, provides a "mask" of the significant bits in an IP address that defines a network.

Switches—Hardware that increases the amount of available bandwidth on a network by limiting traffic to small workgroups.

Telnet—A protocol for communicating with remote text-based network services.

Terminator—Resistor applied to the end of an Ethernet connection to prevent signal reflection.

Thinnet—Common Ethernet coaxial cable wiring, similar to the wiring that your cable box uses.

Time To Live (TTL)—Usually, the length of time a packet will remain alive or active on the network. After the time is exceeded, the packet is no longer passed over the network.

TLD—Top Level Domain. The suffix attached to Internet Domain Names. For example .com is a Top Level Domain.

Transport Layer—The fourth layer in the OSI model, defines the notion of a connection by which devices can communicate. In the OSI TCP/IP model, this is combined with the next layer, the Session Layer.

Trunk Line Level One (T1)—A line capable of carrying large amounts of data that is run directly to a service provider. Cost prohibits this from being used as a "consumer" method of connecting to the Internet.

TTL—See Time To Live.

Tunneling—Provides a means to transmit a protocol over a network that does not support it by means of encapsulating the protocol inside another supported protocol.

Twisted Pair—Ethernet wire, resembling thick phone wire, that connects each node to a hub with its own wire. See also UTP.

UDP—See User Datagram Protocol.

URL—Uniform Resource Locator. Defines a standard way of showing the location of a particular file or resource.

User Datagram Protocol (UDP)—Defines a method of sending data, like TCP, but does not include any error correction.

UTP—Unshielded Twisted Pair. Phone line-like Ethernet cable.

Virtual Hosting—Using a single IP address to provide services for several different hostnames.

Whois—A utility for querying InterNIC registration information.

Windows NT—Microsoft's powerful server platform that provides an incredible amount of TCP/IP services.

Winnuke—A popular Windows "exploit" that crashes Windows computers instantly. The security hole that allows this has since been patched but remains a problem for many unmanaged networks.

WINS—Windows Internet Naming Service. Similar to DNS but specific to the Windows platform.

Index

Symbols

(pound sign), 154

/ (forward slash), 131

3COM, 360

10BASE-2 (thinnet), 21
 BNC (British Naval
  Connectors), 19-20
 disadvantages, 19-20
 problems with, 380-382
 splicing, 383
 terminators, 18

10BASE-T (twisted-pair
 cabling)
 Cat-3 cabling, 21
 Cat-5 cabling, 21
 disadvantages, 21
 hub configuration, 20-22

100BASE-TX, 22

101 Switching Protocols
 message, 138

128-bit addresses, 469-470

200 OK message, 138

251 Non-local user...
 message, 117

301 Moved Permanently
 message, 138

400 Bad Request message,
 138

401 Unauthorized message,
 138

403 Forbidden message,
 138

404 File Not Found
 message, 138

408 Request Timeout
 message, 138

500 Internal Server Error
 message, 138

503 Service Unavailable
 message, 138

505 http Version Not
 Supported message, 138

551 Non-local user...
 message, 117

A

-a option (arp command),
 79

A records (Address), 66

ACAP (Application
 Configuration Access
 Protocol), 388-389

accessing IP (Internet
 Protocol) address
 configuration, 58-59

ACK (acknowledgement)
 messages, 35

ACK flag, 40

Acknowledgement Number
 field (TCP packets), 39

Active Server Pages (ASPs),
 278

ActiveX, 278

Address (A) records, 66

Address Resolution Protocol
 (ARP), 79

addresses
 broadcast, 84
 hardware
  displaying, 25-26
  IP addresses,
   relationship between,
   54-55
  as single network
   address, 52
 IP (Internet Protocol), 29-30,
  55-56, 69
  128-bit addresses,
   469-470
  assigning, 57-58

configuration, 58-59, 89, 92

hardware addresses, relationship between, 54-55

IPng, 468-469

multihoming, 31

numbers, 60

as single network address, 52-53

subnet masks, 61-62

subnets, 60-64

virtual hosts, 31

URLs (Uniform Resource Locators)

defined, 106

future technology, 108

syntax, 107-108

addressing email messages, 116-117

Adleman, Leonard, 368

Adobe Portable Document Format (PDF), 464

advertising spam, 463

agents (SNMP), 83

algorithms, backoff, 27-28

aliases

AppleShare IP, 273

creating, 193

All You Wanted to Know About T1 But Were Afraid to Ask (Web site), 296

analog modems, 290

Anarchie Web site, 162

ANSWERED option (SEARCH command), 125

Apache Web server, 182, 265-269

proxy server capabilities, 329-335

Apple Macintosh. *See* **Macintosh**

AppleScript, 413

AppleShare IP, 186, 190-191, 272-276

AppleShare IP file server, 191

COPSTalk, 207-208

file sharing, 273

FTP (File Transfer Protocol), 273

Internet Aliases, 273

limitations, 275-276

Mac OS, 191-193

MacDNS, 274-275

mail server, 274

PC MACLAN, 208

print server, 275

QuickDNS Pro, 274

ShareWay, 191-193

Windows file sharing, 273-274

AppleTalk, 80, 176, 221

Application Configuration Access Protocol (ACAP), 388-389

application errors, 447-448

Application Gateway firewalls, 358

Application layer (OSI network model), 15. *See also* **applications**

applications

CDDB (CD database), 45-46

Hotline, 44-45

ICQ (I Seek You), 43-44

IPNetMonitor, 34

The Palace, 45

PointCast, 47

Quake, 49

settings, problems with, 388-389

VNC (Virtual Network Computing), 47-48

Arin Web site, 69, 72

ARP (Address Resolution Protocol), 79

arp command (UNIX), 79

ARTICLE command (NNTP), 149-150

Asante Web site, 88

ASDL (Asymmetric Digital Subscriber Line), 291

ASPs (Active Server Pages), 278

assigning IP (Internet Protocol) addresses

DHCP (Dynamic Host Configuration Protocol) servers, 57

dial-in connections, 58

Asymmetric Digital Subscriber Line (ADSL), 291

attacks on security

IP (Internet Protocol) spoofing, 472-473

winnuke program, 354-355, 473

AUI ports, 22

authentication

IMAP (Internet Message Access Protocol), 120-121

Kerberos, 121

POP3 (Post Office Protocol), 111-112

B

backoff algorithm, 27-28

Bad Request message (HTTP), 138

bandwidth, 458-460

banning channel users, 158

BetterTelnet, 104

Billiter Consultants, ipLease, 402-407

BNC (British Naval Connectors), 19-20, 452

BODY command (NNTP), 149-150

BOOTP (Boot Protocol), 57

bots, 151

bridges, 74, 77

Bright Light Technologies, Spam Calculator, 234

British Naval Connectors (BNC), 19-20

BROADCAST setting (ifcfg-eth0 file), 98

broadcasting, 83-84. See also multicasting

Browse Master, 181

browsers
  Internet Explorer, 144
  Netscape, 127, 144
  proxy servers, 300
    Linux browsers, 306-308
    Mac OS browsers, 301-303
    Windows browsers, 303-306

browsing newsgroups messages, 150

bugs. See also error messages
  flood ping, 170
  Ping of Death, 170
  software, 447-448

bulletin boards, Hotline, 44-45

bus topology, 19

C

Cable Modem 101 Web site, 296

cable modems, 291

cable testers, 453

cables
  100BASE-TX, 22
  10BASE-2 (thinnet), 21
    BNC (British Naval Connectors), 19-20, 452
    disadvantages, 19-20
    problems with, 380-382
    splicing, 383
    terminators, 18
  10BASE-T (twisted-pair)
    Cat-3 cabling, 21
    Cat-5 cabling, 21
    disadvantages, 21
    hub configuration, 20-22
    problems with, 382-384
  crossover, 169
  Ethernet cards, 22
  planning, 169
  prices of, 23
  problems, 448-452
  splices, 383

cache (ARP), 79

Canonical Name (CNAME) record, 66

CAP, 221

CAPABILITY command (IMAP), 121

CAs (certifying authorities), 369

Cat-3 cabling, 21

Cat-5 cabling, 21

CDDB (CD database), 45-46

censorship of Internet content
  filtering, 299-300
  LinkCheck program, 298-299
  schools, 298-299
  U.S. government, 298
  workplace, 298

certifying authorities (CAs), 369

CGI (Common Gateway Interface), 256

channels (IRC), 153-154
  # prefix, 154
  connections, limiting, 157
  creating, 156
  customizing, 156-157
  descriptions, 156
  exiting, 155
  joining, 154
  listing, 153-154
  operator, setting, 157
  users
    banning, 158
    forcibly removing, 158
    identifying, 158-159

chat programs
  ICQ (I See You), 43-44
  IRC (Internet Relay Chat)
    bots, 151
    channels, 153-158
    client software, 160
    commands, 153-159
    connections, 152, 155
    server registration, 152-153
  Palace, The, 45

chat rooms. See channels

Checksum field (TCP packets), 40

checksums, 30

Chocolate Chip Cookies Web site, 144

choosing
  packet routes, 79-80
  server solutions
    cost, 284
    ease of use, 283

provided services, 284
scalability, 284
security, 285
stability, 284

Circuit-Level firewalls, 358

CIRCus Web site, 160

classes (subnets), 61-63

client services
AppleTalk (Mac OS), 176
dedicated servers, 183-184
Linux, 182
provided, 284
shared resources
connecting to, 180-182
LMHOSTS file, 181-182
SMB file sharing, 177-181
Web File Sharing,
173-176

client software
FTP (File Transfer
Protocol), 162
IRC (Internet Relay Chat)
bots, 151
channels, 153-158
client software, 160
commands, 153-159
connections, 152, 155
server registration,
152-153
NNTP (Network News
Transfer Protocol) server,
150
NTP (Network Time
Protocol), 164

**client workstations,
configuring, 88**
Linux, 95
/etc/sysconfig/network
file, 96-97
DNS servers, 96
hostnames, 96
ifcfg-eth0 file, 97-98

Mac OS 8.x
connection methods, 89
domain names, 90
Ethernet cards, 88
IP addresses, 89
name server addresses,
90
Windows 95
TCP/IP configuration,
92-95
TCP/IP installation,
91-92
Windows 98
TCP/IP configuration,
92-95
TCP/IP installation,
91-92

**clock synchronization,
163-164**

**CLOSE command (IMAP),
125**

**CLOSE-WAIT state (TCP),
38**

CLOSED state (TCP), 38

closing connections
IMAP (Internet Message
Access Protocol), 125
IRC (Internet Relay Chat),
155
NNTP (Network News
Transfer Protocol), 150
POP3 (Post Office
Protocol), 113
SMTP (Simple Mail
Transfer Protocol), 118

CLOSING state (TCP), 38

**CNAME record (Canonical
Name), 66**

**coaxial cables (10BASE-2),
21**
BNC (British Naval
Connectors), 19-20
disadvantages, 19-20

problems with, 380-382
splicing, 383
terminators, 18

collisions, 27-28

commands
DOS, telnet, 104
File menu (Macintosh), Get
Info, 25
FTP (File Transfer Protocol)
CWD, 161
LIST, 161
PASS, 161
PASV, 162
QUIT, 162
RETR, 162
STOR, 162
TYPE, 162
USER, 161
HTTP (Hypertext Transfer
Protocol)
HEAD, 140-141
GET, 133-134, 140
IMAP (Internet Message
Access Protocol)
CAPABILITY, 121
CLOSE, 125
COPY, 126
CREATE, 126
DELETE, 127
EXAMINE, 121-122
EXPUNGE, 124
FETCH, 122-124
LOGIN, 121
LOGOUT, 125
RENAME, 127
SEARCH, 124-125
SELECT, 121-122
STATUS, 122
STORE, 124
IRC (Internet Relay Chat)
HELP, 159
ISON, 159
JOIN, 154-156
KICK, 158

LIST, 153-154
MODE, 156-157
NICK, 152-153
PART, 155
PASS, 152
PRIVMSG, 155
QUIT, 155
TOPIC, 156
USER, 153
USERHOST, 158-159
WHOIS, 158
netstat -i, 449-450
NNTP (Network News
　Transfer Protocol) servers
　ARTICLE/HEAD/
　　BODY, 149-150
　client software, 150
　GROUP, 148-149
　LIST, 148
　NEWSGROUPS, 148
　NEXT/LAST, 150
　QUIT, 150
　sending, 147-148
POP3 (Post Office Protocol)
　DELE, 113
　LIST, 112
　NOOP, 113
　PASS, 112
　QUIT, 113
　RESET, 113
　RETR, 113
　STAT, 112
　TOP, 114
　UIDL, 114
　USER, 111
SMTP (Simple Mail
　Transfer Protocol)
　DATA, 117
　EXPN, 119
　HELO, 116
　HELP, 118
　MAIL FROM, 116
　QUIT, 118
　RCPT TO, 116-117

RSET, 118
VRFY, 118-119
spray, 450-452
UNIX, arp, 79

**Common Gateway Interface
(CGI), 256**

**Communications Decency
Act, 298**

CommuniGate, 225-235

CommuniGate Pro
　creating accounts, 246-250
　email client, 255-256
　Linux, 236-237
　　communication
　　　protocols, 242-243
　　configuring, 238-239
　　installing, 237
　　Postmaster, 237-238
　　router settings, 239-240
　　security, 241-242
　logs, 253-254
　mailing lists, 250-253
　monitoring system
　　functions, 254
　Remote Queue Starting
　　Command, 244
　RPOP, 244-246
　Windows, 236-238
　　communication
　　　protocols, 242-243
　　configuring, 237-239
　　installing, 237
　　router settings, 239-240
　　security, 241-242

compiling, 331

configuring
　file sharing, 178-179
　IMAP (Internet Message
　　Access Protocol)
　　mailboxes, 126-127
　intranet, 168
　Linux workstations, 95
　　/etc/sysconfig/network
　　file, 96-97

DNS servers, 96
hostnames, 96
ifcfg-eth0 file, 97-98
Linux Configuration and
　Troubleshooting Web
　site, 99
Macintosh workstations,
　88-89
　connection methods, 89
　domain names, 90
　Ethernet cards, 88
　IP addresses, 89
　name server addresses,
　　90
Windows 95 workstations
　TCP/IP configuration,
　　92-95
　TCP/IP installation,
　　91-92
Windows 98 workstations
　TCP/IP configuration,
　　92-95
　TCP/IP installation,
　　91-92
workgroups, 177

conflicts (IP), 386-387

connectivity
　computers, 169
　dial-in connections, 58
　hubs, 169-170
　Internet
　　NAT servers, 338
　　proxy servers, 298
　IRC (Internet Relay Chat)
　　servers, 152
　NNTP (Network News
　　Transfer Protocol) servers,
　　147
　shared resources, 180-182
　tickling connections, 340

Connectix SurfExpress, 300

**content-length field (HTTP
response headers), 139**

content-type field (HTTP response headers), 139

control panels, Users and Groups, 176

controlling Internet content
filtering, 299-300
LinkCheck program, 298-299
schools, 298-299
U.S. government, 298
workplace, 298

Cookie Central Web site, 144

cookies
advantages, 143
Cookie Central Web site, 144
security, 142
setting, 143

COPSTalk, 207-208

COPY command (IMAP), 126

CRC (Cyclic Redundancy Check), 24

CREATE command (IMAP), 126

credit cards and Internet security, 353-354

cross-posting newsgroup messages, 149

crossover cables, 169

cryptography
DES, 367
RSA, 367-368

customizing channels, 156-157

cut-through technology (switched Ethernet), 82

CWD command (FTP), 161

Cyclic Redundancy Check (CRC), 24

D

daemons, 199

DATA command (SMTP), 117

data encryption
DES, 367
email, 366
keys
private key, 366-367
public key, 366-367
laws regarding, 359
PGP (Pretty Good Privacy)
Linux, 376-377
Outlook Express, 373-375
PGPFreeware, 369-373
RSA, 367-368
U.S. government, 359
Web, 366

Data Link layer (OSI network model), 10-11.
See also frames

Data Offset field (TCP packets), 39

data packets. *See* packets

DAVE, 193-198

dedicated servers, 183-184

DELE command (POP3), 113

DELETE command (IMAP), 127

DELETED option (SEARCH command), 125

deleting
email messages
IMAP (Internet Message Access Protocol), 124
POP3 (Post Office Protocol), 113
mailboxes, 127

Denial of Service attacks, 38

DES, 367

Destination Host Unreachable message, 171

Destination Port field (TCP packets), 39

Destination Unreachable message, 33

DEVICE setting (ifcfg-eth0 file), 97

DHCP (Dynamic Host Configuration Protocol) servers, 56-57, 385-388
BOOTP, compared, 57
client configuration
Linux clients, 397-398
Mac OS clients, 394-395
Windows clients, 396-397
IP (Internet Protocol) addresses, assigning, 57
ipLease DHCP server, 402-407
Linux, 408-410
Mac OS, 398-401
Vicom Internet Gateway, 398
Windows, 278, 402-407
Windows NT DHCP server, 402
Wingate for Windows, 398

diagnosing network problems
cabling, 448-453
causes, 438
configuration errors, 441-446
error messages, 439
hardware, 452-453
logs, 439
netstat, 38-39, 449-450
ping, 33-35
protocol analyzers, 453

router configuration errors, 446

software errors, 447-448

spray, 450-452

subnet mask configuration errors, 446-447

user errors, 439-441

dial-in connections, 58

dialog boxes
File and Print Sharing, 178
Select Network Protocol, 92
TCP/IP Configuration
DNS Configuration tab, 93-94
DNS Configuration tab, 93
Gateway tab, 94-95
IP Address tab, 92-93

digests (mailing lists), 224

digital signatures
certifying authorities (CAs), 369
RSA, 368

directories
FTP (File Transfer Protocol), 161
remote directories, viewing, 131-132

directory services
finger, 390
Lightweight Directory Access Protocol (LDAP), 390-392
ph, 390

disabling ports, 169

displaying
ARP (Address Resolution Protocol) cache, 79
hardware addresses
Linux workstations, 26
Macintosh workstations, 25

Windows 95 workstations, 25
Windows 98 workstations, 25

DNS (Domain Name Service), 66
configuration
Linux workstations, 96
Windows 95 workstations, 93-94
Windows 98 workstations, 93-94
domain names, registering, 69
InterNIC, 69
MacDNS (AppleShare IP), 274-275
name resolution, 66
name server records, 66-67
queries, sending, 67-68
QuickDNS Pro, 274
TTL (time to live), 66
whois service, 70-71
Windows NT, 278

document delivery protocols
Gopher
available resources, listing, 131
directories, viewing, 131-132
files, viewing, 132
RFC (Requests for Comment) Web site, 144
server connections, 130-131
HTTP (Hypertext Transfer Protocol)
commands, 140-141
cookies, 142-143
data, uploading to server, 141-142
HTTP v1.0, 136
HTTP v1.1, 136-137
persistent connections, 136-137

requests, 133-134
response headers, 134-139
RFC (Requests for Comment) Web site, 144
S-http, 144
server connections, 133
virtual hosting, 137

Domain Name Service. *See* **DNS**

domain names. *See also* **DNS (Domain Name Service)**
configuration, 90
InterNIC, 69
registering, 69

DOMAINNAME setting (/etc/sysconfig/network file), 97

domains, 65, 277

DOS commands, telnet, 104

drivers, 426

Dynamic Host Configuration Protocol. *See* **DHCP**

E

Echo message (ICMP), 33

echo requests, 33-35

email
encryption, 366
flames, 463
HTML (Hyptertext Markup Language), 464
Linux, 236-256
IMAP (Internet Message Access Protocol) server, 237
POP (Post Office Protocol) server, 237
sendmail, 236

Mac OS, 225-235
mailing lists, 224
messages
    address verification, 118
    addressing, 116-117
    deleting, 113, 124
    forging, 116
    header information,
        returning, 114
    listing, 113
    retrieving, 122-124
    searching, 124-125
    sending, 116
    storing, 126
    unique ID listings, 114
    writing, 117
Outlook Express, 373-375
PDF files, 464
privacy, 465
security, 352
server (AppleShare IP), 274
spam, 233-234, 463
    anti-spam tactics,
        234-235, 240-242
Windows, 236-256

email protocols
IMAP (Internet Message
    Access Protocol), 119-120
    authentication, 120-121
    commands, 121-127
    connections, closing, 125
    deleting messages, 124
    logout procedure, 125
    mailbox configuration,
        121-122, 126-127
    retrieving messages,
        122-124
    RFC (Requests for
        Comment) Web site,
        128
    searching messages,
        124-125
    storing messages, 126

MIME (Multipurpose
    Internet Mail Extensions),
    139
POP3 (Post Office
    Protocol), 110
    advantages, 115
    authentication, 111-112
    commands, 111-114
    connections, closing, 113
    deleting messages, 113
    listing messages, 112
    retrieving messages, 113
    RFC (Requests for
        Comment) Web site,
        128
    unique ID listings, 114
SMTP (Simple Mail Tranfer
    Protocol)
    address verification, 118
    advantages, 119
    commands, 116-119
    connections, closing, 118
    email, sending, 116-117
    help system, 118
    RFC (Requests for
        Comment) Web site,
        128
    SendMail program, 119
    servers, connecting to,
        115-116
    Simple Mail Transfer
        Protocol, 115

email servers, 224
Stalker CommuniGate Pro
    creating accounts,
        246-250
    email client, 255-256
    Linux, 236-243
    logs, 253-254
    mailing lists, 250-253
    monitoring system
        functions, 254
    Remote Queue Starting
        Command, 244

RPOP, 244-246
    Windows, 236-243
Stalker Internet Mail Server
    (SIMS)
    accounts, 228-231
    communication
        protocols, 232-235
    CommuniGator, 225-226
    configuring, 226-228
    logs, 235
    Postmaster, 225
    queues, 235
    router settings, 231-232
    testing, 235

enabling NetBIOS, 177

encryption
DES, 367
email, 366
keys, 366-367
laws regarding, 359
PGP (Pretty Good Privacy)
    Linux, 376-377
    Outlook Express, 373-375
    PGPFreeware, 369-373
RSA, 367-368
U.S. government, 359
Web, 366

EOL (end of line), 162

**error handling, CRC (Cyclic
Redundancy Check), 24**

error messages. *See also*
bugs
document delivery
    protocols, 138
Host Not Found, 440
HTTP (Hypertext Transport
    Protocol), 138
ICMP (Internet Control
    Message Protocol), 33
network problems, 439
Network Unreachable,
    171-172
No Such Host or Domain
    Name, 442

Timeout, 172-173
Unknown Host error, 442

ESTABLISHED state (TCP), 37

Ethernet
100BASE-TX, 22
10BASE-2 (thinnet), 21
BNC (British Naval
Connectors), 19-20, 452
disadvantages, 19-20
problems with, 380-382
splicing, 383
terminators, 18
10BASE-T (twisted-pair)
Cat-3 cabling, 21
Cat-5 cabling, 21
disadvantages, 21
hub configuration, 20-22
problems with, 382-384
cards, 22
prices of, 23
switched Ethernet, 82

EtherTalk (AppleTalk), 80, 176, 221

ethics
bandwidth, 458-460
privacy, 458, 465
sharing information, 458, 461-464

Ethload (Windows), 426-428

Eudora Web site, 127

EXAMINE command (IMAP), 121-122

Exchange Server, 279

exiting IRC (Internet Relay Chat) channels, 155

EXPN command (SMTP), 119

EXPUNGE command (IMAP), 124

F

FETCH command (IMAP), 122-124

Fetch Web site, 162

fields
IP (Internet Protocol)
headers, 31-32
TCP (Transmission Control
Protocol) headers, 39-40

File and Print Sharing dialog box, 178

File menu commands (Macinstosh), Get Info, 25

File Not Found message (HTTP), 138

file servers, AppleShare IP, 191

file sharing
AppleShare IP, 186
configuring, 178-179
FTP (File Transfer
Protocol), 186
Linux, 186
FTP (File Transfer
Protocol), 209-215
Mac OS compatibility, 221
Windows compatibility, 215-221
Mac OS, 186-187
AppleShare IP, 190-193
NetPresenz FTP server, 187-191
Windows compatibility, 193-198
SMB, 186
Windows, 186
Mac OS compatibility, 207-208
War FTPd, 198-207

File Transfer Protocol. *See* **FTP**

files
hosts (DNS server
alternative), 71
HOSTS file, 95
LMHOSTS, 181-182
names, retrieving (FTP), 162
paths, 107
permissions, 210
remote files, viewing, 132
sharing, 177-181
AppleShare IP, 273
configuring, 178-179
connections, 180
Linux, 280
Windows, 273-274, 277
types, 162

filtering Internet content
drawbacks, 299
PICS (Platform for Internet
Content Selection), 299-300

FIN flag, 40

FIN-WAIT-1 state (TCP), 37

FIN-WAIT-2 state (TCP), 38

finger, 390

firewalls, 357-358
3COM, 360
Application Gateway
firewalls, 358
Circuit-Level firewalls, 358
hardware, 365-366
limitations, 358
Linux, 365, 378
Mac Os IPNetRouter, 362-364
packet filter firewalls, 358
proxy firewalls, 358
vendors, 378
Windows WinProxy, 364

flags
IP (Internet Protocol)
headers, 32
TCP (Transmission Control
Protocol) packets, 40

Flags field (IP headers), 32

flaming (email), 463

flood ping, 170

Forbidden message (HTTP), 138

forging email messages, 116

forward slash (/), 131

FORWARD_IPV4 setting (/etc/sysconfig/network file), 97

fragmentation, 31

frames (Ethernet). *See also* **packets**
    collisions, 27-28
    CRC (Cyclic Redundancy Check), 24
    defined, 24

FTP (File Transfer Protocol), 160-161, 186
    AppleShare IP, 273
    client software, 162
    commands
        CWD, 161
        LIST, 161
        PASS, 161
        PASV, 162
        QUIT, 162
        RETR, 162
        STOR, 162
        TYPE, 162
        USER, 161
    connections, closing, 162
    directories, 161
    files, identifying, 162
    Linux, 182
    passive mode, 162
    passwords, 161
    port number, 42
    servers
        Linux, 209-215
        NetPresenz, 187-191
        War FTPd server, 198-207
    storing data, 162

ftp:// syntax (URLs), 108

FTP (File Transfer Protocol) RFC Web site, 163

G

Gamelan Web site, 48

GATEWAY setting (/etc/sysconfig/network file), 97

GATEWAYDEV setting (/etc/sysconfig/network file), 97

gateways, 75. *See also* **routers**

GET command (HTTP), 133-134, 140

Get Info command (File menu), 25

GET method, 141-142

Gopher
    available resources, listing, 131
    directories, viewing, 131-132
    files, viewing, 132
    port number, 42
    RFC (Requests for Comment) Web site, 144
    server connections, 130-131

gopher:// syntax (URLs), 108

GROUP command (NNTP), 148-149

GUIs (graphical user interfaces), K Desktop Environment, 108
    runlevel editor, 281
    Web site, 280

H

hackers. *See also* **attacks on security**

hardware
    bridges, 74, 77
    cables
        10BASE-2, 18-21
        10BASE-T, 20-22
        100BASE-TX, 22
        Ethernet cards, 22
        prices of, 23
        problems, 380-384, 452-453
    defined, 9
    firewalls, 365-366
    gateways, 75
    hubs, 74, 82
    modems
        analog, 290
        cable, 291
    repeaters, 74
    routers, 74-75, 78
        costs, 81
        protocols, 80
        routing tables, 79
        tunneling, 80
    switches, 82

hardware addresses
    displaying, 25-26
    IP addresses, relationship between, 54-55
    as single network address, 52

HEAD command
    HTTP (Hypertext Transfer Protocol)), 140-141
    NNTP (Network News Transfer Protocol) server, 149-150

Header Checksum field (IP headers), 32

headers
    HTTP (Hypertext Transport Protocol)
        content-length field, 139
        content-type field, 139
        example, 134
        last-modified date, 139

version information,
136-137
Web server status, 138
IP (Internet Protocol)
packets
fields, 31-32
IPv4, 471
IPv6, 470-473
TCP (Transmission Control
Protocol) packets, 39-40

**HELO command (SMTP),
116**

HELP command
IRC (Internet Relay Chat),
159
SMTP (Simple Mail
Transfer Protocol), 118

help system (SMTP), 118

**HINFO record (Host
Information), 67**

hops, 75

**Host Information (HINFO)
record, 67**

**Host Not Found error
message, 440**

**HOSTNAME setting (/etc/
sysconfig/network file), 97**

hostnames, 64-66
configuration, 96
DNS (Domain Name
Service) server
domain names,
registering, 69
InterNIC, 69
name resolution, 66
name server records,
66-67
sending queries, 67-68
TTL (time to live), 66
whois service, 70-71
domains, 65
hosts file, 71
TLD (top-level domain),
64-65

hosts, virtual, 31

HOSTS file, 71, 95

Hotline, 44-45

**HTML (Hypertext Markup
Language), 464**

**HTTP (Hypertext Transfer
Protocol)**
commands
GET, 133-134, 140
HEAD, 140-141
cookies
advantages, 143
Cookie Central Web site,
144
security, 142
setting, 143
data, uploading to server
GET method, 141-142
POST method, 142
HTTP v1.0, 136
HTTP v1.1, 136-137
persistent connections,
136-137
port number, 42
requests, 133-134
response headers
content-length field, 139
content-type field, 139
example, 134
last-modified date, 139
version information,
136-137
Web server status, 138
RFC (Requests for
Comment) Web site, 144
S-http, 144
server connections, 133
virtual hosting, 137

http:// syntax (URLs), 107

**http Version Not Supported
message, 138**

hubs, 20-22, 74
cables, 169
connecting, 169-170

intranet, 168-169
prices of, 23
smart hubs, 82

Hypertext Transfer Protocol.
See HTTP

I

I Seek You (ICQ), 43-44

**ICMP (Internet Control
Message Protocol), 32**
messages, 33
requests, sending, 33-35
RFC (Requests for
Comment) Web site, 50

**icons, Network
Neighborhood, 180**

ICQ (I Seek You), 43-44

**Identification field (IP
headers), 32**

identifying
channel users, 158-159
file types, 162

**IIS (Internet Information
Server), 265, 277**

**IMAP (Internet Message
Access Protocol), 119-120**
authentication, 120-121
commands
CAPABILITY, 121
CLOSE, 125
COPY, 126
CREATE, 126
DELETE, 127
EXAMINE, 121-122
EXPUNGE, 124
FETCH, 122-124
LOGIN, 121
LOGOUT, 125
RENAME, 127
SEARCH, 124-125
SELECT, 121-122
STATUS, 122
STORE, 124

connections, closing, 125

email messages
  deleting, 124
  retrieving, 122-124
  searching, 124-125
  storing, 126

logout procedure, 125

mailboxes
  creating, 126
  deleting, 127
  renaming, 127
  selecting, 121-122
  statistics, 122

port number, 42

RFC (Requests for Comment) Web site, 128

installing TCP/IP, 91-92

Integrated Services Digital Network (ISDN), 290-291

intellectual property, 461

InterMapper (Mac OS), 412-418

Internal Server Error message, 138

International Standards Organization (ISO), 8

Internet. *See also* **protocols**
  aliases, 273
  censoring content
    filtering, 299-300
    in schools, 298-299
    in the workplace, 298
    LinkCheck program, 298-299
    U.S. government actions, 298
  connections
    ASDL (Asymmetric Digital Subscriber Line), 291
    cable modems, 291
    IP (Internet Protocol) masquerading, 294

ISDN (Integrated Services Digital Network), 290-291

NAT (Network Address Translation), 293-296, 338

phone-line connections, 290

proxy servers, 292-293, 298

T1 lines, 291

T3 lines, 292

DNS (Domain Name Service) server
  domain names, registering, 69
  InterNIC, 69
  name resolution, 66
  name server records, 66-67
  sending queries, 67-68
  TTL (time to live), 66
  whois service, 70-71

hostnames
  domains, 65
  TLD (top-level domain), 64-65

hosts file, 71

InterNIC, 69

IRC (Internet Relay Chat)
  bots, 151
  channels, 153-158
  client software, 160
  commands, 153-159
  connections, 152, 155
  server registration, 152-153

Internet Control Message Protocol. *See* **ICMP**

Internet Explorer
  proxy server configuration
    Mac OS, 302-303
    Windows, 304-306
  Web site, 144

Internet Information Server (IIS), 265, 277

Internet Message Access Protocol. *See* **IMAP**

Internet Protocol. *See* **IP**

Internet Relay Chat. *See* **IRC**

Internet Software Consortium, 408

InterNIC Web site, 70-72

intranets
  AppleTalk (Mac OS), 176
  cables, 169
  client services, 183
  configuring, 168
  connections
    Network unreachable error message, 171-172
    testing, 170-171
    Timeout error message, 172-173
  dedicated servers, 183-184
  hubs, 168-170
  Linux client services, 182
  shared resources
    connecting to, 180-182
    LMHOSTS file, 181-182
    SMB file sharing, 177-180
    Web File Sharing, 173-176

IP (Internet Protocol), 29-30
  addresses
    128-bit addresses, 469-470
    assigning, 57
    configuration, 58-59, 89, 92
    DHCP (Dynamic Host Configuration Protocol) servers, 56-57
    dial-in connections, 58

hardware addresses,
  relationship between,
  54-55
IPng, 468-469
numbers, 60
as single network
  address, 52-53
subnets, 60-64
conflicts, 386-387
forwarding, 295
IPNetMonitor, 34
IPNetRouter, 338-341
firewall configuration,
  362-364
IPng
  address space, 468-469
  addressing, 469-470
  packet headers, 470-473
  quality of service
    labeling, 473-474
  resources, 475
  security, 473
  transitioning to, 474-475
IPRoute software, 347
IPv4, 468
IPv5, 468
IPv6
  address space, 468-469
  addressing, 469-470
  packet headers, 470-473
  quality of service
    labeling, 473-474
  resources, 475
  security, 473
  transitioning to, 474-475
masquerading, 294
multihoming, 31
packets
  fragmentation, 31
  header fields, 31-32
RFC (Requests for
  Comment) Web site, 50
spoofing, 472-473
virtual hosts, 31

IP (Internet Protocol)
  addresses, 55-56, 69
  128-bit addresses, 469-470
  assigning, 57
  configuration
    accessing, 58-59
    Macintosh workstations,
      89
    Windows 95
      workstations, 92
    Windows 98
      workstations, 92
    windows 98
      workstations, 92
  DHCP (Dynamic Host
    Configuration Protocol)
    servers, 56-57
  dial-in connections, 58
  hardware addresses,
    relationship between,
    54-55
  IPng, 468-469
  numbers, 60
  as single network address,
    52-53
  subnets, 60-61
    classes, 61
    masks, 61-62
    private, 63-64
    routing problems, 62-63

IP Network Browser
  (Windows), 422-425

IPADDR setting (ifcfg-eth0
  file), 97

ipfwadm utility, 365

ipLease DHCP (Dynamic
  Host Configuration
  Protocol) server, 402-407

IPNetMonitor, 34

IPNetRouter, 338-341,
  362-364

IPng
  address space, 468-469
  addressing, 469-470

packet headers, 470-471
  destination address, 472
  destination options, 472
  extensibility, 472-473
  flow label, 471
  fragment headers, 472
  hop limit, 472
  hop-by-hop headers, 472
  IP authentication
    headers, 472
  IP privacy headers, 473
  next header, 472
  payload length, 471
  routing headers, 472
  source address, 472
  version, 471
quality of service labeling,
  473-474
resources, 475
security, 473
transitioning to, 474-475

IPRoute software, 347

IPv4, 468

IPv5, 468

IPv6
  address space, 468-469
  addressing, 469-470
  packet headers, 470-471
    destination address, 472
    destination options, 472
    extensibility, 472-473
    flow label, 471
    fragment headers, 472
    hop limit, 472
    hop-by-hop headers, 472
    IP authentication
      headers, 472
    IP privacy headers, 473
    next header, 472
    payload length, 471
    routing headers, 472
    source address, 472
    version, 471
  quality of service labeling,
    473-474

resources, 475
security, 473
transitioning to, 474-475

**IRC (Internet Relay Chat),
151-152**
bots, 151
channels
banning users, 158
creating, 156
customizing, 156-157
descriptions, 156
forcibly removing users,
158
identifying users, 158-159
joining, 154
leaving, 155
limiting connections, 157
listing, 153-154
lurking, 155
operator, setting, 157
private messages, 155
client software, 160
commands
HELP, 159
ISON, 159
JOIN, 154-156
KICK, 158
LIST, 153-154
MODE, 156-157
NICK, 152-153
PART, 155
PASS, 152
PRIVMSG, 155
QUIT, 155
TOPIC, 156
USER, 153
USERHOST, 158-159
WHOIS, 158
connections, closing, 155
RFC (Requests for
Comment) Web site, 160
server connection, 152
server registration
nicknames, 152-153
passwords, 152
real identity, 153

**ISDN (Integrated Services
Digital Network), 290-291**
**ISO (International
Standards Organization), 8**
ISON command (IRC), 159
InterNIC, 69

J-K

Java, 48
**JOIN command (IRC),
154-156**
**joining IRC (Internet Relay
Chat) channels, 154**

**KDE (K Desktop
Environment), 108**
runlevel editor, 281
Web site, 280
Kerberos, 121
**kernels (operating systems),
330-331**
keys, 366-367
KICK command (IRC), 158

L

label bureaus, 317-318
LADP servers, 391-392
LANs (local area networks).
See **networks**
**LAST command (NNTP),
150**
LAST-ACK state (TCP), 38
**last-modified date (HTTP
response headers), 139**
**layers, OSI network model,
8-9**
Application, 15
Data Link, 10-11

Network, 11-12
Physical, 9-10
Presentation, 14-15, 42
Session, 14, 41-42
Transport, 13-14
**LDAP (Lightweight
Directory Access
Protocol), 390-392**
**licenses, Open Content
License (OCL), 462**
**Lightweight Directory
Access Protocol (LDAP),
390-392**
**limiting channel
connections, 157**
LinkCheck, 298-299
Linux
Apache, 265-269
client services, 182
compatibility, 282
DHCP (Dynamic Host
Configuration Protocol)
servers, 397-398, 408-410
file sharing, 186, 280
FTP (File Transfer
Protocol), 209-215
Mac OS compatibility,
221
Windows compatibility,
215-221
firewalls, 365, 378
hardware addresses, 26
IP (Internet Protocol)
address configuration, 59
KDE (K Desktop
Environment), 280-281
limitations, 282-283
messaging
IMAP (Internet Message
Access Protocol)
server, 237
POP (Post Office
Protocol) server, 237
sendmail, 236

Multi Router Traffic Grapher (MRTG), 428-432
NAT servers, 345-346
PGP (Pretty Good Privacy), 376-377
proxy servers, 306-308, 329-335
security issues, 356-357
Sniffit, 432-435
stability, 284
support, 283
TCP/IP configuration, 95
   DNS servers, 96
   /etc/sysconfig/network file, 96-97
   hostnames, 96
   ifcfg-eth0 file, 97-98
utilities, 281
Web servers, 265-269

Linux Configuration and Troubleshooting Web site, 99

Linux Web site, 182

LIST command
FTP (File Transfer Protocol), 161
IRC, 153-154
NNTP (Network News Transfer Protocol) server, 148

LIST command (POP3), 112

LISTEN state (TCP), 37

listing
IRC (Internet Relay Chat) channels, 153-154
newsgroups
   available number of messages, 148-149
   NNTP (Network News Transfer Protocol) server, 148

LMHOSTS file, 181-182

local area networks (LANs). *See* **networks**

localhost, 176

LOGIN command (IMAP), 121

LOGOUT command (IMAP), 125

log files, 439

lurking, 155

Lynx, 307-308

M

MAC addresses, displaying
Linux workstations, 26
Macintosh workstations, 25
Windows 95 workstations, 25
Windows 98 workstations, 25

MacDNS (AppleShare IP), 274-275

Macintosh, 276
AppleScript, 413
AppleShare IP, 272-276
   file sharing, 273
   FTP (File Transfer Protocol), 273
   Internet Aliases, 273
   limitations, 275-276
   MacDNS, 274-275
   mail server, 274
   print server, 275
   QuickDNS Pro, 274
   Windows file sharing, 273-274
AppleTalk, 80, 176
client workstations, configuring
   connection methods, 89
   domain names, 90
   Ethernet cards, 88

IP (Internet Protocol)
   addresses, 59, 89
   name server addresses, 90
DHCP (Dynamic Host Configuration Protocol) servers, 394-395, 398-401
file paths, 107
file sharing, 186-187
   AppleShare IP, 190-193
   NetPresenz FTP (File Transfer Protocol) server, 187-191
   Windows compatibility, 193-198
hardware addresses, displaying, 25
InterMapper, 412-418
IPNetMonitor application, 34
IPNetRouter, 362-364
messaging, 225-235
NAT servers, 338-341
NetMinder, 418-422
Outlook Express, 373-375
PGPFreeware, 369-373
protected memory, 275
proxy servers
   browsers, 301-303
   SurfExpress, 300
   WebDoubler, 308-321
   WebSTAR, 308
security issues, 355
Sherlock, 462
SimpleText, 174
stability, 284
Telnet, 104
Web File Sharing, 174-176
   security, 175-176
   Web file server mode, 174
   Web server mode, 174
Web servers, 256-262

MacIRC Web site, 160

Mail Exchanger (MX) record, 67

MAIL FROM command (SMTP), 116

mail protocols
IMAP (Internet Message Access Protocol), 119-120
  authentication, 120-121
  commands, 121-127
  connections, closing, 125
  deleting messages, 124
  logout procedure, 125
  mailbox configuration, 121-122, 126-127
  retrieving messages, 122-124
  RFC (Requests for Comment) Web site, 128
  searching messages, 124-125
  storing messages, 126
MIME (Multipurpose Internet Mail Extensions), 139
POP3 (Post Office Protocol), 110
  advantages, 115
  authentication, 111-112
  commands, 111-114
  connections, closing, 113
  deleting messages, 113
  listing messages, 112
  retrieving messages, 113
  RFC (Requests for Comment) Web site, 128
  unique ID listings, 114
SMTP (Simple Mail Tranfer Protocol)
  address verification, 118
  advantages, 119
  commands, 116-119
  connections, closing, 118

email, sending, 116-117
help system, 118
RFC (Requests for Comment) Web site, 128
SendMail program, 119
servers, connecting to, 115-116
Simple Mail Transfer Protocol), 115

mail server (AppleShare IP), 274

mail servers, 224
Stalker CommuniGate Pro
  creating accounts, 246-250
  email client, 255-256
  Linux, 236-243
  logs, 253-254
  mailing lists, 250-253
  monitoring system functions, 254
  Remote Queue Starting Command, 244
  RPOP, 244-246
  Windows, 236-243
Stalker Internet Mail Server (SIMS)
  accounts, 228-231
  communication protocols, 232-235
  CommuniGator, 225-226
  configuring, 226-228
  logs, 235
  Postmaster, 225
  queues, 235
  router settings, 231-232
  testing, 235

mailboxes (IMAP)
creating, 126
deleting, 127
renaming, 127
selecting, 121-122
statistics, 122

mailing lists
benefits, 224
digests, 224
flames, 463
spamming, 463

Majora, 255

managers (SNMP), 83

mapping networks, 412-418

masks (subnets), 61-62

masquerading (IP), 294.
See also NAT (Network Address Translation)

Maxum WebDoubler, 308-319

MBONE (Multicast BackBone), 85-86

memory, protected, 275

Men and Mice Web site, 275

messages
email
  address verification, 118
  addressing, 116-117
  deleting, 113, 124
  forging, 116
  header information, returning, 114
  listing, 112-113
  retrieving, 122-124
  searching, 124-125
  sending, 116
  storing, 126
  unique ID listings, 114
  writing, 117
ICMP (Internet Control Message Protocol), 33

MESSAGES option (STATUS command), 122

messaging. *See* email

methods
GET, 141-142
POST, 142

Microsoft Active Server Pages, 278

Microsoft Exchange Server, 279

Microsoft Outlook and Outlook Express Web site, 150

Microsoft SQL Server, 278

Microsoft Web site
Internet Explorer page, 144, 162
Outlook/Outlook-Express page, 127
Windows Networking page, 99

MIME (Multipurpose Internet Mail Extensions), 139

Mirabilis Communications, ICQ (I Seek You), 43-44

Miramar Systems, PC MACLAN, 208

mIRC Web site, 160

Mischler, David, 347

MODE command (IRC), 156-157

modems
analog, 290
cable, 291

monitoring
networks
Ethload (Windows), 426-428
InterMapper (Mac OS), 412-418
IP Network Browser (Windows), 422-425
Multi Router Traffic Grapher (Linux), 428-432
NetMinder (Mac OS), 418-422

Simple Network Management Protocol (SMTP), 392, 412
Sniffit (Linux), 432-435
users, 465

Monolith Web site, 69

Moved Permanently message (HTTP responses), 138

MRTG (Multi Router Traffic Grapher, 428-432

MS-DOS commands, telnet, 104

Multi Router Traffic Grapher (Linux), 428-432

Multi-Threaded NewsWatcher Web site, 150

Multicast BackBone (MBONE), 85

multicasting, 85

multihoming, 31

multiplexing, 37

Multipurpose Internet Mail Extensions (MIME), 139

MX record (Mail Exchanger), 67

N

name resolution
DNS (Domain Name Service), 66
configuration, 69, 93-94
domain names, registering
InterNIC, 69
MacDNS (AppleShare IP), 274-275
name resolution, 66
name server records, 66-67

queries, sending, 67-68
QuickDNS Pro, 274
TTL (time to live), 66
whois service, 70-71
Windows NT, 278
WINS (Windows Internet Name Service), 94

Name Server (NS) record, 67

name server records, 66-67

NAT (Network Address Translation), 293-296
advantages, 295
IP (Internet Protocol) forwarding, 295
RFC (Requests for Comment) Web site, 296
servers, 362
IPNetRouter, 338-341
IPRoute software, 347
Linux, 345-346
Mac OS, 338-341
NAT32, 341-344
TCP/IP settings, 346
Vicom Internet Gateway, 341
WebRamp, 347
Windows, 341-344

NAT32 NAT server, 341-344

NDIS3PKT program, 426

Neon Software, NetMinder, 418-422

netatalk, 221

NetBIOS, 177

Netcraft survey Web site, 135

netizens, 458

NETMASK setting (ifcfg-eth0 file), 98

NetMinder (Mac OS), 418-422

NetPresenz, 187-191

Netscape
    proxy server configuration
        Linux, 306-307
        Mac OS, 301
        Windows, 303-304
    secure socket layer (SSL),
        366
    Web site, 127, 144, 150, 162

**netstat utility, 38-39,
  449-450**

network addresses
    hardware addresses as, 52
    IP (Internet Protocol)
        addresses as, 52-53

**Network Address
  Translation (NAT),
  293-296**
    advantages, 295
    IP forwarding, 295
    RFC (Requests for
        Comment) Web site, 296

**Network layer (OSI network
  model), 11-12. *See also*
  IP (Internet Protocol)**

**Network Neighborhood
  icon, 180**

**Network News Transfer
  Protocol. *See* NNTP**

**NETWORK setting (ifcfg-
  eth0 file), 98**

**Network Time Protocol
  (NTP), 163-164**

**Network unreachable error
  message, 171-172**

**NETWORKING setting (/
  etc/sysconfig/network
  file), 97**

**networks, 8. *See also*
  Internet; protocols**
    bridges, 74, 77
    broadcasting, 83-84

Browse Master, 181
cables
    100BASE-TX, 22
    10BASE-2 (thinnet),
        18-21, 380-383, 452
    10BASE-T (twisted-pair),
        20-22, 382-384
    crossover, 169
    Ethernet cards, 22
    planning, 169
    prices of, 23
    problems, 448-452
    splices, 383
client services
    AppleTalk (Mac OS), 176
    Web File Sharing (Mac
        OS), 173-176
connections
    Network unreachable
        error message, 171-172
    testing, 170-171
    Timeout error message,
        172-173
dedicated servers, 183-184
ethics
    bandwidth, 458-460
    privacy, 458, 465
    sharing information, 458,
        461-464
gateways, 75
hops, 75
hubs, 74
mapping, 412-418
media, *see* hardware
monitoring
    Ethload (Windows),
        426-428
    InterMapper (Mac OS),
        412-418
    IP Network Browser
        (Windows), 422-425
    Multi Router Traffic
        Grapher (Linux),
        428-432
    NetMinder (Mac OS),

        418-422
    Simple Network
        Management Protocol
        (SMTP), 392, 412
    Sniffit (Linux), 432-435
multicasting, 85
nodes, 11
OSI (Open Systems
  Interconnect) model, 8-9
    Application layer, 15
    Data Link layer, 10-11
    Network layer, 11-12
    Physical layer, 9-10
    Presentation layer, 14-15,
        42
    Session layer, 14, 41-42
    Transport layer, 13-14
packet tunneling, 80
repeaters, 74
routers, 74-75, 78
    costs, 81
    protocols, 80
    routing tables, 79
security, 352-354
    considerations, 359
    credit card transactions,
        353-354
    data encryption, 359
    Denial of Service attacks,
        38
    email, 352
    firewalls, 357-358
    packet sniffers, 352-353
    resources, 360
    SMTP servers, 353
    stability, 354-357
SNMP (Simple Network
  Management Protocol)
    agents, 83
    managers, 83
    RFC (Requests for
        Comment) Web site, 86
subnets
    classes, 61
    masks, 61-62

private, 63-64
routing problems, 62-63
switches, 82
topologies
bus, 19
star, 20
troubleshooting
cabling, 448-453
configuration errors,
441-446
error messages, 439
hardware errors, 380-384,
452-453
logs, 439
netstat, 449-450
protocol analyzers, 453
router configuration
errors, 446
software errors, 384-389,
447-448
spray, 450-452
subnet mask
configuration errors,
446-447
user errors, 390, 439-441

NEW option (SEARCH command), 125

newsgroups
cross-posting, 149
listing, 148
messages
available number of,
148-149
browsing, 150
retrieving, 149-150
NNTP (Network News
Transfer Protocol),
146-150
client software, 150
commands, 147-150
connection, closing, 150
RFC Web site, 150
server connections, 147

NEWSGROUPS command (NNTP), 148

NEXT command (NNTP), 150

NICK command (IRC), 152-153

nicknames (IRC), 152-153

NN-TK Web site, 150

NNTP (Network News Transfer Protocol), 146
client software, 150
commands
ARTICLE/HEAD/
BODY, 149-150
GROUP, 148-149
LIST, 148
NEWSGROUPS, 148
NEXT/LAST, 150
QUIT, 150
sending, 147-148
connection, closing, 150
listing newsgroups, 148
messages
available number of,
148-149
browsing, 150
retrieving, 149-150
RFC Web site, 150
server connections, 147

nntp:// syntax (URLs), 107

No Such Host or Domain Name error message, 442

nodes, 11

NOOP command (POP3), 113

NS record (Name Server), 67

nslookup, 67-68

NTP (Network Time Protocol), 163-164

Nupop email client, 464

O

ODBC (Open Database Connectivity), 282

OK message (HTTP), 138

Olivetti Research Laboratory, VNS (Virtual Network Computing) application, 47-48

OmniHTTPd Web server, 262-265

ONBOOT setting (ifcfg-eth0 file), 98

Open Content group, 462-463

Open Content License (OCL), 462

Open Database Connectivity (ODBC), 282

Open Door Networks, ShareWay, 191-193

Open Link State Protocol (OSLP), 80

Open Systems Interconnect model. *See* **OSI network model**

Open Transport
configuring, 89
connection methods, 89
domain names, 90
IP addresses, 89
name server addresses,
90
Web site, 99

Opera Web site, 144

operating systems
dedicated servers, 183-184
kernels, 330-331
Linux, 280-283
DHCP (Dynamic Host
Configuration Protocol)
servers, 397-398,
408-410

file sharing, 186, 209-221
firewalls, 365, 378
hardware addresses, 26
messaging, 236-256
Multi Router Traffic
   Grapher, 428-432
NAT (Network Address
   Translation) servers,
   345-346
PGP (Pretty Good
   Privacy), 376-377
proxy servers, 306-308,
   329-335
security issues, 356-357
Sniffit, 432-435
TCP/IP configuration,
   95-98
Web servers, 265-269
Macintosh, 276
   AppleScript, 413
   AppleShare IP, 272-276
   AppleTalk, 80, 176
   client workstations,
      configuring, 59, 88-90
   DHCP (Dynamic Host
      Configuration Protocol)
      servers, 394-395,
      398-401
   file paths, 107
   file sharing, 186-198
   hardware addresses,
      displaying, 25
   InterMapper, 412-418
   IPNetMonitor
      application, 34
   IPNetRouter, 362-364
   messaging, 225-235
   NAT servers, 338-341
   NetMinder, 418-422
   Outlook Express, 373-375
   PGPFreeware, 369-373
   protected memory, 275
   proxy servers, 300-303,
      308-321
   security issues, 355

Sherlock, 462
SimpleText, 174
stability, 284
Telnet, 104
Web File Sharing,
   174-176
Web servers, 256-262
UNIX
   KDE desktop system,
      108
   security issues, 355
upgrades, 356
Windows 95/98
   Browse Master, 181
   DHCP (Dynamic Host
      Configuration Protocol)
      servers, 396-397,
      402-407
   Ethload, 426-428
   hardware addresses, 25
   IP Network Browser,
      422-425
   messaging, 236-256
   NAT servers, 341-344
   Outlook Express, 375
   PGPFreeware, 369-373
   proxy servers, 300-306,
      321-329
   security issues, 355
   shared resources,
      177-182, 198-208
   TCP/IP installation/
      configuration, 91-95
   Web servers, 262-265
   winnuke program,
      354-355
   WinProxy, 364
Windows NT
   components, 278
   DHCP (Dynamic Host
      Configuration
      Protocol), 278, 402
   DNS (Domain Name
      Service) server, 278
   file sharing, 277

IIS (Internet Information
   Server), 277
limitations, 279-280
security issues, 355-356
ShareWay IP, 277
stability, 284

Options field
IP (Internet Protocol)
   headers, 32
TCP (Transmission Control
   Protocol) packets, 40

OS. *See* operating systems

**OSI (Open Systems
Interconnect) network
model, 8-9**
Application layer, 15
Data Link layer, 10-11
Network layer, 11-12
Physical layer, 9-10
Presentation layer, 14-15, 42
Session layer, 14, 41-42
Transport layer, 13-14

**Ositis Software, WinProxy,
321-329**

**OSLP (Open Link State
Protocol), 80**

**Outlook Express email
client, 464**
Mac OS, 373-375
Web site, 127
Windows, 375

P

packet sniffers, 352-353
ethical use of, 465
Ethload (Windows), 426-428
IPv6 packet headers, 473
NetMinder (Mac OS),
   418-422
Sniffit (Linux), 432-435

packets. *See also* frames
broadcast packets, 84
drivers, 426

filtering, 358
fragmentation, 31
hops, 75
IPv4, 31-32, 471
IPv6, 470-471
  destination address, 472
  destination options, 472
  extensibility, 472-473
  flow label, 471
  fragment headers, 472
  hop limit, 472
  hop-by-hop headers, 472
  IP authentication
    headers, 472
  IP privacy headers, 473
  next header, 472
  payload length, 471
  routing headers, 472
  source address, 472
  version, 471
routes
  choosing, 79-80
  tracing, 75-77
TCP (Tranmission Control
  Protocol) header fields,
  39-40
tunneling, 80

Padding field
  IP (Internet Protocol)
    headers, 32
  TCP (Tranmission Control
    Protocol) packets, 40

The Palace, 45

**PAP (Password
  Authentication Protocol),
  29**

**Parameter Problem
  message (ICMP), 33**

PART command (IRC), 155

partitioning, 169

PASS command
  FTP (File Transfer
    Protocol), 161

IRC (Internet Relay
  Chat) server registration,
  152
POP3 (Post Office
  Protocol), 112

passive mode (FTP), 162

**Password Authentication
  Protocol (PAP), 29**

passwords
  FTP (File Transfer
    Protocol), 161
  IRC (Internet Relay
    Chat) server registration,
    152

PASV command (FTP), 162

patches, 356

PC MACLAN, 208

**PDF (Portable Document
  Format) files, 464**

permissions, 210

**persistent connections
  (HTTP), 136-137**

**PGP (Pretty Good Privacy),
  366**
  Linux, 376-377
  Outlook Express
    Mac OS, 373-375
    Windows, 375
  PGPFreeware, 369-373

pgpk utility, 376-377

**phone-line connections,
  290**

**Physical layer (OSI network
  model), 9-10.** *See also*
  hardware

**PICS (Platform for Internet
  Content Selection), 299-
  300**
  WebDoubler proxy server,
  315-321

ping
  echo requests, sending,
    33-35
  flood ping, 170
  network connection, 170-171
    Network unreachable
      error message, 171-172
    Timeout error message,
      172-173
  Ping of Death, 170
  problems with, 442

piracy of software, 462

PIRCH Web site, 160

**Platform for Internet
  Content Selection (PICS),
  299-300**
  label bureaus, 317-318
  SafeSurf, 317
  SurfWatch, 317-321
  WebDoubler proxy server,
    315-321

platforms
  kernels, 330-331
  Linux
    DHCP (Dynamic Host
      Configuration Protocol)
      servers, 397-398,
      408-410
    file sharing, 186, 209-221
    firewalls, 365, 378
    hardware addresses, 26
    messaging, 236-256
    Multi Router Traffic
      Grapher, 428-432
    NAT (Network Address
      Translation) servers,
      345-346
    PGP (Pretty Good
      Privacy), 376-377
    proxy servers, 306-308,
      329-335
    security issues, 356-357
    Sniffit, 432-435

TCP/IP configuration, 95-98
Web servers, 265-269
Macintosh, 276
  AppleScript, 413
  AppleShare IP, 272-276
  AppleTalk, 80, 176
  client workstations, configuring, 59, 88-90
  DHCP (Dynamic Host Configuration Protocol) servers, 394-395, 398-401
  file paths, 107
  file sharing, 186-198
  hardware addresses, displaying, 25
  InterMapper, 412-418
  IPNetMonitor application, 34
  IPNetRouter, 362-364
  messaging, 225-235
  NAT servers, 338-341
  NetMinder, 418-422
  Outlook Express, 373-375
  PGPFreeware, 369-373
  protected memory, 275
  proxy servers, 300-303, 308-321
  security issues, 355
  Sherlock, 462
  SimpleText, 174
  stability, 284
  Telnet, 104
  Web File Sharing, 174-176
  Web servers, 256-262
UNIX
  KDE desktop system, 108
  security issues, 355
upgrades, 356
Windows 95/98
  Browse Master, 181
  DHCP (Dynamic Host Configuration Protocol) servers, 396-397,

402-407
  Ethload, 426-428
  hardware addresses, 25
  IP Network Browser, 422-425
  messaging, 236-256
  NAT servers, 341-344
  Outlook Express, 375
  PGPFreeware, 369-373
  proxy servers, 300-306, 321-329
  security issues, 355
  shared resources, 177-182, 198-208
  TCP/IP installation/ configuration, 91-95
  Web servers, 262-265
  winnuke program, 354-355
  WinProxy, 364
Windows NT
  components, 278
  DHCP (Dynamic Host Configuration Protocol), 278, 402
  DNS (Domain Name Service) server, 278
  file sharing, 277
  IIS (Internet Information Server), 277
  limitations, 279-280
  security issues, 355-356
  ShareWay IP, 277
  stability, 284
Point To Point Protocol (PPP), 28-29
PointCast, 47
POP3 (Post Office Protocol), 110
  advantages, 115
  authentication, 111-112
  commands
    DELE, 113
    LIST, 112
    NOOP, 113

PASS, 112
QUIT, 113
RESET, 113
RETR, 113
STAT, 112
TOP, 114
UIDL, 114
USER, 111
  connections, closing, 113
  messages
    deleting, 113
    header information, 114
    listing, 112
    retrieving, 113
    unique ID listings, 114
  port number, 42
Portable Document Format (PDF) files, 464
ports
  AUI ports, 22
  common port numbers, 36-37, 42
  disabling, 169
  proxy servers, 300
  Telnet, 104
POST method, 142
Post Office Protocol. *See* POP3
pound sign (#), 154
PPP (Point To Point Protocol), 28-29, 50
Presentation layer (OSI network model), 14-15, 42
Pretty Good Privacy. *See* PGP
print server (AppleShare IP), 275
privacy, ethical considerations, 458, 465
private key (encryption), 366-367

private messages (IRC), 155

private subnets, 63-64

PRIVMSG command (IRC), 155

problems, troubleshooting
cabling, 380-384, 448-453
causes, 438
configuration errors, 441-446
error messages, 439
hardware, 452-453
IP (Internet Protocol) conflicts, 386-387
Linux, 99
logs, 439
netstat, 38-39, 449-450
Network unreachable error message, 171
ping, 33-35
protocol analyzers, 453
router configuration errors, 446
software errors, 447-448
spray, 450-452
subnet mask configuration errors, 446-447
Timeout error message, 172-173
user errors, 439-441

programs. *See* **applications; utilities**

protected memory, 275

protocol analyzers, 453

Protocol field (IP headers), 32

protocols
AppleTalk, 80
ACAP (Application Configuration Access Protocol), 388-389
ARP (Address Resolution Protocol), 79

common port numbers, 36-37, 42
DHCP (Dynamic Host Configuration Protocol), 56-57, 385-388
BOOTP, compared, 57
client configuration, 394-398
IP (Internet Protocol) addresses, assigning, 57
ipLease DHCP server, 402-407
Linux, 408-410
Mac OS, 398-401
Vicom Internet Gateway, 398
Windows, 278, 402-407
DNS (Domain Name Service)
configuration, 93-96
domain names, registering, 69
InterNIC, 69
MacDNS (AppleShare IP), 274-275
name resolution, 66
name server records, 66-67
queries, sending, 67-68
QuickDNS Pro, 274
TTL (time to live), 66
whois service, 70-71
Windows NT, 278
FTP (File Transfer Protocol), 160-161, 186
client software, 162
commands, 161-162
connections, closing, 162
directories, changing, 161
file types, identifying, 162
passive mode, 162
passwords, 161
port number, 42

storing data, 162
Gopher
available resources, listing, 131
directories, viewing, 131-132
files, viewing, 132
port number, 42
RFC (Requests for Comment) Web site, 144
server connections, 130-131
HTTP (Hypertext Transfer Protocol), 133
commands, 140-141
cookies, 142-143
data, uploading to server, 141-142
HTTP v1.0, 136
HTTP v1.1, 136-137
persistent connections, 136-137
port number, 42
requests, 133-134
response headers, 134-139
RFC (Requests for Comment) Web site, 144
S-http, 144
server connections, 133
virtual hosting, 137
ICMP (Internet Control Message Protocol), 32
messages, 33
requests, sending, 34-35
RFC (Requests for Comment) Web site, 50
IMAP (Internet Message Access Protocol), 119-120
authentication, 120-121
commands, 121-127
connections, closing, 125
deleting messages, 124
logout procedure, 125

mailbox configuration, 121-122, 126-127
port number, 42
retrieving messages, 122-124
RFC (Requests for Comment) Web site, 128
searching messages, 124-125
storing messages, 126
IP (Internet Protocol), 29-30
addresses, 52-64, 89, 92, 468-470
conflicts, 386-387
forwarding, 295
IPNetMonitor, 34
IPNetRouter, 338-341
firewall configuration, 362-364
IPng, 468-475
IPRoute software, 347
IPv4, 468
IPv5, 468
IPv6, 468-475
masquerading, 294
multihoming, 31
packets, 31-32
RFC (Requests for Comment) Web site, 50
spoofing, 472-473
virtual hosts, 31
LDAP (Lightweight Directory Access Protocol), 390-392
limitations, 105-106
MIME (Multipurpose Internet Mail Extensions), 139
NNTP (Network News Transfer Protocol), 146
ARTICLE/HEAD/BODY commands, 149-150
available newsgroup messages (number of), 148-149

browsing messages, 150
client software, 150
commands, 147-150
connection, closing, 150
listing newsgroups, 148
retrieving messages, 149-150
server connections, 147
NTP (Network Time Protocol), 163-164
OSLP (Open Link State Protocol), 80
PAP (Password Authentication Protocol), 29
POP3 (Post Office Protocol), 110
advantages, 115
authentication, 111-112
commands, 111-114
port number, 42
RFC (Requests for Comment) Web site, 128
PPP (Point To Point Protocol), 28-29, 50
RIP (Router Information Protocol), 80
RPC (Remote Procedure Calls), 105
SLIP (Serial Line Internet Protocol), 28, 50
SMTP (Simple Mail Transfer Protocol), 115, 392, 412
address verification, 118
advantages, 119
commands, 116-119
connections, closing, 118
email, sending, 116-117
help system, 118
port number, 42
RFC (Requests for Comment) Web site, 128

SendMail program, 119
servers, connecting to, 115-116
SNMP (Simple Network Management Protocol), 83, 86
TCP (Transmission Control Protocol), 35-36
ACK (acknowledgement) messages, 35
header fields, 39-40
ports, 36-37
RFC (Requests for Comment) Web site, 50
sockets, 37
states, 37-39
Telnet, 104-105
Macintosh platforms, 104
port number, 42, 104
UDP (User Datagram Protocol), 35, 50

proxy firewalls, 358

proxy servers, 292-293, 298-300
advantages, 293
Apache, 329-335
browsers, 300
Linux browsers, 306-308
Mac OS browsers, 301-303
Windows browsers, 303-306
educational applications, 299
filtering, 299-300
limitations, 292
Linux, 329-335
Mac OS, 308-321
ports, 300
SOCKS, 323
SurfExpress, 300
WebDoubler, 308-321
WebSTAR, 308
Windows, 321-329
WinGate, 321
WinProxy, 321-329

PSH flag, 40

public key (encryption), 366-367

push technology, 47

Q-R

Quake, 49

queries (DNS server), sending, 67-68

QuickDNS Pro (DNS server), 274-275

QUIT command
FTP (File Transfer Protocol), 162
IRC (Internet Relay Chat), 155
NNTP (Network News Transfer Protocol) server, 150
POP3 (Post Office Protocol), 113
SMTP (Simple Mail Transfer Protocol), 118

RCPT TO command (SMTP), 116-117

real identity (IRC), 153

records (DNS servers), 66-67

Red Hat Linux. See Linux

Redirect message (ICMP), 33

registering
domain names, 69
IRC (Internet Relay Chat) servers
nicknames, 152-153
passwords, 152
real identity, 153

Remote Procedure Calls. See RPC

removing channel users (IRC), 158

RENAME command (IMAP), 127

repeaters, 74

Request Timeout message (HTTP), 138

requests
HTTP (Hypertext Transport Protocol), 133-134
ICMP (Internet Control Message Protocol), 33-35

Requests for Comment (RFCs), 49-50, 105, 108

Reserved field (TCP packets), 40

RESET command (POP3), 113

resolving names. See name resolution

responses (HTTP)
example, 134
headers
content-length field, 139
content-type field, 139
last-modified date, 139
version information, 136-137
Web server status, 138

RETR command
FTP (File Transfer Protocol), 162
POP3 (Post Office Protocol), 113

retrieving
filenames, 162
newsgroups messages, 149-150

RFCs (Requests for Comment), 49-50, 105, 108

RIP (Router Information Protocol), 80

Rivest, Ron, 368

Rootshell, 356, 473

routers, 74-75, 78
costs, 81
protocols, 80
routing tables, 79
tunneling, 80

routes
choosing, 79-80
tracing, 75-77

routing (network)
defined, 12
subnets, 62-63

Routing on the Internet Web site, 86

routing tables, 79

RPC (Remote Procedure Calls), 105

RSA, 367-368, 378

RSET command (SMTP), 118

RST flag, 40

runlevel editor (KDE), 281

S

S-http, 144

Samba, 215-221

saving email messages, 126

scalability (operating systems), 284

SEARCH command (IMAP), 124-125

search engines, 462

searching email messages, 124-125

Secure Sockets Layer (SSL), 143-144, 366

security, 352-354
  attacks on
    Denial of Service attacks, 38
    IP (Internet Protocol) spoofing, 472-473
    winnuke program, 354-355, 473
  cookies, 142
  credit card transactions, 353-354
  data encryption, 359
  email, 352
  encryption
    DES, 367
    email, 366
    keys, 366-367
    PGP (Pretty Good Privacy), 369-377
    RSA, 367-368, 378
  firewalls, 357-358, 362
    3COM, 360
    Application Gateway firewalls, 358
    Circuit-Level firewalls, 358
    hardware, 365-366
    limitations, 358
    Linux, 365, 378
    Mac OS IPNetRouter, 362-363
    Mac Os IPNetRouter, 362-364
    packet filtering firewalls, 358
    proxy firewalls, 358
    vendors, 378
    Windows WinProxy, 364
  IPv6, 473
  operating systems, 285
    Linux, 356-357
    Mac OS, 355
    UNIX, 355
    Windows, 355
    Windows NT, 355-356
  packet sniffers, 352-353

  resources, 360
  Rootshell, 473
  SMTP (Simple Mail Transfer Protocol) servers, 353
  stability, 354-357
  user groups, 176
  Web connections
    S-http, 144
    SSL (Secure Sockets Layer), 143-144
  Web File Sharing, 175-176
  Web servers, 256

SEEN option (SEARCH command), 125

SELECT command (IMAP), 121-122

Select Network Protocol dialog box, 92

sending
  commands, 147-148
  email, 116-117
  ICMP (Internet Control Message Protocol)
    requests, 33-35
    queries, 67-68

SendMail program, 119

Sequence Number field (TCP packets), 39

Serial Line Internet Protocol (SLIP), 28

server solutions
  AppleShare IP, 272-276
    file sharing, 273
    FTP (File Transfer Protocol), 273
    Internet Aliases, 273
    limitations, 275-276
    MacDNS, 274-275
    mail server, 274
    print server, 275
    QuickDNS Pro, 274
    Windows file sharing, 273-274

  CGI (Common Gateway Interface), 256
  choosing
    cost, 284
    ease of use, 283
    provided services, 284
    scalability, 284
    security, 285
    stability, 284
  Linux
    compatibility, 282
    file sharing, 280
    KDE (K Desktop Environment), 280
    KDE runlevel editor, 281
    limitations, 282-283
    support, 283
    utilities, 281
  Windows NT, 276
    components, 278
    DHCP (Dynamic Host Configuration Protocol), 278
    DNS server, 278
    file sharing, 277
    IIS (Internet Information Server), 277
    limitations, 279-280
    ShareWay IP, 277

servers
  ACAP servers, 389
  Apache, 265-269
  AppleShare IP file server, 191
  daemons, 199
  dedicated, 183-184
  DHCP (Dynamic Host Configuration Protocol) servers, 56-57, 385-388, 394
    BOOTP, compared, 57
    client configuration, 394-398
    IP (Internet Protocol) addresses, assigning, 57

iplease DHCP server, 402-407
Linux, 408-410
Mac OS, 398-401
Vicom server for Mac OS, 398-401
Vicom Internet Gateway, 398
Windows, 402-407
Windows NT DHCP server, 402
Wingate for Windows, 398
DNS (Domain Name Service), 66
configuation, 93-96
domain names, registering, 69
InterNIC, 69
name resolution, 66
name server records, 66-67
sending queries, 67-68
TTL, 66
whois service, 70-71
Windows NT, 278
FTP (File Transfer Protocol) servers
Linux, 209-215
NetPresenz, 187-191
War FTPd, 198-207
Gopher servers, 130-131
IIS (Internet Information Server), 277
IRC (Internet Relay Chat)
bots, 151
channels, 153-158
client software, 160
commands, 153-159
connections, 152, 155
server registration, 152-153
LDAP (Lightweight Directory Access Protocol), 391-392
Linux, 265-269

MacDNS, 274-275
Mac OS, 256-262
NAT servers, 338, 362
IPNetRouter, 338-341
IPRoute software, 347
Linux, 345-346
Mac OS, 338-341
NAT32, 341-344
TCP/IP settings, 346
Vicom Internet Gateway, 341
WebRamp, 347
Windows, 341-344
NNTP (Network News Transfer Protocol)
client software, 150
commands, 147-150
connections, 147, 150
listing newsgroups, 148
messages, 148-150
OmniHTTPd, 262-265
print, 275
proxy servers, 292-293, 298-300
advantages, 293
Apache, 329-335
browsers, 300-308
educational applications, 299
filtering, 299-300
limitations, 292
Linux, 329-335
Mac OS, 308-321
ports, 300
SOCKS, 323
SurfExpress, 300
WebDoubler, 308-321
WebSTAR, 308
Windows, 321-329
WinGate, 321
WinProxy, 321-329
QuickDNS Pro, 274
SMTP (Simple Mail Transfer Protocol)
connecting to, 115-116
security issues, 353

Stalker CommuniGate Pro
creating accounts, 246-250
email client, 255-256
Linux, 236-243
logs, 253-254
mailing lists, 250-253
monitoring system functions, 254
Remote Queue Starting Command, 244
RPOP, 244-246
Windows, 236-243
Stalker Internet Mail Server (SIMS)
accounts, 228-231
communication protocols, 232-235
CommuniGator, 225-226
configuring, 226-228
logs, 235
Postmaster, 225
queues, 235
router settings, 231-232
testing, 235
uploading data to, 141-142
Web Sharing, 257
WebSTAR, 257-262, 355
Windows, 262-265
Windows NT, 265
WINS (Windows Internet Name Service), 181
Service Unavailable message (HTTP), 138
services (client), 183
AppleTalk (Mac OS), 176
dedicated servers, 183-184
Linux, 182
provided, 284
shared resources
connecting to, 180-182
LMHOSTS file, 181-182
SMB file sharing, 177-181
Web File Sharing, 173-176

Session layer (OSI network layer), 14, 41-42. *See also* **sockets**

setting. *See* **configuring**

Shamir, Adi, 368

shared resources
connecting to, 180-182
LMHOSTS file, 181-182
SMB file sharing, 177-181
Web File Sharing, 173-176

ShareWay (Open Door Networks), 191-193, 277

sharing files, 177-181
AppleShare IP, 186, 273
configuring, 178-179
ethical considerations, 458, 461-464
FTP (File Transfer Protocol), 186
Linux, 186, 280
  FTP (File Transfer Protocol), 209-215
  Mac OS compatibility, 221
  Windows compatibility, 215-221
Mac OS, 186-187
  AppleShare IP, 190-193
  NetPresenz FTP (File Transfer Protocol) server, 187-191
  Windows compatibility, 193-198
SMB, 186
Windows, 186, 273-274, 277
  Mac OS compatibility, 207-208
  War FTPd, 198-207

Sherlock, 462

signatures (digital)
certifying authorities (CAs), 369
RSA, 368

Simple Mail Transfer Protocol. *See* **SMTP**

Simple Network Management Protocol (SNMP), 83, 412

SimpleText, 174

SIMS (Stalker Internet Mail Server)
communication protocols, 232-235
CommuniGator, 225-226
configuring, 226-228
creating accounts, 228-231
logs, 235
Postmaster, 225
queues, 235
router settings, 231-232
testing, 235

sites (Web). *See* **Web sites**

slash (/), 131

SLIP (Serial Line Internet Protocol), 28, 50

smart hubs, 82

SMB file sharing, 177-181, 186
configuring, 178-179
Samba, 215-221
shared files, 180
shared resources, 180-182

SMTP (Simple Mail Transfer Protocol), 115, 392
address verification, 118
advantages, 119
commands
  DATA, 117
  EXPN, 119
  HELO, 116
  HELP, 118
  MAIL FROM, 116
  QUIT, 118
  RCPT TO, 116-117
  RSET, 118
  VRFY, 118-119
connections, closing, 118

email, sending, 116-117
help system, 118
port number, 42
security issues, 353
SendMail program, 119
servers, connecting to, 115-116

sniffers, 352-353
ethical use of, 465
Ethload (Windows), 426-428
IPv6 packet headers, 473
NetMinder (Mac OS), 418-422
Sniffit (Linux), 432-435

SNMP (Simple Network Management Protocol), 83, 412

SOA (Start of Authority) record, 67

sockets, 37, 143-144

SOCKS, 323

software. *See* **applications; utilities**

Solar Winds, IP Network Browser, 422-425

Source Port field (TCP packets), 39

Source Quench message (ICMP), 33

Source/Destination Address field (IP headers), 32

Spam Calculator, 234

spamming, 233-234, 463
anti-spam tactics, 234-235, 240-242

spanning trees, 77

spoofing (IP), 472-473

spray, 450-452

SQL Server, 278

SSL (Secure Sockets Layer), 143-144, 366

stability
networks, 354-357
operating systems, 284

Stalker CommuniGate Pro, 236
creating accounts, 246-250
email client, 255-256
Linux, 236-237
communication protocols, 242-243
configuring, 238-239
installing, 237
Postmaster, 237-238
router settings, 239-240
security, 241-242
logs, 253-254
mailing lists, 250-253
monitoring system functions, 254
Remote Queue Starting Command, 244
RPOP, 244-246
Windows, 236-238
communication protocols, 242-243
configuring, 237-239
installing, 237
router settings, 239-240
security, 241-242

Stalker Internet Mail Server (SIMS), 225
communication protocols, 232-235
CommuniGator, 225-226
configuring, 226-228
creating accounts, 228-231
logs, 235
Postmaster, 225
queues, 235
router settings, 231-232
testing, 235

star topology, 20

StarNine Inc., WebSTAR, 257-262

Start of Authority (SOA) record, 67

starting nslookup, 68

STAT command (POP3), 112

states (TCP)
CLOSE-WAIT, 38
CLOSED, 38
CLOSING, 38
displaying, 38-39
ESTABLISHED, 37
FIN-WAIT-1, 37
FIN-WAIT-2, 38
LAST-ACK, 38
LISTEN, 37
SYN-RECEIVED, 37
SYN-SENT, 37
TIME-WAIT, 38

STATUS command (IMAP), 122

STORE command
FTP (File Transfer Ptotocol)), 162
IMAP (Internet Message Access Protocol), 124

store-and-forward technology (switched Ethernet), 82

storing data, 162

storms (broadcast), 84

subnets
filesharing, 181-182
IP (Internet Protocol) addresses, 60-61
classes, 61
masks, 61-62
private, 63-64
routing problems, 62-63

Sun Microsystems, Java language, 48

SurfExpress proxy server, 300

Sustainable Softworks
IPNetMonitor application, 34
IPNetRouter, 338-341

switches, 82

Switching Protocols message (HTTP responses), 138

SYN flag, 40

SYN-RECEIVED state (TCP), 37

SYN-SENT state (TCP), 37

synchronzing clocks, 163-164

T

T1 lincs, 291

T3 lines, 292

tables (routing), 79

TCP (Transmission Control Protocol)
ACK (acknowledgement) messages, 35
packet header fields, 39-40
ports, 36-37
RFC (Requests for Comment) Web site, 50
sockets, 37
states
CLOSE-WAIT, 38
CLOSED, 38
CLOSING, 38
displaying, 38-39
ESTABLISHED, 37
FIN-WAIT-1, 37
FIN-WAIT-2, 38
LAST-ACK, 38
LISTEN, 37
SYN-RECEIVED, 37
SYN-SENT, 37
TIME-WAIT, 38

TCP/IP Configuration dialog box
  DNS Configuration tab, 93-94
  DNs Configuration tab, 93
  Gateway tab, 94-95
  IP Address tab, 92-93

Telnet, 104-105
  Macintosh platforms, 104
  port number, 42, 104

terminators, 18

testing network connections, 170-171
  Network unreachable error message, 171-172
  Timeout error message, 172-173

thinnet (10BASE-2), 21
  BNC (British Naval Connectors), 19-20
  disadvantages, 19-20
  problems with, 380-382
  splicing, 383
  terminators, 18

Thursby Software Systems, 193-198

tickling connections, 340

Time Exceeded message (ICMP), 33

time to live (TTL)
  DNS (Domain Name Service) servers, 66
  IP (Internet Protocol) headers, 32

TIME-WAIT state (TCP), 38

Timeout error message, 172-173

timeouts, 79

TimeStamp message (ICMP), 33

TLD (top level domain), 64-65

tools
  ipfwadm, 365
  Linux, 281
  netstat, 38-39
  pgpk, 376-377
  ping, 33-35
  traceroute, 75-77

TOP command (POP3), 114

top level domain (TLD), 64-65

TOPIC command (IRC), 156

topologies
  bus, 19
  star, 20

Total Length field (IP headers), 32

traceroute utility, 75-77

tracing packet routes, 75-77

Transmission Control Protocol. *See* **TCP**

transparent bridging, 77

Transport layer (OSI network model), 13-14. *See also* **TCP (Transmission Control Protocol)**

trouble spots on networks
  hardware, 380
    thinnet
    twisted pair cabling, 382-384
  software, 384
    application settings, 388-389
    TCP/IP settings, 384-388
  users, 390

troubleshooting network problems
  cabling, 380-384, 448-453
  causes, 438
  configuration errors, 441-446

  error messages, 439
  hardware, 452-453
  IP (Internet Protocol) conflicts, 386-387
  Linux, 99
  logs, 439
  netstat, 38-39, 449-450
  Network unreachable error message, 171
  ping, 33-35
  protocol analyzers, 453
  router configuration errors, 446
  software errors, 447-448
  spray, 450-452
  subnet mask configuration errors, 446-447
  Timeout error message, 172-173
  user errors, 439-441

Trunk Line Level One (TI lines), 291

TTL (time to live)
  DNS (Domain Name Service) servers, 66
  IP (Internet Protocol) headers, 32

tunneling, 80

twisted-pair cabling (10BASE-T)
  Cat-3 cabling, 21
  Cat-5 cabling, 21
  disadvantages, 21
  hub configuration, 20-22

TYPE command (FTP), 162

Type of Service field (IP headers), 32

U

UDP (User Datagram Protocol), 35, 50

UIDL command (POP3), 114

UIDNEXT option (STATUS command), 122

UIDVALIDITY ption (STATUS command), 122

UNANSWERED option (SEARCH command), 125

Unauthorized message (HTTP), 138

Uniform Resource Locators. *See* **URLs**

UNIX. *See also* **Linux**
AppleTalk, 221
KDE desktop system, 108
security issues, 355
stability, 284

Unknown Host error message, 442

UNSEEN option
SEARCH command, 125
STATUS command, 122

unshielded twisted pair cabling (10BASE-T)
Cat-3 cabling, 21
Cat-5 cabling, 21
disadvantages, 21
hub configuration, 20-22

upgrades
IPv6, 474-475
operating systems, 356

uploading data (HTTP)
cookies, 142-143
GET method, 141-142
POST method, 142

URG flag, 40

Urgent pointer (TCP packets), 40

URLs (Uniform Resource Locators)
defined, 106
future technology, 108
syntax, 107-108

USENET (User Network), 146

USER command
FTP (File Transfer Protocol), 161
IRC (Internet Relay Chat) server registration, 153
POP3 (Post Office Protocol), 111

User Datagram Protocol (UDP), 35, 50

User Network (USENET), 146

USERHOST command (IRC), 158-159

users
authentication
IMAP (Internet Message Access Protocol), 120-121
Kerberos, 121
POP3 (Post Office Protocol), 111-112
directory services
finger, 390
LDAP (Lightweight Directory Access Protocol), 390-392
ph, 390
groups, 176
monitoring, 465
problems, 390

Users and Groups control panel, 176

utilities
ipfwadm, 365
Linux, 281
netstat, 38-39
pgpk, 376-377
ping, 33-35
traceroute, 75-77

unshielded twisted-pair cabling (10BASE-T)
Cat-3 cabling, 21
Cat-5 cabling, 21

disadvantages, 21
hub configuration, 20-22

V

verifying email addresses, 118

Verisign, 369

Version field (IP headers), 32

versions, IP (Internet Protocol)
IPng
address space, 468-469
addressing, 469-470
packet headers, 470-473
quality of service labeling, 473-474
resources, 475
security, 473
transitioning to, 474-475
IPv4, 468
IPv5, 468
IPv6
address space, 468-469
addressing, 469-470
packet headers, 470-473
quality of service labeling, 473-474
resources, 475
security, 473
transitioning to, 474-475

Vicom
DHCP server for Mac OS, 398-401
Internet Gateway, 341, 398

viewing
remote directories, 131-132
remote files, 132

virtual hosts, 31, 137

VNC (Virtual Network Computing), 47-48

Vremya Clock Synchronization Web site, 164

VRFY command (SMTP), 118-119

W-Z

Web (World Wide Web). *See also* **Internet; networks; Web sites**
browsers
Internet Explorer, 144
Netscape, 127, 144
proxy servers, 300-308
servers, 256
Apache, 265-269
CGI (Common Gateway Interface), 256
connecting to, 133
cookies, 142-144
IIS (Internet Information Server), 265, 277
Linux, 265-269
Mac OS, 256-262
OmniHTTPd, 262-265
security, 256
uploading data to, 141-142
Web Sharing, 257
WebSTAR, 257-262, 355
Windows, 262-265
URLs (Uniform Resource Locators)
defined, 106
future technology, 108
syntax, 107-108

Web File Sharing, 173-176
security, 175-176
Web file server mode, 174
Web server mode, 174

Web sites
3COM296, 360
Adobe, 464
ADSL Information and Resources, 296

All You Wanted to Know About T1 But Were Afraid to Ask, 296
Anarchie, 162
Arin, 69, 72
Asante, 88
BetterTelnet, 104
Billiter Consultants, 402
Bright Light Technologies, 234
Cable Modem 101, 296
CDDB (CD database), 46
Chocolate Chip Cookies, 144
CIRCus, 160
Cookie Central, 144
COPSTalk, 207
Dartmouth College, 413
Domain Name System RFC, 72
Ethload, 426
Eudora, 127
Fetch, 162
FTP (File Transfer Protocol) RFC, 163
Gamelan, 48
Hotline, 45
ICQ (I Seek You), 44
IMAP (Internet Message Access Protocol), 128
Internet Protocol RFC, 72
InterNIC, 70-72
IRC (Internet Relay Chat)RFC, 160
Ircle, 160
KDE (K Desktop Environment), 108, 280
Kerberos, 121
Linux, 182
Linux Configuration and Troubleshooting, 99
MacIRC, 160
Maxum, 308
MBONE Information Center, 86
Men and Mice, 275

Microsoft
Internet Explorer page, 144, 162
Outlook/Outlook-Express page, 127, 150
Windows Networking page, 99
mIRC, 160
Mischler, David, 347
Monolith, 69
Multi-Threaded NewsWatcher, 150
NDIS3PKT, 426
Neon Software, 418
Netcraft survey, 135
NetPresenz, 187
Netscape, 127, 144
Netscape Navigator/ Communicator, 150, 162
NN-TK, 150
NNTP (Network News Transfer Protocol) RFC, 150
NTP Network Time Protocol) RFC, 164
Omnicron Technologies, 262
Open Content group, 462
Open Door Networks, 192
Open Transport, 99
Opera, 144
The Palace, 45
PC MACLAN, 208
PIRCH, 160
PointCast, 47
POP3 (Post Office Protocol) RFC, 128
Quake, 49
QuickDNS Pro, 275
Red Hat Linux, 356
Rootshell, 356, 473
Routing on the Internet, 86
RSA, 367, 378
Samba, 215
SendMail program, 119
SMTP (Simple Mail Transfer Protocol), 128

Sniffit, 432-435

Solar Winds, 422

SSL (Secure Sockets Layer) FAQ, 144

Stalker CommuniGate Pro, 236

Stalker Internet Mail Server (SIMS), 225

Star Nine Inc., 257

Sustainable Softworks, 34, 338

Thursby Software Systems, 194

USENET history, 146

Verisign, 369

Vicom Internet Gateway, 341

VNC (Virtual Network Computing), 48

Vremya Clock Synchronization, 164

War FTPd, 198

WebRamp, 347

WinGate, 321

WinProxy, 321

WS-FTP, 162

WebDoubler proxy server, 308-321

WebRamp, 347

WebSTAR Web server, 257-262
  proxy module, 308
  security track record, 355

WHOIS command (IRC), 158

whois service (DNS), 70-71

Window field (TCP packets), 40

Windows 95/98
  Browse Master, 181
  DHCP (Dynamic Host Configuration Protocol) servers, 396-397, 402-407
  Ethload, 426-428
  hardware addresses, 25

IP Network Browser, 422-425

messaging, 236-256

NAT servers, 341-344

Outlook Express PGP, 375

PGPFreeware, 369-373

proxy servers
  browsers, 303-306
  SurfExpress, 300
  WinGate, 321
  WinProxy, 321-329

security issues, 355

shared resources
  connecting to, 180-182
  LMHOSTS file, 181-182
  Mac OS compatibility, 207-208
  SMB file sharing, 177-181
  War FTPd, 198-207

TCP/IP
  configuring, 92-95
  installing, 91-92

Web servers, 262-265

winnuke program, 354-355

WinProxy, 364

Windows file sharing (AppleShare IP), 273-274

Windows Internet Name Service (WINS), 94

Windows Internet Naming Service. (WINS), 94, 181

Windows Networking Web site, 99

Windows NT
  components, 278
  DHCP (Dynamic Host Configuration Protocol), 278, 402
  DNS (Domain Name Service) server, 278
  file sharing, 277
  IIS (Internet Information Server), 277
  limitations, 279-280

security issues, 355-356

ShareWay IP, 277

stability, 284

WinGate for Windows, 321, 398

winnuke program, 354-355, 473

WinProxy proxy server, 321-329, 364

WINS (Windows Internet Name Service), 94, 181

wiring. *See* **cables**

workstations, configuring, 88
  Linux, 95
    /etc/sysconfig/network file, 96-97
    DNS servers, 96
    hostnames, 96
    ifcfg-eth0 file, 97-98
  Mac OS 8.x
    connection methods, 89
    domain names, 90
    Ethernet cards, 88
    IP addresses, 89
    name server addresses, 90
  Windows 95
    TCP/IP configuration, 92-95
    TCP/IP installation, 91-92
  Windows 98
    TCP/IP configuration, 92-95
    TCP/IP installation, 91-92

writing email messages, 117

WS-FTP Web site, 162

wu-ftpd, 209-215

Zimmerman, Philip, 366

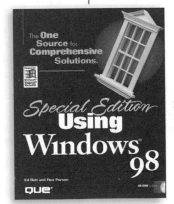